DUTCH SOURCES ON SOUTH ASIA
c. 1600-1825

DUTCH SOURCES ON SOUTH ASIA
c. 1600-1825

VOLUME 2

Archival Guide to the
Repositories
in The Netherlands
Other than
the National Archives

LENNART BES

MANOHAR
2007

This publication has been financed by the Gonda Foundation of the Royal Netherlands Academy of Arts and Sciences (KNAW) and facilitated by the National Archives of the Netherlands.

First published 2007

ISBN 81-7304-370-1 (Set)
ISBN 81-7304-711-1 (Vol. 2)

Published by
Ajay Kumar Jain for
Manohar Publishers & Distributors
4753/23 Ansari Road, Daryaganj
New Delhi 110002

Printed at
Lordson Publishers Pvt Ltd.
Delhi 110007

Distributed in South Asia by
FOUNDATION BOOKS
4381/4 Ansari Road, Daryaganj
New Delhi 110002
and its branches at Mumbai, Hyderabad,
Bangalore, Chennai, Kolkata

Contents

Abbreviations

EIC	(English) East India Company.
GG&C	Governor-General and Council (at Batavia).
VOC	Verenigde Oostindische Compagnie (Dutch East India Company).
VROA	*Verslagen omtrent 's Rijks Oude Archieven.*

Note on Orthography

Repositories, archival collections and specific administrative functions are given in Dutch with an English translation when used for the first time. Abbreviations also refer mostly to current Dutch usage. Only well-known administrative functions such as *Heren XVII* and *Gouverneur(-Generaal) en Raden* are translated as Gentlemen XVII and Governor(-General) and Council. Dutch and English usage of archival terms are based on M.A.P. Meilink-Roelofsz's *The Archives of the Dutch East India Company (1602-1795)* (The Hague, 1992). In general, geographical, personal and technical terms are given in modern transliteration without the use of diacritical marks and according to their current usage. Where the latter is uncertain the Dutch form has been preserved between inverted commas. In the end, dealing with a myriad of different language traditions, a degree of inconsistency cannot be avoided.

Geographical Terms

The geographical scope of the volume comprises the modern states of India, Sri Lanka, Bangladesh, Pakistan, Nepal, Bhutan and the Maldives. When the expression India is used it is usually in its wider, pre-modern meaning of the Indian subcontinent. Other geographical names are often given according to their historical context and relevance: e.g. Ceylon instead of Sri Lanka and Malabar instead of Kerala. The geographical division is based on the administrative organization of the VOC in South Asia. Thus the five regional divisions will be employed which at that time were usually labelled as Surat, Malabar, Ceylon, Coromandel and Bengal. Surat included not only Gujarat (down to Bombay) but also the western parts of Hindustan (e.g. Agra), Malwa (e.g. Burhanpur) and Sind. Although the VOC settlement on the Konkan (Vengurla) had a direct link with Batavia it will be dealt with under Malabar which term refers to the Kanara Coast as well. The settlements on the Fishery Coast as well as the contacts with the Maldives will be treated under Ceylon since they were administered from Colombo. Although Coromandel refers to most of the Indian east coast, the settlements of northern Orissa (Balasore and Pipli) belonged to Bengal. Bengal also included Patna in Bihar.

Preface

This volume is a sequel to *Dutch Sources on South Asia c. 1600-1825. Volume 1: Bibliography and Archival Guide to the National Archives at The Hague (The Netherlands)* (New Delhi: Manohar, 2001), compiled by Jos Gommans, Gijs Kruijtzer and myself. The aim of this second volume is to provide an overview of relevant materials in repositories in the Netherlands other than the National Archives: provincial, regional and municipal archives, libraries of universities and other libraries, ecclesiastical organizations, museums and other public institutions, companies, private organizations and individuals.

As with the previous volume, the focus of this guide is on sources that in one way or another pertain to Indo-Dutch interaction. Nevertheless, it also includes some material deriving from other European backgrounds, chiefly maps. This volume restricts itself to two-dimensional objects: archival texts, maps, drawings, paintings and prints. It also contains descriptions of a small number of very rare printed texts that strictly speaking cannot be considered archival material and are actually often classed as publications, such as pamphlets, occasional poems, proclamations, etc. The sources covered by the guide date from the period roughly between 1600, when the Dutch first appeared in the region, and 1825, when they abandoned the last few remaining settlements formerly belonging to the VOC (Dutch East India Company).

This guide is divided along the lines of the five main administrative divisions of the VOC in South Asia (Chapters 2-6). In addition, Chapter 1 contains general descriptions of all relevant archives and collections, and lists pieces that contain information on more than one region. In the second place, this guide is organized on types of repositories (and, in one case, on the type of document). This results in the following six-point structure, maintained throughout the general and regional chapters:

1 Government archives.
2 Universities.
3 Ecclesiastical organizations.
4 Museums and other public institutions.
5 Companies, private organizations and individuals.
6 Maps and pictures (this section refers to *all* maps and pictures, not only those that are kept separately by the repositories).

Within each section, the repositories are arranged alphabetically on their geographical location, which is given within brackets after the repository if not obvious from its name. The names of repositories are always given in capitals. The materials of each repository are listed according to their creator more or less in the following order: public bodies, ecclesiastical organizations, other institutions, businesses, families, private persons, collections. When items have not been given an inventory number (inv. no.) by the repository keeping them, small letters within brackets are used in this guide.

The guide does not list separate prints and maps that originate from published works. Instead, Appendix I provides a survey of relevant prints and maps to be found in a number of works published between *c.* 1600 and 1825. Separate prints and maps of which the origin is unknown to me, however, have been included in this guide (some prints may accidentally be listed in both the main text and Appendix I). An exception has been made for separate printed maps originating from atlases. As the bibliographies in the present and the previous volumes do not include atlases, both manuscript and separate printed maps are listed in this guide. Maps depicting a much larger area than just South Asia have usually not been included. (With regard to maps and atlases, see also the introductory remarks to the section on maps and pictures, 1.6.)

General information concerning the repositories, such as addresses, web sites, etc., which is often subject to changes, can be found in Appendix II. For a survey of the history and historiography of Indo-Dutch contacts, short introductions and maps on the Dutch presence in various South Asian regions, lists of Dutch chiefs in South Asia and Batavia, and an Indo-Dutch spelling list, the reader should consult Volume 1.

Generally speaking, the nature of the materials described in this volume is somewhat different from the type of documents mentioned in Volume 1. Whereas the previous guide mostly covers the archives of VOC institutions and their legal successors, largely consisting of series of consecutive papers, the present guide rather concerns separate pieces. These were chiefly created by institutions and people whose activities took place literally in the wake of the VOC, like local governments and companies, notaries, orphanages and orphan boards, churches and their missions, artists, scholars and scientific societies, independent travellers and also VOC servants and their relatives in their private capacities. As such, these materials often contain additional information to what can be found in the official Company records and may offer an alternative view. The remark made in 1985 by the Indian historian Ashin Das Gupta with respect to this kind of documents (referring to the work of M.P.H. Roessingh, see the Acknowledgements) still holds true: 'Researches based on the Dutch archives, so far almost exclusively confined to official papers, may now gain important new insights from the private archives ... .'[1]

[1] A. Das Gupta, 'Indian Merchants and the Western Indian Ocean: The Early Seventeenth Century', in idem, *The World of the Indian Ocean Merchant 1500-1800. Collected Essays of Ashin Das Gupta*, eds U. Das Gupta and S. Subrahmanyam (New Delhi, 2001), p. 282, first published in *Modern Asian Studies*, 19 (1985).

Acknowledgements

The content of this volume has been compiled as follows. The unsurpassed but somewhat outdated works by M.P.H. Roessingh, *Sources of the History of Asia and Oceania in the Netherlands. Part I: Sources up to 1796* (Munich, 1982) and F.G.P. Jaquet, *Sources of the History of Asia and Oceania in the Netherlands. Part II: Sources 1796-1949* (Munich, 1983) served as initial guides for setting up the present one. I have visited the relevant repositories mentioned by Roessingh and Jaquet to update their findings and describe the materials in greater detail. In addition, I have contacted all other possibly relevant institutions (totalling to about 400 repositories) listed in various archival surveys and related overviews.[1] In order to trace relevant private archives, I examined the *Centraal Register van Particuliere Archieven*, a card-tray index of such materials in the Netherlands, which is available at the National Archives. For the location of portraits of some of the more well-known Dutchmen serving in South Asia (largely limited to depictions of the chiefs of the five regional establishments, kept at public institutions), I checked the survey compiled by the *Iconografisch Bureau* at The Hague. Finally, I consulted a number of web sites on the Internet (the most useful of which are mentioned in Appendix II).

Obviously, this guide does not pretend to be complete. It is hoped that the list of relevant institutions stated in the Preface provides an idea of where papers pertaining to South Asia are generally to be found. The archives of other orphanages, churches, notaries, etc., than the ones mentioned here may very well refer to Indo-Dutch interaction too.

It should be stressed that this guide is written from the historian's point of view. The descriptions do not claim to meet the standards set by archivists,

[1] These include: *Almanak van het Nederlandse Archiefwezen* (Amsterdam, 2000); H.J.A.H.G. Metselaars (ed.), *Particuliere archieven in Nederland* (*Overzichten van de archieven en verzamelingen in de openbare archiefbewaarplaatsen in Nederland*, Vol. 14) (Houten and Zaventem, 1992); J. Mateboer, *Repertorium bijzondere collecties. Historische en moderne verzamelingen in universiteitsbibliotheken, de Koninklijke Bibliotheek, de bibliotheek van de Koninklijke Nederlandse Akademie van Wetenschappen en de bibliotheken met wetenschappelijke steunfunctie* (The Hague, 1997); *Nederlandse bibliotheek- en documentatiegids '02 '03. Adresboek van in Nederland gevestigde bibliotheken en documentatieinstellingen* (The Hague, 2001); P. van den Brink (ed.), *Almanak verzamelingen topografisch beeldmateriaal. Een overzicht van kaartenverzamelingen en topografisch-historische atlassen in Nederland* (The Hague, 1995); *NCC adres 2000. Bibliotheken en instellingen aangesloten bij de Nederlandse Centrale Catalogus* (The Hague, n.d.); R. Hoekstra and G. Landry (eds), *IIAS Guide to Asian Collections in the Netherlands* (Leiden and Amsterdam, 1997); *Nederland Museumland 2002. Gids langs meer dan 1225 musea, oudheidskamers, kastelen, dierentuinen, hortussen* (Amsterdam and Wormer, 2001); R. Lindeman, Y. Scherf and R. Dekker, *Reisverslagen van Noord-Nederlanders uit de zestiende tot begin negentiende eeuw. Een chronologische lijst* (Rotterdam, 1994).

librarians, art historians, cartography specialists and the like in their respective fields. It should also be kept in mind that the way in which materials are described (and whether or not items are included at all!) depends largely on the available finding aids and the accessibility of these materials. The quality and detail of the host of inventories, checklists, catalogues, card tray indices, data bases, etc., consulted for this volume vary a great deal and have thus significantly influenced its contents. Although the bulk of the descriptions has been based not only on finding aids, but also on sifting through the material itself, I have not been able to personally examine each and every item.

This volume, covering such a wide range of materials in so many repositories, could obviously not have been produced without the invaluable help of a large number of people. I am particularly grateful to Jos Gommans, who initiated the *Dutch Sources on South Asia* series, and who was always ready to give advice and read the first draft of this volume. I would also like to thank Lizette de Koning, who offered ongoing moral support and went through the first draft as well, and Gijs Kruijtzer for his supplementary description of inv. nos 40-3 of the *Hoge Regering Batavia* collection. I wish to express my gratitude to the Gonda Foundation of the Royal Netherlands Academy of Arts and Sciences (KNAW) and the National Archives of the Netherlands for respectively funding and facilitating this project again. Furthermore, I would like to thank the following people, who in one or another way assisted me: Mark de Lannoy, Furoz Ramanand, Alexander Raat, A.G. Menon, Els Jacobs, Remco Raben, Alicia Schrikker, Roelof van Gelder, Femme Gaastra, Paul van Dyke, Marion Peters, Peter Rietbergen, Ikuko Wada, Ian Wendt, Mary Prins, Aryan Klein, Martine Gosselink, Lodewijk Wagenaar, Albert van den Belt, Mieke Beumer, Menno Leenstra, Aart Vos, Christiaan Jörg, Henk Niemeijer, Sebastiaan Derks, Anjana Singh, Nirmal Devasiri, Max de Bruijn, J.F.W. Jansen, Floor Geraedts, Ben Slot, Mahesh Gopalan, Albert van der Zeijden, Marco Ramerini, Erik Löffler and Pim de Vogel.

Naturally, I am very thankful to the staff of all the repositories listed in this guide, especially (in no particular order): Pieter Koenders, Mieke van Leeuwen-Canneman, Jasmijn van den Berg, Dick Kaajan, Diederick Kortlang, Jan Fernhout, Edwin Paar and Erik van der Doe (*Nationaal Archief*), Piet Boon (*Westfries Archief*), Dory Heilijgers (*Universiteit Leiden, Instituut Kern*), Pauline Lunsingh Scheurleer, Marja Stijkel, M.D. Haga, Susan van Gelderen, Kees Zandvliet, Harm Stevens and J.F. Heijbroek (*Rijksmuseum Amsterdam*), B. Woelderink, L.J.A. Pennings, C.J.M. Eymael and H.A. Robaard (*Koninklijk Huisarchief*), G. van der Beek and P.A. Christiaans (*Centraal Bureau voor Genealogie*), W.T. Resida, A. Schoonderbeek and G.J. Weijde (*Gelders Archief*), Lia van Zalinge (*Historisch Informatiecentrum Helmond*), Carl Nix (*Atlas van Stolk*), Arie-Pieter van Nienes and B.H. de Vries (*Tresoar, Frysk Histoarysk en Letterkundich Sintrum*), Dorothée Buur (*Koninklijk Instituut voor Taal-, Land- en Volkenkunde*), Emile Ramakers and Th.J. van Rensch (*Rijksarchief in Limburg*), Marijn van Hoorn, Marijke Besselink, Bert Sliggers and Jeff Borkent (*Teylers Museum*), Albert Meijer, Leo Hollestelle, Katie Heyning and Toon Franken (*Zeeuws Archief*), Lida Ruitinga, Sandra van Daalen and W. Heijting (*Vrije Universiteit Amsterdam*), Arie van der Schoor (*Gemeentearchief Rotterdam*), Han van de Roer-Meijers and Annemieke Hoogeveen-Landsbergen

(*Centrale Bibliotheek Rotterdam*), Jan Wigger and Arnold Gevers (*Historisch Centrum Overijssel*), Jos Biemans, Jan Werner, Wim van Stormbroek and Adri Offenberg (*Universiteit van Amsterdam, Universiteitsbibliotheek*), Irene Jacobs and Sjoerd de Meer (*Maritiem Museum Rotterdam*), Kees Thomassen and Hélène Peeters (*Koninklijke Bibliotheek*), Gerrit Kouwenhoven (*Streekarchivariaat Noord-Veluwe*), Ton van der Meer, Jeroen van de Ven and Gijs Jacobs (*Bibliotheek Universiteit Tilburg*), J. Peijnenburg (*Bisdom 's-Hertogenbosch*), Evert Kwaadgras (*Orde van Vrijmetselaren*), Ineke Sandbrink and Harry de Raad (*Regionaal Archief Alkmaar*), Johan Francke and Liesbeth van der Doe-van der Geest (*Zeeuwse Bibliotheek / Zeeuws Documentatiecentrum*), Rudi van Maanen and Michiel van Halem (*Regionaal Archief Leiden*), Dirk de Vries, A.Th. Bouwman and J.J. Witkam (*Universiteit Leiden, Universiteitsbibliotheek*), Bas de Melker (*Gemeentearchief Amsterdam*), P.J.C. Verhoeven (*Museum Bronbeek*), Karin Booij, Ester de Bruin and Sijbrand de Rooij (*Rijksmuseum voor Volkenkunde*), E. van Deutekom (*Archief van de Nederlandse Provincie der Jezuïeten*), Jan de Ruiter (*Stads- en Streekarchief Zutphen*), Monique van der Pal (*Nederlandsch Economisch-Historisch Archief*), Kees Berg, Dick Brongers and Henk Eijssens (*Haags Gemeentearchief*), David van Duuren and Erwin van Delden (*Koninklijk Instituut voor de Tropen*), Hans van Felius (*Rijksarchief in Noord-Holland*), Joyce Pennings and Douwe Koen (*Utrechts Archief*), J.M.H. van der Hidde (*Koninklijke Nedlloyd*), Koert van der Horst (*Universiteit Utrecht, Universiteitsbibliotheek*), Roelof Oddens (*Universiteit Utrecht, Faculteit Ruimtelijke Wetenschappen*), Jan-Henk van Dijk (*Groninger Museum*), R.J. van den Bergh (*Regionaal Historisch Centrum Bergen op Zoom*), Geeta Bruin, Albert Elen, Saskia de Jong and A.W.F.M. Meij (*Museum Boijmans Van Beuningen*), Freek van Eijk, Theo Tijssen, Lida Sutin and Ans van Schaik (*Technische Universiteit Delft*), G. Verhoeven, B. van der Wulp, M.J.G. Claessens and P.J. Hofland (*Gemeentearchief Delft*), Juliette van Seters (*Stedelijk Museum Alkmaar*), Jos van Heel (*Museum Meermanno*), Henk Dessens, Manon Dujardin and Diederick Wildeman (*Nederlands Scheepvaartmuseum Amsterdam*), Cees Lut and Gerard Thijsse (*Nationaal Herbarium Nederland*), Michaël Lucassen (*Streekarchief Midden-Holland*), Liesbeth Missel (*Bibliotheek Wageningen Universiteit en Researchcentrum*), Hesther van den Donk (*Zeeuws Museum*), Frans Tames and Ed Sewalt (*Archiefdienst voor Kennemerland*), Jaap de Visser (*Universiteit van Amsterdam, Artis Bibliotheek*), Wiljan Puttenstein and Jaap van Gelderen (*Theologische Universiteit Kampen*), Theo Noordermeer and Gineke van der Ree-Scholtens (*Brabants Historisch Informatie Centrum*), Erwin de Leeuw (*Drents Archief*), L.B. Holthuis and Caroline Pepermans (*Naturalis, Nationaal Natuurhistorisch Museum*), J. Six van Hillegom (Six collection), Harry Leechburch (*Museum Boerhaave*), Chris de Bruyn (*Simon van Gijn - Museum aan huis*), Sander Paarlberg and Alicja Rakuzyn (*Dordrechts Museum*), P.H. Riem, J. van Keulen and E. Schut (*Groninger Archieven*), Hester Kuiper (*Slot Zuylen*), Joop Kooiman (*Streekarchivariaat Noordwest-Veluwe*), Jan Feikema, Andre Karting, E. Heyning and the Tutein Nolthenius family. Finally, I would like to thank the many repositories that took the trouble to inform me that they do not keep relevant materials. Obviously, the responsibility for the contents of this guide is entirely mine.

VOLUME 1: SUPPLEMENTS, REVIEWS AND ERRATA

As was to be expected, after the publication of Volume 1, it turned out that both the Bibliography and the Archival Guide were far from comprehensive. Hence, the present volume offers two necessary Supplements with many new titles as well as freshly unearthed documents in the National Archives. As in Volume 1, the Bibliography does not include works that have a wide, Indian-Ocean-like perspective but focuses on Dutch interaction with South Asia only. However, the supplementary Bibliography shows that Volume 1 particularly missed works on Ceylon.

The following reviews of Volume 1 have appeared:

Lakshmi Subramanian, 'Towards a New Frontier', in *The Book Review* (December 2001), p. 13.
Markus Vink, in *Itinerario*, 25, 3-4 (2001), pp. 231-3.
Femme Gaastra, in *Tijdschrift voor Zeegeschiedenis*, 21, 1 (2002), pp. 60-1.
Bhaswati Bhattacharya, in *Journal of the Economic and Social History of the Orient*, 45, 3 (2002), pp. 412-14.
P.J. Marshall, in *The International History Review*, 24, 3 (September 2002), pp. 636-7.

Although generally well received by reviewers, there was some criticism involving the historiographical survey of the Introduction. Obviously, this has been the most personal and theoretical part in what was meant to be an objective and highly practical inventory of sources. Even the Introduction, however, was not intended to disparage either the Indo-centric, economic history of Indian historians or the Hollando-centric tradition of Dutch historians (Bhattacharya). Neither was it meant to claim that every scholar, one way or the other, fits in to this 'simplistic binary model' or to belittle 'the diversity and interdisciplinary nature of contemporary social sciences' (Vink). We did not pretend to cover all possible new directions of the future but merely aimed at showing the main historiographical tendencies of the past.

Furthermore, it should be rectified that it is not H.A.I. Goonetileke but, of course, K.W. Goonewardena who is meant on p. 28 of the Introduction as the most important Sri Lankan historian who was taking up Moreland's and Van Leur's calls for a more Asia-centric perspective. Finally, the first treaty between the Dutch and Kandy was concluded in 1610, instead of 1612 as we erroneously mentioned on p. 221 of the introduction to the Ceylon chapter.

1. GENERAL

1.1. Government Archives

1.1.1. *REGIONAAL ARCHIEF ALKMAAR* REGIONAL ARCHIVES IN ALKMAAR

For general surveys, see *De archieven in Noord-Holland* (*Overzichten van de archieven en verzamelingen in de openbare archiefbewaarplaatsen in Nederland*, Vol. 7) (Alphen aan den Rijn, 1981), pp. 137-74 (somewhat outdated), and the repository's web site (see Appendix II, 1.1).

Van Foreest family

Inv. nos: 1-943
Size: 17 metres
Period: 1422-1979
Inventory: J.H. Rombach, *Inventaris van de archieven van de families Van Foreest, 1422-1979, Van Egmond van de Nijenburg, 1428-1765, De Dieu, Fontein Verschuir, van der Feen de Lille, 1664-1955* (Alkmaar, 1992), pp. 7-122, with introductions, genealogical trees, appendices and indices

The archives of the Alkmaar-based Van Foreest family include papers deriving from Cornelis van Foreest (1704-61), who was Director at the Hoorn Chamber of the VOC among several other functions. For documents concerning Ceylon, see 4.1.

Wollebrand Geleijnsz de Jonghe

Inv. nos: 1-119
Size: 1.4 metres
Period: 1618-1824
Inventory: W.A. Fasel, 'Inventaris van de collectie Wollebrand Geleijnsz de Jonghe' (1986), with introduction and index

In 1623 Wollebrand Geleijnsz de Jonghe (also spelt Wollebrandt Geleynssen de Jongh) came to Surat as a chief-factor. He stayed in Burhanpur for a while and then served as chief-factor of Bharuch from 1624 to 1631. After a spell in the Republic and the South-East Asian archipelago, he was appointed second-in-command at Surat in 1636 and chief of Agra in 1637 where he served until 1640. While on his way from Persia to Batavia, he was taken hostage by the Portuguese at Goa in 1643, after which he spent some time in Vengurla into the year 1644. Later that year he was appointed Rear Admiral to the fleet sailing against Goa but he came to be occupied in Persia again soon after. The bulk of his papers concerning Asia are kept at the *Nationaal Archief*, see *Dutch Sources on South Asia*, Vol. 1 (1.5.2, 1.6.1, 2.5, 2.6, 3.5, 4.5, 5.5 and 6.5) as well as Supplement II, 17 of this volume. The present archives, however, also contain a few references to Goa and Ceylon, see 3.1 and 4.1.

1.1.2. *GEMEENTEARCHIEF AMSTERDAM* MUNICIPAL ARCHIVES OF AMSTERDAM

For general surveys, see J.H. van den Hoek Ostende, P.H.J. van der Laan and E. Lievense-Pelser (eds), *De archieven in Amsterdam* (*Overzichten van de archieven en verzamelingen in de openbare archiefbewaarplaatsen in Nederland*, Vol. 8) (Alphen aan den Rijn, 1981) (somewhat outdated), and the repository's web site (see Appendix II, 1.2). Note that the contents of a great number of inventories are digitally available in the reading room and can thus be searched by keyword.

Burgemeesters; Stukken betreffende lands- en gewestelijk bestuur
Burgomasters; Papers concerning national and provincial government

Access no.: 5030
Inv. nos: unnumbered
Size: 3 metres
Period: 1682-1793
Inventory: not available

These papers were formerly part of the old Amsterdam archives, accessible through the inventory by P. Scheltema, *Inventaris van het Amsterdamsche archief*, 3 vols (Amsterdam, 1866-74). Those archives have been split into several collections, of which the papers of the Burgomasters concerning the national and provincial government appear to be the only collection that includes documents regarding South Asia. Besides the material described below, inv. no. Port 71 also concerns the VOC.

Port 53 Various folders with papers pertaining to the VOC. One bundle. Including:

O 2-12, P 1-7 Papers concerning the VOC, including a report by Daniel Braams, Bookkeeper General at Batavia and Commander of the return fleet, to the States General regarding the state of affairs of the Company in Asia, with sections on Bengal, Coromandel, Ceylon, Malabar and Surat, 1688. One folder (old no. L. O 2, N 12).

Weeskamer en Commissie van Liquidatie der zaken van de voormalige weeskamer
Orphan Board and Commission of Liquidation of the affairs of the former orphan board

Access no.: 5073
Inv. nos: 1-1885
Size: 256 metres
Period: 1309-1853
Inventory: L.P.E. Kretzschmar, 'Voorlopige inventaris van het archief van de weeskamer (1309) 1468-1852' (1985), with introduction

The Orphan Board was probably set up in 1466. After the Board's dissolution in 1811, a commission for the liquidation of its affairs existed until 1852. The archives include a large number of letters exchanged with trustees and other people in South Asia. Inv. nos 11, 16-209, 211-53, 265, 271, 274, 290, 317, 434-5, 468-70 and 482-9 consist of this correspondence and other documents related to the VOC. For papers concerning Surat, Malabar, Ceylon, Coromandel and Bengal, see also 2.1, 3.1, 4.1, 5.1 and 6.1.

211-38 Copies of outgoing papers, 1594-1852, including letters sent to South Asia, mostly Cochin, Colombo, Galle, Jaffna, Pulicat and Nagappattinam. Nine quires, 19 volumes. Inv. no. 225 (1726-47) includes an index to geographical names.

Aalmoezeniers, sinds 1666 regenten van het Aalmoezeniersweeshuis
Almoners, since 1666 trustees of the Almoners' Orphanage

Access no.: 343
Inv. nos: 1-655
Size: 45 metres
Period: 1613-1828
Inventory: E. Lievense-Pelser, 'Inventaris van het archief van het college van Aalmoezeniers, sedert 1666. van Regenten van het Aalmoezeniersweeshuis' (1988, 1993), with introduction and index to personal names

In 1613, a board of almoners was set up to take care of the poor who were not looked after by religious communities or the civil orphanage. The organization existed until 1825. Inv. nos 418-36 concern boys who went overseas in the service of the VOC, chiefly during the eighteenth century. Most of these documents, however, do not specify the boys' destinations.

424-5 Lists of boys (or their fathers and brothers) sent to the East Indies, with financial surveys and destinations, including South Asia, 1750-81. Two folders.

Notarissen ter standplaats Amsterdam
Notaries at Amsterdam

Access no.: 5075
Inv. nos: 1-28620
Size: 3601 metres
Period: 1578-1915
Inventory: for the period 1578-1895: 'Inventaris van de notariële archieven van Amsterdam 1578-1892', 8 vols, with chronological and alphabetical (on notaries) index in separate volume; see also below

The archives consist of acts drawn up by notaries at Amsterdam. These documents cover a very wide range of topics, including South Asia. Relevant acts can be found with the help of several modern indices (available in card trays), but only 5 to 8 per cent of the archives has been made accessible so far. There are indices to geographical names, personal names, professions, commodities and a host of other subjects, with the years 1578-1620 and 1701-10 covered in most detail (the latter period not for personal names). An index to Portuguese Jews is available for the period up to 1640. For personal names in the eighteenth century, there are contemporary indices. A list of the headings in the modern indices is available in the reading room. Even the documents just pertaining to South Asia that are accessible by way of the various indices are too numerous to be described in detail in this guide. Therefore, only the number and period of the index cards found under some of the more obvious headings in the modern indices are mentioned here, in order to give the reader at least an idea of what is available in the notarial archives. Consulted for this guide were the indices to geographical names, professions (VOC servants), Portuguese Jews and a few headings in the topical index, such as Bengal silk and bills of exchange. All index cards thus found are marked with geographical names; these are listed in this guide. For surveys concerning Surat, Malabar, Ceylon, Coromandel and Bengal, see 2.1, 3.1, 4.1, 5.1 and 6.1.

Ganges River	1 index card (1620).
India / Bangladesh	20 index cards (1620, 1641-1768).
'Malapuram / Malapaai / Malapad' (Malappuram east of Calicut or Manapadu on the Fishery Coast?)	2 index cards (1707).

Classis Amsterdam van de Nederlandse Hervormde Kerk
Amsterdam Classis of the Dutch Reformed Church

Access no.:	379
Inv. nos:	1-739
Size:	21 metres
Period:	1582-1951, 1971
Inventory:	G. Verhoeven, 'Inventaris van de archieven van de Classis Amsterdam van de Nederlandse Hervormde Kerk 1582-1951 (1971)' (1989), with introduction

The Amsterdam Classis was established after a decision to do so by the *Particuliere Synode van Noord-Holland* (Private (provincial) Synod of North Holland) made in 1578. The *Deputati ad res exteras*, a committee that functioned from 1636 to 1804, dealt with overseas activities. Inv. nos 157-209, 716, 722 are relevant with regard to Asia.

157-62	Acts of the *Deputati ad res exteras*, 1639-1804. Six volumes. Inv. no. 160 includes extracts of letters received from Colombo, Galle and other places, with index, 1746-58. For a partial index, see inv. no. 174 below.
163-5	Copies of the acts of the Classis, as far as they concern the overseas activities (with some copies of papers sent overseas), partly

regarding South Asia (mostly Ceylon), 1636-1706. Three volumes. For a partial index, see inv. no. 174 below.

166-7 Extracts from received papers, partly concerning South Asia (mostly Ceylon, Malabar and Coromandel), 1759-92. Two volumes.

168-73 Copies of papers sent overseas, including South Asia (mostly Ceylon), 1666-1804. Six volumes.

174 Alphabetical index to inv. nos 157 and 163-4 (see above) and the overseas letters, including references concerning South Asia, *c.* 1650. One volume.

175 List of *Krankenbezoekers* (visitors to patients), appointed on war vessels or dispatched by the VOC, including a few people sent to Ceylon and Bengal, 1781. One piece.

183 Note concerning the reorganization of the Dutch Reformed Church in Asia, by Marinus, partly regarding Ceylon, Cochin and Nagappattinam, eighteenth century. One piece.

185-90 Received papers concerning the Dutch Reformed Church in Asia, partly regarding South Asia, 1630-1791. Six volumes.

201-5 Papers received from Ceylon and, to a lesser extent, Coromandel concerning the Dutch Reformed Church there, 1631-1792. Five volumes. The microfiches kept at the *Centraal Bureau voor Genealogie* (The Hague) referred to as *Overige Archiefbronnen (OA): Noord-Holland*, 'Amsterdam ref', are probably copies of the papers dating from the period 1657-1792, see 4.4.

722 Alphabetical index and glossary of trade regions, persons and commodities, referring to VOC documents, including a number of references pertaining to South Asia, eighteenth century. One volume (no clear relation to the archives of the Amsterdam Classis).

Firma Hope & Co
Firm of Hope & Co

Access no.: 735
Inv. nos: 1-4259
Size: 185 metres
Period: 1679, 1725-1965, 1978
Inventory: A.M. Bendien and J.C.A. Blom, 'Inventaris van de archieven van de firma Hope & Co en van gelieerde bedrijven en personen (1679) 1725-1965 (1978)' (1996), with introduction and appendices

Getting its official name in 1762, Hope & Co started as a family firm in the early eighteenth century. Originally involved in trade, it focused on financing during the second half of the eighteenth century. The Hope family included Thomas (1704-79), representative of Stadtholder William V with the VOC, and Jan (1737-84), Director of the Amsterdam Chamber of the Company. See also *Dutch Sources on South Asia*, Vol. 1 (1.4.3 and 1.5.17). For papers concerning Bengal, see 6.1. Part of the archives has to be consulted on microfilm.

Firma Temminck en Van Twist
Firm of Temminck and Van Twist

Access no.: 188
Inv. nos: 1-144
Size: 0.52 metres
Period: 1781-1804
Inventory: P. Boeijkens, 'Inventaris van de archiefbestanden afkomstig van Cornelis van Twist en Temminck & Van Twist' (1999), with short introduction

The archives consist of documents originating from Cornelis van Twist (*c.* 1740-1823), who functioned as Bookkeeper at the *soldij kantoor* (pay office) and as clerk at the postal services of the Amsterdam Chamber of the VOC, and from Jacob Temminck (*c.* 1748-1822), Cashier at the *Ontvangkamer* (reception office) of the Amsterdam Chamber. They entered into association with each other as merchants under the name Temminck & Van Twist. The archives include documents concerning Diderick Thomas Fretz, *Commandeur* of Galle at the end of the eighteenth century. For these and other papers regarding Ceylon, see 4.1.

Brants family

Access no.: 88
Inv. nos: 1-1849
Size: 48 metres
Period: 1660-1942
Inventory: I.H. van Eeghen, *Inventaris van het familie-archief Brants* (Amsterdam, 1959/1991), with introduction, genealogical trees and indices

The Mennonite Brants family played an important economic role in Amsterdam during the VOC period and invested for instance in a great number of Company ships. Relatives included the Bevel and De Neufville families, members of which received letters from Ceylon and Bengal. See 4.1 and 6.1. The papers have to be consulted on microfilm.

De Graeff family

Access no.: 76
Inv. nos: 1-784
Size: 4 metres
Period: 1258-1863
Inventory: W.R. Veder, 'Het archief der familie De Graeff. Inventaris en regesten' (Amsterdam, 1914), with introduction and index

The De Graeff family of traders and government officials became very influential in Amsterdam during the seventeenth century. The archives include one document deriving from Pieter de Graeff (1638-1707) that seems to concern Bengal, see 6.1.

Sweers family

Access no.: 319
Inv. nos: 1-54
Size: 0.18 metres
Period: 1630-1777
Inventory: P. Boeijkens, 'Inventaris van de familiepapieren Sweers, ca. 1630-1769' (1996)

The archives include papers deriving from Arnout Sweers (born *c.* 1637), who served as VOC factor in Asia. For a document concerning Ceylon, see 4.1.

De Groot Jamin family

Access no.: 7
Inv. nos: 1-79
Size: 0.63 metres
Period: 1733-1813
Inventory: B.F. Schuurman Hess, 'Inventaris van het archief De Groot-Jamin 1733-1813' (1966, 1991)

The archives include documents from Jan de Groot, son of Gerrit de Groot. Both were booksellers. For a document concerning Ceylon, see 4.1.

Jacob de Flines

Access no.: 4
Inv. nos: 1-269 (in 51 folders)
Size: 0.09 metres
Period: 1722-8
Inventory: P. Boeykens, 'Inventaris van het archief van Jacob de Flines & Zonen' (1991), with index

Jacob de Flines possibly belonged to the De Flines family of traders, scholars and poets, chiefly based at Amsterdam. The archives consist entirely of letters received by De Flines and his sons, which are arranged alphabetically according to the place they were sent from. For papers concerning Surat and Ceylon, see 2.1 and 4.1.

Handschriften
Manuscripts

Access no.: 5059
Inv. nos: 1-255
Size: 35 metres
Period: 1303-20th century
Inventory: 'Inventaris van de handschriftenverzameling' (1986-8, 1993)

This collection of miscellaneous documents includes the Huydekoper collection (inv. nos 1-23), 1688-1803, deriving from Jan Elias Huydekoper van Maarseveen (1735-1808), and several other documents partly pertaining to the VOC and South Asia. For papers concerning Malabar, Coromandel and Bengal, see also 3.1, 5.1 and 6.1.

10 Various papers concerning the VOC, with many references to South Asia, originating from Huydekoper, 1726-84. One bundle. Including:
- (a) Report on direct shipping to South Asia, 1773.
- (b) Memorandum by Oudermeulen (?) about the VOC, with sections on South Asia, 1772.
- (c) Letter from Governor Pieter Haksteen of Coromandel (1765-71) to Governor Christiaan Lodewijk Senff of Malabar (1763-8), 1769.
- (d) Translation of a letter from a Jew at Surat to the Jew Ezekiel Rabbi at Cochin, 1769.
- (e) Considerations by Governor-General Jacob Mossel about the VOC, with sections on South Asia, 1752.

11 Various papers concerning the VOC, with many references to South Asia, originating from Huydekoper, 1785-1802. One bundle. Including:
- (a) Appendices to a memorandum by Crayvanger, Falk and Scholten, in reply to Titsingh, with sections on Coromandel, Bengal, Malabar and Surat, mostly concerning bookkeeping, *c.* 1790.

86 Notes of M.A. Beels (1728-89) concerning the VOC, including sections on Ceylon, Coromandel, Bengal, Surat and Malabar. One volume.

146 Various surveys and lists concerning the VOC, including sections on Bengal, Coromandel, Ceylon, Malabar and Surat, after 1765. One volume.

Bibliotheek
Library

Inventory: – data base
– index cards

The collection of the library includes a few items that may be considered archival material. Some of these documents were formerly part of the old Amsterdam archives, accessible through the inventory by P. Scheltema, *Inventaris van het Amsterdamsche archief*, 3 vols (Amsterdam, 1866-74). In addition to the papers described in this guide, there are other documents (mostly printed) concerning the VOC. For papers regarding Bengal, see 6.1.

1.1.3. *GELDERS ARCHIEF* (Arnhem) ARCHIVES OF GUELDERLAND

For general surveys, see G. Verbeek a.o. (eds), *Gelders archievenoverzicht* (Zutphen, 1995), pp. 33-101, 123-47, *De archieven in Gelderland* (*Overzichten van de archieven en verzamelingen in de openbare archiefbewaarplaatsen in Nederland*, Vol. 2) (Alphen aan den Rijn, 1979), pp. 1-74, 86-100, 194-6, 198 (somewhat outdated), and the repository's web site (see Appendix II, 1.3).

Stad Arnhem
Town of Arnhem

Access no.: 2000
Inv. nos: 1-6388
Size: 170 metres
Period: 1255-1851
Inventory: D.P.M. Graswinckel, *Het oud-archief der gemeente Arnhem*, 3 vols (The Hague, 1935), with introduction, appendices and index

The old archives of Arnhem include one item that partly concerns Malabar, see 3.1.

Houses of Waardenburg and Neerijnen

Access no.: 0439
Inv. nos: 1-3082
Size: 38.5 metres
Period: 1288-1970
Inventory: A.P. van Schilfgaarde, 'Inventaris van het archief van de Huizen Waardenburg en Neerijnen' (1980, 1985)

The archives of these Houses, based at Neerijnen (also called Clingelenburch), include papers originating from Isaak Augustijn Rumph, Governor of Ceylon between 1716 and 1723. See 4.1.

Rosendael Castle

Access no.: 0525
Size: 65 metres
Period: 1368-20th century
Inventory: card tray

Also known as House of Rosendael, these archives derive from various families based at Rozendaal. The papers include documents originating from VOC officials such as Willem van Outhoorn (Governor-General 1691-1704) and Joan van Hoorn (Governor-General 1704-9) and correspondence between the Dutch Republic and Asia. For documents relating to Ceylon, see 4.1.

958 Various papers concerning the VOC, 1735-45, including a report regarding the Company's fortifications, with sections on South Asia, 1735. One bundle.

1552 Drafts (?) of letters sent by Lubbert Adolph Torck to various people in Asia, 1740-54, including Lambert van Ruyven, factor at Hooghly, 1742, 1745-6, and Stephanus Rinck, serving at Masulipatam, 1745, 1750. One volume.

Bosch and Van Rosenthal families and relatives

Access no.: 0724

Inv. nos: 1-1187
Size: 7.5 metres
Period: 1418-1952
Inventory: F.F.J.M. Geraedts, 'Inventaris van de archieven van de families Bosch, van (von) Rosenthal en aanverwanten, 1418, 1539, 1484, 1600-1952' (1986)

The archives of the Culemborg-based Bosch and Van Rosenthal families include documents originating from Lucas Bosch (1645-1723), who served as priest in the East Indies. For papers concerning Ceylon and Coromandel, see 4.1 and 5.1.

Brantsen family

Access no.: 0452
Inv. nos: 1-752
Size: 10 metres
Period: 1401-1916
Inventory: R. Wartena, 'Het archief van de familie Brantsen' (1966), with introduction, genealogical trees and supplement

These archives include papers originating from Jacob Mossel and Adriaan Pla (inv. nos 285A1-7G). Mossel (1704-61) served as Governor of Coromandel between 1738 and 1743, and as Governor-General from 1750 to 1761 (among other functions). His granddaughter Andrea Helena Mossel (1774-1840) married Gerhard Brantsen (1772-1814) in 1800. Adriaan Pla (d. 1737), Governor of Coromandel between 1730 and 1733, was the stepfather of Jacob Mossel's wife Adriana Appels (1714-43). For papers and drawings concerning Ceylon and Coromandel, see 4.1, 5.1 and 5.6.

Van Voërst van Lynden family

Access no.: 0491
Inv. nos: 1-195
Size: 1.5 metres
Period: 1557-1930
Inventory: A.P. van Schilfgaarde, 'Inventaris van het archief van de familie Van Voërst van Lynden' (1965), with introduction and genealogical trees

The archives include documents originating from the Van Eck family (inv. nos 92-127), members of which married into the Van Lynden and Vijgh families. Relevant for South Asia are papers relating to Lubbert Jan van Eck, Governor of Coromandel (1758-61) and Ceylon (1761-5). See 4.1 and 5.1.

1.1.4. *DRENTS ARCHIEF* (Assen) ARCHIVES OF DRENTHE

For general surveys, see P. Brood and A.J.M. den Teuling, *De archieven in Drenthe (Overzichten van de archieven en verzamelingen in de openbare archiefbewaarplaatsen in Nederland*, Vol. 1) (Alphen aan den Rijn, 1979) (somewhat outdated), and the repository's web site (see Appendix II, 1.4).

House of Mensinge at Roden

Access no.: 0616
Inv. nos: 1-1830
Size: *c.* 27 metres
Period: 1376-1952
Inventory: J. Bos and W.J. Kuppers, 'Inventaris van het archief van het Huis Mensinge te Roden (1376-1952)' (1986), with introduction, genealogical trees, concordance and indices

From the fourteenth century onward, several families lived in the House of Mensinge at Roden, including (after 1765) the Ellents family, originating from the village of Anloo. One of its members was Coenraad Ellents Junior (1692-1761), a relative of Jan Albert Sichterman (1692-1764), who served the VOC in Bengal between 1717 and 1744. For some letters written by or otherwise pertaining to the latter, see 6.1. For more information on Jan Albert Sichterman, see 1.1.8, *Groninger Archieven*, Sichterman family archives.

Losse publikaties, plakkaten e.d.
Separate publications, proclamations, etc.

Access no.: 0585
Inv. nos: 1-1138
Size: 1.5 metres
Period: 1618-1901
Inventory: M.J.M. de Grauw and J.D. Jansen, 'Plakkaten' (1985), with short introduction and index

This is a collection of pamphlets, edicts, etc., concerning a wide range of subjects. For a document regarding Ceylon, see 4.1.

1.1.5. *REGIONAAL HISTORISCH CENTRUM BERGEN OP ZOOM* REGIONAL HISTORICAL CENTRE BERGEN OP ZOOM

For general surveys, see *De archieven in Noord-Brabant* (*Overzichten van de archieven en verzamelingen in de openbare archiefbewaarplaatsen in Nederland*, Vol. 4) (Alphen aan den Rijn, 1980), pp. 53-69 (somewhat outdated), and the repository's web site (see Appendix II, 1.5).

Notariële archieven
Notarial archives

Inv. nos: 1-1268
Size: 54 metres
Period: 1593-1842
Inventory: J.A. ten Cate, *De notariële archieven in Noord-Brabant* (The Hague,

1957), pp. 342-73, with introduction, appendix and indices to names and residences of notaries; see also below

The archives have been arranged chronologically according to notary. Relevant documents can be found by means of a database (available on Internet), which contains summaries of the notarial acts. Only part of the archives (mostly seventeenth-century documents) has been entered so far. Among other functions, the data base includes the possibility of free text search. For a few documents concerning Ceylon and Coromandel, see 4.1 and 5.1.

1.1.6. *GEMEENTEARCHIEF DELFT*
MUNICIPAL ARCHIVES OF DELFT

For general surveys, see J.A.M.Y. Bos-Rops a.o., *De archieven in Zuid-Holland*, 2 vols (*Overzichten van de archieven en verzamelingen in de openbare archiefbewaarplaatsen in Nederland*, Vol. 10) (Alphen aan den Rijn, 1983), pp. 171-204 (somewhat outdated), and the repository's web site (see Appendix II, 1.6).

Weeshuis der Gereformeerden binnen Delft
Orphanage of the Dutch Reformed Church at Delft

Access no.: 201
Inv. nos: 1-369
Size: 25 metres
Period: 1369-1943
Inventory: in typescript (1996), with introduction, appendices and index

This orphanage developed from the *Heilige Geesthuis* (house of the Holy Spirit), also called the new orphanage. It acquired its present name in the nineteenth century.

205-6 Registers of the names of orphan boys who sailed to the East and West Indies, with financial surveys, including a few references to orphans in South Asia (mostly Colombo), 1620-1793. Two volumes. A data base with these names is available on Internet (see Appendix II, 1.6).

206a Papers concerning orphan boys who went to the East Indies, including a few references to orphans in South Asia (mostly Colombo), 1724-99. One folder.

Weeskamer Delft
Orphan Board of Delft

Access no.: 72
Size: 178 metres
Period: 1550-1920
Inventory: in preparation

At the time of writing, these archives were being inventoried. The inv. nos given below are all provisional.

24 Ia-43 II Papers received from various orphan boards in the East Indies (mostly at Batavia) and the Cape of Good Hope, including some papers received from South Asia, 1700-72, 1774-94, 1796. Inv. nos 7a-10e and 126 may also contain relevant papers.

1.1.7. *STREEKARCHIEF MIDDEN-HOLLAND* (Gouda)
REGIONAL ARCHIVES CENTRAL HOLLAND

For general surveys, see J.A.M.Y. Bos-Rops a.o., *De archieven in Zuid-Holland*, 2 vols (*Overzichten van de archieven en verzamelingen in de openbare archiefbewaarplaatsen in Nederland*, Vol. 10) (Alphen aan den Rijn, 1983), pp. 271-90, 485, 491, 690-1, 702 (somewhat outdated), and the repository's web site (see Appendix II, 1.7).

Varia
Miscellany

Access no.: 200
Inv. nos: *c.* 2500
Size: *c.* 25 metres
Period: 14th century–up to the present
Inventory: data base

This collection consists of miscellaneous papers that cannot be added to any other archives or collection, as well as copies of documents concerning Gouda and environs that are kept elsewhere. For a document partly concerning the Maldives, see 4.1.

1.1.8. *GRONINGER ARCHIEVEN*
ARCHIVES OF GRONINGEN

For general surveys, see J.F.J. van den Broek a.o. (eds), *De archieven in Groningen* (*Overzichten van de archieven en verzamelingen in de openbare archiefbewaarplaatsen in Nederland*, Vol. 5) (Alphen aan den Rijn, 1980), pp. 31-117 (somewhat outdated), and the repository's web site (see Appendix II, 1.8).

Plaatselijke gerechten in het Oldambt
Local courts of justice in the Oldambt

Access no.: 731
Inv. nos: 1-7451
Size: 70.5 metres
Period: 1596-1811
Inventory: 'Inventaris van de archieven van plaatselijke gerechten in het Oldambt' (1994), with introduction and index

These are the archives of several local courts of justice in the region of the Oldambt, in the east of the province of Groningen. The papers deriving from the court of the Wold-Oldambt include some papers pertaining to Bengal, see 6.1.

Van Bolhuis family

Access no.: 493
Inv. nos: 1-527
Size: 3 metres
Period: 17th-19th centuries
Inventory: F.J. Hulst, 'Inventaris van het archief van de families Van Bolhuis, Arkema en Van Zeeburgh te Warffum' (1997), with introduction, genealogical notes, appendices and index

Several members of this family held high administrative and juridical functions in the town of Warffum and its surroundings. The papers originating from Michiel van Bolhuis Junior (1713-64) and his wife Alagonda Beckeringh (1710-80) include correspondence with Ceylon, see 4.1.

Sichterman family

Access no.: 868
Inv. nos: 1-38
Size: 4.75 metres
Period: 17th-20th centuries
Inventory: B.A.C. Velema, 'Plaatsingslijst van het archief van de families Sichterman en Alberda' (1996)

These archives include papers deriving from Jan Albert Sichterman (1692-1764) and his wife Sibilla Volkera Sadelijn (1699-1781), who got married in 1721 at Hooghly. Sichterman took service with the VOC in 1716 and spent most of his career in Bengal. During the years *c.* 1719-21 and 1725-34 he stayed at Cossimbazar. The remaining periods were chiefly spent in Hooghly, between 1734 and 1744 as *Directeur*. Sibilla Volkera Sadelijn, born at Hooghly, was the daughter of *Directeur* Jacob Sadelijn of Bengal (1727-31). Relevant papers all concern Bengal, see 6.1.

1.1.9. ARCHIEFDIENST VOOR KENNEMERLAND (Haarlem) ARCHIVAL SERVICE FOR KENNEMERLAND

For general surveys, see *De archieven in Noord-Holland* (*Overzichten van de archieven en verzamelingen in de openbare archiefbewaarplaatsen in Nederland*, Vol. 7) (Alphen aan den Rijn, 1981), pp. 289-339, 340-2, 345 (somewhat outdated), and the repository's web site (see Appendix II, 1.9). See also 1.6.1.

Van Sypesteyn family

Inv. nos: 1-1676
Size: 10.4 metres
Period: *c.* 1437-1937
Inventory: S.M. van Zanten Jut, 'Inventaris van het familiearchief Van Sypesteyn', 2 vols (1969), with introduction, genealogical trees and indices

These archives include a few papers deriving from Gerrit Reessen Gerritsz Junior (born 1765), who was related to the Van Sypesteyn family and functioned as Book-keeper at the Amsterdam Chamber of the VOC. For a document concerning Ceylon, see 4.1.

1.1.10. *RIJKSARCHIEF IN NOORD-HOLLAND* (Haarlem) STATE ARCHIVES IN NORTH HOLLAND

For general surveys, see H. van Felius (ed.), *Rijksarchief in Noord-Holland. Overzicht van de archieven* (Haarlem, 1995), *De archieven in Noord-Holland* (*Overzichten van de archieven en verzamelingen in de openbare archiefbewaarplaatsen in Nederland*, Vol. 7) (Alphen aan den Rijn, 1981), pp. 89-116 (somewhat outdated), and the repository's web site (see Appendix II, 1.10).

Notarissen in het Rijksarchief in Noord-Holland, 1552-1842
Notaries in the State Archives in North Holland

Access no.: 185
Inv. nos: 1-6581
Period: 1552-1842
Inventory: 'Archieven van notarissen in het Rijksarchief in Noord-Holland, 1552-1842' (1993), with short introduction and appendix; see also below

These archives consist chiefly of notarial protocols, drawn up by notaries from large parts of the province of North Holland. The archives are arranged alphabetically according to the residences and subsequently the surnames of the notaries. All materials up to 1812 have been put on microfilm. The films also cover documents kept elsewhere, including all known papers concerning South Asia (deriving from notaries in Enkhuizen and Zaandam), the originals of which have to be consulted at the *Westfries Archief* (see 1.1.16) and *Gemeentearchief Zaanstad* (see 1.1.17). Geographical and other indices are available for sections of the archives. These include ninety per cent of the materials of notaries from Enkhuizen (the years 1660-80 are mostly not covered), all documents of Zaandam but none of the papers of notaries active in Hoorn. For papers concerning Surat, Malabar, Ceylon, Coromandel and Bengal, see 2.1, 3.1, 4.1, 5.1 and 6.1.

Oud-Katholiek Bisdom Haarlem
Old Catholic Diocese Haarlem

Access no.: 225
Inv. nos: 1-600
Size: 12.5 metres
Period: (1514) 1561-1967 (1981)
Inventory: J.R. Persman, 'Archieven van het Bisdom Haarlem van de Oud-Katholieke kerk (1514) 1561-1967 (1981)' (1985), with introduction, appendices and indices to personal and geographical names

The Diocese of Haarlem was founded in 1559, when Utrecht became an Archbishopric. Both dioceses belong to a group of bishoprics disagreeing with various Papal doctrines issued from Rome in the course of time (see also 1.1.23., *Het Utrechts Archief, Oud-Katholieke Kerk in Nederland (OKN): Oud-Bisschoppelijke Clerezij (OKN / OBC)*). The archives include papers originating from the Chapter of Haarlem, one of which partly concerns South Asia.

366 Papers received by Justus Modersohn, Canon and priest at Amsterdam, 1663-87, including comments by Modersohn (?) on the Dutch Reformed priest Philippus Baldaeus' work *Nauwkeurige beschryvinge van Malabar en Choromandel, derhalver aangrenzende ryken, en het machtige eyland Ceylon. Nevens een omstandige en grondigh doorzochte ontdekking en wederlegginge van de afgoderye der Oost-Indische heydenen* (published in 1672 at Amsterdam), 1672 (?). One folder.

Hollandsche Maatschappij der Wetenschappen
Dutch Society of Sciences

Access no.:	444
Inv. nos:	1-482
Size:	31.2 metres
Period:	1752-1975 (1986)
Inventory:	L. Beelen-Driehuyzen, 'Inventaris van het archief van de Hollandsche Maatschappij der Wetenschappen 1752-1975 (1986)' (1998), with introduction, appendices and index

The Society, founded in 1752, is the oldest scientific society in the Netherlands. It aims at the promotion of sciences, in particular natural sciences, by publishing treatises, awarding prizes and organising meetings. During the VOC period, the Society received a number of scientific treatises with respect to the East Indies, including South Asia. Note that the correspondence of the Society (inv. nos 27-103 concern the years 1752-1825) may include more papers pertaining to South Asia than those described here or mentioned in the appendix of the inventory. The minutes of the Society may also very well include relevant material (inv. nos 12-16 cover the period 1752-1839, inv. no. 22 is a modern-day index to personal names). For papers and drawings regarding Ceylon and Bengal, see 4.1, 4.6 and 6.1.

48 Papers received in 1773, including a Hindustani grammar with a wordlist in Latin and Hindustani and surveys of the Persian and Devanagari alphabet, sent by Iman Willem Falck, with an introductory letter relating to naturalia in South Asia (both to be found in the file 'buitenland'). One bundle. For a short description, see Sliggers and Besselink, *Het verdwenen museum*, pp. 147, 154 (see Supplement I: Bibliography, no. 152).

75 Papers received in 1797, including essays about Hinduism, with accompanying letter, by J. Hafner (Jacob Haafner?). One bundle.

1.1.11. *HAAGS GEMEENTEARCHIEF* MUNICIPAL ARCHIVES OF THE HAGUE

For general surveys, see 'Overzicht van de archieven berustende in het Haags Gemeentearchief' (1998), J.A.M.Y. Bos-Rops a.o., *De archieven in Zuid-Holland*, 2 vols (*Overzichten van de archieven en verzamelingen in de openbare archiefbewaarplaatsen in Nederland*, Vol. 10) (Alphen aan den Rijn, 1983), pp. 293-403 (somewhat outdated), and the repository's web site (see Appendix II, 1.11).

Gemeentebestuur, 'Oud archief'
Town council, 'Old archives'

Access no.: 350
Inv. nos: 46-170, 606-2893, 3726-4220, 4610-21, 4662-6364
Size: 87 metres
Period: 1313-1815
Inventory: G. 't Hart, 'Inventaris van het oud-archief der gemeente 's-Gravenhage' (1957), with introduction, appendices and index

The old archives of the town of The Hague (officially 's-Gravenhage) include one document concerning Bengal, see 6.1.

Weeskamer
Orphan board

Access no.: 402
Inv. nos: 1-3077
Size: 62.6 metres
Period: 1482-1852
Inventory: F.C. van der Meer van Kuffeler, 'Inventaris van het archief van de weeskamer van 's-Gravenhage, 1482-1852' (1939), with introduction and index

The orphan board was set up around 1480, after The Hague was granted the privilege to do so in 1451. During the VOC period, it maintained close relations with the orphan board at Batavia. In addition to the papers described below, inv. nos 18 and 21 also concern the East Indies.

16-17 Letters from orphan boards in the East Indies, including South Asia, mostly Colombo, 1651-1806. Four bundles.

Notarissen ter standplaats 's-Gravenhage I
Notaries at The Hague I

Access no.: 372
Inv. nos: 1-6685
Size: 450 metres
Period: 1597-1842
Inventory: in typescript, with introduction, appendices and index to notaries; see also below

The old notarial archives of The Hague are arranged more or less in chronological order according to notary. They may contain more documents pertaining to South Asia than just the one described below, but only indices to personal names are available.

326, f. 238 Notarial act of Josua de Putter, with signatures of 'Gerrit Mosopatam' (probably from Masulipatam) in Tamil, and of Philippus Baldaeus, 1667. Described and reproduced in Beumer, 'Philippus Baldaeus and Gerrit Mosopatam' (see Supplement I: Bibliography, no. 123).

Waals-Hervormde gemeente te 's-Gravenhage en Voorburg
Walloon Reformed community at The Hague and Voorburg

Access no.: 241
Inv. nos: 1-1566
Size: 49.6 metres
Period: 1563-1963
Inventory: in typescript, with introduction

Initially served from Delft, the Walloon Reformed community at The Hague had its own preacher from 1591 onward. For a document concerning Bengal, see 6.1.

1.1.12. *STREEKARCHIVARIAAT NOORDWEST-VELUWE: HARDERWIJK* REGIONAL ARCHIVES NORTHWEST VELUWE: HARDERWIJK

For general surveys, see G. Verbeek a.o. (eds), *Gelders archievenoverzicht* (Zutphen, 1995), pp. 241-52, *De archieven in Gelderland* (*Overzichten van de archieven en verzamelingen in de openbare archiefbewaarplaatsen in Nederland*, Vol. 2) (Alphen aan den Rijn, 1979), pp. 144-5 (somewhat outdated), and the repository's web site (see Appendix II, 1.12).

Oud-archief der gemeente Harderwijk
Old archives of the municipality of Harderwijk

Inv. nos: 1-2084
Size: *c.* 60 metres
Period: 1190-1853
Inventory: P. Berends, *Het oud-archief der gemeente Harderwijk*, 2 vols (Harderwijk, 1935), with introduction, appendix and index

These archives include papers deriving from Ernst Brinck (*c.* 1582-1649), envoy to Constantinople in 1612 and from 1620 onward *Schepen* (sheriff) or Burgomaster of Harderwijk. In addition to the documents described below, the other papers originating from Brinck (inv. nos 2013-61) may very well contain references to South Asia. For papers concerning Ceylon, see also 4.1.

2052 Extracts by Ernst Brinck from journals and from other texts concerning travels to the East and West Indies, including what seem to be annual news surveys regarding Asia with short references to South Asia, 1640s, and a survey of Dutch and Portuguese possessions in the East Indies with sections on Gujarat and Hindustan, Malabar, Ceylon, Coromandel and Bengal, 1640s (?) (ff. 40-2). One volume.

2055 Two texts, the second of which concerns various currencies and other means of payment in the East Indies, including short sections on Bengal, 'Cattigam' (Chittagong?) and various regions in and around Coromandel, Gujarat and Konkan, as observed by Henrick Jansz. Hollander, *c.* 1620 (?). One volume.

2057 Personal observations and other notes by Ernst Brinck pertaining to birds, arranged according to species, including a few short references to South Asian birds, such as a turkey from Calicut (f. 45v), first half of the seventeenth century. One volume. See also inv. no. 2060, below.

2058 Personal observations and other notes by Ernst Brinck pertaining to mammals, reptiles, amphibians, insects and possibly other animals, arranged according to species, including a few short references to South Asian animals, such as elephants in Surat (f. 5) and a caiman at Batticaloa (f. 96), first half of the seventeenth century. One volume. See also inv. no. 2060, below.

2059 Personal observations and other notes by Ernst Brinck pertaining to fish and other maritime beings and products, arranged according to species, including a few short references to South Asian subjects, such as mermaids off the Coromandel Coast (f. 71) and shells from the Maldives, first half of the seventeenth century. One volume. See also inv. no. 2060, below.

2060 Separate notes by Ernst Brinck concerning various topics, first half of the seventeenth century. 22 folders. Including:

folder II Notes concerning the East Indies, including South Asia, 1615-45.

folder XVII Personal observations and other notes pertaining to various animals, supplementary to inv. nos 2057-9, see above.

1.1.13. *STREEKARCHIVARIAAT NOORD-VELUWE: HATTEM* REGIONAL ARCHIVES NORTH VELUWE: HATTEM

For general surveys, see G. Verbeek a.o. (eds), *Gelders archievenoverzicht* (Zutphen, 1995), pp. 252-8, *De archieven in Gelderland* (*Overzichten van de archieven en verzamelingen in de openbare archiefbewaarplaatsen in Nederland*, Vol. 2) (Alphen aan den Rijn, 1979), pp. 146-8 (somewhat outdated), and the repository's web site (see Appendix II, 1.13).

Oud archief van de stad Hattem
Old archives of the town of Hattem

Inv. nos: 1-1511
Size: 28 metres

Period: 1176-1795
Inventory: J. Rinzema and G. Kouwenhoven, 'Inventaris van het oud archief van de stad Hattem 1176-1795'

The old archives of Hattem include a ship's log by Willem Charles van Braam (1773-1847), who was born at Bengal, served as *Adelborst* (midshipman) and later became Burgomaster of Hattem.

860 Journal by W.C. van Braam of the warship Zephir under captain J.O. Vaillant sailing to the East Indies, including Malabar, Ceylon and Coromandel, 1788-93. One volume.

1.1.14. *HISTORISCH INFORMATIECENTRUM HELMOND* HISTORICAL INFORMATION CENTRE HELMOND

For general surveys, see *De archieven in Noord-Brabant* (*Overzichten van de archieven en verzamelingen in de openbare archiefbewaarplaatsen in Nederland*, Vol. 4) (Alphen aan den Rijn, 1980), pp. 457-66 (somewhat outdated), and the repository's web site (see Appendix II, 1.14).

Van der Brugghen van Croy family

Access no.: 87
Inv. nos: 1-974, 1-55
Size: 4.5 metres
Period: 1522-1905
Inventory: L. van Zalinge-Spooren, 'Archief van de familie Van der Brugghen van Croy (1522-) 1755-1783 (-1905)' (1989), with introduction and genealogical notes

These archives include papers originating from Joan Gideon Loten (1710-89), Governor of Ceylon between 1752 and 1757 (inv. nos 753-79). His daughter Arnoldina Deliana Cornelia (1734-56) married Dirk Willem van der Brugghen (1717-70), who also served the VOC in Asia. For papers concerning Surat and Ceylon, see 2.1 and 4.1. The archives appear to be related to some manuscripts originating from the *Groot-Seminarie* (Great Seminary) at Haaren kept at the *Bibliotheek Universiteit Tilburg* (see 1.2.8) and the *Archief Bisdom 's-Hertogenbosch* (see 1.4.2).

1.1.15. *BRABANTS HISTORISCH INFORMATIE CENTRUM: DEN BOSCH* HISTORICAL INFORMATION CENTRE OF BRABANT: DEN BOSCH

For general surveys, see *De archieven in Noord-Brabant* (*Overzichten van de archieven en verzamelingen in de openbare archiefbewaarplaatsen in Nederland*, Vol. 4) (Alphen aan den Rijn, 1980), pp. 1-51 (somewhat outdated), and the repository's web site (see Appendix II, 1.15).

Aanwinsten
Acquisitions

Access no.: 339

Inv. nos: 1-547
Size: 7 metres
Period: 1280-1981
Inventory: checklist, with indices to subjects, topographical names and persons

This collection consists of separate papers acquired in the course of time. It includes some material concerning Ceylon, see 4.1.

1.1.16. *WESTFRIES ARCHIEF* (Hoorn) ARCHIVES OF WEST FRIESLAND

For general surveys, see *De archieven in Noord-Holland* (*Overzichten van de archieven en verzamelingen in de openbare archiefbewaarplaatsen in Nederland*, Vol. 7) (Alphen aan den Rijn, 1981), pp. 187-237 (somewhat outdated), and the repository's web site (see Appendix II, 1.16).

Stad Hoorn
Town of Hoorn

Inv. nos: 1-*c.* 3182
Size: 100 metres
Period: 1356–1815
Inventory: C.J. Gonnet (and R.D. Baart de la Faille), *Inventaris van het archief der stad Hoorn* (Haarlem, 1918), with introduction and index, additions in manuscript

The old archives of the town of Hoorn, where one of the VOC Chambers was seated, include some papers concerning the Company (inv. nos 1812, 2566, 2852; old nos 443-5), but none of these relate to South Asia.

2321 List of reports with destinations of orphans of the Civil Orphanage who sailed to the East Indies including South Asia, 1685-1797. One volume (old no. 956). (Inv. nos 2458-60 (old nos 1059-61) also concern children who departed to the East Indies but these documents do not mention destinations.)

Stad Enkhuizen
Town of Enkhuizen

Inv. nos: 1-*c.* 2030
Size: 55 metres
Period: 1356-1813
Inventory: C.J. Gonnet, 'Inventaris van het archief der stad Enkhuizen', in *VROA* (1892), with additions in typescript and manuscript

The old archives of the town of Enkhuizen, seat of one of the VOC Chambers, include a number of documents concerning the Company (inv. nos 1150, 1522-89a; old nos 376-426), which originate from Jan Minne, Director at the Enkhuizen Chamber of the Company. Inv. nos 1568-86, 1589 (old no. 423) are ship's logs. For papers concerning Surat, Malabar, Ceylon, Coromandel and Bengal, see also 2.1, 3.1, 4.1, 5.1 and 6.1.

1533 Letters of Jan Minne concerning the VOC, with part B containing notes, descriptions, extracts from other documents, etc., regarding South Asia, 1730-60. Two folders (old no. 387).

1540 Papers concerning or deriving from Jacob Mossel, partly dating from his period as Governor of Coromandel (1738-43). One folder (old no. 394). Including:
- (a) Advice concerning trade and coinage in Coromandel and other parts of India, with list of contents, 1739 (?).

1546 Various papers concerning the VOC. One folder (old no. 401). Including:
- (a) Register of documents received or drawn up at Ceylon and Coromandel, 1682.

1557 Papers concerning cargo for the East Indies, including an *eis* (order for supply) for Ceylon, 1739, and several general *eisen*, 1725-65. Two folders (old no. 412).

1558 Papers concerning cargo from the East Indies, including documents regarding the factories in South Asia, 1624-1768. Two folders (old no. 413).

Oud-notariële archieven Enkhuizen
Old notarial archives of Enkhuizen

Inv. nos: 808-1608
Period: 1557-1842
Inventory: *Inventarissen van Rijks- en Andere Archieven*, 3 (1930), pp. 627-30, with index to names and residences of notaries, modern revision; see also below

The archives have been arranged chronologically according to notary. Relevant documents can be found with the help of geographical and other indices (covering around 90 per cent of the archives) available at the *Rijksarchief in Noord-Holland* at Haarlem (see 1.1.10, *Notarissen in het Rijksarchief in Noord-Holland*, 1552-1842). This repository also keeps microfilms of these archives (as well as microfilms of the notarial archives of Hoorn, which have not been indexed, however). For documents concerning Surat, Malabar, Ceylon, Coromandel and Bengal, see 2.1, 3.1, 4.1, 5.1 and 6.1.

1.1.17. *GEMEENTEARCHIEF ZAANSTAD* (Koog aan de Zaan) MUNICIPAL ARCHIVES OF ZAANSTAD

For general surveys, see *De archieven in Noord-Holland* (*Overzichten van de archieven en verzamelingen in de openbare archiefbewaarplaatsen in Nederland*, Vol. 7) (Alphen aan den Rijn, 1981), pp. 269-86 (somewhat outdated), and the repository's web site (see Appendix II, 1.17).

Oud-notariëel archief Zaandam
Old notarial archives of Zaandam

Inv. nos: 5750-6388
Size: 72.5 metres
Period: 1633-1842
Inventory: *Inventarissen van Rijks- en Andere Archieven*, 3 (1930), pp. 667-9, with index to names and residences of notaries; see also below

The archives have been arranged chronologically according to notary. Relevant documents can be found with the help of geographical and other indices available at the *Rijksarchief in Noord-Holland* at Haarlem (see 1.1.10, *Notarissen in het Rijksarchief in Noord-Holland*, 1552-1842). That repository also keeps microfilms of the archives described here. For documents concerning Ceylon and Bengal, see 4.1 and 6.1.

Library

Size: *c.* 14000 items
Inventory: catalogue on index cards

The library consists chiefly of published works but includes a manuscript pertaining to the Fishery Coast, see 4.1.

1.1.18. *TRESOAR, FRYSK HISTOARYSK EN LETTERKUNDICH SINTRUM* (Leeuwarden) TRESOAR, FRIESIAN HISTORICAL AND LITERARY CENTRE

For general surveys, see P. Nieuwland (ed.), *De archieven in Fryslân* (*Overzichten van de archieven en verzamelingen in de openbare archiefbewaarplaatsen in Nederland*, Vol. 12) (Alphen aan den Rijn, 1987), pp. 19-119 (somewhat outdated), and the repository's web site (see Appendix II, 1.18).

Staten van Friesland, 1580-1795
States of Friesland

Access no.: 5
Inv. nos: 1-7497
Size: *c.* 100 metres
Period: 1580-1795
Inventory: S.P. de Jong, J.A. Schuur and P.M. Peucker, *Inventaris van de archieven van gewestelijke bestuursinstellingen van Friesland, 1580-1795* (Leeuwarden, 1998), with introduction and indices; access no. 5.26 is an eight-volume list of summaries (with indices) of the *resoluties* (proceedings) of the States of Friesland

The States of Friesland were the main government body of the province between 1580 and 1795. The *resoluties* (proceedings) of the meetings of the States occasionally deal with the East Indies. For a document concerning Bengal, see 6.1.

Friese Stadhouders
Friesian Stadtholders

Access no.: 7
Inv. nos: 1-813
Size: *c.* 30 metres
Period: 1584-1777
Inventory: A.P. van Nienes and M. Bruggeman (eds), *Archieven van de Friese stadhouders. Inventarissen van de archieven van de Friese stadhouders van Willem Lodewijk tot en met Willem V, 1584-1795* (Hilversum, The Hague and Leeuwarden, 2002), pp. 355-617, with introduction, genealogical tree, appendices and indices to personal and geographical names and to subjects

The Stadtholders of Friesland (usually serving Groningen and Drenthe as well), whose secretariat was located at the Friesian capital Leeuwarden, belonged to a branch of the Nassau family. The Stadtholders of the western provinces belonged to the Orange branch of this family. After the extinction of that branch, their Friesian counterparts moved to The Hague in 1747 to become Stadtholders of all provinces of the Republic. The secretariat at Leeuwarden, however, continued as a separate administrative body until 1777. The archives contain a few documents concerning the VOC, which probably originate from Artus Gijsels, member of the Council of the Indies in the 1630s. In 1648 he negotiated with Stadtholder Willem Frederik and the States of Friesland (see above) about the possibility to set up a Friesian East India Company. For a paper originating from Malabar, see 3.1.

658 Remonstrance of Artus Gijsels, Commander of the return fleet, to the Gentlemen XVII, including sections on Surat, Goa, Bijapur and Vengurla, Ceylon, Coromandel and Bengal, 1638. One volume.

Van Eysinga-Vegelin van Claerbergen family

Access no.: 323-01
Inv. nos: 1-1343
Size: 40 metres
Period: 1429-1978
Inventory: in typescript, with supplement (revision of S.J. Fockema Andreae, *Huis- en familiearchieven Van Eysinga-Vegelin van Claerbergen* (Leeuwarden, 1965))

Many members of this family were government officials, as a result of which the archives include a great number of documents relating to the functions in question. Inv. nos 715-19 concern the VOC.

716a VOC bookkeeping, including expenses and profits of Bengal (1660-1712),

Coromandel (1660-1712), Ceylon (1661-1713), Malabar (1671-4, 1685-1713) and Surat (1660-1713), *c.* 1720. One volume.

Handschriften, afkomstig van de Provinciale Bibliotheek van Friesland
Manuscripts, originating from the Provincial Library of Friesland

Access no.: 347
Inv. nos: 1-1344
Period: 15th-20th centuries
Inventory: in typescript, with indices

This collection consists of documents that were transferred from the Library because of their possible relevance to the visitors to the present repository. For papers concerning Ceylon, see 4.1.

1.1.19. *REGIONAAL ARCHIEF LEIDEN*
REGIONAL ARCHIVES LEIDEN

For general surveys, see J.A.M.Y. Bos-Rops a.o., *De archieven in Zuid-Holland*, 2 vols (*Overzichten van de archieven en verzamelingen in de openbare archiefbewaarplaatsen in Nederland*, Vol. 10) (Alphen aan den Rijn, 1983), pp. 430-72, 624, 691, 705 (somewhat outdated), and the repository's web site (see Appendix II, 1.19).

Stadsarchief, 1574-1816
Town archives

Access no.: 501A
Inv. nos: 1-10738
Size: 439 metres
Period: 1253-1897
Inventory: R.C.J. van Maanen, *Inventaris van het stadsarchief van Leiden (1253) 1574-1816 (1897)* (Leiden, 1986), with introduction and index

The old archives of Leiden include several documents concerning the VOC (inv. nos 6708-26) because from 1647 the town was entitled to appoint one director in the Amsterdam Chamber of the Company. For papers concerning Bengal, see also 6.1.

6712 Report of the Gentlemen XVII concerning the trade with the East Indies, including sections on Malabar, Surat, Vengurla and Goa, Ceylon, Coromandel, and Pegu and Bengal, 1650. One quire.
6714 Lists of letters sent by the Gentlemen XVII since 1626, including letters to South Asia, 1735. Two pieces.
6721 Papers concerning the VOC and its trade with the East Indies, 1699-1774, with nos 15 and 27 regarding textiles traded by the VOC and the EIC between Bengal, Bombay and other locations, 1728, 1762. One folder.

6723 Notes from correspondence between 1777 and 1778 between the GG&C and the Directors of the VOC, including sections on Bengal, Coromandel, Ceylon, Malabar and Surat, 1779. One folder.

Heilige Geest- of Arme Wees- en Kinderhuis te Leiden
Holy Spirit or Poor Orphanage and Children's Home at Leiden

Access no.: 519
Inv. nos: 1-4854
Size: 83 metres
Period: 1334-1982
Inventory: S.W.M.A. den Haan, *Inventaris van het archief van het Heilige Geest- of Arme Wees- en Kinderhuis te Leiden 1334-1979* (Leiden, 1990), with introduction, appendices and indices

Many boys in the orphanage and poor children's home entered the service of the VOC and went overseas. Inv. nos 2119, 3885-903 and 4531-2 concern the Company. For papers regarding Ceylon and Bengal, see also 4.1 and 6.1.

3886, 3890-2 Various registers of boys (and sometimes their fathers) serving the VOC, stating their departure to the East Indies, career, financial matters and return or decease, with indices, including references to boys who stayed in South Asia, *c.* 1720-90. Three volumes, one bundle.

3894, 3896, 3898 Registers and index of VOC ships, stating their size, captain, departure, itinerary and return, including ships sailing to and from South Asia, 1754-88. Two quires, one volume.

4310 Papers concerning the estates of Willem Switser, who passed away on 7 April 1729 at Cochin, and Andries Switser, who died on 4 October 1732 at Jaffna, 1736. One folder.

Maerten Tersijden

Access no.: 234
Inv. nos: 1-241
Size: 1.2 metres
Period: 1578-1669
Inventory: P.J.M. de Baar, 'Inventaris van de bij zijn overlijden aangetroffen bescheiden (1578-1669) van Maerten Tersijden' (1994), with introduction and genealogical tree

Maerten Tersijden (*c.* 1615-69) was a Notary at Leiden. The papers include some letters he received from his nephew Hugo Adriaensz Tersijden (baptised in 1643), who married a Portuguese woman at Colombo in October 1665, see 4.1.

1.1.20. *RIJKSARCHIEF IN LIMBURG* (Maastricht) STATE ARCHIVES IN LIMBURG

For general surveys, see R.M. Delahaye a.o., *De archieven in Limburg (Overzichten van de archieven en verzamelingen in de openbare archiefbewaarplaatsen in Nederland*, Vol. 13) (Alphen aan den Rijn, 1986), pp. 19-99 (somewhat outdated), and the repository's web site (see Appendix II, 1.20).

Well Castle

Access no.:	16.1112 A/1 (supplements: A/2, B/1 and B/2)
Inv. nos:	1-778 (supplements: 5001-158, 1-630 and 9001-19)
Size:	24 metres, 234 charters (A/1 and A/2)
Period:	14th century-1848 (A/1 and A/2)
Inventory:	A/1: N.L.M. Duijkers, 'Plaatsingslijst van het Huis en Heerlijkheid Well' (1993) (revision of A.F. van Beurden, 'Catalogus van het oud-archief van het Kasteel en der Baronie Well (L.), toebehorende aan "maatschappij Well"' (1906))

The archives of the Well Castle, also known as House of Well, include documents originating from Willem de Liedel (1713-77), who served as surgeon and factor in Asia between approximately 1730 and 1750. He inherited the Well Castle in 1771. Inv. nos 761-78 concern the VOC and consist of letters, reports, bills, insurance papers, powers of attorney and bonds. For papers regarding Bengal, see 6.1.

Handschriften
Manuscripts

Access no.:	18.A
Inv. nos:	1-543
Size:	28.8 metres
Period:	13th-20th centuries
Inventory:	G.J.M. Jägers, 'Catalogus van de handschriftencollectie van het Rijksarchief in Limburg' (Maastricht, 1991), with introduction and index

This collection consists of all kinds of papers acquired in the course of time. Comprising both handwritten and printed materials, they cover a wide range of subjects. For a short note pertaining to Ceylon, see 4.1.

1.1.21. *ZEEUWS ARCHIEF* (Middelburg) ZEELAND ARCHIVES

For general surveys, see J.J.C. van Dijk, R.L. Koops and H. Uil, *De archieven in Zeeland* (*Overzichten van de archieven en verzamelingen in de openbare archiefbewaarplaatsen in Nederland*, Vol. 3) (Alphen aan den Rijn, 1979), pp. 1-39, 86-9, 114 (somewhat outdated), and the repository's web site (see Appendix II, 1.21). For an inventory of documents concerning the VOC kept at the *Zeeuws Archief*, see F. van der Doe, I.J. van Loo and J.H.F. Schwartz, 'VOC-Gids. Overzicht van stukken betreffende de VOC aanwezig in de archieven en verzamelingen van het RAZ [Rijksarchief Zeeland]' (1998), available in the reading room and on Internet.

Staten van Zeeland
States of Zeeland

Access no.: 2.1
Inv. nos: 1-3299
Size: 294 metres
Period: 1574-1799
Inventory: K. Heeringa, *Het archief van de Staten van Zeeland en hunne Gecommitteerde Raden* (The Hague, 1922); the copy at the reading room of the *Zeeuws Archief* includes an index

The States of Zeeland were the main government body of the province in the seventeenth and eighteenth centuries. The *resoluties* (proceedings) of the meetings of the States often deal with the VOC, in particular the Zeeland Chamber, and its activities in the East Indies, including South Asia. Relevant documents can be traced with the help of several types of indices (inv. nos 3220-97), of which inv. nos 3228-67 and 3274-97 appear to be the most useful. References may for instance be found in the rubric 'Oost-Indische Compagnie'.

Walcheren Classis / Middelburg Classis

Access no.: 28.1
Inv. nos: 1-88, 101-44, 201-3
Size: 6.6 metres
Period: 1574-1951
Inventory: J. Grooten, 'Inventaris van de archieven der Classis' (1971) in: *Kerkelijke archieven*, 10 (1978), pp. 3-41, with introduction

At the request of the Zeeland Chamber of the VOC, the Walcheren Classis of the Dutch Reformed Church sent a number of clergymen to the East Indies. Their activities were initially coordinated by the *Comité tot de Oost-Indische Kerkzaken*, or *ad Res Indicas* (Committee regarding East Indian Church affairs), which functioned from 1620 to 1804. In the course of time, this responsibility was taken over by the Amsterdam Classis (see 1.1.2). Inv. nos 65-72 concern the East Indies. For papers regarding Ceylon, see also 4.1.

69 Correspondence between the *Comité tot de Oost-Indische Kerkzaken* and various persons and institutions in the Dutch Republic and the East Indies, 1701-1804, including surveys of church members in the East Indies (including South Asia) and a folder marked as papers concerning the state of affairs of Christianity on Ceylon in the eighteenth century with documents from Colombo and Jaffna. One bundle.

Koninklijk Zeeuwsch Genootschap der Wetenschappen
Royal Zeeland Society of Sciences

Access no.: 26.1
Inv. nos: 1-372
Size: 20 metres

Period: 1769-1969

Inventory:
- G.F. Sandberg, 'Inventaris van het archief van het Koninklijk Zeeuwsch Genootschap der Wetenschappen, 1769-1969' (1997), with introduction, appendices and index
- systematic catalogue on index cards of persons and subjects mentioned in the minutes and received papers during the period 1769-1800

This Society (abbreviated as *KZGW*) focuses on the province of Zeeland and its history. First conceived in 1765, it was recognized by the States of Zeeland in 1769 as the *Zeeuwsch Genootschap der Wetenschappen* and seated at Vlissingen. After a branch was set up at Middelburg in 1784, the Society moved there in 1801. VOC officials donated all kinds of objects from South Asia to the Society. While these objects are nowadays mostly kept at the *Zeeuws Museum* at Middelburg (see 1.4.20) and the *Rijksmuseum voor Volkenkunde* at Leiden (see 1.4.18), the papers registering the donations are still part of the archives of the Society. In addition, the archives include lectures, reports, etc., concerning South Asia, which were presented at the meetings of the Society. Part of these documents has been published or is referred to in the printed proceedings of the Society: *Verhandelingen uitgegeven door het Zeeuwsch Genootschap der Wetenschappen te Vlissingen* (Vlissingen, 1769-92) and successive series. Most of these publications have also been included in the archives of the Society (inv. nos 345-72) and are mentioned in this guide whenever applicable. For documents concerning Surat, Malabar, Ceylon and Bengal, see also 2.1, 3.1, 4.1 and 6.1. The Society's collection of Western manuscripts is kept at the *Zeeuwse Bibliotheek / Zeeuws Documentatiecentrum*, see 1.4.19. For manuscripts in South Asian languages, see 1.4.20, *Rijksmuseum voor Volkenkunde*.

5, p. 208 Minutes concerning an account of the travels of Samuel van de Putte in Asia (including India) printed in 1745 at Batavia (in the periodical *Bataviase Nouvelles*?), 1748. See also no. 59, f. 161 below.

6, pp. 234-5 Minutes concerning the donation by the widow of A.P. Lambrechtsen van Ritthem of horns, shells and other rarities collected by her uncle Samuel van de Putte during his travels in the period 1718-45, with a travel account, 1793. See also no. 133, p. 21 below.

7, p. ? Minutes concerning the donation by A.C. Slicher of five Indian embroideries made of bark and feathers (initially mistaken as Chinese), 5 January 1803.

59, f. 161 Received papers concerning an account of the travels of Samuel van de Putte in Asia (including India) printed in 1745 at Batavia (in the periodical *Bataviase Nouvelles*?), 1748. See also no. 5, p. 208 above.

61, f. 120 Received papers concerning the donation by P. Hofstede of a box with butterflies and other insects from Malabar and Coromandel, with instructions how to conserve this collection, 1777.

62, f. 33 Received papers concerning D. Radermacher, who sends two boxes

	with Indian insects to his cousin I. Winckelman, which will temporarily be kept by Leendert Bomme, 1779. See also no. 133, p. 15 below.
133, p. 15	List of donated naturalia, with references to D. Radermacher, who sends two boxes with Indian insects to his cousin I. Winckelman, which will temporarily be kept by Leendert Bomme, 1779. See also no. 62, f. 33 above.
133, p. 21	List of donated naturalia, with references to the donation by the widow of A.P. Lambrechtsen van Ritthem of horns, shells and other rarities collected by her uncle Samuel van de Putte during his travels in the period 1718-45, with a travel account, 1793. See also no. 6, pp. 234-5 above.

(Snouck) Hurgronje family (I)

Access no.: 98.1
Inv. nos: 1-139
Size: 2 metres
Period: 1641-1893
Inventory: D.A. Felix, 'Stukken afkomstig van of betreffende het geslacht (Snouck) Hurgronje', with introduction, genealogical trees and index to personal names

These papers originate from the Hurgronje family, in 1762 renamed as Snouck Hurgronje, which was based first at Vlissingen and in the second half of the eighteenth century moved to Middelburg. Several members of the family held high governmental positions in the aforementioned towns and the province of Zeeland, as well as functions in the VOC. The papers include some documents concerning the Freemason's lodge at Surat, deriving from the Van Citters family, a member of which married into the Snouck Hurgronje family in 1806. See 2.1.

(Snouck) Hurgronje family II

Access no.: 98.2
Inv. nos: 1-49
Size: 1 metre
Period: 17th century-1807
Inventory: G.F. Sandberg, 'Archivalia afkomstig van enige leden van de family (Snouck) Hurgronje II, (17e eeuw)-(1807)' (1979), with introduction, genealogical trees and indices

These documents can be considered a supplement to the papers of the (Snouck) Hurgronje family (I). For more information, see above. The papers mostly concern the government of Vlissingen, Middelburg and Zeeland. For documents regarding Bengal, see 6.1.

Van de Perre-Schorer family

Access no.: 107
Inv. nos: 1-49
Size: 5.5 metres
Period: 1749-95
Inventory: in typescript, with introduction and index

The collection consists of papers deriving from J.A. van de Perre (d. 1790) and J.H. Schorer, both of whom held high governmental functions. Inv. nos 27-34 concern the VOC. For papers regarding Malabar, Coromandel and Bengal, see also 3.1, 5.1 and 6.1.

27 Papers concerning the VOC, numbered 1-49, with partial table of contents, 1641-1785. One bundle. Including:
  12 *Beknopte historie van het Mogolsche keyzerryk en de zuydelyke aangrensende ryken* (printed by C.C. Renhard at Batavia, 1758), here attributed to François Valentijn, consisting of an introductory description and history of the subcontinent from *c.* the ninth century AD, with genealogy of the Mughals and the Maratha Kings and notes on places and dynasties in Ikkeri, Malabar, Madurai, Ramnad, Thanjavur and Bengal, and copies of recent treaties of the British, French, Nadir Shah, etc., also attributed to Jacobus Mossel (see also *Dutch Sources on South Asia*, Vol. 1, Bibliography, no. 39).
  17 Memorandum concerning means of redress for the factories in Asia, including sections on South Asia, by Sibrandus Collumba, former priest at Batavia, 23 April 1770.
29 Various papers concerning the VOC, numbered 1-39, 40-60, 61-121, *c.* 1780-95. Three bundles. Including:
  36A-B (first bundle) Memorandum concerning the possibility of abandoning the factories in India, with sections on Coromandel, Malabar, Surat and Bengal, *c.* 1790.
30 Various papers concerning the VOC, including bookkeeping with respect to South Asia, 1785-95. One bundle.

Schorer family

Access no.: 157 (supplement: 157.2)
Inv. nos: 1-1244
Size: 10 metres
Period: 1547-1983
Inventory: G.F. Sandberg, 'Inventaris van het familiearchief Schorer, 1547-1983' (1983), with introduction, genealogical notes and appendices

The archives of the Schorer family include papers deriving from Steven Schorer, who was factor in Malabar, and Samuel Radermacher, Director in the Zeeland Chamber of the VOC. For papers concerning Malabar and Ceylon, see 3.1 and 4.1.

1137 Treaty concluded at London between the British and Dutch governments about the possessions in Asia, including India, 17 March 1824. Printed, one folder.

Mathias-Pous-Tak van Poortvliet family

Access no.: 255
Inv. nos: 1-610
Size: *c.* 6 metres
Period: 1386-1944
Inventory: Y.J.A. Welings, 'Inventaris van het familiearchief Mathias-Pous-Tak van Poortvliet, (1386) 1462-1944' (1989), with introduction, genealogical trees, appendices and index

These archives include papers deriving from Johan Constantijn Mathias (1691-1765), his grandson Bonifatius Mathias Pous (1744-97) and Pieter Pous (1777-1851), son of Bonifatius. Among many other high functions, all served as Directors of the VOC or as members of the Zeeland office of the legal successors of the Company, namely the *Comité tot de Zaken van de Oost-Indische Handel en Bezittingen* (1796-1800) and the *Raad der Aziatische Bezittingen en Etablissementen* (1800-6). Inv. nos 15-78, 155-305, 351-74 and 580 concern the VOC and its successors. For papers regarding Surat, Malabar, Ceylon and Bengal, see also 2.1, 3.1, 4.1 and 6.1.

18 Notes made by J.C. Mathias during meetings of the *Haags Besogne* (The Hague Committee), 1738-64, including sections on Bengal, Coromandel, Ceylon, Malabar and Surat, 1738. One folder.
20 Letters concerning the VOC received by J.C. Mathias, 1741-63, from various senders, including P. Blankert at Colombo, 1748 (two letters), Jacob Mossel at Nagappattinam, 1741 (with some bookkeeping), and Julius Valentijn Stein van Gollonesse at Colombo, 1748-9. One bundle.
26 Considerations on the present state of the VOC by Gustaaf Willem van Imhoff, 1741, with table of contents and an index to the minutes of the meetings of the Gentlemen XVII for 1741. One volume.
71 Register containing surveys of profits and losses of VOC offices in Asia and the sale of products from these offices in the Dutch Republic, with ff. 23-32 concerning Bengal, Coromandel, Ceylon, Malabar and Surat, and unnumbered sections dealing with indigo from Coromandel and Ceylon, silk from Bengal, cotton from Surat, Bengal, Tuticorin and Vengurla, cardamom from Malabar and Ceylon, and coffee from Ceylon, 1700-40. One volume.
201 Letters received by B. Mathias Pous from B. Cohen, with drafts of replies and annexes, 1771-96, including price lists of products from Ceylon, the Fishery Coast and Coromandel sold in the Dutch Republic. One bundle.
244 Instructions for the sailing from the Dutch Republic to Ceylon and Bengal (among other destinations), with an extract from a letter and a memorandum by B. Mathias Pous concerning this subject, 1782-3. Printed, one folder.

Van der Feen family

Access no.: 309
Inv. nos: 1-990, 1100-17
Size: *c.* 10 metres
Period: 18th-20th centuries
Inventory: in typescript

The archives of the Van der Feen family include a couple of ship's logs, one of which relates to Bengal, see 6.1.

Pieter van Gote

Access no.: 390
Inv. nos: 1-17
Size: 0.2 metres
Period: 1760-93
Inventory: Y.J.A. Welings, 'Inventaris van het persoonlijk archief van Pieter van Gote, 1760-1793' (1989), with introduction and index

The archives include papers originating from Pieter van Gote (b. 1737), Bookkeeper at the Zeeland Chamber of the VOC, and Adriaan van Es, who deserted the Company as Chief Steers Man. For papers concerning Surat, Malabar and Ceylon, see 2.1, 3.1 and 4.1.

Receuils Van Citters

Access no.: 105
Inv. nos: 1-28
Size: 2.5 metres
Period: 1708-87
Inventory: in typescript, with introduction and indices

The collection consists of papers deriving from Wilhem van Citters (1685-1785) and his son Wilhem (1723-1802), who both held high governmental positions in Zeeland. For documents concerning Ceylon and Bengal, see also 4.1 and 6.1.

17 Papers concerning the VOC, 1741-2, with considerations on the state of the Company by Gustaaf Willem van Imhoff, 1741 (ff. 1-138), including sections on South Asia. One volume.
18 Papers concerning the VOC, ?-1744, including instructions about how to sail to southern India and Ceylon, 1665, and an extract from a letter sent from Colombo by Governor Rijklof van Goens and Council of Ceylon to the GG&C, 1665-8. Printed, one volume.

Handschriftenverzameling
Manuscript collection

Access no.: 33.1
Inv. nos: 1-1639

Size: 43 metres
Period: 1206-1948
Inventory: in typescript (1990), with indices

The collection mostly consists of acquisitions up to 1954 and includes some relevant ship's logs. Inv. nos 355-62, 183-7 and 1623-4b concern the VOC. For papers concerning Malabar, see 3.1.

187 Logs kept by John Isaac Colnet (or Lolnet) of the ship Zuid-Beveland, sailing from Rammekens to Batavia and back to Texel via Colombo and Galle, 1771-3, and of the ship De Bot (or Bodt), sailing from Rammekens via Batavia to Nagappattinam and Jagannathapuram, 1774-5. One volume.

1.1.22. *GEMEENTEARCHIEF ROTTERDAM* MUNICIPAL ARCHIVES OF ROTTERDAM

For general surveys, see J.A.M.Y. Bos-Rops a.o., *De archieven in Zuid-Holland*, 2 vols (*Overzichten van de archieven en verzamelingen in de openbare archiefbewaarplaatsen in Nederland*, Vol. 10) (Alphen aan den Rijn, 1983), pp. 515-622 (somewhat outdated), and the repository's web site (see Appendix II, 1.22).

Oud stadsarchief Rotterdam
Old town archives of Rotterdam

Access no.: 1a and 1b
Inv. nos: 1-3048 (1a), 3049-5325 (1b)
Size: *c.* 50 metres
Period: 1340-1813
Inventory: H. ten Boom and B. Woelderink, *Inventaris van het oud archief van de stad Rotterdam, 1340-1813*, 2 vols (Rotterdam, 1976), with introduction, appendices and indices

The old archives of Rotterdam, seat of one of the VOC chambers, include only one inv. no. concerning the Company. It partly deals with Bengal, see 6.1.

Weeskamer te Rotterdam
Orphan Board of Rotterdam

Access no.: 16
Inv. nos: 1-1502
Size: 85 metres
Period: 1470-1852
Inventory: H.C.H. Moquette, *Het archief van de weeskamer te Rotterdam* (Rotterdam, 1907), with introduction, appendices and index

The archives include papers concerning (orphanages in) the East Indies, which are to be found in inv. nos 90-129, 135-6, 144-6 and 778-81. The inv. nos below contain documents with regard to places such as Cochin, Colombo, Jaffna, Batticaloa, Trincomalee and Hooghly.

90-116 Letters with appendices from the East Indies (with inv. nos 99-100 and 103-116 containing alphabetical indices to personal names), 1668-1807. 27 volumes.
117-28 Letters and other papers from the East Indies, 1663-1833. Twelve bundles.
135-6 Outgoing letters (with alphabetical indices to personal names), 1683-1744, including letters to the East Indies up to 1704. Two volumes.
144-6 Letters to the East Indies (with inv. nos 145-6 containing alphabetical indices to personal names), 1704-1832. Three volumes.

Oude notariële archieven
Old notarial archives

Access no.: 18
Inv. nos: 1-3941
Size: *c.* 520 metres
Period: 1585-1811
Inventory: E. Wiersum, *Archieven der notarissen, die op het tegenwoordig grondgebied der gemeente Rotterdam gefungeerd hebben, 1585-1811* (The Hague, 1920), with introduction and appendices; see also below

The archives contain notarial acts that were drawn up by notaries active in the area nowadays covered by the municipality of Rotterdam. Papers concerning South Asia can be found with the help of a geographical index (in card trays). The documents indexed under 'Surat', 'Ceylon', 'Colombo', 'Coromandel' and 'Bengalen' are described in this guide, see 2.1, 4.1, 5.1 and 6.1. Other relevant papers might be traced through references under 'Oost-Indië' (East Indies) and 'Batavia', or by way of the indices to personal and ship names. The references consist of inv. nos, followed by piece or folio nos.

Voormalige Classis van Schieland en de tegenwoordige Classis van Rotterdam
Former Schieland Classis and the present Rotterdam Classis

Access no.: 24
Inv. nos: 1-575
Size: 20 metres
Period: 1580-1816 (Schieland), 1816–1934 (Rotterdam)
Inventory: in typescript (1936), with introduction

The Schieland Classis and (after 1816) its successor, the Rotterdam Classis, belonged to the Dutch Reformed Church. Inv. nos 479-99 concern the *Deputati ad res Indicas*, the committee dealing with the activities of the church in the East Indies. For papers regarding Ceylon, see 4.1.

Huis ten Donck
House of Donck

Access no.: 30a
Inv. nos: 1-1301 (maps: 1-31)
Size: *c.* 30 metres
Period: 1414-1991
Inventory: B. Woelderink, *Inventaris van het archief van het Huis ten Donck* (Rotterdam, 1968), with introduction, genealogical trees and index

The House of Donck was seated at a castle at Ridderkerk. The archives include papers of Otto Groeninx van Zoelen (1704-58), Director at the Rotterdam Chamber of the VOC from 1740 to 1758. Inv. nos 1200-6 concern the Company.

1204 Considerations on the state of the VOC, including sections on South Asia, drawn up at Amsterdam, 1741. One volume.

Van Teylingen family

Access no.: 37.01
Inv. nos: 1-87
Size: 1 metre
Period: 1702-1813
Inventory: H. ten Boom, 'Inventaris van de collectie Van Teylingen' (1978), with introduction and genealogical tree

These papers include documents deriving from Christiaan van Teylingen (1731-80), who was Governor of Coromandel from 1761 to 1765, see 5.1.

Prins family

Access no.: 329
Inv. nos: 1-480
Size: 0.2 metres
Period: 1692-1802
Inventory: H. ten Boom, 'Inventaris van het familiearchief Prins' (1987), with introduction and genealogical trees

These archives include papers of A.A. Prins, Director at the Rotterdam Chamber of the VOC, Willem Prins, President of the *Hoofdparticipanten* (principal shareholders) of the Company in Rotterdam, and Theodore Lambert Prins, who held many high municipal functions at Rotterdam. Inv. nos 270-1 and 459-67 concern the VOC. See also Supplement II, 48.

461 Papers concerning matters discussed in the meetings of the Rotterdam Chamber of the VOC, including a treatise by Jacob Mossel on the state of the Company with sections on South Asia, 1752. One folder.

Handschriftenverzameling
Collection of manuscripts

Access no.: 33a
Inv. nos: 1-*c.* 10000
Period: 16th-20th centuries
Inventory: J.G.B. Nieuwenhuis, *Catalogus van de handschriftenverzameling*, 3 vols (Rotterdam, 1970-1, 1999), with index to personal and geographical names

The collection includes many documents pertaining to the VOC. For papers concerning Ceylon and Coromandel, see 4.1 and 5.1.

1.1.23. *HET UTRECHTS ARCHIEF* THE ARCHIVES OF UTRECHT

For general surveys, see A.N. Beets, H.L.Ph. Leeuwenberg and J.G. Riphaagen, *De archieven in Utrecht* (*Overzichten van de archieven en verzamelingen in de openbare archiefbewaarplaatsen in Nederland*, Vol. 11) (Alphen aan den Rijn, 1985), pp. 63-121, 169-200 (somewhat outdated), and the repository's web site (see Appendix II, 1.23). See also 1.6.1.

Staten van Utrecht, 1581-1810
States of Utrecht

Access no.: 233
Inv. nos: *c.* 144-12 to 22, 231-2 to 1417-m, 1523
Size: 257 metres
Period: 1581-1810
Inventory: S. Muller Fz, *Catalogus van het archief der Staten van Utrecht 1375-1813* (Utrecht, 1915), with introduction, index and notes added in manuscript

The States of Utrecht were the main government body of the province in the seventeenth and eighteenth centuries. Documents pertaining to the VOC (including inv. nos 284-1 & 2, 333, 364-10-166 & 181) originate from Anthony van Hilten, Secretary of the States of Utrecht. In addition to the papers described below, the *resoluties* (proceedings) of the meetings of the States (inv. nos 231-45, 256-68, 274-7) regularly deal with the VOC, and may occasionally concern South Asia. Relevant documents can be traced with the help of several types of indices (inv. nos 246-55, 269-73). References may for instance be found in the rubric 'Oost-Indische Compagnie'.

364-6-88 Letters brought with the ship Oraengien-Boom, including a letter from the King of Arakan to General Pieter Both (?) concerning the King's conflicts with the Mughals and the Portuguese in Bengal (?), 1619. One folder.

717 Papers concerning the 'wars in the Indies', by Aert Gysels (earlier attributed to Jan Pieterszoon Coen), including sections on Surat and Coromandel, 1622 (?). One volume. Published in *Kroniek van het Historisch Genootschap gevestigd te Utrecht*, 27 (1871), pp. 497-576.

Momboirkamer te Utrecht
Chamber of Guardians at Utrecht

Access no.: 702-3
Inv. nos: 1384-823
Size: 40 metres
Period: 1577-1795
Inventory: S. Muller Fz., *Catalogus van het archief [der stad Utrecht]*, 4 vols (Utrecht, 1880-1914), with introduction and indices in separate volume; updated version in typescript 'Catalogus van het archief [der stad Utrecht], tweede afdeling 1577-1795: archief van de Momboirkamer' (or 'Stadsarchief II', part 3, pp. 135-74) (1994)

These archives are part of a group of archives known as 'Archief der stad Utrecht' (archives of the town of Utrecht). The *Momboirkamer* was an institution looking after orphans or minors, more or less comparable to an orphan board. It maintained relations with some orphan boards in the East Indies. For papers concerning Ceylon, see 4.1.

Notarissen geresideerd hebbende te Utrecht-stad
Notaries having resided at the town of Utrecht

Access no.: 34-4
Inv. nos: U 001 a 001-U 339 b 001
Size: 217 metres
Period: 1560-1905
Inventory: W.B. Heins and J.A.C. Mathijsen, 'Inventaris van de notariële archieven in de provincie Utrecht (1346) 1560-1905' (1982-6), with introduction, appendices and index to notaries; see also below

The old notarial archives of the town of Utrecht are arranged chronologically according to notary. Relevant notarial acts from the period 1640-1789 can be traced by means of a data base (available at the reading room and on Internet), which contains summaries and scanned images of the original acts. Among other possibilities, it can be searched on personal names, professions and places of residence (only in the Dutch Republic). This guide lists relevant acts found under the VOC functions 'Opperkoopman' (senior factor) and 'Onderkoopman' (junior factor). (Explorative searches under other possible Company functions like 'Commandeur' (chief, commander) and 'Bewindhebber' (director) appeared unsuccessful, while documents found under such general professions as 'Koopman' (merchant) and 'Kaartenmaker' (map maker) were much too numerous to be all examined for their possible relevance to South Asia.) Documents that have been scanned for the data base cannot be consulted in the original. For notarial acts concerning Malabar, Ceylon, Coromandel and Bengal, see also 3.1, 4.1, 5.1 and 6.1.

U 106 a 17, act no. 3	Notarial act drawn up by Johannes van Noortdyck, among others involving Mattheus Heck, Margaretha Heck, wife of Adriaen de Mey (priest on Ceylon?), and Sara Heck, wife of Abraham Vinck (factor at Cochin), probably concerning a testament, 1700.

Oud-Katholieke Kerk in Nederland (OKN): Oud-Bisschoppelijke Clerezij OKN/OBC)
Old Catholic Church in the Netherlands: Old Episcopal Clergy

Access no.:	224
Inv. nos:	696-1752
Size:	32.7 metres
Period:	*c.* 1375–1935
Inventory:	J. Bruggeman, *Inventaris van de archieven bij het Metropolitaan Kapittel van Utrecht van de Rooms Katholieke Kerk der Oud Bisschoppelijke Clerezie* (The Hague, 1928), revised edition including supplement (1944), 1997, with introduction and concordance

The so-called Old Catholic Church or Utrecht Church claims to be the legitimate continuation of the Roman Catholic Church after its official expulsion from the Netherlands during the Reformation. As such, it stresses a continued Dutch church hierarchy against the claims of a Papal nuncio governing the Dutch mission from abroad. The final schism occurred in 1723 when the Utrecht chapter elected its own Archbishop against Roman wishes. Only as late as 1853, the Vatican decided to re-establish its own diocesan organization in the Netherlands.

These archives contain various papers regarding the Catholic mission in the East Indies, including correspondence of Balthasar van Wevelinchoven (deceased in 1694), who functioned as Agent at Rome (1662-5, 1670-1), as Secretary of Johannes van Neercassel (see below) and the vicariate of Utrecht, and as priest in Gorinchem.

Tracing relevant documents in the archives is rather complicated. One should first consult the 'Diarium Litterarum O[ud] B[isschoppelijke] C[lerezie]' (six vols, available at the reading room), in which all letters are listed chronologically with date, sender, addressee and a short description of the contents. Vols 3-7 contain the actual list (covering the period 1473-1859); Vol. 2 consists of indices to this list (one of them including geographical names), which refer to the page numbers of Vols 3-7. On the pages thus found, one has to locate the references to the relevant letters. These references may include the former inv. nos of the letters (to be converted to the present inv. nos by means of a concordance), but often the letters can only be located by searching for the names of the senders or addressees in the inventory. It should be noted that most of the relevant letters listed in the 'Diarium Litterarum OBC' have been transferred to the archives of the *Apostolische Vicarissen* (access no. 1003), see below. This guide only lists letters found through references in the index under South Asian geographical names; other relevant letters may be traced through references under 'Indië' and 'Oost-Indië'. For a document concerning Malabar, see 3.1.

Oud-Katholieke Kerk in Nederland (OKN): Apostolische Vicarissen
Old Catholic Church in the Netherlands: Vicars Apostolic

Access no.: 1003
Inv. nos: 1-794
Size: 9.5 metres
Period: 1579-1728
Inventory: J. Bruggeman, 'Inventaris van de archieven van de Apostolische Vicarissen van de Hollandse zending en hun secretarissen 1579-1728' (2001), revised by Y.E. Kortlever, with introduction, glossary, appendices and a concordance

The archives of the Vicars Apostolic of the Dutch mission and their Secretaries were originally part of the archives of the *Oud-Bisschoppelijke Clerezij* of the *Oud-Katholieke Kerk in Nederland* (access no. 224), see above. For an explanation of how to find relevant documents with the help of the 'Diarium Litterarum OBC', see the introductory section of those archives. The correspondence of Johannes van Neercassel (1623-86), who held a large number of ecclesiastical functions and became Vicar Apostolic in 1663, includes several letters concerning Malabar, see 3.1.

Oud-Katholieke Kerk in Nederland (OKN): Verzameling Port Royal
Old Catholic Church in the Netherlands: Port Royal collection

Access no.: 215
Inv. nos: 1-7156
Size: *c.* 38 metres
Period: *c.* 1600-1865
Inventory: J. Bruggeman and A.J. van de Ven, *Inventaire des pièces d'archives françaises se rapportant à l'abbaye de Port-Royal des Champs et son cercle, et à la résistance contre la Bulle Unigenitus et à l'Appèl (ancien fonds d'Amersfoort)* (International Archives of the History of Ideas, 54) (The Hague, 1972), with introduction and indices to personal and geographical names

One part of these archives derives from the abbey of Port-Royal des Champs in France (destroyed in 1709), fugitive Jansenists from France and the southern Netherlands, and antagonists of the Bull Unigenitus. The other part originates from appellants against the Bull Unigenitus. Relevant papers mostly concern French missionaries in Coromandel, see 5.1. Part of the papers has to be consulted on microfiche.

2599 Chronological survey of French bishops and missionaries in the East Indies, including a few references to South Asia, 1658-1722. In French.

3220-1 Various letters, 1667-1719, including remarks on a plan to establish a seminary in the East Indies, with a few references to South Asia, 1694. In French.

3694 74 letters from A. de la Chassaigne, Procurator of the seminary of foreign missions at Paris, possibly including references to South Asia, 1719-38. In French.

7086 Letters from the Capuchin Eusèbe de Bourges about the difficulties of Capuchin missionaries in India and the Patriarch of Tournon with the Jesuits, 1706. One quire, in French and Latin.

Nederlands Hervormde Kerk (NHK): Raad voor de Zending
Dutch Reformed Church: Missionary Council

Access no.: 1102
Inv. nos: 1-1369 (?)
Size: 180 metres
Period: *c.* 1750-1927
Inventory: 'Inventaris van de Raad voor de Zending der Nederlands Hervormde Kerk 1797-1927', with introductions, various supplements (Vols 2-4) and index (Vol. 5)

These archives include documents originating from the *Nederlandsch Zendeling Genootschap* (*NZG*. Dutch Missionary Society), which was founded in 1797 to be the first Reformed missionary corporation in the Netherlands. Among the papers are several documents dating from before the foundation. For papers concerning Ceylon and Bengal, see also 4.1 and 6.1.

146 Various papers concerning missionary activities, 1821-50, including instructions to Johann Christian Timotheus Winckler departing to Coromandel and Bengal, *c.* 1822, and reports by Winckler about his activities in Sadras and other locations in Coromandel, 1824-33. One folder, one bundle (old inv. no. 'kast 19, dossier 1f').

Evangelische Broedergemeente (EBG): Zeister Zendingsgenootschap
Evangelical Community of Moravian Brethren: Missionary Society of Zeist

Access no.: 48-1
Inv. nos: 1-1416
Size: 21.75 metres
Period: 1793-1962
Inventory: C.G.W.M. van Hoogstraten, 'Inventaris van het archief van het Zendingsgenootschap der Evangelische Broedergemeente te Zeist (Zeister Zendingsgenootschap) 1793-1962' (1985), with introduction, appendix and indices

Head-quartered at Herrnhut (Germany), the Community of Moravian Brethren was active in the Dutch Republic from 1734 onward. In 1745 a community was set up at Zeist. As the Community considered mission very important, the Missionary

Society of Zeist was founded in 1793 to support this activity, which was organized from Herrnhut. These archives include eighteenth-century papers from the Deacon Kornelis van Laer, some of which concern Ceylon and Coromandel, see 4.1 and 5.1.

Van Boetzelaer family

Access no.: 32
Inv. nos: 1-1179
Size: 15.1 metres
Period: 1316-1952
Inventory: E.P. de Booy, 'Inventaris van de archieven van de familie Van Boetzelaer, 1316-1952' (1982), with introduction, appendices, genealogical trees and index

The archives of this Kleve-based family include papers deriving from members of the De Groot family, among them Pieter (1615-78), son of the famous Hugo. For papers concerning Ceylon, see 4.1.

Huydecoper family

Access no.: 67
Inv. nos: 1-1431
Size: 21 metres
Period: 1459-1956
Inventory: M.S. Polak, 'Inventaris van het archief van de familie Huydecoper 1459-1956' (1987), with introduction, genealogical tree, appendix and index

This family of merchants, scholars and administrators resided in Amsterdam during the VOC period but in the nineteenth century shifted its attention to the province of Utrecht, where it had bought the manor of Maarsseveen in the early seventeenth century. Relevant papers mostly derive from Sophia Huydecoper (1739-1801) and her husband Jan Boudaen (1735-68), Director at the Amsterdam Chamber of the VOC, and from Jan's cousin Gualterus Petrus Boudaen (1704-81), who was also Director at the Amsterdam Chamber as well as Burgomaster of the city. Other relevant documents originate from Joan Huydecoper (1625-1704), Balthasar Huydecoper (1695-1778), Alderman of Amsterdam among other functions, Jan Elias Huydecoper van Maarsseveen (1735-1808), Burgomaster of Amsterdam among other functions, and Pieter Nuijts (deceased in 1655), member of the Council of the Indies in Batavia. For documents concerning Surat, Malabar, Ceylon, Coromandel and Bengal, see also 2.1, 3.1, 4.1, 5.1 and 6.1.

620 Papers received by Jan Elias Huydecoper in his capacity as *Hoofd-participant* (principal shareholder) of the VOC and Director of the Fifth Department of the Amsterdam Chamber, chiefly concerning efforts to recover the VOC, including references to South Asia, 1776-88. One bundle (old no. 1001?).

621 Papers concerning the VOC, added to the archives by Jan Elias Huydecoper from the papers of Pieter Nuijts and his son Laurens, 1621-38. One bundle. Including:

(a) Report for Governor-General Antonio van Diemen (1636-45) about a voyage from the Sunda Straits to Madagascar, and advice concerning the government of the Indies, probably by Governor-General Hendrik Brouwer (1632-6), including some references to Surat, Bijapur, Goa, Malabar and Coromandel, 1636. One quire (old no. 2072). Partly published in *Bijdragen en mededelingen van het Historisch Genootschap*, 70 (1956), p. 176.

622 Papers concerning the VOC, added to the archives by Jan Elias Huydecoper from the papers of Gualterus Petrus Boudaen, 1670-1760. One bundle. Including:

(a) Two surveys with geographical descriptions of a large number of coastal stretches on Ceylon, in Coromandel, Orissa, Bengal, Pegu and on the Andaman Islands (?), 1670. One folder (old no. 2197).

(b) List of VOC officials in the East Indies, including some *Independent Fiscaals* in South Asia, 1700. One piece (old no. 203).

(c) Correspondence between the VOC and local rulers about the trade to Mocha, including references to Surat and other places in South Asia and Hindu traders in the Middle East, 1707-9. One folder (old no. 1144).

(d) Report of Corporal Johan Andries Bord (?) by order of Governor Steven Vermont of Coromandel (1753-8) concerning the naval battle between the VOC and the Angria 'pirates', 1754 (?). One quire (old no. 2205).

623 Papers concerning the VOC, added to the archives by Jan Elias Huydecoper from the papers of Gualterus Petrus Boudaen, 1762-78. One bundle. Including:

(a) Letters to Boudaen from Pieter Cornelis Hasselaar, including references to Ceylon and Bengal, 1763-5. One folder (old no. 1473b?).

(b) Letters to Boudaen from Governor-General Petrus Albertus van der Parra (1761-75) concerning Ceylon, Bengal and other parts of South Asia, including a treaty concluded in 1766 with Kandy, 1760s (old no. 1473c).

(c) Letters to Boudaen from Jan Schreuder (Governor of Ceylon, 1757-61) at Batavia and Colombo, including references to South Asia, 1765-8, 1776 (?). One folder (old no. 1473d).

(d) Letter from David Kelly at Batavia, with annexes, concerning South Asia, 1766. One folder (old no. 1473e).

(e) Letter to Boudaen from Pieter Haksteen at Nagappattinam, with references to South Asia, 1770. One folder (old no. 1473f).

(f) Report by Schut at Cochin for Jan Boudaen, concerning inspection at Cochin and complaints lodged with the Council of Justice at Batavia against Schut, Abraham Josias Sluysken and N. Holmberg, with references to South Asia, 1769. One quire (old no. 1152).

(g) Papers and extracts of letters by Governor Pieter Haksteen of Coromandel (1765-71), Governor Iman Willem Falck of Ceylon (1765-85) and Jacob Mossel to *Commandeur* Christiaan Lodewijk Senff of

Malabar (1768-70), and letters from Senff to Batavia and from a Jew at Surat to Ezekiel Rabbi in Cochin, all or mostly concerning the disagreement between Senff and Chr. Ernst van Seyffert, *Resident* of 'Adjerhadja' (Sumatra?), about the government of Surat, 1769. One folder (old no. 2213).

Taets van Amerongen van Natewisch family

Access no.: 23
Inv. nos: 1-293
Size: 4 metres
Period: 1438-1937
Inventory: G.M.W. Ruitenberg, 'Inventaris van het archief van de familie Taets van Amerongen van Natewisch, 1438-1937' (1979), with introduction and genealogical trees

These archives include papers deriving from the related Loten and Falck families. For documents concerning Ceylon, see 4.1.

Grothe family and related families

Access no.: 750
Inv. nos: 1-1639
Size: 10.3 metres
Period: 1583-1960
Inventory: J. Gerritsen and A.B.R. du Croo de Vries, 'Inventaris van het archief van de familie Grothe en aanverwante families 1583-1960' (1992), with introduction, appendix and genealogical tree with index

The archives of the Zutphen-based Grothe family (see also under the archives of the Ram family) include papers deriving from relatives such as Joan Gideon Loten (1710-89), Governor of Ceylon from 1752 to 1757 (inv. nos 1374-1417), Joseph Loten (*c.* 1680-1730), who became *Independent Fiscaal* in Bengal in 1709 (inv. nos 1361-4), and Margaretha Pit (1682-1750). For documents concerning Ceylon and Bengal, see 4.1 and 6.1.

Ram family and related families

Access no.: 752
Inv. nos: 1-901
Size: 4.5 metres
Period: 1560-1886
Inventory: S.K. Hazemeijer, J.W.A. van Hengel and J.A.C. Mathijssen, 'Inventaris van de papieren van de familie Ram en enige aanverwante families (1400) 1560-1886' (1988), with introduction, genealogical trees and index on personal names

The archives of the Ram family, many members of which held high functions in the town and province of Utrecht, include papers from related families. Amongst these are documents deriving from Albert van Benthem, VOC Director between 1660 and 1680, and from Laurens Grothe (1708-87; for the Grothe family, see above), who served the VOC in Asia. For papers concerning Ceylon and Bengal, see also 4.1 and 6.1.

845 Papers sent from G. Verhoeven at Amsterdam to Paulus de Crauwler, Provost and Archdeacon of the Oud-Münster Chapter, concerning the estate of Cornelis van der Ham, factor at Cochin, Colombo and Galle from the 1660s to the 1680s, 1787. One folder.

Des Tombe family

Access no.: 26
Inv. nos: 1-1954
Size: *c.* 16.3 metres
Period: 1485-1948
Inventory: C. Dekker, 'Inventaris van het archief van de familie Des Tombe 1485-1948' (1980), with introduction and index to personal and geographical names

The archives of the Des Tombe family, based at Utrecht from 1723 onward, include papers of the related Van Citters family from Middelburg. Jacob van Citters (1708-92) and his wife Anna Sara Boudaen (1718-81) received some letters from Malabar and Ceylon, see 3.1 and 4.1.

Martini Buys family

Access no.: 43
Inv. nos: 1-775
Size: 14.1 metres
Period: 1276-1985
Inventory: G.M.J. de Meij, 'Inventaris van de archieven van de familie Martini Buys 1595-1966 en van het huis en de heerlijkheid Loenersloot (1276) 1569-1954' (1984), with introduction, genealogical trees, appendix and index to personal and geographical names

These archives include papers of the related Casteleijn family, amongst whom Joan Casteleijn (1632-84), factor at Colombo. For papers concerning Ceylon, see 4.1.

De Pesters family

Access no.: 95
Inv. nos: 1-583
Size: 8 metres
Period: 1392-1948
Inventory: L.P.W. de Graaff, 'Inventaris van het archief van de familie De Pesters 1392-1948' (1996), with introduction, appendices and index to personal and geographical names

Part of the archives of the De Pesters family, based at Utrecht from 1678 onward, consists of papers deriving from members of the related Muykens family, including Arnoldus Muykens (deceased in 1702), who was *Directeur* of Bengal between 1688 and 1696. In 1695 he was appointed Governor of Ceylon, but he immediately applied for a dismissal.

338 Deed of appointment of Arnoldus Muykens as *Directeur* of Bengal, drawn up by Hendrik Adriaan van Reede tot Drakenstein at Pulicat, 1689. One piece.

339 Extract from the *resolutie* (proceedings) of the Council of the Indies concerning the dismissal of Arnoldus Muykens as Governor of Ceylon, 1696. One piece.

De Beaufort family

Access no.: 53
Inv. nos: 1-2530
Size: 36.6 metres
Period: 1556-1976
Inventory: E.P. de Booy, 'Inventaris van het archief van de familie De Beaufort 1556-1976' (1985), with introduction, appendices and index to personal and geographical names

The archives of the De Beaufort family, which was initially based in Zeeland but moved to Utrecht in the course of the eighteenth century, include papers regarding the *Westindische Compagnie* (WIC, West India Company), one of which pertains to Malabar, see 3.1. In addition, inv. no. 972 consists of notes, drawings and letters (dating from 1913-31, in English) concerning the grave and epitaph of the chief-factor Henricus Volrad von Söhsten (1754-1824) at Tuticorin by his descendants.

1.1.24. *STADS- EN STREEKARCHIEF ZUTPHEN* TOWN AND REGIONAL ARCHIVES OF ZUTPHEN

This repository keeps a few maps pertaining to South Asia. See 1.6.1.

1.1.25. *HISTORISCH CENTRUM OVERIJSSEL* (Zwolle) HISTORICAL CENTRE OVERIJSSEL

For general surveys, see H. de Beer a.o., *De archieven in Overijssel* (*Overzichten van de archieven en verzamelingen in de openbare archiefbewaarplaatsen in Nederland*, Vol. 6) (Alphen aan den Rijn, 1980), pp. 1-49, 152-70 (somewhat outdated), and the repository's web site (see Appendix II, 1.25).

Rechterlijk archief van het Schoutambt Kamperveen, processtukken
Judicial archives of the function of Bailiff Kamperveen, case files

Access no.: 61.2
Inv. nos: 1-53

Size: *c.* 1.3 metres
Period: 1727-1810
Inventory: checklist in typescript (1920s)

These case files are part of the greater archives of the *Schout* (bailiff) of Kamperveen, an area south of the town of Kampen. In the province of Overijssel, the function of *Schout* ranked as the lowest judicial institution. The *Schout* also served as notary. The case files include a number of letters (formally not belonging to the archives) sent to Eduard Jork (or George) van Slangenburgh (and his wife). He served as priest at Nagappattinam in the 1710s. It seems that one of his descendants functioned as *Schout* of Kamperveen in the late eighteenth century. For documents concerning Ceylon and Coromandel, see also 4.1 and 5.1.

52 Letters chiefly sent by priests in the East Indies to Eduard Jork (or George) van Slangenburgh, his wife Clara Croeuger and their relative Paulus Croeuger, with many references to South Asia, 1711-23. One bundle. Including:
(a) Letter from Cramer at Jaffna to Jacobus Jacobs at Nagappattinam, 1717.

Van Bevervoorden tot Oldemeule family

Access no.: 230.1
Inv. nos: 1-509
Size: *c.* 4 metres
Period: 1345-1974
Inventory: A.J. Gevers, 'Inventaris van de papieren Van Bevervoorden tot Oldemeule' (1974), with introduction, genealogical trees and index

These archives include papers deriving from Bernardus Engelbert van Bevervoorden (1702-63), who served as priest at Nagappattinam. He first married Anna Elisabeth van 's-Gravesand, who passed away at Nagappattinam in 1731. In 1734, in the same town, he married Josina van Zijll, who died in 1747. The archives also include papers originating from Bernardus' sister Euphemia Engelbert (1711-59), who married Diederik van Domburg (*d.* 1737), Governor of Ceylon between 1732 and 1736, and from Bernardus' brother Johannes Engelbert (1713-51), who was factor and Bookkeeper at Jaffna. For documents concerning Coromandel, see also 5.1.

3 Letter to Bernardus Engelbert and Josina van Zijll at Nagappattinam from Johannes Engelbert on Ceylon concerning family matters, including a copy of a note about his birthday, made by their father, 1737. One piece.
4 Will of Bernardus Engelbert, mentioning people in Coromandel and Ceylon, 1759. One piece.
5 Letter to Euphemia Engelbert on Ceylon from Bernardus Engelbert and Josina van Zijll at Nagappattinam concerning family matters, 1739. One piece.
7 Letter to Johannes Engelbert on Ceylon from Bernardus Engelbert at Nagappattinam concerning family matters, *c.* 1740. One piece.

1.2. UNIVERSITIES

1.2.1. *UNIVERSITEIT VAN AMSTERDAM, ARTIS BIBLIOTHEEK* UNIVERSITY OF AMSTERDAM, ARTIS LIBRARY

For general surveys, see J. Mateboer, *Repertorium bijzondere collecties* (The Hague, 1997), pp. 36-8, and the repository's web site (see Appendix II, 2.1).

Artis Bibliotheek
Artis Library

Size: 2000 metres; *c.* 3000 manuscripts and drawings, 13000 prints and 50000 published works
Period: 16th century–up to the present
Inventory:
- systematic catalogue on index cards
- G. Janse, *Catalogus der bibliotheek van het Koninklijk Zoölogisch Genootschap Natura Artis Magistra te Amsterdam* (Amsterdam, 1881)

The collection, consisting of published and unpublished materials, focuses on aspects of zoology, including taxonomy, evolution, animal psychology and various facets of biology. In addition to the materials described in this guide, there are many more depictions of flora and fauna possibly originating from South Asia. For materials concerning Surat, Ceylon and Bengal, see 2.6, 4.2, 4.6 and 6.6. See also 1.6.2.

229: 6 Various texts concerning foreign butterflies, including published works by Pieter Cramer (see Supplement I: Bibliography, no. 10) and Casper Stoll (?), and a manuscript by Stoll in which the butterflies described in the work of Cramer are systematically ordered, with references to butterflies from Coromandel and, to a lesser extent, Bengal, Malabar, Ceylon and possibly Surat, 1787, possibly partly published in *Aanhangsel van het werk, De uitlandsche kapellen, voorkomende in de drie waereld-deelen Asia, Africa en America, door den heer Pieter Cramer ... By een verzameld en beschreeven door Casper Stoll* (Amsterdam, 1791). One volume.

1.2.2. *UNIVERSITEIT VAN AMSTERDAM, UNIVERSITEITSBIBIOTHEEK* UNIVERSITY OF AMSTERDAM, UNIVERSITY LIBRARY

For general surveys, see H.J.A.H.G. Metselaars (ed.), *Particuliere archieven in Nederland* (*Overzichten van de archieven en verzamelingen in de openbare archiefbewaarplaatsen in Nederland*, Vol. 14) (Houten and Zaventem, 1992), pp. 159-66, J. Mateboer, *Repertorium bijzondere collecties* (The Hague, 1997), pp. 20-34, and the repository's web site (see Appendix II, 2.2). See also 1.6.2.

Manuscripts

Size: *c.* 600,000 items

Period: Middle Ages–up to the present

Inventory:
- for documents acquired up to the period *c.* 1902-17: *Catalogus der handschriften (bibliotheek der Universiteit van Amsterdam)*, 7 vols (Amsterdam, 1899-1923); relevant with respect to South Asia:
  - Vol. I, *Schenking-Diederichs, Nederlandse afdeling*, ed. J. Hellendoorn (1899), arranged alphabetically according to author, with list of addressees
  - Vol. II, *De handschriften der stedelijke bibliotheek met de latere aanwinsten*, ed. M.B. Mendes da Costa and C.P. Burger (1902), with index to personal names, geographical terms and subjects
  - Vol. IV (3 parts), *Brieven* (1919), arranged alphabetically according to author, with list of addressees
- for documents acquired after the period *c.* 1902-17: alphabetical and systematic catalogues on index cards

The collection is of a diverse character but mostly pertains to the Netherlands between the fifteenth and twentieth centuries. The bulk consists of letters from scholars, artists, politicians, etc. For documents and drawings concerning Surat, Malabar, Ceylon, Coromandel and Bengal, see also 2.2, 3.2, 3.6, 4.2, 4.6, 5.2, 6.2 and 6.6. See also 1.6.2.

II* A 17 — Ship's log of Samuel Fuller, sailing with the brig Lilly from Boston to India, calling at or passing by Calcutta, Coringa and Madras, 1799-1800, and with the ship Mathilda to the Cape of Good Hope, 1800-1. One volume, in English (catalogue: Vol. II, no. 1309).

IV C 22[1] — Notes concerning the East Indies by a VOC official (probably the Governor of Ceylon), deriving from the papers of Professor C.A. Duker (1670-1752) at Utrecht, seemingly largely dealing with South Asia, *c.* 1720 (?). One folder (catalogue: Vol. II, no. 1292).

VI H 3 — Correspondence in Syriac of Mar Thoma, Bishop of the St. Thomas Christians in Malabar. One bundle (catalogue: Vol. II, no. 1260). Partly published as *Relatio historica ad epistolam Syriacam a Maha Thome ... scriptam ad Ignatium ...* (Leiden, 1714). Including:

G Letter from Christophorus Theodosius Walther at the Jerusalem Church in Tranquebar, on behalf of the Danish missionaries, in Jacobitical script, with a Latin translation, 1725. For the remainder of the correspondence, see 3.2.

Be 1-102, Bf 1-86, 88-100, G 41 — Cuper collection, consisting of correspondence, with annexes and drawings, between Gijsbert Cuper (1644-1716, scholar and Burgomaster of Deventer) and Nicolaas Cornelisz Witsen (1641-1717, VOC Director from 1693 onward and Burgomaster of Amsterdam) concerning ethnology, religion, linguistics, naturalia, history, etc., in many parts of the world including Ceylon and, to a lesser extent, India (mostly Malabar and the Mughals), 1685-1716. Approx. 200 folders. For annexes and drawings, see 1.6.2, 2.2, 3.6, 4.2 and 4.6. For a short, general description of the contents of the letters (then still bound in four volumes), see P. Bosscha, *Opgave en beschrijving van de handschriften nagelaten door Gisbertus Cuperus* (Deventer, 1842) under no. 5, pp. 25-33. For a publication of the majority of the letters from Witsen to Cuper, see J.F. Gebhart, *Het leven van Mr. Nicolaas Cornelisz. Witsen*, 2 vols (Utrecht, 1881-2), Vol. 2, pp. 283-469. For a partial translation and description, see Peters, 'Nicolaes Witsen and Gijsbert Cuper' (see Supplement I: Bibliography, no. 144). Another part of the Cuper collection is kept at the *Koninklijke Bibliotheek*, The Hague, see 1.4.12.

O 32-50 Letters, accounts, powers of attorney and other papers originating from or concerning the Luyken family at Jaffna and Nagappattinam, including documents with regard to Andries Willem Luyken (d. 1754), Gerrit Nicolaas Luyken (Bookkeeper at Nagappattinam), Jan Willem Luyken (Bookkeeper and Minter at Nagappattinam), Anna Jacoba Luyken, Maria Luyken, Gerard Luyken, Johannes Gerardus Luyken, Jan Jacob Kerkenberg (d. 1773, *Vaandrig* (reserve officer candidate) at Jaffna), J.N. Letanche (Lieutenant at Jaffna), Antonius Matthaeus (State *Advocaat-Fiscaal* (judge advocate) of Holland and West-Friesland), Gerrit Willem van Oosten de Bruyn (1727-97, Burgomaster of Haarlem), Johanne Maria van Tuttel, Arnoldus Dix and the Orphan Board at Jaffna, 1744-79. 19 folders (catalogue: Vol. II, no. 1167).

Dortmond collection

Period: 3000 BC–up to the present
Inventory: checklist

The collection of J.A. Dortmond (1912-88) focuses on scripts. It includes manuscripts, *olais* (palm leaf records), copper inscriptions, metal seals, etc. in Sanskrit, Devanagari, Gurmukhi/Panjabi, Bengali, Bihari, Telugu and/or Telinga, Tamil, Malayalam and Sinhalese. One of the *olais* originates from the King of Thanjavur. The date of most items is unknown; some date from the early nineteenth century.

Zeldzame en kostbare werken
Rare and valuable books

Size: *c.* 130,000 items dating from before 1800
Period: up to 1850
Inventory: data base

This collection consists of the printed works of the Library that date from before 1850 as well as later publications deserving special attention because of their contents or workmanship. It includes a few short printed texts concerning Ceylon that are mentioned in this guide because of their rarity, see 4.2.

1.2.3. *VRIJE UNIVERSITEIT AMSTERDAM, BIBLIOTHEEK*
VRIJE UNIVERSITEIT AMSTERDAM, LIBRARY

For general surveys, see J. Mateboer, *Repertorium bijzondere collecties* (The Hague, 1997), pp. 39-43, and the repository's web site (see Appendix II, 2.3). See also 1.6.2.

Handschriften en oude drukken
Manuscripts and early printed books

Size:	*c.* 600 manuscripts, 55000 printed works dating from before 1901 and 1500 prints (among other materials)
Period:	pre-Christian era–up to the present
Inventory:	– data base (on Internet) – various catalogues of parts of the collection

The collection focuses both on the general needs of the university and on Dutch Protestantism. It includes a very rare printed newsletter pertaining to Coromandel. See 5.2.

1.2.4. *BIBLIOTHEEK TECHNISCHE UNIVERSITEIT DELFT*
DELFT UNIVERSITY OF TECHNOLOGY LIBRARY

This repository keeps a number of maps pertaining to South Asia. See 1.6.2.

1.2.5. *THEOLOGISCHE UNIVERSITEIT KAMPEN, BIBLIOTHEEK*
THEOLOGICAL UNIVERSITY OF KAMPEN, LIBRARY

For a general survey, see the repository's web site (see Appendix II, 2.5).

Library

Size:	*c.* 200,000 items
Period:	*c.* 16th century–up to the present
Inventory:	– data base (on Internet) – *Catalogus van de bibliotheek der Theologische School van de Gereformeerde Kerken in Nederland* (Kampen, 1911), with introduction and index

This collection consists of published works as well as manuscripts, pamphlets, etc. It focuses on theology, Semitic religions and others religious studies, philosophy and Semitic languages. It includes some manuscripts pertaining to Hinduism and Sinhalese written by missionaries of the Dutch Reformed Church. For material concerning Ceylon, see 4.2.

101 A 2 'De Godsgeleerthydt der Bramines, die Eswara voor 't Hoogste Voorwerp van hun vertrouwen en dienst stellen. Waar in hunne leerstukken nopens Gods, den Godsdienst, plechtigheden, bijgeloovigheden, volgens hun alden lijfigste boek, den Vedam, kortelijk worden voorgedragen', manuscript concerning the worship of Shiva, or Hinduism as a whole, according to the Vedas, edited by Petrus Sijnjeu, priest and Rector of the Seminary at Colombo, 1711. One volume, last part apparently missing.

101 A 3 'Wetboek der Bramines ofte het eerste goddelijke boek der zelven', i.e. law book or first divine book of the Brahmins (or Hindus), manuscript edited by Petrus Sijnjeu, 1710. One volume.

1.2.6. *UNIVERSITEIT LEIDEN, INSTITUUT KERN*
LEIDEN UNIVERSITY, KERN INSTITUTE

This repository holds a number of maps pertaining to South Asia. See 1.6.2.

1.2.7. *UNIVERSITEIT LEIDEN, UNIVERSITEITSBIBLIOTHEEK*
LEIDEN UNIVERSITY LIBRARY

For general surveys, see S.M. Gieling, P.G. Hoftijzer and J.J. Witkam (eds), *Special Collections. A Guide to the Collections of Leiden University Library and Neighbouring Institutions* (Leiden, 2002), J. Mateboer, *Repertorium bijzondere collecties* (The Hague, 1997), pp. 79-91, and the repository's web site (see Appendix II, 2.7). See also 1.6.2. Note that some of the Library's materials listed in the section on maps and pictures also include texts, see 3.6, 4.6 and 5.6 in particular.

Maatschappij der Nederlandse Letterkunde te Leiden
Society of Netherlands Literature at Leiden

Inv. nos: 1-*c.* 2258
Period: Middle Ages–up to the present
Inventory:
- 'Catalogus der bibliotheek van de Maatschappij der Nederlandsche Letterkunde te Leiden (Hss Ltk. 1-1084)' (1887), covering inv. nos 1-1084, with introduction and table of contents
- 'Journaal Ltk (1085-1599/1600-2050)', 2 vols, handwritten, covering inv. nos 1085-2050
- 'Catalogus compendiarus ... Pars III ... naamlijst van de brievencollectie in het bezit van de Maatschappij der Nederlandsche Letterkunde (Ltk brieven)' (1936), with indices to senders and addressees of the letters in this collection
- 'Catalogus compendiarus ... Pars IV ... handschriften in het bezit van de Maatschappij der Nederlandsche Letterkunde (Ltk Codices)' (1937), covering inv. nos 1-1874, with index to personal names
- 'Brievencatalogus UB Leiden', 12 vols (1989), referring to all letters kept at the University Library, covering various collections including the *Maatschappij der Nederlandse Letterkunde te*

Leiden, with indices to senders and addressees, also available as data base
- alphabetical catalogue of authors of manuscripts and systematic catalogue of anonymous manuscripts, both on index cards

Founded in 1766, the Society focuses on (the publication of works concerning) literature, linguistics, archaeology, Dutch history and rhetoric. Its collection is of a varied character. For documents concerning Surat, Ceylon and Coromandel, see 2.2, 4.2 and 5.2.

Ltk 591 Abstract from a manuscript composed by a VOC Director, containing an alphabetical list of words and expressions in Asian languages that are relevant for the VOC, including South Asian terms, and explanations, *c.* 1750, with a nineteenth-century review by H.C. Millies. One volume.

Ltk 592 Survey of the Tamil script, undated (eighteenth century?). One piece.

Bibliotheca Publica Latina
Latin Public Library

Inv. nos: 1-*c.* 3500
Period: Middle Ages–up to the present
Inventory:
- 'Catalogi manuscriptorum bibliothecae Lugduno Bataviae. Bibliotheca Publica Latina', 3 vols, partly handwritten, covering inv. nos 1-2782, partly in Latin
- 'Catalogus compendiarius ... Pars I. Codices manuscripti bibliotheca academiae Lugduno-Batavae. (UB Codices)' (1932), pp. 97-161, covering inv. nos 1-2267, in Latin, with index
- 'Codices Bibliothecae Publicae Latini (BPL Codices)' (1912), covering most inv. nos between 1 and 2012, in Latin, with indices
- 'Brievencatalogus UB Leiden', 12 vols (1989), referring to all letters kept at the University Library, covering various collections including *Bibliotheca Publica Latina*, with indices to senders and addressees, also available as data base
- alphabetical catalogue of authors of manuscripts and systematic catalogue of anonymous manuscripts, both on index cards
- data base (not for general use)

The collection is of varied nature, the sole common characteristic of all papers being their Roman (Latin) script. It includes all documents that do not make up substantial collections themselves. In addition to the papers described in this guide, several other documents pertain to the VOC. Inv. no. BPL 3042 concerns a folder with early twentieth-century papers regarding VOC remains at Surat, Bharuch, Ahmadabad, Chinsura, Murshidabad or Cossimbazar ("Kalkapur'), Chhapra, Calcutta and Balasore, including texts of epitaphs. Inv. no. BPL 1882 consists of a copy in typescript of a plan regarding the administration of justice by Alexander Higginson, secretary at the Revenue Department at Calcutta, 1772. For documents and drawings concerning Surat, Malabar, Ceylon, Coromandel and Bengal, see 2.2, 3.2, 3.6, 4.2, 4.6, 5.2, 5.6 and 6.2. See also 1.6.2.

BPL 126D	'Icones Plantarum Malabaricum [*sic*], adscriptis nominibus et viribus', manuscript containing 262 descriptions and drawings of plants growing on Ceylon and in south India, with names in Tamil (?) and Sinhalese, *c.* late seventeenth century (?). Two volumes.
BPL 616	Papers originating from H.G. Nahuys van Burgst (1782-1858), high functionary in the South-East Asian Archipelago between 1805 and 1839. 22 items. Including: Portfolio 8, no. 14 Letter from Rammohun Roy, 1824. One piece.
BPL 617	*Resoluties* (proceedings), letters, memorandums and other papers concerning the VOC, with list of contents, 1687-1769, probably deriving from Augustinus van Son (1722-89), who became Secretary of the representatives of the Stadtholder with the VOC in 1750, and Lawyer of the VOC in 1755. 32 folders. Including: 10 Papers concerning the return fleet of 1762-3, including sections on Bengal, Coromandel, Ceylon, Malabar and Surat. 28 Memorandums concerning conflicts with the French in South Asia, in particular at Masulipatam, Sadras, Thanjavur, Pondicherry and Chandernagore, partly in connection with a number of ships, 1760-2. Partly in French.
BPL 622, ff. 1-10	Dissertation concerning the state of the VOC by Governor-General Jacob Mossel, including sections on South Asia, 1752.
BPL 622, ff. 17-54	Memorandum regarding the state of the VOC by Mossel, including sections on Bengal, Coromandel, Ceylon, Malabar and Surat (ff. 28v-36), 1753.
BPL 930	Notes of a servant of the Zeeland Chamber of the VOC (Jan de Mauregnault?) concerning his voyage to Java in 1722, his appointment as *Fiscaal* of Colombo and his journey to Ceylon via Malabar in 1727, with ff. 7-20 largely dealing with Cochin, Quilon, Travancore and religious matters in Malabar. One volume.
BPL 932	Report for the States General by Mattheus van den Broeck, Commander of the return fleet, including sections on Bengal, Coromandel, Ceylon, Madurai, Malabar, Kanara, Vengurla and Surat, 1670. One volume.
BPL 933	Treatise in two parts on the causes of the decay of the VOC and the means for recovery, including a section suggesting to abandon Surat and shift its trade to Cochin (ff. 111-16), 1773. One volume.
BPL 952	Journals of Pieter van den Broecke's voyages to Africa and Asia, 1608-40, including sections on Ceylon, Surat,

Ahmadabad, Calicut, the Deccan, Pulicat and other parts of Coromandel, with some drawings (see 5.6). One volume. The parts concerning Asia are published in *Pieter van den Broecke in Azië*, 2 vols, ed. W.Ph. Coolhaas (Werken Linschoten Vereniging, 63-4) (The Hague, 1962-3). For an adapted version, see Pieter van den Broecke, *Korte historiael ende journaelsche aenteyckeninghe* (Haarlem, 1634).

BPL 1218 — Register of priests and parishes in the Dutch Republic and its overseas settlements, deriving from J.G. de Waldkirch Ziepprecht. Including:

- o Priests in the East Indies, including South Asia, 1629-1794. One folder.
- q Parishes and their ministers in the East Indies, including sections on Galle, Colombo, Negombo, Jaffna, Matara, Pulicat, Nagappattinam and Cochin. One folder.

BPL 2881 — 't Leven der Heydense Benjanen', unfinished manuscript (323 ff.) concerning Hinduism, including sections on Ganesha, Mahadeva/Shiva and the ten incarnations of Vishnu, probably written by a VOC missionary. One volume.

Bibliotheca Thysiana
Thysius Library

Inv. nos: manuscripts: 1-23, 100-293
Size: *c.* 3000 books
Period: 16th-20th centuries
Inventory:
- R. van Roijen, 'Bibliotheca Thysiana. Catalogus archief, familiepapieren en koopmansboeken' (1941), with introduction
- H. de Jonge, 'Inventaris van het archief van de Bibliotheca Thysiana' (*c.* 2002)
- L.D. Petit and H.J.A. Ruys, *Bibliotheek van Nederlandsche pamfletten: verzamelingen van de bibliotheek van Joannes Thysius en de bibliotheek der Rijks-Universiteit te Leiden*, 4 vols (The Hague, 1882-4, Leiden, 1925-34).
- *Catalogus der bibliotheek van Joannes Thysius*, ed. P.A. Thiele (Leiden, 1879)

This collection comprises a private library that was left by the jurist Johannes Thysius (1621-53). In addition to books, it consists mostly of pamphlets, some of which concern Ceylon or Bengal, see 4.2 and 6.2. It also includes a number of manuscripts, some of which relate to the *Voorcompagnieën* (early or pre-companies) and the early years of the VOC.

215 Letters from Jacques de Velaer Senior and Junior at Amsterdam to Anthoine l'Empereur, textile trader at Leiden, with appendices, partly concerning trade with the East Indies, including a few references to South Asia, 1601-12. Partly in French, two folders.

Oosterse Handschriften (Legatum Warnerianum)
Oriental Manuscripts (Warner's Legacy)

Inv. nos: 1-*c.* 28000
Size: *c.* 160 metres
Period: 500 BC–up to the present
Inventory:
- catalogues according to language (none on South Asian languages), of which the following mentions some relevant documents: E.P. Wieringa (ed.), *Catalogue of Malay and Minangkabau Manuscripts in the Library of Leiden University and Other Collections in the Netherlands. Volume One: Comprising the Acquisitions of Malay Manuscripts in Leiden University Library up to the Year 1896* (Leiden, 1998), with introduction and indices
- J.J. Witkam, 'Inventory of the Oriental Manuscripts in the Legatum Warnerianum in the Library of the University of Leiden and Other Collections in the Netherlands', with index (in preparation; a provisional digital version has been consulted for this guide)

The collection grew around the Middle Eastern manuscripts collected by Levinus Warner (1619-65), envoy to the Ottoman Empire. The present-day collection covers manuscripts originating from the area roughly between West Africa and the Far East, with the greater part coming from Indonesia. It includes a number of manuscripts from South Asia, some of which were received or otherwise acquired by or through VOC officials. Note that in addition to the documents described in this guide, there are many other manuscripts in various South Asian languages (such as Persian, Sanskrit, Pali, Malayalam, Tamil, Telugu, Dakhni and Sinhalese, the latter including Christian texts), of which a connection to the Dutch presence in South Asia is uncertain or which have not been properly described yet (for Sinhalese palm leaves, see P.H.D.H. de Silva, *A Catalogue of Antiquities and Other Cultural Objects from Sri Lanka (Ceylon) Abroad* (Colombo, 1975), pp. 396-9 (somewhat outdated and occasionally inaccurate)). For papers concerning Surat, Malabar, Ceylon, Coromandel and Bengal, see also 2.2, 3.2, 4.2, 5.2 and 6.2.

Or. 1204 The four Gospels in Syriac, copied in Malabar and received from Ceylon, donated by Wolpherdus Senguerdius in 1724. One volume.

Or. 1216 b Survey of the Tamil script, compiled by a European, donated by Gerard Riemersma in 1748. One volume.

Or. 1425-7 Various studies and notes on Sanskrit and comparisons with other languages such as Persian and German, by H.A. Hamaker (1789-1835), Professor of Sanskrit at Leiden. Partly in Latin.

Or. 1687-8 Two so-called 'Leiden charters', texts in Tamil and Sanskrit of various Chola rulers, brought from India by Florentius Camper, clergyman at Batavia from 1702 to 1713, later owned by H.A. Hamaker. 24 copper plates. Reproduced, transcribed and translated in K.V. Subrahmanya Aiyer, *Epigraphia Indica*, 22 (1934), pp. 213-81. Or. 1688a consists of later and related material.

Or. 1926 Unidentified text in Tamil, formerly owned by Isaac Vossius (1618-89). Palm leaf.

Or. 1927 Fragment of the Tamil classic Tirukkural by Tiruvalluvar, formerly owned by Jacobus Perizonius (1651-1715). Palm leaf.

Or. 3090 Various papers, largely in Persian and Bengali (mostly in Arabic script), probably chiefly originating from Bengal and consisting of documents concerning slaves and passes sent to an unknown Dutch addressee, 1691, *c.* 1750-4 (?). One folder. Including:

- 1 Letter from Muhammad Karim Beg, merchant at Surat, to Muhammad Zahid Bey Tabrizi at Cranganur (?), 1691. In Persian, note in Dutch on the back.
- 2, 5, 11, 13-15 Various documents in Persian (?), *c.* 1750-4 (?).
- 4 Document concerning a female slave (?), *c.* 1750-4 (?). In Persian, note in Dutch on the back.
- 8 Part of a letter in Persian, with a note in Dutch on the back reading 'gegertzeets', *c.* 1750-4 (?).
- (unnumbered) Six fragments with parts of texts, seal prints and an address, *c.* 1750-4 (?), including one piece with a note in Dutch seemingly saying it was sent by Saiyid Abdulla by order of Nawab Siraj-ud-Daula to prepare a garden, 1754.

Or. 5008 Collection of short texts in Tamil, Telugu and possibly Sinhalese. 34 palm leaves. Including:

- (c) The Lord's Prayer in Tamil and the Tamil alphabet, with a few short Dutch notes. Two palm leaves.

1.2.8. *BIBLIOTHEEK UNIVERSITEIT TILBURG* TILBURG UNIVERSITY LIBRARY

For a general survey, see the repository's web site (see Appendix II, 2.8)

Handschriften
Manuscripts

Size: *c.* 200 items
Period: *c.* 13th-18th centuries
Inventory: J. van de Ven, *Handschriften en handschriftfragmenten in het bezit van de Theologische Faculteit Tilburg* (Tilburg, 1990)

The major part of the collection, including the papers relevant for South Asia, originates from the *Groot-Seminarie* (Great Seminary) at Haaren. Inv. nos TF-HS 54-5, 59-60 and 74-9 concern the VOC. For papers pertaining to Ceylon, Coromandel and Bengal, see also 4.2, 5.2 and 6.2. The documents deriving from the Seminary appear to be related to some papers in the Van der Brugghen van Croy family archives at the *Historisch Informatiecentrum Helmond* (see 1.1.14) and to manuscripts originating from the Seminary kept at the *Archief Bisdom 's-Hertogenbosch* (see 1.3.1).

TF-HS 60 Secret papers concerning conflicts with other Europeans, mostly regarding Ceylon, Coromandel and other places in South Asia, including correspondence between Colombo, Trincomalee, Jaffna, Batticaloa, Nagappattinam, Galle, Fort St. David (Teganapatam) and Pondicherry, 1748-50. Partly in English and French, one volume (catalogue no. 51).

1.2.9. *UNIVERSITEIT UTRECHT, FACULTEIT RUIMTELIJKE WETENSCHAPPEN*
UTRECHT UNIVERSITY, FACULTY OF GEOSCIENCES

This repository keeps a number of maps pertaining to South Asia. See 1.6.2.

1.2.10. *UNIVERSITEIT UTRECHT, UNIVERSITEITSBIBLIOTHEEK*
UTRECHT UNIVERSITY LIBRARY

For general surveys, see K. van der Horst, L.C. Kuiper-Brussen and P.N.G. Pesch, *Handschriften en oude drukken van de Utrechtse Universiteitsbibliotheek* (Utrecht, 1984), H.J.A.H.G. Metselaars (ed.), *Particuliere archieven in Nederland* (*Overzichten van de archieven en verzamelingen in de openbare archief-bewaarplaatsen in Nederland*, Vol. 14) (Houten and Zaventem, 1992), pp. 470-5, J. Mateboer, *Repertorium bijzondere collecties* (The Hague, 1997), pp. 112-19, and the repository's web site (see Appendix II, 2.10).

Handschriften
Manuscripts

Inv. nos: Hs. 1-1907 (acquisitions up to 1909), Hs. 0.A.1-29.C.18 (acquisitions after 1909)
Size: *c.* 2850 manuscripts, 100,000 letters and 2000 lecture notes
Period: third century–up to the present
Inventory:
- for acquisitions up to 1909: P.A. Tiele (Vol. I) and A. Hulshof (Vol. II), *Catalogus codicum manu scriptorum bibliothecae Universitatis Rheno-Trajectinae* (Utrecht, 1887, 1909), with index; partly updated in the so-called 'Addenda'
- for acquisitions after 1909: catalogue on index cards in the so-called 'Supplement'
- data base

The collection is of a varied character, but focuses on the *c.* 350 medieval manuscripts originating from the libraries of the Utrecht monasteries and convents, other medieval works (mostly of religious content such as books of hours and prayer and liturgical books) and manuscripts concerning the history of Utrecht and its University. In addition to the materials described separately in this guide, the collection includes Sanskrit and Persian manuscripts that do not seem to have a clear connection to the VOC presence in South Asia. Inv. nos Hs. 1704 (8*.E.27), Hs. 1712-14 (8*.C.1) and Hs. 8.C.2-4 consist of nineteenth-century notes, extracts and index cards made by H.C. Millies pertaining to the VOC, the Dutch

Reformed Church in the East Indies, etc., including references to South Asia, mostly Ceylon. Inv. nos Hs. 1165 (3.G.5), Hs. 4*.F.25 (Wttewaal collection no. 74) and Hs. 3. L.19 also concern the VOC. For papers, drawings and maps regarding Surat, Ceylon, Coromandel and Bengal, see 2.2, 4.2, 4.6, 5.2 and 6.2.

Hs. 1314 (4.L.10)	Letters from Reverent G. Reinking at Batavia and the Cape of Good Hope to B.C. van Lijnden van Lunenburg, mostly concerning the propagation of Christianity in the East Indies, including a few references to South Asia, 1776-9. One folder.
Hs. 1479 (1.E.22)	Description of the Tamil script and grammar (referred to as 'Malabarese'), including comparisons to other languages, seventeenth century. One volume (originating from Adriaan Reland).

1.2.11. *BIBLIOTHEEK WAGENINGEN UNIVERSITEIT EN RESEARCHCENTRUM* WAGENINGEN UNIVERSITY AND RESEARCH CENTRE LIBRARY

This repository keeps a number of drawings pertaining to South Asia. See 1.6.2.

1.3. Ecclesiastical Organizations

Note that most archival materials of ecclesiastical organizations (or private papers deriving from people involved in Christian affairs) are kept at governmental archives, universities and other institutions. See for example *Gemeentearchief Amsterdam* (1.1.2), *Rijksarchief in Noord-Holland* (1.1.10), *Haags Gemeentearchief* (1.1.11), *Zeeuws Archief* (1.1.21), *Gemeentearchief Rotterdam* (1.1.22), *Het Utrechts Archief* (1.1.23), *Historisch Centrum Overijssel* (1.1.25), *Theologische Universiteit Kampen* (1.2.5), *Bibliotheek Universiteit Tilburg* (1.2.8), *Centraal Bureau voor Genealogie* (1.4.11), *Koninklijk Huisarchief* (1.5.6) and *Nationaal Archief* (Supplement II).

1.3.1. *ARCHIEF BISDOM 'S-HERTOGENBOSCH* ARCHIVES DIOCESE 'S-HERTOGENBOSCH

For a general survey, see the repository's web site (see Appendix II, 3.1).

Groot-Seminarie Haaren
Great Seminary Haaren

Inv. nos:	1-680
Size:	*c.* 40 metres
Period:	13th-20th centuries
Inventory:	in typescript

After several seminaries outside the Dutch Republic were closed, the Great Seminary was founded in 1798 at 's-Hertogenbosch to provide education for Roman Catholic priests. From 1839 to its dissolution in 1967 it had its seat in

Haaren. The archives include some papers regarding Ceylon, see 4.3. The documents appear to be related to some manuscripts deriving from the same Seminary kept at the *Bibliotheek Universiteit Tilburg* (see 1.2.8) and to some papers in the Van der Brugghen van Croy family archives at the *Historisch Informatiecentrum Helmond* (see 1.1.14).

1.3.2. *ARCHIEF VAN DE NEDERLANDSE PROVINCIE DER JEZUÏETEN (NIJMEGEN)* ARCHIVES OF THE NETHERLANDS PROVINCE OF THE JESUITS

For general surveys, see H.J.A.H.G. Metselaars (ed.), *Particuliere archieven in Nederland (Overzichten van de archieven en verzamelingen in de openbare archiefbewaarplaatsen in Nederland*, Vol. 14) (Houten and Zaventem, 1992), pp. 332-8, and the repository's web site (see Appendix II, 3.2).

Handschriften
Manuscripts

Inv. nos:	A. 1-Z. 354
Size:	*c.* 80 metres
Period:	1389–up to the present
Inventory:	G. Gorris, 'Cataloog van de historische handschriftenverzameling berustende in het archief van de Nederlandse Provincie der Jezuieten' (1962-70), with later additions

This miscellaneous collection includes papers deriving from the 'Old Society of Jesus' in general and the Dutch Jesuit mission and the 'Province Flandro-Belgica' in particular. Among these are some documents concerning Jesuits in India, which are mostly copies of papers kept at the National Archives of Belgium at Brussels. In addition to the documents described in this guide, inv. no. A.D. 1 contains documentation and modern handwritten copies of papers partly concerning Jesuits in India. For documents concerning Surat, Malabar, Coromandel and Bengal, see 2.3, 3.3, 5.3 and 6.3.

A.D. 3 (box 21)	Letters sent by Jesuits in India to Jesuits in Europe. Photocopies and contemporary manuscript copies, with recent documentation and notes pertaining to these letters and Jesuits in India, one folder. Including: (a) Letter to Le Gobien at Paris.

1.4. Museums and Other Public Institutions

1.4.1. *STEDELIJK MUSEUM ALKMAAR* MUNICIPAL MUSEUM OF ALKMAAR

This repository keeps some paintings pertaining to South Asia. See 1.6.4.

1.4.2. *KONINKLIJK INSTITUUT VOOR DE TROPEN (KIT)* (Amsterdam) ROYAL TROPICAL INSTITUTE

For general surveys, see H.J.A.H.G. Metselaars (ed.), *Particuliere archieven in Nederland (Overzichten van de archieven en verzamelingen in de openbare archiefbewaarplaatsen in Nederland*, Vol. 14) (Houten and Zaventem, 1992), pp. 115-16, and the repository's web site (see Appendix II, 4.2). See also 1.6.4.

Kenniscentrum
Resource Centre

Size: *c.* 270,000 books and journals, 25000 maps and 850 atlases
Period: 16th century–up to the present
Inventory: data base

Also known as the KIT Library, this is the main library of the Institute. It focuses on developing countries and chiefly consists of published works but includes a few relevant manuscripts and drawings. For materials concerning Ceylon, Coromandel and Bengal, see also 4.4, 4.6, 5.6 and 6.6.

RG-176 Regulations (extracts) concerning the reduction of VOC personnel and rations in Asia, with sections on Bengal, Coromandel, Ceylon, Malabar and Surat (ff. 13-34), 1680. One volume.

Tropen Museum
Tropical Museum

Size: *c.* 280,000 items
Period: prehistory–up to the present
Inventory:
- data base
- geographical and other catalogues on index cards

The collection of the Museum includes anthropological objects, works of art, prints and manuscripts pertaining to the tropics and adjacent regions (for materials concerning Ceylon, see P.H.D.H. de Silva, *A Catalogue of Antiquities and Other Cultural Objects from Sri Lanka (Ceylon) Abroad* (Colombo, 1975), pp. 382-95 (somewhat outdated and occasionally inaccurate)). Part of the collection originates from the Artis Zoo in Amsterdam; the inv. nos of the objects in question begin with 'A'. In addition to the items described in this guide, the Museum also keeps Indian paintings and manuscripts in Sinhalese, Tamil and other Indian languages that do not seem to have a clear connection with the presence of the VOC in South Asia. Besides, the collection includes relevant prints originating from published works (see also Appendix I). For materials concerning Malabar, Ceylon, Coromandel and Bengal, see 3.6, 4.4, 5.4, 5.6 and 6.4. See also 1.6.4.

3710 / 46a-b Letter from James Balfour in India to his accountants, 1821-2. In English.

3710 / 47 Letter from Jane R. Sneyd to Scott concerning a war in India in which Captain Sneyd is partaking, 1825. In English.

3710 / 50 Letter from Lionel Darell (?) concerning the appointment of officials in India, 1801. In English.

1.4.3. *NEDERLANDSCH ECONOMISCH-HISTORISCH ARCHIEF (NEHA)* (Amsterdam) NETHERLANDS ECONOMIC-HISTORICAL ARCHIVES

For general surveys, see H.J.A.H.G. Metselaars (ed.), *Particuliere archieven in Nederland* (*Overzichten van de archieven en verzamelingen in de openbare archiefbewaarplaatsen in Nederland*, Vol. 14) (Houten and Zaventem, 1992), pp. 117-18, J. Lucassen, *Tracing the Past. Collections and Research in Social and Economic History* (Amsterdam, 1989), pp. 82-3, and the repository's web site (see Appendix II, 4.3). For materials concerning Asia, see E. Schwidder and E. Vermeij (eds), *Guide to the Asian Collections at the International Institute of Social History* (Amsterdam, 2001) (with introduction and index), which includes the holdings of the NEHA.

Bijzondere collecties
Special collections

Size: 112 metres
Period: 13th century–up to the present
Inventory: – P. Boorsma and J. Lucassen, *Gids van de collecties van het Nederlandsch Economisch-Historisch Archief te Amsterdam* (Amsterdam, 1992), with introduction, appendices and index
– data base

These collections focus on all aspects of economic history, including trade and commerce, insurance, management, accountancy, finance and monetary policy. Inv. nos 119-27, 132, 543-4 concern the VOC and other companies. For documents concerning Ceylon, see 4.4.

121 Considerations about the state of the VOC and proposals to reorganise it, by Governor-General Gustaaf Willem van Imhoff, with sections on South Asia, 1741. One volume.
122 Two sets of sailing instructions, with the second part including sections on the stretches from Masulipatam to Batavia (f. 99) and from the Cape of Good Hope to Ceylon (f. 112-18), 1744-86. Two volumes, mostly printed.
125 Auction lists with prices and buyers of textiles sold at Amsterdam and Middelburg, including textiles from South Asia, in particular Bengal, Coromandel, the Fishery Coast and Surat, 1763. One volume, mostly printed.
127 Financial administration and correspondence of Jacob Temminck and Cornelis van Twist (see 1.1.2, *Gemeentearchief Amsterdam, Firma Temminck en Van Twist*), 1788-1813. Including:
    8 Notes concerning the auction of textiles at Amsterdam, including textiles from South Asia, in particular Bengal, 1794. One volume, printed.

1.4.4. *NEDERLANDS SCHEEPVAARTMUSEUM AMSTERDAM* NETHERLANDS MARITIME MUSEUM AMSTERDAM

For general surveys, see H.J.A.H.G. Metselaars (ed.), *Particuliere archieven in Nederland* (*Overzichten van de archieven en verzamelingen in de openbare archiefbewaarplaatsen in Nederland*, Vol. 14) (Houten and Zaventem, 1992), pp. 157-8, and the repository's web site (see Appendix II, 4.4). See also 1.6.4.

Library

Size: *c.* 50000 items
Period: 1451–up to the present
Inventory:
- data base (on Internet)
- catalogue on index cards
- W. Voorbeytel Cannenburg, *Catalogus der bibliotheek van het Nederlandsch Historisch Scheepvaartmuseum*, 2 vols (Amsterdam, 1960), with index

This collection consists of both manuscripts and published works, and focuses on Dutch maritime history. Around 40 per cent of the collection dates from before 1850. Among these materials, there are many papers concerning the VOC, including ship's logs, nautical guides, travel accounts and printed documents. For papers and drawings concerning Malabar, Ceylon, Coromandel and Bengal, see also 3.4, 3.6, 4.4, 4.6, 5.4, 5.6, 6.4 and 6.6.

A-IV-2-234 a Various texts concerning the sailing to and trade in Asia, collected as part of the preparation for the first Dutch expedition to the East Indies in 1595, based on Dutch and Portuguese sources, 1594-5. One volume. For a detailed description, see H. Hazelhoff Roelfzema, 'Een handschrift uit 1594, bevattende gegevens ten behoeve van de voorgenomen handel en scheepvaart op Oost-Indië', *Nederlandsch Historisch Scheepvaart Museum, Jaarverslag 1971-1972*, pp. 72-5 (inv. no. A-IV-2-234 b is a modern-day transcription). Including:

- ff. 1-11 Short descriptions of regions, kingdoms, ports, etc., on the sailing route to the East Indies, apparently a summary of the information collected by Cornelis de Houtman in Lisbon, including sections on Cambay, Calicut, the Maldives, Ceylon, Coromandel and Bengal.
- ff. 59-63 Survey of commodities traded by the Portuguese in the East Indies, including South Asia (see also ff. 11-14).
- ff. 73, 106-7 Descriptions of the overland route between Goa and Cochin and Venice and the accompanying expenses.

B-III-391 Papers concerning the career of Librecht Hooreman, including his appointment as factor at Nagappattinam, 1739, promotion from *Opperhoofd* of Masulipatam to *Commandeur* of Jaffna, 1746, appointment as Governor of Coromandel, 1748, and documents regarding his salary increase because of his promotions to *Opperhoofd* of Masulipatam, 1743, and Governor of Coromandel, 1747. One folder.

B-III-499 Various printed proclamations, instructions, extracts from *resoluties* (proceedings), cargo lists, etc., all pertaining to the VOC, 1747. One bundle. Including:

11 Regulations for ships sailing in the East Indies, with section 36 containing short instructions to sailors in Bengal, Malabar and Surat (among other locations). One quire.

1.4.5. *RIJKSMUSEUM AMSTERDAM*
RIJKSMUSEUM AMSTERDAM

This repository keeps a great number of maps and pictures (and a few manuscripts) pertaining to South Asia. See 1.6.4.

1.4.6. *MUSEUM BRONBEEK* (Arnhem)
BRONBEEK MUSEUM

This repository keeps a painting concerning South Asia. See 1.6.4.

1.4.7. *DORDRECHTS MUSEUM*
MUSEUM OF DORDRECHT

This repository keeps a painting pertaining to South Asia. See 1.6.4.

1.4.8. *SIMON VAN GIJN - MUSEUM AAN HUIS* (Dordrecht)
SIMON VAN GIJN - MUSEUM AT HOME

This repository keeps a painting pertaining to South Asia. See 1.6.4.

1.4.9. *GRONINGER MUSEUM*
MUSEUM OF GRONINGEN

This repository keeps some paintings concerning South Asia. See 1.6.4.

1.4.10. *TEYLERS MUSEUM* (Haarlem)
TEYLER'S MUSEUM

For general surveys, see H.J.A.H.G. Metselaars (ed.), *Particuliere archieven in Nederland* (*Overzichten van de archieven en verzamelingen in de openbare archiefbewaarplaatsen in Nederland*, Vol. 14) (Houten and Zaventem, 1992), pp. 284-5, and the repository's web site (see Appendix II, 4.10). See also 1.6.4.

Teylers Stichting
Teyler's Foundation

Inv. nos: 1-2386

Size: *c*. 70 metres
Period: 1606–up to the present
Inventory: C.J. van Ronnen, 'Inventaris van de archieven van Teylers Stichting te Haarlem, 1606-1945' (1977), with introduction, annexes and indices, and with supplement

The Teyler's Foundation was established in 1778 as a result of a testamentary disposition of the Haarlem silk manufacturer and merchant Pieter Teyler van der Hulst (1702-78). The archives include manuscripts that were submitted as part of prize contests hold by the Foundation. The archives may also contain information about the drawings kept by the Foundation (see 1.6.4).

1120 Manuscript submitted by Jacob Haafner as part of a prize contest dealing with the question what has been the contribution by missionaries to the propagation of the 'true' Christianity in the seventeenth and eighteenth centuries, partly concerning South Asia, 1803. One volume. Published as *Onderzoek naar het nut der zendelingen en zendelingsgenootschappen* (Haarlem, 1807); reprint edited by J.A. de Moor and P.G.E.I.J. van der Velde (Hilversum, 1993). Described in J. de Moor and P. van der Velde, 'De "heilige tale des lands". Jacob Haafner als voorloper van de studie van het Sanskrit in Nederland', in H.J. 't Hart-van den Muyzenberg and Th. de Bruin (eds), *Waarom Sanskrit? Honderdvijfentwintig jaar Sanskrit in Nederland* (Kern Institute miscellanea, 4) (Leiden, 1991), pp. 88-9, and J.A. de Moor and P.G.E.I.J. van der Velde, *De werken van Jacob Haafner*, Vol. 1 (Werken Linschoten Vereniging, 91) (Zutphen, 1992), pp. 30, 33.

1.4.11. *CENTRAAL BUREAU VOOR GENEALOGIE (CBG)* (The Hague) CENTRAL OFFICE FOR GENEALOGY

For general surveys, see C.W. Delforterie, *Overzicht van de verzamelingen berustende bij het Centraal Bureau voor Genealogie en het Iconographisch Bureau* (The Hague, 1986), H.J.A.H.G. Metselaars (ed.), *Particuliere archieven in Nederland* (*Overzichten van de archieven en verzamelingen in de openbare archiefbewaarplaatsen in Nederland*, Vol. 14) (Houten and Zaventem, 1992), pp. 175-82, and the repository's web site (see Appendix II, 4.11). In addition to the materials described below and in the regional chapters, the *CBG* keeps documents that probably partly concern South Asia up to 1825 but fall outside the scope of this guide because they date from after 1825. These include genealogical notes in the collections of W. Wijnaendts van Resandt, P.C. Bloys van Treslong (Prins) and Van Beresteyn. Furthermore, besides the microfiches listed separately here, the *CBG* holds fiches of genealogical VOC documents (such as muster rolls) kept at the *Nationaal Archief* in The Hague, and of Ceylonese so-called *tombo registers* (referred to as *kerkelijk archief* but in fact concerning land ownership), the originals of which are kept at Colombo. The latter microfiches can only be consulted with special permission.

Doop-, Trouw-, Begraaf- en Lidmatenregisters (DTBL): voormalige Nederlandse koloniën (on microfiche)
Baptismal, Marriage, Funeral and Church Member registers: former Dutch colonies

Period: 17th-20th centuries
Inventory: catalogue in typescript (1995)

The collection consists entirely of microfiches. It includes baptismal, marriage and funeral registers of the Dutch Reformed Church on Ceylon, the originals of which are to be found in the Wolvendaal Church at Colombo, and correspondence between churches on Ceylon and the Dutch Republic, the originals of which are possibly kept at the *Nationaal Archief* in The Hague, see Supplement II, 13. The microfiches with material of the Wolvendaal Church appear to be part of a larger collection that is available on microfilm at the *Nationaal Archief*, see Supplement II, 52. Because the microfiches are unnumbered, the references at the top of the fiches are listed in this guide (with 'ref' denoting the Dutch Reformed Church). See 4.4.

Overige Archiefbronnen (OA): Noord-Holland (on microfiche)
Other Archival sources: North Holland

Inventory: catalogue in typescript (1996)

The collection consists entirely of microfiches. It includes archival materials of the Amsterdam Classis, with letters or reports from the Dutch Reformed Church on Ceylon (among other places, such as 'Oost-Indië' (East Indies), 1630-1791). The originals are kept in the *Gemeentearchief Amsterdam* (see 1.1.2). Because the microfiches are unnumbered, the references at the top of the fiches are listed in this guide (with 'ref' denoting the Dutch Reformed Church). See 4.4.

Van Boecop family

Access no.: FA 00031
Inv. nos: 01.1.01-199.30
Size: 2.1 metres
Period: 1518-1926
Inventory: W. Wijnaendts, 'Inventaris van het familiearchief Van Boecop (1518-1926)' (1988), with introduction, genealogical notes and indices to geographical and personal names

These archives are actually kept by the *Koninklijk Nederlandsch Genootschap voor Geslachts- en Wapenkunde* (Royal Dutch Society for Genealogy and Heraldry), to which the papers have been given on loan by the family. All the holdings of this Society are presently being managed by the *CBG*, however. Part of the archives consists of papers deriving from several members of the related Schwendler family, including Johan (born 1734), who served the VOC in Bengal between *c.* 1754 and 1764, and his uncle Justinus. For papers concerning Bengal, see also 6.4.

67.5.01 Report (15 ff.) of the 'unfortunate' journey of Justinus (or Tinus) Schwendler from Batavia via Malabar, Ceylon and Coromandel to Bengal, eighteenth century. One quire, one piece, slightly damaged.

Bybau family

Access no.: FA 00055
Inv. nos: 1-15
Size: *c.* 3 metres
Period: 1750-1853
Inventory: in typescript

These archives are actually kept by the *Koninklijk Nederlandsch Genootschap voor Geslachts- en Wapenkunde* (Royal Dutch Society for Genealogy and Heraldry) but all the holdings of this Society are presently being managed by the *CBG*. A large part of the papers concerns the Van Haeften family, of which some members served in Asia and which was related to the Bybau family. For documents regarding Ceylon and Coromandel, see 4.4 and 5.4.

Dossier Loten [CBG]
Loten file [CBG]

Size: *c.* 0.01 metre; 1 item
Period: 18th-20th centuries

This collection concerns the Loten family, including Joan Gideon Loten (1710-89). He left the Dutch Republic as VOC servant in 1731 and held several functions in the South-East Asian Archipelago until 1752. He was Governor of Ceylon between 1752 and 1757. For a letter from Colombo, see 4.4.

1.4.12. *KONINKLIJKE BIBLIOTHEEK (KB)* (The Hague) ROYAL LIBRARY

For general surveys, see H.J.A.H.G. Metselaars (ed.), *Particuliere archieven in Nederland* (*Overzichten van de archieven en verzamelingen in de openbare archiefbewaarplaatsen in Nederland*, Vol. 14) (Houten and Zaventem, 1992), pp. 214-24, J. Mateboer, *Repertorium bijzondere collecties* (The Hague, 1997), pp. 49-59, and the repository's web site (see Appendix II, 4.12). See also 1.6.4.

Handschriften
Manuscripts

Size: *c.* 150,000 items
Period: Middle Ages–up to the present
Inventory: relevant for this guide:
- shelf list (most extensive descriptions)
- systematic catalogue
- alphabetical index to authors, title (when anonymous) or addressee (in case of letters)
- data base (on Internet) in preparation

The collection mostly consists of letters from scholars, artists and politicians, and focuses on Dutch history and literature. It includes documents deriving from private persons, such as the scholar and statesman Gijsbert Cuper (1644-1716, see also 1.2.2, *Universiteit van Amsterdam, Universiteitsbibliotheek*). For papers concerning Surat, Malabar, Ceylon, Coromandel and Bengal, see 2.4, 3.4, 4.4, 5.4 and 6.4. For a map belonging to a manuscript, see 2.6.

129 D 17 Various papers including a letter from the GG&C to the western factories (including India), 1755, and two memorandums by Governor-General Jacob Mossel concerning the state of the VOC, one with sections on the factories in Ceylon (ff. 93-111), Coromandel (ff. 112-27), Bengal (ff. 127v-40), Malabar (ff. 140v-50) and Surat (ff. 151-3), 1755. One volume.

135 K 4 'Catalogus linguarum et rariorum dialectorum', 206 texts in various languages and scripts, 1612-35, collected by Ernst Brinck (*c.* 1582-1649), envoy to Constantinople in 1612 and from 1620 onward *Schepen* (sheriff) or Burgomaster of Harderwijk. One volume. Described in E. Bergvelt and R. Kistemaker (eds), *De wereld binnen handbereik. Nederlandse kunst- en rariteitenverzamelingen, 1585-1735* (Zwolle, 1992), pp. 137-8. Including:

f. 183v Example of Telugu or Kannada (?), with an accompanying note in Latin.

Handschriften der Koninklijke Nederlandse Akademie van Wetenschappen
Manuscripts of the Royal Netherlands Academy of Arts and Sciences

Inv. nos: KA 1-62, KA 110-343
Period: 14th-19th centuries
Inventory: D.J.H. ter Horst, *Catalogus van de handschriften der Koninklijke Nederlandse Akademie van Wetenschappen, in bruikleen in de Koninklijke Bibliotheek* (The Hague, 1938), with an index to authors

These manuscripts originate from the collection of the *Koninklijke Nederlandse Akademie van Wetenschappen* (*KNAW*) and have been given on loan. The bulk of that collection is kept by the *Nederlands Instituut voor Wetenschappelijke Informatiediensten* (*NIWI*, Dutch Institute for Scientific Information Services) at Amsterdam. For documents concerning Ceylon and Coromandel, see 4.4 and 5.4.

KA 144 Instruction for Jacob Joriszn Pits, newly appointed Governor of Coromandel, also concerning Bengal, with index, October 1680. One volume

KA 145 Memorandums, instructions, reports, etc., concerning Ceylon, Malabar and the Fishery Coast, 1650-1721 (copy from *c.* 1800). One volume. Including:

Part 1, ff. 169-227 Report by Jacob Hustaert concerning Ceylon, Malabar and the Fishery Coast, 1664.

Oude drukken
Early printed works

Size: *c.* 7000 metres; *c.* 150,000 works, including *c.* 30000 pamphlets
Period: 1541-1800; pamphlets: 1486-1853
Inventory:
- W.P.C. Knuttel, *Catalogus van de pamfletten-verzameling berustende in de Koninklijke Bibliotheek* (The Hague, 1889-1920); reprint H. van der Hoeven (ed.) (Utrecht, 1978), with introduction
- alphabetical and systematic catalogue on index cards
- data base (on Internet)

The collection consists of incunabula, post-incunabula, songbooks, popular prose, occasional poetry, pamphlets, edicts and book sales catalogues. Initially, it was of a general character and focused on subjects such as religion and ecclesiastical history, law and government publications, history and geography (including subdivisions such as travel and topography), and literature and other arts. In the course of time, the emphasis has shifted to Dutch cultural heritage. Although printed works are usually not considered to be archival material, this collection includes a few very rare pieces with regard to South Asia. For works concerning Surat and Ceylon, see 2.4, 4.4 and 4.6. See also 1.6.4.

298 A 48 Sailing instructions for the route from the Cape of Good Hope to Malabar, the Fishery Coast and Ceylon (in particular the bays of Galle and Nilwala), 1665-8, printed at Middelburg. One volume.

7452 Short newsletter from Aleppo, partly concerning the VOC fighting against the Portuguese near Goa and Ceylon, with woodcut depicting a naval battle, 1653. One piece.

1.4.13. *MUSEUM MEERMANNO* (The Hague)
MEERMANNO MUSEUM

For general surveys, see J. Mateboer, *Repertorium bijzondere collecties* (The Hague, 1997), pp. 60-4, and the repository's web site (see Appendix II, 4.13).

Van Westreenen family

Size: *c.* 6.5 metres
Period: *c.* 17th century-1848
Inventory: J.H. Kernkamp, *Inventaris der familiepapieren Meerman, Van Westreenen, Dierkens en Van Damme aanwezig in het Museum Meermanno-Westreenianum* (The Hague, 1948), with introduction, genealogical tree and index to personal names

Part of these archives consists of papers of Willem Hendrik Jacob Baron van Westreenen van Thiellandt (1783-1848), who was a scholar and founded the Meermanno Museum. The archives include documents deriving from Jacobus Mersen (1706-73), merchant at Batavia, who married Maria Aletta de Joncheere (1708-85) in 1749. She had earlier been married to Gerrit van Westreenen (1708-

42), Master of the warehouse at Batavia, who was a son of Governor Gerrit van Westreenen of Coromandel (1719-23) and the grandfather of Willem Hendrik Jacob. For papers concerning Surat, Ceylon and Coromandel, see 2.4, 4.4 and 5.4.

Handschriften
Manuscripts

Size: *c.* 350 items
Period: 14th-19th centuries
Inventory:
- P.H.J. Vermeeren and A.F. Dekker, *Inventaris van de handschriften van het Museum Meermanno-Westreenianum* (The Hague, 1960), with index
- P.C. Boeren, *Catalogus van de handschriften van Rijksmuseum Meermanno-Westreenianum* (The Hague, 1979), with introduction and indices

This collection mostly derives from Willem Hendrik Jacob van Westreenen van Thiellandt (see above). It is of a miscellaneous character and includes only one relevant document, which concerns Ceylon, see 4.4.

1.4.14. *KONINKLIJK INSTITUUT VOOR TAAL-, LAND- EN VOLKENKUNDE (KITLV)* (LEIDEN) ROYAL INSTITUTE OF LINGUISTICS AND ANTHROPOLOGY

For a general survey, see the repository's web site (see Appendix II, 4.14). See also 1.6.4.

Collectie in westerse talen
Collection in Western languages

Inv. nos: 1-*c.* 1350
Size: *c.* 80 metres
Period: *c.* 17th-20th centuries
Inventory:
- data base (on Internet)
- H.J. de Graaf, *Catalogus van de handschriften in Westerse talen, toebehorende aan het Koninklijk Instituut voor Taal-, Land- en Volkenkunde* (The Hague, 1963), supplements published in *Bijdragen van het Instituut voor Taal-, Land- en Volkenkunde*, 123 (1967), 125 (1969), 127 (1971), 129 (1973) and 131 (1975), geographically arranged, with indices to personal, ship and geographical names

Apart from miscellaneous documents, the collection includes papers deriving from people such as Joan van Hoorn (Governor-General 1704-9), J. Hageman JCz., J.B. van Herwerden, J.F.W. van Nes, G.P. Rouffaer, W.L. de Sturler and J.W.J. Wellan. In addition to the papers described in this guide, many other documents pertain to the VOC. Inv. nos H 685 and H 760 consist of twentieth-century drafts of glossaries with respect to the Company. Inv. nos H 695 and H 697 contain late nineteenth-century copies of sixteenth-century documents in Portuguese, Spanish and Latin (by Duarte Barbosa a.o.) concerning the Portuguese in Malabar and the rest of Asia, which are kept at Lisbon, Rome and Munich. For papers, maps, drawings and prints regarding Surat, Malabar, Ceylon, Coromandel and Bengal, see also 2.4, 3.4, 4.4, 4.6, 5.4, and 6.4. For drawings, see also 1.6.4.

H 6 Collection of 112 mounted letters and separate notes about various subjects, including South Asia (mostly Ceylon), deriving from Isaac de l'Ostal de Saint-Martin, member of the Council of the Indies, and other persons, 1683-96. One volume.

H 9 Report of Isaac van Schinne, Deputy Commander of the return fleet, for the Directors of the VOC at Middelburg, concerning the state of the Company in Asia, with sections on Bengal, Coromandel, Ceylon, Malabar, Kanara and Surat (ff. 43-68), 1685. One volume.

H 10 Reports for the Gentlemen XVII by Commanders of the return fleets, Cornelis Valckenier, Constantijn Ranst and Rijklof van Goens Junior, 1675, 1678, 1681, with sections on Bengal, Coromandel, Ceylon, Malabar, Vengurla, Surat, Galle and Madurai (ff. 7-12, 29-33, 51-5). One quire.

H 12 Discourses about Ceylon and Malabar by Hendrik Adriaan van Reede tot Drakenstein, 1677. One volume. For a partial translation, see *Reisebeschreibungen von deutschen Beamten und Kriegsleuten im Dienst der niederländischen West- und Ost-Indischen Kompagnien*, ed. S.P. l'Honoré Naber (The Hague, 1930), Vol. V, pp. 247-85.

H 45 Extracts from letters of the Gentlemen XVII to the GG&C, including sections on South Asia, 1629-97. One volume.

H 48 Extracts and copies of letters, reports, etc., of the Gentlemen XVII, GG&C and other VOC servants, 1665-93. One volume. Including:

- A Letter of Rijcklof van Goens, Governor of Ceylon, to Ludolph van Coulster, *Commandeur* of Malabar, 1665.

H 49 Various letters and other documents, 1613-91. One volume. Including:

- EE Report of Wilhelm Volger concerning his activities in Melaka, Bengal and Surat, 1672 (13 ff.).
- GG Remonstrance of Rijklof van Goens and Marten Pit concerning direct shipping from South Asia, 1685 (13 ff.).

H 62 Historical surveys of various VOC establishments sent to the GG&C, with ff. 71-100 concerning Coromandel, Ceylon and Malabar, 1707-9. One volume.

H 74 Report concerning the state of affairs of the VOC in Asia by Joan Pietersz. van Hoorn, including sections on South Asia, 1710. One volume.

H 77 Considerations about the present state of the VOC by Gustaaf Willem van Imhoff, including references to South Asia, with annexes, 1741. One volume.

H 206 Report concerning the state of affairs of the VOC in Asia by Joan Pietersz. van Hoorn, including sections on South Asia, 1710 (two copies). One volume.

H 209 Survey of bills of exchange, including sections on South Asia, 1691-1708. One piece.

H 314 Memorandum concerning money lent at interest at the expense of the VOC at factories other than Batavia, including sections on Colombo, Jaffna, Galle, Cochin, Hooghly, Cossimbazar, Patna, Agra, Nagappattinam, Fort Geldria (Pulicat) and Sadras, 1700. One quire.

H 315 Note concerning received bills of exchange and capital sent to Asia, including sections on South Asia, 1691-1709. One volume.

H 336 Survey of VOC personnel arrived at Batavia from Ceylon via Coromandel, 1705 (?). One piece.

H 445 Abstract in Dutch from the travel accounts of Jean Baptiste Tavernier, including sections on the Mughal Empire, Golkonda, Goa and Malabar, late seventeenth century. One volume.

H 468 'Lapidarium', various papers, photographs, drawings, etc., regarding (inscriptions on) remains of the VOC in Ceylon (folder 8) and Coromandel (folder 19), including rubbings and other copies of memorial tablets and gravestones in Colombo and Draksharama (of Johannes Caulier and Johanna Petronella de Peyster van Uytrecht), 1889-91, with separate inventory (with introduction) by M.P.H. Roessingh (1976). 19 folders. The material concerning Draksharama described and reproduced in Peters and André de la Porte, *In steen geschreven*, p. 155 (see Supplement I: Bibliography, no. 848).

H 496 Memorandum about coins, weights and measures in Asia, including sections on a large number of factories in Coromandel, Bengal, Surat, Ceylon and Malabar, *c.* 1665 (?). One volume. For more details, see 2.4, 3.4, 4.4, 5.4 and 6.4.

H 571 Signatures of the Governors-General of the VOC, 1610-1811, cut from other documents, around 1850, including former chiefs in South Asia: Carel Reniers (Coromandel, 1636-8), Joan Maetsuyker (Ceylon, 1646-50), Rijcklof van Goens Senior (Ceylon, 1662-3, 1665-75), Cornelis Janszoon Speelman (Coromandel, 1663-5), Hendrik Zwaardecroon (Surat, 1699-1701), Dirck van Cloon (Coromandel, 1723-30), Abraham Patras (Bengal, 1724-7), Gustaaf Willem van Imhoff (Ceylon, 1736-40) and Jacob Mossel (Coromandel, 1738-43)

H 604 Historical and geographical survey of the VOC factories, drawn up by the *Haags Besogne* (The Hague Committee), with detailed sections on Bengal, Coromandel, Ceylon, Malabar and Surat (ff. 67-111), *c.* 1750. One volume.

H 771 'Deex-Avtaars', treatise about the ten incarnations of Vishnu by merchant Phil. Angel, with a dedication to *Directeur-Generaal* Carel Hartsinck, a frontispiece, a poem in explanation of this and ten drawings after Indian miniatures of Vishnu's incarnations, 1658. Photocopy of record kept in the Norbertine Abbey of Postel at Mol (Belgium), one bundle of 295 folios.

H 1232 Daily report by Frederik Knotzer of a campaign at Java in 1811 and his subsequent journey as a prisoner of war of the British via Melaka, Penang, Bengal, Ceylon and St. Helena to England, 1822. One volume.

1.4.15. *MUSEUM BOERHAAVE* (Leiden) BOERHAAVE MUSEUM

This repository keeps a few prints pertaining to South Asia. See 1.6.4.

1.4.16. *NATIONAAL HERBARIUM NEDERLAND - UNIVERSITEIT LEIDEN* NATIONAL HERBARIUM OF THE NETHERLANDS - LEIDEN UNIVERSITY

For a general survey, see the repository's web site (see Appendix II, 4.16). See also 1.6.4 (including some manuscripts).

Library

Size: 4800 metres; *c.* 350,000 items
Period: 1542–up to the present
Inventory:
- data base
- catalogue on index cards

The library focuses on botany. In addition to books and journals, the library includes plant illustrations and a number of manuscripts. For material concerning Ceylon, see 4.4.

1.4.17. *NATURALIS, NATIONAAL NATUURHISTORISCH MUSEUM* (Leiden) NATURALIS, NATIONAL MUSEUM OF NATURAL HISTORY

This repository keeps a drawing pertaining to South Asia. See 1.6.4.

1.4.18. *RIJKSMUSEUM VOOR VOLKENKUNDE* (Leiden) NATIONAL MUSEUM OF ETHNOLOGY

For a general survey, see the repository's web site (see Appendix II, 4.18). In addition to the materials described in this guide, the holdings of the Museum comprise ethnological objects and works of art pertaining to non-western cultures, including South Asia (for some of the materials concerning Ceylon, see P.H.D.H. de Silva, *A Catalogue of Antiquities and Other Cultural Objects from Sri Lanka (Ceylon) Abroad* (Colombo, 1975), pp. 399-417 (somewhat outdated and occasionally inaccurate)).

Papiercollectie
Paper collection

Size: *c.* 24000 items
Period: *c.* 17th century–up to the present
Inventory:
- data base
- the following works cover (at least) all ethnographic objects and manuscripts in non-Western languages originating from the *Koninklijk Zeeuwsch Genootschap der Wetenschappen*, regardless of the repository where they are presently kept:
  - F. Nagtglas, *Catalogus der oud- en zeldzaamheden, schilderijen, teekeningen en portretten in het kabinet van het Zeeuwsch Genootschap der Wetenschappen* (Middelburg, 1869)

- *Catalogus van de oudheidkundige verzamelingen van het Zeeuwsch Genootschap der Wetenschappen* (1890)
- 'Catalogus ethnografica KZGW', geographically arranged
- C.E. Heyning a.o., 'Kunst of konst, de verzamelingen van het Zeeuws Genootschap', *Zeeland. Tijdschrift van het Koninklijk Zeeuwsch Genootschap der Wetenschappen*, 10, 0 (Special Issue) (2001)

The collection includes a relevant painting as well as a number of manuscripts in South Asian languages (such as Sinhalese, Tamil and Malayalam). Most of these manuscripts are inscribed on palm leaves. Some of them have been given on loan by the *Koninklijk Zeeuwsch Genootschap der Wetenschappen* (*KZGW*, Royal Zeeland Society of Sciences), which was founded in the 1760s and focuses on the province of Zeeland and its history (for more information, see 1.1.21, *Zeeuws Archief*). Only a few manuscripts seem to have a clear connection with the early-modern Dutch presence in South Asia. For materials concerning Malabar and Ceylon, see 3.4, 4.4 and 4.6.

3600-BEV-Z-104 Letter from an Indian sender (?) to the VOC, originating from south India. Palm leaf, in Tamil (deriving from the *Koninklijk Zeeuwsch Genootschap der Wetenschappen*).

1.4.19. *ZEEUWSE BIBLIOTHEEK / ZEEUWS DOCUMENTATIECENTRUM* (Middelburg) ZEELAND LIBRARY / ZEELAND DOCUMENTATION CENTRE

For general surveys, see H.J.A.H.G. Metselaars (ed.), *Particuliere archieven in Nederland* (*Overzichten van de archieven en verzamelingen in de openbare archiefbewaarplaatsen in Nederland*, Vol. 14) (Houten and Zaventem, 1992), pp. 327-31, J. Mateboer, *Repertorium bijzondere collecties* (The Hague, 1997), pp. 97-8, and the repository's web site (see Appendix II, 4.19). See also 1.6.4.

Handschriften
Manuscripts

Inv. nos: 1-*c.* 8000
Size: 23 metres
Period: 16th-20th centuries
Inventory:
- data base
- catalogue of authors on index cards
- J.P. van Visvliet, *Inventaris der handschriften van het Zeeuwsch Genootschap der Wetenschappen* (Middelburg, 1861); see also C.E. Heyning a.o., 'Kunst of konst, de verzamelingen van het Zeeuws Genootschap', *Zeeland. Tijdschrift van het Koninklijk Zeeuwsch Genootschap der Wetenschappen*, 10, 0 (Special Issue) (2001)

The collection focuses on Zeeland and its history. The manuscripts belong mostly to the *Koninklijk Zeeuwsch Genootschap der Wetenschappen* (*KZGW*, Royal

Zeeland Society of Sciences), founded in the 1760s (for more information as well as the Society's archives, see 1.1.21, *Zeeuws Archief*). The *KZGW* received several letters and other papers regarding South Asia from VOC officials. For documents concerning Surat, Malabar and Ceylon, see 2.4, 3.4 and 4.4. For maps and drawings, see 1.6.4. For manuscripts of the Society in South Asian languages, see 1.4.18, *Rijksmuseum voor Volkenkunde*, Leiden.

Hs. 3388 Various papers regarding or deriving from Samuel van de Putte, traveller from Vlissingen, including captions written by Van de Putte (as well as lists compiled later on) referring to his lost naturalia collection, which partly concerned Nepal and Tibet, *c.* 1726-39, *c.* 1803, also including a copy of the Batavia periodical *Bataviase Nouvelles* containing an obituary of Van de Putte, 5 October 1745. Partly Italian, one folder.[1]

Hs. 3531 Various papers concerning or originating from Samuel van de Putte, including a fragment of a letter sent by him from Cochin to Madras, May 1725, a note regarding politics in Nepal, a short note concerning politics in Peddapuram and Mogalturu (northern Coromandel) and maps with notes on Nepal and Tibet, *c.* 1730 and undated (*c.* 1730?). Partly French and Italian, one folder.[1]

Hs. 6115 Treatise concerning the invasion of the Mughal Empire by Nadir Shah in 1738-9, written by order of *Directeur* Jan Albert Sichterman of Bengal (1734-44), based on Persian reports, including translations of Persian documents. One volume.

Hs. 6443 Notes concerning VOC ships sailing to and from the East Indies, including South Asia, with destinations and noteworthy events, 1684-1794. One volume.

[1] Described and reproduced in F. Lequin and A. Meijer, *Samuel van de Putte, een Mandarijn uit Vlissingen (1690-1745)* (Middelburg, 1989), especially pp. 16, 20, 41-100.

1.4.20. *ZEEUWSE MUSEUM* (Middelburg) ZEELAND MUSEUM

For a general survey, see the repository's web site (see Appendix II, 4.20).

Collectie Koninklijk Zeeuwsch Genootschap der Wetenschappen
Royal Zeeland Society of Sciences collection

Period: prehistory–up to the present

Inventory: the following works cover all ethnographic objects and manuscripts in non-Western languages originating from the *Koninklijk Zeeuwsch Genootschap der Wetenschappen*, regardless of the repository where they are presently kept:

- F. Nagtglas, *Catalogus der oud- en zeldzaamheden, schilderijen, teekeningen en portretten in het kabinet van het Zeeuwsch Genootschap der Wetenschappen* (Middelburg, 1869)
- *Catalogus van de oudheidkundige verzamelingen van het Zeeuwsch Genootschap der Wetenschappen* (1890)

- 'Catalogus ethnografica KZGW', geographically arranged
- C.E. Heyning a.o., 'Kunst of konst, de verzamelingen van het Zeeuws Genootschap', *Zeeland. Tijdschrift van het Koninklijk Zeeuwsch Genootschap der Wetenschappen*, 10, 0 (Special Issue) (2001)

The *Koninklijk Zeeuwsch Genootschap der Wetenschappen* (*KZGW*), founded in the 1760s, focuses on the province of Zeeland and its history (for more information as well as the Society's archives, see 1.1.21, *Zeeuws Archief*). The *KZGW*'s collection (consisting of books, manuscripts, prints, drawings, art, ethnological objects, naturalia, etc.) is scattered over several repositories, including the *Zeeuws Museum*, which keeps arts and crafts, historical objects and folk art. Materials regarding or originating from South Asia have usually been received from VOC officials. For documents and paintings concerning Surat, Malabar and Ceylon, see 2.6, 3.3, 3.6 and 4.6. Most ethnological objects of the Society are kept at the *Rijksmuseum voor Volkenkunde* at Leiden (1.4.18). The manuscripts collection of the Society is kept at the *Zeeuwse Bibliotheek / Zeeuws Documentatiecentrum*, see 1.4.19.

1.4.21. *SLOT ZUYLEN* (Oud-Zuilen)
ZUYLEN CASTLE

This repository keeps a drawing pertaining to South Asia. See 1.6.4.

1.4.22. *ATLAS VAN STOLK* (Rotterdam)
VAN STOLK ATLAS

This repository keeps a number of drawings and prints pertaining to South Asia. See 1.6.4.

1.4.23. *CENTRALE BIBLIOTHEEK ROTTERDAM*
CENTRAL LIBRARY OF ROTTERDAM

For general surveys, see J. Mateboer, *Repertorium bijzondere collecties* (The Hague, 1997), pp. 107-8, and the repository's web site (see Appendix II, 4.23). See also 1.6.4.

Manuscripts

Size: *c.* 300 items
Inventory: systematic and alphabetical catalogue on index cards

The collection is of a general character. Around ten manuscripts concern the VOC.

14 B 40: 2 Considerations about the present state of the VOC by Gustaaf Willem van Imhoff, Elias de Haze and Isaac van Schinne, drawn up at Amsterdam, with sections on South Asia, 1741. Together with other documents in one volume.

14 B 41 Description of the best seasons to sail between various places in Asia and the Dutch Republic, including sections on South Asia, in particular Coromandel, Bengal, Ceylon and Goa, eighteenth century (?). One volume.

1.4.24. *MARITIEM MUSEUM ROTTERDAM* MARITIME MUSEUM ROTTERDAM

For a general survey, see the repository's web site (see Appendix II, 4.24). See also 1.6.4.

Handschriften
Manuscripts

Inv. nos: 1-*c.* 1750
Period: *c.* 1650–up to the present
Inventory: – data base (on Internet)
– systematic catalogue on index cards

The collection consists of handwritten and personal documents, including ship's logs. For documents concerning Surat, Malabar, Ceylon, Coromandel and Bengal, see also 2.4, 3.4, 4.4, 5.4 and 6.4.

H55 Passport for Captain William Ingram of the ship Escape, given by the EIC for a voyage from Fort St. George at Madras to Jaffna, 1782. In English, one piece.

1.4.25. *MUSEUM BOIJMANS VAN BEUNINGEN* (Rotterdam) BOIJMANS VAN BEUNINGEN MUSEUM

This repository keeps some drawings pertaining to South Asia. See 1.6.4.

1.5. Companies, Private Organizations and Individuals

1.5.1. FEIKEMA (Amersfoort)

Canter Visscher

Size: *c.* 0.05 metres; 1 item
Period: 17th-18th centuries

This manuscript originates from Adrianus Canter Visscher (1707-82, born at Harlingen), who entered the service of the VOC in 1731. From 1734 to 1743 he functioned as Cashier and *Fiscaal* at Masulipatam. Thereafter he probably stayed at Nagappattinam and returned to the Dutch Republic (Friesland) in 1745. For material concerning the Mughals and Coromandel, see also 1.6.5, 5.5 and 5.6.

(a) Letter (207 ff.) from Adrianus Canter Visscher, most probably addressed to the Gentlemen XVII, joining in the debate about possible means of redress, as a result of the memorandum of Governor-General Jacob Mossel concerning the state of affairs of the VOC, *c.* 1753. One volume. Including:

ff. 1-13 Discussion of the state of affairs in the Dutch Republic.

ff. 13-77 History of the Mughal Empire, with a section based on existent stories and traditions (ff. 13-62), and a section concerning political developments with regard to the Deccan as observed in Masulipatam (ff. 62-77).

ff. 167-207 Discussions of private trade, the *Amfioen Sociëteit* (opium trade association), and the direct shipping of tea.

1.5.2. SIX COLLECTION (Amsterdam)

Six collection

Size: *c.* 100 metres
Period: 1032–up to the present
Inventory: in preparation

The collection of the Six (or Six van Hillegom) family comprises all kinds of papers. Part of it consists of *c.* 6000 eighteenth-century letters deriving from the related Van Winter family (numbered 1-61), which include material concerning Coromandel, see 5.5.

1.5.3. TUTEIN NOLTHENIUS (Doorn)

Tutein Nolthenius family

Size: *c.* 10 boxes
Period: *c.* 1712-1930
Inventory: checklist in typescript

These family papers include documents deriving from Balthazar Nolthenius (1701-55), who served as Bookkeeper of the Amsterdam Chamber of the VOC (among other functions), and his wife Johanna Boel (1697-1768). For material concerning Malabar, Ceylon, Coromandel and Bengal, see 3.5, 4.5, 5.5 and 6.5. In the future, these archives may be transferred to the *Gemeentearchief Amsterdam* (see 1.1.2).

1.5.4. DE LANNOY (Deventer)

De Lannoy family

Inv. nos: 1-96
Size: *c.* 1.5 metres
Period: 16th century–up to the present
Inventory: M. de Lannoy, 'Inventaris van het familiearchief De Lannoy' (1999), with introduction and index

These archives include papers deriving from Carel Wybrandus de Lannoy, who moved to Colombo as a VOC official in 1760. His descendants left for Java in the early nineteenth century. For a document concerning Ceylon, see 4.5.

1.5.5. HEYNING (The Hague)

Heijning family

Size: 1 box
Period: 18th century–up to the present

These materials include a drawing pertaining to the period between 1769 and 1817 when members of the Heijning family stayed in Bengal, see 6.6. Note that this collection may also include some portraits of members of the family who lived in Bengal. For more information on the family and a description of the papers deriving from it, see Supplement II, 42.

1.5.6. *KONINKLIJK HUISARCHIEF* (The Hague)
ARCHIVES OF THE ROYAL FAMILY

For general surveys, see E. Pelinck, *Het Koninklijk Huisarchief. Geschiedenis en overzicht* (The Hague, 1971), B. Woelderink and M. Loonstra, *Het Koninklijk Huisarchief te 's-Gravenhage* (The Hague, 1989) H.J.A.H.G. Metselaars (ed.), *Particuliere archieven in Nederland (Overzichten van de archieven en verzamelingen in de openbare archiefbewaarplaatsen in Nederland*, Vol. 14) (Houten and Zaventem, 1992), pp. 225-56, and the repository's web site (see Appendix II, 5.6). A list of documents pertaining to the VOC in the archives of William IV and William V can be found in A.E. Wassing, 'Inventarisatie van stukken in het Koninklijk Huisarchief betreffende de relatie van Stadhouders prins Willem IV en prins Willem V met de VOC en de WIC', which is available at the reading room. See also 1.6.5.

Maria Louise van Hessen-Kassel

Access no.: A 10
Inv. nos: 1-555
Period: 1709-65
Inventory: A.P. van Nienes and M. Bruggeman (eds), *Archieven van de Friese stadhouders. Inventarissen van de archieven van de Friese stadhouders van Willem Lodewijk tot en met Willem V, 1584-1795* (Hilversum, The Hague and Leeuwarden, 2002), pp. 294-335, with introduction, appendices, genealogical tree and indices to personal and geographical names and to subjects

Maria Louise van Hessen-Kassel (1688-1765) married Johan Willem Friso van Nassau-Dietz (1687-1711), Stadtholder of the Provinces of Friesland and Groningen, in 1709. Shortly after her husband's death, she gave birth to Willem Karel Hendrik Friso, the future Stadtholder William IV (see below). Between 1711 and 1731, she acted as Regent on behalf of her son. The archives include a few documents concerning Ceylon and Coromandel, see 4.5 and 5.5.

Prince William IV

Access no.: A 17
Inv. nos: 1-527
Size: 16 metres
Period: 1711-66
Inventory: in manuscript and typescript

Prince William IV of Orange (1711-51) became Stadtholder of the Provinces of Friesland, Groningen and Drenthe when he reached adulthood and Hereditary Stadtholder of the Dutch Republic in 1747. He was honoured with the function of *Opperbewindhebber* (chief director) of the VOC in 1749, and in this capacity oversaw the elections and appointments of the Company's Directors and of the high officials in Asia. The archives consist mostly of his personal documents, several of which relate to South Asia. For papers concerning Surat and Ceylon, see 2.5 and 4.5. For the archives of his office, the *Stadhouderlijke Secretarie*, which are kept in the *Nationaal Archief* at The Hague, see *Dutch Sources on South Asia*, Vol. 1 (1.4.3).

173: 4 Correspondence of William IV with A. Bergsma, 1742-7, including a letter by Bergsma concerning French landings on the Malabar and Coromandel Coasts, 17 July 1742. One bundle.

266 Considerations on the present state of the VOC by Gustaaf Willem van Imhoff, Elias de Haze and Isaac van Schinne, drawn up at Amsterdam, including sections on the factories in South Asia, 1741. One volume, copy belonging to the papers of the Privy Councillor J. van der Lühe.

323 Inventory of the papers and books kept at the office of William IV, with p. 62 very briefly referring to Coromandel, Ceylon, Bengal and Malabar (nos 7, 8, 11, 13), *c.* 1760-80. One folder.

Prince William V

Access no.: A 31
Inv. nos: 1-339
Size: 70 metres
Period: 1748-1806
Inventory: in manuscript and typescript (a new inventory with a concordance is in preparation)

Prince William V of Orange (1748-1806) was Hereditary Stadtholder of the Dutch Republic between 1766 and 1795. Like his father, William IV, he functioned as *Opperbewindhebber* of the VOC (see above). The archives largely comprise his personal papers, a number of which deal with South Asia. At the time of writing, the archives were being rearranged. As a consequence, all inv. nos are provisional. For papers concerning Malabar, Ceylon, Coromandel and Bengal, see 3.5, 4.5, 5.5 and 6.5. For the archives of his office, the *Stadhouderlijke Secretarie*, which are kept in the *Nationaal Archief* at The Hague, see *Dutch Sources on South Asia*, Vol. 1 (1.4.3).

291: IV Papers concerning naval matters, *c.* 1760-1800. One bundle. Including:
(a) Ship's log of the brig De Vlieg sailing under the command of Captain J.B. Zeegers to Malabar and Ceylon, 1791-2.

333: I a Correspondence of William V's representative with the VOC, Thomas Hope, and the Duke of Brunswijk, 1765-6. One bundle. Including:
(a) Letters from Governor Iman Willem Falck of Ceylon to *Commandeur* Cornelis Breekpot of Malabar, 19 and 26 February 1766.

1.5.7. *ORDE VAN VRIJMETSELAREN ONDER HET GROOTOOSTEN DER NEDERLANDEN* (The Hague) FRATERNITY OF FREEMASONS UNDER THE GRAND EAST OF THE NETHERLANDS

For a general survey, see H.J.A.H.G. Metselaars (ed.), *Particuliere archieven in Nederland* (*Overzichten van de archieven en verzamelingen in de openbare archiefbewaarplaatsen in Nederland*, Vol. 14) (Houten and Zaventem, 1992), pp. 260-4.

Groot Oosten der Nederlanden
Grand East of the Netherlands

Inv. nos: 2001-416, 2501-728, 3001-4963
Size: *c.* 275 metres
Period: 1747–up to the present
Inventory: in manuscript; an inexhaustive register of letters received and sent by the Grand Lodge of the Freemasons during the period 1747-1843 is also available

These are the main archives of the *Groot Oosten*, formerly called *Groote Loge* (Grand Lodge), which is the umbrella organization of the Freemasons' lodges in the Netherlands. In the second half of the eighteenth century, at least eight Masonic lodges were set up by Dutchmen in South Asia: St. Jean la Concorde (1775-88?) at Surat; De Getrouwigheid or La Fidélité (1770-88?), La Réunion Neuchâtelloise (1790-6) and De Vereeniging or Virtus Nostra Ductrix (1794-1806?) at Colombo; De Opregtheid or La Candeur (1772-1814?) at Galle; De Langgewenschte (1773-88?) at Nagappattinam; and La Concorde (1768-?) and De Standvastigheid or La Constance (1772-1815?) at Hooghly. Another lodge, called Salomon (1759-83?), was established at a location that may be present-day Taldangra (near Bankura) in Bengal.

Inv. nos 2001-186 (old nos R1-209) are the *resoluties* (proceedings) of the *Groote Loge*. Between 1757 and 1806, these documents regularly deal with the lodges in South Asia. The *resoluties* of the years 1756-1816 have been published in E.A. Boerenbeker (ed.), *De Resolutiën van de Groote Loge*, 3 vols (The Hague, 1979, 1991), with introductions and various indices. Other papers concerning South Asia may be found throughout the archives.

Constitutie dossiers
Constitution files

Inv. nos: 2401-16
Size: *c.* 2 metres
Period: 1735–up to the present
Inventory: none; E. Kwaadgras a.o. (eds), *Overzicht van loges die onder het Grootoosten der Nederlanden en zijn voorlopers gewerkt hebben of werken* (The Hague, 2002), with indices to persons, lodges and geographical names, is used as a reference guide

This collection consists of papers taken from the archives of the *Groot Oosten der Nederlanden* and filed separately per lodge. The documents mostly concern official occasions, such as the foundation of the lodges. For papers concerning Surat, Ceylon, Coromandel and Bengal, see 2.5, 4.5, 5.5 and 6.5.

Bibliotheek
Library

Size: *c.* 1000 metres
Inventory: – systematic and alphabetical catalogue on index cards
– data base

The collection consists mostly of books and magazines but includes a few manuscripts concerning Ceylon, see 4.5.

1.5.8. *STICHING KUNSTBEZIT KONINKLIJKE NEDLLOYD* (Rotterdam) ROYAL NEDLLOYD ART COLLECTION FOUNDATION

This repository keeps a few maps pertaining to South Asia. See 1.6.5.

1.5.9. KARTING (Voorburg)

Hallegua family (photocopies)

Size: 2 items
Period: 1761, 1781

This collection consists of photocopies of juridical VOC documents presently kept by the Jewish Hallegua (traditionally spelt Alewa) family living at Cochin. Since the Dutch presence in Malabar, members of this family have been holding the hereditary office of *Mudaliar*, leader of the Jewish community in Cochin. See 3.5.

1.6. Maps and Pictures

As has been explained in the Preface, the sections on maps and pictures include many separate printed maps originating from atlases published between *c.* 1600 and 1825. For a survey of such atlases involving Dutchmen, see C. Koeman, *Atlantes Neerlandici. Bibliography of Terrestrial, Maritime and Celestial Atlases and Pilot-Books, Published in the Netherlands (and by Dutch Cartographers) up to 1880*, 5 vols (Amsterdam, 1967-72), and P. van der Krogt, *Koeman's Atlantes Neerlandici*, Vols 1-? ('t Goy-Houten, 1997-?). For an overview of repositories keeping particular atlases, see C. Koeman, *Collections of Maps and Atlases in the Netherlands. Their History and Present State* (Leiden, 1961). For a general survey of collections of maps and atlases, see P. van den Brink (ed.), *Almanak verzamelingen topografisch beeldmateriaal. Een overzicht van kaartenverzamelingen en topografisch-historische atlassen in Nederland* (The Hague, 1995). A number of prints and drawings listed in this guide and in Vol. 1 (as well as a number of relevant pictures outside the Netherlands) can be viewed on Internet: www.atlasmutualheritage.nl.

1.6.1. Government Archives

ARCHIEFDIENST VOOR KENNEMERLAND (Haarlem)
ARCHIVAL SERVICE FOR KENNEMERLAND

See also 1.1.9.

Kennemer Atlas
Kennemerland Atlas

Size: *c.* 25000 prints and drawings
Period: 16th century–up to the present
Inventory: – data base (on Internet)
– catalogue on index cards

This collection consists of drawings, prints, photos, etc., regarding the history of Haarlem and its environs. It includes several drawings of the Haarlem-based artist Cornelis van Noorde (1731-95), one of which pertains to Bengal. See 6.6.

HET UTRECHTS ARCHIEF
THE ARCHIVES OF UTRECHT

See also 1.1.23.

Evangelische Broedergemeente (EBG): collectie prenten, tekeningen, kaarten en foto's, Zeist

Evangelical Community of Moravian Brethren: collection of prints, drawings, maps and photos, Zeist

Access no.: 46
Inv. nos: 1-921
Period: *c.* 1700-1982
Inventory: C.M.P.F. van den Broek, 'Inventaris van de collectie prenten, tekeningen, kaarten en foto's van de Evangelische Broedergemeente te Zeist ca. 1700-1982' (1985), with introduction, appendix and index to personal names

This collection of the Community of the Moravian Brethren at Zeist (see 1.1.23, *Het Utrechts Archief, Evangelische Broedergemeente (EBG): Zeister Zendingsgenootschap*) consists of miscellaneous materials; it was not built up on purpose. For a print concerning Coromandel, see 5.6.

STADS- EN STREEKARCHIEF ZUTPHEN
TOWN AND REGIONAL ARCHIVES OF ZUTPHEN

For general surveys, see G. Verbeek a.o. (eds), *Gelders archievenoverzicht* (Zutphen, 1995), pp. 421-48, *De archieven in Gelderland* (*Overzichten van de archieven en verzamelingen in de openbare archiefbewaarplaatsen in Nederland*, Vol. 2) (Alphen aan den Rijn, 1979), pp. 224-45 (somewhat outdated), and the repository's web site (see Appendix II, 1.24).

Topografisch-Historische Atlas
Topographic-Historical Atlas

Inv. nos: 1-*c.* 3000
Period: 17th-20th centuries
Inventory: – data base
– in typescript

This collection focuses on materials concerning Zutphen, but includes a number of printed maps pertaining to Asia.

555 Map of South Asia and adjacent regions, with special reference to the Maldives and the Andaman Islands, published by Pierre Mortier at Amsterdam, eighteenth century. In French.
556 Map of South Asia, published by Covens and Mortier at Amsterdam, eighteenth century. In French.
562 Map of South Asia, with a few remarks concerning commodities, politics and European settlements, by J. van Jagen, Eman. Bowen and W.A. Bachiene, *c.* 1774. Print.

1.6.2. Universities

UNIVERSITEIT VAN AMSTERDAM, ARTIS BIBLIOTHEEK
UNIVERSITY OF AMSTERDAM, ARTIS LIBRARY

Artis Bibliotheek
Artis Library

See 1.2.1

Legkast 238 'Wonderen der natuur', collection of *c.* 180 pencil drawings, water colours, gouaches and prints (as well as some texts) of special and exotic animals and people as seen in the menagerie at the hostelry of Blauw Jan (Jan Westerhof) in Amsterdam and some other locations, including several animals (possibly) originating from South Asia, such as elephants, monitors, rhinoceroses, flying squirrels, spider monkeys ('satyrs'), other mammals and birds, by Jan Velten, *c.* 1695-1709. Seven boxes. Described and partly reproduced in F.F.J.M. Pieters and H. Veldhuijzen van Zanten (eds), *Wonderen der natuur in de menagerie van Blauw Jan te Amsterdam, zoals gezien door Jan Velten rond 1700 / Wonders of Nature in the Menagerie of Blauw Jan in Amsterdam, as Observed by Jan Velten around 1700* (Amsterdam, 1998), W. de Bell, 'Flora en fauna', in the *Catalogus* accompanying E. Bergvelt and R. Kistemaker (eds), *De wereld binnen handbereik. Nederlandse kunst- en rariteitenverzamelingen, 1585-1735* (Amsterdam, 1992), and F.F.J.M. Pieters, 'De dieren in de menagerie van "De Witte Oliphant" te Amsterdam zoals gezien door Jan Velten rond 1700', in K. van der Horst, P.A. Koolmees and A. Monna (eds), *Over beesten en boeken* (Rotterdam, 1995); also entirely reproduced on CD. Including:

99 South Asian monitor, referred to as 'Campergoo' in Tamil (?). Woodcut (23 x 15 cm).[1]

100 Man with an Indian pangolin. Pen drawing (55 x 62 cm).[1]

[1] Reproduced in F.F.J.M. Pieters, 'The Menagerie of "The White Elephant" in Amsterdam, with Some Notes on Other 17th and 18th Century Menageries in The Netherlands', in H. v. Lothar Dittrich, D. v. Engelhardt and A. Rieke-Müller (eds), *Die Kulturgeschichte des Zoos* (Berlin, 2001), pp. 49-50.

UNIVERSITEIT VAN AMSTERDAM, UNIVERSITEITSBIBLIOTHEEK
UNIVERSITY OF AMSTERDAM, UNIVERSITY LIBRARY

See also 1.2.2.

Kaarten en Atlassen
Maps and Atlases

Size: *c.* 150,000 items
Period: *c.* 1500–up to the present
Inventory:
- geographic and systematic catalogue on index cards (inexhaustive), with a separate section for the Muller collection
- data base (on Internet) (inexhaustive)

Consisting of maps, atlases and globes, the collection is of a varied character but focuses on Amsterdam, the Netherlands and its overseas settlements. It includes a large number of maps and atlases dating from the seventeenth and eighteenth centuries. All maps in this collection that concern South Asia are printed, except where indicated. Part of the collection has been given on loan by the *Koninklijk Nederlands Aardrijkskundig Genootschap* (*KNAG*, Royal Dutch Geographical Society). This includes the Muller collection (named after Frederik Muller), consisting of about ten thousand maps that originate from atlases produced between 1570 and the early nineteenth century (the inv. nos of those described in this guide beginning with 33). For maps concerning Surat, Malabar, Ceylon, Coromandel and Bengal, see 2.6, 3.6, 4.6, 5.6 and 6.6.

1-2-A-9 (27a)	Map of Persia, Gujarat and Malabar, made after a French map by order of the Lord of Maurepas, Amsterdam, 1773. Copper engraving, coloured, partly in French, scale 1:14,000,000. Identical to no. 108-01-01, see below.
33-12-51 to 53	Three identical maps of the Mughal Empire, with printed text at the back concerning the Mughals, by Henr. Hondius and Joan. Janssonius. One coloured, Dutch, French and Latin editions (old inv. nos 9988M-90M). Identical to nos 33-12-54 & 55 and 33-13-14, see below.
33-12-54 & 55	Two identical maps of the Mughal Empire (no text at the back). Coloured (old inv. nos 9991M-2M). Identical to nos 33-12-51 to 53 and 33-13-14, see above and below.
33-12-56 to 62	Seven identical maps of the Mughal Empire, some with printed Dutch text at the back concerning the Mughals, by Johannes Huydekoper. Five coloured (old inv. nos 9998M-10001M, 10003M, 10006M-7M).
33-12-63 & 64	Three identical maps of the Bay of Bengal, including Ceylon and the coasts of Malabar (partly), Coromandel, Orissa, Bengal, Arakan and Pegu, published at Amsterdam by Hendrick Doncker. Coloured (old inv. nos 10010M-11M).
33-12-65 to 68	Four identical maps of the Bay of Bengal, including Ceylon, Coromandel, Orissa, Bengal, Arakan and Pegu, at least two published at Amsterdam by G. Valk and P. Schenk. Three coloured (old inv. nos 10012M-13M, 10015M, 10017M).
33-12-69	Map of South Asia, by J. Keyser, published at Amsterdam by Isaak Tirion, 1730. Coloured (old inv. no. 10019M).
33-13-01	Map of south India, including parts of Gujarat and Bengal, by Guillaume de l'Isle, published at Amsterdam by J. Covens and C. Mortier. Coloured, in French (old inv. no. 10023M). See also no. 33-13-02 below.
33-13-02	Map of south India, including parts of Gujarat and Bengal, by Guillaume de l'Isle (Delisle), published at Amsterdam by Pierre Schenk. Coloured, in French (old inv. no. 10032M). See also no. 33-13-01 above.
33-13-03	Map of the Mughal Empire, published at Amsterdam by P. Schenk and G. Valk. Coloured (old inv. no. 10035M).

33-13-04 to 06	Three identical maps of the Mughal Empire, by F. de Witt, published by P. Mortier and J. Covens. In Latin (old inv. nos 10038M, 10041M, 10045M).
33-13-07 & 08	Two identical maps of south India and north Ceylon, by Hadrianus Relandus, published at Amsterdam by Gerard van Keulen. One coloured (old inv. nos 10046M, 10050M).
33-13-09 & 10	Two identical maps of south India, showing the political divisions according to the treaty of Sriranga-patnam, 1792, by J. Rennell, London, 1792. Coloured, in English (old inv. nos 10055M-6M).
33-13-11	Map of the Bay of Bengal, including Ceylon and the coasts of Malabar (partly), Coromandel, Orissa, Bengal, Arakan and Pegu, 1740 (?). Coloured, in German (old inv. no. 10071M).
33-13-14	Map of the Mughal Empire (no text at the back) (old inv. no. 10074M). Identical to nos 33-12-51 to 53 and 33-12-54 & 55, see above.
33-13-20	Map of the coasts of south Konkan, Kanara and north Malabar and the northern Maldives, published at Amsterdam by Johannes van Keulen. Coloured (old inv. no. 10085M).
33-13-21	Map of South Asia, published at Amsterdam by Covens and Mortier. Coloured, in French. (old inv. no. 10090M).
33-13-22	Map of south India and Ceylon, by De l'Isle, published by Homanniani Heredes, 1733 (?). Coloured, in Latin (old inv. no. 10092M).
33-13-23	Map of the Mughal Empire, by Matth. Seutter. Coloured, in Latin (old inv. no. 10093M).
33-13-26	Map of India and parts of South-East Asia and Central Asia, by R. and J. Ottens. Coloured, in French (old inv. no. 10096M).
33-13-28	Map of the Indian Ocean, including Ceylon and the Maldives, with one inset showing the kingdoms of Cranganur, Cochin, Purakkad, Kayankulam and Quilon, and another showing the surroundings of Colombo and Negombo up to Sitawake and 'Arandery', by R. and J. Ottens, Amsterdam, 1750. Coloured, in French (old inv. no. 10099M).
33-13-29	Map of the coasts of Konkan and Gujarat. Coloured, in English (old inv. no. 10100M).
33-13-30	Map of the Bay of Bengal, including Ceylon and the coasts of Coromandel, Orissa, Bengal, Arakan and Pegu, 1740 (?). Coloured, in English (old inv. no. 10101M).

33-13-52	Map of India and parts of South-East Asia and Central Asia, published at Amsterdam by Jan Bt. Elwe, 1792. Coloured, in French (old inv. no. 10134M).
69-10-07	Map of the Indian Ocean, including Ceylon and the Maldives, with one inset showing the kingdoms of Cranganur, Cochin, Purakkad, Kayankulam and Quilon, and another showing the surroundings of Colombo and Negombo up to Sitawake and 'Arandery', by R. and J. Ottens, Amsterdam, 1750. Copper engraving, coloured, in French.
71-30-06	Map of north India, by F. de Witt (1721-78), Amsterdam, published by J. Covens and C. Mortier. Copper engraving, coloured, scale 1:8,000,000.
72-01-03 (a to f)	Map of India, by A. Arrowsmith, London, 1804. Copper engraving, coloured, scale 1:1,780,000. Six sheets.
108-01-01	Map of Persia, Gujarat and Malabar, made after a French map by order of the Lord of Maurepas, Amsterdam, 1773. Copper engraving, coloured, partly in French, scale 1:14,000,000. Identical to no. 1-2-A-9 (27a), see above.
108-01-16A & B	Map of India, with details concerning the European presence, by N. Bellin, published at Amsterdam in 1773. Copper engraving, coloured, largely in French, scale 1:10,000,000. Two sheets.

Manuscripts

See 1.2.2

VI G 1-9	So-called 'Moninckx Atlas', consisting of drawings of foreign plants growing in the Hortus Botanicus at Amsterdam, including plants originating from South Asia, mostly painted by Johan and Maria Moninckx (by order of J. Huydecoper and J. Commelin, Commissioners of the Hortus), 1687-92, 1749. Nine volumes, coloured. Described and partly reproduced in D.O. Wijnands, *The Botany of the Commelins. A Taxonomical, Nomenclatural and Historical Account of the Plants Depicted in the Moninckx Atlas and in the Four Books by Jan and Caspar Commelin on the Plants in the Hortus Medicus Amstelodamensis, 1682-1710* (Rotterdam, 1983), and Akveld and Jacobs, *De kleurrijke wereld / The Colourful World*, pp. 65-6 (see Supplement I: Bibliography, no. 61).
Bf 98b1-13	Drawings of eighth- to twelfth-century bronze statues of Buddhist deities found near the fort of Nagappattinam at a sanctuary called 'Chinese pagoda' (possibly a remnant of a thirteenth-century Buddhist temple complex built by order of Chinese) in 1687, and of sixteenth- to seventeenth-century bronze statues of Hindu (and

Christian?) deities taken by the VOC from a temple in Malabar in 1691, sent to Nicolaas Cornelisz Witsen in the 1710s, including depictions of Buddha, Tara, Ganesha, Subrahmanya, Garuda, Durga (?), Varaha (Vishnu's third incarnation) and various mythical animals, among which a dog-faced man (*c.* 41 x 30 cm and 32 x 19 cm). Part of the correspondence between Witsen and Gijsbert Cuper, 1685-1716 (inv. nos Be 1-102, Bf 1-86, 88-100, G 41, see 1.2.2). Partly reproduced and described in E. Bergvelt and R. Kistemaker (eds), *De wereld binnen handbereik. Nederlandse kunst- en rariteitenverzamelingen, 1585-1735* (Zwolle, 1992), pp. 144-5, the accompanying *Catalogus*, pp. 189-92, and Peters, 'Nicolaes Witsen and Gijsbert Cuper', between pp. 132-3 (see Supplement I: Bibliography, no. 144). Drawing of Ganesha published in *Epithalamia in auspicatissimas nuptias ... Francisci Witsen ... nec non ornatissimae virginis Estherae Cuperi* (1715), and with some of the other drawings in the edition of 1785 of Witsen's *Noord en Oost Tartarye* (Amsterdam). The correspondence also includes drawings of animals that are possibly South Asian.

VRIJE UNIVERSITEIT AMSTERDAM, BIBLIOTHEEK
VRIJE UNIVERSITEIT AMSTERDAM, LIBRARY

See also 1.2.3.

Kaartenverzameling
Map collection

Size: *c.* 40000 maps, *c.* 3000 atlases
Period: 1515–up to the present
Inventory: – data base (on Internet)
– geographical catalogue on index cards

The collection is of a general character and includes a couple of maps concerning South Asia. The maps described in this guide that are not part of the so-called 'Atlas du Sr. d'Anville', originate from the collection of Mr H. Bos, a former director of the University. For maps of Ceylon, Coromandel and Bengal, see 4.6, 5.6 and 6.6.

LL.04763gk: 000/od/1760 'Atlas du Sr. [Jean Baptiste Bourguignon] d'Anville', consisting of 24 separate copper engravings by Guill. de la Haye, compiled at Paris after 1760. In French, partly coloured, one folder. Including:

1 Part of a map of Asia, showing south India, Ceylon and Arabia, 1751. Scale 1:6,650,000.

10a Part of a map of South Asia, showing north India, made for the French Compagnie des Indes, 1752. Scale 1:3,400,000.

	10b Part of a map of South Asia, showing south India, Ceylon, Lakshadweep and the Andaman and Nicobar Islands, with insets of Goa and the Hooghly River between Hooghly and the Bay of Bengal, made for the French Compagnie des Indes, 1752. Scale 1: 3,400,000.
LL.05784gk: 324/od/1720	'Magni Mogol infeniutus', map of the Mughal Empire and adjacent regions, with political divisions, possibly by Joan F. van Essen at Antwerp around 1720, but seemingly showing the state of affairs in the late sixteenth, early seventeenth century (?). Manuscript, coloured, in Latin, scale 1:5,000,000.

BIBLIOTHEEK TECHNISCHE UNIVERSITEIT DELFT
DELFT UNIVERSITY OF TECHNOLOGY LIBRARY

For general surveys, see J. Mateboer, *Repertorium bijzondere collecties* (The Hague, 1997), pp. 46-7, and the repository's web site (see Appendix II, 2.4).

Kaarten
Maps

Size: *c.* 20000 maps
Period: 16th century–up to the present
Inventory: data base

The collection is of a miscellaneous character and mainly consists of maps pertaining to the Netherlands. Most maps concerning South Asia originate from the department of Geodetic Engineering. For maps regarding Coromandel and Bengal, see 5.6 and 6.6.

H-7321-11	Map of Konkan, Kanara, Malabar, Fishery Coast, Coromandel and part of Ceylon, by Hadrianus Relandus, published by Gerard van Keulen, 1728. Copper engraving, coloured, scale *c.* 1:2,000,000 (48 x 60 cm).
TRL 5.1.1.23	Map of South Asia and the Indian Ocean, according to which the fleet of Admiral Watson was equipped, depicting the route of Commander James from Madras to Bombay in the years 1754-5 against the 'country winds', with inset of part of Bengal with the Hooghly and Ganges Rivers up to Patna, 1780 (?). Engraving, coloured, scale *c.* 1: 21,000,000 (old inv. no. P-9621-02).
TRL 6.4.1 L 14	Two identical maps of India, by F. de Witt, published by Covens and Mortier at Amsterdam, *c.* 1740. Copper engraving, coloured, in Latin, scale *c.* 1:7,000,000 (42 x 52 cm) (old inv. no. H-7321-01).
TRL 6.4.1 L 16	Three identical maps of India, by Johannes Huydekoper

and Johannes and Cornelis Blaeu (?) at Amsterdam, with text on the back, 1642. Copper engraving, one coloured, scale *c.* 1:7,000,000. (42 x 52 cm) (old inv. no. H-7321-03).

TRL 6.5.2.04 Map of India, by S. Gerolamo Correr (?) and Coronelli (?), *c.* 1700. Copper engraving, coloured, in Italian, scale *c.* 1:5,500,000 (46 x 61 cm) (old inv. no. H-7321-02).

TRL 6.5.2.05 Map of the Indian peninsula up to Gujarat and Bengal, and of northern Ceylon, with references to European settlements, by Guillaume de l'Isle at Amsterdam, published by I. Covens and C. Mortier, *c.* 1730. Copper engraving, coloured, in French, scale *c.* 1:4,000,000 (46 x 56 cm) (old inv. no. H-7321-08).

TRL 6.5.2.07 Map of South Asia in four parts, by Jakob (James) Rennell, published by F.A. Schreambl, 1788. Copper engraving, partly coloured, in German, scale *c.* 1:2,600,000, four sheets (117 x 142 cm) (old inv. no. H-7321-07).

UNIVERSITEIT LEIDEN, INSTITUUT KERN
LEIDEN UNIVERSITY, KERN INSTITUTE

For general surveys, see D. Heilijgers, 'The Kern Institute', in S.M. Gieling, P.G. Hoftijzer and J.J. Witkam (eds), *Special Collections. A Guide to the Collections of Leiden University Library and Neighbouring Institutions* (Leiden, 2002), H.J. 't Hart-van den Muyzenberg, 'De collecties in het Instituut Kern' (1990) (available at the reading room), and the repository's web site (see Appendix II, 2.6).

Old maps

Size: *c.* 10 items
Period: 17th-19th centuries (?)
Inventory: shelf list

The collection consists only of printed maps. Because they are unnumbered, their captions are given literally here in order to facilitate their identification.

(a) 'Nieuwe kaart van 't Keyzerrijk van den grooten Mogol ...', map of India and Ceylon, by Jacob Keyser (?), published by Isaak Tirion at Amsterdam, 1730 (?). Coloured.
(b) 'Magni Mogolis imperium de novo correctum et divisum ...', map of north and part of south India, by F. de Witt (?) at Amsterdam, published by I. Covens and C. Mortier (?), *c.* 1725-50 (?). Coloured, in Latin.
(c) 'Nova Tabula terrarum Cucan, Canara, Malabaria, Madura & Coromandelia, cum parte Septentrionali Insulae Ceylon, in mari Indica Orientali ...', map (in Dutch) of Konkan, Kanara, Malabar, Madurai, Coromandel and part of Ceylon, by Hadrianus Relandus, printed by Gerard van Keulen at Amsterdam, 1700 (?).
(d) 'Imperii Magni Mogolis sive Indica Padschach ...', map of north and most of south India, by Matthias Seutter (or Seutteri). Coloured, in Latin.

(e) 'Orarum Malabariae, Coromandelae & Tabula accuratissima. Carte des Côtes de Malabar et de Coromandel présentée au Roy ...', map of Malabar, Coromandel, and parts of Gujarat, Orissa and Bengal, showing European settlements, by Guillaume de l'Isle, at Amsterdam, published by I. Covens and I. Mortier, second half seventeenth century (?). Coloured, in French. Reproduced in D. Heilijgers, 'The Kern Institute', in S.M. Gieling, P.G. Hoftijzer and J.J. Witkam (eds), *Special Collections. A Guide to the Collections of Leiden University Library and Neighbouring Institutions* (Leiden, 2002), p. 88.

(f) 'Ad antiquam Indiae geographiam tabulam ...', map of India and part of South-East Asia, showing locations known to Ptolemy on an eighteenth-century geographical background, with inset of Ceylon and south India according to Ptolemy, by d'Anville (?), 1765. (The collection also includes a map that is solely or mostly based on Ptolemy, entitled: 'Tab. X Asiae, complectens Indiam intra Gangem ...'.)

(g) 'A map of the East-Indies and the adjacent countries ...', map of India and South-East Asia, with European settlements and remarks concerning geography, flora, fauna, politics, commodities, etc., with insets showing maps of Madras, Batavia and Bantam, and views of Goa and Surat, by Herman Moll, second half of the seventeenth century (?). In English.

UNIVERSITEIT LEIDEN, UNIVERSITEITSBIBLIOTHEEK
LEIDEN UNIVERSITY LIBRARY

See also 1.2.7.

Collectie Bodel Nijenhuis
Bodel Nijenhuis collection

Size: *c.* 60000 maps, *c.* 1500 atlases, *c.* 1600 drawings, *c.* 24000 prints
Period: *c.* 1515–up to the present
Inventory:
- maps:
    - geographical catalogue on index cards (old and new sections), covering maps that were acquired early as well as latest acquisitions
    - printed geographical catalogue, covering relatively recent acquisitions
    - D. de Vries, *Uit de kaartenwinkel van de VOC. Catalogus van zeekaarten van de Verenigde Oostindische Compagnie in de Collectie Bodel Nijenhuis* (Alphen aan den Rijn, 1996), covering sea charts of the VOC, with introduction (also on Internet)
- prints and drawings:
    - alphabetic catalogue to geographical and artist names
    - systematic catalogue to subjects

The collection, consisting of maps, drawings and prints, was started by Johannes Tiberius Bodel Nijenhuis (1797-1872). It focuses on the Netherlands, its neighbouring countries, former Dutch colonies and overseas settlements, sea charts and plans of towns and fortifications, among other subjects. With regard to South Asia, the collection includes a substantial number of manuscript maps originating from the VOC, beside many printed maps from the Dutch Republic and abroad. In addition to the prints described in this guide, the collection includes a great number of relevant prints originating from published works (see also Appendix I). For material concerning Surat, Malabar, Ceylon, Coromandel and Bengal, see 2.6, 3.6, 4.6, 5.6 and 6.6.

002-09-038	Map (in two sections) of the entire course of the Ganges and Ghaghara Rivers, *c.* 1810. Manuscript, coloured, in German, scale *c.* 1:3,300,000 (42 x 34 cm, 26 x 42 cm) (old no. Port 176 N 116).
006-14-028	Sea chart of Ceylon, the Fishery Coast, the Maldives and Malabar up to Cranganur, with soundings, some landfalls and Dutch settlements, second quarter of the eighteenth century. Pen and brush drawing, coloured, scale *c.* 1: 1,400,000 (102 x 109 cm) (no. 75 in catalogue of sea charts).[1]
054-09-001	Map of the Indian Ocean, showing in pencil the itinerary of a ship in the waters around India and Ceylon in 1738. Manuscript, coloured, scale 1:11,500,000 (70 x 94 cm).
054-10-002	Map of the Indian Ocean and the adjacent coasts, by Isaak de Graaf at Amsterdam, 1740, showing in pencil the itinerary of a ship in the waters around India and Ceylon. Manuscript, coloured, scale 1:10,800,000 (70 x 93 cm).
Port 172 N 96	Map of the Indian Ocean with Ceylon, the Maldives and the Andaman Islands (among other areas), by P. Mortier at Amsterdam, *c.* 1700. Copper engraving, in French (57 x 85 cm). Identical to Port 175 N 5 & N 6, see below.
Port 175 N 5 & N 6	Two identical maps of the Indian Ocean with Ceylon, the Maldives and the Andaman Islands (among other areas), by P. Mortier at Amsterdam, *c.* 1700. Copper engraving, one coloured, in French (57 x 85 cm). Identical to Port 172 N 96, see above.
Port 175 N 7	Sea chart of South Asia and the Indian Ocean, with reference to the fleet of Admiral Watson in 1754-5, with inset of Bengal. Copper engraving, coloured (41 x 50 cm).
Port 175 N 8 & N 9	Two charts of the currents and winds in the Indian Ocean during various monsoon seasons, by Grenier, 1776. Printed, in French.

Port 175 N 10	Sea chart of the Arabian Sea with the coasts of Gujarat, Konkan, Kanara and Malabar, the Fishery Coast, the Maldives and the Lakshadweep. Copper engraving, in French (47 x 65 cm). Related to Port 175 N 11, see below.
Port 175 N 11	Sea chart of the Bay of Bengal with the coasts of Ceylon, Coromandel and Bengal, the Fishery Coast and the Andaman and Nicobar Islands. Copper engraving, in French (47 x 65 cm). Related to Port 175 N 10, see above.
Port 175 N 23	Map of South Asia, by Covens and Mortier at Amsterdam, *c.* 1750. Copper engraving, coloured, in French (52 x 48 cm).
Port 175 N 24	Map of India, detailing the Ganges River area, west and south India and Ceylon, by d'Anville (and G. de la Haye?), with two insets of the Hooghly River up to Hooghly (with soundings) and the vicinity of Goa, 1752. Copper engraving, in French, two sheets (46 x 100 cm). Identical to Port 202 N 23a & b, see below.
Port 175 N 25	Map of South and South-East Asia, with a few remarks concerning trade and politics in South Asia, by Eman. Bowen and W.A. Bachiene, 1774. Printed (33 x 40 cm).
Port 175 N 26	Map of South Asia and Burma, by J.D. Barbié du Bocage, *c.* 1800. Printed (34 x 38 cm).
Port 175 N 31	Map of South Asia, by J. Rennell, published at London, 1788. Copper engraving, coloured, four sheets (51 x 61 cm).
Port 176 N 1	Map of the Mughal Empire, by N. Sanson d'Abbeville, 1652. Copper engraving, coloured (18 x 24 cm). Closely resembling Port 176 N 2, see below.
Port 176 N 2	Map of the Mughal Empire, by N. Sanson d'Abbeville, *c.* 1652. Copper engraving (18 x 23 cm). Closely resembling Port 176 N 1, see above.
Port 176 N 3	Map of the Indian peninsula up to Bengal and Gujarat, and north Ceylon, with inset of Malabar, by N. Sanson d'Abbeville, 1652. Copper engraving, coloured (18 x 24 cm). Closely resembling Port 176 N 4, see below.
Port 176 N 4	Map of the Indian peninsula up to Bengal and Gujarat, and north Ceylon, with inset of Malabar, by N. Sanson d'Abbeville, *c.* 1652. Copper engraving (18 x 24 cm). Closely resembling Port 176 N 3, see above.

Port 176 N 10 & N 11	Two identical maps of the Mughal Empire, by F. de Wit, published by Covens and Mortier, *c.* 1750. Copper engraving, one coloured, in Latin (40 x 50 cm). Almost identical to Port 176 N 12 and N 13, see below.
Port 176 N 12 & N 13	Two identical maps of the Mughal Empire, by F. de Wit, published by P. Mortier, Amsterdam, *c.* 1700. Copper engraving, one coloured, in Latin (40 x 50 cm). Almost identical to Port 176 N 10 & 11, see above.
Port 176 N 15	Map of the Mughal Empire, by Sanson d'Abbeville, published by Pierre Mariette, Paris, 1703. Copper engraving, coloured, in French (33 x 53 cm).
Port 176 N 22 & N 23	Two identical maps of the Indian peninsula up to Gujarat and Orissa, by G. Delisle, Paris, 1723. Copper engraving, coloured, in French (42 x 55 cm).
Port 176 N 24	Map of north India and most of the peninsula, by M. and A.C. Seutter, *c.* 1740. Copper engraving, coloured, in Latin (48 x 55 cm).
Port 176 N 26	Map of south and most of north India, by Pierre van der Aa, *c.* 1710. Printed (21 x 29 cm).
Port 176 N 27	Map of the Indian peninsula up to Gujarat and Orissa and north Ceylon, by Guillaume de l'Isle, published by J. Covens and C. Mortier, Amsterdam. Copper engraving, coloured, in French (*c.* 42 x 55 cm). Identical to Port 176 N 134 & N 135, see below.
Port 176 N 29	Map of south India up to Konkan and northern Coromandel, with remarks concerning the Europeans in the area and a table of their settlements, originating from the 'Atlas Guendeville' (?), 1726. Copper engraving, coloured, in French (35 x 42 cm).
Port 176 N 30 & N 31	Two identical maps of South Asia, by J. Keyser, 1730, published by I. Tirion. Copper engraving, coloured (27 x 35 cm).
Port 176 N 32	Map of south India up to Konkan and northern Coromandel, with print of some South Asians with an elephant, 1733. Copper engraving, coloured, in Latin (53 x 47 cm).[2]
Port 176 N 33 & N 34	Two identical maps of the coast of Persia and the west coast of South Asia, indicating European settlements and locations where

astronomical observations were made on which the map was based, with legend, by J. van der Schley (?), 1740. Copper engraving, one coloured, partly in French (23 x 19 cm).

Port 176 N 34a — Map of the coast of Persia and the west coast of South Asia, indicating locations where astronomical observations were made on which the map was based, 1740. Copper engraving, in French (23 x 19 cm).

Port 176 N 35 — Map of the Bay of Bengal and adjacent coasts, indicating European settlements, by J. van der Schley, 1740. Copper engraving, partly in French (20 x 25 cm).

Port 176 N 40, N 42 to N 44 — Four virtually identical maps of north India, by Hr. Bellin (?) and J. van der Schley, 1752. Copper engraving, two coloured (20 x 32 cm). Related to Port 176 N 41, see below.

Port 176 N 41 — Map of south India, by Hr. Bellin (?) and J. van der Schley, 1752. Copper engraving, coloured (20 x 32 cm). Related to Port 176 N 40, N 42 to N 44, see above.

Port 176 N 47 (I & II) — Map of South Asia, showing British possessions and the Maratha confederacy, by Thomas Jefferys, 1768. Copper engraving, coloured, in English, two sheets (56 x 139 cm).

Port 176 N 49 — Map of Bengal, Bihar and eastern Hindustan, with legend, by Jefferys and Faden, London, 1773. Copper engraving, coloured, in English (57 x 100 cm).

Port 176 N 52 & N 109 — Two identical maps of north India, with sailing directions (?) and inset of the mouths of the Ganges River. Copper engraving (20 x 30 cm). Related to Port 176 N 53, see below.

Port 176 N 53 — Map of south India and Ceylon, with sailing directions (?). Copper engraving (20 x 30 cm). Related to Port 176 N 52 & N 109, see above.

Port 176 N 54 (I to III) — Map of South Asia, by J. Rennell, 1782, 1785. Copper engraving, three sheets (37 x 39 cm).

Port 176 N 55 — Map of south India, with special reference to Mysore under Haidar Ali Khan, by J.R. Forster, 1784. Copper engraving, in German (36 x 27 cm).

Port 176 N 56 — Map of South Asia, by C. Mannert, published at Nürnberg, 1797. Copper engraving, coloured, in German (52 x 69 cm).

Port 176 N 57	Map of South Asia, with political divisions and European possessions, by the Lotter brothers after J. Rennell, *c.* 1760. Copper engraving, coloured, in German (52 x 46 cm).
Port 176 N 58	Map of India, by Endner, late eighteenth century (?). Copper engraving, in German (34 x 34 cm).
Port 176 N 59	Map of South Asia, by W. Palmer (?) and L.S. de la Rochette, published by W. Faden at London, 1788. Printed, coloured, in English (68 x 57 cm).
Port 176 N 60	Map of South Asia, with political divisions, published by W. Faden at London, 1788. Copper engraving, coloured, in English (33 x 28 cm).
Port 176 N 61	Map of India south of Madras and northern Ceylon, describing the routes of the armies under Col. Fullarton and Humberston, showing geographical features such as mountains and woods, with legend, published by W. Faden at London, 1788. Copper engraving, coloured, in English (86 x 100 cm).
Port 176 N 62 & N 171	Two identical maps of the former possessions of Tipu Sultan of Mysore and the present division of the area, with legend, after Colin Mackenzie, 1799. Copper engraving, coloured, in German (22 x 29 cm).
Port 176 N 63 & N 64	Two identical maps of south India and northern Ceylon, with political divisions, by B. Baker, 1792, published by W. Faden at London, 1800. Steel engraving, coloured, in English (97 x 80 cm).
Port 176 N 65 to N71, N 73, N 75, N 76, N 104, N 110, N 114	Various maps and plans of British battles and sieges at least partly under General Gerard Lake against the Marathas (and others?) chiefly in north India, including Delhi, Bharatpur, Deeg, Aligarh, Laswari, Assyae and Perron's camp, in the period 1803-6, with legends and explanations, mainly by E. Cullan, mostly published by J. Stockdale at Picadilly. Copper engravings, coloured, in English, thirteen sheets.
Port 176 N 72	Map of South Asia, by J. Rausch and F.G. Canzler after J. Rennell, 1798, republished by the Homann heirs at Nürnberg, 1804. Copper engraving, coloured, in German (51 x 52 cm).
Port 176 N 74	Map of the territories of the Marathas and the

	Nizam of Hyderabad, Bengal and Awadh, with explanations, by J. Leeffman, London, 1804. Copper engraving, coloured (33 x 49 cm).
Port 176 N 78	Map of South Asia, 1809. Copper engraving, coloured, in French (24 x 19 cm).
Port 176 N 80	Map of the area north and south of Kathmandu, by Kirkpatrick, published by the Geographical Institute at Weimar, 1818. Printed, in German and English (42 x 30 cm).
Port 176 N 108	Maps of the Mughal Empire and Kashmir, with political and ethnological descriptions of these regions, genealogical tree of the Mughal Emperors and views of an elephant fight, the weighing of a king and the burning of dead bodies. Copper engraving, coloured, in French, one sheet (37 x 43 cm).
Port 176 N 129	Map of the Bay of Bengal with adjacent coasts, published by G. Valk and P. Schenk, Amsterdam, *c.* 1700. Copper engraving, coloured, in Latin (46 x 52 cm). Almost identical to Port 176 N 172, see below.
Port 176 N 131 to N 133	Three identical maps of Konkan, Kanara, Malabar, the Fishery Coast, part of Coromandel and Ceylon north of Colombo, with soundings, by Hadrianus Relandus, *c.* 1700, published by Gerard van Keulen at Amsterdam. Copper engraving, two coloured, partly in Latin (47 x 59 cm).
Port 176 N 134 & N 135	Two identical maps of the Indian peninsula up to Gujarat and Orissa and north Ceylon, by Guillaume de l'Isle, published by J. Covens and C. Mortier, Amsterdam. Copper engraving, coloured, in French (42 x 55 cm). Identical to Port 176 N 27, see above.
Port 176 N 138	Map of India south of Bombay and Ceylon, by J. van der Schley (?). Copper engraving, partly in French (20 x 23 cm).
Port 176 N 139	Map of India south of Dabhol, Ceylon and the Maldives, with sailing directions (?). Copper engraving (20 x 31 cm).
Port 176 N 140	Map of the Konkan, Kanara, Malabar, Coromandel and Fishery Coasts, after De l'Isle and Bruzen la Matiniere. Copper engraving (29 x 28 cm).
Port 176 N 141	Map of India south of the Krishna River, with the division of the lands of Tipu Sultan of

	Mysore according to the treaties of 1792 (by Cornwallis) and 1799 (by Wellesley), with legend, by J. Rennell, Weimar, 1804. Copper engraving, coloured, in German (46 x 37 cm).
Port 176 N 142	Map of the coasts of Ceylon, Malabar and the Maldives, with two landfalls of Cape Comorin, soundings and explanatory notes. Copper engraving, in French (49 x 66 cm).
Port 176 N 148	Map of the coasts of Gujarat, Konkan and Kanara, with soundings and inset of the vicinity of the Tapti River from the coast to Surat with soundings, by Guill. de la Haye. Copper engraving, in French (67 x 48 cm).
Port 176 N 172	Map of the Bay of Bengal with adjacent coasts, *c.* 1700 (?). Copper engraving, coloured, in Latin (46 x 52 cm). Almost identical to Port 176 N 129, see above.
Port 176 N 181	Map of India's east coast from Pondicherry to Hooghly, with soundings and landfalls of the Jagannath Temple at Puri, the 'Black Temple' (Konarka?) and 'Montercota'. Copper engraving, in French (47 x 67 cm).
Port 176 N 188	Map of the Mughal Empire, published by Joannus Janssonius at Amsterdam. Copper engraving, in Latin (*c.* 35 x 47 cm). Almost identical to Port 176 N 189 & N 190, see below.
Port 176 N 189 & N 190	Two identical maps of the Mughal Empire, by P. Schenk and G. Valk, Amsterdam, *c.* 1700. Copper engraving, coloured, in Latin (35 x 47 cm). Almost identical to Port 176 N 188, see above.
Port 176 N 191	Map of South Asia, by Covens and Mortier at Amsterdam, *c.* 1750 (?). Copper engraving, coloured, in French (52 x 48 cm).
Port 202 N 23a & b	Map of India, detailing the Ganges River area, west and south India and Ceylon, by d'Anville and G. de la Haye, with two insets of the Hooghly River up to Hooghly (with soundings) and the vicinity of Goa, 1752. Copper engraving, in French, two sheets (40 x 102 cm). Identical to Port 175 N 24, see above.
Port 202 N 69	Map of India, after James Rennell, 1788. Printed, in French, small part missing (16 x 13 cm).
Port 202 N 70a to d	Map of the Indian Ocean, with N 70a & b showing the coasts of South Asia, with soundings, climatic and nautical remarks and routes of

	some British ships, by A. Arrowsmith, 1802 (?). Printed, in English, four sheets (64 x 96 cm).
Port 204 N 46	Map of the kingdoms of Cranganur, Cochin, Purakkad, Kayankulam and Quilon, and a map of the surroundings of Colombo and Negombo up to Sitawake and 'Arandery', *c.* 1750 (?). Printed, coloured, in French (16 x 38 cm). Originally insets of another map, see 1.6.4, *Koninklijk Instituut voor Taal-, Land- en Volkenkunde*, Maps, inv. nos A 4,5 Blad 2 (or 3) & A 4,7 Blad 3.
Port 222 N 9	Map of the Bay of Bengal, including the coasts of Ceylon, Coromandel and Bengal, with some remarks concerning trade and commodities in Bengal, by J. Janssonius, Amsterdam, *c.* 1650. Copper engraving, coloured (47 x 54 cm).

[1] Reproduced and described in Paranavitana and De Silva, *Maps and Plans of Dutch Ceylon*, p. 37 (see Supplement I: Bibliography, no. 655).

[2] A (virtually) identical map has been reproduced and described in Paranavitana and De Silva, *Maps and Plans of Dutch Ceylon*, p. 45 (see Supplement I: Bibliography, no. 655).

Bibliotheca Publica Latina
Latin Public Library

See 1.2.7

BPL 126D	'Icones plantarum Malabaricum, adscriptis nominibus et viribus', manuscript containing 262 coloured drawings and descriptions of plants growing on Ceylon and in south India, *c.* late seventeenth century (?). Two volumes.

UNIVERSITEIT UTRECHT, FACULTEIT RUIMTELIJKE WETENSCHAPPEN
UTRECHT UNIVERSITY, FACULTY OF GEOSCIENCES

For a general survey, see the repository's web site (see Appendix II, 2.9).

Main collection

Size:	*c.* 120,000 maps, 5000 atlases
Period:	16th century–up to the present
Inventory:	– catalogue on index cards, arranged according to region and theme
	– data base (inexhaustive at the time of writing)

The collection focuses on maps concerning the Netherlands and its (former) overseas possessions, Europe and the United States of America. It includes about 5500 maps that date from before 1850. For maps regarding Ceylon, see 4.6.

VIII G.h.1 Map of South Asia, published by Covens and Mortier at Amsterdam. Coloured, in French.

VIII G.h.2 Map of the Indian peninsula south of Gujarat and Bengal, and of northern Ceylon, indicating places with European settlements, by G. de l'Isle, published by I. Covens and C. Mortier at Amsterdam. Coloured, in French.

VIII G.h.4 Map of South Asia, showing political divisions, by H.C. Albers, after Arrowsmith, 1806. Coloured, in German.

Ackersdijck

Inv. nos: 1-1035, supplement: 1-27
Size: 40 metres
Period: 16th-19th centuries
Inventory: G.G. Schilder, 'Lijst van kaarten in de Ackersdijck-Collectie van de Rijksuniversiteit Utrecht' (1975), geographically arranged, with introduction and index to personal names

These maps were collected by Jan Ackersdijck (1790-1861), Professor of Law, Economics and Statistics at the University of Utrecht. The collection has been given on loan by the University Library. It consists of seventeenth- and eighteenth-century printed maps as well as geographical and thematic maps from the first half of the nineteenth century. Most maps originate from atlases. For maps concerning Ceylon, see 4.6.

842 Map of the Indian peninsula up to Gujarat and Bengal, and of northern Ceylon, by G. Delisle, published by Pierre Schenk at Amsterdam. Copper engraving, coloured, in French, scale *c.* 1:3,800,000 (43 x 56 cm).

BIBLIOTHEEK WAGENINGEN UNIVERSITEIT EN RESEARCHCENTRUM
WAGENINGEN UNIVERSITY AND RESEARCH CENTRE LIBRARY

For general surveys, see J. Mateboer, *Repertorium bijzondere collecties* (The Hague, 1997), pp. 120-1, and the repository's web site (see Appendix II, 2.11).

Speciale collecties
Special collections

Size: *c.* 200,000 items
Period: 15th century–up to the present
Inventory: data base

These collections focus on agriculture, horticulture, forestry, livestock farming, garden and landscape design, and land use. They include manuscripts, printed works, magazines, maps, drawings, prints and photos. For drawings concerning Ceylon and Bengal, see 4.6 and 6.6.

1.6.3. Ecclesiastical Organizations

No relevant materials found in the inventories.

1.6.4. Museums and other public institutions

STEDELIJK MUSEUM ALKMAAR
MUNICIPAL MUSEUM OF ALKMAAR

For a general survey, see the repository's web site (see Appendix II, 4.1).

Schilderijen
Paintings

Size: *c.* 840 items
Period: 16th century–up to the present
Inventory:
- data base
- for paintings dating from the 16th and 17th centuries: S. de Vries (ed.), *De zestiende- en zeventiende-eeuwse schilderijen van het Stedelijk Museum Alkmaar. Collectie-catalogus* (Alkmaar and Zwolle, 1997), with introduction and index to personal names

This collection focuses on the history of the town of Alkmaar and the surrounding region of northern Kennemerland, in particular the seventeenth century. It includes two paintings pertaining to Surat, see 2.6.

KONINKLIJK INSTITUUT VOOR DE TROPEN (KIT) (Amsterdam)
ROYAL TROPICAL INSTITUTE

See also 1.4.2.

Tropen Museum
Tropical Museum

See 1.4.2

4304 / 4 Map of the Indian peninsula south of Goa and northern Ceylon, showing European (chiefly Dutch) settlements, by Hadrianus Relandus, published by Gerard van Keulen at Amsterdam, 1718 (?). Engraving, coloured, partly in Latin.

NEDERLANDS SCHEEPVAARTMUSEUM AMSTERDAM
NETHERLANDS MARITIME MUSEUM AMSTERDAM

See also 1.4.4.

Zeevaartkundige collectie
Navigational collection

Size: *c.* 4080 maps
Period: 16th century–up to the present
Inventory:
- data base (on Internet)
- systematic catalogue on index cards

This collection consists of nautical instruments, maps and globes. The bulk of the collection is kept in a separate depot, which can only be visited by appointment. Note that some plans are part of the iconographic collection, see below. For maps concerning Surat, Malabar, Ceylon and Bengal, see also 2.6, 3.6, 4.6 and 6.6.

A.0145 (127) (1-5)	Five maps of the Indian Ocean, showing in pencil the itineraries of ships in South Asian waters, by Isaac de Graaf at Amsterdam, 1709 (?), *c.* 1728-31. Manuscripts, coloured, scale *c.* 1:10,000,000 and 1:5,000,000 (*c.* 75 x 100 cm). Map from 1729 probably reproduced in P. van Mil and M. Scharloo, *De VOC in de kaart gekeken. Cartografie en navigatie van de Verenigde Oostindische Compagnie 1602-1799* (The Hague, 1988), p. 60.
A.2629 (05)	Sea chart of the Bay of Bengal and surrounding waters, by an unidentified Frenchman, second half of the seventeenth century. Coloured, scale *c.* 1:5,000,000 (57 x 70 cm).
A.3845 (094)	Map of south India and north Ceylon, by Adriaan Reland, published by Gerard van Keulen at Amsterdam, 1728 (?). Partly in Latin, scale 1:2,000,000 (55 x 66 cm).
S.1012 (1)	Map of the Indian Ocean, with inset showing Ceylon, the Maldives and south India, by Joan Blaeu at Amsterdam, *c.* 1680. Manuscript, coloured (20 x 41 cm), probably incomplete.

Iconografische collectie
Iconographic collection

Size:	*c.* 450 paintings, 3000 drawings, 4000 prints
Period:	16th century–up to the present
Inventory:	data base (on Internet)

This collection, consisting of paintings, drawings and prints as well as photographs, focuses on Dutch maritime history. Note that the collection includes some plans as well as texts accompanying drawings. The bulk of the collection is kept in a separate depot, which can only be visited by appointment. For materials concerning Surat, Malabar, Ceylon, Coromandel and Bengal, see 2.6, 3.6, 4.6, 5.6 and 6.6.

RIJKSMUSEUM AMSTERDAM
RIJKSMUSEUM AMSTERDAM

For a general survey, see the repository's web site (see Appendix II, 4.5). In addition to the materials described below and in the regional chapters, the Museum keeps a number of artefacts and works of art pertaining to South Asia that fall outside the scope of this guide. These include weaponry, ceremonial objects, furniture, textiles, coins and medals (for objects concerning Ceylon, see P.H.D.H. de Silva, *A Catalogue of Antiquities and Other Cultural Objects from Sri Lanka*

(Ceylon) Abroad (Colombo, 1975), pp. 375-81 (somewhat outdated and occasionally inaccurate)).

Afdeling Nederlandse Geschiedenis
Department of Dutch History

Size: *c.* 40000 items (?)
Period: Middle Ages–up to the present
Inventory: relevant for this guide:
- data base (partly on Internet)
- for paintings: P.J.J. van Thiel a.o (eds), *Alle schilderijen van het Rijksmuseum te Amsterdam. Volledig geïllustreerde catalogus / All the Paintings of the Rijksmuseum in Amsterdam. A Completely Illustrated Catalogue* (Amsterdam and Maarssen, 1976); *All the Paintings of the Rijksmuseum in Amsterdam. First Supplement, 1976-91* (Amsterdam and The Hagüe, 1992), with introductions, appendices, indices and miniature reproductions of most paintings
- *Bulletin van het Rijksmuseum* (1953-)

This Department focuses on objects documenting Dutch History, among which are Asian materials produced for the Dutch market. The collection includes paintings, drawings, prints, maps and also some manuscripts. For materials concerning Surat, Malabar, Ceylon, Coromandel and Bengal, see 2.6, 3.6, 4.4, 4.6, 5.6 and 6.6.

NG-20-C Views of Surat, Goa and Calicut (?) (among other locations), by Frederick de Wit, 1700. Engravings, one sheet (54 x 45 cm).[1]

NG-20-F Views of Ahmadabad, Cranganur, Cochin, Colombo, Pulicat and Masulipatam (among other locations), by Frederick de Wit, 1700. Engravings, one sheet (55 x 44 cm).[1]

NG-20-K Views of Cannanore and Tuticorin (among other locations), by Frederick de Wit, 1700. Engravings, one sheet (22 x 29 cm).[1]

NG-501-65 Map of India and the west coast of Arakan, Pegu, Siam and Melaka, with insets of the surroundings of Goa and the mouth of the Ganges (among other locations), by Jean Baptiste Bourguignon d'Anville, Johannes Covens and Cornelis Mortier, 1752 (?). Printed, coloured (87 x 106 cm).

NG-501-67 Map of north and central India, by Cornelis and Johannes Willemszoon Blaeu, 1640. Printed, coloured (42 x 52 cm).

NG-501-68 Map of India and Ceylon, by Jacob Keyser, published by Isaak Tirion at Amsterdam, 1730 (?). Coloured (28 x 36 cm).

NG-501-70 Map showing the course of the Ganges River from Hardwar to the Bay of Bengal, by W. Faden and James Rennell (1742-1830), 1786. Printed, coloured, in English (72 x 106 cm).

NG-501-71 Map of Konkan, Kanara, Malabar, Madurai, Coromandel and part of Ceylon, by Adriaan Reland (1676-1718), printed by Gerard van Keulen at Amsterdam, 1700. Coloured (60 x 50 cm).

NG-1985-7-1 Album (20 x 17 cm) in which 152 drawings are bound, partly concerning Asia, mostly with explanatory notes, by Rev. Jan Brandes (1743-1808). Partly described and reproduced in De Bruijn and Raben, *The World of Jan Brandes 1743-1808* (see Supplement I: Bibliography, no. 125). For the second part of the album, see 3.6 and 4.6, *Rijksmuseum Amsterdam, Afdeling Nederlandse Geschiedenis*, NG-1985-7-2. Including:

–1 Self portrait of Brandes at the age of 42, made at Galle, 1786. Grey wash.[2]

SK-A-1299 Portrait of Philippus Baldaeus (?) and 'Gerrit Mosopatam' (probably from Masulipatam, earlier thought to belong to the Ceylonese Velala community) in a Ceylonese landscape, with in the background the Dutch Reformed church and church house of Pandattarippu, North-East of Jaffna, by Johan de la Rocquette, 1668. Oil on canvas (141 x 176 cm).[2]

[1] Originally part of a world map by Frederick de Wit, Amsterdam.

[2] Described and reproduced in R.K. de Silva and W.G.M. Beumer, *Illustrations and Views of Dutch Ceylon, 1602-1796. A Comprehensive Work of Pictorial Reference with Selected Eye-witness Accounts* (Leiden, 1988), pp. 357, 463; inv. no. SK-A-1299 also described and reproduced in Beumer, 'Philippus Baldaeus and Gerrit Mosopatam' (see Supplement I: Bibliography, no. 123), Zandvliet, *De Nederlandse ontmoeting met Azië / The Dutch Encounter with Asia*, pp. 212-14 (Bibl., no. 98), and Peters and André de la Porte, *In steen geschreven*, pp. 58-9 (Bibl., no. 848).

Rijksprentenkabinet
Print Room

Size: *c.* 1,000,000 drawings, prints and photos
Period: Middle Ages–up to the present
Inventory: relevant for this guide:

- data base
- *Gids voor het Rijksprentenkabinet. Een overzicht van de verzamelingen met naamlijsten van graveurs en tekenaars* (Amsterdam, 1964), with extensive introduction and summary in English
- *Bulletin van het Rijksmuseum* (1953-)
- F. Muller, *De Nederlandse geschiedenis in platen, beredeneerde beschrijving van Nederlandse historieplaten, zinneprenten en historische kaarten*, 4 vols (Amsterdam, 1863-82), with indices
- geographical catalogue on index cards

The holdings of the *Rijksprentenkabinet* can be considered the principal collection of drawings and prints in the Netherlands. The objects are largely arranged according to artist. Part of the collection (mostly anonymous works and duplicates depicting specific locations) is kept separately and referred to as 'collectie topografie'. In this guide such items are indicated by 'topo. col.' following the inv. no. In addition to the items described in this guide, the holdings of the *Rijksprentenkabinet* include many relevant prints originating from published works (see also Appendix I). Of the Indian miniature paintings, this guide describes only those that clearly relate to Indo-Dutch relations, for instance paintings to which Dutch texts have been added. Note that there are many other Indian miniatures showing Indian rulers, religious representations, scenes from everyday life, etc. For pictures concerning Surat, Malabar, Ceylon, Coromandel and Bengal, see 2.6, 3.6, 4.6, 5.6 and 6.6.

RP-P-OB-47.483 (topo. col.)	Views of Diu and Goa (among other locations). Prints, possibly originating from a work by Hogenberg (?).
RP-T-1930-42	Indian with arrow and bow, by Rembrandt Harmensz van Rijn (1606-69), *c.* 1655. Pen and wash drawing, coloured (19 x 13 cm). Free adaptation of an Indian miniature painting. Described and reproduced in O. Benesch, *The Drawings of Rembrandt*, Vol. 5 (London, 1957), p. 341 (no. 1202) and plate no. 1427.
RP-T-1972-24	Portrait of Muhammad Amin Khan (son of Mir Jumla), with a poem in Dutch, produced in Golkonda and purchased by a VOC official, *c.* 1680. Coloured, Indian miniature painting (23 x 18 cm).

MUSEUM BRONBEEK (Arnhem)
BRONBEEK MUSEUM

For a general survey, see the repository's web site (see Appendix II, 4.6).

Koninklijk Tehuis voor Oud-Militairen en Museum Bronbeek
Royal Home for Retired Military Personnel and Bronbeek Museum

Size:	*c.* 25000-30000 objects
Period:	16th century–up to the present
Inventory:	data base

This collection, consisting of various kinds of objects, focuses on the *Koninklijk Nederlands-Indisch Leger* (KNIL, Royal Dutch East Indian Army) and mostly concerns the period 1830-1950. The museum keeps one painting that pertains to Malabar, see 3.6.

DORDRECHTS MUSEUM
MUSEUM OF DORDRECHT

For a general survey, see the repository's web site (see Appendix II, 4.7).

Schilder-, teken- en prentkunst
Paintings, drawings and prints

Size: *c.* 3500 items
Period: 16th century–up to the present
Inventory: data base (in preparation)

The collection focuses on materials pertaining to the Netherlands, with the older works mostly concerning the town of Dordrecht. It includes a painting of Mattheus van den Broucke, see 6.6. Van den Broucke took service with the VOC in 1648 and was sent to Bengal in 1652 as Chief-merchant. In 1653 he became *Opperhoofd* at Cossimbazar and in 1655 he was appointed as second-in-command at Hooghly. During the years 1658-63, he functioned as *Directeur* of Bengal. He returned to the Dutch Republic in 1669 as Commander of the return fleet to become Director of the VOC at Amsterdam and Burgomaster of Dordrecht.

SIMON VAN GIJN - MUSEUM AAN HUIS (Dordrecht)
SIMON VAN GIJN - MUSEUM AT HOME

For a general survey, see the repository's web site (see Appendix II, 4.8).

Main collection

Inv. nos: 1-*c.* 16000
Period: prehistory–up to the present
Inventory: systematic catalogue on index cards

This collection consists of various types of objects and focuses on the town of Dordrecht and its history. Part of it has been given on loan by the *Dordrechts Museum* (see above), including a painting of Mattheus van den Broucke, see 6.6. For more information on Van den Broucke, see again the *Dordrechts Museum.*

GRONINGER MUSEUM
MUSEUM OF GRONINGEN

For a general survey, see the repository's web site (see Appendix II, 4.9).

Schilderijen
Paintings

Size: *c.* 1735 paintings
Period: Middle Ages–up to the present
Inventory:
- catalogue on index cards, arranged according to artist and inv. no.
- data base

The collection focuses on the town and province of Groningen and their history. It includes some paintings of *Directeur* Jan Albert Sichterman of Bengal and his wife, see 6.6. For more information on the people depicted, see 1.1.8, *Groninger Archieven*, Sichterman family archives.

TEYLERS MUSEUM (Haarlem)
TEYLER'S MUSEUM

See also 1.4.10.

Kunstverzameling
Art collection

Size: *c.* 11000 drawings, 31000 prints and 350 paintings
Period: 16th century–up to the present
Inventory:
- drawings: catalogue on index cards according to date and artist
- prints: data base

In addition to the items described separately in this guide, the collection includes a number of Indian (or some possibly Persian) miniatures, partly originating from the Teding van Berkhout family. For plans and drawings concerning Ceylon and Coromandel, see 4.6 and 5.6.

Natuurwetenschappelijke Bibliotheek
Scientific Library

Size: *c.* 125,000 items
Period: *c.* 16th-20th centuries
Inventory: alphabetical and systematic catalogues on index cards

The collection incorporates the library of the *Hollandsche Maatschappij der Wetenschappen* (for the archives of this scientific society, see 1.1.10, *Rijksarchief in Noord-Holland*). It mainly consists of books and magazines, but includes some drawings concerning Ceylon. See 4.6.

KONINKLIJKE BIBLIOTHEEK (KB) (The Hague)
ROYAL LIBRARY

See also 1.4.12.

Cartografische collectie
Cartographic collection

Size: *c.* 25000 items
Period: Middle Ages (?)–up to the present
Inventory: data base

Since maps, atlases, globes, etc., are scattered over different collections, they have not yet been described or made accessible as a separate collection. At present, all collections of the *Koninklijke Bibliotheek* are being examined for cartographic materials. A separate inventory may be available in the future.

78 B 31 Map in four parts of the coasts of Gujarat, Konkan, Kanara and Malabar, showing European settlements, sepulchral monuments, landfalls, etc., by John Friend, 1708-9. Manuscript, in English, coloured (90 x 66 cm, 80 x 66 cm).

Oude drukken
Early printed works

See 1.4.12

7452 Newsletter with woodcut depicting a naval battle, probably between the VOC and the Portuguese near Goa or Ceylon, 1653. One piece.

KONINKLIJK INSTITUUT VOOR TAAL-, LAND- EN VOLKENKUNDE (KITLV)
(Leiden)
ROYAL INSTITUTE OF LINGUISTICS AND ANTHROPOLOGY

See also 1.4.1.

Maps

Size: *c.* 2000 items
Period: 18th-20th centuries
Inventory: data base (on Internet)

In addition to the maps described in this guide, the collection includes various British maps from the early nineteenth century. For maps of Ceylon, see 4.6.

A 4,5 Blad 2 (or 3) &
A 4,7 Blad 3 Map of the Indian Ocean, including Ceylon and the Maldives, with one inset of the kingdoms of Cranganur, Cochin, Purakkad, Kayankulam and Quilon, and another of the surroundings of Colombo and Negombo up to Sitawake and 'Arandery', *c.* 1750. Printed, coloured, in French.

Images

Size: *c.* 3500 items
Period: 17th-20th centuries
Inventory:
- data base (on Internet)
- J.H. Maronier, *Pictures of the Tropics. A Catalogue of Drawings, Water-colours, Paintings and Sculptures in the Collection of the Royal Institute of Linguistics and Anthropology in Leiden* (The Hague, 1967)

In addition to the images described in this guide, the collection includes some relevant prints originating from published works (see also Appendix I), a number of early nineteenth-century paintings and drawings of British and French origin, 49 water colours made by John Leonard Kalenberg van Dort in 1888-9, which depict existing or extinct remains of VOC buildings, canals, tombstones, etc., on Ceylon,[1] as well as photographs of Company remains. For images concerning Surat, Malabar, Ceylon and Coromandel, see 2.6, 3.6, 4.6 and 5.6.

[1] Many of these have been reproduced in R.K. de Silva and W.G.M. Beumer, *Illustrations and Views of Dutch Ceylon, 1602-1796. A Comprehensive Work of Pictorial Reference with Selected Eye-witness Accounts* (Leiden, 1988).

Collectie in westerse talen
Collection in Western languages

See 1.4.14

H 771 'Deex-Avtaars', treatise about the ten incarnations of Vishnu by merchant Phil. Angel, with a dedication to *Directeur-Generaal* Carel Hartsinck, a frontispiece, a poem in explanation of this and ten drawings after Indian miniatures of Vishnu's incarnations, 1658. Photocopy of record kept in the Norbertine Abbey of Postel at Mol (Belgium), one bundle of 295 folios.

MUSEUM BOERHAAVE
BOERHAAVE MUSEUM

For general surveys, see H.J.A.H.G. Metselaars (ed.), *Particuliere archieven in Nederland* (*Overzichten van de archieven en verzamelingen in de openbare archiefbewaarplaatsen in Nederland*, Vol. 14) (Houten and Zaventem, 1992), pp. 296-312, and the repository's web site (see Appendix II, 4.15).

Prentencollectie
Print collection

Size: *c.* 7000 items
Period: *c.* 1600–up to the present
Inventory: data base

This collection consists of portraits of physicians and scholars, and of depictions pertaining to medical and scientific subjects. For two prints concerning Bengal, see 6.6.

NATIONAAL HERBARIUM NEDERLAND - UNIVERSITEIT LEIDEN
NATIONAL HERBARIUM OF THE NETHERLANDS - LEIDEN UNIVERSITY

See also 1.4.16.

Icones

Size: *c.* 40000 items
Period: 15th century–up to the present
Inventory: – data base
– catalogue on index cards

This is a pictorial collection focusing on botany. About 3000 drawings, water colours and prints date from before *c.* 1850. Many of these are anonymous or copies and are usually filed under the collectors' names. For drawings possibly concerning Surat, see 2.6.

Herbarium collection

Size: *c.* 4,000,000 items
Period: 16th century–up to the present
Inventory: data base

This collection consists principally of plant specimens and focuses on the Netherlands, Europe and South-East Asia. It also includes some manuscripts. Two historical sub-collections are relevant with regard to Ceylon. One of these originates from Paul Hermann (1646-95), who served the VOC and collected plants on Ceylon from 1672 to 1679, and later became Professor of Medicine and Botany at Leiden University as well as Prefect of the Hortus Botanicus in Leiden. Carolus Linnaeus' *Flora Zeylanica* (1748) was based in this collection. (Other parts of the Hermann collection are kept at the National History Museum in London and at Gotha, Germany.) The other relevant collection was put together by Adriaan van Royen and his cousin or nephew David van Royen, both eighteenth-century Leiden-based Professors of Botany and employed at the Hortus. See 4.4 and 4.6.

NATURALIS, NATIONAAL NATUURHISTORISCH MUSEUM (Leiden)
NATURALIS, NATIONAL MUSEUM OF NATURAL HISTORY

For a general survey, see the repository's web site (see Appendix II, 4.17).

Prentencollectie
Print collection

Size: *c.* 7000 items
Period: *c.* 18th century–up to the present
Inventory: data base

This collection, which includes manuscript drawings, consists of pictures that are related to the history and activities of the museum itself and concern natural-historical subjects. For a drawing pertaining to Ceylon, see 4.6.

ZEEUWSE BIBLIOTHEEK / ZEEUWS DOCUMENTATIECENTRUM (Middelburg)
ZEELAND LIBRARY / ZEELAND DOCUMENTATION CENTRE

See also 1.4.19.

Handschriften
Manuscripts

See 1.4.19

Hs. 3531 Various papers concerning or originating from Samuel van de Putte, traveller from Vlissingen, including a manuscript map of the Kathmandu Valley, geopolitical notes regarding a lost map of Nepal, both *c.* 1730, and a late nineteenth-century map of Nepal and Tibet drawn after a lost map by Van de Putte. In Italian, one folder. Described and reproduced in F. Lequin and A. Meijer, *Samuel van de Putte, een Mandarijn uit Vlissingen (1690-1745)* (Middelburg, 1989), pp. 41-53, 56-7, and Ormeling Sr., 'De reizen van Samuel van de Putte' (see Supplement I: Bibliography, no. 143).

SLOT ZUYLEN (Oud-Zuilen)
ZUYLEN CASTLE

For general surveys, see K. Verboeket, *Slot Zuylen, Oud-Zuilen* (Amsterdam, 2003), and the repository's web site (see Appendix II, 4.21).

Collectie Slot Zuylen
Zuylen Castle collection

Size: *c.* 11000 items
Period: Middle Ages–1952
Inventory: portraits: S. Kuus, 'Bestandscatalogus', in A. van der Goes and J. de Meyere (eds), *Op stand aan de wand. Vijf eeuwen familieportretten in Slot Zuylen* (Maarssen, 1996), pp. 108-66, with introduction, genealogical trees and index

The collection consists of all kinds of objects amassed in the course of time by nobles who lived in the castle. It includes about 200 portraits of the former inhabitants of the castle and their relatives. One of these is Hendrik Adriaan van Reede tot Drakenstein (1636-91), who entered the service of the VOC in 1657. From 1661 onward he stayed at Cochin, Quilon and Colombo and was *Commandeur* of Malabar between 1670 and 1677. After some years in Batavia and the Dutch Republic, he was appointed *Commissaris-Generaal* in 1684 and charged with the task to carry through reforms in the East Indian establishments. In this capacity he visited Bengal in 1685, Ceylon in 1686 and Coromandel in 1687, where he had the Nagappattinam fort built. In 1690 he founded the seminary at Nallur on Ceylon and 1691 saw him in Malabar. In December of that year, he died on the way to Surat, where he was buried in January 1692. He was also the author of the botanical work *Hortus Indicus Malabaricus*, published in twelve volumes at Amsterdam between 1678 and 1703.

S 192 Portrait of Hendrik Adriaan van Reede tot Drakenstein. Chalk drawing, coloured (20 x 15 cm) (no. 106 in the catalogue). Reproduced and described in R. Ekkart, S. Kuus and K. Schaffers-Bodenhausen, 'De portretgalerij van Slot Zuylen. Het karakter van een particuliere portretgalerij', in A. van der Goes and J. de Meyere (eds), *Op stand aan de wand. Vijf eeuwen familieportretten in Slot Zuylen* (Maarssen, 1996), p. 15.

ATLAS VAN STOLK (Rotterdam)
VAN STOLK ATLAS

For a general survey, see the repository's web site (see Appendix II, 4.22).

Atlas van Stolk

Size: *c.* 100,000 items
Period: 16th century–up to the present
Inventory:
- events up to *c.* 1850, acquired up to *c.* 1895-1933: *Catalogus der historie-, spot- en zinneprenten betrekkelijk de geschiedenis van Nederland, verzameld door A. van Stolk, gerangschikt en beschreven door G. van Rijn* (10 vols, with index in Vol. 11) (The Hague, 1895-1933)
- entire collection: data base (on Internet) (limited description for items listed in the above-mentioned catalogue)

The drawings, prints and maps that were collected by Abraham van Stolk, his son and grandson from 1835 onward have been the basis of this collection, which focuses on Dutch history. In addition to the items described in this guide, the collection includes some relevant prints originating from published works (see also Appendix I). For drawings, prints and maps concerning Malabar, Ceylon and Bengal, see 3.6, 4.6 and 6.6.

CENTRALE BIBLIOTHEEK ROTTERDAM
CENTRAL LIBRARY OF ROTTERDAM

See also 1.4.23.

Maps

Period: 17th-20th centuries
Inventory: catalogue on index cards

The collection is of a general character. Items numbered from 86 K to P concern Asia. For maps, drawings and prints pertaining to Malabar and Ceylon, see 3.6 and 4.6.

86 L 2 Map of South Asia, by Covens and Mortier at Amsterdam, eighteenth century (?). Printed, coloured, in French.
86 L 3 Map of South Asia, with legend, by I. Rennel and the Lotter brothers, eighteenth century (?). Printed, coloured, in German.

MARITIEM MUSEUM ROTTERDAM
MARITIME MUSEUM ROTTERDAM

See also 1.4.24.

Cartografische collectie
Cartographic collection

Inv. nos: *c.* 2300 items
Period: 1500–up to the present
Inventory:
- data base (on Internet)
- geographical catalogue on index cards

The collection consists of maps, atlases and globes. Some of the maps originate from the former collections of Willem Anton Engelbrecht (1874-1965, inv. nos beginning with WAE), and C. de Jonge (State Archivist between 1831 and 1853, inv. nos beginning with CdJ), both of which concerned the history of shipping, discoveries and cartography. For maps of Ceylon, see 4.6.

CdJ858	Map of south India, including parts of Gujarat and Bengal, and north Ceylon, by Guillaume de l'Isle, published at Amsterdam by Johannes Covens and Cornelis Mortier. Engraving, in French. Identical to inv. no. K181, see below.
K134	Map of the Bay of Bengal, including the coasts of Ceylon, Coromandel, Orissa, Bengal, Arakan and Pegu, by Joannes Janssonius. Coloured, engraving.
K181	Map of south India, including parts of Gujarat and Bengal, and north Ceylon, by Guillaume de l'Isle, published at Amsterdam by Johannes Covens and Cornelis Mortier, 1721. Coloured, engraving, in French (43 x 59 cm). Identical to inv. no. CdJ858, see above.
K212-1 & 2	Map of south India up to the nineteenth degree north latitude, and north Ceylon, by William Faden, London, 1795. Copper engraving, two sheets (49 x 81 cm).
K277-5 & 6	Maps of the 'system' (currents and winds?) of the northern Indian Ocean during the monsoon, by Chevallier de Grenier, 1776. Coloured, two sheets (with four other maps in a paper case).
WAE 49-111	Map of India, by Hendricus Hondius, published at Amsterdam by Joannes Janssonius, 1636. Engraving.

Picturalia
Pictures

Size: *c.* 5500 items
Period: 1550–up to the present
Inventory:
- data base (on Internet)
- geographical catalogue on index cards

The collection includes paintings, prints, drawings, water colours, etc. In addition to the items described in this guide, the collection includes some relevant prints originating from published works (see also Appendix I). For pictures concerning Surat, Malabar and Ceylon, see 2.6, 3.6 and 4.6.

MUSEUM BOIJMANS VAN BEUNINGEN (Rotterdam)
BOIJMANS VAN BEUNINGEN MUSEUM

For a general survey, see the repository's web site (see Appendix II, 4.25).

Prentenkabinet
Print Room

Size: *c.* 100,000 prints and 10000 drawings
Period: *c.* 1400–up to the present
Inventory: data base

This collection consists of drawings, with examples of almost all West European schools until *c.* 1900 and a number of twentieth-century works, as well as prints from the fifteenth century onward (focusing on the sixteenth and nineteenth centuries). It includes drawings pertaining to the Mughals and Ceylon, see 2.6 and 4.6.

1.6.5. Companies, private organizations and individuals

FEIKEMA (Amersfoort)

Canter Visscher

See 1.5.1

(a) Letter (207 ff.) from Adrianus Canter Visscher, most probably addressed to the Gentlemen XVII, joining in the debate about possible means of redress, as a result of the memorandum of Governor-General Jacob Mossel concerning the state of affairs of the VOC, *c.* 1753. One volume. Including:

following f. 207 Two series of portraits of various Mughal Emperors and their relatives, including Timur and other ancestors, Babur, Humayun, Akbar, Jahangir, Shah Jahan, Aurangzeb, Bahadur Shah, Farrukh Siyar, Parviz (son of Jahangir), Mumtaz Mahal, Dilras Begam (?), and depictions of Akbar, Jahangir and Shah Jahan on their thrones with their *Wazirs*, Jahangir riding an elephant and being attacked by a tiger, princes visiting a *sufi*, courtesans in the rooms and gardens of the harem, and a Persian prince locked up in the fort of Gwalior (?), made in the Deccan for the Dutch market, second half of the seventeenth century and early eighteenth century, with Dutch (and occasionally Persian) captions, probably purchased by Canter Visscher in the Dutch Republic. 28 Indian miniature paintings, coloured (one of the series *c.* 4 x 3 cm).[1] For a short description and partial reproduction, see P. Lunsingh Scheurleer, 'Het Witsenalbum. Zeventiende-eeuwse Indiase portretten op bestelling', *Bulletin van het Rijksmuseum*, 44, 3 (1996), pp. 224-5.

[1] Information kindly provided by Pauline Lunsingh Scheurleer (*Rijksmuseum Amsterdam*).

KONINKLIJK HUISARCHIEF (The Hague)
ARCHIVES OF THE ROYAL FAMILY

See also 1.5.6.

Maps

Size: *c.* 2000 items
Period: 16th century–up to the present
Inventory: data base

717 Map of South Asia, with political divisions, by J. Rennell, 1788. Coloured, three sheets (one part appears to be missing).

STICHTING KUNSTBEZIT KONINKLIJKE NEDLLOYD (Rotterdam)
ROYAL NEDLLOYD ART COLLECTION FOUNDATION

For a general description, see J. Horstink, *Uit de schatkamer van Koninklijke Nedlloyd* (Rotterdam, 2001), especially pp. 5-9.

Kunst en historische collectie
Art and historical collection

Inv. nos: *c.* 1-1500
Period: 17th century–up to the present
Inventory: in typescript, alphabetically arranged

This collection derives from several shipping companies (mostly set up in the nineteenth century) that in the course of time merged into Koninklijke Nedlloyd. It consists of maps, drawings, prints, paintings, ship models, nautical instruments, etc. In the future, part of the collection may be transferred to the *Maritiem Museum Rotterdam* (see 1.4.24).

55 Map of India south of Gujarat and Bengal, and north Ceylon, by Guillaume de l'Isle at Amsterdam, published by I. Covens and C. Mortier, eighteenth century. Partly coloured, in French.

163 Map of the Indian Ocean, including Ceylon and the Maldives, with one inset showing the kingdoms of Cranganur, Cochin, Purakkad, Kayankulam and Quilon, and another showing the surroundings of Colombo and Negombo up to Sitawake and 'Arandery', published by Jan Bt. Elwe at Amsterdam, 1792. Partly coloured, in French.

2. SURAT
(including Sind and Hindustan)

2.1. Government Archives

GEMEENTEARCHIEF AMSTERDAM
MUNICIPAL ARCHIVES OF AMSTERDAM

Weeskamer en Commissie van Liquidatie der zaken van de voormalige weeskamer
Orphan Board and Commission of Liquidation of the affairs of the former orphan board

See 1.1.2
Access no.: 5073

209 Papers received from private persons in various places in Asia and the Cape of Good Hope, 1687-1789, including Surat, 1722-3. One bundle.

Notarissen ter standplaats Amsterdam
Notaries at Amsterdam

See 1.1.2
Access no.: 5075

Geographical names on index cards found under some of the more obvious headings in the modern indices:

Ahmadabad	2 index cards (1704).
Bombay	4 index cards (1670, 1705).
'Sandroe' (30 km north of Bombay)	3 index cards (1705).
Surat	72 index cards (1670-98, 1701-10).

Jacob de Flines

See 1.1.2
Access no.: 4

14-15 Letters received from Middelburg regarding Surat (?) textiles ('sourats') among other products, 1724. Two pieces (old no. 8). Inv. no. 140 (old no. 35) also seems to concern Surat textiles.

144, 177 Letters received from Gilbert de Flines at London concerning the sailing of some EIC ships to and from Bombay, 1723-8. Two pieces (old no. 35).

RIJKSARCHIEF IN NOORD-HOLLAND (Haarlem)
STATE ARCHIVES IN NORTH HOLLAND

Notarissen in het Rijksarchief in Noord-Holland, 1552-1842
Notaries in the State Archives in North Holland

See 1.1.10

Access no.: 185

943, no. 200 Notarial act drawn up by Jan van Conincxvelt at Enkhuizen, concerning shipping between Surat and the Red Sea, 1633 (microfilm no. 882).

977, no. 63 Notarial act drawn up by Reijer Claesz. Sampson at Enkhuizen, concerning the Surat factory, 1641 (microfilm no. 130).

HISTORISCH INFORMATIECENTRUM HELMOND
HISTORICAL INFORMATION CENTRE HELMOND

Van der Brugghen van Croy family

See 1.1.14
Access no.: 87

755 Letter received in 1744 by Joan Gideon Loten from C. (Jan?) Schreuder at Surat, concerning the birth of a daughter, 1743. One piece.

WESTFRIES ARCHIEF (Hoorn)
ARCHIVES OF WEST FRIESLAND

Stad Enkhuizen
Town of Enkhuizen

See 1.1.16

1532 Papers received by the Enkhuizen Chamber of the VOC, including a letter from Batavia concerning Joris Stevensz serving Mughal Emperor Aurangzeb in Daulatabad, 1666, and a letter on the state of affairs at the Surat factory, 1742. One folder (old no. 386).

Oud-notariële archieven Enkhuizen
Old notarial archives of Enkhuizen

See 1.1.16

943, no. 200 Notarial act drawn up by Jan van Conincxvelt, concerning shipping between Surat and the Red Sea, 1633.

977, no. 63 Notarial act drawn up by Reijer Claesz. Sampson, concerning the Surat factory, 1641.

ZEEUWS ARCHIEF (Middelburg)
ZEELAND ARCHIVES

Koninklijk Zeeuwsch Genootschap der Wetenschappen
Royal Zeeland Society of Sciences

See 1.1.21
Access no.: 26.1

7, p. 333 — Minutes with regard to J. Stavorinus presenting the account of his father's travels in 1783 to Surat and other places, 1803.

130, p. 24 &
133, pp. 13-14 — Lists of donated books and naturalia, including references to donations by J. Boekhout, which include an eye of a wild cat and a piece of agate, both from Surat, 1777.

(Snouck) Hurgronje family (I)

See 1.1.21
Access no.: 98.1

120 Charter of foundation of the Freemason's lodge St. Jean la Concorde at Surat, issued at The Hague, 1775. One piece.

121 Certificate of the Freemason's lodge St Jean la Concorde at Surat, declaring Cornelis van Citters Aarnoutszoon to be the *Grand Elu des Quinzes* of the lodge, 1776. In French, one piece.

Mathias-Pous-Tak van Poortvliet family

See 1.1.21
Access no.: 255

57 Letter of W. van der Laar to the Zeeland Chamber of the VOC concerning complaints about *Directeur* Jan Schreuder, 1742. One piece.

58 Memorandum by W. van der Laar concerning the poor financial situation of the *Directie* of Surat, held against *Directeur* Jan Schreuder and his second-in-command Johannes Pecock, 1742. One piece.

Pieter van Gote

See 1.1.21
Access no.: 390

4 Letters received by Pieter van Gote and his wife Johanna Bekker from Adriaan van Es and his wife Adriana de Cauw, partly with drafts of replies and annexes, 1773-93. One bundle. Including:
  (a) Papers concerning the years 1775-80, including three letters from Surat, 1780. One folder.

5 Letters received by Pieter van Gote and his wife Johanna Bekker from various people, partly with drafts of replies and annexes, 1773-93, with the folder concerning Bonifas Freres including a letter from Surat, 1780. One folder.

GEMEENTEARCHIEF ROTTERDAM
MUNICIPAL ARCHIVES OF ROTTERDAM

Oude notariële archieven
Old notarial archives

See 1.1.22

Access no.: 18

2418: 90 Notarial act concerning merchandise on the ship 't Wapen van Hoorn, 18 March 1741.

HET UTRECHTS ARCHIEF
THE ARCHIVES OF UTRECHT

Huydecoper family

See 1.1.23
Access no.: 67

621 Papers concerning the VOC, added to the archives by Jan Elias Huydecoper from the papers of Pieter Nuijts and his son Laurens, 1621-38. One bundle. Including:
- (a) Letter from the chief-factor Wouter ten Haeff, departing from Batavia to Surat with the ship Brouwershaven, to Pieter Nuijts, containing a copy of Ten Haeff's memorandum for Governor-General Jacques Specx (1629-32) concerning the private trade in Surat and Persia, and correspondence between VOC officials in the Surat *Directie*, 1630. One quire (old no. 2067).

622 Papers concerning the VOC, added to the archives by Jan Elias Huydecoper from the papers of Gualterus Petrus Boudaen, 1670-1760. One bundle. Including:
- (a) Calculation of the debts of the Mughal Governor of Surat and the merchants Abdul Ghafur and Mia Muhammad Hazin (?) to the VOC, 1703. One quire (old no. 2202).
- (b) Translations of *farmans* of Mughal Emperor Bahadur Shah to *Directeur* Johan Grotenhuys (1707-8), 1709 (?), and of Mughal Emperor Jahandar Shah to *Directeur* Johan Joshua Ketelaar (1711-15), 1712. One quire.
- (c) Decrees issued at the roadstead of Surat, 1690-1713. One quire (old no. 2201).
- (d) Extract from the Surat *dagregister* (diary) by Ketelaar concerning a *sadhu* doing penance and the resultant complications, May 1714, and account of the heavy rainfall and storms at Ahmadabad, July 1714. One quire (old no. 1147).
- (e) Epitaphs of a large number of Dutch men and women, buried at Surat from the seventeenth century to 1713, with a list of high VOC officials in the Surat *Directie* from 1639 to 1713. One quire (old no. 1146).

2.2. UNIVERSITIES

UNIVERSITEIT VAN AMSTERDAM, UNIVERSITEITSBIBLIOTHEEK
UNIVERSITY OF AMSTERDAM, UNIVERSITY LIBRARY

Manuscripts

See 1.2.2

Bf 74c Extract from the daily record of the embassy of Johan Joshua Ketelaar to Mughal Emperor Bahadur Shah at Lahore, containing a description of the Mughal throne, by E.C. Graeff, Delhi 12 July 1712. One folder. Part of the correspondence between Gijsbert Cuper and Nicolaas Cornelisz Witsen, 1685-1716 (inv. nos Be 1-102, Bf 1-86, 88-100, G 41, see 1.2.2). See also J.J. Ketelaar, *Journaal van J.J. Ketelaar's hofreis naar den Groot Mogol te Lahore 1711-1713*, ed. J.Ph. Vogel (Werken Linschoten Vereniging, 41) (The Hague, 1937); part. trans. D. Kuenen-Wicksteed, 'Embassy of Mr. Johan Josua Ketelaar', *Journal of the Panjab Historical Society*, 10 (1929).

UNIVERSITEIT LEIDEN, UNIVERSITEITSBIBLIOTHEEK
LEIDEN UNIVERSITY LIBRARY

Maatschappij der Nederlandse Letterkunde te Leiden
Society of Netherlands Literature at Leiden

See 1.2.7

Ltk 589 Dutch-Hindustani-Persian dictionary written in Roman and Arabic script, largely concerning botany and navigation, late seventeenth century (with explanation by Leopold van Alstein and review by H.E. Wijers from 1841). One volume.

Bibliotheca Publica Latina
Latin Public Library

See 1.2.7

BPL 622, ff. 83-92 Bookkeeping concerning Surat, 1662-1774, with various types of surveys, including overviews per year, decade and *Directeur.*

Oosterse Handschriften (*Legatum Warnerianum*)
Oriental Manuscripts (Warner's Legacy)

See 1.2.7

Or. 2241 IV Eleven letters in Arabic and Persian, all in Arabic script, sent from the Middle East and India mostly to the GG&C, 1793-8. One folder. Including:

258 Dutch translation of inv. no. Or. 2241 IV, 272 (see below), by P. Kool in accordance with the information of the Persian interpreter Amien Hassan (no. 5b in the catalogue by Wieringa).

272 Letter in Persian from Nuruz Bahramji, Tiranji (son of Bahramji) and Hurmuzji (son of Ratanji), all at Surat, to Governor-General Pieter Gerardus van Overstraten (1796-1801), received at Batavia in 1800 (no. 5a in catalogue by

Wieringa). For a translation, see inv. no. Or. 2241 IV, 258 (above).

UNIVERSITEIT UTRECHT, UNIVERSITEITSBIBLIOTHEEK
UTRECHT UNIVERSITY LIBRARY

Handschriften
Manuscripts

See 1.2.10

Hs. 1478 (1.E.21) Dutch-Hindustani-Persian glossary, arranged according to subject, sections on grammar, comparison of Hindustani and Dutch weights and measures, explanation of Muslim names, the Persian alphabet, Christian texts translated into Hindustani, with index to Dutch words, *c.* 1700. One volume (probably originating from Adriaan Reland).

2.3. Ecclesiastical Organizations

ARCHIEF VAN DE NEDERLANDSE PROVINCIE DER JEZUÏETEN (Nijmegen)
ARCHIVES OF THE NETHERLANDS PROVINCE OF THE JESUITS

Handschriften
Manuscripts

See 1.3.2

A.D. 2 (box 21) Three letters (part of an annual series) from the College at Agra and the 'Mughal mission' (marked 'Goa 46^{II}, fol. 201-fol. 251'), 1648-9. Photocopies, in Latin and Italian, one folder.

A.D. 3 (box 21) Letters sent by Jesuits in India to Jesuits in Europe. Photocopies and contemporary manuscript copies, with recent documentation and notes pertaining to these letters and Jesuits in India, one folder. Including:

- (a) Letter from Henricus Busaeus (1618-67) at Agra, 1649. In Latin, photocopy.
- (b) Letter from Gollet at Surat, 1700. In French.

2.4. Museums and Other Public Institutions

KONINKLIJKE BIBLIOTHEEK (KB) (The Hague)
ROYAL LIBRARY

Handschriften
Manuscripts

See 1.4.12

76 D 39 Letter concerning the famine and high mortality in Surat in 1631 (with a modern transcription). Published in 'Hongersnood in Suratta anno 1631' (see Supplement I: Bibliography, no. 166).

129 B 3 Remonstrance by Franciscus Pelsaert concerning the empire of the Great Mughal (copy), with map, *c.* 1625. Published as Franscisco Pelsaert, *De geschriften van Francisco Pelsaert over Mughal Indië, 1627. Kroniek en remonstrantie*, eds D.H.A. Kolff and H.W. van Santen (Werken Linschoten Vereniging, 81) (The Hague, 1979); part. trans. W. Moreland and P. Geyl, *Jahangir's India. The Remonstrantie of Francisco Pelsaert* (Cambridge, 1925); part. trans. B. Narain and S.R. Sharma, *A Contemporary Dutch Chronicle of Moghul India* (Calcutta, 1957).

Oude drukken
Early printed works

See 1.4.12

7453 Extract from a letter written at Agra containing a description of the Mughal court at Delhi, possibly by Joan Berckhout and Joan Tack, 1653, printed as a kind of newsletter. One piece.

MUSEUM MEERMANNO (The Hague)
MEERMANNO MUSEUM

Van Westreenen family

See 1.4.13

S 72-3 Correspondence (chiefly received letters) and some accompanying papers of Jacobus Mersen, his wife and a few others, partly with copies, alphabetically arranged, 1748-61. Seven folders (each containing several files) in two boxes (inv. no. 43 in the inventory by Kernkamp). Including:
72.1: II Including a letter from J. Drabbe at Surat, 1753.

KONINKLIJK INSTITUUT VOOR TAAL-, LAND- EN VOLKENKUNDE (KITLV) (Leiden)
ROYAL INSTITUTE OF LINGUISTICS AND ANTHROPOLOGY

Collectie in westerse talen
Collection in western languages

See 1.4.14

H 49 Various letters and other documents, 1613-91. One volume. Including:
J Oath of allegiance of the *Directeur* and Council (including the chief-factor Johan van Teylingen) at Surat, 1647 (two ff.).

H 127 *Memorie van overgave* (final report) by *Directeur* Jan Schreuder (to Johannes Pecock), 1750 (only from chapter V onwards). One volume.

H 333 Letter of *Directeur* Cornelis Besuyen to Governor-General Joan van Hoorn, 1708. One piece.

H 496 Memorandum about coins, weights and measures in Asia, including sections on Surat, Ahmadabad, Bharuch and Agra, *c.* 1665 (?). One volume.

ZEEUWSE BIBLIOTHEEK / ZEEUWS DOCUMENTATIECENTRUM
(Middelburg)
ZEELAND LIBRARY / ZEELAND DOCUMENTATION CENTRE

Handschriften
Manuscripts

See 1.4.19

Hs. 472 Letter from Martin, court physician of the Mughal Emperor at Delhi, to Samuel van de Putte, traveller from Vlissingen, 1756. In French, one piece. For a description and partial reproduction, see F. Lequin and A. Meijer, *Samuel van de Putte, een Mandarijn uit Vlissingen (1690-1745)* (Middelburg, 1989), pp. 27, 32. For the Indian miniature paintings originally accompanying the letter, see 2.6, *Zeeuws Museum* (Middelburg), inv. nos G 1860-1.

MARITIEM MUSEUM ROTTERDAM
MARITIME MUSEUM ROTTERDAM

Handschriften
Manuscripts

See 1.4.24

H595 Autobiography of George Naporra (1731-93) from East Prussia, who served the VOC between 1752 and 1756 as sailor, 1757. In German, in Gothic script, one volume. Including:

ff. 425-85 Notes concerning his stay with the ship De Drie Papagaaien at the roadstead of Surat in 1753-4, including references to the population of Surat, their customs, dressing and attacks of the Angria 'pirates'. Partly described in Van Gelder, *Naporra's omweg*, chapters 17-18 (see Supplement I: Bibliography, no. 175).

2.5. Companies, Private Organizations and Individuals

KONINKLIJK HUISARCHIEF (The Hague)
ARCHIVES OF THE ROYAL FAMILY

Prince William IV

See 1.5.6
Access no.: A 17

46: III N14 & N17 a-b (alternative nos 78 and 219) — Inventories of the collections of naturalia and antiquities of William IV, including a memorandum of curiosities originating from Surat, sent by *Directeur-Generaal* Julius Valentijn Stein van Gollonesse through Van der Vorm and received by William IV in 1754, consisting of jewellery usually worn by Hindu and Muslim women, 1760. One folder. The actual jewellery is kept at the Department of Asiatic Art of the *Rijksmuseum Amsterdam*, inv. nos NM 7050-4, NM 7056-73, NM 7075-81, NM 7086-9, NM 7121. Reproduced and described in P. Lunsingh Scheurleer, 'Rich Remains from Social Anthropological Fieldwork in Eighteenth-Century India', *Journal of the History of Collections*, 8, 1 (1996); also described in idem, 'Jewels for the Stadholder', in S. Strong (ed.), *The Jewels of India* (Bombay, 1995); see also idem, 'Twee Oosterse sieraden uit de stadhouderlijke verzameling', *Bulletin van het Rijksmuseum*, 44, 1 (1996).

ORDE VAN VRIJMETSELAREN ONDER HET GROOTOOSTEN DER NEDERLANDEN (The Hague)
FRATERNITY OF FREEMASONS UNDER THE GRAND EAST OF THE NETHERLANDS

Constitutie dossiers
Constitution files

See 1.5.7

2401-4 Files concerning Masonic lodges. Including:
(a) St.Jean la Concorde at Surat, 1775. One folder.

2.6. Maps and Pictures

UNIVERSITEIT VAN AMSTERDAM, ARTIS BIBLIOTHEEK
UNIVERSITY OF AMSTERDAM, ARTIS LIBRARY

Artis Bibliotheek
Artis Library

See 1.2.1

Legkast 238 'Wonderen der natuur', collection of *c.* 180 depictions of special and exotic animals and people as seen in the menagerie at the hostelry of Blauw Jan (Jan Westerhof) in Amsterdam and some other locations, by Jan Velten, *c.* 1695-1709. Seven boxes. Reproduced on CD. Including:

7 *Sadhu*, who in 1702 had been sitting in the same position for two years near the village of 'Oxkaij', one mile from Surat, probably copied from another picture. Pen drawing. Reproduced in F.F.J.M. Pieters and H. Veldhuijzen van Zanten (eds), *Wonderen der natuur in de menagerie van Blauw Jan te Amsterdam, zoals gezien door Jan Velten rond 1700 / Wonders of Nature in the Menagerie of Blauw Jan in Amsterdam, as Observed by Jan Velten around 1700* (Amsterdam, 1998), p. 60.

106 Mughal prince or noble (?). Pen drawing.

UNIVERSITEIT VAN AMSTERDAM, UNIVERSITEITSBIBLIOTHEEK
UNIVERSITY OF AMSTERDAM, UNIVERSITY LIBRARY

Kaarten en Atlassen
Maps and Atlases

See 1.6.2

33-13-18 & 19 Map of Bombay and surroundings, published at Amsterdam by Johannes van Keulen. Coloured (old inv. nos 10083M-4M).

33-13-37 Maps of the mouth of the Tapti River and the surroundings of Surat, published by J. van Keulen. Coloured (old inv. no. 10109M).

71-28-15 Map of Baluchistan and parts of the Punjab and Sind, by A. Arrowsmith, London, 1813. Copper engraving, coloured.

UNIVERSITEIT LEIDEN, UNIVERSITEITSBIBLIOTHEEK
LEIDEN UNIVERSITY LIBRARY

Collectie Bodel Nijenhuis
Bodel Nijenhuis collection

See 1.6.2

F43 : 7 : 002903 : 110/3 View of the bay and town of Surat, with explanation, originating from the 'Atlas Guendeville' (?). Print, in French.

F43 : 7 : 002903 : 110/4 Portrait of a couple from Surat, with the town in the background, by I. de Ram. Print.

H44 : 19 : 002019 : 100/1, 110/2, 710/1 to 3 Five prints pertaining to Agra, date unknown. Missing at the time of research.

Port 176 N 151 — Map of Bombay and its vicinity, with soundings, by J. van der Schley. Copper engraving, mostly in French (19 x 26 cm).

Port 176 N 152 — Map of Bombay and its vicinity, with soundings. Copper engraving, in French (48 x 33 cm).

Port 176 N 153 — Map of Bombay island, by G.H. Koning. Copper engraving, partly in French (20 x 16 cm).

STEDELIJK MUSEUM ALKMAAR
MUNICIPAL MUSEUM OF ALKMAAR

Schilderijen
Paintings

See 1.6.4

20925 Portrait of Wollebrandt Geleynssen de Jongh (1594-1674), 1664. Oil on canvas (85 x 70 cm).[1]

20926 Portrait of Wollebrandt Geleynssen de Jongh, depicted as VOC official and Commander of the return fleet, by Caesar van Everdingen, 1674. Oil on canvas (215 x 182 cm).[1]

[1] Reproduced in Van Santen, *VOC-dienaar in India*, p. 31 and cover (see Supplement I: Bibliography, no. 185); inv. no. 20926 also reproduced and described in P. van Mil and M. Scharloo, *De VOC in de kaart gekeken. Cartografie en navigatie van de Verenigde Oostindische Compagnie 1602-1799* (The Hague, 1988), p. 85, A.J. de Koning, 'Wollebrandt Geleynssen de Jongh. Drager van de Commandeurs penning', *Beeldenaar*, 18, 1 (1994), and E.M. Jacobs, *De Vereenigde Oost-Indische Compagnie* (Zeist, 1997), p. 87. For information on Geleynssen de Jongh, see 1.1.1.

NEDERLANDS SCHEEPVAARTMUSEUM AMSTERDAM
NETHERLANDS MARITIME MUSEUM AMSTERDAM

Zeevaartkundige collectie
Navigational collection

See 1.6.4

S.0521 (107) Map of the harbour of Bombay in 1803-4, published by James Horsburgh at London, 1806. In English (67 x 99 cm).

Iconografische collectie
Iconographic collection

See 1.6.4

A.0145 (211) (4) — View of a tank and the grave of three of the last 'kings' of Surat at Sarkhej (6 miles from Ahmadabad), by A.P., *c.* 1675. Pen and pencil drawing (17 x 25 cm).

A-III-318 — Album containing 80 affixed prints depicting views and maps of cities, probably originally marginal decorations of wall

maps, by Frederick de Wit, with index, *c.* 1690. Including:
26 Surat.
37 Ahmedabad.

RIJKSMUSEUM AMSTERDAM
RIJKSMUSEUM AMSTERDAM

Afdeling Nederlandse Geschiedenis
Department of Dutch History

See 1.6.4

NG-20-A View of Surat (among other locations), by Frederick de Wit, 1700. Originally part of a world map by De Wit, Amsterdam. Engraving (45 x 53 cm).

NG-1987-7 View from above of the reception of VOC envoy Johan Joshua Ketelaar and his company by Maharana Sangram Singh II of Udaipur, made by order of the Maharana, *c.* 1711. Painting on cotton (168 x 272 cm).[1]

SK-A-3773 Portrait of *Directeur* Hendrik Zwaardecroon (1699-1701), depicted as Governor-General, by Hendrick van den Bosch, 1723. Panel (99 x 81 cm). (SK-A-4542 is a copy. Copper, 34 x 26 cm). Described in J. de Loos-Haaxman, *De landsverzameling schilderijen in Batavia*, 2 vols (Leiden, 1941) and F.W. Stapel, *De gouverneurs-generaal van Nederlandsch-Indië in beeld en woord* (The Hague, 1941).

SK-A-4778 View of the harbour and town of Surat, with a (probably) Dutch official (*Directeur* Leonard Winnincx?) in an Indian carriage, possibly by Johannes Vingboons, *c.* 1670. Oil on canvas (80 x 119 cm).[1]

[1] Described and reproduced in Akveld and Jacobs, *De kleurrijke wereld / The Colourful World*, pp. 18-19, 176-8 (see Supplement I: Bibliography, no. 61), Zandvliet, *De Nederlandse ontmoeting met Azië / The Dutch Encounter with Asia*, pp. 44-6, 98, 124-6 (Bibl., no. 98), and Jacobs, *Koopman in Azië*, pp. 82, 84 (Bibl., no. 104); inv. no. NG-1987-7 also described and reproduced in J. Bautze, 'Maharana Sangram Singh of Udaipur Entertaining Members of the Dutch East India Company Led by Johan Josua Ketelaar', *Bulletin van het Rijksmuseum*, 36, 2 (1988), and Lunsingh Scheurleer, 'De Maharana van Udaipur' (Bibl., no. 179); inv. no. SK-A-4778 also described and reproduced in Zandvliet, *Mapping for Money*, p. 235 (Bibl., no. 96), and P. van Mil and M. Scharloo, *De VOC in de kaart gekeken. Cartografie en navigatie van de Verenigde Oostindische Compagnie 1602-1799* (The Hague, 1988), p. 10.

Rijksprentenkabinet
Print Room

See 1.6.4

RP-P-OB-67.345 Portrait of *Directeur* Hendrik Zwaardecroon (1699-1701), depicted as Governor-General, by Jacobus van der Schley. Engraving.

RP-T-00-3186 So-called 'Witsen-Album', consisting of 49 Indian miniature paintings (20 x 14 cm), depicting Mughal, Bijapur, Maratha, Golkonda and Persian rulers and officials, produced at Golkonda and probably purchased by a VOC official, *c.* 1680, with notes in Persian, Portuguese and Dutch, acquired by Nicolaas Cornelisz Witsen (1641-1717, VOC Director from 1693 onward and Burgomaster of Amsterdam). Coloured, one folder. Described and reproduced (together with other Indian miniature paintings) in P. Lunsingh Scheurleer, 'Het Witsenalbum. Zeventiende-eeuwse Indiase portretten op bestelling', *Bulletin van het Rijksmuseum*, 44, 3 (1996), and Goetz, *The Indian and Persian Miniature Paintings* (see Supplement I: Bibliography, no. 131). Including:

1A Timur (no. 1 in Goetz).
1B Babur, Mughal Emperor (no. 2 in Goetz).
2 Fath (or Firoz) Jang Khan, *Wazir* under Aurangzeb (no. 13 in Goetz).
3 Akbar, Mughal Emperor (no. 4 in Goetz).
4 Jahangir, Mughal Emperor (no. 5 in Goetz).
5 Shah Jahan, Mughal Emperor (no. 6 in Goetz).
6 Aurangzeb, Mughal Emperor (no. 7 in Goetz). Reproduced in Akveld and Jacobs, *De kleurrijke wereld / The Colourful World*, pp. 166-7, 179 (Bibl., no. 61).
7 Murad Bakhsh, son of Shah Jahan (no. 10 in Goetz).
8 Dara Shukoh, son of Shah Jahan (no. 8 in Goetz).
9 Shuja, son of Shah Jahan (no. 9 in Goetz).
10 Muhammad Sultan, son of Aurangzeb (no. 11 in Goetz).
11 Bahadur Shah, Mughal Emperor (Shah Alam, Muazzam) (no. 12 in Goetz).
12 Humayun, Mughal Emperor (no. 3 in Goetz).
13 Raja Bhao Singh of Bundi, *Wazir* under Aurangzeb (no. 17 in Goetz).
14 Raja Man Singh (of Gwalior?), *Wazir* under Aurangzeb (no. 19 in Goetz).
15 Qilij (or Ilich) Khan, *Wazir* under Aurangzeb (no. 14 in Goetz).
16 Raja Karan Singh of Bikaner, *Wazir* under Aurangzeb (no. 18 in Goetz).
17 Dalil (or Diler) Khan, Grand *Wazir* under Aurangzeb (no. 15 in Goetz).
18 Saf-shikan Khan, *Wazir* under Aurangzeb (no. 16 in Goetz).

RP-T-1930-41 Portrait of Mughal Emperor Shah Jahan, by Rembrandt Harmensz van Rijn (1606-69), *c.* 1657. Pen and brush drawing, coloured (7 x 7 cm). Free adaptation of an Indian miniature painting. Described and reproduced in O. Benesch, *The*

	Drawings of Rembrandt, Vol. 5 (London, 1957), pp. 339-40 (no. 1195) and plate no. 1419.
RP-T-1961-82	Portrait of Mughal Emperor Jahangir, by Rembrandt van Rijn, *c.* 1657. Pen and brush drawing, coloured (18 x 12 cm). Free adaptation of an Indian miniature painting. Described and reproduced in P. Lunsingh Scheurleer, 'Mogolminiaturen door Rembrandt nagetekend', in *De Kroniek van het Rembrandthuis*, 32, 1 (1980), p. 23, and O. Benesch, *The Drawings of Rembrandt*, Vol. 5 (London, 1957), p. 338 (no. 1191) and plate no. 1415.[1]
RP-T-1961-83	Portrait of Mughal Emperor Shah Jahan and one of his sons, by Rembrandt van Rijn, *c.* 1657. Pen and brush drawing, coloured (9 x 9 cm). Free adaptation of an Indian miniature painting. Described and reproduced in P. Lunsingh Scheurleer, 'De Moghul-miniaturen van Rembrandt', *Museum Magazine Vitrine*, 4, 1 (1991), p. 7, idem, 'Hoofse Snuisterijen uit India', p. 8 (see Supplement I: Bibliography, no. 141), and O. Benesch, *The Drawings of Rembrandt*, Vol. 5 (London, 1957), p. 340 (no. 1196) and plate no. 1420.[1]
RP-T-1969-1	View of Bharuch, 1678. Brush drawing (42 x 53 cm).[2]
RP-T-1969-2	View of a tank outside Ahmadabad, 1678. Brush drawing (42 x 52 cm).[2]
RP-T-1969-3	View of Cambay, 1679. Brush drawing (42 x 52 cm).[2]
RP-T-1969-4	View of a tank and a grave at Sarkhej (6 miles from Ahmadabad), 1678. Brush drawing (42 x 53 cm).[2]
RP-T-1969-5	View of Ahmadabad, 1679. Brush drawing (42 x 53 cm).[2]

[1] Also reproduced (inv. no. RP-T-1961-82 only) and described in J.Q. van Regteren Altena, 'De tekeningen [schenking De Bruijn-van der Leeuw]', *Bulletin van het Rijksmuseum*, 9, 2/3 (1961), pp. 70, 76, 86.

[2] Reproduced (inv. no. RP-T-1969-1 only) and described in Terwen-de Loos, *Nederlandse schilders en tekenaars*, pp. 17-18, 57 (see Supplement I: Bibliography, no. 153).

KONINKLIJKE BIBLIOTHEEK (KB) (The Hague)
ROYAL LIBRARY

Handschriften
Manuscripts

See 1.4.12

129 B 3	Map of the empire of the Great Mughal, belonging to the remonstrance of Franciscus Pelsaert, *c.* 1625. Coloured.

KONINKLIJK INSTITUUT VOOR TAAL-, LAND- EN VOLKENKUNDE (KITLV) (Leiden)
ROYAL INSTITUTE OF LINGUISTICS AND ANTHROPOLOGY

Images

See 1.6.4

37 B-629 Portrait of *Directeur* Hendrik Zwaardecroon (1699-1701), depicted as Governor-General, by Balen, *c.* 1750. Copper engraving (31 x 19 cm).

37 C-11 View of Surat and its fortifications, with various vessels and some fish in the foreground, *c.* 1750. Engraving (22 x 29 cm).

47 A-49 Portrait of *Directeur* Pieter van den Broecke (1620-8), by Hals and Ledeboer, *c.* 1720. Copper engraving (30 x 19 cm).

NATIONAAL HERBARIUM NEDERLAND - UNIVERSITEIT LEIDEN
NATIONAL HERBARIUM OF THE NETHERLANDS - LEIDEN UNIVERSITY

Icones

See 1.6.4

(a) Depictions of the trees, twigs and fruits of different kinds of 'Garioffel' cloves and nutmeg in Surat (?), with explanatory notes, originating from the estate of *Directeur* Johan van Teylingen (1648-51). Manuscript, coloured, one sheet. Reproduced in Baas, 'De VOC in Flora's Lusthoven', p. 126 (see Supplement I: Bibliography, no. 120), and M. Witteveen, *Een onderneming van landsbelang. De oprichting van de Verenigde Oost-Indische Compagnie in 1602* (Amsterdam, 2002), p. 66.

ZEEUWS MUSEUM (Middelburg)
ZEELAND MUSEUM

Collectie Koninklijk Zeeuwsch Genootschap der Wetenschappen
Royal Zeeland Society of Sciences collection

See 1.4.20

G 1860-1 Portraits of 'two mistresses of the Mughal Emperor' (?), originating from Samuel van de Putte, traveller from Vlissingen, sent to him in 1756 by Martin, court physician of the Mughal Emperor at Delhi, *c.* 1750 (?). Coloured, two Indian miniature paintings (no. 404b in the catalogue of 1890) (25 x 18 cm). Reproduced and described on pp. 170-1 of the *Catalogus* accompanying E. Bergvelt and R. Kistemaker (eds), *De wereld binnen handbereik. Nederlandse kunst- en rariteitenverzamelingen, 1585-1735* (Zwolle, 1992). For the accompanying letter, see 2.4, *Zeeuwse Bibliotheek / Zeeuws Documentatiecentrum* (Middelburg), *Handschriften*, inv. no. Hs. 472.

MARITIEM MUSEUM ROTTERDAM
MARITIME MUSEUM ROTTERDAM

Picturalia
Pictures

See 1.6.4

P1604 Portrait of *Directeur* Pieter van den Broecke (1620-8), by Adriaen Matham after Frans Hals, 1633. Engraving.

MUSEUM BOIJMANS VAN BEUNINGEN (Rotterdam)
BOIJMANS VAN BEUNINGEN MUSEUM

Prentenkabinet
Print Room

See 1.6.4

R 35 (PK) Portrait of an Indian woman with some jewellery, by Rembrandt Harmensz van Rijn (1606-69), *c.* 1656. Pen drawing, coloured (8 x 7 cm). Free adaptation of an Indian miniature painting.[1]

R 36 (PK) Glorification of the Mughal Emperors Akbar and Jahangir, by Rembrandt Harmensz van Rijn, *c.* 1656. Pen drawing, coloured (21 x 18 cm). Free adaptation of an Indian miniature painting.[1]

[1] Described and reproduced in P. Lunsingh Scheurleer, 'Mogol-miniaturen door Rembrandt nagetekend', *De Kroniek van het Rembrandthuis*, 32, 1 (1980), pp. 24, 37, J. Giltaij, *De tekeningen van Rembrandt en zijn school in het Museum Boymans-van Beuningen* (Rotterdam, 1988), pp. 94-7, and O. Benesch, *The Drawings of Rembrandt*, Vol. 5 (London, 1957), pp. 337, 342 (nos 1189, 1206) and plates nos 1413, 1421; inv. no. R 36 (PK) also described and reproduced in Lunsingh Scheurleer, 'De Moghul-miniaturen van Rembrandt', *Museum Magazine Vitrine*, 4, 1 (1991), p. 8, and on p. 170 of the *Catalogus* accompanying E. Bergvelt and R. Kistemaker (eds), *De wereld binnen handbereik. Nederlandse kunst-en rariteitenverzamelingen, 1585-1735* (Zwolle, 1992).

3. MALABAR
(including Kanara and Konkan)

3.1. GOVERNMENT ARCHIVES

REGIONAAL ARCHIEF ALKMAAR
REGIONAL ARCHIVES ALKMAAR

Wollebrand Geleijnsz de Jonghe

See 1.1.1

53 Correspondence of Wollebrandt Geleynssen with his agents (and some of their relatives), including Jacob Cornelisz Baert, 1623, 1634-48, concerning Geleynssen's controversial stay at Goa, August 1644. 47 Pieces.

GEMEENTEARCHIEF AMSTERDAM
MUNICIPAL ARCHIVES OF AMSTERDAM

Weeskamer en Commissie van Liquidatie der zaken van de voormalige weeskamer
Orphan Board and Commission of Liquidation of the affairs of the former orphan board

See 1.1.2
Access no.: 5073

182 Papers received from the trustees at Cochin, 1685-1790. One bundle.
183 Copies of papers received from the trustees at Cochin, 1687-1790. One folder.
209 Papers received from private persons in various places in Asia and the Cape of Good Hope, 1687-1789, including Cochin, 1697-1764. One bundle.
245 Papers sent to the trustees at Cochin, 1695-1764. One folder.

Notarissen ter standplaats Amsterdam
Notaries at Amsterdam

See 1.1.2
Access no.: 5075

Geographical names on index cards found under some of the more obvious headings in the modern indices:

Cochin 23 index cards (1613-21, 1701-10, 1724).
Goa 64 index cards (1613-21, 1647-1744).
Malabar 4 index cards (1703-6, 1724).
Vengurla 3 index cards (1705).

Handschriften
Manuscripts

See 1.1.2
Access no.: 5059

10 Various papers concerning the VOC, with many references to South Asia, originating from Huydekoper, 1726-84. One bundle. Including:
(a) Letter from Cochin to G.P. Boudaen, 1769.

GELDERS ARCHIEF (Arnhem)
ARCHIVES OF GUELDERLAND

Stad Arnhem
Town of Arnhem

See 1.1.3
Access no.: 2000

5519 Reply of the States General to Sir George Downing, envoy of England to the Dutch Republic, concerning disagreements between England and the VOC, including a section regarding the ships Hoopwel and Luypaerd at Purakkad, 1644. Printed, one volume.

RIJKSARCHIEF IN NOORD-HOLLAND (Haarlem)
STATE ARCHIVES IN NORTH HOLLAND

Notarissen in het Rijksarchief in Noord-Holland, 1552-1842
Notaries in the State Archives in North Holland

See 1.1.10
Access no.: 185

1015, nos 142, 145 Notarial act drawn up by Siewert Koeckebacker at Enkhuizen, concerning shipping between Goa and the Sunda Straits, 1643 (microfilm no. 138).

WESTFRIES ARCHIEF (Hoorn)
ARCHIVES OF WEST FRIESLAND

Stad Enkhuizen
Town of Enkhuizen

See 1.1.16

1547 Printed letter from the Gentlemen XVII and abstracts from letters and *resoluties* (proceedings) concerning a claim by the *Westindische Compagnie* (WIC, West India Company) of three million guilders over the possession of Cochin and Cannanore to the VOC or the States General,

1704; letter from Enkhuizen regarding trade in Malabar, 1739; letter from Wijbrand Blom, member of the Batavia Council, to the Gentlemen XVII concerning the trade in Malabar (and the rest of South Asia), 1732. One folder (old no. 402).

Oud-notariële archieven Enkhuizen
Old notarial archives of Enkhuizen

See 1.1.16

1015, nos 142, 145 Notarial act drawn up by Siewert Koeckebacker, concerning shipping between Goa and the Sunda Straits, 1643.

TRESOAR, FRYSK HISTOARYSK EN LETTERKUNDICH SINTRUM
(Leeuwarden)
TRESOAR, FRIESIAN HISTORICAL AND LITERARY CENTRE

Friese Stadhouders
Friesian Stadtholders

See 1.1.18
Access no.: 7

660 Account of the fall of Isfahan, written by Alexander ab Sigismundi at Cochin, 1724 (or 1729?). One quire. Copy made by Petrus Laan for Stadtholder William IV of Orange or his mother Maria Louise van Hessen-Kassel.

ZEEUWS ARCHIEF (Middelburg)
ZEELAND ARCHIVES

Koninklijk Zeeuwsch Genootschap der Wetenschappen
Royal Zeeland Society of Sciences

See 1.1.21
Access no.: 26.1

4, p. 236 Minutes concerning a report about the Jews in Malabar, accompanied by a copy of the patent granted to the Jews at Cochin by King Cheruman Perumal and a painting of Ezekiel Rabbi, all donated by A. 's Gravezande, 1774.[1] For the actual copy of the patent and the painting of Ezekiel Rabbi, see respectively 3.4 and 3.6, *Zeeuws Museum* (Middelburg), inv. nos G 1797a-b. See also no. 135, p. 7 (a).

5, p. 6 Minutes concerning the donation by A 's Gravezande of some papers concerning the Jews in Malabar, 1782.[1]

5, p. 229 Minutes regarding papers donated by A. 's Gravezande concerning the Jews in Malabar and a translation relating to the

	same topic included in a work by Bussing, 1777, 1780, 1785.[1] See also no. 55, pp. 143, 152 and no. 130, pp. 29, 40.
5, p. 239	Minutes concerning the donation by Adriaan Moens of a mug from Mozambique made of the horn of an elephant and acquired by Moens in Malabar, 1785.
6, pp. 13-14	Minutes concerning the donation by Adriaan Moens of a mug from Mozambique made of the horn of a rhinoceros and acquired by Moens in Malabar, 1787-8. The actual mug is kept at the *Rijksmuseum voor Volkenkunde* (Leiden), inv. no. Z-8051.
55, p. 134	Index to the minutes over the period 1769-1811, dating from *c.* 1815, with references to L. Bomme concerning the note sent by Adriaan Moens about the location of Cochin, 1778.
55, pp. 143, 152	Index to the minutes over the period 1769-1811, dating from *c.* 1815, with references to A. 's Gravezande concerning the Jews in Malabar and a translation relating to the same topic included in a work by Bussing, 1777, 1780, 1785.[1] See also no. 5, p. 229 and no. 130, pp. 29, 40.
55, p. 147	Index to the minutes over the period 1769-1811, dating from *c.* 1815, with references to the donation by Adriaan Moens of the astronomical observations of Cochin by the Briton W. Smith, 1778.[2] See also no. 56, p. 34 and no. 61, ff. 179-80.
56, p. 34	List of lectures and received papers, including references to the donation by Adriaan Moens of the astronomical observations of Cochin by the Briton W. Smith, 1778.[2] See also no. 55, p. 147 and no. 61, ff. 179-80.
61, ff. 179-80	Papers received from Adriaan Moens concerning a British astronomer (W. Smith?) who has determined the degrees of latitude and longitude of Cochin with the help of a quadrant, a telescope and a watch, 1777. See also no. 55, p. 147 and no. 56, p. 34.
61, ff. 240-1	Papers received from A. 's Gravezande concerning Gillissen's treatise and objects regarding the Jews at Cochin, and Gillissen's wish to have all these returned to him, 1778.[1]
62, ff. 68-9	Papers received from Governor Adriaan Moens (1770-80) concerning a missing piece of radix 'lopeziana' and wood from Cochin, including two wooden mugs with medicinal qualities, 1779. Published or referred to in *Verhandelingen*, VIII (1782) (inv. no. 352), p. xxv. The actual mugs are kept at the *Rijksmuseum voor Volkenkunde* (Leiden), inv. nos BEV-Z-67a & b. See also no. 133, p. 115.
62, f. 269	Papers received from Radermacher and Metzlar, partly concerning a mummy from Malabar, donated by Adriaan Moens, 1780.
130, pp. 29, 40	List of donated books, including references to donations by

A. 's Gravezande concerning the Jews in Malabar and a translation relating to the same topic, included in a work by Bussing, 1777, 1780, 1785.[1] See also no. 5, p. 229 and no. 55, pp. 143, 152.

133, p. 15 List of donated naturalia, including references to papers received from Governor Adriaan Moens concerning a missing piece of radix 'lopeziana' and wood from Cochin, including two wooden mugs with medicinal qualities, 1779. Published or referred to in *Verhandelingen*, VIII (1782) (inv. no. 352), p. xxv. The actual mugs are kept at the *Rijksmuseum voor Volkenkunde* (Leiden), inv. nos BEV-Z-67a & b. See also no. 62, ff. 68-9.

135, p. 7 List of donated antiquities and rarities, including:

(a) Reference to a copy (of a copperplate print?), originating from the Jewish synagogue at Cochin, of the patent granted to Joseph Rabbi and the Jews at Cochin by King Cheruman Perumal, and reference to a painting of the Jew Ezekiel Rabbi at Cochin and to a piece of wood (from a Portuguese crucifix?) originating from the Jews at Cochin, all objects deriving from Adriaan Moens and donated by A. 's Gravezande, 1778.[1] For the actual copy of the patent and the painting of Ezekiel Rabbi, see respectively 3.4 and 3.6, *Zeeuws Museum* (Middelburg), inv. nos G 1797a-b. The piece of wood is kept at the *Zeeuws Museum*, inv. no. G 2170. See also no. 4, p. 236.

(b) Reference to a palm leaf letter from Malabar donated by H.J. Krom, 1779. For the actual letter, see 3.4, *Rijksmuseum voor Volkenkunde* (Leiden), inv. no. 3600-BEV-Z-101.

[1] Published or referred to in *Verhandelingen*, VI (1778) (inv. no. 350), p. 517; IX (1782) (inv. no. 353), p. 515.

[2] Published or referred to in *Verhandelingen*, VI (1778) (inv. no. 350), p. 625. See also Supplement I: Bibliography, no. 200.

Van de Perre-Schorer family

See 1.1.21
Access no.: 107

27 Papers concerning the VOC, numbered 1-49, with partial table of contents, 1641-1785. One bundle. Including:

  32 Short note about the struggle between the EIC and Haidar Ali Khan of Mysore.

29 Various papers concerning the VOC, numbered 1-39, 40-60, 61-121, *c.* 1780-95. Three bundles. Including:

  83 (third bundle) Extract from the journal by Captain Stavorinus

concerning the state of defence of the factories in Malabar, 1792.

Schorer family

See 1.1.21
Access no.: 157

132 Deed of promotion of Steven Schorer from Middelburg to factor in Malabar under *Commissaris* Marten Huijsman, 1678. One piece.

Mathias-Pous-Tak van Poortvliet family

See 1.1.21
Access no.: 255

66 Memorandum of the Directors of the VOC concerning a claim by the *Westindische Compagnie* (WIC, West India Company) of three million guilders over the possession of Cochin and Cannanore to the VOC or the States General, 1705. Printed, one quire.

Pieter van Gote

See 1.1.21
Access no.: 390

4 Letters received by Pieter van Gote and his wife Johanna Bekker from Adriaan van Es and his wife Adriana de Cauw, partly with drafts of replies and annexes, 1773-93. One bundle. Including:
(a) Papers concerning the year 1781, including a letter from Goa. One folder.

Handschriftenverzameling
Manuscript collection

See 1.1.21
Access no.: 33.1

185 Fragment of the journal of the flute De Samaritaan, sailing from Gombroon to Cochin and running ashore on the Malabar coast, kept by Gerrit de Somer, 1729 (among some other papers). One folder.

HET UTRECHTS ARCHIEF
THE ARCHIVES OF UTRECHT

Notarissen geresideerd hebbende te Utrecht-stad
Notaries having resided at the town of Utrecht

See 1.1.23
Access no.: 34-4

U 118 a 6, act no. 182 Notarial act drawn up by Thomas Vosch van Avezaat, among others involving Lambert van Gessel (factor at Cochin) and Lambertus de Jager, concerning the collection of payment at the Delft Chamber of the VOC, 1728.

Oud-Katholieke Kerk in Nederland (OKN): Oud-Bisschoppelijke Clerezij (OKN/OBC)
Old Catholic Church in the Netherlands: Old Episcopal Clergy

See 1.1.23
Access no.: 224

751 Letters received by Balthasar van Wevelinchoven, 1662-88, including a letter from C.F. Airoldi (Internuncio at Brussels) partly concerning Cochin, 8 August 1669, in Italian (?). One folder.

Oud-Katholieke Kerk in Nederland (OKN): Apostolische Vicarissen
Old Catholic Church in the Netherlands: Vicars Apostolic

See 1.1.23
Access no.: 1003

224 Letters and papers received by Johannes van Neercassel, 1669-70, including two letters from C.F. Airoldi (Internuncio at Brussels) partly concerning (a Bishop in) Cochin, 27 June and 28 October 1669 (numbered 1084 and 1146 respectively), in Latin. One volume.

227 Letters and papers received by Van Neercassel, 1675-6, including a letter from Sebastiano Antonio di Tanara (Internuncio at Brussels) partly concerning the mission at Cochin, 2 December 1675 (numbered 2001), in Latin. One volume.

238 Copies of letters sent by Van Neercassel to Rome and the Nuncio at Brussels, 1660-70, including seven letters to Airoldi partly concerning Cochin, 18 January (ff. 145-52, second numeration), 5 February (ff. 157-60), 14 March (ff. 185-6), 1 April (ff. 190-4), 17 September (ff. 5-6, third numeration), 10 October (ff. 28-32) and 4 November 1669[1] (ff. 51-2), in Latin. One volume.

239 Copies of letters sent by Van Neercassel to Rome and the Nuncio at Brussels, 1670-78, including two letters to Di Tanara partly concerning Cochin, 27 September[1] (ff. 379-82) and 25 November 1675 (f. 389), in Latin. One volume.

240 Copies of letters sent by Van Neercassel to Rome and the Nuncio at Brussels, 1678-83, including a letter to Di Tanara concerning the mission in Malabar, 14 June 1678,[1] in Latin. One volume.

[1] Published in *Romeinsche bronnen voor den kerkelijken toestand der Nederlanden onder de apostolische vicarissen 1592-1727*, ed. R.R. Post, Vol. II: 1651-86 (Rijksgeschiedkundige Publikatiën, Grote Serie, 84) (The Hague, 1941), pp. 594, 844, 899.

Huydecoper family

See 1.1.23
Access no.: 67

622 Papers concerning the VOC, added to the archives by Jan Elias Huydecoper from the papers of Gualterus Petrus Boudaen, 1670-1760. One bundle. Including:
(a) Account of the fall of Isfahan, written by Alexander ab Sigismundi at Cochin, 1729 (or 1724?). One quire (old no. 1148).

623 Papers concerning the VOC, added to the archives by Jan Elias Huydecoper from the papers of Gualterus Petrus Boudaen, 1762-78. One bundle. Including:
(a) Correspondence of R. van Harn at Cochin, 1774.

Des Tombe family

See 1.1.23
Access no.: 26

832 Letters received by Jacob van Citters and Anna Sara Boudaen, 1723-92. One bundle. Including:
(a) Letter from Cornelis Arnoudsz. van Citters at Cochin, 1773.

De Beaufort family

See 1.1.23
Access no.: 53

2291 Reply of the Directors of the VOC to a claim of thirty tons of gold, submitted to the States General by the *Westindische Compagnie* (WIC, West India Company), as compensation for the VOC's occupation of places in Malabar (Cochin and Cannanore), which has disturbed the WIC's relations with the Portuguese, 1704. One quire, printed.

3.2. Universities

UNIVERSITEIT VAN AMSTERDAM, UNIVERSITEITSBIBLIOTHEEK
UNIVERSITY OF AMSTERDAM, UNIVERSITY LIBRARY

Manuscripts

See 1.2.2

IV F 32h Notes concerning the history of the St. Thomas Christians in Malabar and their relations with the VOC, the Jews and other communities, probably by a (former) Dutch Governor, *c.* 1773 (?). One folder (catalogue: Vol. II, no. 694).

VI H 3 Correspondence in Syriac of Mar Thoma, Bishop of the St. Thomas

Christians in Malabar. One bundle (catalogue: Vol. II, no. 1260). Partly published as *Relatio historica ad epistolam Syriacam a Maha Thome ... scriptam ad Ignatium ...* (Leiden, 1714). For one of the letters, see 1.2.2. See also 3.2, *Universiteit Leiden, Universiteitsbibliotheek, Oosterse Handschriften*, inv. nos Or. 1212-15. Including:

A Two letters to Ignatius, Patriarch of Antioch, in Estrangelo script, 1709, 1721, of which the first was delivered to *Commandeur* Adam van der Duijn of Malabar (1708-9), with a transcription of the first letter in Jacobitical script and translations (with notes) of that letter into Latin and Dutch by Carolus Schaaf (1646-1729), Professor at Leiden (who received a copy from Van der Duijn).

B Six letters to Carolus Schaaf, one of which appears to have been shown to the VOC Directors at Amsterdam, in Estrangelo and Jacobitical script, 1715-28, and a letter in Jacobitical script concerning the 'miraculous temple building' by the apostle Thomas, undated.

C Letter to the Governor-General at Batavia, including a request to Carolus Schaaf for recommendation, in Estrangelo script, 1728.

D Letter to the VOC, with a request to Carolus Schaaf for recommendation, in Estrangelo script, 1728.

E Letter from Carolus Schaaf at Leiden, with five copies in Jacobitical script, two copies of a Latin translation and two copies of a Dutch translation, 1713.

F Letter from Joh. Henr. Schaaf, in Jacobitical script, 1720.

H The address of Mar Thoma written in Syriac by Carolus Schaaf.

UNIVERSITEIT LEIDEN, UNIVERSITEITSBIBLIOTHEEK
LEIDEN UNIVERSITY LIBRARY

Bibliotheca Publica Latina
Latin Public Library

See 1.2.7

BPL 617 — *Resoluties* (proceedings), letters, memorandums and other papers concerning the VOC, with list of contents, 1687-1769, probably deriving from Augustinus van Son (1722-89), who became Secretary of the representatives of the Stadtholder with the VOC in 1750, and Lawyer of the VOC in 1755. 32 folders. Including:

2c Advice and considerations concerning changes with respect to the coinage in Malabar, 1766.

BPL 622, ff. 75-82 — Extracts from the *memorie van overgave* (final report) of *Commandeur* Frederik Cunes to his successor Casparus de Jong, December 1756, secret considerations concerning Malabar by De Jong, 1757, and notes regarding the state of Malabar by Governor-General Jacob Mossel, 1758.

BPL 2013 — Papers deriving from the linguist H.A. Hamaker (1789-1835), including a letter by A.H. Anquetil du Perron concerning and accompanied by an unidentified text from Malabar, 1790.

BPL 2030 — Descriptions of the coasts of Ceylon and south India, consisting of sailing instructions, soundings and landfalls of 85 locations, including nos 74-84: 'Kerripattenam' (Kadiapattanam?), Tengapattanam, Anjengo, Vilinjam, Kayankulam, Purakkad, Manakkodam, Cochin, Chetwai and Ponnani (ff. 39-44), *c.* 1750 (?). One volume.

Oosterse Handschriften (Legatum Warnerianum)
Oriental Manuscripts (Warner's Legacy)

See 1.2.7

Or. 1212-15 — Collection of texts in Syriac and Malayalam, donated in 1720 by Gabriel, the Metropolite of the Syrian Christians in Malabar, to Carolus Schaaf (1646-1729), Professor at Leiden. See also 3.2, *Universiteit van Amsterdam, Universiteitsbibliotheek*, Manuscripts, inv. no. VI H 3. Including:

- 1212 a-b — Syriac New Testament, in Nestorian script. Two volumes. Described in H.E. Weijers, *Orientalia*, 1 (1840), pp. 322-3, and A.G.P. Janson, *Summiere beschrijvingen* (1991), p. 3.
- 1213 — Texts in Syriac, in Nestorian script, concerning the history of the Syrian Christians in Malabar (?). Described and translated into Latin in J.P.N. Land, *Anecdota Syriaca*, Vol. 1 (Leiden, 1862), pp. 7, 24-30, 123-7.
- 1214 — Texts in Syriac and Malayalam, in Malayalam script, concerning the history of the Syrian Christians in Malabar (?). Described in Land, *Anecdota Syriaca*, Vol. 1, pp. 7-8.
- 1215 — Liturgical treatises in Syriac and Malayalam. One volume. Described in Land, *Anecdota Syriaca*, Vol. 1, pp. 8-12, and Janson, *Summiere beschrijvingen*, pp. 3-4. Including:
  - ff. 1-51v — Texts in Syriac with rubrics in Malayalam, in Nestorian script.
  - ff. 52v-end — Text in Syriac concerning the order of the Mass.

Or. 1352 a-b — 'Le Guide persan ou le munschy', manuscript Persian grammar in eight parts (with a copy and translation of the Persian epitaph of Tipu Sultan of Mysore in part VII (1), p. 16), by the French Colonel J.C.H. Bonnel, dedicated to Colonel V.-J.E. Jouy, 1810, written in Malabar after a campaign against Tipu Sultan of Mysore until 1795. Two volumes, in French.

Or. 4735 Apocalypse of St. John, in Syriac, copied at Rome in 1580 by a Syrian Christian from Malabar. Described in Janson, *Summiere beschrijvingen*, p. 3.

Or. 4804 'Megilat Ahashverosh', text in Hebrew, with a note in French from 1822 saying that the Boas family of bankers at The Hague received it from Jews at Cochin around 1792. For a reference to translations into Tamil at Cochin in 1757 (?), see M. Steinschneider, *Catalogus codicum hebraeorum bibliothecae academiae Lugduno-Batavae* (Leiden, 1858), pp. 299-300.

3.3. Ecclesiastical Organizations

ARCHIEF VAN DE NEDERLANDSE PROVINCIE DER JEZUÏETEN (Nijmegen)
ARCHIVES OF THE NETHERLANDS PROVINCE OF THE JESUITS

Handschriften
Manuscripts

See 1.3.2

A.D. 3 (box 21) Letters sent by Jesuits in India to Jesuits in Europe. Photocopies and contemporary manuscript copies, with recent documentation and notes pertaining to these letters and Jesuits in India, one folder. Including:

(a) Letter from Henricus Busaeus (1618-67) at Goa, 1647. In Latin, photocopy.

3.4. Museums and Other Public Institutions

NEDERLANDS SCHEEPVAARTMUSEUM AMSTERDAM
NETHERLANDS MARITIME MUSEUM AMSTERDAM

Library

See 1.4.4

A-III-278 Nautical guide consisting of sailing instructions and landfalls of locations in Europe, Africa, and the East and West Indies, by Hans N. Lunge, on board various ships, 1756-66, including instructions concerning (the surroundings of) Quilon,

'Coeijland' (Quilon or Kayankulam?), Anjengo and Vilinjam. One volume (alternative inv. no. B.0208 (03)).

A-IV-2-234 a — Various texts concerning the sailing to and trade in Asia, collected as part of the preparation for the first Dutch expedition to the East Indies in 1595, based on Portuguese and Dutch sources, 1594-5. One volume. For a detailed description, see H. Hazelhoff Roelfzema, 'Een handschrift uit 1594, bevattende gegevens ten behoeve van de voorgenomen handel en scheepvaart op Oost-Indië', *Nederlandsch Historisch Scheepvaart Museum, Jaarverslag 1971-1972*, pp. 72-5 (inv. no. A-IV-2-234 b is a modern-day transcription). Including:

- ff. 108-13 — Copy of letter written by Jan Huygen van Linschoten in 1584 at Goa to his father, with notes about India and a description of the overland route Van Linschoten would like to travel back to the Dutch Republic. Partly published in Lucas Jansz Waghenaer, *Thresoor der zeevaert* (Leiden, 1592); reprint R.A. Skelton (ed.) (Amsterdam, 1965).
- ff. 158-87 — Astronomic treatise including a description of the magnetic variation when sailing to Goa and notes concerning the shipping from Cochin to Lisbon.

B-I-0069-IV — Various printed texts. One box. Including:

(a) Treatise on the relations between the VOC and the EIC, concerning trade and politics in Malabar, in particular Cochin and Purakkad, printed by P. Guldemont, 1664. One quire.

(b) Reply of the States General to the request of the King of Portugal for the restitution of Cochin and other places, printed by L. Lambertsen, 1664. One quire.

B-III-502 — Letter of the Directors of the VOC about a claim of thirty tons of gold, submitted to the States General by the *Westindische Compagnie* (WIC, West India Company), as compensation for the VOC's occupation of Cochin and Cannanore, which has disturbed the WIC's relations with the Portuguese, *c.* 1705. One quire, printed.

B-III-629 & 726 — Accounts of the battle between the ship Vrouwe Geertruida, sailing from Surat to Batavia under the command of Captain Willem Bruelle, and a number of Maratha ships in January 1775 near Danda Rajapuri (Janjira), inv. no. B-III-726 printed by Johannes van Zeggeren at Amsterdam. Two quires, printed.

KONINKLIJKE BIBLIOTHEEK (KB) (The Hague)
ROYAL LIBRARY

Handschriften
Manuscripts

See 1.4.12

72 C 14 Various papers collected by Gijsbert Cuper, including an extract from a letter by *Commandeur* Hendrik Adriaan van Reede tot Drakenstein (1670-7) concerning the Roman and St. Thomas Christians at Cochin, 1674. One volume

KONINKLIJK INSTITUUT VOOR TAAL-, LAND- EN VOLKENKUNDE (KITLV) (Leiden)
ROYAL INSTITUTE OF LINGUISTICS AND ANTHROPOLOGY

Collectie in westerse talen
Collection in Western languages

See 1.4.14

H 49 Various letters and other documents, 1613-91. One volume. Including:

- D Survey of the (financial) state of affairs at Malabar, 1681 (56 ff.).
- E Account by A. Paviljoen and H. van Rheede (Hendrik Adriaan van Reede tot Drakenstein?) about the report of Willem Volger concerning financial matters at Vengurla, 1677 (three ff.).
- K Oath of allegiance of five Franciscans at Cochin, 1663 (four ff.).
- N Contract with the Ali Raja (in the territory of the Kolathiri), signed at Cannanore, 13 December 1664 (eight ff.). Published in *Corpus diplomaticum Neerlando-Indicum. Verzameling van politieke contracten en verdere verdragen door de Nederlanders in het oosten gesloten, van privilegebrieven aan hen verleend, enz.*, Vol. 2, ed. J.E. Heeres (The Hague, 1931), pp. 297-301; also in *Bijdragen tot de Taal-, Land- en Volkenkunde van Nederlandsch-Indië*, 87 (1931), pp. 297-301.
- P Note regarding financial aspects of Dutch troops in Cochin or Quilon, seventeenth century (?) (three ff.).
- S Treaty between Adam Westerwolt, Commander of the VOC fleet in the bay of Goa, and Viceroy Pedro da Silva of Goa, 1637 (three ff.).
- W Oath of allegiance, to be sworn by natives who are allowed

to stay in Cochin after its conquest, 1663 (three ff.).

X-AA Treaties with the Zamorin of Calicut, regents of Parur and the Kings of Cochin and Purakkad, 1663 (ten ff.).

H 454 One volume containing five documents, including:

a *Memorie van overgave* (final report) by *Commandeur* Hendrik Adriaan van Reede tot Drakenstein of Malabar to Jacob Lobs, 1677.

b Instruction for *Commandeur* Magnus Wichelman and Council of Malabar, drawn up by Hendrik Zwaardecroon, Commissioner for Malabar and *Commandeur* of Jaffna, at Cochin, 1697.

H 496 Memorandum about coins, weights and measures in Asia, including sections on Vengurla, Kanara, Cochin, Cannanore, Purakkad, Kayankulam, Quilon and Tengapattanam, *c.* 1665 (?). One volume.

RIJKSMUSEUM VOOR VOLKENKUNDE (Leiden)
NATIONAL MUSEUM OF ETHNOLOGY

Papiercollectie
Paper collection

See 1.4.18

3600-BEV-Z-101 Letter from Malabar, donated by H.J. Krom in 1779 (?). Six palm leaves, in Malayalam (?) (no. 4 and 402 in the KZGW catalogues of 1869 and 1890 respectively). For papers referring to the donation, see 3.1, *Zeeuws Archief, Koninklijk Zeeuwsch Genootschap der Wetenschappen*, inv. no. 135, p. 7 (b).

ZEEUWSE BIBLIOTHEEK / ZEEUWS DOCUMENTATIECENTRUM
(Middelburg)
ZEELAND LIBRARY / ZEELAND DOCUMENTATION CENTRE

Handschriften
Manuscripts

See 1.4.19

Hs. 474, 485-6 Three letters from *Commandeur* Adriaan Moens (1770-80) at Cochin to J. Tsjeenk (?), 1777-9. Three pieces.

Hs. 498 Fragment of a letter from Adriaan Moens, possibly at Cochin. One piece.

Hs. 1979, 1982 Two (identical?) letters from Adriaan Moens at Batavia to Jona Willem te Water (?), Secretary of the *Zeeuwsch Genootschap*, partly concerning Malabar, 1783. Two pieces.

Hs. 3266 Various notes concerning Malabar, originating from A. 's Gravezande (?), including a short geopolitical description of Malabar on the basis of a map by Joh. Wilh. de Graaf, 1772, and letters to Job Basler and to or regarding the Jews at Cochin, 1753. Partly in English, one quire.

Hs. 4185 Letter from Adriaan Moens at Cochin to J. Tsjeenk (?), 1778. One piece (identical to Hs. 485?).

ZEEUWS MUSEUM (Middelburg)
ZEELAND MUSEUM

Collectie Koninklijk Zeeuwsch Genootschap der Wetenschappen
Royal Zeeland Society of Sciences collection

See 1.4.20

G 1797b Copy (of a copperplate print?), originating from the Jewish synagogue at Cochin, of the patent granted to Joseph Rabbi and the Jews at Cochin by King Cheruman Perumal, originating from Adriaan Moens and donated by A. 's Gravezande, 1778. Partly in Malayalam, one piece (no. 3b and 407b in the catalogues of 1869 and 1890 respectively). For papers referring to the donation, see 3.1, *Zeeuws Archief, Koninklijk Zeeuwsch Genootschap der Wetenschappen*, inv. no. 4, p. 236 and inv. no. 135, p. 7 (a).

MARITIEM MUSEUM ROTTERDAM
MARITIME MUSEUM ROTTERDAM

Handschriften
Manuscripts

See 1.4.24

H595 Autobiography of George Naporra (1731-93) from East Prussia, who served the VOC between 1752 and 1756 as sailor, 1757. In German, in Gothic script, one volume. Including:

ff. 425-85 Notes concerning his stay with the ship De Drie Papagaaien at the roadstead of Surat in 1753-4, including references to a battle of the Angria 'pirates' near Cochin (against the Dutch?). Partly described in Van Gelder, *Naporra's omweg*, Chapters 17-18 (see Supplement I: Bibliography, no. 175).

H736 Letters by Claas Bichon (and his wife Elisabeth Lucasz) to various people, with register, 1694-7. One volume. Including:

f. 2 Letter to Lieutenant Sero at Cochin, 1694.

3.5. Companies, Private Organizations and Individuals

TUTEIN NOLTHENIUS (Doorn)

Tutein Nolthenius family

See 1.5.3

(a) Approx. 130 letters (and a few other documents), chiefly received by Balthazar Nolthenius and Johanna Boel from relatives and friends at various locations in the East Indies, 1737-42. One volume. With early twentieth-century transcriptions and summaries. Described in Tutein Nolthenius, 'De brieven van Overzee', pp. 453-63 (see Supplement I: Bibliography, no. 57). Including:

33-4, 63-4, 76, 96, 123	Seven letters from *Commandeur* Julius Valentijn Stein van Gollonesse (1734-42) at Cochin, 1738-42. Summarized and partly transcribed in Tutein Nolthenius, 'Verdere brieven van overzee', pp. 1051-5 (see Supplement I: Bibliography, no. 44).

KONINKLIJK HUISARCHIEF (The Hague)
ARCHIVES OF THE ROYAL FAMILY

Prince William V

See 1.5.6
Access no.: A 31

171 (alternative no. 333: 60)	Correspondence with various rulers, including a letter from King Rama Varma of Cochin, requesting support of Dutch soldiers, with duplicate. Two envelopes, two bags with seals, in Dutch and Malayalam.
333: I b	Correspondence of William V's representative with the VOC, Thomas Hope, and the Duke of Brunswijk, 1766. One bundle. Including: (a) Letter from Hope to the Duke of Brunswijk, 9 November 1766, with an extract from a letter from Cochin, 1766.
333: II	Correspondence of Thomas Hope and the Duke of Brunswijk, 1767-8. One bundle. Including: (a) Letter from Hope to the Duke of Brunswijk, 12 May 1767, with an extract from a letter from Cochin, 1766.
333: VI b	Correspondence of William V with Willem Jacob van de Graaff, Johan Gerard van Angelbeek,

Adriaan Moens, D.D. (Count) van Ranzou and others, concerning the VOC, 1773-95. One bundle. Including:

file 36 Five letters from *Commandeur* Johan Gerard van Angelbeek (1780-93) at Cochin, with some papers concerning the strength of the military troops in Malabar, 1787-92.

file 37 Four letters from *Commandeur* Adriaan Moens (1770-80) at Cochin, with some papers concerning the strength of the military troops in Malabar, 1775-80.

KARTING (Voorburg)

Hallegua family (photocopies)

See 1.5.9

(a) Document concerning the transfer of premises in Cochin, signed by Jacob Calkoen and Louis Quintin Martinsart, 1761. One piece.

(b) Will of David Alewa at Cochin, drawn up by Johan Andries Daimichen, 1781. Two copies.

3.6. Maps and Pictures

UNIVERSITEIT VAN AMSTERDAM, UNIVERSITEITSBIBLIOTHEEK
UNIVERSITY OF AMSTERDAM, UNIVERSITY LIBRARY

Kaarten en Atlassen
Maps and Atlases

See 1.6.2

30-10-07 Map of Malabar between Cochin and Cannanore, by A. Arrowsmith, London, 1809. Copper engraving, coloured, scale 1:234,000.

33-13-31 Map of the Kanara and Malabar Coasts and the Lakshadweep. Coloured, in English (old inv. no. 10102M).

33-13-36 Map of the surroundings of Cranganur and Azhikkodu, with explanatory notes, published by Johannes van Keulen. Coloured (old inv. no. 10108M).

Manuscripts

See 1.2.2

Bf 58b1 Drawing of a pilgrim from Malabar (with another figure). Coloured. Part of the correspondence between Gijsbert Cuper and Nicolaas Cornelisz Witsen, 1685-1716 (inv. nos Be 1-102, Bf 1-86, 88-100, G 41, see 1.2.2). Reproduced and described in E. Bergvelt and R. Kistemaker (eds), *De wereld binnen handbereik. Nederlandse kunst- en rariteitenverzamelingen, 1585-1735* (Zwolle, 1992), p. 155, and the accompanying *Catalogus*, p. 154.

UNIVERSITEIT LEIDEN, UNIVERSITEITSBIBLIOTHEEK
LEIDEN UNIVERSITY LIBRARY

Collectie Bodel Nijenhuis
Bodel Nijenhuis collection

See 1.6.2

002-09-030	Plan of the fort at Quilon, with cross-section of the wall, explanatory notes and legend, by Engineer Hans Georg Laarant on orders from Commander Adriaan van Ommen, 1687. Manuscript, coloured, scale *c.* 1:850 (52 x 73 cm) (old no. Port 176 N 9).
002-09-035	Map of the coastal area between Cochin and Chetwai, eighteenth century. Manuscript, coloured, scale *c.* 1:95000 (36 x 72 cm) (old no. Port 176 N 36).
002-11-023 & 024	Map of Cannanore, including the Dutch fort, bazaar and forts of the Ali Raja, with separate short explanation of the military and commercial significance of the fort, *c.* 1770. Manuscript, coloured, scale *c.* 1:8200 (23 x 37 cm), two sheets (old nos Port 176 N 156 & N 158).
002-11-025 & 026	Map of Chetwai, including the Dutch Fort Wilhelmus, with legend and separate short explanation of the military and commercial significance of the fort, with plan, *c.* 1770. Manuscript, coloured, scale *c.* 1:8200 (24 x 38 cm), two sheets (old no. Port 176 N 159).
002-11-027 & 028	Map of the fort at Cranganur and surroundings, with separate short explanation of the military and commercial significance of the fort, *c.* 1770. Manuscript, coloured, scale *c.* 1:5500 (23 x 37 cm), two sheets (old no. Port 176 N 160).
002-11-029 & 030	Map of Cochin, with legend and separate short explanation of its military and commercial significance, *c.* 1770. Manuscript, coloured, scale

	c. 1:5500 (25 x 39 cm), two sheets (old nos Port 176 N 164 & N 165).
002-11-031 & 032	Map of the fort at Quilon and surroundings, with separate short explanation of the military and commercial significance of the fort, *c.* 1770. Manuscript, coloured, scale *c.* 1:10000 (23 x 38 cm), two sheets (old no. Port 176 N 166).
002-12-041	Plan of the Dutch fort at Cannanore, with legend, second quarter of the eighteenth century. Manuscript, coloured, scale *c.* 1:1350 (35 x 51 cm) (old no. Port 176 N 157).
002-12-042	Plan of the fort at Quilon, with legend, second quarter of the eighteenth century. Manuscript, coloured, scale *c.* 1:1950 (34 x 51 cm) (old no. Port 176 N 167).
006-14-009	Sea chart (in two sections) of the Coasts of Malabar, Kanara and Konkan up to Surat, with soundings, some landfalls and European settlements, second quarter of the eighteenth century. Pen and brush drawing, coloured, scale *c.* 1:1,000,000 (66 x 92 cm) (no. 70 in catalogue of sea charts).
006-14-010	Sea chart of the Coasts of Malabar, Kanara and Konkan up to Surat, with soundings, some landfalls and European settlements, second quarter of the eighteenth century. Pen and brush drawing, coloured, scale *c.* 1: 1,000,000 (55 x 159 cm) (no. 71 in catalogue of sea charts). Reproduced in P. van Mil and M. Scharloo, *De VOC in de kaart gekeken. Cartografie en navigatie van de Verenigde Oostindische Compagnie 1602-1799* (The Hague, 1988), pp. 76-7.
C43 : 11 : 100227 : 110/1	View of Cochin, with legend. Engraving.
C43 : 22 : 009432 : 110/4	View of the bay and town of Cannanore, by J. van der Schley. Print. Closely resembling but slightly different from Baldaeus, *Nauwkeurige beschryvinge*, p. 100, see Appendix I.
D43 : 20 : 5947 : 110/1	View of the bay and town of Goa, by J. van der Schley. Print. Closely resembling but slightly different from Baldaeus, *Nauwkeurige beschryvinge*, p. 574, see Appendix I.
Port 176 N 18	Plan of the fort at Cranganur, 1709. Copper engraving, partly in French (16 x 52 cm).
Port 176 N 79	Map of Bombay harbour and its vicinity, with soundings and insets of landfalls, by R. Blachford,

	London, 1816. Copper engraving, in English (61 x 91 cm).
Port 176 N 154	Map of the town of Goa, with legend, by Pierre van der Aa, Leiden. Copper engraving, in Latin (33 x 45 cm).
Port 176 N 155	Map of the town of Goa, with legend, by J. van der Schley. Copper engraving, partly in French (20 x 35 cm).
Port 176 N 158 (b)	Plan of the fort at Cannanore. Copper engraving (16 x 25 cm). Closely resembling but slightly different from Valentijn, *Oud en nieuw Oost-Indiën*, Vol. V, part 2, 1st section, p. 8 (a), see Appendix I.
Port 176 N 165 (b)	Map of Cochin, by J. van der Schley. Copper engraving, partly in French (16 x 25 cm). Closely resembling but slightly different from Valentijn, *Oud en nieuw Oost-Indiën*, Vol. V, part 2, 1st section, p. 12 (a), see Appendix I.
Port 176 N 169	Plan of the fort at Quilon, by J. van der Schley. Copper engraving, partly in French (16 x 25 cm). Closely resembling but slightly different from Valentijn, *Oud en nieuw Oost-Indiën*, Vol. V, part 2, 1st section, p. 12 (b), see Appendix I.

Bibliotheca Publica Latina
Latin Public Library

See 1.2.7

BPL 2030 Descriptions of the coasts of Ceylon and south India, with coloured landfalls of 85 locations, including nos 74-84: 'Kerripattenam' (Kadiapattanam?), Tengapattanam, Anjengo, Vilinjam, Kayankulam, Purakkad, Manakkodam, Cochin, Chetwai and Ponnani (ff. 39-44), *c.* 1750 (?). One volume.

KONINKLIJK INSTITUUT VOOR DE TROPEN (KIT) (Amsterdam)
ROYAL TROPICAL INSTITUTE

Tropen Museum
Tropical Museum

See 1.4.2

1638/1	View of Goa. Engraving.
Haarlem 3114	View of Goa, 1509. Engraving, coloured, in Latin.

NEDERLANDS SCHEEPVAARTMUSEUM AMSTERDAM
NETHERLANDS MARITIME MUSEUM AMSTERDAM

Zeevaartkundige collectie
Navigational collection

See 1.6.4

A.2444 Map of Malabar between Cranganur and Quilon, with a great number of drawings of buildings such as forts and palaces of Malabar rulers, temples and churches as well as VOC forts and factories, *c.* 1720. Manuscript, coloured (70 x 294 cm).

A.2629 (04) Map of the Konkan, Kanara and Malabar Coasts between Vengurla and Quilon, in two sections, by Blaeu at Amsterdam, second half of the seventeenth century. Manuscript, coloured, scale 1:500,000 (104 x 61 cm), possibly incomplete.

Iconografische collectie
Iconographic collection

See 1.6.4

A-III-318 Album containing 80 affixed prints depicting views and maps of cities, probably originally marginal decorations of wall maps, by Frederick de Wit, with index, *c.* 1690. Including:
27 Cochin.
33 Cannanore.
34 Calicut.
35 Cranganur.

Library

See 1.4.4

A-III-278 Nautical guide consisting of sailing instructions and landfalls of locations in Europe, Africa, and the East and West Indies, by Hans N. Lunge, on board various ships, 1756-66, including landfalls of (the surroundings of) Quilon, 'Coeijland' (Quilon or Kayankulam?), Anjengo and Vilinjam. Coloured, one volume (alternative inv. no. B.0208 (03)).

RIJKSMUSEUM AMSTERDAM
RIJKSMUSEUM AMSTERDAM

Afdeling Nederlandse Geschiedenis
Department of Dutch History

See 1.6.4

NG-380 — View of Cranganur, attributed to Rev. Jan Brandes (1743-1808), 1785. Watercolour (27 x 41 cm) (possibly copied from a work by C.F. Reimer).[1]

NG-1985-7-2 — Album (20 x 17 cm) in which 146 drawings are bound, partly concerning Asia, mostly with explanatory notes (partly in Swedish), by Jan Brandes. For the first part of the album, see 1.6.4 and 4.6, *Rijksmuseum Amsterdam, Afdeling Nederlandse Geschiedenis*, NG-1985-7-1. Including:

- -46 Drawing of 'a Malabar officer and an ordinary rider', two Indian cavalrymen in the service of the VOC, *c.* 1780. Coloured.[1]

NG-1985-7-3-139 — View of Cochin, seen from the sea, by Jan Brandes, 1785. Brush drawing (24 x 81 cm) (probably based on an unidentified work).[1]

SK-A-2126 — Dutch squadron under the command of Cornelis Simonsz van der Veer attacking three Portuguese galleons by surprise on 30 September 1639 in the bay of Goa, by Hendrick van Anthonissen in 1653. Canvas (152 x 275 cm). Described and reproduced in De Balbian Verster, 'De verrassing van Goa' (see Supplement I: Bibliography, no. 201); also reproduced in J.C. Mollema, *Geschiedenis van Nederland ter Zee* (Amsterdam, 1942), Vol. IV, pp. 380, 383.

SK-A-2665 — Portrait of Adam van Westerwolt (Westerholt?), Commander of the Dutch fleet at Goa, attributed to Michiel Jansz van Miereveld, 1636. Oil on panel (106 x 76 cm). Described and reproduced in R.K. de Silva and W.G.M. Beumer, *Illustrations and Views of Dutch Ceylon, 1602-1796. A Comprehensive Work of Pictorial Reference with Selected Eye-witness Accounts* (Leiden, 1988), p. 429.

SK-A-3879 — View of the VOC envoy Johan van Twist returning from Bijapur in 1637, accompanied by a Bijapuri official, with the blockade of Goa in the background, by Jan Baptist Weenix (1621-63), *c.* 1650. Canvas (104 x 182 cm). Described and reproduced in R. van Luttervelt, 'Een nieuwe aanwinst' (see Supplement I: Bibliography, no. 210), Akveld and Jacobs, *De kleurrijke wereld / The Colourful World*, pp. 168-9 (Bibl., no. 61), and Zandvliet, *De Nederlandse ontmoeting met Azië / The Dutch Encounter with Asia*, pp. 108-9 (Bibl., no. 98).

SK-A-4471 — View of Cochin, attributed to Johannes Vingboons, *c.* 1650. Oil on canvas (97 x 140 cm). Reproduced in Zandvliet, *Mapping for Money*, p. 219 (see Supplement I: Bibliography, no. 96), and Gaastra, *De geschiedenis van de VOC* (only in reprint of 2002), between pp. 69-70 (Bibl., no. 71).

SK-A-4472 — View of Cannanore, attributed to Johannes Vingboons,

	c. 1650. Oil on canvas (97 x 140 cm). Reproduced in Zandvliet, *Mapping for Money*, p. 220 (see Supplement I: Bibliography, no. 96), Putten, *Ambitie en onvermogen*, pp. 130-1 (Bibl., no. 83), and Jacobs, *Koopman in Azië*, p. 56 (Bibl., no. 104).
SK-A-4473	View of Raybag, attributed to Johannes Vingboons, *c.* 1650. Oil on canvas (97 x 140 cm). Reproduced in Zandvliet, *Mapping for Money*, p. 221 (see Supplement I: Bibliography, no. 96).
SK-A-4947	Representation of various aspects of the Amsterdam trade with the East Indies, including depictions of the King of Cochin on an elephant, some Portuguese, a mosque and a Hindu temple, based on prints in Jan Huygen van Linschoten, *Itinerario. Voyage ofte schipvaert* (Amsterdam, 1596), and idem, *Icones* (see Supplement I: Bibliography, no. 26), by Pieter Isaaksz assisted by Karel van Mander, *c.* 1606. Panel (80 x 166 cm), originally the cover of the town harpsichord of Amsterdam (alternative no. NG-1999-19). Described and reproduced in Miedema, 'Het stadsklavecimbel van Amsterdam' (see Supplement I: Bibliography, no. 211), Akveld and Jacobs, *De kleurrijke wereld / The Colourful World*, pp. 39-41 (Bibl., no. 61), and Zandvliet, *De Nederlandse ontmoeting met Azië / The Dutch Encounter with Asia*, pp. 159-61 (Bibl., no. 98).

[1] Described and reproduced in De Bruijn and Raben, *The World of Jan Brandes 1743-1808* (see Supplement I: Bibliography, no. 125); inv. no. NG-380 also reproduced in Jacobs, *Koopman in Azië*, p. 62 (Bibl., no. 104); inv. no. NG-1985-7-2-46 also reproduced in Stevens, *De VOC in bedrijf / Dutch Enterprise and the VOC*, p. 73 (Bibl., no. 85).

Rijksprentenkabinet
Print Room

See 1.6.4

RP-P-1896-A-19368/397	Sea battle at Goa, by Jan Luyken. Engraving.
RP-P-1988-28 (topo. col.)	Map of Cochin, eighteenth century. Printed (9 x 14 cm).
RP-P-1988-31 (topo. col.)	Views of Calicut and Cannanore (among other locations). Print (34 x 47 cm), possibly originating from a work by Hogenberg (?).
RP-P-OB-47.383 (topo. col.)	View of Goa. Print.
RP-P-OB-47.386 (topo. col.)	View of Cannanore and its harbour, *c.* 1680-1750. Engraving (17 x 12 cm).
RP-P-OB-47.388 (topo. col.)	View of Cochin, with legend, eighteenth century. Engraving (17 x 28 cm).

RP-P-OB-75.345 — Bird's-eye view of Malabar (and part of Coromandel) and the Dutch conquest of Cochin, with a general description of Malabar, by P. v.d. Voorde, published by Pieter Arentsz, 1663. Print (17 x 27 cm) (Frederik Muller no. 2191).

RP-T-00-3186 — So-called 'Witsen-Album', consisting of 49 Indian miniature paintings (20 x 14 cm), depicting Mughal, Bijapur, Maratha, Golkonda and Persian rulers and officials, produced at Golkonda and probably purchased by a VOC official, *c.* 1680, with notes in Persian, Portuguese and Dutch, acquired by Nicolaas Cornelisz Witsen (1641-1717, VOC Director from 1693 onward and Burgomaster of Amsterdam). Coloured, one folder.[1] Including:

- 39 Sultan Ibrahim Adil Shah of Bijapur (no. 20 in Goetz).
- 40 Sultan Muhammad Adil Shah of Bijapur (no. 21 in Goetz).
- 41 Sultan Ali Adil Shah II of Bijapur (no. 22 in Goetz).
- 42 Khawwas Khan, *Peshwa* (commander-in-chief) under Muhammad Adil Shah (no. 23 in Goetz).
- 43 Mustafa Khan, *Peshwa* under Muhammad Adil Shah (no. 24 in Goetz).
- 44 Bahlul Khan, *Peshwa* under Sikandar Adil Shah (no. 25 in Goetz).
- 45 Sayyid Makhdum Sharza Khan, *Wazir* of Bijapur (no. 26 in Goetz).
- 46 Shivaji, Maratha ruler (no. 27 in Goetz).

RP-T-1883-A-214 — View of the naval battle at Goa between the VOC under Adam Westerwolt and the Portuguese, with legend, 1638. Pen drawing (Frederik Muller no. 1782A).

RP-T-1960-103 — Plover from Malabar, possibly by Aert Schouman, eighteenth century. Water colour (21 x 17 cm).

RP-T-1972-25 — Portrait of Shivaji, with a poem in Dutch, produced in Golkonda and purchased by a VOC official, *c.* 1680. Coloured, Indian miniature painting (24 x 19 cm).[1]

RP-T-1995-25 — Portrait of Sultan Muhammad Adil Shah of Bijapur, with caption in Persian and Dutch at the back, produced in Golkonda and probably purchased by a VOC official, *c.* 1685. Coloured, Indian miniature painting (12 x 9 cm).[1]

[1] Described and reproduced (together with other Indian miniature paintings) in P. Lunsingh Scheurleer, 'Het Witsenalbum. Zeventiende-eeuwse Indiase portretten op bestelling', *Bulletin van het Rijksmuseum*, 44, 3 (1996), and Goetz, *The Indian and Persian Miniature Paintings* (see Supplement I: Bibliography, no. 131).

MUSEUM BRONBEEK (Arnhem)
BRONBEEK MUSEUM

Koninklijk Tehuis voor Oud-Militairen en Museum Bronbeek
Royal Home for Retired Military Personnel and Bronbeek Museum

See 1.6.4

1195 View of the Dutch squadron under the command of Cornelis Simonsz van der Veer surprising three Portuguese galleons on 30 September 1639 in the bay of Goa, by Abraham van Beerstraten. Painting (110 x 162 cm). Described and reproduced in De Balbian Verster, 'De zeeslag voor Goa' (see Supplement I: Bibliography, no. 202); also reproduced in J.C. Mollema, *Geschiedenis van Nederland ter Zee* (Amsterdam, 1942), p. 380.

KONINKLIJK INSTITUUT VOOR TAAL-, LAND- EN VOLKENKUNDE (KITLV) (Leiden)
ROYAL INSTITUTE OF LINGUISTICS AND ANTHROPOLOGY

Images

See 1.6.4

36 C-5 View of Cochin, by H.B. Hoppenstok, *c.* 1816. Pen drawing (9 x 15 cm).

37 C-12 View of Goa, *c.* 1750. Engraving (19 x 33 cm).

ZEEUWS MUSEUM (Middelburg)
ZEELAND MUSEUM

Collectie Koninklijk Zeeuwsch Genootschap der Wetenschappen
Royal Zeeland Society of Sciences collection

See 1.4.20

G 1797a Portrait of the Jew Ezekiel Rabbi at Cochin, originating from Adriaan Moens and donated by A. 's Gravezande, 1778. Coloured, miniature painting on paper (7 x 9 cm) (no. 3a and 407a in the catalogues of 1869 and 1890 respectively). For papers referring to the donation, see 3.1, *Zeeuws Archief, Koninklijk Zeeuwsch Genootschap der Wetenschappen*, inv. nos 4, p. 236 and 135, p. 7 (a).

ATLAS VAN STOLK (Rotterdam)
VAN STOLK ATLAS

Atlas van Stolk

See 1.6.4

2299 Bird's-eye view of Malabar (and part of Coromandel) and the Dutch conquest of Cochin, with a general description of Malabar, 1663, by P. v.d. Voorde, published by Pieter Arentsz. Print.

Top. 1071 View of Cochin, with some ships in the foreground, published by P. Schenk, *c.* 1700. Engraving (22 x 27 cm).

CENTRALE BIBLIOTHEEK ROTTERDAM
CENTRAL LIBRARY OF ROTTERDAM

Maps

See 1.6.4

86 L 5 Four depictions of fort 'Geriah' (Janjira?), south of Bombay, and the inscriptions there, eighteenth century (?). Prints, two sheets.

MARITIEM MUSEUM ROTTERDAM
MARITIME MUSEUM ROTTERDAM

Picturalia
Pictures

See 1.6.4

P2623 View of the bay and town of Dabhol. Engraving.

4. CEYLON
(including Fishery Coast and Maldives)

4.1. Government Archives

REGIONAAL ARCHIEF ALKMAAR
REGIONAL ARCHIVES ALKMAAR

Van Foreest family

See 1.1.1

149 Letters received by Cornelis van Foreest, 1741-59, including a letter from A. de la Rij on Ceylon (with genealogy of the Schilperoort family), 1759. One folder.

Wollebrand Geleijnsz de Jonghe

See 1.1.1

5 Correspondence of Wollebrandt Geleynssen at Galle with Cornelis Lourensz Rijckeboom, husband of the daughter of Geleynssen's brother Jochem, at 'Allecan' (Alutgama?), 1647. Two pieces.

GEMEENTEARCHIEF AMSTERDAM
MUNICIPAL ARCHIVES OF AMSTERDAM

Weeskamer en Commissie van Liquidatie der zaken van de voormalige weeskamer
Orphan Board and Commission of Liquidation of the affairs of the former orphan board

See 1.1.2
Access no.: 5073

184-6 Papers received from the trustees at Colombo, 1675-1804. Three bundles.
187 Copies of papers received from the trustees at Colombo, 1684-1804. One bundle.
190 Papers received from the trustees at Galle, 1682-1791. One bundle.
191 Copies of papers received from the trustees at Galle, 1688-1785. One bundle.
193 Papers received from the trustees at Jaffna, 1683-1766. One bundle.
194 Copies of papers received from the trustees at Jaffna, 1693-1726. One folder.
209 Papers received from private persons in various places in Asia and the Cape of Good Hope, 1687-1789, including Colombo, 1695-1789, Galle,

1687-1721, Jaffna, 1698-1700, and Trincomalee, 1730-47. One bundle.

246 Papers sent to the trustees at Colombo, 1693-1768. One bundle.

247 Papers sent to the trustees at Galle, 1694-1772. One folder.

248 Papers sent to the trustees at Jaffna, 1693-1765. One folder.

435 Papers concerning the current account of the orphan boards at Colombo and the Cape of Good Hope, 1712, 1787. One folder.

Notarissen ter standplaats Amsterdam
Notaries at Amsterdam

See 1.1.2
Access no.: 5075

Geographical names on index cards found under some of the more obvious headings in the modern indices:

Colombo	37 index cards (1680-1739).
Galle	22 index cards (1701-10).
Jaffna	5 index cards (1702-7).
Madurai	4 index cards (1702-9).
Manapadu	1 index card (1707) (see also Chapter 1).
Matara	1 index card (1706).
Sri Lanka	68 index cards (1647-1782).
Trincomalee	3 index cards (1708-10).
Tuticorin	16 index cards (1702-10).
Varshalai River	1 index card (1702).

Firma Temminck en Van Twist
Firm of Temminck and Van Twist

See 1.1.2
Access no.: 188

124 Papers concerning a batch of 'hanekaatjes' (textiles) from Madurai, sent by Diderick Thomas Fretz at Galle per the ship De Gerechtigheid to Cornelis van Twist and the merchant Justus Hendrik Pfeil, 1793. Two pieces.

125 Papers drawn up at Colombo concerning a request by Fretz to count the money in the VOC's till, 1792-3. Partly printed, one folder.

126 *Eis* (order for supply), including a drawing of some jewellery, sent by Fretz at Galle to Pfeil and Van Twist, 1793-4. Two pieces.

127 Letters to Pfeil and Van Twist from Fretz at Galle, with appendices, 1794-1800. 21 pieces.

128 Drafts of letters from Pfeil and Van Twist to Fretz at Galle, with appendices, 1794-1800. Ten pieces.

129 Bills of exchange, receipts, etc., concerning Fretz, partly drawn up at Galle, 1795-7. Ten pieces.

130 Application of Fretz at Galle for the function of Governor of Ceylon, sent to Batavia, 1799. One piece.
131 Current account of Fretz with Pfeil and Van Twist, drawn up at Amsterdam, 1800. One piece.
132 Papers concerning H.F. Meijer (widow of M.J. Gratiaen), drawn up or sent to Galle, 1800-1. Six pieces.
144 Letters to Temminck and Van Twist, mostly sent from Colombo by J.L. van Plomann (?), Lieutenant of the Würtenberg Regiment, and P. Wühlenbeet (?), Captain of the National Infantry, 1792-9. Eleven pieces.

Brants family

See 1.1.2
Access no.: 88

1215 Letters to Jan Isaak de Neufville (1706-72) and company, with part B consisting of letters from Jan van Grieken, partly sent from Trincomalee, 1752, 1754. One bundle (part B) (microfilm nos 8393-6).
1616 Letters to Simon Bevel (1669-1736) and Reyna de Vries (d. 1727) from close relatives including David Bonte at Colombo, 1728 (microfilm nos 8421-2).

Sweers family

See 1.1.2
Access no.: 319

35 Testament of Arnout Sweers drawn up at Colombo, 1669, with an extract from a civil roll in connection with the Court of Justice at Colombo, 1671. One quire.

De Groot Jamin family

See 1.1.2
Access no.: 7

39 Insurance policy of Jan de Groot for goods loaded in the ship Velsen, sailing under Captain Cornelis Bosch from Amsterdam to Ceylon, with receipt, 1767. Two pieces.

Jacob de Flines

See 1.1.2
Access no.: 4

9 Letter received from Beauck at Delft, with an appendix regarding an account of textiles from Matara, among other products, 1725. One piece (old no. 6). Inv. nos 18, 21, 146, 148, 154, 269 (old nos 8, 35, 51) also seem to concern Matara textiles.

GELDERS ARCHIEF (Arnhem)
ARCHIVES OF GUELDERLAND

Houses of Waardenburg and Neerijnen

See 1.1.3
Access no.: 0439

488 Correspondence of Governor Isaak Augustijn Rumph and Gijsberta Johanna Blesius-Rumph with their brothers in Stockholm (and other places?), 1717-21. Partly in French, one folder.

Rosendael Castle

See 1.1.3
Access no.: 0525

1551 Drafts (?) of letters sent by Petronella Willemina van Hoorn and her husband Jan Trip de Jonge to various people in Asia, 1721-40, including Governors Stephanus Versluys and Gustaaf Willem van Imhoff, 1729-40. One volume.

Bosch and Van Rosenthal families and relatives

See 1.1.3
Access no.: 0724

15 Sealed will of Lucas Bosch and his wife Angenita Nolet, drawn up and signed at Jaffna, 1676. One piece.

Brantsen family

See 1.1.3
Access no.: 0452

287 A 1 Kind of law book with orders, prohibitions and penalties pertaining to the 'kingdom of Jaffna', 1659. One folder.

Van Voërst van Lynden family

See 1.1.3
Access no.: 0491

104 Deed of appointment of Lubbert Jan van Eck as Governor of Ceylon, 1761. One piece.

105 Papers concerning the career of Lubbert Jan van Eck, 1735-66, including his death on Ceylon, 1765-6. One folder.

106 Papers concerning the estate of Lubbert Jan van Eck at Colombo, 1765-77, including a printed peace treaty between the VOC and Kandy, 1766, and Van Eck's death announcement, 1765. One folder.

DRENTS ARCHIEF (Assen)
ARCHIVES OF DRENTHE

Losse publikaties, plakkaten e.d.
Separate publications, proclamations, etc.

See 1.1.4
Access no.: 0585

516 Announcement of a general exemption from the import of cinnamon from Ceylon on payment of one per cent of its value, 1803. One piece.

REGIONAAL HISTORISCH CENTRUM BERGEN OP ZOOM
REGIONAL HISTORICAL CENTRE BERGEN OP ZOOM

Notariële archieven
Notarial archives

See 1.1.5

366, act no. 54 Power of attorney drawn up by Michiel de Pottere, among other people involving Janna Lonckhuijsen of Bergen op Zoom and Jan Scholten of the Amsterdam Chamber of the VOC (?), concerning the ship Den Voetboogh at Colombo, 1695 (microfiche no. 1385).

STREEKARCHIEF MIDDEN-HOLLAND (Gouda)
REGIONAL ARCHIVES CENTRAL HOLLAND

Varia
Miscellany

See 1.1.7
Access no.: 200

2004 Account of the second voyage of Frederik de Houtman (born at Gouda *c.* 1540) in 1598-1601 to Aceh, including a description of the Maldives, *c.* 1602 (?). One volume. Published in Frederick de Houtman, *Cort verhael vant' gene wederuaren is Frederick de Houtman tot Atchein, enz.* (Gouda, 1880), and W.S. Unger, *De oudste reizen van de Zeeuwen naar Oost-Indië 1598-1604* (Werken Linschoten Vereniging, 51) (The Hague, 1948), pp. 64-111.

GRONINGER ARCHIEVEN
ARCHIVES OF GRONINGEN

Van Bolhuis family

See 1.1.8

Access no.: 493

205 Correspondence of Michiel van Bolhuis Junior and his wife Alegonda Beckeringh with Daniel Overbeek (Governor 1742-3) and his wife Geertruida Overbeek-Brengman, 1740-7, including letters sent to and from Ceylon, 1740-2. One folder.
206 Correspondence of Van Bolhuis and Beckeringh with Jonas Leenderts, 1741-3, including letters sent to and from Colombo, 1741-2. One folder.

ARCHIEFDIENST VOOR KENNEMERLAND (Haarlem)
ARCHIVAL SERVICE FOR KENNEMERLAND

Van Sypesteyn family

See 1.1.9

1268 Letter from A.M. van Charlet, widow of Hermanus Meier, to Gerrit Reessen Gerrits Junior, concerning the death of her husband at Colombo, 1794. One piece.

RIJKSARCHIEF IN NOORD-HOLLAND (Haarlem)
STATE ARCHIVES IN NORTH HOLLAND

Notarissen in het Rijksarchief in Noord-Holland, 1552-1842
Notaries in the State Archives in North Holland

See 1.1.10
Access no.: 185

913, nos 92-3 Notarial acts drawn up by Olbrant Smetius at Enkhuizen, concerning the killing of *Bosschieter* (gunner) Wouter Reijnersz Vos by the Portuguese near Galle as witnessed by Hercke Lambertsz, 1643 (microfilm no. 880).
6035, no. 118 Notarial act drawn up by Jacob Pet at Zaandam, concerning the goods of the *Kwartiermeester* Jan Sinvet (?), deceased on board the ship Withenburgh, deposited at Colombo, 1736 (microfilm no. 847).

Hollandsche Maatschappij der Wetenschappen
Dutch Society of Sciences

See 1.1.10
Access no.: 444

35 Papers received in 1760, including a description of the various species of cinnamon trees on Ceylon. One bundle.
51 Papers received in 1776, including a translation of a Sinhalese treatise from 1766 on Buddhism and the founding of the Pahala Vihara Temple at

Mulgirigala (erroneously referred to as being on Adam's Peak), with a drawing of the Temple, sent by Iman Willem Falck. One folder. For a short description, see Sliggers and Besselink, *Het verdwenen museum*, p. 147 (see Supplement I: Bibliography, no. 152).

STREEKARCHIVARIAAT NOORDWEST-VELUWE: HARDERWIJK
REGIONAL ARCHIVES NORTHWEST VELUWE: HARDERWIJK

Oud-archief der gemeente Harderwijk
Old archives of the municipality of Harderwijk

See 1.1.12

2052 Extracts by Ernst Brinck from journals and from other texts concerning travels to the East and West Indies, including essays and letters by Governor-General Jan Pietersz. Coen with short notes about Colombo, Trincomalee, Batticaloa and Matara, 1620s (?) (ff. 10-11). One volume.

HISTORISCH INFORMATIECENTRUM HELMOND
HISTORICAL INFORMATION CENTRE HELMOND

Van der Brugghen van Croy family

See 1.1.14
Access no.: 87

6 Testament of the chief-factor Dirk Willem van der Brugghen and Arnoldina Deliana Cornelia van der Brugghen née Loten, drawn up at Colombo, 1755. One folder.

475 Papers concerning the estates of Deliana Blesius, Isabella Sara Becker, Captain Arnout van Beaumont and Mrs Van Cuyk van Meteren née Van Beaumont, including extracts from the testaments of I.S. Becker and Ms Althusius, concerning Frans van Beaumont, *Dispencier* on Ceylon, 1722. One folder.

779 Papers of Joan Gideon Loten related to his period as Governor (1752-7), including: judicial documents, 1756; paper concerning the state of defence of Ceylon, undated; letters of complaint, 1752, 1757; bookkeeping, 1753, 1755-6. One folder.

BRABANTS HISTORISCH INFORMATIE CENTRUM: DEN BOSCH
HISTORICAL INFORMATION CENTRE OF BRABANT: DEN BOSCH

Aanwinsten
Acquisitions

See 1.1.15

Access no.: 339

24 Notes (four ff.) of Joan Casteleijn (1632-84), factor on Ceylon, concerning family matters, mostly with regard to his wife Lucretia Elisabeth Nijkerck and daughter Maria Elisabeth Casteleijn, 1675-84. Two pieces.

WESTFRIES ARCHIEF (Hoorn)
ARCHIVES OF WEST FRIESLAND

Stad Enkhuizen
Town of Enkhuizen

See 1.1.16

1540 Papers concerning or deriving from Jacob Mossel, partly dating from his period as Governor of Coromandel (1738-43). One folder (old no. 394). Including:
  (a) Considerations by Governor Van Imhoff of Ceylon concerning the textile trade on the Fishery Coast with regard to the local coinage, 1738.

1546 Various papers concerning the VOC. One folder (old no. 401). Including:
  (a) Judicial document concerning Ceylon and Batavia, 1731.
  (b) Letter by Jan Minne at Enkhuizen regarding Ceylon, 1737.

1549 Extract from the considerations of Governor Gustaaf Willem van Imhoff concerning the trade on the Fishery Coast, 1738. One folder (old no. 404).

1556 Papers concerning the trade in the East Indies of other Europeans, including a letter from Colombo to Batavia regarding the Ostend Company, 1742. One folder (old no. 411).

Oud-notariële archieven Enkhuizen
Old notarial archives of Enkhuizen

See 1.1.16

913, nos 92-3 Notarial act drawn up by Olbrant Smetius, concerning the killing of *Bosschieter* (gunner) Wouter Reijnersz Vos by the Portuguese near Galle as witnessed by Hercke Lambertsz, 1643.

GEMEENTEARCHIEF ZAANSTAD (Koog aan de Zaan)
MUNICIPAL ARCHIVES OF ZAANSTAD

Oud-notariëel archief Zaandam
Old notarial archives of Zaandam

See 1.1.17

6035, no. 118 Notarial act drawn up by Jacob Pet, concerning the goods of the *Kwartiermeester* Jan Sinvet (?), deceased on board the ship Withenburgh, deposited at Colombo, 1736.

Library

See 1.1.17

00761 Ship's log kept by the factor Gerrit Blaauw Nicolaasz of the ship Vliedlust under Captain Jacobus Swart, sailing from the Cape of Good Hope to Tuticorin in 1757-8, copy from 1780. One volume.

TRESOAR, FRYSK HISTOARYSK EN LETTERKUNDICH SINTRUM (Leeuwarden)
TRESOAR, FRIESIAN HISTORICAL AND LITERARY CENTRE

Handschriften, afkomstig van de Provinciale Bibliotheek van Friesland
Manuscripts, originating from the Provincial Library of Friesland

See 1.1.18
Access no.: 347

213 Letter from D. van Domburg (Governor Diederik van Domburg (1732-6)?) at Matara to Colonel Albert Emilius van Coenders at Leeuwarden, concerning Van Domburg's adventures and including a reply to Van Coenders' recommendation of a certain Mr Overman, 1726. One folder.

REGIONAAL ARCHIEF LEIDEN
REGIONAL ARCHIVES LEIDEN

Heilige Geest- of Arme Wees- en Kinderhuis te Leiden
Holy Spirit or Poor Orphanage and Children's Home at Leiden

See 1.1.19
Access no.: 519

3895 List of ships, with their sizes, sailing for the Amsterdam Chamber to the East Indies at Easter 1755, including the ship Roozenburg leaving for Ceylon at Christmas 1754. Printed, one piece.

4696 Deed in which the Directors of the VOC declare the death of sailor Dirk Bleykersveld (born 1758) on 11 March 1780 at the hospital in Colombo, October 1783. One piece.

Maerten Tersijden

See 1.1.19
Access no.: 234

13 Letters received by Maerten Tersijden from Hugo Adriaensz Tersijden,

1658-67, including three letters (nos 6-8) sent from Colombo, 1665-7. Eight pieces.

RIJKSARCHIEF IN LIMBURG (Maastricht)
STATE ARCHIVES IN LIMBURG

Handschriften
Manuscripts

See 1.1.20
Access no.: 18.A

3 Various papers concerning several subjects, with index, collected by the Bailiff August. Godefr. Collette, eighteenth century. Six volumes (numbered 2-7). Including:

Vol. 5, ff. 611-12 Short description of the tricks performed at Maastricht in 1648 by the elephant Hanske (or Hansken, not to be confused with the elephant Hans), shipped from Ceylon to the Dutch Republic in 1630. Published in Vos, 'Hanske', p. 167 (see Supplement I: Bibliography, no. 159).

ZEEUWS ARCHIEF (Middelburg)
ZEELAND ARCHIVES

Walcheren Classis / Middelburg Classis

See: 1.1.21
Access no.: 28.1

68 Correspondence between the *Comité tot de Oost-Indische Kerkzaken* and various persons and institutions in the Dutch Republic and the East Indies, 1681-1700, including a great number of letters and other papers to and from Colombo, Jaffna and Galle; document no. 29 is a treatise on Christianity in Dutch and Sinhalese, *c.* 1700 (?).

70 Register of papers received and dispatched by the *Comité tot de Oost-Indische Kerkzaken*, bound with many of these papers themselves, 1723-1802, including letters to and from Colombo. One volume.

Koninklijk Zeeuwsch Genootschap der Wetenschappen
Royal Zeeland Society of Sciences

See 1.1.21
Access no.: 26.1

4, p. 197 Minutes concerning the donation by A. Vosmaer of a plate with a description of a rare Ceylonese *boshond* (wild or wood dog?), 1773.

5, p. 238 Minutes concerning the treatise by Carl Peter Thunberg on Ceylonese cinnamon, with notes by M. Houttuyn, 1785. Published or referred to in *Verhandelingen*, XII (1786) (inv. no. 356), p. 296 (see Supplement I: Bibliography, no. 368).

55, p. 159 Index to the minutes over the period 1769-1811, dating from *c*. 1815, including some remarks by Johan Gerard van Angelbeek, *Opperhoofd* at Tuticorin, concerning the propagation of Christianity in that region (Ceylon?), 1779.

130, p. 20 List of donated books, including a reference to the donation by *Krankenbezoeker* (visitor to patients) P. van Esch of the Gospel of Mathew in Tamil (?), printed in 1741 at Colombo, 1775.

Schorer family

See 1.1.21
Access no.: 157

509 Minutes of the Council of Justice at Batavia concerning the detention of members of the so-called Ceylonese emergency council or court-martial, with accompanying papers, 1733-43. One folder.

Mathias-Pous-Tak van Poortvliet family

See 1.1.21
Access no.: 255

61 Instructions of the GG&C to the crew of the ship Woitkensdorp for the journey from Ceylon to the Dutch Republic, 1741. One piece.

Pieter van Gote

See 1.1.21
Access no.: 390

4 Letters received by Pieter van Gote and his wife Johanna Bekker from Adriaan van Es and his wife Adriana de Cauw, partly with drafts of replies and annexes, 1773-93. One bundle. Including:
(a) Papers concerning the years 1775-80, including two letters from Galle, 1779. One folder.

Receuils Van Citters

See 1.1.21
Access no.: 105

28 Papers concerning the VOC, 1740-?, including a copy of a treaty with the King of Kandy, 1766. One volume.

GEMEENTEARCHIEF ROTTERDAM
MUNICIPAL ARCHIVES OF ROTTERDAM

Oude notariële archieven
Old notarial archives

See 1.1.22
Access no.: 18

750: 106	Notarial act concerning the ship De Leeuw, 15 May 1662.
1262: 46, 48	Notarial act concerning the ship Honselaersdijk, 27 February and 1 March 1690.
1719: 11-12, 15	Notarial act concerning the ship Abbekerk, 13 April 1739.
1729: 6	Notarial act concerning the ship Vosmaer, 12 January 1703.
1968: 40	Notarial act concerning the ship Berckvliet, 13 September 1729.
2392: 72-3	Notarial act concerning the ship Stadwijk, 12 and 14 July 1725.
2769: 193	Notarial act concerning the ship Loverdaal, 27 July 1741.
2897: 344, 346-51, 363-4, 368	Notarial act concerning the ship De Gouverneur Generaal, 5 and 9 July 1763.
2905: 538	Notarial act concerning the ship De Damzicht, 25 November 1766.
3012: 58	Notarial act concerning the ship Wolthemade den Helt, 18 March 1783.
3097: 81-2	Notarial act concerning the ship De Gouverneur Generaal, 1 July 1763.
3099: 127	Notarial act concerning the ship Dantzigt, 20 August 1766.

Voormalige Classis van Schieland en de tegenwoordige Classis van Rotterdam
Former Schieland Classis and the present Rotterdam Classis

See 1.1.22
Access no.: 24

479 Proceedings of the *Deputati ad res Indicas*, including letters to the Church Council of Colombo, 1681-1816. One volume.

480 Papers received by the *Deputati ad res Indicas* concerning the churches in the East Indies, including letters from Colombo and Jaffna, 1762-1803. One bundle.

485 Proceedings of the Synod of South Holland, 1794-1810, with one of the volumes containing proceedings of 1796 destined for Ceylon. One bundle.

Handschriftenverzameling
Collection of manuscripts

See 1.1.22
Access no.: 33a

399 Letter from Gijsbert de Spruijt, Master of the shipyard on the island 'Allelande' near Tuticorin, to his wife Gijsbertha Burghout at Rotterdam, 1763. One piece.

HET UTRECHTS ARCHIEF
THE ARCHIVES OF UTRECHT

Momboirkamer te Utrecht
Chamber of Guardians at Utrecht

See 1.1.23
Access no.: 702-3

1401 Letters chiefly received from the Orphan Board at Batavia, with appendices, including a few papers originating from or referring to Colombo and Jaffna, 1697, 1714-94. 11 bundles.

1414 Current account book of the *Momboirkamer* with the Orphan Boards at Batavia and (in one case) Colombo, mostly concerning minors raised at Utrecht yet entitled to remittances from estates in the East Indies, 1771-1805. One volume.

Notarissen geresideerd hebbende te Utrecht-stad
Notaries having resided at the town of Utrecht

See 1.1.23
Access no.: 34-4

U 151 a 9, act no. 16 Notarial act drawn up by Abel de Coole, among others involving Joan Benjamin Vernatti (factor and Secretary of the Council of Justice at Galle) and Anna van Hardenbergh, concerning the estate of Anna Helena van Campen, widow of Benjamin de Boham, 1727.

U 169 a 6, act no. 100 Notarial act drawn up by Wernard van Vloten, among others involving Iman de Jonge (factor and *Dissave* of Colombo) and Ysbrand Ysbrandse, concerning the collection of payment at the Zeeland Chamber of the VOC, 1735 (related to a power of attorney for Anthony Leermans at Colombo, 1735).

U 188 a 33, act no. 46 Notarial act drawn up by Dirk Oskamp, among others involving Ernestine Henriette van Bronckhorst, Adriaan Storm van 's Gravesanden and Jacob Lambert van Gessel (factor on Ceylon), seemingly concerning a testament, 1777.

U 195 a 4, act no. 62 — Notarial act drawn up by Anthonie van den Doorslagh, among others involving Ernestine Henriette van Bronckhorst, Adriaan Storm van 's Gravesanden and Jacob van Gessel (factor on Ceylon), 1758.

U 205 a 7, act no. 125 — Notarial act drawn up by Luyt van der Pauw, among others involving Albert Burgart de Jonckheere (factor and *Fiscaal* at Jaffna) and Dirk de Visser, concerning the collection of payment at the Zeeland Chamber of the VOC, 1752 (related to a power of attorney for Justinus Panneel at Jaffna, 1751).

U 205 a 9, act no. 77 — Notarial act drawn up by Luyt van der Pauw, among others involving Albert Burgard de Jonckheere and Dirk de Visser, concerning the collection of payment at the Zeeland Chamber of the VOC, 1754 (related to a power of attorney for Justinus Panneel at Jaffna, 1753).

U 205 a 11, act no. 109 — Notarial act drawn up by Luyt van der Pauw, among others involving Albert Burgard de Jonckheere and Johan Simon Willemsz Vermeulen, concerning the collection of payment at the Zeeland Chamber of the VOC, 1756 (related to a power of attorney for Joan Hugonis at Jaffna, 1754).

Nederlands Hervormde Kerk (NHK): Raad voor de Zending
Dutch Reformed Church: Missionary Council

See 1.1.23
Access no.: 1102

66 Various papers concerning the VOC and missionary activities in the East Indies in the eighteenth and nineteenth centuries, with references to South Asia, mostly Ceylon, including documents regarding the seminary at Colombo, 1770s, remonstrance pertaining to the harmful growth of Roman Catholicism on Ceylon, 1758, and a letter of Governor Iman Willem Falck (1765-85) at Colombo, 1777. One bundle (old inv. no. 'kast 8, dossier 11').

444 Various papers concerning missionary activities, eighteenth and twentieth centuries, including a short speech about the attendance of the schools at the annual examination of the seminary at Colombo, made by Rector Jan Jacob Meijer, 1759, and letters from Johan Gerard van Angelbeek, *Opperhoofd* at Tuticorin, to Guillaume Titsingh at Amsterdam, with a treatise of Van Angelbeek regarding the propagation of Christianity on Ceylon, 1777-9. One box (old inv. nos 'kast 53, dossiers 2-3'). Missing at the time of research; the treatise of Van Angelbeek is probably identical to Hs. 6120 of the *handschriften* collection at the *Zeeuwse Bibliotheek / Zeeuws Documentatiecentrum* (Middelburg), see 4.4. For a description of Van Angelbeek's treatise, see Hofstede, *Oost-Indische Kerkzaken*, Vol. 2, pp. 198-221 (see Supplement I: Bibliography, no. 292).

Evangelische Broedergemeente (EBG): Zeister Zendingsgenootschap
Evangelical Community of Moravian Brethren: Missionary Society of Zeist

See 1.1.23
Access no.: 48-1

1188 Bookkeeping of the Deaconate, 1755-60, and the missions in Asia, including Ceylon, 1758-61. One folder.

Van Boetzelaer family

See 1.1.23
Access no.: 32

1100 'Dissertatio de territorio Gallensi', treatise by Pieter de Groot about Galle, in which he refutes Portuguese claims, 1667. One quire, in Latin.

Huydecoper family

See 1.1.23
Access no.: 67

51 Letters received by Joan Huydecoper, 1644-1704, including three letters from Hendrik Adriaan van Reede tot Drakenstein (referred to as A. Vreede) at Jaffna and Galle, 1689-91. One bundle.

622 Papers concerning the VOC, added to the archives by Jan Elias Huydecoper from the papers of Gualterus Petrus Boudaen, 1670-1760. One bundle. Including:
(a) Decree of Commissioner Hendrik Adriaan van Reede tot Drakenstein against 'the forbidden trade' at Jaffna, 1690. One piece (old no. 2200).

623 Papers concerning the VOC, added to the archives by Jan Elias Huydecoper from the papers of Gualterus Petrus Boudaen, 1762-78. One bundle. Including:
(a-b) Advice for the Council of the Indies concerning the war (with Kandy?) in Ceylon, 1762, 1765. One quire, one piece (old nos 2208-9).

Taets van Amerongen van Natewisch family

See 1.1.23
Access no.: 23

160 Letters received by Margaretha G. Falck (1761-1843, wife of Johan Karel Gideon van der Brugghen), including a letter from her cousin Otto Wilhelm Falck in which he mentions his brother-in-law Schuler as factor on Ceylon, 1787. Two pieces.

183 Funeral oration in memory of Anna Henriette van Beaumont, wife of

Governor Joan Gideon Loten (1752-7) and deceased at Colombo in 1755, by priest Matthias Wermelskircher. One volume, printed at Colombo.

Grothe family and related families

See 1.1.23
Access no.: 750

1377 Astronomic calculations, notes and drawings by Joan Gideon Loten, including references to Colombo (for instance on f. 99), *c.* 1750. One volume.
1378 Papers concerning the death and funeral at Colombo of Anna Henriëtta van Beaumont, wife of Loten, including two copies of a funeral oration by priest Matthias Wermelskircher (printed at Colombo), invitations for the funeral, epitaph (in Latin) and extract of the Colombo *dagregister* (diary) and notes concerning the funeral procession, 1755. One folder. See also inv. no. 1380, below.
1379 Letter from Loten at Colombo to his parents concerning the sickness and death of Van Beaumont, 1755. One quire.
1380 Extract of the Colombo *dagregister* concerning the death and funeral of Van Beaumont and the subsequent mourning, 1755. One quire. See also inv. no. 1378, above.
1381 List of people in the Dutch Republic who have received news about Van Beaumont's death, 1755. One folder.
1382 Genealogical notes concerning the Van Beaumont family, by Loten at Colombo, 1755. One quire.
1398 Personal notes written by Loten concerning the years 1755-6 on Ceylon, mostly consisting of lists of place or ship names and a few remarks regarding people and naturalia, 1785 (?). One volume.
1399 Drafts of letters from Van Beaumont to her husband Loten and other relatives, possibly partly written on Ceylon. One folder.
1402 Letter from Dirk Willem van der Brugghen to his father-in-law Loten concerning financial interests on Ceylon and other places in the East Indies, with a copy of Loten's reply, 1759. One piece.
1415 Two copies of a poem by Adriaan Moens on the occasion of Loten's arrival on Ceylon in the capacity of Governor, 1753. One folder, printed.

Ram family and related families

See 1.1.23
Access no.: 752

794 Papers deriving from Hendrik Brouwer, Director of the VOC (1661-83) and Burgomaster of Leiden, including six letters from the factor Cornelis van der Ham at Galle and Colombo, 1697-83. One folder.

Des Tombe family

See 1.1.23
Access no.: 26

832 Letters received by Jacob van Citters and Anna Sara Boudaen, 1723-92. One bundle. Including:
(a) Letter from C.S. van Citters (widow of one Castelijn) at Jaffna, 1758.
(b) Letter from G. Frankena and H.J. Frankena (née Castelijn) at Colombo, 1775.
(c) Letter from cousin Governor Gustaaf Willem van Imhoff (1736-40) at Colombo, 1738.

Martini Buys family

See 1.1.23
Access no.: 43

519 Extracts from the baptismal register of the Reformed congregation at Colombo concerning the baptism in 1676 of Joan Casteleijn's daughter Maria Elisabeth, 1683. One piece.

520 Act drawn up at Colombo in which Joan Casteleijn appoints the *Cranckbesoeker* (Visitor to patients) Burrit Cornelisz. Aart (van Koehorn) and his wife as companions of his daughter Maria Elisabeth during her voyage from Colombo to the Dutch Republic, with a list of her goods, 1684. One piece.

HISTORISCH CENTRUM OVERIJSSEL (Zwolle)
HISTORICAL CENTRE OVERIJSSEL

Rechterlijk archief van het Schoutambt Kamperveen, processtukken
Judicial archives of the function of Bailiff Kamperveen, case files

See 1.1.25
Access no.: 61.2

52 Letters chiefly sent by priests in the East Indies to Eduard Jork (or George) van Slangenburgh, his wife Clara Croeuger and their relative Paulus Croeuger, with many references to South Asia, 1711-23. One bundle. Including:
(a) Letter from Cramer at Nallur to Van Slangenburgh (?) at Amsterdam, 1713.
(b) Four letters from Cramer at Jaffna to Van Slangenburgh and Clara Croeuger at Amsterdam, 1716-18.
(c) Three letters from Cramer at Negombo to Van Slangenburgh and Clara Croeuger at Kampen, 1720-1.

4.2. Universities

UNIVERSITEIT VAN AMSTERDAM, ARTIS BIBLIOTHEEK
UNIVERSITY OF AMSTERDAM, ARTIS LIBRARY

Artis Bibliotheek
Artis Library

See 1.2.1

Legkast 238 'Wonderen der natuur', collection of *c.* 180 depictions and some texts of special and exotic animals and people as seen in the menagerie at the hostelry of Blauw Jan (Jan Westerhof) in Amsterdam and some other locations, by Jan Velten, *c.* 1695-1709. Seven boxes. Reproduced on CD. Including:

99 Text (with picture) concerning a pangolin, caught on Ceylon in 1702 and referred to as 'Negombo devil'. Printed. Reproduced in F.F.J.M. Pieters, 'The Menagerie of "The White Elephant" in Amsterdam, with Some Notes on Other 17th and 18th Century Menageries in The Netherlands', in H. v. Lothar Dittrich, D. v. Engelhardt and A. Rieke-Müller (eds), *Die Kulturgeschichte des Zoos* (Berlin, 2001), p. 49.

UNIVERSITEIT VAN AMSTERDAM, UNIVERSITEITSBIBLIOTHEEK
UNIVERSITY OF AMSTERDAM, UNIVERSITY LIBRARY

Manuscripts

See 1.2.2

Be 74b Extract of a description (regarding Ceylon and Madurai) based on reports of Rijklof van Goens (1675) and the chief-factor Huysman, concerning an ancient deserted city on Ceylon, probably Anuradhapura. One folder. Part of the correspondence between Gijsbert Cuper and Nicolaas Cornelisz Witsen, 1685-1716 (inv. nos Be 1-102, Bf 1-86, 88-100, G 41, see 1.2.2).

Bf 75b Description of Adam's Peak (?) and the 'grave of Adam and Eve' on it, with a drawing of the inscription on the grave. Two pieces. Part of the correspondence between Gijsbert Cuper and Nicolaas Cornelisz Witsen, 1685-1716 (inv. nos Be 1-102, Bf 1-86, 88-100, G 41, see 1.2.2). Described and reproduced on p. 186 of the *Catalogus* accompanying E. Bergvelt and R. Kistemaker (eds), *De wereld binnen handbereik. Nederlandse kunst- en rariteitenverzamelingen, 1585-1735* (Zwolle, 1992); see also *De wereld binnen handbereik* itself, p. 138.

Died 8 Bd Current account of Gommert van der Peer van Lier, drawn up at Colombo, 1678, signed by Rijklof van Goens Junior. One piece.

Zeldzame en kostbare werken
Rare and valuable books

See 1.2.2

OG 74-26 (1) New Year's poem presented to Governor Iman Willem Falck (1765-85), printed at Colombo, 1779.
(2) Poem on the occasion of Iman Willem Falck's 43rd birthday, by Salomom Tjellin Erichson (?), printed at Colombo, 1779.
(3) Poem in praise of Iman Willem Falck (?), by Ennus Belgicus (?), printed at Colombo, 1779.

OG 99-716 Poetic sermon on the occasion of the inauguration of Governor Jan Schreuder (1757-91), presented by Minister Gerard Potken, printed at Colombo, 1757. Missing at the time of research.

THEOLOGISCHE UNIVERSITEIT KAMPEN, BIBLIOTHEEK
THEOLOGICAL UNIVERSITY OF KAMPEN, LIBRARY

Library

See 1.2.5

101 A 1 'Grammatica off Singalese Taal-kunst, zijnde eene korte methode om de voornaamste fondamenten van de Singaleese spraak te leeren', manuscript Sinhalese grammar by Joannes Ruëll (d. 1701), Vicar and Rector of the Seminary at Colombo, with explanations in Dutch and conjugations, declensions, etc., in the Sinhalese script, *c.* 1699. One volume (old no. 23 A 1). Published under the same title at Amsterdam in 1708 with financial assistance of the Amsterdam Chamber of the VOC.

UNIVERSITEIT LEIDEN, UNIVERSITEITSBIBLIOTHEEK
LEIDEN UNIVERSITY LIBRARY

Maatschappij der Nederlandse Letterkunde te Leiden
Society of Netherlands Literature at Leiden

See 1.2.7

Ltk 523 'Horatius', tragedy written by Montanier at Colombo and dedicated to Governor Rijcklof van Goens Senior (1665-75), 1674. One volume.

Ltk 732 Secret *resoluties* (proceedings) concerning the surrender to the British, July 1795-February 1796; extract from a draft of a secret letter to the GG&C concerning the coastal strips of Ceylon ceded to the VOC in 1766; extracts of private letters from Governor Johan Gerard van Angelbeek (1794-6) to *Directeur-Generaal* W.J. van de Graaff concerning the surrender to the British, 1796. One volume.

Bibliotheca Publica Latina
Latin Public Library

See 1.2.7

BPL 246 Various correspondence, alphabetically arranged, mostly according to sender, with index. Approx. 30 folders. Including:
- (a) Letter from Governor Iman Willem Falck (1765-85) to the physician Arnout Vosmaer, 1780.
- (b) Letter from Governor Gustaaf Willem van Imhoff (1736-40) to Joan François de Witte van Schooten, 1738. Filed under 'Schooten'.
- (c) Two letters from Governor Isaak Augustijn Rumph (1716-23) to his brother, 1722.

BPL 617 *Resoluties* (proceedings), letters, memorandums and other papers concerning the VOC, with list of contents, 1687-1769, probably deriving from Augustinus van Son (1722-89), who became Secretary of the representatives of the Stadtholder with the VOC in 1750, and Lawyer of the VOC in 1755. 32 folders. Including:
- 17 Summaries of the letters from the Gentlemen XVII to the GG&C concerning Ceylon, 1700-59, with a glossary of Sinhalese words pertaining to matters of government and land control.

BPL 902 Astronomical treatise by Jacob van Veen, entitled 'De loopende werelt', with a preface dedicating it to Governor Rijcklof van Goens Senior, 1670. One volume.

BPL 1204 Log of the VOC ship Polanen, sailing from Amsterdam to Ceylon, by Captain D. den Back, April 1669-January 1670. One quire.

BPL 2030 Descriptions of the coasts of Ceylon and south India, consisting of sailing instructions, soundings and landfalls of 85 locations, including nos 1-58, 64-73, 85: Mannar, 'Kaimelle' (near Negombo), Adam's Peak, Kalpitiya, Negombo, Colombo, Galkissa (Mount Lavinia), Kalutara, Maggona, Beruwala Island, Alutgama, Bentota, Ambalangoda, Haycock, 'Tottegamme', Ragama, Galle, 'Aardewatte' (Unawatuna?), Weligama, Matara, Dondra, Nilwala, Kudawella, Walawe, 'Mago', Great and Little Basses reefs, 'Agaus', 'Paugamme', 'Sineklattedelle', Batticaloa, Vandeloos Bay, 'Ellentiture', Kottiyar, Trincomalee, Talaimannar, Vembar, Baipar (Vaypar), Punneikayal, Manapadu, 'east and west cape' (Cape Comorin?), Amsterdam Island (Karaitivu) and various unidentified mountains, islands, reefs etc. (ff. 2-31, 33v-8v, 45), *c.* 1750 (?). One volume.

BPL 2108 Three treatises by one or various persons known as Don Samuel Lanerolles Nanklar de Lay (?), *Apuhami* of the King of Kandy, concerning several subjects, including a conspiracy against the King in 1760 and the arrival of a British ambassador in Kandy in 1761-2; essay concerning the governmental system, laws and customs of

Kandy by the *Maha Mohottiar Mudaliyar*, interpreter of the *Dissave* of Matara, 1771; treatise regarding Ceylonese trees, fruits, etc., translated from Sinhalese and signed by B. Rodrigo and H.D. Dias de Fonseca, Colombo, 1771. One volume.

Bibliotheca Thysiana
Thysius Library

See 1.2.7

13916 'Kort en naaukeurig verhaal van 't leven en opkomst van den heer en Mr. Petrus Vuyst', pamphlet concerning the atrocities committed by Governor Vuyst (1726-9), with the names of people executed by him, 1733. One piece (number 6079 in the catalogue by Petit and Ruys).

13953 'De onregtveerde justitie uytgevoert door den Gouverneur Petrus Vuyst', pamphlet concerning the unjust administration of law by Vuyst on Ceylon and the sentence passed on him by the Judicial Council at Batavia, 1733. One piece (number 6105 in the catalogue by Petit and Ruys).

Oosterse Handschriften (Legatum Warnerianum)
Oriental Manuscripts (Warner's Legacy)

See 1.2.7

Or. 1216 a Survey of the Sinhalese script, compiled by a European, donated by Gerard Riemersma in 1748. One volume.

Or. 2221 Fragment of a Pali grammar, in Sinhalese script, with a note in Dutch on the back saying it was received from Lieutenant Reidt in 1769. One palm leaf.

Or. 2240 Ia 85 letters from various places to the Governor-General, 1786-1808. Including:

- 71 Letter from *Cucanda* Prince Major Bacan Sandaralam and Gagugu Bacan Kecil Naimuddin at Colombo to the GG&C, 1792 (no. 11 in the catalogue by Wieringa).

Or. 2241 I 23 letters in Malay, Persian and Arabic, all in Arabic script, sent from various places to Batavia, 1790-1807. Including:

- 520 Letter in Malay from the exiled *Pangéran Mas Dipati* Mangkurat at Colombo to the GG&C, 1806 (no. 23 in the catalogue by Wieringa).
- 521 Letter in Malay from the exiled *Cucanda Raden Tumenggung* Wirakusuma of Surakarta at Colombo to the GG&C, 1806 (no. 24 in the catalogue by Wieringa).
- 526 Letter in Malay from Sitti Hapipa at Ceylon, widow of the exiled Sultan Fakhruddin of Goa (in the Southeast Asian Archipelago), to the GG&C, 1807 (no. 25 in the catalogue by Wieringa).

Or. 2242 II 39 letters in Malay, Arabic and Turkish, all in Arabic script, written to and by various Dutch officials, 1790-1850. Including:

522 Letter in Malay from the Princes Wahu Kicil Muhammad Masyud and Muhammad Safiuddin, sons of Sultan Iskandar Alami, in exile on Ceylon, to the GG&C, 1806 (no. 24 in the catalogue by Wieringa).

Or. 3066 Manuscript copy of the Heidelberg Catechism (of the Dutch Reformed Church) in Sinhalese and Dutch, Sinhalese translation made by Revd J.M.S. Glennie in 1825 (?). One volume.

Or. 3067 Manuscript exercises for reading the Sinhalese script, in Sinhalese and Dutch, eighteenth century (?). One quire.

Or. 3194 Reply from the nobles of the Kandy court to a complaint made to the King of Kandy by Governor Johannes Hertenberg (1723-5) that the chiefs in Puttalam and 'Munnesvaram' (Chilaw) have been obstructing Dutch transport of cinnamon, with references to an albino mouse-deer and a civet cat presented to Hertenberg, 1724. Palm leaf, in Sinhalese. Described and transcribed in P.H.D.H. de Silva, *A Catalogue of Antiquities and Other Cultural Objects from Sri Lanka (Ceylon) Abroad* (Colombo, 1975), pp. 396-8.

Or. 4997 (7) Specimens of various non-West European scripts, including the Acts of the Apostles in Tamil, translated by Adrianus de Meij at Jaffna and Simon Kat at Colombo, *c.* 1697 (?). One folder.

BIBLIOTHEEK UNIVERSITEIT TILBURG
TILBURG UNIVERSITY LIBRARY

Handschriften
Manuscripts

See 1.2.8

TF-HS 59 Secret *resoluties* (proceedings) of the Governor and Council of Ceylon concerning Kandy, 1737 (ff. 1-28), and Ramnad and Rameswaram Island, 1739 (ff. 29-46). One volume (catalogue no. 50).

TF-HS 75 Correspondence of Joan Gideon Loten (1710-89) at Semarang, 1736-7. One volume (catalogue no. 56). Including:

- ff. 37-8 Letter from his cousins Frans Willem and Adriana Falk at Colombo, 1736.
- ff. 106-7 Letter from Frans Willem and Adriana Falk at Matara, 1737.
- f. 247 Letter from his cousins Gustaaf Willem and Ms Van Imhoff (?) at Colombo, 1737.

TF-HS 76 Ledger of Ceylon (copy for Batavia), with index, 1754-5. One volume (catalogue no. 57).

TF-HS 77 Correspondence of Joan Gideon Loten (mostly concerning Bantam), including an extract from a *resolutie* regarding his appointment as Governor of Ceylon (ff. 97-8v), 1752. One volume (catalogue no. 58).

TF-HS 78 Letters from Colombo to Batavia, Mannar, Galle and unknown places, 1754-5. One volume (catalogue no. 59).

TF-HS 79 Copy of Lopo de Abreu's *Summa theologiae* (translation of his *Suma de moral*), which, according to a note on the title page, fell to Philippus Baldaeus after the conquest of Jaffna in 1658. One volume (catalogue no. 60).

UNIVERSITEIT UTRECHT, UNIVERSITEITSBIBLIOTHEEK
UTRECHT UNIVERSITY LIBRARY

Handschriften
Manuscripts

See 1.2.10

Hs. 1058 (6.K.11) Correspondence and notes of the Almeloveen family, mainly the priest Johannes Almeloveen (*c.* 1618-78), including a letter by him to the priest Johannes Bogardus at Ceylon, in Latin, 1649 (no. 24). One box.

Hs. 6.A.23 Descriptions of the coasts, bays and anchorage locations of Ceylon, consisting of sailing instructions, soundings and landfalls of *c.* 80 locations, including Mannar, Mannar Channel, Talaimannar, Kalpitiya, 'Kaimelle' (near Negombo), Adam's Peak, Negombo, Colombo, Kalutara, Galkissa (Mount Lavinia), Haycock, Beruwala Island, 'Amellegotte' (Ambalangoda?), 'Tottegamme', Ragama, Galle, 'Aardewatte' (Unawatuna?), Weligama, Matara, Dondra, Nilwala, Kudawella, Walawe, 'Mago', Great and Little Basses reefs, 'Agaus', 'Paugamme', 'Sineklattedelle', Batticaloa, Vandeloos Bay, 'Ellentiture', Kottiyar, Trincomalee and various unidentified mountains, islands, reefs, etc., as well as some maps, eighteenth century. One volume.

4.3. Ecclesiastical Organizations

ARCHIEF BISDOM 'S-HERTOGENBOSCH
ARCHIVES DIOCESE 'S-HERTOGENBOSCH

Groot-Seminarie Haaren
Great Seminary Haaren

See 1.3.1

654 Papers concerning Asia, 1736-58, including a judicial document regarding a financial dispute between *Mudaliyar* Don Philip Caralesinga of Jaffna and the chief-factor Dirk Willem van der Brugghen (1717-70), with an

account, drawn up at Colombo, 1755, and an extract from a *resolutie* (proceedings) concerning the resignation of Joan Gideon Loten as Governor of Ceylon and the appointment of his successor, Jan Schreuder, 1756. One folder.

4.4. Museums and Other Public Institutions

KONINKLIJK INSTITUUT VOOR DE TROPEN (KIT) (Amsterdam)
ROYAL TROPICAL INSTITUTE

Kenniscentrum
Resource Centre

See 1.4.2

RP-31 & 32 Description of 'the most important matters concerning the land service, consisting of the differentiation and customs of the castes ...', relating to Sinhalese people in the service of the VOC, trade, administration, etc., by P. Sluysken at Colombo, 1784, with abstracts concerning the customs and laws of Jaffna, as noted by Claas Isaacsz, with glossaries, summaries of indigenous products, etc. Two volumes.

Tropen Museum
Tropical Museum

See 1.4.2

4847/11a Letter by the Chief *Dissave* of Colombo, appointing Hendrick Perera Appuhamy, son of *Muhandiram* Abraham Preruwardhane Jayasundera, as *Muhandiram*, 1785. Palm leaf, in Sinhalese (old no. 1322 / 143a).[1]

4847/11b Proclamation by the Chief *Dissave* of Colombo, prohibiting the illicit sale of coffee, chillies, lime and eggs by transporting them through secret routes to Slave Island instead of using approved roads, 1785. Palm leaf, in Sinhalese (old no. 1322 / 143b).[1]

4847/11c Proclamation by the Chief *Dissave* of Colombo, prohibiting the sale of arrack after 9 p.m., *c.* 1785 (?). Palm leaf, in Sinhalese (old no. 1322 / 143c).[1]

4847/12 Letter from Warnasuriya Wijetunga Samarasekara, *Mahavidane* of Totamune, Kalutara, to the Chief *Dissave* of Colombo, stating that the accused referred to is ill and will be sent as soon as she recovers from her illness, *c.* 1785 (?). Palm leaf, in Sinhalese (old no. 1322 / 146).[1]

A 9018 Envelope (contents missing) sent by the King of Kandy to Governor Cornelis Jan Simonsz (1702-7) (?). Palm leaf, in Sinhalese.[1]

[1] Described, translated and reproduced in P.H.D.H. de Silva, *A Catalogue of Antiquities and Other Cultural Objects from Sri Lanka (Ceylon) Abroad* (Colombo, 1975), pp. 385-94.

NEDERLANDSCH ECONOMISCH-HISTORISCH ARCHIEF (NEHA)
(Amsterdam)
NETHERLANDS ECONOMIC-HISTORICAL ARCHIVES

Bijzondere collecties
Special collections

See 1.4.3

127 Financial administration and correspondence of Jacob Temminck and Cornelis van Twist (see 1.1.2, *Gemeentearchief Amsterdam, Firma Temminck en Van Twist*), 1788-1813. Including:

3 Correspondence with various people (with index), including Baron van Ploman, Lieutenant of the Würtenberg Regiment at Colombo, 1795, 1799, Henricus (Volaard?) van Sohsten, factor at Colombo, 1794-9, and Johannes Adriaan Vollenhoven, factor and *Fiscaal* at Colombo, 1794-9. One volume.

4 Correspondence with various people (with index), including H. von Sohsten at Colombo, 1800, and J.A. Vollenhoven at Colombo, 1800-1. One volume.

6 Correspondence, bills of exchange and receipts concerning the account of J.A. Vollenhoven and H.V. von Sohsten at Colombo, 1793-1800. One folder.

NEDERLANDS SCHEEPVAARTMUSEUM AMSTERDAM
NETHERLANDS MARITIME MUSEUM AMSTERDAM

Library

See 1.4.4

A-III-278 Nautical guide consisting of sailing instructions and landfalls of locations in Europe, Africa, and the East and West Indies, by Hans N. Lunge, on board various ships, 1756-66, including instructions concerning (the surroundings of) Negombo, Adam's Peak, 'Amsterdam Island' (Karaitivu near Ceylon?), Cape Comorin, Punneikayal, Manapadu, island of 'Allelande' (near Tuticorin), Talaimannar, house of Bakenburg (eastern Mannar Island), Kalpitiya, Chilaw, 'Kaimelle' (near Negombo), Colombo, Galkissa (Mount Lavinia), 'Bantoera' (Panadura?), Kalutara, Maggona, Beruwala Island, Haycock, Alutgama River (Bentota Ganga?), Ambalangoda, Bentota, 'Tellegamme', Ragama, Galle, 'Oelewatte', 'Aardewatte' (Unawatuna?), Weligama, 'Murezee' (Mirissa?), Matara, Dondra, Nilwala, 'Calwettij' (Kudawella?), 'Magamme', Basses reefs, 'Agaus', 'Pauwgamme', 'Sinecalette', Batticaloa, Vandeloos Bay, 'Ellentijture', Kottiyar, Trincomalee, Point Pedro, 'Moeliwakelle' and various unidentified mountains, islands, reefs, etc. One volume (alternative inv. no. B.0208 (03)).

B-I-0069-IV Various printed texts. One box. Including:

(a) Conditions of the capitulation of the Portuguese in Colombo to the Dutch in 1656, printed at The Hague by C. Calamirus, 1657. One quire.

B-III-006 Various papers concerning the VOC, 1703-1809. One bundle. Including:

7 Letter sent along with the ship Zuydpool to *Commandeur* Diderick Thomas Fretz of Galle, mostly concerning financial matters on Ceylon, 1794.

B-III-515 Instructions for the sailing from the Cape of Good Hope to Ceylon during all seasons, 1783 (?). Printed.

B-III-550 Claim filed with the Council of Justice at Batavia on behalf of the Orphan Board at Colombo, concerning the estate of Governor Johannes Hertenberg (1723-5), printed at Batavia, 1726. One quire, incomplete.

B-III-810 Letter of credit, in Dutch, Sinhalese and Tamil, printed at Colombo, 1795, with a great number of handwritten notes about cessions and interest, running up to 1910. Reproduced in Veeger, 'Het verlies van Ceylon aan de Engelsen', p. 98 (see Supplement I: Bibliography, no. 779).

B-III-852 Penalty imposed by the GG&C upon the former Governor Petrus Vuyst (1726-9), 1732. One piece, printed.

B-III-870 Various printed papers concerning the VOC, with register. Three largely identical volumes. Including:

7 Sailing instructions for the route from the Cape of Good Hope to Ceylon, 1783.

GR-79-120 Instruction to the foremen of ship's carpenters, craftsmen and Javanese workers at Batavia, the island of Onrust and on Ceylon to service the VOC vessels carefully, 1728. Printed.

GR-82-051 Instructions for the sailing from the Cape of Good Hope to Ceylon during all seasons, 1783. Printed.

I-036 Ship's log of the ship De Unie sailing under the command of Captain S. Laurentius from Middelburg to Colombo and back, with stops at Punneikayal and Galle, by J. Jansen, 1790-1. One volume.

RIJKSMUSEUM AMSTERDAM
RIJKSMUSEUM AMSTERDAM

Afdeling Nederlandse Geschiedenis
Department of Dutch History

See 1.6.4

NG-1985-7-6-3 Papers deriving from Jan Brandes (1743-1808), including letters sent from Galle to Bartlo, *Vice-praeses* of the bench of Sheriffs (at Batavia?), and to Governor-General Willem Arnold Alting (1780-96), about a conflict with Popkes, *Procureur* (solicitor), and Harringa, former chief-factor in Japan, about the education of Bartlo's children during the voyage from Batavia to Ceylon, 1786. One folder.

NG-1985-7-6-9 Drafts of letters written by Jan Brandes during his voyage from Batavia to the Dutch Republic, 1785-7, including letters sent from Colombo and Galle to Dowager Van der Parra (?), Governor-General Alting and Captain Hogendorp of the ship Stavenisse among others, 1785-6. One folder.

CENTRAAL BUREAU VOOR GENEALOGIE (CBG) (The Hague)
CENTRAL OFFICE FOR GENEALOGY

Doop-, Trouw-, Begraaf- en Lidmatenregisters (DTBL): voormalige Nederlandse koloniën (on microfiche)
Baptismal, Marriage, Funeral and Church member registers: former Dutch colonies

See 1.4.11

'Ceylon ref' — Correspondence of churches on Ceylon (mostly Colombo), chiefly with the Delft and Schieland Classes, with register, 1700-40. Eight microfiches. (Inv. no. 320 of the archives of the *Nederlandse Hervormde Kerk, Synode, 1566-1816*, kept at the *Nationaal Archief* (The Hague), is probably the original, (see Supplement II, 13.)

'Caliture ref' — Baptismal registers of Kalutara, Negombo, Kalpitiya and Tuticorin, 1702-1806. 23 microfiches.

'Colombo (Wolvendaalkerk) ref' — Registers of the Wolvendaal Church at Colombo, 1736-1981. Including:

(a) Baptismal and marriage register, 1736-57. 24 microfiches.
(b) Baptismal register, 1743-1803. 22 microfiches.
(c) Baptismal and marriage register, 1757-67. 13 microfiches.
(d) Baptismal and marriage register, 1767-1803. 36 microfiches.
(e) Baptismal register, 1801-46. 50 microfiches.
(j) Marriage register, 1743-1810. 23 microfiches.

(k) Marriage register, 1802-39. 33 microfiches.
(l) Marriage register, 1804-38. 16 microfiches.
(s) Funeral register, 1803-51. 47 microfiches.

'Jaffnepatnam ref' Registers of Jaffna, 1806-77. Including:
(a) Baptismal register, 1806-23. 23 microfiches.

Overige Archiefbronnen (OA): Noord-Holland (on microfiche)
Other Archival sources: North Holland

See 1.4.11

'Amsterdam ref' Archives of the Amsterdam Classis. (Inv. nos 201-5 of the archives of the *Classis Amsterdam van de Nederlandse Hervormde Kerk*, kept at the *Gemeentearchief Amsterdam*, are probably the originals, see 1.1.2.) Including:
(a) Letters from Ceylon, 1657-93. 23 microfiches.
(b) Letters from Ceylon, 1694-9. 20 microfiches.
(c) Letters from Ceylon, 1699-1737. 27 microfiches.
(d) Letters from Ceylon, 1737-50. 29 microfiches.
(e) Letters from Ceylon, 1750-92. 31 microfiches.

Bybau family

See 1.4.11
Access no.: FA 00055

Port. 8 Papers partly concerning Johan van Haeften, naval officer, who was taken prisoner by the British in 1797 and released in 1800. One bundle. Including:
(a) Report about the events on the ship Susanna Amalia (bound for Tranquebar) in the Bay of Galle in 1797, drawn up by order of Lieutenant Colonel Robert Croker.
(b) Letter sent to Van Haeften in Colombo, 1798.
(c) Papers concerning Van Haeften's wedding at Mannar in 1799.

Dossier Loten [CBG]
Loten file [CBG]

See 1.4.11

(a) Various papers deriving from or concerning the Loten family, eighteenth to twentieth centuries, including a letter from Joan Gideon Loten at Colombo to Apollonia Rendorp (Dowager of Balthazar Boreel) at Amsterdam, concerning the donation of some tea and textiles, 1755. One folder.

KONINKLIJKE BIBLIOTHEEK (KB) (The Hague)
ROYAL LIBRARY

Handschriften
Manuscripts

See 1.4.12

76 D 42	Letters received by Cornelis Wilhelmus van der Sleijden (1744-1817, born at Colombo) from various people, including his aunt Susanna Petronella Visboom-Schmidt at Colombo, 1771. One folder.
76 D 43	Letters from Jacobus van der Sleijden (1711-61) and Arnoldine van der Sleijden-Konijn to various people, including Jan van der Kool and Johanna van der Kool-van der Sleijden at Colombo, 1745 (notarial copy, signed in conformity by C. Onderdewijngaart, 1764). One folder.
129 B 4	Papers in justification of the court martial called in 1729 at Colombo by Governor Petrus Vuijst, 1729-31. One volume.
134 A 6	Letter from Jacobus op den Akker on behalf of the clergymen and elders of the Dutch Reformed Parish at Colombo to the Walcheren Classis (Zeeland) of the Dutch Reformed Church, 1686. One piece.

Handschriften der Koninklijke Nederlandse Akademie van Wetenschappen
Manuscripts of the Royal Netherlands Academy of Arts and Sciences

See 1.4.12

KA 144a — *Memorie van overgave* (final report) by Governor Gustaaf Willem van Imhoff to Willem Maurits Bruininck, March 1740 (copy from *c.* 1800). One volume. For a translation, see S. Anthonisz-Pieters (Colombo, 1911).

KA 145 — Memorandums, instructions, reports, etc., concerning Ceylon, Malabar and the Fishery Coast, 1650-1721 (copy from *c.* 1800). One volume. Including:

Part 1, ff. 1-27	Instruction for Governor Jacob van Kittensteyn (1650-3), 1650.
Part 1, ff. 28-55	Exposition concerning the state of Ceylon by Governor Adriaan van der Meijden (1653-62), 1660.
Part 1, ff. 56-78	Considerations concerning Ceylon by Rijcklof van Goens, 1661.
Part 1, ff. 79-168	*Memorie van overgave* (final report) by Governor Rijcklof van Goens Senior to Jacob Hustaert, December 1663. For a translation, see E. Reimers (Selections from the Dutch Records of Ceylon Government/Government of Sri Lanka, 3) (Colombo, 1932).

Part 1, ff. 228-396	Considerations concerning Ceylon by Rijcklof van Goens, 1675.
Part 2, ff. 1-184	Considerations concerning Ceylon by Hendrik Adriaan van Reede tot Drakenstein, 1667.
Part 2, ff. 185-7	Treaty with Kandy, undated.
Part 2, ff. 188-217	Instruction for the *Dissave* of Colombo by Governor Cornelis Jan Simonsz (1702-7), 1707.
Part 2, ff. 218-37	Considerations concerning the service of the *Dissave* of Colombo by Governor Cornelis Jan Simonsz, 1707.
Part 2, ff. 238-69	Instruction for the Captain of the cinnamon by Governor Cornelis Jan Simonsz, 1707.
Part 2, ff. 270-321	'Visit' of the *Dissave* Bolscho, 1707.
Part 2, ff. 322-63	*Memorie van overgave* (final report) by Governor Cornelis Jan Simonsz to Hendrik Bekker, December 1707. For a translation, see S. Anthonisz-Pieters (Colombo, 1914).
Part 2, ff. 364-90	Report of an envoy (Cornelis Takel?) to Kandy, May 1721.
Part 2, ff. 391-2	Proclamation concerning the introduction of the German language, 1659.
Part 2, ff. 393-5	Extract from a *resolutie* (proceedings) by the Gentlemen XVII concerning the seminary on Ceylon, June 1703.

Oude drukken
Early printed works

See 1.4.12

82 H 9 Tamil translation of the Lord's Prayer, printed at Colombo, 1739. One piece. Reproduced in Schutte, *Het Indisch Sion*, p. 240 (see Supplement I: Bibliography, no. 151).

676 C 135 Various printed VOC instructions, resolutions, etc., One volume. Including:

4th section, p. 37	Sailing instructions for the route between the Cape of Good Hope and Ceylon, 1741.
9th section, 2nd part	Instruction to the foremen of ship's carpenters, craftsmen and Javanese workers at Batavia, the island of Onrust and on Ceylon to service the VOC vessels caresfully, printed at Amsterdam, 1728 (?).

853 E 267 Elegy for Governor Gerard Johan van Vreelandt (1751-2), by Adriaan Moens, printed at Colombo, 1752.

853 G 85 Poem on the occasion of the commencement of Joan Gideon Loten's Government, by Adriaan Moens, printed at Middelburg, 1753.

3145 B 44 Lamentation in memory of Governor Isaak Augustijn Rumph (1716-

23), by Minister Gerard Potken, and instructions for the funeral procession, by Joan Beekman and Adriaan Maten, 1723.

16824 List of 'summoned' or dismissed VOC servants, including Governors Stephanus Versluys (1729-32) and Diederik van Domburgh (1732-6), and Jan de Mauregnault, with a satiric poem, 1731.

16915 Penalty inflicted upon Petrus Vuyst, former Governor of Ceylon (1726-9), at Batavia in June 1732, printed at Batavia, 1733.

16916 Pamphlet concerning the unjust administration of law by Petrus Vuyst at Ceylon and the sentence passed on him by the Judicial Council at Batavia, 1733.

MUSEUM MEERMANNO (The Hague)
MEERMANNO MUSEUM

Van Westreenen family

See 1.4.13

S 72-3 Correspondence (chiefly received letters) and some accompanying papers of Jacobus Mersen, his wife and a few others, partly with copies, alphabetically arranged, 1748-61. Seven folders (each containing several files) in two boxes (inv. no. 43 in the inventory by Kernkamp). Including:

72.1: II Including two letters from J. Hemmingson (?) at Colombo, 1756-7.

72.2: IV Including twelve letters from B. and B.W. de Joncheere and B.W.A. Potken (?) at Jaffna, 1753-5, and Colombo, 1756-7.

73.3: VI Including one letter from Susanna Petronella Visboom (widow of Vreelandt) at Colombo, 1752.

Handschriften
Manuscripts

See 1.4.13

10 B 35 Letter from the King of Kandy to Governor Iman Willem Falck of Ceylon (1765-85), 1772 (?). Palm leaf (unopened), with decorative embroidery and seal depicting a lion or a mythological animal, in Sinhalese (old no. 332).

KONINKLIJK INSTITUUT VOOR TAAL-, LAND- EN VOLKENKUNDE (KITLV) (Leiden)
ROYAL INSTITUTE OF LINGUISTICS AND ANTHROPOLOGY

Collectie in westerse talen
Collection in Western languages

See 1.4.14

H 1 Report by Joan van Hoorn for the GG&R concerning Ceylon and the relations with Kandy, 1700, with annexes including extracts from letters received from patria concerning Ceylon, 1668, and a list of treaties with the King of Kandy. One volume.

H 3 Various papers concerning Ceylon, consisting of extracts from letters; *resoluties* (proceedings), 1681-2; *resoluties* and annexes of the GG&C, 1696; extract from letters from Batavia to Ceylon concerning fortifications on Ceylon; *verbaal* of secret letters of the GG&C given to Governor Gerrit de Heere, 1696. One volume.

H 4a-b Extracts from papers originating from the GG&R concerning Ceylon, 1696; draft of a treaty between King Rajasinga of Kandy and the VOC, probably seventeenth century. One folder.

H 47 Daily record by Governor Gerrit de Heere of Ceylon of his journey to Galle, Jaffna and other places, 1698. With maps, plans and drawings by engineer J.C. Toorzee (see 4.6). One volume. For a partial translation, see Gerrit de Heere, *Diary of Occurrences during the Tour of Gerrit de Heere, Governor of Ceylon, from Colombo to Jaffna, July 9 to Sept. 3, 1697*, trans. S. Anthonisz-Pieters (Colombo, 1914).

H 48 Extracts and copies of letters, reports, etc., of the Gentlemen XVII, GG&C and other VOC servants, 1665-93. One volume. Including:
- B Extract of a letter of the GG&C to Rijcklof van Goens Senior and Junior, 1673.

H 49 Various letters and other documents, 1613-91. One volume. Including:
- BB Report of the mission to Kandy by Henricus Bijstervelt, 1671 (51 ff.).
- FF Message of Joan 't Suirien van Chiangane, living at Jaffna, to *Dissave* M. Huijsman, 1672 (ten ff.).

H 57 Nine extracts from the *generale missiven* (annual reports of the GG&C) concerning Ceylon in general and occasionally Tuticorin in particular, correspondence between Batavia and Colombo, 1668-98. One quire.

H 131 Letter from J.F.C. Dorheim, printer at Colombo, to the Bloos van Amstel brothers, type founders at Amsterdam, concerning the supply of types, the low wages and how to improve them, 1778. One piece.

H 208 Survey of what has been spent on the purchase of textiles on the Fishery Coast between 1670 and 1708, with sections on Tuticorin, Alwar Tirunagarai, Manapadu and Kilakkarai, 1708. One piece.

H 454 Five documents concerning the VOC. One volume. Including:
- c *Memorie van overgave* (final report) by *Commandeur* D. van der Duijn of Galle to J. van Velse, 1708.

H 496 Memorandum about coins, weights and measures in Asia, including sections on Colombo, Galle, Tuticorin, Jaffna and Mannar, *c.* 1665 (?). One volume.

H 656 Inscription on the so-called grave of Adam and Eve on the island of 'Samara', 22 miles from Colombo, with an explanation in Dutch, eighteenth century. One piece.

NATIONAAL HERBARIUM NEDERLAND - UNIVERSITEIT LEIDEN
NATIONAL HERBARIUM OF THE NETHERLANDS - LEIDEN UNIVERSITY

Library

See 1.4.16

(a) 'Catalogus Horti Leidensis', manuscript catalogue of the Hortus Botanicus at Leiden, including descriptions of Ceylonese plants, by Paul Hermann (see 1.6.4, *Nationaal Herbarium Nederland-Universiteit Leiden, Herbarium collection*), 1681. In Latin, one volume.

Herbarium collection

See 1.6.4

(a) Van Royen collection, including two letters from Governor Iman Willem Falck (1765-85) to David van Royen concerning the collection of plants on Ceylon (with a remark that this has been frustrated by the activities of Haidar Ali Khan of Mysore), a list of medicinal herbs from Ceylon, drawn up at Colombo, 1780, and specimens of Ceylonese plants (originating from EIC employee J.G. König among others).

RIJKSMUSEUM VOOR VOLKENKUNDE (Leiden)
NATIONAL MUSEUM OF ETHNOLOGY

Papiercollectie
Paper collection

See 1.4.18

2749-2 Almost certainly a letter issued by Maha Mudiyanse Siriwardhana Jayatilake Seneviratne of Colombo to Mudiyanse Ralahamy Abhayasundera Seneviratne of the two Udukahagangabada Pattu of Siyane Korale, instructing him to supply two Sapu tree trunks, with a cover and two seals, 1773. Palm leaf, in Sinhalese. Most probably described and transcribed in P.H.D.H. de Silva, *A Catalogue of Antiquities and Other Cultural Objects from Sri Lanka (Ceylon) Abroad* (Colombo, 1975), pp. 412-13, erroneously under no. 2479.2.

ZEEUWSE BIBLIOTHEEK / ZEEUWS DOCUMENTATIECENTRUM (Middelburg)
ZEELAND LIBRARY / ZEELAND DOCUMENTATION CENTRE

Handschriften
Manuscripts

See 1.4.19

Hs. 4186 Comments by Adriaan Moens (*Commandeur* of Malabar, 1770-80) on the treatise by Johan Gerard van Angelbeek (*Commandeur* of Malabar, 1780-93, Governor of Ceylon, 1794-6) concerning the propagation of Christianity on Ceylon, with a reply of Van Angelbeek and a response by Moens, *c.* 1778. Three pieces. See also Hs. 6120 below.

Hs. 6120 Treatise by Johan Gerard van Angelbeek concerning the propagation of Christianity on Ceylon, written at Tuticorin, 1778, with a roll of indigenous Christians on Ceylon and their slaves, 1777. One volume, one piece. See also Hs. 4186 above. For a description of Van Angelbeek's treatise, see Hofstede, *Oost-Indische Kerkzaken*, Vol. 2, pp. 198-221 (see Supplement I: Bibliography, no. 292).

MARITIEM MUSEUM ROTTERDAM
MARITIME MUSEUM ROTTERDAM

Handschriften
Manuscripts

See 1.4.24

H26 List of goods that can always be imported in Ceylon at a profit, eighteenth century (?). One piece (originating from the archives of Rear Admiral C. de Jong van Rodenburgh).

H736 Letters by Claas Bichon (and his wife Elisabeth Lucasz) to various people, with register, 1694-7. One volume. Including:

- f. 40 Letter to Captain Melckert de Vos at Tuticorin, 1696.
- f. 41 Letter to *Commandeur* Carel Bolner at Galle, 1696.
- ff. 42-3 Letter to Captain Bruijn Jansz. at Tuticorin, 1696.
- ff. 46-7 Letter to Governor Gerrit de Heere (1696-1702) at Colombo, 1697.
- f. 49 Letter to Governor Gerrit de Heere at Colombo, 1697.

H737 Letters by Claas Bichon, mostly sent from Batavia to people in the Dutch Republic, but also including four letters sent from Rotterdam to Governor Gerrit de Heere, 1698-9, *c.* 1702, with incomplete register. One volume.

4.5. Companies, Private Organizations and Individuals

TUTEIN NOLTHENIUS (Doorn)

Tutein Nolthenius family

See 1.5.3

(a) Approx. 130 letters (and a few other documents), chiefly received by Balthazar Nolthenius and Johanna Boel from relatives and friends at various locations in the East Indies, 1737-42. One volume. With early twentieth-century transcriptions and summaries. Described in Tutein Nolthenius, 'De brieven van Overzee', pp. 453-63 (see Supplement I: Bibliography, no. 57). Including:

35, 97 Two letters from priest Johannes Philippus Wetzelius at Colombo, 1738, 1741. Summarised in Tutein Nolthenius, 'Verdere brieven van overzee', pp. 1055-6 (see Supplement I: Bibliography, no. 44).

DE LANNOY (Deventer)

De Lannoy

See 1.5.4

A/33 Papers concerning the branch of the family that moved from the Dutch Republic to Colombo, seventeenth to twentieth centuries. One bundle. Including:

K Genealogical notes concerning the descendants of VOC official Carel Wybrandus de Lannoy between 1760 and 1794, early nineteenth century.

KONINKLIJK HUISARCHIEF (The Hague)
ARCHIVES OF THE ROYAL FAMILY

Maria Louise van Hessen-Kassel

See 1.5.6
Access no.: A 10

211 Letter from J. Guillot Junior at Amsterdam (not addressed to Maria Louise) concerning the death of Philip Hendrik Meisenbuch van Kassel at Colombo in 1739 and the settlement of his estate, 1748. One piece.

Prince William IV

See 1.5.6
Access no.: A 17

173: 24 Correspondence of William IV with Gustaaf Willem van Imhoff (and a copy of the latter's will), 1737-48, including letters sent by Van Imhoff from Colombo, 1737-9. Approx. 30 letters, partly in French, one bundle.

Prince William V

See 1.5.6
Access no.: A 31

291: IV Papers concerning naval matters, *c.* 1760-1800. One bundle. Including:
(a) Ship's log of the brig De Diane sailing under the command of Lieutenant Helleman to the Cape of Good Hope and Ceylon, 1787-9.

333: I a Correspondence of William V's representative with the VOC, Thomas Hope, and the Duke of Brunswijk, 1765-6. One bundle. Including:
(a) Various papers concerning the VOC, including a document regarding Ceylon and piracy (put in a separate file, no. 2?).

333: I b Correspondence of Thomas Hope and the Duke of Brunswijk, 1766. One bundle. Including:
(a) Letter from Hope to the Duke of Brunswijk, 19 July 1766, with an extract from a letter from the 'secret committee' at Colombo to the Gentlemen XVII, 1766.
(b) Letter from Hope to the Duke of Brunswijk, 20 July 1766, with a letter from Governor Iman Willem Falck (1765-85) at Colombo to Hope concerning the inheritance of a cannon of Governor Lubbert Jan van Eck (1761-5), 1765.
(c) Letter from Hope to the Duke of Brunswijk, 3 August 1766, with the preliminary contents of the peace treaty between Kandy and the VOC.
(d) Letter from Hope to the Duke of Brunswijk, 13 August 1766, with instructions for Pierre Duflo, at Colombo, 1766. In French.
(e) Letter from Hope to the Duke of Brunswijk, 27 September 1766, with an extract from a letter from Ceylon to Hope (?), 1765.
(f) Letter from Hope to the Duke of Brunswijk, 23 October 1766, with a copy of the peace treaty of the States General and the VOC with Rajasinga of Kandy.

333: II Correspondence of Thomas Hope and the Duke of Brunswijk, 1767-8. One bundle. Including:
(a) Letter from Hope to the Duke of Brunswijk, 18 July 1767, with a letter from Iman Willem Falck at Colombo to William V, 1767.
(b) Instruction to Lieutenant Adrianus van den Bergh, 31 January 1768 (?), with a copy from a translated Sinhalese text ('sanmas ola') made for Arnoldus de Lij, 1768 (?), and a paper concerning the expedition near Walawe under the command of Van den Bergh, 1768 (?).

333: VI a Correspondence of William V with J.C. van Metzlar, Paringauw, Iman Willem Falck and others, concerning the VOC, 1774-93. One bundle. Including:
file 34 18 letters from Governor Iman Willem Falck at Colombo, with document concerning the strength of the troops on Ceylon, 1775-84 (formerly filed under no. 333: VIII e?).

333: VI b Correspondence of William V with Willem Jacob van de Graaff, Johan Gerard van Angelbeek, Adriaan Moens, D.D. (Count) van Ranzou and others, concerning the VOC, 1773-95. One bundle.

Including:

(a) (in file 35) Around 18 letters from Governor Willem Jacob van de Graaff (1785-94) at Colombo, with papers concerning the strength of the troops on Ceylon and (extracts from) letters exchanged between Van de Graaff, L. de Souillac, J. Reintous, C.F. Schreuder, Conway at Trincomalee, Jacques Fabrice van Senden at Trincomalee, Amsterdam Chamber, Gentlemen XVII, S. Nederburgh and others, 1786-95. Partly in French.

(b) (in file 38) Letter from J.G.D. Fedder at Trincomalee, 29 October 1788.

(c) (in file 38) Letter from J.C. von Hermes at Colombo, 26 January 1788. In German.

(d) (in file 38) Three letters from D.D. van Ranzou at Galle, 1780, Mannar, 1789, and Negombo, 1791, with (extracts from) letters exchanged between Van Ranzou, A. de Lij, Governor-General Willem Arnold Alting, Adriaan Moens and the Gentlemen XVII, 1784, 1789-91.

(e) (in file 38) Letter received from Galle, 1787, with some bills of lading, 1784.

ORDE VAN VRIJMETSELAREN ONDER HET GROOTOOSTEN DER NEDERLANDEN (The Hague)
FRATERNITY OF FREEMASONS UNDER THE GRAND EAST OF THE NETHERLANDS

Constitutie dossiers
Constitution files

See 1.5.7

2401-4 Files concerning Masonic lodges. Including:

(a) De Getrouwigheid (La Fidélité) at Colombo, with some letters from Hooghly, 1772. One folder.
(b) De Opregtheid (La Candeur) at Galle, 1772-4. One folder.
(c) La Réunion Neuchâtelloise at Colombo, 1790. In French, one piece.

Bibliotheek
Library

See 1.5.7

123.C.59-60 Speeches given in the Masonic lodge De Vereeniging (Virtus Nostra Ductrix) at Colombo, 1795, 1800. Two volumes.

123.E.29 Regulations for the Masonic lodge De Opregtheid or Opregtigheijd (La Candeur) at Galle, *c.* 1805. One volume.

4.6. Maps and Pictures

GEMEENTEARCHIEF AMSTERDAM
MUNICIPAL ARCHIVES OF AMSTERDAM

Firma Temminck en Van Twist
Firm of Temminck and Van Twist

See 1.1.2
Access no.: 188

126 Drawing of some earrings and a bracelet set with diamonds, accompanying an *eis* (order for supply) sent by Diderick Thomas Fretz at Galle to Justus Hendrik Pfeil and Cornelis van Twist, 1793-4. Two pieces.

RIJKSARCHIEF IN NOORD-HOLLAND (Haarlem)
STATE ARCHIVES IN NORTH HOLLAND

Hollandsche Maatschappij der Wetenschappen
Dutch Society of Sciences

See 1.1.10
Access no.: 444

51 Papers received in 1776, including a view of the Pahala Vihara Temple at Mulgirigala (erroneously referred to as being on Adam's Peak), with legend (belonging to a treatise on Buddhism and the founding of the Temple, sent by Iman Willem Falck). Water colour.

UNIVERSITEIT VAN AMSTERDAM, ARTIS BIBLIOTHEEK
UNIVERSITY OF AMSTERDAM, ARTIS LIBRARY

Artis Bibliotheek
Artis Library

See 1.2.1

C 1 Depictions of two Ceylonese elephants called Hans and Parkie (the latter also known as Greetje, the former not to be confused with the elephant Hanske), by the Physician Petrus Camper (1722-89), 1786. Coloured, three red chalk drawings (20 x 32 cm). Reproduced or described in B.C. Sliggers and A.A. Wertheim (eds), *Een vorstelijke dierentuin. De Menagerie van*

Willem V / Le zoo du prince. La Ménagerie du stathouder Guillaume V (Haarlem and Paris, 1994), p. 55, Bruggen and Pieters, 'Notes on a Drawing of Indian Elephants' (see Supplement I: Bibliography, no. 480), F.F.J.M. Pieters, 'Diergaarden in de Nederlanden 1750-1850 en hun betekenis voor de Zoologie', in *Acta Octavi Conventus Historiae Scientiae Medicinae Matheseos Naturaliumque Excolendae* (Amsterdam, 1978), p. 63, idem, 'De menagerie van Stadhouder Willem V. Een vorstelijke dierentuin', *Dieren*, 11, 5 (1995), p. 137. A contemporary copy of one of these drawings is kept at *Naturalis, Nationaal Natuurhistorisch Museum* (see 4.4).

Legkast 238 'Wonderen der natuur', collection of *c.* 180 depictions of special and exotic animals and people as seen in the menagerie at the hostelry of Blauw Jan (Jan Westerhof) in Amsterdam and some other locations, by Jan Velten, *c.* 1695-1709. Seven boxes. Reproduced on CD. Including:

99 Pangolin, caught on Ceylon in 1702 and referred to as 'Negombo devil' (with accompanying text). Woodcut. Reproduced in F.F.J.M. Pieters, 'The Menagerie of "The White Elephant" in Amsterdam, with Some Notes on Other 17th and 18th Century Menageries in The Netherlands', in H. v. Lothar Dittrich, D. v. Engelhardt and A. Rieke-Müller (eds), *Die Kulturgeschichte des Zoos* (Berlin, 2001), p. 49.

S Two drawings of a pigeon and parrot from Ceylon (?), by Aart Schouman. Aquatint and pencil (21 x 16 cm, 20 x 16 cm). Drawn for Aernout Vosmaer, *Natuurkundige beschryving eener uitmuntende verzameling van zeldsaame gedierten, bestaande in Oost- en Westindische viervoetige dieren, vogelen en slangen, weleer leevend voorhanden geweest zijnde buiten den Haag op het Kleine Loo van Z.D.H. den Prins van Oranje Nassau* (Amsterdam, 1766-1804) (?) (see also Appendix I).

VV 1 Depiction of a plant from Ceylon, by Carel Borchart Voet (1671-1743). Water colour (42 x 27 cm).

unnumbered Collection of *c.* 70 depictions of plants from Ceylon, mostly with names in Sinhalese and Tamil (?) (in Roman script) and descriptions in German or Dutch. Water colours, one folder (*c.* 30 x 20 cm).

UNIVERSITEIT VAN AMSTERDAM, UNIVERSITEITSBIBLIOTHEEK
UNIVERSITY OF AMSTERDAM, UNIVERSITY LIBRARY

Kaarten en Atlassen
Maps and Atlases

See 1.6.2

1-2-A-9 (24)	Map of Ceylon, with details concerning the European presence, by N. Bellin, Amsterdam, 1750. Copper engraving, scale 1:1,800,000. Identical to no. 108-02-89, see below.
25-32-12	Map of Ceylon, by Nicolaus Visscher, Amsterdam. Copper engraving, scale 1:300,000.
33-13-17	Map of the Maldives, depicting safe channels between the southern atolls, with explanatory notes, by James Horsburgh, 1814. In English (old inv. no. 10082M).
33-13-34	Map of an atoll near or in the Maldives, published by Johannes van Keulen. Coloured (old inv. no. 10106M).
33-13-35	Map of the 'Aria' (Ari?) Atoll in the western part of the Maldives, published by Johannes van Keulen. Coloured (old inv. no. 10107M).
33-13-38	Map of the surroundings of Tuticorin and a map of the surroundings of Kayalpatnam and Punneikayal, with explanatory notes, published by Johannes van Keulen (old inv. no. 10110M).
33-13-40 & 43	Two identical maps of Ceylon, with printed Latin text at the back concerning Ceylon, by Cypriano Sanchez, *c.* 1600 (?). Coloured, in Latin (old inv. nos 10112M, 10116M).[1]
33-13-41 & 42	Two identical maps of Ceylon, one with printed Latin text at the back concerning Ceylon, by Cypriano Sanchez, *c.* 1600 (?). One coloured, in Latin (old inv. nos 10113M-14M).[1]
33-13-44 & 45	Two partly identical maps of Ceylon, published by Johannes van Keulen, 1681 (?). Coloured (51 x 59 cm) (old inv. nos 10117M-18M).[2]
33-13-46 to 48	Three identical maps of Ceylon, with a print depicting an elephant and some people, published at Amsterdam by Nicolaas Visscher. Two coloured (old inv. nos 10119M, 10121M, 10126M).[2]
33-13-49	Map of Ceylon and the Fishery Coast, by Guillaume de l'Isle, published at Amsterdam by Jean Covens and Corneille Mortier. Coloured, in French (old inv. no. 10128M).
33-13-50 & 51	Two identical maps of Ceylon and the Fishery Coast, published at Amsterdam by R. and J. Ottens, *c.* 1750 (?). One coloured (50 x 60 cm) (old inv. nos 10131M-2M).[2]
72-01-06	Map of Ceylon, by A. Arrowsmith, London, 1805. Copper engraving, scale 1:500,000.
80-25-10	Map of the Maldives, with details concerning the European presence, 1750. Copper engraving, coloured, scale 1:1,700,000.
102-11-02	Map of Ceylon, by Gerard van Keulen, 1681 (?). Copper engraving, scale: 1:775,000 (51 x 59 cm).[2] Pasted on the back of another map of Ceylon, by Pieter van der Aa, Leiden, 1706-7. Copper engraving, scale 1:2,884,000.
108-02-89	Map of Ceylon, with details concerning the European presence, by N. Bellin, Amsterdam, 1750. Copper engraving, scale 1:1,800,000. Identical to no. 1-2-A-9 (24), see above.

L.K. VI 5 Map of the 'Aria' (Ari?) Atoll in the western part of the Maldives, as observed by Anthonij Klink, Shipmaster on the ship Ravenstijn that sunk there in 1726, with explanatory notes, *c.* 1730. Manuscript, coloured, scale 1:85000 (52 x 68 cm).

L.K. VI 8 Map of the bay of Nilwala, with explanatory notes, *c.* 1750. Manuscript, coloured, scale 1:12500 (41 x 51 cm).

L.K. VII 7 Map of the Bay of Galle and the 'false bay' (immediately west of Galle), with explanatory notes, *c.* 1750. Manuscript, coloured (37 x 85 cm).[2]

L.K. VII 8 Map of the 'Aria' (Ari?) Atoll in the western part of the Maldives, as observed by Anthonij Klink, Shipmaster on the ship Ravenstijn that sunk there in 1726, with explanatory notes, by Abraham Anias at Middelburg, 1728. Manuscript, coloured, scale 1:85000 (62 x 77 cm).

[1] One of these reproduced and described in Paranavitana and De Silva, *Maps and Plans of Dutch Ceylon*, p. 14 (see Supplement I: Bibliography, no. 655).

[2] Reproduced and described in Paranavitana and De Silva, *Maps and Plans of Dutch Ceylon*, pp. 33-5, 46, 118 (see Supplement I: Bibliography, no. 655).

Manuscripts

See 1.2.2

IV B 28 d'Acquet collection, mostly consisting of water colours of trees, plants, etc., from all over the world, with descriptions in Latin and table of contents, after specimens in the collection of Hendrik d'Acquet (1632-1706), Burgomaster of Delft. Coloured, 192 sheets (*c.* 16 x 20 cm). Other parts of this collection are kept at the *Bibliotheek Wageningen Universiteit en Researchcentrum* (1.2.11), and the *Koninklijk Instituut voor de Tropen* (1.4.2). Together described in Bergvelt, Jonker and Wiechman, *Burgers verzamelen*, pp. 112-20 (see Supplement I: Bibliography, no. 122), and E. Bergvelt and R. Kistemaker (eds), *De wereld binnen handbereik. Nederlandse kunst- en rariteitenverzamelingen, 1585-1735* (Zwolle, 1992), pp. 223-30. Including:

ff. 137, 142, 155, 167[1] Plants from Ceylon, 1677, 1681-2.

Bf 71* Drawings of statues of 'Adam and Eve and their children', their grave and its surroundings (on Adam's Peak?). Seven sheets. Part of the correspondence between Gijsbert Cuper and Nicolaas Cornelisz Witsen, 1685-1716 (inv. nos Be 1-102, Bf 1-86, 88-100, G 41, see 1.2.2). Including:

a Statue of 'Adam' in a lying posture (reclining Buddha).[1]

b Statue of 'Eve' in a lying posture (reclining Buddha).

c Statues of 'Adam's children' (Buddhist deities).

d Statues of 'Eve's children' (Buddhist deities).

e Statue of a Buddhist deity carved from a cliff, and its surroundings, east of Weligama.

f Mountain (Adam's Peak?) on which the 'grave of Adam and Eve' is located with stairs leading up, with legend.

g Mountain top with the rooms or caves containing the 'grave of Adam and Eve' with an inscription in an unidentified language, with legend.[1]

Bf 75b Drawing of the inscription on the 'grave of Adam and Eve' on Adam's Peak (?), with a description. Two pieces.[1] Part of the correspondence between Gijsbert Cuper and Nicolaas Cornelisz Witsen, 1685-1716 (inv. nos Be 1-102, Bf 1-86, 88-100, G 41, see 1.2.2).

[1] Described and reproduced on pp. 127, 186 of the *Catalogus* accompanying E. Bergvelt and R. Kistemaker (eds), *De wereld binnen handbereik. Nederlandse kunst- en rariteitenverzamelingen, 1585-1735* (Zwolle, 1992).

VRIJE UNIVERSITEIT AMSTERDAM, BIBLIOTHEEK
VRIJE UNIVERSITEIT AMSTERDAM, LIBRARY

Kaartenverzameling
Map collection

See 1.6.2

LL.05783gk: 374/od/1720 Map of Ceylon, with political divisions and notes in Portuguese and Dutch, by Joan F. van Essen at Antwerp, *c.* 1630. Manuscript, coloured, scale 1:1,000,000 (44 x 49 cm). Reproduced and described in Paranavitana and De Silva, *Maps and Plans of Dutch Ceylon*, p. 20 (see Supplement I: Bibliography, no. 655).

UNIVERSITEIT LEIDEN, UNIVERSITEITSBIBLIOTHEEK
LEIDEN UNIVERSITY LIBRARY

Collectie Bodel Nijenhuis
Bodel Nijenhuis collection

See 1.6.2

001-11-088 & 011-04-031 Two identical maps of Ceylon, with geographical explanation in German and view of some Sinhalese, a European and an elephant, by Tobias Conrad Lotter, between 1756 and 1777. Copper engraving, coloured, partly in Latin, scale *c.* 1:900,000 (50 x 58 cm) (old no. Port 175 N 167). Virtually identical to no. 011-04-032, see below.

002-09-003 Map of the Bay of Trincomalee, second half of the eighteenth century. Manuscript, coloured, scale

	c. 1:17000 (38 x 55 cm) (old no. Port 175 N 142).
002-09-017	Map of Ceylon, by G.H. Uhlenbeck, first quarter of the nineteenth century. Manuscript, coloured, scale *c.* 1:780,000 (67 x 45 cm) (old no. Port 175 N 158).[1]
002-09-031	Map of Ceylon, depicting the district borders as well as a number of elephants and other animals (cows and deer?), with a list of the districts, *c.* 1765. Manuscript, coloured, scale *c.* 1:680,000 (47 x 73 cm) (old no. Port 175 N 159).[1]
002-09-033	Map of the Muturajawela province and adjacent areas through which water is directed to this province, by Baltus van Lier, 1767. Manuscript, coloured, scale *c.* 1:25000 (53 x 75 cm) (old no. Port 175 N 124).[1]
002-09-036	Map of Kandy and surroundings, depicted circularly (based on an indigenous map?), with the routes of the military expedition in 1765 under Governor Lubbert Jan van Eck (1761-5), *c.* 1770. Manuscript, coloured (76 x 55 cm) (old no. Port 175 N 154).[1]
002-09-040	Map of the routes of the military expedition to Kandy in 1765 under Governor Lubbert Jan van Eck, by J.L. Guijard on orders from Governor Iman Willem Falck (1765-85), 1766. Manuscript, coloured, scale *c.* 1:380,000 (38 x 71 cm) (old no. Port 175 N 156).[1]
002-11-033 & 034	Map of Tuticorin and surroundings, with separate short explanation of its military and commercial significance, with plan of the fortifications, *c.* 1770. Manuscript, coloured, scale *c.* 1:45000 (23 x 38 cm), two sheets (old no. Port 176 N 173).
002-11-037 & 038	Map of Hanwella and surroundings, with separate short explanation of its military and commercial significance, *c.* 1770. Manuscript, coloured, scale *c.* 1:3500 (23 x 38 cm), two sheets (old no. Port 175 N 130).[1]
002-11-039 & 040	Map of Negombo and surroundings, with legend and separate short explanation of its military and commercial significance, with plan of the fort, *c.* 1770. Manuscript, coloured, scale *c.* 1:33000 (22 x 37 cm), two sheets (old no. Port 175 N 131).[1]
002-11-041 & 042	Map of the fort at Kalpitiya and surroundings, with separate short explanation of the military and commercial significance of the fort, with plan, *c.* 1770. Manuscript, coloured, scale *c.* 1:22000 (26 x 40 cm), two sheets (old no. Port 175 N 132).[1]

02-11-043 & 044	Map of the fort at Arippu and surroundings, with separate short explanation of the military and commercial significance of the fort, with plan, *c.* 1770. Manuscript, coloured, scale *c.* 1:2800 (26 x 40 cm), two sheets (old no. Port 175 N 133).[1]
002-11-045 & 046	Map of the fort at Mannar and surroundings, with soundings and separate short explanation of the military and commercial significance of the fort, with plan, *c.* 1770. Manuscript, coloured, scale *c.* 1:17000 (25 x 40 cm), two sheets (old no. Port 175 N 134).[1]
002-11-047 & 048	Map of the fort at Pooneryn and surroundings, with separate short explanation of the military and commercial significance of the fort, *c.* 1770. Manuscript, coloured, scale *c.* 1:1800 (25 x 39 cm), two sheets (old no. Port 175 N 135).[1]
002-11-049 & 050	Map of the fort at Hammenhiel and surroundings, with separate short explanation of the military and commercial significance of the fort, with plan, *c.* 1770. Manuscript, coloured, scale *c.* 1:5500 (24 x 39 cm), two sheets (old no. Port 175 N 136).
002-11-051 & 052	Map of the fort and town of Jaffna and surroundings, with separate short explanation of the military and commercial significance of the fort, *c.* 1770. Manuscript, coloured, scale *c.* 1:11000 (25 x 39 cm), two sheets (old no. Port 175 N 138).
002-11-053 & 054	Map of the fort and Bay of Trincomalee and surroundings, with separate short explanation of the military and commercial significance of the fort, with plan, *c.* 1770. Manuscript, coloured, scale *c.* 1:22000 (25 x 39 cm), two sheets (old no. Port 175 N 141 & N 143).[1]
002-11-055 & 056	Map of the fort at Batticaloa and surroundings, with separate short explanation of the military and commercial significance of the fort, with plan, *c.* 1770. Manuscript, coloured, scale *c.* 1:11000 (24 x 38 cm), two sheets (old no. Port 175 N 148).
002-11-057 & 058	Map of the fort at Katuwana and surroundings, with separate short explanation of the military and commercial significance of the fort, with plan, *c.* 1770. Manuscript, coloured, scale *c.* 1:5500 (24 x 38 cm), two sheets (old no. Port 175 N 149).[1]
002-11-059 & 060	Map of the fortifications at Matara and surroundings, with separate short explanation of the military and commercial significance of the

	fortifications, *c.* 1770. Manuscript, coloured, scale *c.* 1:5500 (23 x 38 cm), two sheets (old no. Port 175 N 150).[1]
002-11-061 & 062	Map of the town and Bay of Galle and surroundings, with separate short explanation of the military and commercial significance of the town, *c.* 1770. Manuscript, coloured, scale *c.* 1:17000 (24 x 38 cm), two sheets (old no. Port 175 N 151).[1]
002-11-063 & 064	Map of the fort at Kalutara and surroundings, with separate short explanation of the military and commercial significance of the fort, *c.* 1770. Manuscript, coloured, scale *c.* 1:5500 (25 x 39 cm), two sheets (old no. Port 175 N 152).[1]
002-11-065 & 066	Map of the fort and town of Colombo and surroundings, with legend and separate short explanation of the military and commercial significance of the fort, *c.* 1770. Manuscript, coloured, scale *c.* 1:22000 (25 x 39 cm), two sheets (old no. Port 175 N 155).[1]
002-12-002	Sketch and five soundings and measurements of the width of the waterway behind Company's Island in the Bay of Trincomalee, by Lieutenant Van Stralen, 1785. Manuscript (34 x 22 cm) (old no. Port 175 N 142a).
002-14-001	Map of Ceylon, by Petrus Plancius at Amsterdam, between 1633 and 1650, adaptation of a map by Mercator from the early seventeenth century. Copper engraving, coloured, scale *c.* 975,000 (35 x 50 cm) (old no. Port 300 N 146).
006-12-001	Plan of the royal palace at Kandy, with legend, *c.* 1750 (?). Manuscript, coloured, scale *c.* 1:100 (71 x 74 cm).
006-14-002	Sea chart of Ceylon, with soundings, some landfalls and Dutch settlements, *c.* 1660 (?). Pen and brush drawing, coloured, scale *c.* 1:720,000 (74 x 52 cm) (no. 72 in catalogue of sea charts).[1]
006-14-005	Sea chart of Ceylon and the Fishery Coast, with soundings, some landfalls and Dutch settlements, second quarter of the eighteenth century. Pen and brush drawing, coloured, scale *c.* 1:720,000 (73 x 76 cm) (no. 73 in catalogue of sea charts).[1]
006-14-014	Sea chart of Ceylon and the Fishery Coast, with soundings, some landfalls and Dutch settlements, second quarter of the eighteenth century. Pen and brush drawing, coloured, scale *c.* 1:720,000 (83 x 97 cm) (no. 74 in catalogue of sea charts).

009-01-044	Map of Ceylon, with short printed Latin text at the back concerning Ceylon, by Johannes Theodorus and Johannes Israël de Bry at Frankfurt, 1606. Copper engraving, in German, scale 1:1,750,000 (28 x 20 cm).
011-04-032	Map of Ceylon, with geographical explanation in German and drawing of some Sinhalese, a European and an elephant, by Matthaeus Seutter, *c.* 1730. Copper engraving, coloured, scale 1:900,000 (50 x 58 cm) (old no. Port 175 N 168). Virtually identical to nos 001-11-088 and 011-04-031, see above.
048-23-027 (1 to 3)	Three maps by A. Dalrymple after Van Keulen, 1782, published by Dalrymple at London, *c.* 1792. Copper engraving, one sheet. Including: (1) Vicinity of Kayalpatnam, with soundings and landfall. Scale 1:180,000 (16 x 21 cm). (2) Vicinity of Tuticorin, with soundings. Scale 1:45000 (14 x 21 cm). (3) Colombo harbour, with soundings. Scale 1:11000 (29 x 20 cm).
048-23-035	Map of the Bay of Trincomalee, with soundings, by J. van der Schley, *c.* 1760. Copper engraving, scale 1:50000 (27 x 36 cm).
054-10-001	Sea chart of the 'Aria' (Ari?) Atoll in the western part of the Maldives, as observed by Anthony Klink, Shipmaster on the ship Ravenstijn that sunk there in 1726, with some explanatory notes, possibly by Isaak de Graaf at Amsterdam, *c.* 1730. Pen and brush drawing on parchment, coloured, scale *c.* 1:85000 (62 x 66 cm) (no. 76 in catalogue of sea charts).
B44 : 22 : 008725 : 110/2	View of two Ceylonese soldiers (?) with Batticaloa in the background, by J. de Ram, seventeenth century. Engraving (15 x 19 cm). Reproduced and described in R.K. de Silva and W.G.M. Beumer, *Illustrations and Views of Dutch Ceylon, 1602-1796. A Comprehensive Work of Pictorial Reference with Selected Eye-witness Accounts* (Leiden, 1988), p. 476.
C44 : 1 : 008172 : 110/2	View of the pearl fishery off the coast of Tuticorin, by Jan Caspar Philips, 1730. Etching.
C44 : 4 : 000000 : 110/1	View of the production of cinnamon, nutmeg, mace and nuts, and the catching of elephants, monkeys and birds, with explanation, by P. van der Aa at Leiden, originating from the 'Atlas Guendeville' (?). Print, partly in French.

Port 175 N 114	Map of Ceylon, by P. Kaerius, published by J. Janssonius, Amsterdam, 1634. Copper engraving (13 x 17 cm).
Port 175 N 115	Map of Ceylon, by Sanson d'Abbeville, 1652. Copper engraving, coloured (12 x 8 cm). Identical to the inset of Port 175 N 116, see below. Possibly originating from Port 202 N 67, see below.
Port 175 N 116	Map of the Maldives, Ceylon and part of south India, with inset of Ceylon, by Sanson d'Abbeville, 1651. Copper engraving, scale *c.* 1:6,000,000 (17 x 22 cm), in French. Main map identical to Port 202 N 67, see below; inset identical to Port 175 N 115, see above.
Port 175 N 117 & N 118	Two identical maps of Ceylon and the Fishery Coast, by De l'Isle, published by De l'Isle at Paris, 1722. Copper engraving, coloured (40 x 55 cm).
Port 175 N 119	Map of Ceylon, with historical notes, 1726, originating from the 'Atlas Guendeville' (?). Copper engraving, coloured, in French (35 x 43 cm).
Port 175 N 120 to N 122	Three largely identical maps of Ceylon (two with Dutch names), by M. Bellin, 1750. Copper engraving, one coloured, mostly in French (25 x 23 cm).
Port 175 N 123	Map of the Bay and harbour of Trincomalee, with soundings, legend, geographical remarks and sailing instructions, by Nicholson, 1762. Copper engraving (49 x 65 cm). See also Port 175 N 125, below.
Port 175 N 125	Map of Ceylon and part of a historical description, originally part of a page from the newspaper *Vaderlandsche Na-courant* of 12 May 1783. Copper engraving (23 x 16 cm).[1]
Port 175 N 126	Map of the Bay and harbour of Trincomalee, with soundings, legend, geographical remarks and sailing instructions, by W. Nicholson, published by W. Gilbert, 1790. Copper engraving (46 x 60 cm). Apparently an English version of Port 175 N 123, see above.
Port 175 N 127 & N 128	Two identical maps of Ceylon, showing its provinces and districts, after A. Arrowsmith, published at Weimar, 1803. Copper engraving, one coloured (32 x 19 cm).
Port 175 N 129	Map of Ceylon, showing its provinces and districts, by A. Arrowsmith, 1805. Copper engraving, coloured (91 x 57 cm).
Port 175 N 160 to N 162	Three identical maps of Ceylon and part of the Fishery Coast, published by Isaak Tirion at

	Amsterdam, *c.* 1750. Copper engraving, two coloured (27 x 35 cm).
Port 175 N 165	Map of Ceylon and a small part of the Fishery Coast, by François Valentijn, published by Joannes Braam at Dordrecht, *c.* 1726. Originating from Valentijn's *Oud en Nieuw Oost-Indien*, hand-coloured, scale *c.* 1:900,000 (44 x 54 cm).[1]
Port 175 N 166	Map of Ceylon, published by Johannes van Keulen, *c.* 1681 (?). Copper engraving (56 x 94 cm).[1]
Port 175 N 169 to N 171	Three identical maps of Ceylon and the Fishery Coast, with soundings, by De l'Isle, published by C. Mortier and J. Covens at Amsterdam, *c.* first half of the eighteenth century. Copper engraving, two coloured, in French (40 x 55 cm).
Port 175 N 172	Map of Ceylon and the Fishery Coast, with soundings, by De l'Isle, published by P. Mortier at Amsterdam, *c.* 1700. Copper engraving, coloured, in French (40 x 55 cm).
Port 175 N 173 & N 174	Two identical maps of Ceylon and the Fishery Coast, by R. and J. Ottens, Amsterdam, *c.* 1750. Copper engraving, coloured, in French (48 x 57 cm).
Port 175 N 175	Map of Ceylon, with legend and drawing of some Sinhalese with an elephant, and added drawing of Dutchmen meeting with Sinhalese, published by Nicolaas Visscher at Amsterdam, 1681 (?). Copper engraving, coloured, one sheet (48 x 57 cm), in Latin. Largely identical to Port 175 N 176 to N 179, see below.[1]
Port 175 N 176 to N 179	Four identical maps of Ceylon, with drawing of some Sinhalese with an elephant, by N. Visscher, Amsterdam, *c.* 1675. Copper engraving, three coloured, in Latin (48 x 57 cm). Largely identical to Port 175 N 175, see above.
Port 175 N 180	Map of Ceylon, with soundings, published by Van Keulen at Amsterdam, *c.* 1715. Copper engraving (50 x 59 cm).
Port 175 N 183	Map of Ceylon, published by P. Schenk and G. Valk at Amsterdam, *c.* 1700 (?). Copper engraving, coloured (34 x 50 cm). Almost identical to Port 175 N 184, see below.
Port 175 N 184	Map of Ceylon, *c.* 1700 (?). Copper engraving (34 x 50 cm). Almost identical to Port 175 N 183, see above.
Port 176 N 37 & N 39	Two identical maps of the Maldives, 1750. Copper engraving, one coloured, partly in French (21 x

	15 cm). Closely resembling Port 176 N 38, see below.
Port 176 N 38	Map of the Maldives, 1750. Copper engraving, in French (21 x 15 cm). Closely resembling Port 176 N 37 & N 39, see above.
Port 202 N 67	Map of the Maldives, Ceylon and part of south India, by Sanson d'Abbeville, 1651. Copper engraving, scale *c.* 1:6,000,000 (17 x 23 cm), in French. Identical to main map of Port 175 N 116, see above; inset missing, possibly Port 175 N 115, see above.

[1] Reproduced and described in Paranavitana and De Silva, *Maps and Plans of Dutch Ceylon*, pp. 33, 36, 43-4, 53, 60, 63-4, 82, 93, 99, 102, 106, 116, 126, 140, 150, 163-4, 167, 171, 176-7 (see Supplement I: Bibliography, no. 655); inv. no. 002-09-031 also reproduced in Vermeulen, 'Op het tapijt gebragt', p. 93 (Bibl., no. 781); inv. no. 002-09-036 also reproduced in L. Blussé and I. Ooms (eds), *Kennis en Compagnie. De Verenigde Oost-Indische Compagnie en de moderne Wetenschap* (Leiden, 2002), p. 6; inv. no. 006-14-005 also reproduced in the catalogue of sea charts, p. 32.

Bibliotheca Publica Latina
Latin Public Library

See 1.2.7

BPL 2030	Descriptions of the coasts of Ceylon and south India, with coloured landfalls of 85 locations, including nos 1-58, 64-73, 85: Mannar, 'Kaimelle' (near Negombo), Adam's Peak, Kalpitiya, Negombo, Colombo, Galkissa (Mount Lavinia), Kalutara, Maggona, Beruwala Island, Alutgama, Bentota, Ambalangoda, Haycock, 'Tottegamme', Ragama, Galle, 'Aardewatte' (Unawatuna?), Weligama, Matara, Dondra, Nilwala, Kudawella, Walawe, 'Mago', Great and Little Basses reefs, 'Agaus', 'Paugamme', 'Sineklattedelle', Batticaloa, Vandeloos Bay, 'Ellentiture', Kottiyar, Trincomalee, Talaimannar, Vembar, Baipar (Vaypar), Punneikayal, Manapadu, 'east and west cape' (Cape Comorin?), Amsterdam Island (Karaitivu) and various unidentified mountains, islands, reefs, etc. (ff. 2-31, 33v-8v, 45), *c.* 1750 (?). One volume.

UNIVERSITEIT UTRECHT, FACULTEIT RUIMTELIJKE WETENSCHAPPEN
UTRECHT UNIVERSITY, FACULTY OF GEOSCIENCES

Main collection

See 1.6.2

VIII G.h.3	Map of Ceylon and the Fishery Coast, with soundings, by G. de l'Isle, published by J. Covens and C. Mortier. Coloured, in French.

Ackersdijck

See 1.6.2

844 Map of Ceylon and the Fishery Coast, with a few geographical remarks, by R. and J. Ottens at Amsterdam. Copper engraving, scale *c.* 1:1,000,000 (50 x 59 cm).

845 Map of Ceylon, with a few geographical remarks, explanatory text in German and view of a European, some Sinhalese and an elephant, mid-eighteenth century (?), by Tobias Conrad Lotter. Copper engraving, coloured, scale *c.* 1:825,000 (50 x 59 cm).

846 Map of Ceylon, with soundings and coats of arms of eleven VOC settlements on Ceylon, made by order of Rijcklof van Goens and edited (?) by David Hill, Professor of Theology at Utrecht, published by Joannes van Keulen at Amsterdam. Copper engraving, coloured, scale *c.* 1:550,000 (58 x 98 cm).

847 Map of Ceylon, by the widow of Esveldt and Holtrop. Copper engraving, coloured, scale *c.* 1:5,000,000 (10 x 13 cm).

UNIVERSITEIT UTRECHT, UNIVERSITEITSBIBLIOTHEEK
UTRECHT UNIVERSITY LIBRARY

Handschriften
Manuscripts

See 1.2.10

Hs. 6.A.23 Descriptions of the coasts, bays and anchorage locations of Ceylon, with 73 coloured landfalls of Mannar, Mannar Channel, Talaimannar, Kalpitiya, 'Kaimelle' (near Negombo), Adam's Peak, Negombo, Colombo, Kalutara, Galkissa (Mount Lavinia), Haycock, Beruwala Island, 'Amellegotte' (Ambalangoda?), 'Tottegamme', Ragama, Galle, 'Aardewatte' (Unawatuna?), Weligama, Matara, Dondra, Nilwala, Kudawella, Walawe, 'Mago', Great and Little Basses reefs, 'Agaus', 'Paugamme', 'Sineklattedelle', Batticaloa, Vandeloos Bay, 'Ellentiture', Kottiyar, Trincomalee and various unidentified mountains, islands, reefs, etc., as well as affixed coloured printed (?) maps of Colombo, Galle and surroundings, bay of Nilwala, bay of 'Aproeretotte' (near Panama), coast south of Batticaloa (not coloured), Vandeloos Bay and the Bay of Trincomalee, with soundings, eighteenth century. One volume.

BIBLIOTHEEK WAGENINGEN UNIVERSITEIT EN RESEARCHCENTRUM
WAGENINGEN UNIVERSITY AND RESEARCH CENTRE LIBRARY

Speciale collecties
Special collections

See 1.6.2

R 362 D 01 d'Acquet collection, mostly consisting of water colours of trees, plants, etc., from all over the world, including South Asia, after specimens in the collection of Hendrik d'Acquet (1632-1706), Burgomaster of Delft, *c.* 1670-1706. Coloured, 149 sheets (*c.* 16 x 20 cm). Described in detail in D.O. Wijnands, 'Planten uit de collectie van Henricus d'Acquet', in J. Kuijlen, C.S. Oldenburger-Ebbers and D.O. Wijnands, *Paradisus Batavus. Bibliografie van plantencatalogi van onderwijstuinen, particuliere tuinen en kwekerscollecties in de Noordelijke en Zuidelijke Nederlanden (1550-1839)* (Wageningen, 1983). Other parts of this collection are kept at the *Universiteit van Amsterdam, Universiteitsbibliotheek* (1.2.2), and the *Koninklijk Instituut voor de Tropen* (1.4.2). Together described in Bergvelt, Jonker and Wiechman, *Burgers verzamelen*, pp. 112-20 (see Supplement I: Bibliography, no. 122) and E. Bergvelt and R. Kistemaker (eds), *De wereld binnen handbereik. Nederlandse kunst- en rariteitenverzamelingen, 1585-1735* (Zwolle, 1992), pp. 223-30. Including:

ff. 21, 124	Plants from Ceylon, 1679, 1681.
f. G (unnumbered)	Leaf skeleton of the *Ficus religiosa* or so-called Buddha tree, on which five insects have been painted, serving as a pilgrimage souvenir (from Ceylon?). For a reproduction and short description, see Bergvelt and Kistemaker, *De wereld binnen handbereik*, p. 145, and the accompanying *Catalogus*, p. 126.

KONINKLIJK INSTITUUT VOOR DE TROPEN (KIT) (Amsterdam)
ROYAL TROPICAL INSTITUTE

Kenniscentrum
Resource Centre

See 1.4.2

RG-84 Drawings of insects (such as beetles, flies, grasshoppers and butterflies), spiders, scorpions, amphibians, reptiles and molluscs from Asia, after specimens in the gallery of Hendrik d'Acquet (1632-1706), Burgomaster of Delft, partly with names of suppliers, *c.* 1680-1710. Coloured, 183 sheets (*c.* 31 x 21 cm). Other parts of this collection are kept at the *Universiteit van Amsterdam, Universiteitsbibliotheek* (1.2.2), and the *Bibliotheek Wageningen Universiteit en Researchcentrum* (1.2.11). Together described in Bergvelt, Jonker and Wiechman, *Burgers verzamelen*, pp. 112-20 (see Supplement I: Bibliography, no. 122) and

E. Bergvelt and R. Kistemaker (eds), *De wereld binnen handbereik. Nederlandse kunst- en rariteitenverzamelingen, 1585-1735* (Zwolle, 1992), pp. 223-30. Including:
part 1, f. 68 Spider from Colombo, 1704.

NEDERLANDS SCHEEPVAARTMUSEUM AMSTERDAM
NETHERLANDS MARITIME MUSEUM AMSTERDAM

Zeevaartkundige collectie
Navigational collection

See 1.6.4

A.3845 (057)	Map of Ceylon, with geographical remarks and print of some Ceylonese and an elephant, published by Nicolaas Johannes Visscher at Amsterdam, *c.* 1698. Partly in Latin, scale 1:300,000 (56 x 67 cm).
A.4692 (15)	Map of Ceylon and the Maldives, with inset depicting Ceylon, probably by Antony de Winter after Nicolas Sanson, *c.* 1700. Engraving, in French (22 x 30 cm).
S.0128	Map of the Indian Ocean, showing in pencil the itinerary of a ship through the waters around Ceylon, by Isaac de Graaf at Amsterdam, *c.* 1740. Manuscript, coloured, scale 1:10,000,000 (71 x 90 cm). Reproduced in Akveld and Jacobs, *De kleurrijke wereld / The Colourful World*, p. 122 (see Supplement I: Bibliography, no. 61), and in E. Jacobs, *Varen om peper en thee. Korte geschiedenis van de Verenigde Oostindische Compagnie / In Pursuit of Pepper and Tea. The Story of the Dutch East India Company* (Zutphen, 1991, 1996), p. 63.

Iconografische collectie
Iconographic collection

See 1.6.4

A.0145 (7 or 13?)	Portrait of Joris van Spilbergen, by A. Stok, *c.* 1620 (?). Print (10 x 8 cm).
A.0145 (179) (9)	Portrait of Governor Gustaaf Willem van Imhoff (1736-40), depicted as Governor-General. Print (52 x 35 cm).
A.1656 (37)	Portrait of Governor Gustaaf Willem van Imhoff, depicted as Governor-General, by P. van Dyk and P. Tanjé, 1745. Print.
A.1656 (38)	Portrait of Governor Gustaaf Willem van Imhoff, depicted as Governor-General, by J. Houbraken. Print.
A-III-204	Landfalls with accompanying texts of various locations, including landfalls of Adam's Peak, Talaimannar,

'Bakenburg' (eastern Mannar Island?), bay of Kalpitiya, and possibly other places on Ceylon, and landfalls with descriptions and sailing instructions of Adam's Peak, Talaimannar, 'Bakenburg', Kalpitiya, Chilaw, 'Caimelle' (near Negombo), Negombo, Colombo, Kalutara, Haycock, Beruwala, Bentota, Alutgama, 'Tottegamme', Ambalangoda, Ragama, Galle, 'Oelewatte', 'Aardewatte' (Unawatuna?), Weligama, Matara, Dondra, Nilwala, 'Calwettij' (Kudawella?), 'Mago', 'Agaus', 'Pauwgamme', 'Sinnekalette', Batticaloa, Vandeloos Bay, Kottiyar, Trincomalee and various unidentified mountains, islands, reefs, etc., by L. Woutersen, 1793. Coloured, one box.

A-III-318 Album containing 80 affixed prints depicting views and maps of cities, probably originally marginal decorations of wall maps, by Frederick de Wit, with index, *c.* 1690. Including:
39 Jaffna.
40 Galle.
64 Tuticorin.
65 Colombo.

S.0597 (0001) Bird's-eye view of the town and Bay of Galle, probably drawn during the homeward journey of the squadron under the command of Jacob Pieter van Braam, 1785. Coloured (44 x 56 cm). Reproduced in Jacobs, *Koopman in Azië*, p. 41 (see Supplement I: Bibliography, no. 104).

Library

See 1.4.4

A-III-278 Nautical guide consisting of sailing instructions and landfalls of locations in Europe, Africa, and the East and West Indies, by Hans N. Lunge, on board various ships, 1756-66, including landfalls of (the surroundings of) Negombo, Adam's Peak, 'Amsterdam Island' (Karaitivu near Ceylon?), Cape Comorin, Manapadu, Talaimannar, house of Bakenburg (eastern Mannar Island), Kalpitiya, Chilaw, 'Kaimelle' (near Negombo), Colombo, Galkissa (Mount Lavinia), 'Bantoera' (Panadura?), Kalutara, Maggona, Beruwala Island, Haycock, Alutgama river (Bentota Ganga?), Ambalangoda, Bentota, 'Tellegamme', Ragama, Galle, 'Oelewatte', 'Aardewatte' (Unawatuna?), Weligama, 'Murezee' (Mirissa?), Matara, Dondra, Nilwala, 'Calwettij' (Kudawella?), 'Magamme', Basses reefs, 'Agaus', 'Pauwgamme', 'Sinecalette', Batticaloa, Vandeloos Bay, 'Ellentijture', Kottiyar, Trincomalee, Point Pedro, 'Moeliwakelle' and various unidentified mountains, islands, reefs, etc., and a map of the bay between Punneikayal and the island of 'Allelande' (near Tuticorin). Coloured, one volume (alternative inv. no. B.0208 (03)).

Page depicting Galle, Haycock and Adam's Peak reproduced in R. Daalder, *Tekenen op zee. Reizende kunstenaars en creatieve zeelieden (1750-2000)* (Amsterdam and Zutphen, 1999), p. 99; page depicting Colombo, Negombo and Adam's Peak reproduced in Akveld and Jacobs, *De kleurrijke wereld / The Colourful World*, p. 123 (see Supplement I: Bibliography, no. 61), and Jacobs, *Koopman in Azië*, p. 50 (Bibl., no. 104).

RIJKSMUSEUM AMSTERDAM
RIJKSMUSEUM AMSTERDAM

Afdeling Nederlandse Geschiedenis
Department of Dutch History

See 1.6.4

NG-20-L	View of Galle (among other locations), by Frederick de Wit, 1700. Originally part of a world map by De Wit, Amsterdam. Engraving (22 x 29 cm).
NG-20-M	View of Jaffna (among other locations), by Frederick de Wit, 1700. Originally part of a world map by De Wit, Amsterdam. Engraving (22 x 29 cm).
NG-362	View of a *stupa* and adjacent buildings at Kelaniya, two hours from Colombo, by Rev. Jan Brandes (1743-1808), 1785. Watercolour (29 x 40 cm).[1,6]
NG-364	View of a white mosque (or temple?) and a grave under a big rock, by Jan Brandes, 1785. Watercolour (20 x 27 cm) (copied from an anonymous work?).[1,6]
NG-365	View of a sanctuary under a rock next to a tank 'near Colombo' (?) (at Mulgirigala?), by Jan Brandes, 1785. Watercolour (26 x 39 cm).[1,6]
NG-377	View of the reception hall in the palace of Kandy, with kneeling VOC officials in front of the King on his throne, the King's guards and the VOC envoy Cornelis de Cock (?) with his retinue, March 1785 (?), by Jan Brandes, *c.* 1785. Watercolour (30 x 27 cm).[1,3,4,5,6]
NG-378	View of Colombo from the north, seen from the sea, including a VOC ship, by Jan Brandes, 1785. Watercolour (26 x 41 cm).[1,5,6]
NG-379	View of Colombo, seen from the Slave Island, by Jan Brandes, *c.* 1785. Watercolour (10 x 75 cm) (copied from an anonymous work?).[1,6]
NG-400-X	View of the city and castle of Colombo, by A. de Nelly or Johannes Rach, second half eighteenth century. Washed Indian ink drawing (32 x 49 cm).[1]

NG-501-72 Map of Ceylon, by Nicolaus Visscher, second half of the seventeenth century. Printed, coloured (49 x 59 cm).

NG-1985-7-1 Album (20 x 17 cm) in which 152 drawings are bound, partly concerning Asia, with (apart from the drawings described below) many depictions of plants and animals that cannot be associated with a particular region, but possibly belong to Ceylon, mostly with explanatory notes, by Jan Brandes.[6] For the second part of the album, see NG-1985-7-2 (below). Including:

-2 Three *Laskars* or Ceylonese soldiers, with another indigenous man and two women, *c.* 1785. Coloured.

-5 Ceylonese butter trader, his assistant and a woman, *c.* 1785. Coloured.[5]

-6 Reformed church and flagpole house at Galle, *c.* 1785.

-8 VOC emblem surrounded by Sinhalese VOC soldiers and servants as well as envoys from the King of Kandy, 1785. Coloured.[1]

-9 *Dissave* of Colombo administering justice at his residence, with 'captains of the Ceylonese people', people seeking justice and a sleeping dog, 1785. Coloured.[4,5]

-10 Group of people awaiting the *Dissave's* administration of justice, and a 'hennikap' (free servant) at Colombo, 1785 (with another drawing). Coloured.[4]

-37 Ceylonese squirrel, 1785. Coloured.[1]

-38 Ceylonese bird, 1785. Coloured.

-39 Ceylonese bird, 1785. Coloured.

-48 Small Ceylonese bird (and four fruits), 1785. Coloured.

-53 Small Ceylonese parrot in various positions, *c.* 1785. Coloured.

-64 Ceylonese coconut tree and a shawm, 1785. Coloured.

-66 Tower at Colombo, 1785. Coloured.

-68 Ceylonese merchant, another man and women or slaves (and female heads with particular hair styles) *c.* 1785. Coloured.

-69 Ceylonese beggars, one of them singing and playing the violin, and a barber, *c.* 1785. Coloured.

-70 Ceylonese 'Rolleway' monkey in various positions, *c.* 1785 (inv. nos NG-1985-7-1-61 and NG-1985-7-2-102 also depict 'Rolleway' monkeys, probably from Ceylon).

-73 Part of flagpole house at Galle, *c.* 1785. Coloured.
-129 Ceylonese sloth (or sluggard), 1786. Coloured.

NG-1985-7-2 Album (20 x 17 cm) in which 146 drawings are bound, partly concerning Asia, with (apart from the drawings described below) many depictions of plants and animals that cannot be associated with a particular region, but possibly belong to Ceylon, mostly with explanatory notes (partly in Swedish), by Jan Brandes.[6] For the first part of the album, see NG-1985-7-1 (above). Including:

-16 Ceylonese tree and the surrounding landscape, *c.* 1785. Coloured.
-17 Group of European men and women (probably including Brandes in black on the right) playing cards near an elephant corral, 1785. Coloured.
-18 Countryhouse of the Count of Randzow (D.D. van Ranzou?) (on Ceylon?), 1758. Coloured.
-23 King Rajadhi Rajasinga of Kandy on the throne, 1785. Coloured.[3]
-24 Tankard of the King of Kandy, made of a shell with silver parts, 1786. Coloured.
-25 Cross-cut of the tankard of the King of Kandy, 1786. Coloured.
-26 Details and ornaments of the tankard of the King of Kandy, 1786.
-27 Stem of the tankard of the King of Kandy, 1786.
-38 Anchored East Indiaman, possibly at Colombo, 1785. Coloured.
-49 Two eating pigs without hind legs at Colombo, 1785. Coloured.
-50 Ox-cart and some Ceylonese, including a police officer, on a road passing by a lake, a house and palm trees, 1785. Coloured.[1,5]
-62 Sketch of the reception of VOC envoys by the King of Kandy, 1785.
-78 Elephant just caught in a bamboo frame between two trees, with the elephant's head on a separate revolving piece of paper affixed with a string, 1786. Coloured.
-79 Part of a deadfall used for catching elephants, and some buildings with spectators and a carriage, 1786. Coloured.
-80 Part of a deadfall used for catching elephants, with a Ceylonese about to lock it, 1786. Coloured.
-81 Large group of Ceylonese with torches and drums putting up running elephants behind a bamboo fence, 1786. Coloured.

-82 Sketch of a herd of running elephants, 1785.
-83 Elephant getting tied up, with three Ceylonese on its back, 1785. Coloured.
-84 Bamboo corral where Ceylonese tie up elephants, 1785. Coloured.
-85 Elephants being taken out from the corral where they have been tied up, 1785. Coloured.
-86 Elephants taken out from the corral and getting further tied up, 1785. Coloured.[1]
-87 Bird's-eye view of elephants getting tied up and washed or baptised, with VOC officials being protected from the sun by servants, 1785. Coloured.[1]
-88 Bamboo framework in which three elephants are tied up, with Ceylonese busy with ropes and washing or baptising one of the elephants, front view, 1785. Coloured.[1]
-89 Bamboo framework in which three elephants are tied up, with Ceylonese busy with ropes, view from behind, 1785. Coloured.[1]
-90 Ceylonese carrying a sun screen, and the screen folded up, with a sketch of the harnessed back of an elephant, 1785. Partly coloured.
-91 Ceylonese on the back of an elephant, 1785.
-92 Two drawings of a Ceylonese standing on and hacking at a lying elephant, views from two sides, 1785. Coloured.
-93 Bamboo framework for keeping elephants, with a Ceylonese holding a staff, 1758.
-94 European travelling in a palanquin through an area with termite hills to 'Jaele' (Galle?), 1785. Coloured.[5]
-95 Young (Ceylonese?) elephant tied to a tree, and some sketches of its head, 1785.
-96 Young (Ceylonese?) elephant, and some sketches of its head and one of its paws, 1785.
-97 Young (Ceylonese?) elephant, and a sketch of its trunk and one of its paws, 1785.
-98 Harnessed (Ceylonese?) elephant standing and lying, with its tamer carrying a staff, 1785. Coloured.
-99 Wild elephant tied between two trees and a Ceylonese with a staff, 1785. Coloured.
-100 VOC officials in a hut watching an elephant hunt, 1785. Coloured.[5]
-101 Bird's-eye view of an elephant corral, 1785. Coloured.

-103	*Thonies* (fishing boats) at Galle, 1786. Coloured.[5]
-104	View of Galle, depicting the *Commandeur's* residence, reformed church, warehouse and Adam's Peak, *c.* 1786. Coloured.[5]
-114	View of Galle fort, *c.* 1786. Coloured.[5]
-115	View of Galle and part of its walls, *c.* 1786.[5]
NG-1985-7-3-123	View of a *stupa* and a small adjacent building at 'Moegerikalle' (Mulgirigala?), and the statues to be found in the *stupa*, by Jan Brandes, *c.* 1785. Brush and pencil drawing, coloured (33 x 41 cm).[6]
NG-1985-7-3-124	Various depictions of the reception of the envoys from Kandy, with Governor Willem Jacob van de Graaff (1785-94) greeting the envoys, portrait of *Mudaliyar* (interpreter) Nicolas Dias Abayasinha Amarasekara (1719-94), Ceylonese flag-bearers, soldiers, guns and musical instruments, by Jan Brandes, *c.* 1785. Brush and pencil drawing, coloured (33 x 42 cm).[4,6]
NG-1985-7-3-125	View of a dark space with a large lying statue (reclining Buddha?) and some Ceylonese, close to Colombo, by Jan Brandes, 1785. Brush and pencil drawing, coloured (21 x 33 cm).[6]
NG-1985-7-3-126	View of the front of the royal palace at Kandy, guarded by soldiers, by Jan Brandes, 1785. Pen and pencil drawing (51 x 33 cm).[6]
NG-1985-7-3-127	View of the reception of the envoys of Kandy by high VOC officials and an interpreter standing around a table, with captions referring to those present, by Jan Brandes, 1785. Brush and pencil drawing, coloured (33 x 42 cm).[4,6]
NG-1985-7-3-128	Various depictions of VOC envoys at the annual audience in Kandy, with captions, by Jan Brandes, 1785. Pencil drawing (52 x 38 cm).[6]
NG-1996-6	117 depictions concerning Ceylon, including portraits of Ceylonese people and VOC servants, street scenes, interiors and animals (including elephants and crocodiles), with some notes, by Esaias Boursse, *c.* 1670. One volume, graphite, chalk and brush drawings, coloured (16 x 21 cm).
SK-A-3103	Portrait of Gerard Pietersz Hulft, Commander of the troops sent to Ceylon and envoy to Kandy in 1655-6 (?), by Govert Flinck, 1654. Canvas (130 x 103 cm).[1]
SK-A-3765	Portrait of Governor Joan Maetsuyker (1646-50), depicted as Governor-General, by Jacob Jansz Coeman, *c.* 1670. Panel (98 x 78 cm).[1,2] (SK-A-4535 is a copy. Panel, 33 x 25 cm.)
SK-A-3766	Portrait of Governor Rijcklof van Goens Senior (1662-3, 1665-75), depicted as Governor-General, attributed to

	Martin Palin, *c.* 1680. Panel (98 x 79 cm).[1,2] (SK-A-4536 is a copy. Panel, 33 x 25 cm.)
SK-A-3780	Portrait of Governor Gustaaf Willem Baron van Imhoff (1736-40), depicted as Governor-General, copy after Philip van Dijk and Jan Maurits Quinkhard, *c.* 1745. Brass (110 x 93 cm).[2] See also no. SK-A-4549, below.
SK-A-4162	Portrait of Isaac de l'Ostal de Saint-Martin (1629-96), serving on Ceylon in the 1660s, attributed to Jan de Baen. Canvas (132 x 102 cm).
SK-A-4549	Portrait of Governor Gustaaf Willem Baron van Imhoff (1736-40), depicted as Governor-General, by Jan Maurits Quinkhard, 1742. Copper (34 x 27 cm).[2] See also no. SK-A-3780, above.

[1] Described and reproduced in R.K. de Silva and W.G.M. Beumer, *Illustrations and Views of Dutch Ceylon, 1602-1796. A Comprehensive Work of Pictorial Reference with Selected Eye-witness Accounts* (Leiden, 1988), pp. 200-1, 233-5, 267, 343, 350, 395, 401, 412-15, 431, 435-6; inv. no. SK-A-3103 also described and reproduced in Akveld and Jacobs, *De kleurrijke wereld / The Colourful World*, pp. 124-5 (see Supplement I: Bibliography, no. 61); inv. nos NG-362, NG-377, NG-1985-7-1-8, NG-1985-7-2-86 & 87 and SK-A-3103 also described and reproduced in Zandvliet, *De Nederlandse ontmoeting met Azië / The Dutch Encounter with Asia*, pp. 156, 160-1, 254-62 (Bibl., no. 98); inv. no. SK-A-3766 also reproduced in Van Goor, 'De V.O.C. op Ceylon', p. 23 (Bibl., no. 547); inv. nos NG-377 and NG-1985-7-2-87 also reproduced in Jacobs, *Koopman in Azië*, pp. 39, 45 (Bibl., no. 104); inv. nos NG-1985-7-2-88 & 89 also reproduced in Gaastra, 'Ceylon als "handelscomptoir"', p. 34 (Bibl., no. 534); inv. nos NG-1985-7-1-8 and NG-1985-7-2-88 & 89 also reproduced in H. Visser, 'Jan Brandes, de Lutherse predikant-tekenaar', *Bulletin van het Rijksmuseum*, 34, 2 (1986), pp. 73, 75.

[2] Described in J. de Loos-Haaxman, *De landsverzameling schilderijen in Batavia*, 2 vols (Leiden, 1941), and F.W. Stapel, *De gouverneurs-generaal van Nederlandsch-Indië in beeld en woord* (The Hague, 1941); inv. no. SK-A-3780 also described and reproduced in Zandvliet, *De Nederlandse ontmoeting met Azië / The Dutch Encounter with Asia*, pp. 82-3 (see Supplement I: Bibliography, no. 98), Stevens, *De VOC in bedrijf / Dutch Enterprise and the VOC*, p. 34 (Bibl., no. 85), and H. Stevens, 'De VOC-galerij in het Rijksmuseum: een vroeg-modern bedrijf tentoongesteld', *Bulletin van het Rijksmuseum*, 43, 4 (1995), p. 267.

[3] Described and reproduced in Akveld and Jacobs, *De kleurrijke wereld / The Colourful World*, pp. 126-9 (see Supplement I: Bibliography, no. 61); inv. no. NG-1985-7-2-23 also described and reproduced in Zandvliet, *De Nederlandse ontmoeting met Azië / The Dutch Encounter with Asia*, pp. 256-7 (Bibl., no. 98).

[4] Described and reproduced in G.P. Sanders, 'Joan Aalwis Widjejewarddene Senewiratne en *de uijtgebreidheid van een mostaart Zaatje*. Een Ceylonese beloningspenning uitgereikt door de Verenigde Oostindische Compagnie in 1762', *Bulletin van het Rijksmuseum*, 42, 1 (1994), pp. 18, 20-1, 30-1; inv. nos NG-1985-7-1-9 & 10 also reproduced in Vroom, 'Jan Brandes' (see Supplement I: Bibliography, no. 804); inv. no. NG-1985-7-1-9 also reproduced in Van den Horst and Hovy, 'Recht en rechtspraak', p. 46 (Bibl., no. 562); inv. no. NG-1985-7-3-124 also described and reproduced in Zandvliet, *De Nederlandse ontmoeting met Azië / The Dutch Encounter with Asia*, pp. 257-9 (Bibl., no. 98); inv. no. NG-1985-7-3-127 also reproduced in Schrikker, 'Een ongelijke strijd?', p. 380 (with erroneous reference to the inv. no.) (Bibl., no. 729).

[5] Described and reproduced in L. Wagenaar, *Galle: VOC-vestiging in Ceylon. Beschrijving van een koloniale samenleving aan de vooravond van de Singalese opstand tegen het Nederlandse gezag, 1760* (Amsterdam, 1994), pp. 18-19, 42, 71, 73, 81, 117, 120, 169.

[6] A substantial part of the works by Brandes is described and reproduced in De Bruijn and Raben, *The World of Jan Brandes 1743-1808* (see Supplement I: Bibliography, no. 125).

Rijksprentenkabinet
Print Room

See 1.6.4

Frederik Muller no. 1854	Elephant called Hanske (or Hansken, not to be confused with the elephant Hans), shipped from Ceylon to the Dutch Republic in 1630, with 16 insets showing Hanske doing tricks, with short poems. Engraving (30 x 38 cm). Described and reproduced in Slatkes, 'Rembrandt's Elephant' (see Supplement I: Bibliography, no. 739) and P. Schatborn, "Beesten nae 't leven", *De Kroniek van het Rembrandthuis*, 29, 2 (1977), p. 20.
RP-P-1886-A-10499	Reception of three ambassadors from Kandy by Governor Falck, by Chirurgeon Carl Friedrich Reimer, 1772. Engraving (31 x 44 cm) (Frederik Muller no. 4271B).
RP-P-1909-1658	View of the pearl fishery off the coast of Tuticorin, by Jan Caspar Philips, 1730. Etching (18 x 29 cm).
RP-P-OB-12.952	Sea battle between the British and the French in the Ceylonese waters in May 1783, by Reinier Nooms, *c.* early nineteenth century. Etching (9 x 21 cm).
RP-P-OB-47.381 (topo. col.)	Map of the Maldives and part of Ceylon, with some ships, *c.* 1550-1650. Coloured, engraving (9 x 12 cm).
RP-P-OB-47.453	View of the fort at Colombo from the north, with a VOC ship, by Chirurgeon Carl Friedrich Reimer, *c.* 1772-5 (?). Etching (18 x 41 cm).[1]
RP-P-OB-67.337	Portrait of Governor Joan Maetsuyker (1646-50), depicted as Governor-General, by Jacobus van der Schley. Engraving.
RP-P-OB-67.341	Portrait of Governor Rijcklof van Goens Senior (1662-3, 1665-75), depicted as Governor-General, by Jacobus van der Schley. Engraving.
RP-P-OB-67.353	Portrait of Governor Gustaaf Willem van Imhoff (1736-40), depicted as Governor-General, by Jacobus van der Schley. Engraving.
RP-T-00-829	View of Galle, from Haycock to Unawatuna, seen from the sea, by Pieter Cornelisz de Bevere, *c.* 1753-5 (?). Indian ink drawing (21 x 82 cm).[1]
RP-T-00-830	View of Colombo, seen from the sea, by Pieter Cornelisz de Bevere, 1755. Indian ink drawing (20 x 29 cm).[1,3]
RP-T-00-898	Women of the Velala community at Jaffna

	making butter, by Jean Covitré, eighteenth century. Pen and brush drawing (15 x 20 cm).
RP-T-00-899	Men of the Velala community at Jaffna, engaged in farming, by Jean Covitré, eighteenth century. Pen and brush drawing (18 x 24 cm).
RP-T-00-913 (topo. col.)	View of the ferry and reinforcement of the Grote Pas ('great narrows') of 'Nagalagam' at the Kelani River, possibly by Pieter Cornelisz de Bevere or Balthus Jacobsz van Lier, mid-eighteenth century. Water colour (35 x 45 cm).[1,2,3]
RP-T-00-914 (topo. col.)	View of the fort at Kalutara, seen from the north across the Kalu Ganga, possibly by Pieter Cornelisz de Bevere or Balthus Jacobsz van Lier, mid-eighteenth century. Water colour (35 x 51 cm).[1,2]
RP-T-00-915	View of Governor Joan Gideon Loten and his company fishing in the river at Negombo, by Pieter Cornelisz de Bevere, *c.* 1754. Indian ink drawing (24 x 37 cm).[1,2,3]
RP-T-00-3226 (topo. col.)	View of the fort at Matara, seen from the Nilwala River, second half eighteenth century. Water colour (19 x 31 cm).[1,3]
RP-T-00-3247 (topo. col.)	View of the country house of the Governor at the Grote Pas ('great narrows') near Colombo, possibly by Pieter Cornelisz de Bevere or Balthus Jacobsz van Lier, mid-eighteenth century. Water colour (32 x 52 cm).[1,2]
RP-T-00-3248 (topo. col.)	View of the fort at Kalutara, seen from the south, possibly by Pieter Cornelisz de Bevere or Balthus Jacobsz van Lier, mid-eighteenth century. Water colour (32 x 48 cm).[1,2,3]
RP-T-00-3249 (topo. col.)	View of the fort at Negombo, seen from the river, 1753. Water colour (30 x 53 cm).[1]
RP-T-00-3250 (topo. col.)	View of the country house De Uytvlught at Beira Lake in Colombo, with several Sinhalese and Europeans, possibly by Balthus Jacobsz van Lier or Pieter Cornelisz de Bevere, *c.* 1755. Water colour (40 x 70 cm).[1,2]
RP-T-00-3251 (topo. col.)	View of the Baygam area, north of Matara, second half eighteenth century. Water colour (44 x 64 cm).[1,2]
RP-T-1898-A-3698	Four Ceylonese birds, by A. Schouman, eighteenth century. Water colour.
RP-T-1902-A-4661	View of the square at the fort of Jaffna, by C. Steiger, *c.* 1706. Water colour (29 x 49 cm).[1]
RP-T-1902-A-4662	View of the castle at Colombo, seen from the

	'de Beer' sluice, by C. Steiger, *c.* 1706. Water colour (34 x 50 cm).[1]
RP-T-1902-A-4663	View of Colombo, seen from the roadstead, by C. Steiger, *c.* 1706. Water colour (34 x 50 cm).[1,3]
RP-T-1902-A-4664	View of the interior of the church at Jaffna, seen from the south side, by C. Steiger, *c.* 1706. Water colour (24 x 27 cm).[1]
RP-T-1902-A-4665	View of the fort Hammenhiel, seen from the sea, by C. Steiger, *c.* 1706. Water colour (28 x 45 cm).[1]
RP-T-1902-A-4666	View of the fort Hammenhiel, seen from the quay, by C. Steiger, *c.* 1706. Water colour (29 x 44 cm).[1]
RP-T-1902-A-4667	View of Mannar, seen from the mainland, by C. Steiger, *c.* 1706. Water colour (28 x 45 cm).[1]
RP-T-1902-A-4668	View of the fort at Kalutara, seen from the river side, by C. Steiger, *c.* 1706. Water colour (24 x 43 cm).[1,2]
RP-T-1902-A-4669	View of Galle, seen from the land road, by C. Steiger, *c.* 1706. Water colour (34 x 50 cm).[1,3]
RP-T-1902-A-4670	View of the fort at Jaffna, seen from the land side, by C. Steiger, *c.* 1706. Water colour (37 x 48 cm).[1]
RP-T-1902-A-4671	View of the Governor's residence at Colombo, seen from the back garden, by C. Steiger, *c.* 1706. Water colour (27 x 44 cm).[1]
RP-T-1904-18	Reception of three ambassadors from Kandy by Governor Falck, by Chirurgeon Carl Friedrich Reimer, 1772. Water colour (28 x 43 cm).[1,3]

[1] Described and reproduced in R.K. de Silva and W.G.M. Beumer, *Illustrations and Views of Dutch Ceylon, 1602-1796. A Comprehensive Work of Pictorial Reference with Selected Eye-witness Accounts* (Leiden, 1988), pp. 159, 170-1, 177, 203, 207, 213, 225, 233-4, 239, 241, 269, 273-4, 288, 295-6, 299, 306-7, 315; inv. nos RP-T-1902-A-4661 to 4671 also partly reproduced in 'In the days of the Dutch in Ceylon' (see Supplement I: Bibliography, no. 563), and Reimers, 'Early Dutch Views of Ceylon' (Bibl., no. 712); inv. nos RP-T-1902-A-4661, 4664, 4666 & 4671 and RP-T-1904-18 also reproduced in Temminck Groll a.o., *The Dutch Overseas*, pp. 249, 257, 259 (Bibl., no. 87); inv. nos RP-T-00-3226 and RP-T-1904-18 also reproduced in G.P. Sanders, 'Joan Aalwis Widjejewarddene Senewiratne en *de uijtgebreidheid van een mostaart Zaatje*. Een Ceylonese beloningspenning uitgereikt door de Verenigde Oostindische Compagnie in 1762', *Bulletin van het Rijksmuseum*, 42, 1 (1994), pp. 27, 29; inv. no. RP-T-00-3226 also reproduced in Paranavitana and De Silva, *Maps and Plans of Dutch Ceylon*, p. 124 (Bibl., no. 655); inv. nos RP-T-1902-A-4661 and RP-T-1904-18 also described and reproduced in Akveld and Jacobs, *De kleurrijke wereld / The Colourful World*, pp. 120-1, 133-4 (Bibl., no. 61); inv. nos RP-T-00-3247, RP-T-1902-A-4662 & 4667 also reproduced in Putten, *Ambitie en onvermogen*, pp. 88-9, 134-5 (Bibl., no. 83); inv. no. RP-T-00-915, RP-T-00-3250 and RP-T-1904-18 also reproduced and described in Zandvliet, *De Nederlandse ontmoeting met Azië / The Dutch Encounter with Asia*, pp. 130-1, 235-6 (Bibl., no. 98); inv. no. RP-T-1902-A-4671 also reproduced in Van Goor, 'De V.O.C. op Ceylon', p. 23 (Bibl., no. 547); inv. no. RP-T-00-913 also reproduced in Jacobs, *Koopman in Azië*, p. 42 (Bibl.,

no. 104); RP-T-1904-18 also described in Terwen-de Loos, *Nederlandse schilders en tekenaars*, p. 22 (Bibl., no. 153).

[2] Described and reproduced in J.R. van Diessen and A. van den Belt (eds), 'Een toelichting op zes topografische aquarellen van Ceylon in het Prentenkabinet', *Bulletin van het Rijksmuseum*, 35 (1987); inv. no. RP-T-00-3251 also reproduced in P. van Mil and M. Scharloo, *De VOC in de kaart gekeken. Cartografie en navigatie van de Verenigde Oostindische Compagnie 1602-1799* (The Hague, 1988), p. 12.

[3] Described and reproduced in L. Wagenaar, *Galle: VOC-vestiging in Ceylon. Beschrijving van een koloniale samenleving aan de vooravond van de Singalese opstand tegen het Nederlandse gezag, 1760* (Amsterdam, 1994), pp. 16, 23, 26, 70, 108, 131, 151, 156, 167, 171, 176.

TEYLERS MUSEUM (Haarlem)
TEYLER'S MUSEUM

Kunstverzameling
Art collection

See 1.6.4

(a) Depictions of 13 Ceylonese birds and a plant, in all probability by Pieter Cornelisz de Bevere (1722-81?), by order of Governor Joan Gideon Loten (1752-7), 1750s. 12 water colours (*c.* 30 x 20 cm). This collection is apparently incomplete.[1] Other parts of the original collection are kept at another department of the *Teylers Museum* (see below), in the *Rijksmuseum Amsterdam* (see 1.6.4) and in the Natural History Museum at London.

[1] Information kindly provided by Alexander Raat.

Natuurwetenschappelijke Bibliotheek
Scientific Library

See 1.6.4

(a) Depictions of naturalia from Ceylon, Java and Makassar (with a manuscript concerning Makassar), including Ceylonese plants, fruit (referred to as 'Godha Para'), crustaceans, birds and a langur (monkey, referred to as 'Rolleway' or 'Wandoera'), by Pieter Cornelisz de Bevere (1722-81?) and Joan Gideon Loten (Governor of Ceylon 1752-5) among others, put together by Loten, 1732-69. Coloured, 37 numbered and unnumbered drawings, water colours and engravings in one box.[1] Described and partly reproduced in Sliggers and Besselink, *Het verdwenen museum*, pp. 84-9, 135 (see Supplement I: Bibliography, no. 152), and R.K. de Silva and W.G.M. Beumer, *Illustrations and Views of Dutch Ceylon, 1602-1796. A Comprehensive Work of Pictorial Reference with Selected Eye-witness Accounts* (Leiden, 1988), p. 397. Other parts (or copies) of the original collection are kept at another department of the *Teylers Museum* (see above), in the *Rijksmuseum Amsterdam* (see 1.6.4) and in the Natural History Museum at London.

[1] Information kindly provided by Alexander Raat.

KONINKLIJKE BIBLIOTHEEK (KB) (The Hague)
ROYAL LIBRARY

Oude drukken
Early printed works

See 1.4.12

17332 Portrait of Governor Gustaaf Willem van Imhoff (1736-40), with coat of arms, by J.C. Philips and H. Besseling, belonging to a homage to Van Imhoff in his capacity as Governor-General, by Dikaiophilus, 1742. One quire (17 x 12 cm).

KONINKLIJK INSTITUUT VOOR TAAL-, LAND- EN VOLKENKUNDE (KITLV) (Leiden)
ROYAL INSTITUTE OF LINGUISTICS AND ANTHROPOLOGY

Maps

See 1.6.4

A 23,4 Map of Ceylon, showing its mountains, rivers, ports, provinces, cinnamon areas, towns and forts in 1666, drawn in Batavia in 1670, and copied at Middelburg in 1683 by Johan Roggeveen. Black and white photographic reproduction.

Images

See 1.6.4

36 C-13 View of Adam's Peak (Haycock?) from the Bay of Galle, by H.B. Hoppenstok, *c.* 1816. Pen drawing (9 x 14 cm).[1]

36 C-362 Profile (and coat of arms?) of Governor Gustaaf Willem van Imhoff (1736-40), 1742. Engraving (20 x 16 cm).

36 C-363 Portrait of Governor Gustaaf Willem van Imhoff, depicted as Governor-General, by Mij and Bleyswyck, with Dutch poem by Henr. Snakenburg, *c.* 1745. Engraving (20 x 16 cm). Reproduced in F.S. Gaastra, 'Succesvol ondernemerschap, falend bestuur? Het beleid van de bewindhebbers van de VOC, 1602-1795', in L. Blussé and I. Ooms, *Kennis en Compagnie. De Verenigde Oost-Indische Compagnie en de moderne Wetenschappen* (Leiden, 2002), p. 64.

36 C-367 Portrait of Governor Joan Maetsuyker (1646-50), depicted as Governor-General, by Buys and Vinkeles, 1790. Engraving (17 x 9 cm).

36 D-15 Portrait of Governor Gustaaf Willem van Imhoff, depicted as Governor-General, with French caption, by Zuinkhard and Houbraken, published by F. Changuion at Amsterdam, *c.* 1742. Copper engraving (14 x 9 cm).

37 B-619 Portrait of Governor Rijcklof van Goens Senior (1662-3, 1665-75), depicted as Governor-General, by Balen, *c.* 1750. Engraving (32 x 21 cm).

37 B-622 Portrait of Governor Joan Maetsuyker, depicted as Governor-General, by Balen and Iongman (Dirk Jongman?), *c.* 1750. Engraving (30 x 19 cm).

37 C-13 View of the roadstead of Galle, with some Dutch and Ceylonese vessels in the foreground, *c.* 1750. Engraving (20 x 29 cm).

47 A-2 Portrait of Governor Gustaaf Willem van Imhoff, depicted as Governor-General, by Dijk and Tanjé, 1745. Engraving (47 x 35 cm). Proof, see 47 A-3.

47 A-3 Portrait of Governor Gustaaf Willem van Imhoff, depicted as Governor-General, by Dijk and Tanjé, 1745. Engraving (50 x 33 cm). See 47 A-2.

47 A-7 Portrait of Governor Gustaaf Willem van Imhoff, depicted as Governor-General, by Zuinkhard and Houbraken, published by Isaac Tirion at Amsterdam, 1742. Engraving (37 x 24 cm).

48 M-7 View of the new hospital of Colombo from the north, possibly by Johannes Rach or Carl Friedrich Reimer, *c.* 1800. Water colour (42 x 55 cm).[1]

48 M-8 View of the new hospital of Colombo from the south, possibly by Johannes Rach or Carl Friedrich Reimer, *c.* 1800. Water colour (41 x 54 cm).[1]

[1] Reproduced and described in R.K. de Silva and W.G.M. Beumer, *Illustrations and Views of Dutch Ceylon, 1602-1796. A Comprehensive Work of Pictorial Reference with Selected Eye-witness Accounts* (Leiden, 1988), pp. 170, 248, 251; inv. no. 48 M-7 also reproduced in Gaastra, *De geschiedenis van de VOC*, p. 93 (see Supplement I: Bibliography, no. 71); inv. no. 48 M-8 also reproduced in Temminck Groll a.o., *The Dutch Overseas*, p. 250 (Bibl., no. 87).

Collectie in westerse talen
Collection in Western languages

See 1.4.14

H 47 Daily record by Governor Gerrit de Heere of Ceylon of his journey to Galle, Jaffna and other places, 1698. With coloured maps, plans and views by engineer J.C. Toorzee of the surroundings of Colombo (31 x 38 cm);[1] Negombo; Hanwella; Kalutara (water colour, 39 x 33 cm);[1,2] *Commandement* (district) of Galle;[1] Galle; constructions in the Gintota river; Matara (31 x 65 cm);[1] Katuwana; coast between Batticaloa and Trincomalee; Batticaloa; Trincomalee, with two insets depicting views from the sea (water colours, 17 x 35 cm);[1,2] Fort Oostenburg; Bay of Trincomalee (two parts); northern Ceylon including the Jaffna peninsula, Vanni up to Mannar Island and Kalpitiya (31 x 22 cm);[1] Jaffna; surveys of land plots near Jaffna (52 x 70 cm);[1,3] redoubts Pijl, Beschutter and Eliphant (east Vanni); Pooneryn; Hammenhiel; tank of 'Catchaij'; Mannar and Kalpitiya.

H 656 Inscription on the so-called grave of Adam and Eve, on the island of 'Samara' (Ceylon?), 22 miles from Colombo, with an explanation in Dutch, eighteenth century. One piece.

[1] Reproduced and described in Paranavitana and De Silva, *Maps and Plans of Dutch Ceylon*, pp. 88, 104, 119, 125, 136, 143, 147 (see Supplement I: Bibliography, no. 655).

[2] Reproduced and described in R.K. de Silva and W.G.M. Beumer, *Illustrations and Views of Dutch Ceylon, 1602-1796. A Comprehensive Work of Pictorial Reference with Selected Eye-witness Accounts* (Leiden, 1988), pp. 142, 204.

[3] Reproduced in Zandvliet, *Mapping for Money*, p. 153 (see Supplement I: Bibliography, no. 96).

NATIONAAL HERBARIUM NEDERLAND - UNIVERSITEIT LEIDEN
NATIONAL HERBARIUM OF THE NETHERLANDS - LEIDEN UNIVERSITY

Herbarium collection

See 1.6.4

(a) 'Herbar. Vivus Ceylonens', 157 sheets (54 x 31 cm) in two volumes with specimens of Ceylonese plants, collected by Paul Hermann in the second half of the seventeenth century, with names in Latin and often in Sinhalese or Tamil script. Described and partly reproduced in Oostroom, 'Hermann's Collection of Ceylon Plants' (see Supplement I: Bibliography, no. 650), and Baas, 'De VOC in Flora's Lusthoven', p. 128 (Bibl., no. 120). With two volumes containing surveys and indices of the specimens, one compiled by David van Royen in the eighteenth century.

NATURALIS, NATIONAAL NATUURHISTORISCH MUSEUM (Leiden)
NATURALIS, NATIONAL MUSEUM OF NATURAL HISTORY

Prentencollectie
Print collection

See 1.6.4

S 31 194 Depictions of two Ceylonese elephants called Hans and Parkie (the latter also known as Greetje, the former not to be confused with the elephant Hanske), by the Physician Petrus Camper (1722-89), 1786. Red chalk or crayon drawings, one sheet (*c.* 21 x 32 cm). Reproduced and described in Bruggen and Pieters, 'Notes on a Drawing of Indian Elephants' (see Supplement I: Bibliography, no. 480). A contemporary copy is kept at the *Universiteit van Amsterdam, Plantage Bibliotheek* (see 4.4).

RIJKSMUSEUM VOOR VOLKENKUNDE (Leiden)
NATIONAL MUSEUM OF ETHNOLOGY

Papiercollectie
Paper collection

See 1.4.18

5964-1 View of a five-year old Ceylonese elephant (shipped to Japan by the British, donated to the Japanese authorities by the Dutch) and his two attendants (probably also from Ceylon) with the Bay of Nagasaki in the background, by Watanabe Kakushu (1778-1830), *c.* 1813. Ink and pigments on silk, coloured (42 x 56 cm). Described and reproduced in Forrer, 'Vijfjarige Ceylonese olifant' (see Supplement I: Bibliography, no. 533).

ZEEUWS MUSEUM (Middelburg)
ZEELAND MUSEUM

Collectie Koninklijk Zeeuwsch Genootschap der Wetenschappen
Royal Zeeland Society of Sciences collection

See 1.4.20

G 1645 Portrait of Governor Stephanus Versluys (1729-32), with Galle in the background, 1729. Coloured, oil on canvas (98 x 70 cm) (no. 8 in an inventory of 1961). Described and reproduced in J. de Loos-Haaxman, 'Het portret van Stephanus Versluys, Gouverneur en Directeur van Ceylon', *Tijdschrift voor Indische taal-, land- en volkenkunde*, 83 (1949) and R.K. de Silva and W.G.M. Beumer, *Illustrations and Views of Dutch Ceylon, 1602-1796. A Comprehensive Work of Pictorial Reference with Selected Eye-witness Accounts* (Leiden, 1988), p. 439.

ATLAS VAN STOLK (Rotterdam)
VAN STOLK ATLAS

Atlas van Stolk

See 1.6.4

Supplement anno 1772 — Reception of three ambassadors from Kandy by Governor Falck, by Chirurgeon Carl Friedrich Reimer, 1772. Engraving. Described and reproduced in R.K. de Silva and W.G.M. Beumer, *Illustrations and Views of Dutch Ceylon, 1602-1796. A Comprehensive Work of Pictorial Reference with Selected Eye-witness Accounts* (Leiden, 1988), p. 276.

Top. Ceylon (1995-55) — Map of Ceylon, published by Isaak Tirion, mid-eighteenth century.

Top. Ceylon roltekening Dose — View of the procession of three ambassadors of Kandy on their way to the VOC Governor at Colombo, accompanied by Dutch troops including VOC officials Jan Hendrik Borwater

(*Fiscaal*), Van Kleef (?), D. Burnat and A. Moens, with inset showing the ambassadors, their clothing, a Sinhalese coolie and Burnat, Borwater and Moens, with legend, by A. Dose after Guyard, *c.* 1766 (?). Coloured manuscript drawing, partly in French (12 x 253 cm). Reproduced and described in L. Wagenaar, *Galle: VOC-vestiging in Ceylon. Beschrijving van een koloniale samenleving aan de vooravond van de Singalese opstand tegen het Nederlandse gezag, 1760* (Amsterdam, 1994), p. 21, and *Bulletin Historisch Museüm Rotterdam*, 4 (1992).

CENTRALE BIBLIOTHEEK ROTTERDAM
CENTRAL LIBRARY OF ROTTERDAM

Maps

See 1.6.4

86 L 7 Map of Ceylon, by Tobias Conradus Lotterus, with notes in German and Dutch, eighteenth century (?). Printed, coloured.

86 L 8 Map of the fort and town of Colombo, with insets of Anguruwatota (north-east of Kalutara), Kalpitiya, Sitawake, Kalutara, Hanwella, 'Koudangelle' (north-east of Anguruwatota), 'Maluane' and Walcheren, 1688. Manuscript, coloured.

86 L 9 Map of Galle, undated. Manuscript, coloured.

MARITIEM MUSEUM ROTTERDAM
MARITIME MUSEUM ROTTERDAM

Cartografische collectie
Cartographic collection

See 1.6.4

CdJ854 Map of Ceylon, published by Johannes van Keulen. Engraving.

K120 Map of Ceylon, by Nicolaas Visscher, Amsterdam. Printed.

Picturalia
Pictures

See 1.6.4

P117A-B Identical portraits of Gerard Hulft (1621-56), Commander of the troops sent to Ceylon and envoy to Kandy in 1655-6 (?), by Abraham Bloteling, *c.* 1656. Two engravings.

P120 Portrait of Governor Gustaaf Willem van Imhoff (1736-40), depicted as Governor-General, with family arms, by J. Houbraken, 1742. Engraving.

P2255 Portrait of Governor Gustaaf Willem van Imhoff, depicted as Governor-General. Water colour (27 x 21 cm?).

P2635 View of Colombo, *c.* 1800 (?). Engraving.

P2732 Portrait of Governor Rijcklof van Goens, depicted as Governor-General. Painting (42 x 34 cm).

P2842 View of the naval battle between the British and the French near Trincomalee, 1782. Oil painting (*c.* 145 x 241 cm).

MUSEUM BOIJMANS VAN BEUNINGEN (Rotterdam)
BOIJMANS VAN BEUNINGEN MUSEUM

Prentenkabinet
Print Room

See 1.6.4

JPK 1 (PK) Portrait of Rijcklof van Goens Senior, depicted as Governor-General, with his wife Jacobena Bartholomeusz, his two sons, including Rijcklof van Goens Junior (14 years old, on the right), and a servant, by Johan Philips Koelman (1818-93), nineteenth century. Water colour (28 x 38 cm). Copy of a painting made by Bartholomeus van der Helst (1613-70) in 1656, which burnt up in 1864. Copy reproduced in G.D. Winius and M.P.M. Vink, *The Merchant-Warrior Pacified. The VOC (The Dutch East India Co.) and its Changing Political Economy in India* (Delhi, 1991), between pp. 86-7.

5. COROMANDEL

5.1. Government Archives

GEMEENTEARCHIEF AMSTERDAM
MUNICIPAL ARCHIVES OF AMSTERDAM

Weeskamer en Commissie van Liquidatie der zaken van de voormalige weeskamer
Orphan Board and Commission of Liquidation of the affairs of the former orphan board

See 1.1.2
Access no.: 5073

188 Papers received from the trustees at Coromandel, 1699-1792 (Nagappattinam, 1699-1784, and Pulicat, 1787-92). One bundle.
189 Copies of papers received from the trustees at Coromandel, 1699-1787 (Nagappattinam, 1699-1784, and Pulicat, 1787). One folder.
200 Papers received from the trustees at Nagappattinam, 1683-1700. One folder.
201 Papers received from the trustees at Pulicat, 1648-88. One bundle.
202 Copies of papers received from the trustees at Pulicat, 1686. One folder.
209 Papers received from private persons in various places in Asia and the Cape of Good Hope, 1687-1789, including Nagappattinam, 1721. One bundle.
251 Papers sent to the trustees at Nagappattinam, 1694-1751. One folder.
252 Papers sent to the trustees at Pulicat, 1693. One folder.

Notarissen ter standplaats Amsterdam
Notaries at Amsterdam

See 1.1.2
Access no.: 5075

Geographical names on index cards found under some of the more obvious headings in the modern indices:

Bimlipatam	2 index cards (1708).
Coromandel	22 index cards (1623-1773).
Fort St. George	1 index card (1707).
Golkonda	3 index cards (1670, 1705).
Kanchipuram	4 index cards (1707).
Madras	3 index cards (1713-69).
Masulipatam	6 index cards (1701-10).
Nagappattinam	12 index cards (1702-10, 1765).

Pondicherry	1 index card (1760).
Pulicat	12 index cards (1701-8).
Tranquebar	2 index cards (1724-60).

Handschriften
Manuscripts

See 1.1.2
Access no.: 5059

10 Various papers concerning the VOC, with many references to South Asia, originating from Huydekoper, 1726-84. One bundle. Including:
   (a) Consideration concerning British demands, in particular with respect to Nagappattinam, eighteenth century (?). Printed.

11 Various papers concerning the VOC, with many references to South Asia, originating from Huydekoper, 1785-1802. One bundle. Including:
   (a) Considerations of a *Hoofdparticipant* (principal shareholder) of the VOC concerning the possession of Nagappattinam, *c.* 1788.

GELDERS ARCHIEF (Arnhem)
ARCHIVES OF GUELDERLAND

Bosch and Van Rosenthal families and relatives

See 1.1.3
Access no.: 0724

16 Deed, in which Lucas Bosch states in the presence of Daniel Cartié, Secretary at Nagappattinam, that the sealed will of himself and his deceased wife Angenita Nolet (d. 1678) dating from 1676 is opened, 1679. One piece.

Brantsen family

See 1.1.3
Access no.: 0452

285 A 1 Extracts from papers concerning Jacob Mossel, including: marriage register of Coromandel, 1730; book of deeds of the Coromandel church, confirming Mossel as member, 1730; baptismal register of Nagappattinam, concerning Mossel's son, 1739. One folder.

285 B Funeral oration, funeral song, epitaph and other related documents concerning Adriana Appels who passed away at Nagappattinam in June 1743. Partly printed, one folder. Partly published in Peters and André de la Porte, *In steen geschreven*, pp. 105-7 (see Supplement I: Bibliography, no. 848).

286 A Deed of appointment of Jacob Mossel as Governor of Coromandel, 1738. One piece.

287 B Deed of appointment of Adriaan Pla as Governor of Coromandel, 1729, with annex and papers concerning his salary as merchant and chief-merchant, 1721, 1728. One folder and one piece.

Van Voërst van Lynden family

See 1.1.3
Access no.: 0491

103 Letter of commission for Lubbert Jan van Eck as Governor of Coromandel, 1758. One piece.

REGIONAAL HISTORISCH CENTRUM BERGEN OP ZOOM
REGIONAL HISTORICAL CENTRE BERGEN OP ZOOM

Notariële archieven
Notarial archives

See 1.1.5

45, act no. 66, ff. 211-12 Power of attorney drawn up by Jan van Wesel, among other people involving Johan Pender, Chirurgeon at Masulipatam, and Anthonij Quirijnssen and Andries van Wielen, Directors of the Zeeland Chamber of the VOC (?), 1651.

RIJKSARCHIEF IN NOORD-HOLLAND (Haarlem)
STATE ARCHIVES IN NORTH HOLLAND

Notarissen in het Rijksarchief in Noord-Holland, 1552-1842
Notaries in the State Archives in North Holland

See 1.1.10
Access no.: 185

977, no. 63 Notarial act drawn up by Reijer Claesz. Sampson at Enkhuizen, concerning Masulipatam (?), 1629, 1641 (microfilm no. 130).
1013, no. 57 Notarial act drawn up by Siewert Koeckebacker at Enkhuizen, concerning Fort Geldria at Pulicat, 1651 (microfilm no. 884).

WESTFRIES ARCHIEF (Hoorn)
ARCHIVES OF WEST FRIESLAND

Stad Enkhuizen
Town of Enkhuizen

See 1.1.16

1540 Papers concerning or deriving from Jacob Mossel, partly dating from his period as Governor of Coromandel (1738-43). One folder (old no. 394). Including:
- (a) Letters from Nagappattinam to Batavia and the Gentlemen XVII, 1739-40.
- (b) Notes regarding the textile trade in Coromandel, 1740.

1545 Papers concerning trade in Coromandel, 1682, 1707, and a defence by Governor Dirk Coomans, 1729-33, 1739. Partly printed, one folder (old no. 400).

Oud-notariële archieven Enkhuizen
Old notarial archives of Enkhuizen

See 1.1.16

977, no. 63 Notarial act drawn up by Reijer Claesz. Sampson, concerning Masulipatam (?), 1629, 1641.

1013, no. 57 Notarial act drawn up by Siewert Koeckebacker, concerning Fort Geldria at Pulicat, 1651.

ZEEUWS ARCHIEF (Middelburg)
ZEELAND ARCHIVES

Van de Perre-Schorer family

See 1.1.21
Access no.: 107

27 Papers concerning the VOC, numbered 1-49, with partial table of contents, 1641-1785. One bundle. Including:
- 43 Letter from the Amsterdam Chamber of the VOC concerning the Company's contacts with Thanjavur.

GEMEENTEARCHIEF ROTTERDAM
MUNICIPAL ARCHIVES OF ROTTERDAM

Oude notariële archieven
Old notarial archives

See 1.1.22
Access no.: 18

946: 201 Notarial act concerning the ship De Blauwe Hulck, 4 February 1677.
2328: 24 Notarial act concerning the ship De Gulde Leeuw, 1 February 1734.

Van Teylingen family

See 1.1.22

Access no.: 37.01

11 Three congratulatory poems on the occasion of the appointment of Christiaan van Teylingen as Governor of Coromandel, printed at Batavia, 1761. One quire.

12 *Memorie van overgave* (final report) by Governor Jacob Mossel to his successor Galenus Mersen, 1744. One volume.

13 Papers concerning Coromandel, particularly the unlawful activities and the dismissal of Governor Christiaan van Teylingen, including correspondence with the courts of Thanjavur and Arcot and the British at Madras, with table of contents, 1763-5. One bundle.

Handschriftenverzameling
Collection of manuscripts

See 1.1.22
Access no.: 33a

219 Papers concerning the ancestors and descendants of Didericus Lulius and his wife Quirina Adriana Vosmaer, 1746-1836, including an extract from the baptismal register of the Reformed Church in Fort Geldria at Pulicat concerning the birth of Quirina on 29 May 1735 as daughter of Adriaan Vosmaer (factor, *Fiscaal* and Cashier) and Agatha Keijser, 20 April 1746. One folder.

HET UTRECHTS ARCHIEF
THE ARCHIVES OF UTRECHT

Notarissen geresideerd hebbende te Utrecht-stad
Notaries having resided at the town of Utrecht

See 1.1.23
Access no.: 34-4

U 118 a 6, act no. 440 Notarial act drawn up by Thomas Vosch van Avezaat, among others involving Allardus Stipel van 's Gravenhage, Daniel Bernard Guilliams (formerly Governor of Coromandel, 1710-16) and Stephanus Courallet, concerning the collection of payment at the Zeeland Chamber of the VOC, 1731.

U 123 a 6, act no. 135 Notarial act drawn up by Matthijs van Lobrecht, among others involving Diderick van Westrenen and Gerrit van Westrenen (*Opperhoofd* at Masulipatam), concerning the collection of payment from Dirk Both at Pulicat, 1718.

U 123 a 6, act no. 220 Notarial act drawn up by Matthijs van Lobrecht, among others involving Adriana van Westrenen and Gerard (Gerrit?) van Westrenen (*Opperhoofd* at Masulipatam),

	concerning the estate of Sara van Westrenen, 1720.
U 126 a 3, act no. 83	Notarial act drawn up by Aaron Duerkant, among others involving Gerrit van Westrenen, concerning the estate of Wouterus van Westrenen and his wife Adriana Meerman, 1715 (related to a power of attorney for Thomas van Thest at Masulipatam, 1713).
U 126 a 3, act no. 84	Notarial act drawn up by Aaron Duerkant, among others involving Dirk van Westrenen, Gerrit van Westrenen and Judit van Westrenen, concerning the estate of Catharina van Royesteyn, 1715 (related to a power of attorney for Thomas van Thest, 1713).
U 139 a 2, act no. 104	Notarial act drawn up by Jacob van den Doorslagh, among others involving Gerrit van Westrenen (factor at Nagappattinam) and Johannes van Steelandt (Governor of Coromandel, 1705-10), concerning two bonds, 1708.
U 142 a 3, act no. 176	Notarial act drawn up by Joannes Both, involving Daniel Bernard Guilliams (formerly Governor of Coromandel) and Arnoldus Abeleven, 1723.
U 162 a 18, act no. 201	Notarial act drawn up by Cornelis Frederic Pronckert, involving the heirs of Frederick Elliot (factor at Nagappattinam) and Wynand Stant, concerning the collection of payment at the Amsterdam Chamber of the VOC, 1737.
U 162 a 24, act no. 118	Notarial act drawn up by Cornelis Frederic Pronckert, among others involving the Frederick Elliot heirs and Otto Ruysch, concerning a bill of exchange, 1743.
U 169 a 12, act no. 86	Notarial act drawn up by Wernard van Vloten, involving Constantia Margaretha Meinertzhagen, widow of Ottho Willem Falk (Otto Willem Falck?), and Dirk van den Enden, concerning money sent by George Tamme Falk (Falck?) (factor at Nagappattinam) through David Mullem, 1748.
U 205 a 6, act no. 86	Notarial act drawn up by Luyt van der Pauw, among others involving Nicolaas de Jonckheere (factor at Nagappattinam) and Dirk de Visser, concerning the collection of payment at the Zeeland Chamber of the VOC, 1751 (related to a power of attorney for Paulus Looman in Coromandel, 1750).

Oud-Katholieke Kerk in Nederland (OKN): Verzameling Port Royal
Old Catholic Church in the Netherlands: Port Royal collection

See 1.1.23
Access no.: 215

3067 Letters from the Vicars Apostolic in Pondicherry, 'Mahapram', Siam, Tonkin and China to the Directors of the foreign missions at Paris (and others?), 1673-1734. One bundle, in French and Latin.

3739 Five letters from the Capuchin Thomas at Madras about the missions in China, 1719-24. In French (?).

6208 Correspondence of the Capuchin Norbert at Pondicherry and accompanying papers, partly concerning his stay in India, including letters from Madras, 1740-5. One folder, in French.

7147 Various letters, including an extract of a letter from 'Virapatnam' near Pondicherry about the destruction of the College of St. Anges Gardiens and the Seminary of St. Joseph of the foreign missions because of the war in Siam, dated 6 October 1771. One folder, in French.

Evangelische Broedergemeente (EBG): Zeister Zendingsgenootschap
Evangelical Community of Moravian Brethren: Missionary Society of Zeist

See 1.1.23
Access no.: 48-1

1170 Correspondence of Kornelis van Laer, 1756-61, including a letter by Van Laer to his father referring to the Danes at Tranquebar, 1759. One folder, in German.

Huydecoper family

See 1.1.23
Access no.: 67

340 Notes by Balthasar Huydecoper concerning medieval and early-modern European history, including notes entitled 'Begin en Voortgang van de Vereenigde Nederlandsche Geoctroyeerde Oost-Indische Compagnie' (summary of Isaac Commelin's *Begin ende voortgangh van de Vereenighde Nederlantsche Geoctroyeerde Oost-Indische Compagnie* published at Amsterdam in 1645?), which contain references to Steven van der Hage's journey from Bantam to Coromandel in 1605-6. One folder (old no. 650).

HISTORISCH CENTRUM OVERIJSSEL (Zwolle)
HISTORICAL CENTRE OVERIJSSEL

Rechterlijk archief van het Schoutambt Kamperveen, processtukken
Judicial archives of the function of Bailiff Kamperveen, case files

See 1.1.25
Access no.: 61.2

52 Letters chiefly sent by priests in the East Indies to Eduard Jork (or George) van Slangenburgh, his wife Clara Croeuger and their relative

Paulus Croeuger, with many references to South Asia, 1711-23. One bundle. Including:
(a) Letter from Batavia to Van Slangenburgh at Nagappattinam, 1711.
(b) Letter from Hermanus Kolde de Horn (?) at Batavia to Van Slangenburgh (at Nagappattinam?), 1711.
(c) Letter from Godefridus van Holten at Batavia to Van Slangenburgh at Nagappattinam, 1711.
(d) Letter from Joh. Kiezenga (?) at Batavia to Van Slangenburgh at Nagappattinam, 1712.
(e) Letter from Westrenen at Masulipatam to Van Slangenburgh (at Nagappattinam?), 1712.
(f) Letter from Nagappattinam to Van Slangenburgh at Amsterdam, 1713.
(g) Letter from Jacobus Jacobs at Nagappattinam to Van Slangenburgh (at Amsterdam?), 1714.
(h) Letter from Dirck van Cloon and Jacobus Jacobs (?) at Nagappattinam to Van Slangenburgh at Amsterdam, 1716.
(i) Two letters from Jacobus Jacobs at Nagappattinam to Van Slangenburgh at Amsterdam, 1717-18.

Van Bevervoorden tot Oldemeule family

See 1.1.25
Access no.: 230.1

1 Letter (apparently unsent) from Bernardus Engelbert at Nagappattinam to Ambrosius van der Nol and Nicolaas Munnix at Batavia, partially announcing his wedding with Josina van Zijll, 1734. One piece.

2 Letter to Bernardus Engelbert and Josina van Zijll at Nagappattinam from Bernardus' brother at Rotterdam concerning family matters and genealogy, 1735. One piece.

6 Letter to Johannes Engelbert from his brother Bernardus and Josina van Zijll at Nagappattinam, in which he announces the birth of his son Henricus Johannes, 1737. One piece.

5.2. UNIVERSITIES

UNIVERSITEIT VAN AMSTERDAM, UNIVERSITEITSBIBLIOTHEEK
UNIVERSITY OF AMSTERDAM, UNIVERSITY LIBRARY

Manuscripts

See 1.2.2

Bc 128 Letter from Trembley at Nagappattinam, with a reference to the Maratha attack on Bimlipatam, 1754. In French, one piece.

Died 4 V — Letter from Brant Jzn at Nagappattinam to his uncle (?), 1711. One piece (catalogue: Vol. I, p. 29).

Died 128 Bx 1, 2 — Two letters from George Pocock at Nagappattinam to Governor Lubbert Jan van Eck (1758-61), 1759. Two pieces.

VRIJE UNIVERSITEIT AMSTERDAM, BIBLIOTHEEK
VRIJE UNIVERSITEIT AMSTERDAM, LIBRARY

Handschriften en oude drukken
Manuscripts and early printed books

See 1.2.3

XW.07161.- Report about eight wives of 'Werra Teuver', Commander-in-Chief of King Ekoji of Thanjavur, committing *sati* in 1678 near Nagappattinam, printed as a kind of newsletter, *c.* 1680. One quire.

UNIVERSITEIT LEIDEN, UNIVERSITEITSBIBLIOTHEEK
LEIDEN UNIVERSITY LIBRARY

Maatschappij der Nederlandse Letterkunde te Leiden
Society of Netherlands Literature at Leiden

See 1.2.7

Ltk 451 Poem (*c.* 1200 lines) about the position of the VOC at Pulicat and the behaviour of VOC officials, late eighteenth century. One volume.

Bibliotheca Publica Latina
Latin Public Library

See 1.2.7

BPL 617 *Resoluties* (proceedings), letters, memorandums and other papers concerning the VOC, with list of contents, 1687-1769, probably deriving from Augustinus van Son (1722-89), who became Secretary of the representatives of the Stadtholder with the VOC in 1750, and Lawyer of the VOC in 1755. 32 folders. Including:

- 2b Documents concerning coinage, weights and measures in Asia, including sections on Pulicat, Masulipatam, Teganapatam, Nagappattinam, Golkonda, Palakollu, Draksharama, Bimlipatam, Sadras, Porto Novo and Coromandel in general, 1687.
- 26 Summaries of the letters from the Gentlemen XVII concerning Coromandel, 1700-58, with a *radicale beschrijving* (official review) of Coromandel by Jacob van der Waaijen, 1757.

BPL 623 Dissertation concerning the state of the VOC, including an extensive section on Coromandel (ff. 351-97v), with its Dutch establishments, commodities, religions and a historical survey from 1552 to 1723.

BPL 935 Papers concerning the VOC and its successor the *Comité tot de Zaken van de Oost-Indische Handel en Bezittingen* (Committee regarding East Indian Trade and Possessions), including an agreement and correspondence between Governor Jacob Eilbracht (1790-5), Governor-General Willem Arnold Alting (1780-96), the Gentlemen XVII and Lord Hobard of the EIC concerning the surrender of the VOC settlements in Coromandel to the British (ff. 12-32), 1795-6. One bundle.

BPL 2030 Descriptions of the coasts of Ceylon and south India, consisting of sailing instructions, soundings and landfalls of 85 locations, including nos 60-3: Point Calimere, 'Sinjeur Soudij', Nagappattinam and Karaikal (ff. 31v-3), *c.* 1750 (?). One volume.

BPL 2223 Rubbings of Dutch inscriptions on the walls of a temple at Tirukkalukundram and of a commemorative stone from 1749 at the fort of Sadras. Two boxes. Described and reproduced in Peters and André de la Porte, *In steen geschreven*, pp. 22-35, 236-42 (see Supplement I: Bibliography, no. 848), and F.W. Stapel, 'A Dutch Memorial Slab in India', *Epigraphica Indica*, 24, pp. 123-6. See also 5.4, *Koninklijk Instituut voor de Tropen, Tropen Museum*, inv. no. 3440 / 4, and 5.4, *Koninklijk Instituut voor Taal-, Land- en Volkenkunde, Collectie in westerse talen*, inv. no. H 825.

Oosterse Handschriften (Legatum Warnerianum)
Oriental Manuscripts (Warner's Legacy)

See 1.2.7

Or. 1343 'Tarikh-i Sultan Muhammad Qutbshahi', text in Persian concerning the history of Golkonda, dating from 1617, acquired by a European in 1680, including a lengthy description of the contents by N.W. Schroeder (1721-98).

BIBLIOTHEEK UNIVERSITEIT TILBURG
TILBURG UNIVERSITY LIBRARY

Handschriften
Manuscripts

See 1.2.8

TF-HS 75 Correspondence of Joan Gideon Loten (1710-89) at Semarang, 1736-7. One volume (catalogue no. 56). Including:

ff. 249-50 Letter from Loten's cousin Louis Gravia (?) at Nagappattinam, 1737.

UNIVERSITEIT UTRECHT, UNIVERSITEITSBIBLIOTHEEK
UTRECHT UNIVERSITY LIBRARY

Handschriften
Manuscripts

See 1.2.10

Hs. 1473 (1.B.7) Collection of copies of *farmans* and other official documents in Persian, all granted by or submitted to the Kings of Golkonda (mainly Abdullah Qutb Shah) to and by the VOC, dating from the period *c.* 1627-79, concerning or drawn up at places such as Golkonda, Masulipatam, Palakollu, 'Condewar' and 'Condepillij' (Kondapalle?), made by 'Shah Qasim' for VOC official Daniel Havart and mostly translated by the latter into Dutch, with a reference to Herbert de Jager, 1679. One volume.

5.3. Ecclesiastical Organizations

ARCHIEF VAN DE NEDERLANDSE PROVINCIE DER JEZUÏETEN (Nijmegen)
ARCHIVES OF THE NETHERLANDS PROVINCE OF THE JESUITS

Handschriften
Manuscripts

See 1.3.2

A.D. 3 (box 21) Letters sent by Jesuits in India to Jesuits in Europe. Photocopies and contemporary manuscript copies, with recent documentation and notes pertaining to these letters and Jesuits in India, one folder. Including:

(a) Letter from Pondicherry, *c.* 1700 (?). In French.
(b) Letter from (Pierre?) Martin at Pondicherry to Dolu, 1700. In French.

5.4. Museums and Other Public Institutions

KONINKLIJK INSTITUUT VOOR DE TROPEN (KIT) (Amsterdam)
ROYAL TROPICAL INSTITUTE

Tropen Museum
Tropical Museum

See 1.4.2

3440 / 4 Rubbing of a commemorative stone from 1749 at the fort of Sadras. Described and reproduced in Peters and André de la Porte, *In steen geschreven*, pp. 28-9 (see Supplement I: Bibliography, no. 848), and F.W. Stapel, 'A Dutch Memorial Slab in India', *Epigraphica Indica*, 24, pp. 123-6. See also 5.2, *Universiteit Leiden, Universiteitsbibliotheek, Bibliotheca Publica Latina*, inv. no. BPL 2223, and 5.4, *Koninklijk Instituut voor Taal-, Land- en Volkenkunde, Collectie in westerse talen*, inv. no. H 825.

3710 / 58 Letter of attorney for a debt collection, drawn up by the Notary at Pondicherry, late eighteenth century. In French.

NEDERLANDS SCHEEPVAARTMUSEUM AMSTERDAM
NETHERLANDS MARITIME MUSEUM AMSTERDAM

Library

See 1.4.4

A-III-278 Nautical guide consisting of sailing instructions and landfalls of locations in Europe, Africa, and the East and West Indies, by Hans N. Lunge, on board various ships, 1756-66, including instructions concerning (the surroundings of) Nagappattinam, Point Calimere, Nagore and the coastal stretch between 'Calangepatnam' and Pondicherry (?). One volume (alternative inv. no. B.0208 (03)).

CENTRAAL BUREAU VOOR GENEALOGIE (CBG) (The Hague)
CENTRAL OFFICE FOR GENEALOGY

Bybau family

See 1.4.11
Access no.: FA 00055

Port. 8 Papers partly concerning Johan van Haeften, naval officer, who was taken prisoner by the British in 1797 and released in 1800. One bundle. Including:
- (a) Reports drawn up at Jagannathapuram concerning Van Haeften's journey to Pegu, *c.* 1788.
- (b) Papers concerning Van Haeften's wedding at Palakollu in 1799.

KONINKLIJKE BIBLIOTHEEK (KB) (The Hague)
ROYAL LIBRARY

Handschriften
Manuscripts

See 1.4.12

72 D 36 Sixteen letters from William Burke (cousin of Edmund Burke), agent of the King of Thanjavur, mostly to Lord Macartney, Governor of Fort St. George at Madras, sent from Basra, Thanjavur, Tranquebar, Nagappattinam and unknown places, written during the wars of the British with the Dutch and Haidar Ali Khan, 1781-3 and undated. In English, one folder.

79 J 70 *Album amicorum* (album of friends) of Hieronymus Christoph Wilhelm Eschenbach (1764-97), mathematician and astronomer, who in 1791 joined the Württemberg Regiment (which served the VOC) and passed away at Madras, including a short note from Friederich v. Franquemont, Madras, 1797 (f. 9), and three engravings of Hindu gods (ff. 32-4). One volume.

133 M 36 Correspondence of Frederik Godard and Johan Frederik van Reede tot de Parkeler with various people, 1720-1807. Including:

folder 3, no. 36 Bill of exchange drawn up at Tranquebar (copy), 1797.

Handschriften der Koninklijke Nederlandse Akademie van Wetenschappen
Manuscripts of the Royal Netherlands Academy of Arts and Sciences

See 1.4.12

KA 143 Reports, memorandums, instructions, considerations, descriptions, correspondence, etc., concerning all kinds of subjects and locations pertaining to the Dutch in Coromandel, such as textiles and other merchandise, coinage, bookkeeping, civil and military personnel, VOC buildings, diamonds, church matters, contacts with other VOC establishments, Golkonda, Pulicat, Nagappattinam, Masulipatam, Bimlipatam, Teganapatam, Sadras, Thanjavur, Draksharama, Petapoli, Irikam, Karaikal, Neknam Khan, etc., with a table of contents, 1663-80 (copy from *c.* 1800). One volume.

MUSEUM MEERMANNO (The Hague)
MEERMANNO MUSEUM

Van Westreenen family

See 1.4.13

S 72-3 Correspondence (chiefly received letters) and some accompanying papers of Jacobus Mersen, his wife and a few others, partly with copies, alphabetically arranged, 1748-61. Seven folders (each containing several files) in two boxes (inv. no. 43 in the inventory by Kernkamp). Including:

72.1: I Including one letter each from Anth. Bout (?), 1748, J. Campie, 1759, N. Campie, 1756, and Leonora de Vos (widow of Campie), 1754, all at Nagappattinam.

72.1: II Including two letters from J. Haselkamp, 1755-6, one each from J. Dumon, 1757, and L. and C.R. Hooreman, 1752, all at Nagappattinam, and two from J. Hoffland (d'Lafosse) at Pulicat, 1756-7.

72.2: III Including *c.* 15 letters from J. Jansz at Pulicat, 1751-5, 1758, and Nagappattinam, 1756, and two exchanged by Jansz at Pulicat with Everaad and François Ravellet (?) at Batavia, 1752.

72.3: VI Including 26 letters from the factor Nicolaas de Joncheere and his wife Adriana van Son (1737-63) at Nagappattinam, 1751-6, and Pulicat, 1756-9.

73.1: I Including three letters from F.J. Keijser (widow of Nebbens), 1753-4, two from Jacoba Keijser (widow of Serrat), 1754, one from Theodora Keijser (1720-89, widow of Pieter van Son), 1754, and ten from F.A. van Someren van Vrijenes (widow of Lons), 1753-7, all at Nagappattinam.

73.1: II Including eight letters from F.J. Lovenaar at Pulicat, 1755-7, and Nagappattinam, 1758-9.

73.2: IV Including one letter from S. Seloover (?) at Nagappattinam, 1755, and one from J.F. de Ravellet (at Batavia?) to Jan Campie at Nagappattinam, 1752.

73.2: V Including three letters from Marten Snel at Pulicat, 1751-3.

73.3: VI Including one letter from S. Vermont at Pulicat, 1750, and one from F. Canter Visscher at Nagappattinam, 1752.

73.3: VII Including 16 letters from F. Canter Visscher at Nagappattinam, 1752-4, and Sadras, 1754-8.

73.3: VIII Including one letter from S.C. Ziek (or Vick?), 1756, one from a cousin, 1753, and one from a friend, 1758, all at Nagappattinam.

KONINKLIJK INSTITUUT VOOR TAAL-, LAND- EN VOLKENKUNDE (KITLV) (Leiden)
ROYAL INSTITUTE OF LINGUISTICS AND ANTHROPOLOGY

Collectie in westerse talen
Collection in Western languages

See 1.4.14

H 49 Various letters and other documents, 1613-91. One volume. Including:
A Papers drawn up (by the war council) at St. Thome, Pulicat and 'Tiroewellikeri', 1673-4 (127 ff.).

H 72 Extracts and copies of letters of Governor-General Antonio van Diemen, 1636. One quire. Including:

6 Letter to Governor Carel Reniers (1636-8), 1636.

H 169 Letters and other papers received from the East Indies by Quirijn de Blau, Judge of the Court of Justice at Leeuwarden, including correspondence and other papers from or concerning Governor Reynier van Vlissingen (1771-80), partly sent from Nagappattinam, 1769-75. One bundle.

H 496 Memorandum about coins, weights and measures in Asia, including sections on Pulicat, Masulipatam, Nagappattinam, Teganapatam, Golkonda, Draksharama, Palakollu, Bimlipatam, Petapoli, Nagulvancha, Sadras and Jamshedpet, *c.* 1665 (?). One volume.

H 825 Rubbing of a memorial tablet from 1749 at the fort of Sadras, 1911. Described and reproduced in Peters and André de la Porte, *In steen geschreven*, pp. 28-9 (see Supplement I: Bibliography, no. 848), and F.W. Stapel, 'A Dutch Memorial Slab in India', *Epigraphica Indica*, 24, pp. 123-6. See also 5.2, *Universiteit Leiden, Universiteitsbibliotheek, Bibliotheca Publica Latina*, inv. no. BPL 2223, and 5.4, *Koninklijk Instituut voor de Tropen, Tropen Museum*, inv. no. 3440 / 4.

MARITIEM MUSEUM ROTTERDAM
MARITIME MUSEUM ROTTERDAM

Handschriften
Manuscripts

See 1.4.24

H482 Ship's logs by Claas Bichon, 1681-5, including a journal of the ship Japan sailing from 'Poeloe Timaon' via Masulipatam to Batavia, November 1681-June 1682, and a journal of the yacht Castricum sailing from Melaka via Coromandel to Batavia, December 1684-April 1685. One volume.

5.5. Companies, Private Organizations and Individuals

FEIKEMA (Amersfoort)

Canter Visscher

See 1.5.1

(a) Letter (207 ff.) from Adrianus Canter Visscher, most probably addressed to the Gentlemen XVII, joining in the debate about possible means of redress, as a result of the memorandum of Governor-General Jacob Mossel concerning the state of affairs of the VOC, *c.* 1753. One volume. Including:

ff. 62-77 History of political developments with regard to the Mughals in the Deccan, as observed from Masulipatam in the 1730s and 1740s.

ff. 77-191 Extensive survey of the VOC settlements in Coromandel in the 1730s and 1740s (such as Nagappattinam, Porto Novo, Teganapatam, Sadras, Pulicat, Masulipatam, Palakollu, Draksharama, Jagannathapuram and Bimlipatam), including sections on political intrigues at Masulipatam, relations with local merchants, and the organization and mobility of textile labourers, also containing a detailed description and map of Divi island (near Divi Point south of Masulipatam) (ff. 136-44), eyewitness accounts and a drawing of sieges of Masulipatam in 1734 and 1742 (ff. 155-67), and references to Indian kingdoms (Hyderabad, Marathas, Arcot and Thanjavur) and other European Companies such as the French (Karaikal, Pondicherry), British (Fort St. David, Madras), Portuguese (St. Thome) and Danish (Tranquebar).

SIX COLLECTION (Amsterdam)

Six collection

See 1.5.2

50 A (Van Winter section) One or several letters from G. Brandt Junior at Nagappattinam to his sisters, 1711.

TUTEIN NOLTHENIUS (Doorn)

Tutein Nolthenius family

See 1.5.3

(a) Approx. 130 letters (and a few other documents), chiefly received by Balthazar Nolthenius and Johanna Boel from relatives and friends at various locations in the East Indies, 1737-42. One volume. With early twentieth-century transcriptions and summaries. Described in Tutein Nolthenius, 'De brieven van Overzee', pp. 453-63 (see Supplement I: Bibliography, no. 57). Including:

6, 32, 62, 77, 90-1, 120-2 Nine letters from Nolthenius' cousin chief-factor Pieter van Son (1708-53) and partly also from the latter's wife Theodora van Son (née Keyser, 1720-89) at Nagappattinam, 1737-42.[1]

78 Letter from Nolthenius' cousin Book-keeper Ewout van Son (1720-86) at Nagappattinam, 1740.[1]

125 Letter from Nolthenius' relative G.E. Brandt at Nagappattinam, 1742.[1]

[1] Summarized in Tutein Nolthenius, 'Verdere brieven van overzee', pp. 1039, 1049-51 (see Supplement I: Bibliography, no. 44).

KONINKLIJK HUISARCHIEF (The Hague)
ARCHIVES OF THE ROYAL FAMILY

Maria Louise van Hessen-Kassel

See 1.5.6
Access no.: A 10

135 Two letters from priest Carel Willem Gebhard at Nagappattinam to Maria Louise van Hessen-Kassel expressing his devotion to her, 1762, 1765. Two pieces.

Prince William V

See 1.5.6
Access no.: A 31

333: I a Correspondence of William V's representative with the VOC, Thomas Hope, and the Duke of Brunswijk, 1765-6. One bundle. Including:
- (a) Letter from Hope to the Duke of Brunswijk, 22 April 1766, with an extract from a letter from the GG&C to the Gentlemen XVII concerning Coromandel, 1765.
- (b) Letters to the Bailiff of Rotterdam, Paulus Boogaert, and the Burgomaster of Rotterdam, requesting the arrest of former Governor Christiaan van Teylingen (1761-5) and others who fled with the help of an EIC ship, 30 April 1766, with a letter from 'Ferumani Setti' to the Gentlemen XVII complaining about Van Teylingen, 1765.

333: I b Correspondence of Thomas Hope and the Duke of Brunswijk, 1766. One bundle. Including:
- (a) Letter from C. van der Hoog to Hope (?), 3 May 1766, with a note concerning Van Teylingen at Nagappattinam. In French.
- (b) Letter from Hope to the Duke of Brunswijk, 13 August 1766, with a letter in which 'Hoeclum' (?) states to Hope that he was appointed as Governor (?) of Coromandel, also concerning Van Teylingen.
- (c) Letter from Hope to the Duke of Brunswijk, 2 September 1766, with an extract from a letter from Van Teylingen at Madras to Governor Pieter Haksteen (1765-71) and Council, 1765.

333: II Correspondence of Thomas Hope and the Duke of Brunswijk, 1767-8. One bundle. Including:
- (a) Letter from Hope to the Duke of Brunswijk, 5 January 1767, with an extract from a letter from the Gentlemen XVII (?) to the States General concerning Van Teylingen.

333: III Correspondence of Thomas Hope and the Duke of Brunswijk, 1768-71. One bundle. Including:
- (a) (in file 1) Letter from Hope to the Duke of Brunswijk, 21 May 1768, with an extract from a letter from Nagappattinam, 1767.

(b) (in file 2) Extract from a private letter from Coromandel, arrived on 4 December 1768.

333: VI b Correspondence of William V with Willem Jacob van de Graaff, Johan Gerard van Angelbeek, H. (Adriaan?) Moens, D.D. (Count) van Ranzou and others, concerning the VOC, 1773-95. One bundle. Including:

(a) (in file 38) Letter from J. Accama at Nagappattinam, 15 August 1773.

(b) (in file 38) Letter from J.L. Beggle at Madras, 31 July 1788.

(c) (in file 38) Letter from C.H. Horst at Madras, 2 April 1788. In French.

(d) (in file 38) Letter from H. van Someren van Vrijenes (?) at Jagannathapuram, 11 January 1790.

(e) (in file 38) Letter from Galenus Jacobus Vick at Nagappattinam, 23 August 1779, with letters and other papers from Vick, Governor Reynier van Vlissingen (1771-80), Governor-General Petrus Albertus van der Parra, H.F. Vick, Van Zeuthem, J.W. Luken and J. Obdam, partly drawn up at Nagappattinam and Tranquebar, 1765, 1774-9.

ORDE VAN VRIJMETSELAREN ONDER HET GROOTOOSTEN DER NEDERLANDEN (The Hague)
FRATERNITY OF FREEMASONS UNDER THE GRAND EAST OF THE NETHERLANDS

Constitutie dossiers
Constitution files

See 1.5.7

2401-4 Files concerning Masonic lodges. Including:
(a) De Langgewenschte at Nagappattinam, 1772-4. One folder.

5.6. Maps and Pictures

GELDERS ARCHIEF (Arnhem)
ARCHIVES OF GUELDERLAND

Brantsen family

See 1.1.3
Access no.: 0452

TK 43 Drawing of the obelisk on the grave of Adriana Appels at Nagappattinam, and of the headstones of Governor Adriaan Pla, Adriana Catharina

Pla and Catharina Johanna Mossel, *c.* 1743. Coloured, one sheet (old no. 285 C).

HET UTRECHTS ARCHIEF
THE ARCHIVES OF UTRECHT

Evangelische Broedergemeente (EBG): collectie prenten, tekeningen, kaarten en foto's, Zeist
Evangelical Community of Moravian Brethren: collection of prints, drawings, maps and photos, Zeist

See 1.6.1
Access no.: 46

592 View of the settlement of the Community of Moravian Brethren near Tranquebar, with legend, by J. Noüal, third quarter of the eighteenth century. Engraving, in German (15 x 22 cm).

UNIVERSITEIT VAN AMSTERDAM, UNIVERSITEITSBIBLIOTHEEK
UNIVERSITY OF AMSTERDAM, UNIVERSITY LIBRARY

Kaarten en Atlassen
Maps and Atlases

See 1.6.2

33-13-16 Map of the theatre of war in south Coromandel, with legend. Partly in French (old inv. no. 10081M).

33-13-33 Map of the surroundings of Pulicat and a map of the surroundings of Teganapatam and Thiruppapuliyar, published by Johannes van Keulen. Coloured (old inv. no. 10105M).

VRIJE UNIVERSITEIT AMSTERDAM, BIBLIOTHEEK
VRIJE UNIVERSITEIT AMSTERDAM, LIBRARY

Kaartenverzameling
Map collection

See 1.6.2

LL.04763gk: 000/od/1760 'Atlas du Sr. [Jean Baptiste Bourguignon] d'Anville', consisting of 24 separate copper engravings by Guill. de la Haye, compiled at Paris after 1760. In French, partly coloured, one folder. Including:

11a Part of a map of Coromandel, showing in detail the area roughly between Pulicat,

Nagappattinam, Tiruchirappalli and Arcot, 1753. Scale 1:555,000.

11b Part of a map of Coromandel, showing in detail the area roughly between Golkonda, Tirupati and Masulipatam, 1753. Scale 1:555,000.

BIBLIOTHEEK TECHNISCHE UNIVERSITEIT DELFT
DELFT UNIVERSITY OF TECHNOLOGY LIBRARY

Kaarten
Maps

See 1.6.2

TRL 6.5.2.08 Map in two parts of Coromandel between Nagappattinam, Tiruchirappalli, Golkonda and Narasapur, by d'Anville, published by F.A. Schreamble at Vienna, *c.* 1785. Copper engraving, in German, scale *c.* 1:800,000, two sheets (95 x 50 cm) (old inv. no. H-7321-06). German edition of inv. no. TRL 6.5.2.09, see below.

TRL 6.5.2.09 Map of Coromandel between Nagappattinam, Tiruchirappalli, Golkonda and Narasapur, by d'Anville and Guillaume de la Haye, 1753. Copper engraving, coloured, in French, scale *c.* 1:800,000, two sheets glued together (95 x 50 cm) (old inv. no. H-7321-05). See also inv. TRL 6.5.2.08, above.

UNIVERSITEIT LEIDEN, UNIVERSITEITSBIBLIOTHEEK
LEIDEN UNIVERSITY LIBRARY

Collectie Bodel Nijenhuis
Bodel Nijenhuis collection

See 1.6.2

002-09-034 Map of Bimlipatam, the Dutch factory and surroundings, with the plan of a projected fort and legend, by C.P. Keller, 1756. Manuscript, coloured, scale *c.* 1:1700 (52 x 74 cm) (old no. Port 176 N 46). Partly reproduced in Jacobs, *Koopman in Azië*, p. 79 (see Supplement I: Bibliography, no. 104). Related to no. 002-12-040, see below.

002-11-035 & 036 Map of the fort and town of Nagappattinam, with separate short explanation of the military and commercial significance of the fort, *c.* 1770. Manuscript, coloured, scale *c.* 1:11000 (23 x

	38 cm), two sheets (old no. Port 176 N 176).
002-12-040	Plan of a fort projected at Bimlipatam, showing various optional designs by means of movable parts, by C.P. Keller, 1756. Manuscript, coloured, scale *c.* 1:1480 (33 x 33 cm) (old no. Port 176 N 185). Related to no. 002-09-034, see above.
006-14-030	Sea chart of the coast of Golkonda from Masulipatam to Palmyras Point, first quarter of the eighteenth century. Pen and brush drawing, coloured, scale *c.* 1:780,000 (39 x 115 cm) (no. 69 in catalogue of sea charts).
C44 : 20 : 000933 : 722/1	View of the settlement of the Community of Moravian Brethren near Tranquebar, with legend, by J. Noüal, third quarter of the eighteenth century. Engraving, in German (15 x 22 cm).
Port 176 N 16	Plan of Pondicherry, with legend, by N. de Fer and A. Coquart, Paris, 1705. Copper engraving, in French (23 x 35 cm).
Port 176 N 45 (I & II)	Map of south and north Coromandel between Tiruchirappalli, Nagappattinam, Golkonda and Narasapur, by d'Anville, 1753. Copper engraving, two sheets (48 x 49 cm), in French. Almost identical to Port 202 N 24a & b, see below. See also Port 219 N 40, below.
Port 176 N 174	Map of the theatre of war in south Coromandel, with political divisions and European settlements, by J. van der Schley. Copper engraving, partly in French (31 x 23 cm). See also Port 176 N 175, below.
Port 176 N 175	Map of the theatre of war in south Coromandel, with political divisions and European settlements, by Fourez and Th. Jefferys. Copper engraving, coloured, in French (44 x 35 cm). Apparently a French version of Port 176 N 174, see above.
Port 176 N 177	Map of the town and district of Tranquebar, with extensive explanatory notes, by Matthaeus Seutter. Copper engraving, coloured, in German (48 x 55 cm).
Port 176 N 178	Map of the district of Tranquebar, with legend, by J. van der Schley (?). Copper engraving, partly in French (29 x 30 cm).
Port 176 N 179	Plan of the fort and town of Tranquebar, by J. van der Schley. Copper engraving, partly in French (18 x 27 cm).
Port 176 N 180	Plan of the fort and town of Tranquebar, with legend and landfall of the fort and town, by Matthaeus

	Seutter. Copper engraving, coloured, in German (49 x 55 cm).
Port 176 N 182	Map of Pondicherry in 1741, by J. van der Schley (?). Printed, partly in French (18 x 15 cm).
Port 176 N 183	Map of the vicinity of Pondicherry. Copper engraving, in French (10 x 9 cm).
Port 176 N 186	Map of Fort St. George, Madras and surroundings as taken by the French in 1746, by J. van der Schley (?). Copper engraving, partly in French (18 x 31 cm).
Port 176 N 187	Map of Fort St. George, Madras and surroundings as taken by the French in 1746, with legend. Copper engraving, in French (37 x 57 cm).
Port 177 N 49	Map of the Nicobar Islands, with inset of the waters between Nancowry and Trinkat Island, by De la Haye (?). Copper engraving, in French (45 x 29 cm).
Port 202 N 24a & b	Map of south and north Coromandel between Tiruchirappalli, Nagappattinam, Golkonda and Narasapur, by d'Anville and Guillaume de la Haye, 1753. Copper engraving, two sheets (49 x 49 cm), in French. Almost identical to Port 176 N 45 (I & II), see above. See also Port 219 N 40, below.
Port 219 N 40	Map of north Coromandel between Armagon, Golkonda and Narasapur, published by F.A. Schraembl, *c.* 1780. Copper engraving, in German (48 x 50 cm). Apparently a German version of Port 176 N 45 and Port 202 N 24b, see above.

Bibliotheca Publica Latina
Latin Public Library

See 1.2.7

BPL 952	Journals of Pieter van den Broecke's voyages to Africa and Asia, 1608-40, including three drawings of the VOC factories at Pulicat and possibly Masulipatam (at the back of the volume), *c.* 1617. Reproduced in *Pieter van den Broecke in Azië*, Vol. I, ed. W.Ph. Coolhaas (Werken Linschoten Vereniging, 63) (The Hague, 1962), pp. 171-3, and in Peters and André de la Porte, *In steen geschreven*, p. 13 (see Supplement I: Bibliography, no. 848).
BPL 2030	Descriptions of the coasts of Ceylon and south India, with coloured landfalls of 85 locations, including nos 60-3: Point Calimere, 'Sinjeur Soudij', Nagappattinam and Karaikal (ff. 31v-3), *c.* 1750 (?). One volume.

KONINKLIJK INSTITUUT VOOR DE TROPEN (KIT) (Amsterdam)
ROYAL TROPICAL INSTITUTE

Kenniscentrum
Resource Centre

See 1.4.2

RG-84 Drawings of insects (such as beetles, flies, grasshoppers and butterflies), spiders, scorpions, amphibians, reptiles and molluscs from Asia, after specimens in the gallery of Hendrik d'Acquet (1632-1706), Burgomaster of Delft, partly with names of suppliers, *c.* 1680-1710. Coloured, 183 sheets (*c.* 31 x 21 cm). Other parts of this collection are kept at the *Universiteit van Amsterdam, Universiteitsbibliotheek* (1.2.2), and the *Bibliotheek Wageningen Universiteit en Researchcentrum* (1.2.11). Together described in Bergvelt, Jonker and Wiechman, *Burgers verzamelen*, pp. 112-20 (see Supplement I: Bibliography, no. 122) and E. Bergvelt and R. Kistemaker (eds), *De wereld binnen handbereik. Nederlandse kunst- en rariteitenverzamelingen, 1585-1735* (Zwolle, 1992), pp. 223-30. Including:

part 1, ff. 8, 34, 38, 44, 57	Various insects from Coromandel, 1688-94. Folio 44 described and reproduced in Bergvelt and Kistemaker, *De wereld binnen handbereik*, p. 145, and the accompanying *Catalogus*, p. 128.
part 1, f. 28	Two insects from Coromandel, supplied by Van Schravesande ('s Gravesande?) and Jan Braijne, 1690-1.
part 2, f. 39	Various butterflies from Coromandel, supplied by Mr Swammerdam, 1690.
part 3, f. 18	Rattlesnake from Coromandel, 1697.

Tropen Museum
Tropical Museum

See 1.4.2

A 9584 View of the encampment of the Dutch envoy Johannes Bacherus at Golkonda, *c.* 1686-90, showing him twice, resting in his camp and as part of a procession, made at Golkonda by order of the envoy (earlier thought to depict Ketelaar at Udaipur or the Mughal court or Laurens Pit). Painting on cloth, coloured (240 x 103 cm). Described and reproduced in P. Lunsingh Scheurleer, 'Het Witsenalbum. Zeventiende-eeuwse Indiase portretten op bestelling', *Bulletin van het Rijksmuseum*, 44, 3 (1996), pp. 200-1, 209, idem, 'De Maharana van Udaipur', pp. 244-5 (see Supplement I: Bibliography, no. 179), E.M. Jacobs, *De Vereenigde Oost-Indische Compagnie* (Zeist, 1997), p. 178 (only partially), and P. Lunsingh Scheurleer and G. Kruijtzer, 'Camping with the Mughal Emperor. A Golkonda Artist Portrays a Dutch Ambassador in 1689', *Arts of Asia*, 35, 3 (2005).

NEDERLANDS SCHEEPVAARTMUSEUM AMSTERDAM
NETHERLANDS MARITIME MUSEUM AMSTERDAM

Iconografische collectie
Iconographic collection

See 1.6.4

A.0145 (211) (3)	Map of Nagappattinam and surroundings, indicating Dutch defensive works, with legend, 1773-4. Manuscript, coloured (55 x 113 cm).
A.1007	Portrait of Governor Cornelis Janszoon Speelman (1663-5), depicted as Governor-General, *c.* 1700. Oil on canvas (42 x 34 cm). Reproduced in Gaastra, *De geschiedenis van de VOC* (only in reprint of 2002), between pp. 58-9 (see Supplement I: Bibliography, no. 71), and E. Jacobs, *Varen om peper en thee. Korte geschiedenis van de Verenigde Oostindische Compagnie / In Pursuit of Pepper and Tea. The Story of the Dutch East India Company* (Zutphen, 1991, 1996), p. 87.
A.2275 (07)	View of the burning of the British ship Duke of Athol in the roadstead of Madras in 1783, with explanatory text, by James Gilray (or R. Wilkinson?), 1783. Engraving, in English (45 x 56 cm).
A-III-318	Album containing 80 affixed prints depicting views and maps of cities, probably originally marginal decorations of wall maps, by Frederick de Wit, with index, *c.* 1690. Including: 36 Pulicat. 38 Masulipatam.

Library

See 1.4.4

A-III-278 Nautical guide consisting of sailing instructions and landfalls of locations in Europe, Africa, and the East and West Indies, by Hans N. Lunge, on board various ships, 1756-66, including landfalls of (the surroundings of) Nagappattinam, Point Calimere, Nagore and the coastal stretch between 'Calangepatnam' and Pondicherry (?). Coloured, one volume (alternative inv. no. B.0208 (03)).

RIJKSMUSEUM AMSTERDAM
RIJKSMUSEUM AMSTERDAM

Afdeling Nederlandse Geschiedenis
Department of Dutch History

See 1.6.4

NG-363 View of a sanctuary at Nagappattinam, consisting of a statue (of the Hindu deity Aiyanar?), a temple and a tower called 'Chinese pagoda' (possibly a remnant of a thirteenth-century Buddhist temple complex built by order of Chinese), by Rev. Jan Brandes (1743-1808), 1785. Water colour (21 x 29 cm) (copy of an anonymous work dating from 1733?). Described and reproduced in De Bruijn and Raben, *The World of Jan Brandes 1743-1808* (see Supplement I: Bibliography, no. 125).

NG-501-69 Map of the Coromandel Coast between Nagappattinam and Narasapur, by Guillaume Nicolas Delahaye, Jean Baptiste Bourguignon d'Anville, Johannes Covens and Cornelis Mortier, 1753. Printed (96 x 50 cm).

NG-BR-943 Portrait of Governor Cornelis Janszoon Speelman (1663-5), depicted as Governor-General, with his coat of arms on the back, by Gerrit van Goor, 1680. Oil on porcelain (5 x 4 cm). Described and reproduced in Zandvliet, *De Nederlandse ontmoeting met Azië / The Dutch Encounter with Asia*, p. 43 (see Supplement I: Bibliography, no. 98).

SK-A-3764 Portrait of Governor Carel Reniers (1636-8), depicted as Governor-General, mid-seventeenth century. Panel (98 x 78 cm).[1] (SK-A-4534 is a copy. Panel, 33 x 25 cm.)

SK-A-3767 Portrait of Governor Cornelis Janszoon Speelman, depicted as Governor-General, attributed to Martin Palin, 1680s. Panel (100 x 79 cm).[1] (SK-A-4537 is a copy. Panel, 33 x 25 cm.)

SK-A-3776 Portrait of Governor Dirck van Cloon (1723-30), depicted as Governor-General, by Hendrick van den Bosch, 1733. Panel (99 x 82 cm).[1] (SK-A-4545 is a free copy. Copper, 34 x 27 cm.)

SK-A-3781 Portrait of Governor Jacob Mossel (1738-43), depicted as Governor-General, *c.* 1755. Canvas (113 x 96 cm).[1] See also no. SK-A-4550, below.

SK-A-4550 Portrait of Governor Jacob Mossel, depicted as Governor-General. Copper (34 x 27 cm).[1] See also no. SK-A-3781, above.

[1] Described in J. de Loos-Haaxman, *De landsverzameling schilderijen in Batavia*, 2 vols (Leiden, 1941), and F.W. Stapel, *De gouverneurs-generaal van Nederlandsch-Indië in beeld en woord* (The Hague, 1941).

Rijksprentenkabinet
Print Room

See 1.6.4

RP-P-1988-54 (topo. col.) Map of the fort and town of Pondicherry in 1741, by Jacobus van der Schley. Printed (21 x 17 cm).

RP-P-OB-67.338 Portrait of Governor Cornelis Janszoon Speelman (1663-5), depicted as Governor-General, by Jacobus van der Schley. Engraving.

RP-P-OB-67.340 — Portrait of Governor Carel Reniers (1636-8), depicted as Governor-General, by Jacobus van der Schley. Engraving.

RP-P-OB-67.350 — Portrait of Governor Dirck van Cloon (1723-30), depicted as Governor-General, by Jacobus van der Schley. Engraving.

RP-P-OB-67.354 — Portrait of Governor Jacob Mossel (1738-43), depicted as Governor-General, by Jacobus van der Schley. Engraving.

RP-T-00-3186 — So-called 'Witsen-Album', consisting of 49 Indian miniature paintings (20 x 14 cm), depicting Mughal, Bijapur, Maratha, Golkonda and Persian rulers and officials, produced at Golkonda and probably purchased by a VOC official, *c.* 1680, with notes in Persian, Portuguese and Dutch, acquired by Nicolaas Cornelisz Witsen (1641-1717, VOC Director from 1693 onward and Burgomaster of Amsterdam). Coloured, one folder. Described and reproduced (together with other Indian miniature paintings) in P. Lunsingh Scheurleer, 'Het Witsenalbum. Zeventiende-eeuwse Indiase portretten op bestelling', *Bulletin van het Rijksmuseum*, 44, 3 (1996), Goetz, *The Indian and Persian Miniature Paintings* (see Supplement I: Bibliography, no. 131), and Kruijtzer, 'Madanna, Akkanna and the Brahmin Revolution', p. 239 (Bibl., no. 844). Including:

19A Sultan Quli Qutb Shah of Golkonda (no. 28 in Goetz).

19B Sultan Ibrahim Qutb Shah of Golkonda (no. 29 in Goetz).

20 Sultan Muhammad Quli Qutb Shah of Golkonda (no. 30 in Goetz).

21 Sultan Muhammad Qutb Shah (?) of Golkonda (no. 31 in Goetz).

22 Sultan Abdullah Qutb Shah of Golkonda (no. 32 in Goetz).

23 Sultan Abul-Hasan Qutb Shah of Golkonda (no. 33 in Goetz).

24 Mirza Ahmad, *Wazir* under Abdullah Qutb Shah (no. 34 in Goetz).

25 Neknam Khan, *Wazir* and *Sar-lashkar* (head of the cavalry, governor) under Abdullah Qutb Shah (no. 35 in Goetz).

26 Musa Khan, page (?) and *Sar-lashkar* of Abdullah Qutb Shah (no. 40 in Goetz).

27 Shah Mirza, *Sar-khail* (troop commander) under Abul-Hasan Qutb Shah (no. 41 in Goetz).

28 Sayyid Muzaffar, *Peshwa* (commander-in-chief) under Abul-Hasan Qutb Shah (no. 39 in Goetz).

29 Muhammad Ibrahim, *Sar-lashkar* and *Sar-khail* of Golkonda (no. 45 in Goetz).

30 Shah Raju, *Pir* (spiritual guide) of Abul-Hasan Qutb Shah (no. 42 in Goetz).

31 Mulla Tayfur, *Ustad* (teacher) of Abdullah Qutb Shah (no. 38 in Goetz).

32 Mulla Abd al-Samad, *Dabir* (secretary) of Abdullah Qutb Shah (no. 37 in Goetz).

33 Muhammad Amin, *Qiladar* (commander of the fort) of Golkonda (no. 48 in Goetz).

34 Abd al-Jabbar, *Wazir* under Abdullah Qutb Shah (no. 36 in Goetz).

35 Sharza Khan, *Wazir* under Abdullah and Abul-Hasan Qutb Shah (no. 46 in Goetz).

36 Abd al-Aziz, brother of Bahlul Khan who was *Wazir* under Abul-Hasan Qutb Shah (no. 47 in Goetz).

37 Madanna Pandit, *Majmudar* (revenue auditor) under Abul-Hasan Qutb Shah (no. 43 in Goetz).

38 Akkanna Pandit, *Shahnawis-ikull* (secretary-in-chief) under Abul-Hasan Qutb Shah (no. 44 in Goetz).

RP-T-1904-19 View of the Shiva temple at Chidambaram and some Indians in front of it, by Chirurgeon Carl Friedrich Reimer, 1774. Water colour (24 x 47 cm).[1]

RP-T-1904-20 View of a Muslim cemetery (possibly with a few European graves), with a procession, including *devadasis* (female temple dancers), musicians, wrestlers and possibly an Indian VOC servant, probably near the Shiva temple at Chidambaram, by Carl Friedrich Reimer, 1773. Water colour (20 x 43 cm).[1]

[1] Described and reproduced in Zandvliet, *De Nederlandse ontmoeting met Azië / The Dutch Encounter with Asia*, pp. 239-41 (see Supplement I: Bibliography, no. 98), and Terwen-de Loos, *Nederlandse schilders en tekenaars*, pp. 22-3, 61 (inv. no. RP-T-1904-20 only described) (Bibl., no. 153); inv. no. RP-T-1904-20 also partly reproduced in Van Goor, *Indische avonturen*, p. 73 (Bibl., no. 74).

TEYLERS MUSEUM (Haarlem)
TEYLER'S MUSEUM

Kunstverzameling
Art collection

See 1.6.4

(a) Three sets of drawings and accompanying texts pertaining to a number of Hindu temples (referred to as 'Saodoloue', 'Pedagarjar', 'Tchebool', 'Sandeste' and 'Sheembolone'?), collected at different times by three Europeans probably in north Coromandel. Partly coloured, one portfolio.[1] For a short description and a reproduction of one of the drawings of Hindu deities, see Sliggers and Besselink, *Het verdwenen museum*, pp. 146-7, 154 (see Supplement I: Bibliography, no. 152). Consisting of:
  (a) Plans and cross sections of two south Indian Shiva temples, made by an Indian craftsman by order of a Frenchman, with notes in French, probably late eighteenth century. Five sheets, French paper.
  (b) 56 drawings (numbered A-Z, AA-ZZ, 1-16) of Hindu deities and scenes from the *Ramayana* (in Vijayanagara style) appearing in Shiva temples, made in European style by an Indian craftsman by order of a European (probably a Dutchman), with notes about the depicted figures in Telugu and a Dutch translation, probably late eighteenth century. French paper.
  (c) Ten miniatures of Hindu deities and scenes from the *Ramayana*, with a description of 40 miniatures in Telugu and a Dutch translation, probably made by an Indian craftsman at Rajahmundry by order of a Dutchman, between 1755 and 1765. Indian paper pasted on European paper.

[1] Information kindly provided by Pauline Lunsingh Scheurleer (*Rijksmuseum Amsterdam*).

KONINKLIJK INSTITUUT VOOR TAAL-, LAND- EN VOLKENKUNDE (KITLV) (Leiden)
ROYAL INSTITUTE OF LINGUISTICS AND ANTHROPOLOGY

Images

See 1.6.4

37 B-624 Portrait of Governor Carel Reniers (1636-8), depicted as Governor-General, by Balen, *c.* 1750. Engraving (29 x 19 cm).

37 B-627 Portrait of Governor Cornelis Janszoon Speelman (1663-5), depicted as Governor-General, by Balen, *c.* 1750. Engraving (31 x 19 cm).

37 C-80 View of the French storehouses and the Governor's residence at

Pondicherry, with some ships in the foreground, *c.* 1800. Coloured, engraving (24 x 39 cm).

47 A-1 Portrait of Governor Cornelis Janszoon Speelman, depicted as Governor-General, by Blooteling, with an ode by Jacob Steendam, 1670. Copper engraving (28 x 19 cm).

FEIKEMA (Amersfoort)

Canter Visscher

See 1.5.1

(a) Letter (207 ff.) from Adrianus Canter Visscher, most probably addressed to the Gentlemen XVII, joining in the debate about possible means of redress, as a result of the memorandum of Governor-General Jacob Mossel concerning the state of affairs of the VOC, *c.* 1753. One volume. Including:
  - (a) Map of Divi island (near Divi Point south of Masulipatam), indicating villages and forts, with explanatory notes. Coloured (*c.* 70 x 50 cm).
  - (b) Bird's-eye view of Masulipatam, fortified by the VOC, besieged by a Maratha army with banners, elephants, dromedaries and horses, with Dutch and other ships in the background. Coloured (*c.* 60 x 50 cm).

6. BENGAL
(including Bihar)

6.1. Government Archives

GEMEENTEARCHIEF AMSTERDAM
MUNICIPAL ARCHIVES OF AMSTERDAM

Weeskamer en Commissie van Liquidatie der zaken van de voormalige weeskamer
Orphan Board and Commission of Liquidation of the affairs of the former orphan board

See 1.1.2
Access no.: 5073

192 Papers received from the trustees at Hooghly, 1787. One folder.
209 Papers received from private persons in various places in Asia and the Cape of Good Hope, 1687-1789, including Hooghly, 1698-1721. One bundle.

Notarissen ter standplaats Amsterdam
Notaries at Amsterdam

See 1.1.2
Access no.: 5075

Geographical names on index cards found under some of the more obvious headings in the modern indices:

Bengal	70 index cards (1637, 1668-1787).
Calcutta	8 index cards (1779-81).
Chinsura	2 index cards (1770-1).
Cossimbazar	6 index cards (1708, 1754, 1761).
Dhaka	2 index cards (1780).
Frederiksnagore / Serampore	2 index cards (1767, 1785).
Hooghly	49 index cards (1698-1787).
'Kalihati'	1 index card (1755).
Patna	1 index card (1780).

Firma Hope & Co
Firm of Hope & Co

See 1.1.2
Access no.: 735

1513 Papers concerning a claim of W. Paxton in Bengal against the VOC in Bengal through the agency of Hope & Co, 1780-5. One folder.

Brants family

See 1.1.2
Access no.: 88

1158 Letters to Isaac (1692-1738) and Pieter (1694-1740) de Neufville from Leendert Mijndersz at Banquibazar, 1728-36. Four pieces (microfilm no. 8392).

De Graeff family

See 1.1.2
Access no.: 76

166 Letter from Pieter de Witt at The Hague requesting Pieter de Graeff to replace him at a meeting of the Directors of the VOC, as De Witt is 'involved in Bengal', 1703. One piece.

Handschriften
Manuscripts

See 1.1.2
Access no.: 5059

95 Extracts from letters, sent from *Directeur* Constantijn Ranst (1669-73) at Hooghly to the factor Pieter Hofmeester at Dhaka, from Pieter Hofmeester to Constantijn Ranst, Harman Fentzel, Van der Schepen and Elias van den Brouck, and from Harman Fentzel at Cossimbazar to Elias van den Brouck and Mattheus van den Brouck, Director of the VOC at Dordrecht, 1672-3. One volume.

Bibliotheek
Library

See 1.1.2

N 20.01.72/01-13 Various papers listing goods (including cotton, silk and tea) from Bengal and Canton brought by ships of the VOC and various other Companies, 1778-88. Mostly printed, one folder.

DRENTS ARCHIEF (Assen)
ARCHIVES OF DRENTHE

House of Mensinge at Roden

See 1.1.4
Access no.: 0616

90 Letters from Jan Albert Sichterman to Coenraad Ellents Junior, sent from various places, including Hooghly and Cossimbazar, 1720-5. Four pieces.

91 Letter from Coenraad Ellents Junior to *Directeur-Generaal* Anthony Huysman at Batavia, concerning a certain case to be addressed to Jan Albert Sichterman at Hooghly, undated (probably late 1720s). One piece.

454 Letters from Jan Albert Sichterman at Hooghly to his nephew Andreas Conring at Groningen, 1739, 1741. Two pieces.

GRONINGER ARCHIEVEN
ARCHIVES OF GRONINGEN

Plaatselijke gerechten in het Oldambt
Local courts of justice in the Oldambt

See 1.1.8
Access no.: 731

5677 Papers concerning the administration by Alderts of the goods of the *Equipagemeester* (master of the equipage) Lucas Jurriaans Zuidland in Bengal, 1765-82. One folder.

Sichterman family

See 1.1.8
Access no.: 868

25 Various papers including a descriptive list of the children of Jan Albert Sichterman and Sibilla Volkera Sadelijn, some of whom were born at Hooghly or Cossimbazar, eighteenth century (?). One box.

35 Various papers including correspondence of Jan Albert Sichterman (often together with Sibilla Volkera Sadelijn) at Cossimbazar and Hooghly with his sons Gerard Jan and Anthonij Ewouts, cousin Coenraad Ellents at Anloo, nephew Andreas Conring, Mr Burnand at The Hague and Jacob Helmolt, 1720, 1725-7, 1737-43, with modern transcriptions. One box, partly in French.

RIJKSARCHIEF IN NOORD-HOLLAND (Haarlem)
STATE ARCHIVES IN NORTH HOLLAND

Notarissen in het Rijksarchief in Noord-Holland, 1552-1842
Notaries in the State Archives in North Holland

See 1.1.10
Access no.: 185

1119, no. 58 Notarial act drawn up by Jacob Tjallis at Enkhuizen, concerning the Hooghly factory, 1669 (microfilm no. 888).

1310, nos 33-5 Notarial act drawn up by Jan Meun at Enkhuizen, concerning Bengal, 1752 (microfilm no. 202).

1380, nos 73, 81 Notarial act drawn up by Abel van der Willige at Enkhuizen,

	concerning trade and shipping of textiles between Bengal and Enkhuizen, 1752 (microfilm no. 222).
1381, no. 52	Notarial act drawn up by Abel van der Willige at Enkhuizen, concerning trade and shipping of textiles between Bengal and Enkhuizen, 1755 (microfilm no. 222).
1386, no. 153	Notarial act drawn up by Abel van der Willige at Enkhuizen, concerning trade and shipping of textiles between Bengal and Enkhuizen, 1768 (microfilm no. 224).
6071, no. 124	Notarial act drawn up by Joannes Arnoldus Lette at Zaandam, concerning the dissolution of the trading partnership at Chinsura between Dirk Schoon and Jan Frederik Volmer, 1775 (microfilm no. 1002).
6078, nos 25, 67	Notarial act drawn up by Albert Booker at Zaandam, concerning shipping between Bengal and Amsterdam, 1777 (microfilm no. 856).
6104, no. 96	Notarial act drawn up by Albert Booker at Zaandam, concerning the payment of the crew and other financial matters (?) of the ships Eyk en Linden, Anthoinetta and Engel van de Stad, sailing between Bengal and Amsterdam, 1796 (microfilm no. 1006).
6135, no. 90	Notarial act drawn up by Albert Booker at Zaandam, concerning the sale of the ship De Goede Intentie by Oostzaandam to Serampore, 1806 (microfilm no. 857).

Hollandsche Maatschappij der Wetenschappen
Dutch Society of Sciences

See 1.1.10
Access no.: 444

43 Papers received in 1768, including observations of the weather conditions and the temperature at 'Kalkapur' (Cossimbazar) over the period June 1766-October 1768, carried out by Johannes Bacheracht with the help of the 'thermometer of At. Tessa'. One bundle.

45 Papers received in 1770, including observations of the weather conditions and the temperature at Cossimbazar over the period November 1768-October 1769, carried out by Johannes Bacheracht with the help of the 'thermometer of At. Tessa', and letters by Bacheracht sent from Hooghly, 1769-70, and Cossimbazar, 1769, to C.C.H. van der Aa, priest at Haarlem. One bundle.

46 Papers received in or concerning 1771, including notes about a meteorological experiment carried out with the help of a thermometer (Fahrenheit scale) of C. Buspinus at Chinsura over the period September-December 1771. One bundle.

48 Papers received in 1773, including an extract from a letter from Patna (by *Directeur* Johannes Bacheracht?) concerning ammonia (?). One bundle.

HAAGS GEMEENTEARCHIEF
MUNICIPAL ARCHIVES OF THE HAGUE

Gemeentebestuur, 'Oud archief'
Town council, 'Old archives'

See 1.1.11
Access no.: 350

5801 Notarial act, drawn up by Cornelis Veenendael, concerning a security of *Directeur* Willem de Roo (1705-10) for his brother Otto de Roo, Cashier of the *bank van lening* (pawnshop) at The Hague, 1705. One piece.

Waals-Hervormde gemeente te 's-Gravenhage en Voorburg
Walloon Reformed community at The Hague and Voorburg

See 1.1.11
Access no.: 241

441 Testament, executed before Andries Jurgen Schultz at Hooghly, of Jacques Lateur, second-in-command at Patna, and his wife Cornelia Borwater, in which they bequeath a sum of money to the parish at The Hague, 1753, notarial copy from 1761. One piece.

WESTFRIES ARCHIEF (Hoorn)
ARCHIVES OF WEST FRIESLAND

Stad Enkhuizen
Town of Enkhuizen

See 1.1.16

1531 Papers received by the Gentlemen XVII, 1722-63, including a letter from Johannes Bacheracht at Cossimbazar concerning theft from the cash box in the factory at Hooghly, 1763. One folder (old no. 385).

1542 Papers received by officials and other employees of the VOC, 1649-1776; part B includes papers concerning the financial interests of Jacob Eilbracht, Casher and Secretary at Hooghly, 1744-70. Two folders (old no. 396).

Oud-notariële archieven Enkhuizen
Old notarial archives of Enkhuizen

See 1.1.16

1119, no. 58 Notarial act drawn up by Jacob Tjallis, concerning the Hooghly factory, 1669.

1310, nos 33-5	Notarial act drawn up by Jan Meun, concerning Bengal, 1752.
1380, nos 73, 81	Notarial act drawn up by Abel van der Willige, concerning trade and shipping of textiles between Bengal and Enkhuizen, 1752.
1381, no. 52	Notarial act drawn up by Abel van der Willige, concerning trade and shipping of textiles between Bengal and Enkhuizen, 1755.
1386, no. 153	Notarial act drawn up by Abel van der Willige, concerning trade and shipping of textiles between Bengal and Enkhuizen, 1768.

GEMEENTEARCHIEF ZAANSTAD (Koog aan de Zaan)
MUNICIPAL ARCHIVES OF ZAANSTAD

Oud-notariëel archief Zaandam
Old notarial archives of Zaandam

See 1.1.17

6071, no. 124	Notarial act drawn up by Joannes Arnoldus Lette, concerning the dissolution of the trading partnership at Chinsura between Dirk Schoon and Jan Frederik Volmer, 1775.
6078, nos 25, 67	Notarial act drawn up by Albert Booker, concerning shipping between Bengal and Amsterdam, 1777.
6104, no. 96	Notarial act drawn up by Albert Booker, concerning the payment of the crew and other financial matters (?) of the ships Eyk en Linden, Anthoinetta and Engel van de Stad, sailing between Bengal and Amsterdam, 1796.
6135, no. 90	Notarial act drawn up by Albert Booker, concerning the sale of the ship De Goede Intentie by Oostzaandam to Serampore, 1806.

TRESOAR, FRYSK HISTOARYSK EN LETTERKUNDICH SINTRUM
(Leeuwarden)
TRESOAR, FRIESIAN HISTORICAL AND LITERARY CENTRE

Staten van Friesland, 1580-1795
States of Friesland

See 1.1.18
Access no.: 5

184, f. 86v	*Resolutie* (proceedings) concerning the suggestion of the States of Holland to raise the export duties on Bengal silk imported by the VOC, 9 May 1777.

REGIONAAL ARCHIEF LEIDEN
REGIONAL ARCHIVES LEIDEN

Stadsarchief, 1574-1816
Town archives

See 1.1.19
Access no.: 501A

6716 Report by David van Royen concerning the VOC in connection with the renewal of its charter, 1740, with appendices, including printed extracts of a letter from Bengal to the Gentlemen XVII (?) regarding the damage caused by bad weather, 1737. One volume.

Heilige Geest- of Arme Wees- en Kinderhuis te Leiden
Holy Spirit or Poor Orphanage and Children's Home at Leiden

See 1.1.19
Access no.: 519

851 Notarial act concerning the estate of former *Directeur* George Lodewijk Vernet (1763-9), with appendices, May 1793. One folder.

RIJKSARCHIEF IN LIMBURG (Maastricht)
STATE ARCHIVES IN LIMBURG

Well Castle

See 1.1.20
Access no.: 16.1112 A/1

762 Case file of VOC official Elso Herrenberg against his wife Metta Christina Woordenberg accusing her of adultery, tried by the judicial council at Hooghly under the chief-factor Cornelis de Jonge (deceased in 1743), 1738-9 (designated as 'immoral' in the inventory). One volume.

ZEEUWS ARCHIEF (Middelburg)
ZEELAND ARCHIVES

Koninklijk Zeeuwsch Genootschap der Wetenschappen
Royal Zeeland Society of Sciences

See 1.1.21
Access no.: 26.1

6, pp. 143, 275 Minutes concerning the lecture by J. Stavorinus about a journey in 1769-70 to Bengal, 1790, 1794. See also no. 63, ff. 46-50, below.

6, p. 167 — Minutes concerning the lecture by I. Winckelman citing from the treatise by J. Stavorinus (Johan Splinter) regarding religion in Bengal, 1790.

8, p. ? — Minutes concerning the donations by J.R. Vos at Calcutta and Van Hugenholtz of various objects from Bengal, including three statues of Buddha and one of Shiva, two fans and a drum, 7 December 1825 (and 1807, 17 November 1819 and 3 May 1820). See also nos 55 and 341. The actual objects are kept at the *Provinciaal Archeologisch Centrum Zeeland / Stichting Cultureel Erfgoed Zeeland* in Middelburg (Shiva statue) and at the *Rijksmuseum voor Volkenkunde* in Leiden (other objects), inv. nos BEV-Z-72 & 73, Z-8049 (?) and unnumbered.

63, ff. 46-50 — Received papers concerning the lecture by J. Stavorinus about a journey in 1769-70 to Bengal, undated (*c.* 1790s). See also no. 6, pp. 143, 275, above.

(Snouck) Hurgronje family II

See 1.1.21
Access no.: 98.2

42 Description of the invasion of Bengal by the Marathas, undated (1740s?). One quire.

Van de Perre-Schorer family

See 1.1.21
Access no.: 107

29 Various papers concerning the VOC, numbered 1-39, 40-60, 61-121, *c.* 1780-95. Three bundles. Including:
31 (first bundle) Papers concerning Robert Charnock at Calcutta, 1789.

Mathias-Pous-Tak van Poortvliet family

See 1.1.21
Access no.: 255

50 Memorandum by former *Directeur* Jan Kersseboom of Bengal (1750-5) for the GG&C, defending his activities in connection with accusations by Bengal servants, with accompanying letter, 1757. One volume and one piece.

51 Protest of *Directeur* Adriaan Bisdom and the Council in Fort Gustavus at Hooghly concerning the damage of the Dutch trade inflicted by the British during the seven-year war, 1759. One piece. (The first few folios were formerly filed under inv. no. 360.)

52 Papers concerning the complaints of the Minister-Plenipotentiary York of the British King about the hostile attitude of the Dutch at Bengal, 1761. Printed, one volume.

190 Petitions addressed to Bonifatius Mathias Pous, 1770-92, from various senders, including Gregorius Herklots at Chinsura, 1783, 1786. One folder.

191 Letters received by the Gentlemen XVII, 1770-89, including an extract from a letter from Bengal concerning dyes, 1781. One folder.

243 Extracts from *resoluties* (proceedings) of the States General concerning a memorandum by J.C. van der Hoop with regard to the trade in Bengal, 1791. Printed, one quire.

Van der Feen family

See 1.1.21
Access no.: 309

7 Two ship's logs, including one of the ship Raadhuis van Middelburg, sailing for the Zeeland Chamber of the VOC under the command of Pieter Buijs from Rammekens via Batavia and Melaka to Bengal and back, March 1717-August 1719. One folder.

Receuils Van Citters

See 1.1.21
Access no.: 105

22 Papers concerning the VOC (among other matters), 1747-68, including documents regarding conflicts with the EIC in Bengal, 1761-2, with copies of treaties between the EIC and the Nawab of Bengal. One volume.

GEMEENTEARCHIEF ROTTERDAM
MUNICIPAL ARCHIVES OF ROTTERDAM

Oud stadsarchief Rotterdam
Old town archives of Rotterdam

See 1.1.22
Access no.: 1a

3024 Papers concerning the VOC, 1613-1792, including a document regarding contacts in Bengal with the British, the French and the Nawab, second half eighteenth century (?). One folder.

Oude notariële archieven
Old notarial archives

See 1.1.22
Access no.: 18

976: 747 Notarial act concerning the ship Stavenisse, 4 July 1688.
1433: 22 Notarial act concerning the ship Donckervliet, 22 January 1698.
1900: 210 Notarial act concerning the ship Francis, 29 September 1729.

2343: 129 Notarial act concerning wine and arrack on the ship Wiltrijk, 9 October 1748.

2522: 91 Notarial act concerning the ship Witsburg, 23 October 1751.

2524: 76, 84 Notarial act concerning the ship De Erfprins, 8 July 1753.

2626: 223-4 Notarial act concerning the ship De Vrouw Elisabeth, 18 July 1768.

2626: 281 Notarial act concerning the ship De Vrouw Elisabeth, 14 September, 1768.

2748: 181 Notarial act concerning the ship De Osdorp, 20 July 1753.

2885: 45, 47 Notarial act concerning goods on the ship–'t Huis ten Donck, 4 March 1758.

2918: 412-13 Notarial act concerning the ship De Zilveren Leeuw, 27 August 1771.

2934: 280-1 Notarial act concerning the ship 't Huis te Krooswijk, 6 July 1779.

3024: 225 Notarial act concerning the ship Rotterdam, 27 September 1760.

3876: 52 Notarial act concerning the ship Amazone, 22 September 1718.

HET UTRECHTS ARCHIEF
THE ARCHIVES OF UTRECHT

Notarissen geresideerd hebbende te Utrecht-stad
Notaries having resided at the town of Utrecht

See 1.1.23
Access no.: 34-4

U 124 a 2, act no. 49 Notarial act drawn up by Johannes Munster, among others involving Alida Pelius, widow of Herman Fensel (second-in-command in Bengal), and Elisabeth Fensel, concerning some goods, 1703.

U 169 a 14, act no. 93 Notarial act drawn up by Wernard van Vloten, among others involving Adriaan Bisdom (second-in-command in Bengal) and Arend Leliveld, concerning the collection of money from an estate at the Amsterdam Chamber of the VOC, 1754 (related to a power of attorney for George Lodewijk Vernet at Cossimbazar, 1753).

U 173 a 1, act no. 157 Notarial act drawn up by Arnold Herman van Munster, among others involving Jacob Sadelyn (*Opperhoofd* at Cossimbazar) and Pieter Houtuyn, concerning the collection of payment at the Amsterdam Chamber of the VOC, 1726 (related to a power of attorney for Huybert de Haze at Cossimbazar, 1725).

U 174 a 5, act no. 44 Notarial act drawn up by Willem Jacob van

	Overmeer, among others involving Abraham Ormea and Maurits Coeno (both factors in Bengal), and Jan van Vlooten, concerning the collection of payment at the Amsterdam Chamber of the VOC, 1734.
U 184 a 26, act nos 1, 167	Notarial acts drawn up by Hendrik van Dam, among others involving Geertruyd Alida de Leeuw, Gerardus Ewout de Leeuw and Andreas Franciscus Immens (factor and *Fiscaal* in Bengal), concerning an estate, 1763-4.
U 188 a 22, act no. 129	Notarial act drawn up by Dirk Oskamp, among others involving Pieter van de Weert and Willem van Staveren, concerning textiles from Bengal, 1761.
U 188 a 24, act no. 137	Notarial act drawn up by Dirk Oskamp, among others involving Otto Willem Falck (factor in Bengal) and Cornelis Harthals, concerning the collection of payment at the Amsterdam Chamber of the VOC, 1765 (related to a power of attorney for D.F. de Bary in Bengal, 1763).

Nederlands Hervormde Kerk (NHK): Raad voor de Zending
Dutch Reformed Church: Missionary Council

See 1.1.23
Access no.: 1102

341 Various papers concerning missionary activities, nineteenth and twentieth centuries, including reports about the mission in Bengal, 1825. One bundle, two folders (old inv. no. 'kast 38, dossier 1').

Huydecoper family

See 1.1.23
Access no.: 67

622 Papers concerning the VOC, added to the archives by Jan Elias Huydecoper from the papers of Gualterus Petrus Boudaen, 1670-1760. One bundle. Including:
- (a) Report by P.C.D. Veld (?) at Batavia, probably for Boudaen, concerning the situation in Bengal and Melaka, with a note of Huydecoper at the back, 1758. One quire (old no. 1149).

623 Papers concerning the VOC, added to the archives by Jan Elias Huydecoper from the papers of Gualterus Petrus Boudaen, 1762-78. One bundle. Including:
- (a) Extract of a letter from Batavia concerning the British and the Nawab of Bengal, 1763. One piece.

Grothe family and related families

See 1.1.23
Access no.: 750

365 Certificate of baptism of Margaretha Pit, issued by Joannes Evans of the English church at Cossimbazar, 1682. One piece, in Latin.

1361 Testament of Joseph Loten and his wife Alberta Pierraerd (deceased in 1716), drawn up at Hooghly, 1716. One quire.

Ram family and related families

See 1.1.23
Access no.: 752

812 Fragment of a letter from Johannes Vos to his cousin or nephew Philips Ram about his life in the East Indies, including a reference to Bengal, 1759. One piece.

6.2. Universities

UNIVERSITEIT VAN AMSTERDAM, UNIVERSITEITSBIBLIOTHEEK
UNIVERSITY OF AMSTERDAM, UNIVERSITY LIBRARY

Manuscripts

See 1.2.2

IV B 27 Journal of the ship Kooningh van Pruissen of the Prussian Bengal Company, kept by Captain Pieter Londt on the voyage from Emden to Calcutta and back, 1760, with several drawings (see 6.6). One volume (catalogue: Vol. II, no. 1308).

VIII G 60, 233-4 Letter from A. Bogaardt at Chinsura to Johan van Hoogstraten, 1778. One piece.

UNIVERSITEIT LEIDEN, UNIVERSITEITSBIBLIOTHEEK
LEIDEN UNIVERSITY LIBRARY

Bibliotheca Publica Latina
Latin Public Library

See 1.2.7

BPL 246 Various correspondence, alphabetically arranged, mostly according to sender, with index. Approx. 30 folders. Including:

(a) Two letters from the chief-factor Cornelis de Jonge (deceased in 1743) at Hooghly to Joan François de Witte van Schooten, 1738-9. Possibly filed under 'Schooten'.

BPL 328 Essay concerning East Indies affairs, beginning with an extract from the history of Dirk van Hogendorp (1761-1822) who stayed in Patna from *c.* 1786 to 1789, deriving from H. van Roijen, 1801. One folder.

BPL 617 *Resoluties* (proceedings), letters, memorandums and other papers concerning the VOC, with list of contents, 1687-1769, probably deriving from Augustinus van Son (1722-89), who became Secretary of the representatives of the Stadtholder with the VOC in 1750, and Lawyer of the VOC in 1755. 32 folders. Including:

29 Memorandums concerning conflicts with the British, partly regarding Bengal, the Nawab and saltpetre, 1711-63.

BPL 623 Dissertation concerning the state of the VOC, including an extensive section on Bengal (ff. 334v-51), with its Dutch establishments, commodities and a historical survey from 1552 to 1724.

Bibliotheca Thysiana
Thysius Library

See 1.2.7

5845 Report about a great fire at Patna in June 1651, which destroyed the royal palace, printed as a kind of newsletter. One piece (number 2627 in the catalogue by Petit and Ruys).

Oosterse Handschriften (Legatum Warnerianum)
Oriental Manuscripts (Warner's Legacy)

See 1.2.7

Or. 3090 Various papers, largely in Persian and Bengali (mostly in Arabic script), probably chiefly originating from Bengal and consisting of documents concerning slaves and passes sent to an unknown Dutch addressee, 1691, *c.* 1750-4 (?). One folder. Including:

3 Letter in Bengali (?), in Arabic script (?), *c.* 1750-4 (?).

6 Document in Bengali, in Bengali script, *c.* 1750-4 (?).

7 Document in Persian, with a note in Dutch on the back stating it is a *dastak* (pass) issued by Nawab 'Zeidamat ...', *c.* 1750-4 (?).

9 'Panciho de Notario', document in Persian related to Naib Khadim Shar Qadi Muhammad Hamid Allah, with a note in Dutch on the back reading 'slave letters and passports / in Bengal from 1750 to 54'.

10 Document in Persian (?), 1753, with a note in Dutch on the back stating it is a *dastak* for a 'Bassora', 'Cassimier' and 'oelak' accompanying Chief Chirurgeon Gerrit Moss departing from Hooghly, drawn up at Cossimbazar in 1754, signed by Adriaan Bisdom.

12 Document in Persian (?), with a note in Dutch on the back saying it was sent by Nawab 'Serate Daula' (Siraj-ud-Daula?), *c.* 1750-4 (?).

BIBLIOTHEEK UNIVERSITEIT TILBURG
TILBURG UNIVERSITY LIBRARY

Handschriften
Manuscripts

See 1.2.8

TF-HS 75 Correspondence of Joan Gideon Loten (1710-89) at Semarang, 1736-7. One volume (catalogue no. 56). Including:

ff. 125-6 Letter from his cousins Mr and Ms Huijghens at Hooghly, 1737.

UNIVERSITEIT UTRECHT, UNIVERSITEITSBIBLIOTHEEK
UTRECHT UNIVERSITY LIBRARY

Handschriften
Manuscripts

See 1.2.10

Hs. 1480 (1.E.25) Various papers deriving from the Dutch official and traveller Jacob Haafner (1755-1809), late eighteenth century. 13 folders. Described in J. de Moor and P. van der Velde, 'De "heilige tale des lands". Jacob Haafner als voorloper van de studie van het Sanskrit in Nederland', in H.J. 't Hart-van den Muyzenberg and Th. de Bruin (eds), *Waarom Sanskrit? Honderdvijfentwintig jaar Sanskrit in Nederland* (Kern Institute miscellanea, 4) (Leiden, 1991), pp. 90-1. Including:

1, 3, 5, 7-12 Letters, notes and lists in Bengali, including bookkeeping and a philosophical text by the early ninth-century philosopher Shankara (?) (incorrectly bound).

2 Bengali words for insects and a note to Haafner by a Briton at Calcutta concerning the rent for a house, in English, 1785.

4 Notes in Bengali with English translations concerning ceremonies to be executed if a Bengali is possessed by the devil or a witch.

6 Texts in Bengali and Persian (?).

6.3. Ecclesiastical Organizations

ARCHIEF VAN DE NEDERLANDSE PROVINCIE DER JEZUÏETEN (Nijmegen)
ARCHIVES OF THE NETHERLANDS PROVINCE OF THE JESUITS

Handschriften
Manuscripts

See 1.3.2

A.D. 3 (box 21) Letters sent by Jesuits in India to Jesuits in Europe. Photocopies and contemporary manuscript copies, with recent documentation and notes pertaining to these letters and Jesuits in India, one folder. Including:
- (a) Letter from Pierre Martin at Balasore to Villette, 1699. In French.
- (b) Letter from Chandernagore, 1701. In French.
- (c) Letter from Quenein at Chandernagore to Le Gobien at Paris, 1702.

6.4. Museums and Other Public Institutions

KONINKLIJK INSTITUUT VOOR DE TROPEN (KIT) (Amsterdam)
ROYAL TROPICAL INSTITUTE

Tropen Museum
Tropical Museum

See 1.4.2

3710 / 44b Letter from Professor Wilson, Secretary of the Asiatic Society at Calcutta, requesting the sending of some pages of the *Rig Veda*, 1811. In English.

3710 / 45 Letter from Reverent D. Wilson, Bishop at Calcutta, 1820. In English.

NEDERLANDS SCHEEPVAARTMUSEUM AMSTERDAM
NETHERLANDS MARITIME MUSEUM AMSTERDAM

Library

See 1.4.4

A-III-278 Nautical guide consisting of sailing instructions and landfalls of locations in Europe, Africa, and the East and West Indies, by Hans

N. Lunge, on board various ships, 1756-66, including instructions concerning (the surroundings of) Balasore and the 'Jangarnat' Temple in Orissa (Jagannath Temple at Puri?). One volume (alternative inv. no. B.0208 (03)).

B-III-616 Memorandum by Robert Voute to the States General declaring that the trade of the ship Antoinetta in Calcutta (of Robert Charnock?) is not violating the monopoly of the VOC, *c.* 1790. Printed, one volume.

B-III-870 Various printed papers concerning the VOC, with register. Three largely identical volumes. Including:

8 Sailing instructions for the route from the Cape of Good Hope to Bengal, 1783.

J-199 Papers deriving from or concerning Jacob Pieter van Braam (1737-1803), 1758-94. One folder. Including:

(3) Appointment of Braam as *Equipagemeester* (master of the equipage) of Bengal, 1761.

CENTRAAL BUREAU VOOR GENEALOGIE (CBG) (The Hague) CENTRAL OFFICE FOR GENEALOGY

Van Boecop family

See 1.4.11
Access no.: FA 00031

61.2.01 Various papers, including *c.* ten letters from Johan Schwendler at Hooghly to his father Cornelis (born 1701) and mother, 1754-62, a letter from H.P. Faure (?) at Batavia to Johan Schwendler, 1757, and a paper concerning the estate of someone in Bengal. One folder.

63.2.01 Various papers, including *c.* five letters from Johan Schwendler at Hooghly to his brother Iman Bonifacius (born 1730) and his wife, 1757-63. One folder.

64.4.01 Payment accounts of Johan Schwendler at Hooghly, with appendices, including a letter received from Batavia, 1756-61. One folder.

64.5.01 Diary or *dagregister* (*c.* 100 ff.) kept by Johan Schwendler at Hooghly, including translations from Persian texts such as a report by a VOC *Wakil* (representative) at Cossimbazar concerning events at Murshidabad since the death of Nawab Alivardi Khan, and *parwanas* (official orders) and letters exchanged with Nawab Siraj-ud-Daula and other Indian officials, *c.* April-July 1756. One folder.

65.2.01 Various papers, including *c.* ten letters from Johan Schwendler at Hooghly to his sister Geertruid (1743-1810, married to Henricus Justus Michael van Boecop), 1755-64. One folder

67.2.01 Letter from Johan Schwendler at Hooghly to his uncle Justinus, 1762. One piece.

KONINKLIJKE BIBLIOTHEEK (KB) (The Hague)
ROYAL LIBRARY

Handschriften
Manuscripts

See 1.4.12

72 E 17 Eleven letters from Thomas Stamford Raffles to N. Wallich, botanist at Calcutta, sent from Penang, Singapore and Bengkulu, 1819-24. In English, one volume.

76 A 8 Correspondence between VOC officials in Bengal, mostly concerning trade, 1673-6. One volume. Including:

ff. 1-35v Letters to *Directeur* Constantijn Ranst Junior (1669-73), from Daniel Keskes and E. van Jonasz at Mirzapur, and Jacob Verburgh, Herman Fentzel, Jan Pit, Joan van Lieve and David van den Hemel at Cossimbazar.

ff. 35v-89v Letters to Jacob Verburgh, chief-factor, and Herman Fentzel, factor and second-in-command, from Hendrik Canzius, David van den Hemel and Jan Pit at Cossimbazar.

ff. 89v-212 Letters to *Directeur* François de Haze (1674-6), from David van den Hemel, Jan Pit and Jacob Verburgh at Cossimbazar.

ff. 213-14v Chronological list of the letters.

KONINKLIJK INSTITUUT VOOR TAAL-, LAND- EN VOLKENKUNDE (KITLV) (Leiden)
ROYAL INSTITUTE OF LINGUISTICS AND ANTHROPOLOGY

Collectie in westerse talen
Collection in Western languages

See 1.4.14

H 496 Memorandum about coins, weights and measures in Asia, including sections on Hooghly, Cossimbazar, Rajmahal, Pipli, Balasore, Dhaka, Patna, Sherpur and Khanakul, *c.* 1665 (?). One volume.

H 562 Correspondence between Thomas Stamford Raffles and Thomas Horsfield, 1813-23. One folder. Including:

7 Letter from Raffles at Calcutta to Horsfield, 1819 (three ff.).

H 990 Letters of Thomas Stamford Raffles to Lord Minto, 1810-14. Photocopies of the originals kept in the India Office Library at London, four volumes. Including:

Vol. 1, ff. 6-11 Letter sent from Calcutta, 1810.

MARITIEM MUSEUM ROTTERDAM
MARITIME MUSEUM ROTTERDAM

Handschriften
Manuscripts

See 1.4.24

H25 Notes regarding ships of the EIC, partly concerning ships in Bengal, *c.* 1799. One piece (originating from the archives of Rear Admiral C. de Jong van Rodenburgh).

H456 Ship's logs by Albert Bichon, 1690-8, including journals of the ship Walenburgh, sailing five times to Bengal (from other locations in Asia), 1692-7. One volume.

H618 Survey of Otto Willem Falck's receipts and expenses during his stay in Asia, 1756-75, including sections concerning Hooghly, 1757-74. One volume.

H692 Ship's logs, 1785-90, including a journal by J.G. Drees on board the vessel d'Goede Trouw sailing from Batavia to Melaka and Bengal, October 1787-January 1788, and a journal by J. Arkenhout on board the ship Verwagting sailing under the command of J.G. Drees from Bengal to Batavia, March-July 1788. One volume.

H736 Letters by Claas Bichon (and his wife Elisabeth Lucasz) to various people, with register, 1694-7. One volume. Including:

ff. 3-4, 8	Two letters to Commander Simon van der Bergh in Bengal, 1694.
ff. 7, 10, 22, 27	Four letters to *Independent Fiscaal* Dirck van Bleijswijck in Bengal, 1694-5.
f. 37	Letter to *Directeur* Pieter van Dishoeck (1696-1701), 1696.
ff. 50-1	Letter to Benjamin Burlamachi, second-in-command in Bengal, 1697.

6.5. Companies, Private Organizations and Individuals

TUTEIN NOLTHENIUS (Doorn)

Tutein Nolthenius family

See 1.5.3

(a) Approx. 130 letters (and a few other documents), chiefly received by Balthazar Nolthenius and Johanna Boel from relatives and friends at various locations in the East Indies, 1737-42. One volume. With early twentieth-century transcriptions and summaries. Described in Tutein

Nolthenius, 'De brieven van Overzee', pp. 453-63 (see Supplement I: Bibliography, no. 57). Including:

48-50 Three letters from Nolthenius' brother-in-law Nicolaas Paradijs at Hooghly, 1739. Summarized in Tutein Nolthenius, 'Verdere brieven van overzee', pp. 1045-6 (see Supplement I: Bibliography, no. 44).

KONINKLIJK HUISARCHIEF (The Hague)
ARCHIVES OF THE ROYAL FAMILY

Prince William V

See 1.5.6
Access no.: A 31

217: V 24 a Correspondence with various people including W. (Count) van Hogendorp, 1784-9. One bundle. Including:
- (a) Letter from G.W. de Haven, 23 April 1789, with a letter from Dirk van Hogendorp at Patna, 1788. In French.
- (b) Two letters from Dirk van Hogendorp at Patna and Hooghly, concerning the opium policy of the EIC and related privileges granted by the Mughals, and Van Hogendorp's departure to Batavia, 20 August 1787 and 5 April 1788. Partly in French.

333: II Correspondence of Thomas Hope and the Duke of Brunswijk, 1767-8. One bundle. Including:
- (a) Letter from Hope to the Duke of Brunswijk, 4 October 1767, with lètters from *Directeur* George Lodewijk Vernet (1763-9) at Hooghly to Hope, 1767.

333: III Correspondence of Thomas Hope and the Duke of Brunswijk, 1768-71. One bundle. Including:
- (a) (in file 1) Extract from a letter from Hooghly, 8 January 1768.
- (b) (in file 1) Letter from Hope to the Duke of Brunswijk, 23 December 1768, with a letter from Vernet and Council to Hope and the Gentlemen XVII, concerning complaints about the EIC trade in Bengal, 1768.
- (c) (in file 2) Letter from Bengal to the Gentlemen XVII, 21 November 1769.

333: VI b Correspondence of William V with Willem Jacob van de Graaff, Johan Gerard van Angelbeek, H. (Adriaan?) Moens, D.D. (Count) van Ranzou and others, concerning the VOC, 1773-95. One bundle. Including:
- (a) (in file 35) Letter from Bengal concerning local affairs, 1788. In French.
- (b) (in file 38) Letter from *Directeur* Johannes Bacheracht

(1771-6) at Hooghly concerning the donation of 'Hindustan' weaponry, 7 January 1776.

(c) (in file 38) Letter from Hooghly, 10 January 1789.

F1-22 (?) Papers concerning the share of William V in the *Amfioen Sociëteit* (opium trade association), with a table of contents, *c.* 1745-93. One bundle. Including:

27 Extracts from two letters from *Directeur* Louis Taillefert (1760-3) and the factor M. Isink at Hooghly to the GG&C, concerning the opium trade and the EIC activities in this respect, 1762.

ORDE VAN VRIJMETSELAREN ONDER HET GROOTOOSTEN DER NEDERLANDEN (The Hague)
FRATERNITY OF FREEMASONS UNDER THE GRAND EAST OF THE NETHERLANDS

Constitutie dossiers
Constitution files

See 1.5.7

2401-4 Files concerning Masonic lodges. Including:

(a) Salomon at Taldangra (?), 1758-75. Partly in French, one folder.

(b) De Standvastigheid (La Constance) at Hooghly, 1772-3. One folder.

6.6. Maps and Pictures

ARCHIEFDIENST VOOR KENNEMERLAND (Haarlem)
ARCHIVAL SERVICE FOR KENNEMERLAND

Kennemer Atlas
Kennemerland Atlas

See 1.6.1

53-999001-1k Around 80 sketches by Cornelis van Noorde, 1756-83, including on p. 150 a chalk drawing depicting a rhinoceros named Clara (caught in Assam in 1738, presented to *Directeur* Jan Albert Sichterman and shipped to Rotterdam in 1741 by Captain Douwemout van der Meer) on a fair in Haarlem, 1756. One volume (15 x 24 cm) (old no. 232). Described and reproduced in Verheij, *Op reis met Clara*, p. 46 (see Supplement I: Bibliography, no. 886) and B. Sliggers (ed.), *Het schetsboek van Cornelis van Noorde, 1731-1795. Het leven van een veelzijdig Haarlems kunstenaar* (Haarlem, 1982), pp. 146-7.

UNIVERSITEIT VAN AMSTERDAM, ARTIS BIBLIOTHEEK
UNIVERSITY OF AMSTERDAM, ARTIS LIBRARY

Artis Bibliotheek
Artis Library

See 1.2.1

H — Tiger and tigress from Bengal, drawn by J. v. Haastert (1753-1834) at Delft, 1806. Water colour (22 x 34 cm).

Legkast 238 — 'Wonderen der natuur', collection of *c.* 180 depictions of special and exotic animals and people as seen in the menagerie at the hostelry of Blauw Jan (Jan Westerhof) in Amsterdam and some other locations, by Jan Velten, *c.* 1695-1709. Seven boxes. Reproduced on CD. Including:

- 95 — Tree with amadavats (birds) from Bengal. Water colour or gouache.
- 135 — Munia from Bengal. Water colour or gouache. Reproduced in F.F.J.M. Pieters and H. Veldhuijzen van Zanten (eds), *Wonderen der natuur in de menagerie van Blauw Jan te Amsterdam, zoals gezien door Jan Velten rond 1700 / Wonders of Nature in the Menagerie of Blauw Jan in Amsterdam, as Observed by Jan Velten around 1700* (Amsterdam, 1998), p. 101.

S 1b — Sloth from Bengal, in the menagerie of Prince William V of Orange, by Aart Schouman. Washed pen drawing (16 x 16 cm). Reproduced in B.C. Sliggers and A.A. Wertheim (eds), *Een vorstelijke dierentuin. De Menagerie van Willem V / Le zoo du prince. La Ménagerie du stathouder Guillaume V* (Haarlem and Paris, 1994), p. 27, and F.F.J.M. Pieters, 'Diergaarden in de Nederlanden 1750-1850 en hun betekenis voor de Zoologie', in *Acta Octavi Conventus Historiae Scientiae Medicinae Matheseos Naturaliumque Excolendae* (Amsterdam, 1978), p. 62.

UNIVERSITEIT VAN AMSTERDAM, UNIVERSITEITSBIBLIOTHEEK
UNIVERSITY OF AMSTERDAM, UNIVERSITY LIBRARY

Kaarten en Atlassen
Maps and Atlases

See 1.6.2

1-2-A-9 (28) — Map of the Bengal 'kingdom', Amsterdam, 1773. Copper engraving, coloured, in French, scale 1:4,000,000. Identical to no. 108-01-120, see below.

25-32-16 — Map of the Bengal 'kingdom', made by Joh. van Leenen by order of Mattheus van den Broucke, Dordrecht (?), *c.* 1700. Copper engraving, scale 1:2,340,000.

33-13-12 & 13 Two identical maps of the Bengal 'kingdom', made by Joh. van Leenen by order of Mattheus van den Broucke, published by J. van Braam and G. onder de Linden. One coloured (old inv. nos 10072M-3M).

108-01-120 Map of the Bengal 'kingdom', Amsterdam, 1773. Copper engraving, coloured, in French, scale 1:4,000,000. Identical to no. 1-2-A-9 (28), see above.

Manuscripts

See 1.2.2

IV B 27 Landfalls of the coasts of Orissa and Bengal, including landfalls of 'Jan Garnaat' (Jagannath Temple at Puri?) and the 'Black Pagoda' (Konarka?), in the journal of the ship Kooningh van Pruissen of the Prussian Bengal Company, kept by Captain Pieter Londt on the voyage from Emden to Calcutta and back, 1760. One volume (catalogue: Vol. II, no. 1308).

Port. A X Drawings, notes and correspondence concerning rhinoceroses by the Physician Petrus Camper (1722-89), 1739-88. One folder. Including:

(a) Four sketches of a rhinoceros named Clara (caught in Assam in 1738, presented to *Directeur* Jan Albert Sichterman and shipped to Rotterdam in 1741 by Captain Douwemout van der Meer), 1748 (?). Chalk drawings. Described and re-produced in Verheij, *Op reis met Clara*, pp. 31-3 (see Supplement I: Bibliography, no. 886).

(b) Rhinoceros caught at Patna by the EIC and shipped to London, 1739. Print.

VRIJE UNIVERSITEIT AMSTERDAM, BIBLIOTHEEK
VRIJE UNIVERSITEIT AMSTERDAM, LIBRARY

Kaartenverzameling
Map collection

See 1.6.2

LL.04763gk: 000/od/1760 'Atlas du Sr. [Jean Baptiste Bourguignon] d'Anville', consisting of 24 separate copper engravings by Guill. de la Haye, compiled at Paris after 1760. In French, partly coloured, one folder. Including:

2b Part of a map of Asia, showing Bengal, northeast India and east Asia, 1751. Scale 1:6,650,000.

BIBLIOTHEEK TECHNISCHE UNIVERSITEIT DELFT
DELFT UNIVERSITY OF TECHNOLOGY LIBRARY

Kaarten
Maps

See 1.6.2

TRL 6.4.1 L 13 Map of Bengal, by J. v. Schley, *c.* 1780. Copper engraving, coloured, partly in French, scale *c.* 1:4,000,000 (29 x 35 cm) (old inv. no. H-7321-09).

UNIVERSITEIT LEIDEN, UNIVERSITEITSBIBLIOTHEEK
LEIDEN UNIVERSITY LIBRARY

Collectie Bodel Nijenhuis
Bodel Nijenhuis collection

See 1.6.2

006-14-016 Sea chart (in two sections) of the Bengal coast from Balasore to Sagar Island and the Hooghly River up to Hooghly, with soundings, fourth quarter of the seventeenth century. Pen and brush drawing, coloured, scale *c.* 1:260,000 and 1:350,000 (72 x 101 cm) (no. 66 in catalogue of sea charts).

006-14-017 Sea chart (in two sections) of the Bengal coast from Palmyras Point to Sagar Island and the Hooghly River up to Calcutta, with soundings, second quarter of the eighteenth century. Pen and brush drawing, coloured, scale *c.* 1:260,000 and 1:160,000 (71 x 99 cm) (no. 67 in catalogue of sea charts).

006-14-018 Sea chart (in two sections) of the Bengal coast from Palmyras Point to Sagar Island and the Hooghly River up to Calcutta, with soundings, second quarter of the eighteenth century. Pen and brush drawing, coloured, scale *c.* 1:260,000 and 1:160,000 (74 x 103 cm) (no. 68 in catalogue of sea charts).

010-07-036 Map of the Bengal coast between Palmyras Point and Sagar Island and the Hooghly River up to Baranagar, by Tho. Greg. Warren and William Wood, published by W. Mount and T. Page at London, 1748. Copper engraving, coloured, scale 1:440,000 (47 x 71 cm).

Port 176 N 48	Sea chart of the Bay of Bengal from Orissa to Chittagong, with soundings and legend, by G. de la Haye, published by A. Dalrymple, 1772. Copper engraving, in English (44 x 58 cm).
Port 176 N 50	Map of the Brahmaputra River from the head of the Lakhya or Banar River to Assam, with insets of view and plan of the 'Dellamcotta' fort in Bhutan, published by J. Rennell, 1780. Copper engraving, in English (25 x 59 cm).
Port 176 N 51	Map of the Ganges River from the 'Calligonga' to its confluence with the Meghna River and the Meghna River from there to the head of the Lakhya River, with inset showing a cross-section of the Jalangi River, published by J. Rennell, 1780. Copper engraving, in English (24 x 60 cm).
Port 176 N 77	Map of the course of the Ganges River from 'Colgong' to 'Hurrisonker', with insets of specific sectors and cross-sections, by R.H. Colebrooke, published by the Geographical Institute at Weimar, 1805. Copper engraving, coloured, in German (25 x 56 cm).
Port 176 N 117	Map of Bengal, by W. Bolts. Copper engraving, in French (36 x 52 cm).
Port 176 N 118	Map of Bengal, with soundings, by Joh. van Leenen by order of *Directeur* Mattheus van den Broucke, published by J. van Braam and G. onder de Linden. Copper engraving, coloured (44 x 54 cm). Closely resembling but slightly different from Valentijn, *Oud en nieuw Oost-Indiën*, Vol. V, part 1, 1st section, p. 146, see Appendix I.
Port 176 N 122 & N 123	Two identical maps of Bengal, by J. van der Schley. Copper engraving, one coloured, mostly in French (27 x 33 cm). Closely resembling but slightly different from Valentijn, *Oud en nieuw Oost-Indiën*, Vol. V, part 1, 1st section, p. 146, see Appendix I.
Port 176 N 124	Plan of the palace and gardens of 'Prince Cha-Sousa' of Rajmahal, and map of Monghyr, by J. van der Schley (?). Copper engraving, partly in French (17 x 12 cm).
Port 176 N 125	Map of the Hooghly River up to Hooghly and the Bengal coast down to Palmyras Point, with soundings, by d'Anville, 1752. Copper engraving, in French (32 x 23 cm).
Port 176 N 126 & N 127	Two identical maps of the Hooghly River and its vicinity from the Bay of Bengal to Bandel, with special reference to European settlements and a

few explanatory notes, based on the memory and observations of Jacque André Cobbé, by Eugene Henry Friex, Brussels, 1726. Copper engraving, one coloured, in French (46 x 66 cm).

Port 177 N 58 — Sea chart of the Bay of Bengal including the coast of east Bengal, with soundings, by Guillaume de la Haye. Copper engraving (48 x 32 cm).

Port 314-I N 107 to N 110 — Views by Nicolaes de Graaff, made during his journey in Bengal in 1671. Four pen drawings and water colours (filed under no. 20506-23). Including:

N 107 VOC saltpetre factory at Chhapra (77 x 50 cm).[1]

N 108 VOC garden at Chhapra (71 x 40 cm).

N 109 Bay of Sultanganj with the 'Jangira' rock (72 x 38 cm).[1]

N 110 Monghyr, seen from the Ganges River (72 x 38 cm).[1]

[1] Described and reproduced in Barend-van Haeften, *Oost-Indië gespiegeld*, pp. 43-7 and cover (see Supplement I: Bibliography, no. 121); inv. no. N 107 also reproduced in Gaastra, *De geschiedenis van de VOC*, p. 76 (Bibl., no. 71), and partially in Jacobs, *Koopman in Azië*, p. 97 (Bibl., no. 104).

BIBLIOTHEEK WAGENINGEN UNIVERSITEIT EN RESEARCHCENTRUM
WAGENINGEN UNIVERSITY AND RESEARCH CENTRE LIBRARY

Speciale collecties
Special collections

See 1.6.2

R 362 D 01 — d'Acquet collection, mostly consisting of water colours of trees, plants, etc., from all over the world, including South Asia, after specimens in the collection of Hendrik d'Acquet (1632-1706), Burgomaster of Delft, *c.* 1670-1706. Coloured, 149 sheets (*c.* 16 x 20 cm). Described in detail in D.O. Wijnands, 'Planten uit de collectie van Henricus d'Acquet', in J. Kuijlen, C.S. Oldenburger-Ebbers and D.O. Wijnands, *Paradisus Batavus. Bibliografie van plantencatalogi van onderwijstuinen, particuliere tuinen en kwekerscollecties in de Noordelijke en Zuidelijke Nederlanden (1550-1839)* (Wageningen, 1983). Other parts of this collection are kept at the *Universiteit van Amsterdam, Universiteitsbibliotheek* (1.2.2), and the *Koninklijk Instituut voor de Tropen* (1.4.2). Together described in Bergvelt, Jonker and Wiechman, *Burgers verzamelen*, pp. 112-20 (see Supplement I: Bibliography, no. 122) and E. Bergvelt and R. Kistemaker (eds), *De wereld binnen handbereik. Nederlandse kunst- en rariteitenverzamelingen, 1585-1735* (Zwolle, 1992), pp. 223-30. Including:

f. 114 Plant from Bengal (and Africa), 1680.

KONINKLIJK INSTITUUT VOOR DE TROPEN (KIT) (Amsterdam)
ROYAL TROPICAL INSTITUTE

Kenniscentrum
Resource Centre

See 1.4.2

RG-84 Drawings of insects (such as beetles, flies, grasshoppers and butterflies), spiders, scorpions, amphibians, reptiles and molluscs from Asia, after specimens in the gallery of Hendrik d'Acquet (1632-1706), Burgomaster of Delft, partly with names of suppliers, *c.* 1680-1710. Coloured, 183 sheets (31 x 21 cm). Other parts of this collection are kept at the *Universiteit van Amsterdam, Universiteitsbibliotheek* (1.2.2), and the *Bibliotheek Wageningen Universiteit en Researchcentrum* (1.2.11). Together described in Bergvelt, Jonker and Wiechman, *Burgers verzamelen*, pp. 112-20 (see Supplement I: Bibliography, no. 122) and E. Bergvelt and R. Kistemaker (eds), *De wereld binnen handbereik. Nederlandse kunst- en rariteitenverzamelingen, 1585-1735* (Zwolle, 1992), pp. 223-30. Including:

part 1, f. 15	Two insects from Bengal, partly supplied by Rich. Meuster (?), 1695, 1698.
part 1, ff. 25, 27, 33, 35, 45, 58, 60-1	Various insects from Bengal, 1690-1706.[1]
part 1, f. 66	Scorpion from Bengal, supplied by Professor Hermans, 1688.[1]
part 2, f. 36, 45-6	Various insects from Bengal, 1694-6.
part 3, f. 39	'Sourijkatie' (rodent or lizard?) from Bengal, 1695.

[1] Folios 33, 66 described and reproduced on pp. 128-9 of the *Catalogus* accompanying Bergvelt and Kistemaker, *De wereld binnen handbereik*; f. 66 also in *De wereld binnen handbereik* itself, p. 223.

NEDERLANDS SCHEEPVAARTMUSEUM AMSTERDAM
NETHERLANDS MARITIME MUSEUM AMSTERDAM

Zeevaartkundige collectie
Navigational collection

See 1.6.4

S.0521 (088) Map of part of the Bengal coast, by John Ritchie in 1768-70, published by Aaron Arrowsmith at London, 1806. In English (67 x 77 cm).

Iconografische collectie
Iconographic collection

See 1.6.4

RB.0568 Bird's-eye view of a 'Dutch plantation' in Bengal, probably the VOC factory at Cossimbazar, and its surroundings, including Bengali villages, a visiting English official, merchandise, cows, horses, birds, etc., by Hendrik van Schuylenburgh, *c.* 1665. Oil on canvas (133 x 205 cm). Given on loan by the *Rijkmuseum Amsterdam*, see 1.6.4. Originally inv. no. SK-A-4283, pendant to inv. no. SK-A-4282, see *Rijkmuseum Amsterdam, Afdeling Nederlandse Geschiedenis*, below. Described and reproduced in Gosselink, 'Schilderijen van Bengaalse VOC-loges' (see Supplement I: Bibliography, no. 875), and E. Jacobs, *Varen om peper en thee. Korte geschiedenis van de Verenigde Oostindische Compagnie / In Pursuit of Pepper and Tea. The Story of the Dutch East India Company* (Zutphen, 1991, 1996), p. 80.

Library

See 1.4.4

A-III-278 Nautical guide consisting of sailing instructions and landfalls of locations in Europe, Africa, and the East and West Indies, by Hans N. Lunge, on board various ships, 1756-66, including landfalls of (the surroundings of) Balasore and the 'Jangarnat' Temple in Orissa (Jagannath Temple at Puri?). Coloured, one volume (alternative inv. no. B.0208 (03)).

RIJKSMUSEUM AMSTERDAM
RIJKSMUSEUM AMSTERDAM

Afdeling Nederlandse Geschiedenis
Department of Dutch History

See 1.6.4

NG-105 to 118 Fourteen epitaph panels showing arms, initials and dates of death (and sometimes birth) of VOC personnel in Bengal, 1665-1783. Indian wood or metal. Originating from the church at Chinsura and presented by the bishop of Calcutta in 1949. Partly published in Epen, 'Grafschriften in Voor-Indië' (see Supplement I: Bibliography, no. 69). Including:

- NG-105 *Directeur* Rogier van Heyningen (d. 1665) (122 x 121 cm).
- NG-106 "W.A.', probably deputy *Directeur* Arnoldus van Wachtendonck (d. 1668) (115 x 115 cm).
- NG-107 *Directeur* Nicolaas Baukes (d. 1683) (119 x 119 cm).
- NG-108 *Directeur* Marten Huysman (d. 1685) (125 x 129 cm).

NG-109 *Directeur* Pieter van Dishoeck (d. 1701) (128 x 130 cm).

NG-110 *Directeur* Rogier Beernaards (d. 1733) (120 x 119 cm).

NG-111 Probably Jeronimo Isinck (152 x 150 cm).

NG-112 Theodora Hendrica Piekenbroek (d. 1770), wife of *Directeur* Boudewijn Versewel Faure (100 x 100 cm).[2]

NG-113 *Directeur* Boudewijn Versewel Faure (d. 1770) (101 x 100 cm).[2]

NG-114 Theodora Antoinette Bodle (d. 1774) (124 x 123 cm).

NG-115 *Directeur* George Lodewijk Vernet (d. 1775) (100 x 100 cm).

NG-116 Tammerus Canter Visscher, *Opperhoofd* at Cossimbazar (d. 1778) (135 x 136 cm).

NG-117 *Directeur* François de Haze (d. 1676) (123 x 125 cm).

NG-118 Pieter de Brueys, chief-factor at Chinsura (d. 1783) (104 x 103 cm).

NG-400-C View of the south and west sides of Fort Gustavus at Chinsura, by Johannes Rach (1720-83) or an imitator, 1762. Washed Indian ink drawing (34 x 49 cm).

SK-A-158 Portrait of *Directeur* Mattheus van den Broucke (1658-63), depicted as Commander of the return fleet, by Samuel van Hoogstraten (1627-78), *c.* 1672. Canvas (142 x 111 cm). Described and reproduced in Akveld and Jacobs, *De kleurrijke wereld / The Colourful World*, p. 174 (see Supplement I: Bibliography, no. 61), Zandvliet, *De Nederlandse ontmoeting met Azië / The Dutch Encounter with Asia*, pp. 187-9 (Bibl., no. 98), Kalff, 'Een Indisch portret' (Bibl., no. 880), and G.P. Sanders, 'Joan Aalwis Widjejewarddene Senewiratne en *de uijtgebreidheid van een mostaart Zaatje.* Een Ceylonese beloningspenning uitgereikt door de Verenigde Oostindische Compagnie in 1762', *Bulletin van het Rijksmuseum*, 42, 1 (1994), p. 14.

SK-A-3777 Portrait of *Directeur* Abraham Patras (1724-7), depicted as Governor-General, by Theodorus Justinus Rheen, *c.* 1737. Copper (102 x 85 cm). (SK-A-4546 is a copy. Copper, 34 x 27 cm.) Described in J. de Loos-Haaxman, *De landsverzameling schilderijen in Batavia*, 2 vols (Leiden, 1941) and F.W. Stapel, *De gouverneurs-generaal van Nederlandsch-Indië in beeld en woord* (The Hague, 1941).

SK-A-4282 Bird's-eye view of the VOC factory at Hooghly and its surroundings, including a procession of a VOC envoy (to Cossimbazar?), a camp of an Indian official (sent by the Nawab of Bengal?), merchandise, Dutch and Indian vessels on the Hooghly River, a woman committing *sati*, Hindus doing penance, Indian musicians, part of a Muslīm graveyard, elephants, horses, dromedaries, cows, etc., by Hendrik van Schuylenburgh (*c.* 1620-89), possibly by order of *Directeur* Pieter Sterthemius (1655-8), 1665. Oil on canvas (203 x 316 cm).[1,2] Pendant to SK-A-4283, see below.

SK-A-4283 Bird's-eye view of a 'Dutch plantation' in Bengal, probably the VOC factory at Cossimbazar, and its surroundings, including Bengali villages, a visiting English official, merchandise, cows, horses, birds, etc., by Hendrik van Schuylenburgh, *c.* 1665. Oil on canvas (133 x 205 cm).[1] Pendant to SK-A-4282, see above. At the time of writing given on loan to the *Nederlands Scheepvaartmuseum Amsterdam*, see 1.4.4.

[1] Described and reproduced in Gosselink, 'Schilderijen van Bengaalse VOC-loges' (see Supplement I: Bibliography, no. 875), and J.C. Mollema, *Geschiedenis van Nederland ter Zee* (Amsterdam, 1942), Vol. IV; inv. no. SK-A-4282 also described and reproduced in Akveld and Jacobs, *De kleurrijke wereld / The Colourful World*, pp. 170-3 (Bibl., no. 61), and Zandvliet, *De Nederlandse ontmoeting met Azië / The Dutch Encounter with Asia*, pp. 189-92 (Bibl., no. 98); inv. no. SK-A-4283 also reproduced in E. Jacobs, *Varen om peper en thee. Korte geschiedenis van de Verenigde Oostindische Compagnie / In Pursuit of Pepper and Tea. The Story of the Dutch East India Company* (Zutphen, 1991, 1996), p. 87.

[2] Reproduced in Stevens, *De VOC in bedrijf / Dutch Enterprise and the VOC*, pp. 90-1, 95 (see Supplement I: Bibliography, no. 85); inv. no. NG-113 also in Peters and André de la Porte, *In steen geschreven*, p. 102 (Bibl., no. 848), and Jacobs, *Koopman in Azië*, p. 85 (Bibl., no. 104).

Rijksprentenkabinet
Print Room

See 1.6.4

Frederik Muller no. 3786B Rhinoceros named Clara (caught in Assam in 1738, presented to *Directeur* Jan Albert Sichterman and shipped to Rotterdam in 1741 by Captain Douwemout van der Meer) and an archer, with explanatory text in German. Print (new inv. no. RP-P-A-23739?).

RP-P-1896-A-19368/240 Bengali bridegroom on horseback being led to his bride, by Jan Luyken. Etching.

RP-P-A-23739 Rhinoceros named Clara, with inset showing Douwemout van der Meer and explanatory notes in various languages. Print (Frederik Muller no. 3786B).

RP-P-OB-67.347 Portrait of *Directeur* Abraham Patras (1724-7), depicted as Governor-General, by Jacobus van der Schley. Engraving.

RP-P-OB-75362 Rhinoceros named Clara at Mannheim in 1747, with inset showing Douwemout van der Meer, explanatory notes in various languages and a poem in German. Print (Frederik Muller no. 3786). Reproduced in Verheij, *Op reis met Clara*, pp. 11, 24 (see Supplement I: Bibliography, no. 886), and W. Kühne-van Diggelen, *Jan Albert Sichterman. VOC-dienaar en 'koning' van Groningen* (Groningen, 1995), p. 44.

DORDRECHTS MUSEUM
MUSEUM OF DORDRECHT

Schilder-, teken- en prentkunst
Paintings, drawings and prints

See 1.6.4

DM/890/499 Portrait of *Directeur* Mattheus van den Broucke (1658-63), with references to his period as VOC official, by Samuel van Hoogstraten (1627-78), 1676. Oil on canvas (89 x 71 cm). Described and reproduced in P. Marijnissen a.o. (ed.), *De zichtbaere werelt. Schilderkunst uit de Gouden Eeuw in Hollands oudste stad* (Zwolle and Dordrecht, 1992), pp. 206-7, and A. Tamvaki and S. Paarlberg, *The Golden Age of Dutch Painting from the Collection of the Dordrechts Museum* (Athens, 2002), pp. 196-7.

SIMON VAN GIJN - MUSEUM AAN HUIS (Dordrecht)
SIMON VAN GIJN - MUSEUM AT HOME

Main collection

See 1.6.4

1754 Portrait of *Directeur* Mattheus van den Broucke (1658-63), portrayed as Burgomaster of Dordrecht, by Godfried Schalcker, *c.* 1680-5. Oil on canvas (44 x 36 cm).

GRONINGER MUSEUM
MUSEUM OF GRONINGEN

Schilderijen
Paintings

See 1.6.4

1991.0205 Portrait of *Directeur* Jan Albert Sichterman (1734-44), by C.L. Havercamp, 1755. Oil on canvas (70 x 87 cm).[1]

1991.0206 Portrait of Sibilla Volkera Sadelijn, wife of Sichterman, by C.L. Havercamp, 1755. Oil on canvas (70 x 87 cm).[1]

1992.0212 Portrait of Jan Albert Sichterman with his son Jan Albert and a servant, by Philip van Dijk, 1745. Oil on canvas (149 x 117 cm).[1]

1992.0213 Portrait of Sibilla Volkera Sadelijn with her daughters Sibilla Volkera (1735-1803) and Christina Elisabeth, by Philip van Dijk, 1745. Oil on canvas (149 x 117).[1]

[1] Reproduced in W. Kühne-van Diggelen, *Jan Albert Sichterman. VOC-dienaar en 'koning' van Groningen* (Groningen, 1995), pp. 18-19, 68-9; inv. no. 1991.0205 also in Jacobs, *Koopman in Azië*, p. 217 (see Supplement I: Bibliography, no. 104); inv. nos 1992.0212-13 also in E.A.J. Ast-Boiten, *De terugkeer van twee portretten van Philip van Dijk* (1993).

MUSEUM BOERHAAVE (Leiden)
BOERHAAVE MUSEUM

Prentencollectie
Print collection

See 1.6.4

P00410-11 Depictions of a rhinoceros named Clara (caught in Assam in 1738, presented to *Directeur* Jan Albert Sichterman and shipped to Rotterdam in 1741 by Captain Douwemout van der Meer) in Dresden, by M. Bodenehr, 1747, and in Stuttgart (with Clara fighting against an elephant in the background). Partly in German, French and English, two prints (44 x 58 cm, 32 x 42 cm) (old nos B1229, B662). Described and reproduced in Verheij, *Op reis met Clara*, pp. 13, 20, 26 (see Supplement I: Bibliography, no. 886).

ATLAS VAN STOLK (Rotterdam)
VAN STOLK ATLAS

Atlas van Stolk

See 1.6.4

29 P Atlas published by Joan Blaeu in 1665 (part 11, concerning Asia and Africa), containing an affixed view of 'Setegam', mentioned as being located in 22 degrees and 17 minutes north latitude, possibly referring to Chittagong. Pencil drawing (*c.* 20 x 45 cm).

3674 Depiction of a rhinoceros named Clara, caught in Assam in 1738, presented to *Directeur* Jan Albert Sichterman and shipped to Rotterdam in 1741 by Captain Douwemout van der Meer, with inset showing Van der Meer and explanatory notes in various languages, 1747. Engraving. Reproduced in Verheij, *Op reis met Clara*, p. 22 (see Supplement I: Bibliography, no. 886), and J. Beijerman-Schols a.o., *Geschiedenis in beeld* (Zwolle, 2000), p. 182.

HEYNING (The Hague)

Heijning family

See 1.5.5

(a) View of Fort Gustavus at Chinsura, with some people and animals in front of it, undated (*c.* 1800?). Manuscript drawing. Reproduced in Heyning, *Een Hollandse familie overzee*, p. 53 (see Supplement I: Bibliography, no. 876).

Appendices

Appendix I: Prints and Maps in Works Published Between *c.* 1600 and 1825

This inexhaustive overview covers the works listed below (in chronological order). Note that page numbers may be different in later editions. For modern reprints, translations, etc., see Supplement I and *Dutch Sources on South Asia*, Vol. 1, Bibliography. For a detailed survey of prints and maps in virtually all works concerning the VOC printed between *c.* 1600 and 1800, see J. Landwehr and P. van der Krogt (eds), *VOC. A Bibliography of Publications Relating to the Dutch East India Company, 1602-1800* (Utrecht, 1991).

- Jan Huygen van Linschoten, *Itinerario. Voyage ofte schipvaert* (Amsterdam, 1596).
- *'t Historiael journael van tghene ghepasseert is van weghen dry schepen, ghenaemt den Ram, Schaep, ende 't Lam* (Delft, 1605).
- Johan Theodor and Johan Israel de Bry, *Achter Theil der Orientalische Indien* (Frankfurt, 1606).
- Joannes de Laet, *De Imperio Magni Mogolis sive India vera commentarius e variis auctoribus congestus* (Leiden, 1631).
- Pieter van den Broecke, *Korte historiael ende journaelsche aenteyckeninghe* (Haarlem, 1634).
- Isaac Commelin (ed.), *Begin ende voortgangh van de Vereenighde Nederlantsche Geoctroyeerde Oost-Indische Compagnie*, 2 vols (Amsterdam, 1645).
- *Journael van de Voyagie gedaen met drie schepen, uyt Zeelandt, naer Oost-Indien, onder het beleydt van den Commandeur Joris van Spilbergen, zijn eerste reyse, uytghevaren in de jare 1601, 1602, 1603, en 1604* (Amsterdam, *c.* 1648?).
- Johan van Twist, *Generaele beschrijvinghe van Indiën. Ende in 't bysonder kort verhael van de regering, ceremonien, handel, vruchten en gelegentheyt van 't koninckrijck van Gusuratten ...* (Hendrick Doncker's 2nd edn., Amsterdam, 1650).
- Abraham Rogerius, *De open-deure, tot het verborgen heydendom ofte waerachtigh vertoogh van het leven ende zeden, mitsgaders de religie, ende gods-dienst der Bramines, op de Cust Chormandel, ende de Landen daar ontrent* (Leiden, 1651).
- Cornelis Claesz van Purmerendt, *Journael, ofte een Oost-Indische reys-beschrijvinghe ... verhalende veel besondere vreemdigheden van landen, lieden het belegeren van Mosambiecke en Goa ...* (Amsterdam, 1651).
- David Pieterszoon de Vries, *Korte historiael en journaels aenteykeninge*

van verscheyden voyagiens in de vier deelen des wereltsronde, als Europa, Africa Asia, ende Americka gedaen (Hoorn, 1655).

- Johann Jacob Saar, *Ost-indianische funfzehen-jährige Kriegs-Dienst, und wahrhaftige Beschreibung* (Nürnberg, 1662).
- *Journael van de Voyagie, gedaen met twaelf scheepen naer Oost-Indien, onder 't beleydt van den Heer Admirael Steven van der Hagen, waer in verhaelt wordt ... de reyse van 't schip Delft ... van Bantam naer de kuste van Choromandel* (Amsterdam, *c.* 1663-70).
- Johann von der Behr, *Diarium, oder Tage-Büch* (Jena, 1668).
- Albrecht Herport, *Eine kurtze Ost-Indianische Reisz-Beschreibung* (Bern, 1669).
- Jürgen Andersen and Volquard Iversen, *Orientalische Reisebeschreibunge* (Schleszwig, 1669).
- Georg Andriesz, *De beschrijving der reizen van Georg Andriesz deur Oostindiën en d'eilanden, deur Sina, Tartarijen, Persiën ... sedert 1644*, trans. J.H. Glazemaker, ed. A. Olearius (Amsterdam, 1670).
- Johann Jacob Saar, Volckert Evertsz and Albrecht Herport, *Verhaal van drie voorname reizen naar Oost-Indien*, trans. J.H. Glazemaker (Amsterdam, 1671).
- Philippus Baldaeus, *Nauwkeurige beschryvinge van Malabar en Choromandel, derhalver aangrenzende ryken, en het machtige eyland Ceylon. Nevens een omstandige en grondigh doorzochte ontdekking en wederlegginge van de afgoderye der Oost-Indische heydenen*, 3 vols (Amsterdam, 1672).
- Olfert Dapper, *Asia, of naukeurige beschrijving van het rijk des grooten Mogols, en een groot gedeelte van Indiën* (Amsterdam, 1672).
- Frans Janszoon van der Heiden and Willem Kunst, *Vervarelyke schip-breuk van 't oost-indisch jacht Ter Schelling, onder het landt van Bengale; ... en voorts in 't velt-leger van den Grooten Mogol, tot in 't koningrijk van Assam landewaerts opgevoert zijn. Beneffens een bondige beschrijving der koningrijken van Arrakan, Bengale, Martavan, Tanassery, &c.* (Amsterdam, 1675).
- Wouter Schouten, *Oost-Indische voyagie*, 2 vols in 1 (Amsterdam, 1676).
- Jacob Breynius, *Jacobi Breynii Gedanensis exoticarum aliarmque minus cognitarum plantarum centuria prima, cum figuris aeneis summo studio elaboratis* (Gdansk, 1678).
- Hendrik Adriaan van Reede tot Drakestein, *Hortus Indicus Malabaricus, continens regni Malabarici apud Indos celeberrimi omnis generis plantas rariores*, 12 vols (Amsterdam, 1678-1703).
- Johann Nieuhof, *Gedenkwaerdige zee- en lant-reize door verscheide gewesten van Oost-Indien* (Amsterdam, 1682).
- Simon de Vries, *Curieuse aenmerckingen der bijsonderste Oost- en West-Indische verwonderens-waerdige dingen*, 4 vols in 2 parts (Utrecht, 1682).
- Lambert van den Bos, *Leeven en daden der doorlughtige zee-helden* (Amsterdam, 1683).
- Johann Sigmund Wurffbain, *Vierzehen Jährige Ost-Indianische Krieg- und*

Ober-Kauffmanns-Dienste in einem richtig geführten Journal- und Tage-Buch (Sultzbach, 1686).

- Paul Hermann, *Horti academici Lugduno-Batavi catalogus* (Leiden, 1687).
- Christoph Schweitzer, *Journal- und Tage-Buch Seiner Sechs-Jährigen Ost-Indianische Reise* (Tubingen, 1688).
- Robert Knox, *'t Eyland Ceylon in sijn binnenste, of 't koningrijck Candy, geopent en nauwkeuriger dan oyt te vooren ontdeckt door Robert Knox, Scheeps-Capitein der Engelsche Oost-Indische Compagnie ... behelsende een eygentlijcke beschrijvingh, soo van 't landschap in sich selven als der inwoonderen politie, regeeringh, godsdienst, zeeden, konsten, en meenigerley seldsame gewoonten*, trans S. de Vries (Utrecht, 1692).
- Daniel Havart, *Op- en ondergang van Cormandel*, 3 vols (Amsterdam, 1693).
- Christophorus Frikius, Elias Hesse and Christophorus Schweitzer, *Drie seer aenmercklijcke reysen nae en door veelerley gewesten in Oost-Indien* (Utrecht, 1694).
- Carel Allard, *Orbis habitabilis oppida et vestitus* (Amsterdam, *c.* 1695).
- Johan Commelin, Frederik Ruysch and François Kiggelaar, *Horti Medici Amstelodamensis rariorum tam Orientalis, quam Occidentalis Indiae, aliarumque peregrinarum plantarum / Beschryvinge en curieuse afbeeldingen van rare vreemde Oost-, West-Indische en andere gewassen vertoont in den Amsterdamsche Kruyd-hof*, 2 vols [Vol. 2 slightly different title] (Amsterdam, 1697, 1701-2).
- Daniel Parthey, *Ost-Indianische und Persianische Neun-jährige Kriegs-Dienste* (Nürnberg, 1698).
- Paul Hermann, *Paradisus Batavus* (Leiden, 1698).
- Nicolaus de Graaff, *Reisen van Nicolaus de Graaff, na de vier gedeeltens des werelds, als Asia, Africa, America en Europa* (Hoorn, 1701).
- Frederick Ruysch, *Thesaurus animalium primus / Het eerste cabinet der dieren* (Amsterdam, 1710).
- Abrahamus Bógaert, *Abraham Bógaerts historische reizen door d'oostersche deelen van Asia* (Amsterdam, 1711).
- Cornelis de Bruin, *Reizen over Moskovie, door Persie en Indie* (Amsterdam, 1711).
- Engelbert Kaempfer, *Amoenitatum exoticarum politico-physico-medicarum fasciculi V, quibus continentur variae relationes, observationes & descriptiones rerum Persicarum & Ulterioris Asiae* (Lemgoviae, 1712).
- Francois Valentijn, *Oud en nieuw Oost-Indiën*, 5 vols in 8 parts (Dordrecht, 1724-6).
- Bernard Picart, *Naaukeurige beschryving der uitwendige godtsdienst-plichten, kerk-zeden, gewoontens van alle volkeren der waereldt, in een historisch verhaal ... en in kunstige tafereelen afgemaalt*, 6 vols, trans. Abraham Moubach (The Hague, Amsterdam and Rotterdam, 1727-38), Vols 3-4: *Naaukeurige beschryving der uitwendige godtsdienst-plichten, tempel-zeden en gewoontens der afgodische volkeren.*
- Albertus Seba, *Naaukeurige beschryvinge van het schatryke kabinet der voornaamste seldzaamheden der natuur / Locupletissimi rerum naturalium*

thesauri accurata descriptio, 4 vols (Amsterdam, 1734-65).

- Joannes Burmannus, *Thesaurus Zeylanicus, exhibens plantas in Insula Zeylana nascentes* (Amsterdam, 1737).
- Hendrik Velse, *Naauwkeurige berigten nopens de grondvesting des Christendoms onder de Heidenen op de kust van Choromandel en Malabaar, door de Deensche missionarissen op Tranquebar; behelzende ook veel aanmerckelyke byzonderheden aangaande het land, den aart, godsdienst, gewoontens, kunsten en wetenschappen der Malabaaren* (The Hague, 1739).
- Johann Wolfgang Heydt [or Heijdt], *Allerneuester geographisch- und topographischer Schau-platz von Africa und Ost-Asien oder ausführliche und wahrhafte Vorstellung und Beschreibung, von den wichtigsten, der Holländische-Ost-Indischen Compagnie in Africa und Asia zugehörigen Ländere, Küsten und Insulen* (Willhermsdorff, 1744).
- Jacob de Bucquoy, *Aanmerkelyke ontmoetingen in de zestien jaarige reize naa de Indiën, gedaan door Jacob De Bucquoi* (Haarlem, 1744).
- Johann Gottlieb Worms, *Ost-Indian- und Persianische Reisen*, 2nd edn. (Frankfurt and Leipzig, 1745).
- J.P.J. du Bois, *Historische beschryving der reizen of nieuwe en volkoome verzameling van de aller-waardigste en zeldsaamste zee- en landtochten* (The Hague and Amsterdam, 1747-67).
- Jan de Marre and Joannes van Keulen, *De nieuwe groote lichtende zee-fakkel, het sesde deel, vertoonende de zee-kusten, eylanden en havens van Oost-Indiën* (Amsterdam, 1753).
- Jacob Mossel (?), *Beknopte historie van het Mogolsche keyzerryk en de zuydelyke aangrensende ryken* (Batavia, 1758).
- *Defence de la Compagnie Unie, de Marchands d'Angleterre Commerçans aux Indes Orientales, et de ses employés (particulièrement de ceux au Bengale) contre les plaintes de la Compagnie Hollandoise des Indes Orientales* ... (The Hague, 1762).
- Pieter Cramer, *De uitlandsche kapellen voorkomende in de drie waereld-deelen Asia, Africa en America*, 4 vols (Amsterdam and Utrecht, 1779-82).
- *Het Heylige Evangelium Onses Heeren en Zaligmakers Jesu Christi, na de beschreyvinge van de Mannen Gods en H. Evangelisten Mattheus, Marcus, Lucas en Joannes, uyt het oirspronkelyke Grieks in de Singaleesche tale overgebragt*, ed. Johan Joachim Fybrants and Henricus Philipsz (Colombo, 1780).
- Casper Stoll, *Natuurlyke en naar 't leeven naauwkeurig gekleurde afbeeldingen en beschryvingen der cidaden en wantzen ... / Représentation exactement colorée d'après nature des cigales et des punaises ...*, 4 vols [with slightly different titles] (Amsterdam, 1780-1813).
- *Nederlandsche reizen, tot bevordering van den koophandel, na de meest afgelegen gewesten des aardkloots*, 14 vols, eds. Petrus Conradi and V. van der Plaats (Amsterdam and Harlingen, 1784-7).
- Johannes Splinter Stavorinus, *Reize van Zeeland over de Kaap de Goede Hoop, naar Batavia, Bantam, Bengalen, enz. gedaan in de jaaren MDCCLXVIII tot MDCCLXXI* (Leiden, 1793).

- Aernout Vosmaer, *Natuurkundige beschryving eener uitmuntende verzameling van zeldsaame gedierten, bestaande in Oost- en Westindische viervoetige dieren, vogelen en slangen, weleer leevend voorhanden geweest zijnde buiten den Haag op het Kleine Loo van Z.D.H. den Prins van Oranje Nassau* (Amsterdam, 1766-1804).
- Jacob Haafner, *Lotgevallen op eene reize van Madras over Tranquebaar naar het eiland Ceilon* (Haarlem, 1806).
- Jacob Haafner, *Reize in eenen palanquin of Lotgevallen en merkwaardige aanteekeningen op een reize langs de kusten Orixa en Choromandel*, 2 vols (Amsterdam, 1808).
- Jacob Haafner, *Reize te voet door het eiland Ceilon* (Amsterdam, 1810).
- Jacob Haafner, *Lotgevallen en vroegere zeereizen van Jacob Haafner*, ed. C.M. Haafner (Amsterdam, 1820).
- Jacob Haafner, *Reize naar Bengalen en terugreize naar Europa*, ed. C.M. Haafner (Amsterdam, 1822).

1. General

Van Linschoten, *Itinerario*

title page	Portrait of Van Linschoten, with inset depicting a view of Goa.	
p. 58	(a)	Indian trader, a *Bania* from Cambay and a Brahmin couple.
	(c)	Burning of a dead Brahmin and his wife committing *sati*, with onlookers.
	(d)	Family from Kanara, an Indian soldier (*Lascorin*) and an Indian prostitute.
p. 66	Worshipping of a Hindu deity and a mosque.	
p. 76	Asian fruits and trees, including mango, pineapple and ginger.	
p. 80	Asian fruits and trees, including coconut, pepper and areca.	
p. 86	(a)	Asian fruits and trees, including bamboo, durian and 'root tree'.
	(b)	Asian flower tree in a village courtyard.

De Laet, *De Imperio Magni Mogolis*

p. 96 or 100 Twig of a plant.

Van den Broecke, *Korte historiael*

title page? Portrait of Van den Broecke, by A. Matham, after F. Hals, 1663.

Van Twist, *Generaele beschrijvinghe*

p. 32 Ambassador of Bijapur presenting gifts to the Mughal Emperor.

Rogerius, *De open-deure*

title page Views of a temple, hook-swinging, widow-burning, processions, a ceremony and self-chastisement.

p. 358	Ten incarnations of Vishnu (only in the French edition of 1670).

Saar, *Ost-indianische funfzehen-jährige Kriegs-Dienst*

title page	Portrait of Saar, by V. Sommer, 1661.
p. 22	Indian satyrs (?). Only in the edition of 1672.

Journael van ... Steven van der Hagen

p. 2	Portrait of Van der Hagen.

Von der Behr, *Diarium*

title page	Portrait of Von der Behr.

Baldaeus, *Nauwkeurige beschryvinge*

part 1, title page	South Asian people, elephant and other animals.
part 1, title page	Portrait of Baldaeus, by Sijdervelt and Blooteling (?).
part 1, title page	Map of Malabar, Kanara, Konkan and parts of the Fishery Coast, Gujarat and the Maldives, partly with soundings, scale *c.* 1:5,000,000.
part 1, p. 154	(a) Map of Coromandel, north Ceylon and parts of the Fishery Coast and Orissa, with soundings, scale *c.* 1:5,000,000.
part 1, p. 190	Tamil alphabet, and Our Father and the Creed in Tamil.
part 1, p. 193	Indians writing in the sand.
part 3, p. 11	Worship of a Shiva statue.
part 3, p. 20	Worship of a Ganesha statue.
part 3, p. 45	Mythological scene with Vishnu and Brahma.
part 3, p. 51	Removal of the mount 'Meeperwat'.
part 3, p. 52	Varaha, Vishnu's third incarnation.
part 3, p. 57	Narasimha, Vishnu's fourth incarnation.
part 3, p. 61	'Mavaly' giving the world to Vishnu.
part 3, p. 66	Mythological scene with 'Camdoge', the Cow of Plenty.
part 3, p. 77	Demon Ravana and Hanuman (?).
part 3, p. 89	Deliverance of Krishna.
part 3, p. 127	Worship of Buddha.
part 3, p. 128	Kalki, Vishnu's tenth incarnation, and the Winged Horse.

Dapper, *Asia*

title page	Elephant with attendants (in South Asia?).
title page	Map of north India.
p. 37	Three *sadhus*.
p. 45	Wedding ceremony (?).
p. 56	Widow-burning.
p. 86	(a) Matsya, Vishnu's first incarnation, with Brahma.

	(b) Kurma, Vishnu's second incarnation.
p. 88	(a) Varaha, Vishnu's third incarnation.
	(b) Narasimha, Vishnu's fourth incarnation.
p. 90	(a) Vamana, Vishnu's fifth incarnation.
	(b) Parashurama, Vishnu's sixth incarnation.
p. 96	Rama, Vishnu's seventh incarnation.
p. 134	Krishna, Vishnu's eighth incarnation.
p. 136	(a) Buddha, Vishnu's ninth incarnation.
	(b) Kalki, Vishnu's tenth incarnation.
pp. 146-7, 149, 156, 158	Views of Hindu temples, worshipping of Hindu deities and *sadhus* doing penance.
p. 175	Muslim burial.
p. 176	Muslim clothing.
p. 188	Mounted elephants.
p. 277	View of a battle.
p. 302	Some Parsis (?).
p. 306	Parsi wedding (?).
p. 310	War troops and elephant.
p. 353	Muslim ruler with servants and dromedaries (?).

Schouten, *Oost-Indische voyagie*

part 1, title page	Portrait of Schouten.

Van Reede tot Drakestein, *Hortus Indicus Malabaricus*

occasionally in one of the volumes	Portrait of Van Reede.

Nieuhof, *Gedenkwaerdige zee- en lant-reize*

p. 82	'Goegijs' (*yogis?*) or Hindu saints (near Gombroon?), by Gilliam vander Gouwen.
p. 107	Map of Konkan, Kanara, Malabar, the Fishery Coast and Coromandel, with soundings, by J.N., scale *c.* 1:4,000,000.

De Vries, *Curieuse aenmerckingen*

Vol. 1, p. 68	Map of the Maldives, Ceylon and south India, with inset of Ceylon, by N. Sanson d'Abbeville.
Vol. 2, p. 532	Various animals, including species from South Asia.
Vol. 2, p. 540	Map of India south of Gujarat and Bengal, and north Ceylon, by N. Sanson d'Abbeville.
Vol. 2, p. 946	Diamond mine in India (?).
Vol. 2, pp. 988-9	Various diamonds, rubies and other gemstones, possessed by the Mughal Emperor or originating from Ahmadabad, Golkonda, Bijapur and other places in India.

Vol. 3, p. 2	Wedding ceremonies from various places, including Hindustan.
Vol. 3, p. 88	Various religious rituals and other scenes, including Brahmins washing themselves.
Vol. 4, p. 750 (or 592?)	Various deities, including Hindu gods, and debating Brahmins.

Frikius, Hesse and Schweitzer, *Drie seer aenmercklijcke reysen*

p. 388	Catching of fish in the 'Malabarese' way (referring to Tamils in north Ceylon?).

Bógaert, *Abraham Bógaerts historische reizen*

title page?	Portrait of Bógaert, by D. van der Haes and A. de Blois, with poem by A. Moonen.

De Bruin, *Reizen over Moskovie*

title page	(a)	Portrait of De Bruin.
	(b)	Map showing the itinerary of De Bruin.

Valentijn, *Oud en nieuw Oost-Indiën*, Vol. Ia

title page	Portrait of Valentijn.

Valentijn, *Oud en nieuw Oost-Indiën*, Vol. V, part 1

1st section, p. 2	Map of Konkan, Kanara, Malabar, the Fishery Coast, Coromandel and north Ceylon, by François Valentijn, J. van Braam and G. onder de Linden, scale *c.* 1:2,400,000.

Picart, *Naaukeurige beschryving*

Vol. 3, part 2, p. 146	Four depictions of 'Brahmins' (*sadhus*?) doing penance, by Picart, 1723.
Vol. 3, part 2, p. 193 or 194	Brahma, by Picart, 1723.
Vol. 3, part 2, p. 195 or 196	Depictions of Shiva and Ganesha, both with worshippers, by Picart, 1722.
Vol. 3, part 2, p. 200	Matsya, Kurma, Varaha and Narasimha, first four incarnations of Vishnu, by Picart, 1721.
Vol. 3, part 2, p. 202 or 203	Vamana, Parashurama, Rama and Krishna, fifth to eighth incarnations of Vishnu, by Picart, 1722.
Vol. 3, part 2, p. 206	Buddha and Kalki, ninth and tenth incarnation of Vishnu, and Shiva appearing as Mahadeva (*lingam*?), by Picart, 1722.
Vol. 3, part 2, p. 207	Ten incarnations of Vishnu.
Vol. 3, part 2, p. 212	View of the interior of a temple dedicated to 'Kamaetsma' (Parvati) and a procession for Vishnu, by Picart, 1722.

Vol. 3, part 2, p. 215	Two female and two male 'Brahmins' (*sadhus*?) doing penance, and a female 'Brahmin' (Hindu) pilgrim, by Picart, 1723.
Vol. 3, part 2, p. 216	Various kinds of penance and other acts by *yogis* and 'Brahmins', by Picart, 1722.
Vol. 3, part 2, p. 218	Procession dedicated to Ganga and the festival of Holi, by Picart, 1723.
Vol. 4, p. 7	Various *sadhus*, performing different religious acts and doing penance, and temples dedicated to Rama and 'Mamaniva', by Picart, 1729.
Vol. 4, p. 20	Ceremonies observed when a 'Baniya' (Hindu?) child is born and given a name, by Picart, 1728.
Vol. 4, p. 22	Burning of a dead man and his wife performing *sati*, and the burial of a dead man together with his still living wife, by Picart, 1729.
Vol. 4, p. 24	Ill people brought into the presence of Shiva (or Brahma?) to be cured, and being sprinkled with the urine of a cow, by Picart, 1728.
Vol. 6, p. 316	'Pulleyar' (Ganesha?) and the signs to be found on various part of his body.

Seba, *Naaukeurige beschryvinge*

Vol. 2, plate 114, no. 21	'Composed snake stone' of Brahmans (in South Asia?).

Velse, *Naauwkeurige berigten*

4th section, p. 3	Map of Konkan, Kanara, Malabar, the Fishery Coast, Coromandel and north Ceylon, after De l'Isle and Bruzen la Martiniere, scale *c.* 1:4,000,000.

Heydt, *Allerneuester Geographisch- und Topographisher Schau-Platz*

p. 283	Map of Ceylon, the Fishery Coast and parts of Coromandel and Malabar, by Heydt, scale *c.* 1:3,300,000.

De Bucquoy, *Aanmerkelyke ontmoetingen*

title page	Portrait of De Bucquoy. Only in the edition of 1757.

Du Bois, *Historische beschryving*

Vol. 1, p. 41	Map of the Indian coasts bordering the Arabian Sea and the Maldives, showing European settlements, by J. van Schley after a French map.

Vol. 15, p. 90 (a) Map of north India, by Bellin and J. van Schley, (1752?).
(b) Map of south India and Ceylon, by Bellin and J. van Schley, (1752?).
Vol. 15, p. 383 Portrait of Brahma, by J. v. Schley.
Vol. 15, p. 392 (a) Vishnu, by J. v. Schley.
(b) 'Isuren' (Shiva?), by J. v. Schley.
Vol. 15, p. 395 Various *sadhus*, by J. v. Schley.

De Marre and Van Keulen, *De nieuwe groote lichtende zee-fakkel*

p. 76 (no. 49) Map of the northern Arabian Sea, including the coasts of Gujarat and Konkan, with soundings.

Cramer, *De uitlandsche kapellen*

throughout Vols 2 and 4 Foreign butterflies, including types originating from Coromandel, Ceylon, Bengal, Malabar and possibly Surat.

Stoll, *Natuurlyke en naar 't leeven naauwkeurig gekleurde afbeeldingen*

throughout the vols Insects, including species originating from Coromandel, Bengal, Ceylon and Malabar.

Conradi and Van der Plaats, *Nederlandsche reizen*

Vol. 10, p. 90 Various types of *sadhus* or *yogis*.

Haafner, *Reize in eenen palanquin*

part 1 and 2, title page Haafner in a palanquin, by R. Vinkeles.

Haafner, *Lotgevallen en vroegere zeereizen*

title page Portrait of Haafner, by Dalin and Velyn.

2. Surat
(including Sind and Hindustan)

Van den Broecke, *Korte historiael*

p. 78 Bird's-eye view of the barricade 'Ten Broeck' near Daman.
p. 128 Deer and hare hunt with the help of leopards and dogs.
p. 152 Bird's-eye view of the factory at Surat.
p. 153 Bird's-eye view of Surat.

Commelin, *Begin ende voortgangh*, Vol. 2

part 5, p. 68 Bird's-eye view of the barricade 'Ten Broeck' near Daman.
part 5, p. 98 Hunting of deer near Surat (?).
part 5, p. 102 One-horned goat and two birds in Hindustan (?).
part 5, p. 106 (b) View of Surat from the sea.
(c) View of the factory at Surat.

Van Twist, *Generaele beschrijvinghe*

title page, p. 13 View of Surat.
p. 29 Festivities at the Mughal court in Agra.
p. 39 *Banias* from Gujarat.
p. 43 Widow-burning in Gujarat.
p. 64 Muslim wedding ceremony in Gujarat.
p. 66 Muslim and servant in Gujarat.

Andersen and Iversen, *Orientalische Reisebeschreibunge*

p. 202 Parsis at Surat worshipping fire amid the Towers of Silence.
p. 205 Naked *Banias* or *sadhus* (?) in or near Surat washing themselves and being fed (?).

Andriesz, *De beschrijving der reizen*

p. 21 Riders under a miraculous tree near Surat.
p. 32 Men fighting against lions and tigers in the arena in Agra in the presence of the Mughal Emperor.
p. 34 Execution of two noblemen by skinning in Ahmadabad.
p. 41 Dance of naked women at Ahmadabad, and bodies of some beheaded dancers.

Baldaeus, *Nauwkeurige beschryvinge*

part 1, p. 2 View of Ahmadabad, with dromedaries and other animals in the forefront.
part 1, p. 12 View of Surat, with animals and people in the forefront.
part 1, p. 20 Murder committed in the presence of the Mughal Emperor.
part 1, p. 36 Bird's-eye view of Diu.
part 1, p. 61 Seizure of Diu by the Portuguese.
part 1, p. 70 (a) Two views from the land side and the seaside of the English fort at Bombay.

Dapper, *Asia*

p. 178 (a) Horseman and elephant fighting.
(b) View of the Mughal court, with nobles, elephants, horses and dromedaries.
p. 182 Men fighting against lions, tigers and elephants in an arena in the presence of the Mughal Emperor.

p. 187	Mughal carriages drawn by oxen.
p. 196	Portrait of the Mughal Emperor Jahangir (Selim).
p. 198	Portrait of Nur Jahan (referred to as Nur Mahal).
p. 202	Portrait of Mughal Emperor Shah Jahan.
p. 204	(a) Portrait of Mughal Emperor Aurangzeb.
	(b) Portrait of Begam Sahib.
p. 206	Portrait of Raushanara Begam (daughter of Mughal Emperor Shah Jahan).
p. 284	View of Surat from the river.
p. 290	View of Bharuch.
p. 291	View of Ahmadabad from a temple or a mosque.

De Vries, *Curieuse aenmerckingen*

Vol. 2, p. 1167	View of the Mughal court at Agra, with a procession of dromedaries, horses and elephants.
Vol. 2, p. 1185	Thomas Roe at the Mughal court.

Wurffbain, *Vierzehen Jährige*

p. 138 (or 128)	View of the Dutch fleet nearing Surat, by L.C. Glotsch.
p. 174	Fight with robbers near Surat.

Havart, *Op- en ondergang*

part 3, p. 89	View of the funeral procession of Hendrik Adriaan van Reede tot Drakenstein at Surat, January 1692.

Allard, *Orbis habitabilis*

plate 49	View of Surat, by Allard.
plate 50	View of a man and woman from Surat, with town in the background, by A. Meijer.

Bógaert, *Abraham Bógaerts historische reizen*

p. 311	Zodiac rupees and Nur Jahan (referred to as Nur Mahal) distributing these among the poor (?).

Valentijn, *Oud en nieuw Oost-Indiën*, Vol. IV, part 2

1st section, p. 144	Map of the Tapti River between Surat and Suvali, with soundings, scale *c.* 1:200,000.
1st section, p. 165	Seal of the Mughal Emperor Aurangzeb.
1st section, pp. 173, 175-7, 185, 187	Portraits of ancestors of the Mughal Emperors.
1st section, p. 193	Portrait of the Mughal Emperor Babur.
1st section, p. 202	Portrait of the Mughal Emperor Humayun.

1st section, p. 212	Portrait of Padmana, Queen of Chittaurgarh, by J. Lamsveld.
1st section, p. 217	Portrait of the Mughal Emperor Akbar.
1st section, p. 223	View of a military expedition of *Directeur* Pieter van den Broecke, by M. Balen and I.C. Philips.
1st section, p. 224	(a) Portrait of *Directeur* Pieter van den Broecke (1620-8), by F. Hals and J. Ledeboer. (b) Portrait of Nur Jahan, wife of Mughal Emperor Jahangir, and female attendants, by J. Lamsveld.
1st section, p. 229	Portrait of the Mughal Emperor Jahangir.
1st section, p. 231	Portrait of Mumtaz Mahal, wife of Mughal Emperor Shah Jahan.
1st section, p. 247	Portrait of Rauchanara Begam, daughter of Mughal Emperor Shah Jahan.
1st section, p. 248	(b) Portrait of Murad Bakhsh, fourth son of Mughal Emperor Shah Jahan.
1st section, p. 250	Portrait of Rana Deva, daughter of Rana Raja (of Udaipur).
1st section, p. 255	Portraits of Mughal Prince Dara Shukoh and his grandson 'Sepe Sjecoer'.
1st section, p. 258	(a) Portrait of 'Noer El Tadjoe', daughter of Mughal Prince Dara Shukoh, and portrait of Begam Sahib, eldest sister of Mughal Emperor Aurangzeb. (b) Portraits of Nur Begam and 'Hhamed Mahal'.
1st section, p. 260	Portrait of the Mughal Emperor Shah Jahan.
1st section, p. 264	Portrait of Mir Jumla, who (having washed himself) enjoys himself with his wives and concubines in his *zenana* (harem), by I. Folkema.
1st section, p. 275	Portrait of the Mughal Emperor Aurangzeb, with buildings and tents being blown away in the background.
1st section, p. 290	Portraits of Shah Alam and his wife.
1st section, p. 294	(a) Portrait of Mulla Muhammad Ali, *Sar-khail* of the Mughal Emperor's mother, and portrait of Karim-ud-din, first son of Muhammad Azim. (b) Portraits in medallions of Saadullah Khan Mutaqad and Zafar Khan, friends of Mughal Emperor Muizz-ud-din, by Wouter Jongman. (c) Portraits in medallions of 'Souraat' Khan Bahadur and Bahramand Khan, friends of Mughal Emperor Muizz-ud-din, by Wouter Jongman. (d) Portraits in medallions of Khwaja Hasan Khan and Zulfiqar Khan, friends of Mughal Emperor Muizz-ud-din, by Wouter Jongman. (e) Portraits in medallions of Khan-i-Dauran Bahadur and Murtaza Khan Bahadur, friends of Mughal Emperor Muizz-ud-din, by Wouter Jongman.

	(f) Portraits in medallions of Asad Khan and Khan-i-Jahan, friends of Mughal Emperor Muizz-ud-din, by Wouter Jongman.
1st section, p. 297	Portrait of Shah Shuja, second son of Mughal Emperor Shah Jahan, and portrait of Dona Juliana.
1st section, p. 304	(a) Portrait of Mughal Emperor Muizz-ud-din, by J. Lamsveld.
	(b) Portraits of the Mughal Emperors Rafi-ud-Darjat and Farrukh Siyar.

Valentijn, *Oud en nieuw Oost-Indiën*, Vol. V, part 1

1st section, p. 172	View of a tank and the graves of the last three 'kings' of Gujarat at Sarkhej, seen from within.

Picart, *Naaukeurige beschryving*

Vol. 6, p. 256	Weighing of the Mughal Emperor (?), by Dubourg and Duflos.

Du Bois, *Historische beschryving*

Vol. 1, p. 188	Bird's-eye view of Diu, by J. v. Schley.
Vol. 1, p. 210	Siege of Diu, by J. v. Schley.
Vol. 13, p. 296	View of Surat from the river, by J. v. Schley.
Vol. 13, p. 325	Map of Bombay and surroundings, with soundings, by J. v. Schley.
Vol. 15, p. 175	View of the Mughal court, with elephants, horses and dromedaries, by J. v. Schley.
Vol. 15, p. 200	(a) Rauchanara Begam (daughter of Mughal Emperor Shah Jahan) with her retinue, by J. v. Schley.
	(b) Begam Sahib with some servants, by J. v. Schley.
Vol. 15, p. 331	Mughal Emperor Shah Jahan with some servants, by J. v. Schley.
Vol. 15, p. 332	(a) Portrait of Mir Jumla, enjoying himself with his wives in his *zenana* (harem), by J. v. Schley.
	(b) Seal of the Mughals, by J. v. Schley.
Vol. 15, p. 334	Mughal carriages drawn by oxen, by J. v. Schley.
Vol. 20, p. 330	Portrait of *Directeur* Hendrik Zwaardecroon (1699-1701), depicted as Governor-General, by J. v. Schley.

De Marre and Van Keulen, *De nieuwe groote lichtende zee-fakkel*

p. 14 (no. 18)	Map of Bombay and the surrounding islands, with soundings, scale *c.* 1:100,000.

Mossel (?), *Beknopte historie*

p. 33	Seal of Mughal Emperor Aurangzeb.

p. 36	Seal of Mughal Emperor Bahadur Shah.
p. 39	Seal of Mughal Emperor Muhammad Shah.

Conradi and Van der Plaats, *Nederlandsche reizen*

Vol. 7, p. 104	View of Surat from the river.
Vol. 10, p. 76	View of the Mughal court, with elephants, horses and dromedaries.

3. Malabar
(including Kanara and Konkan)

Van Linschoten, *Itinerario*

p. 42	Map of the town of Goa and immediate surroundings, by Baptista (?).	
p. 44	(a)	Village people, animals and dwellings near Goa.
	(b)	View of the market at the town of Goa, by Van Linschoten.
p. 46	(a)	Portuguese civilians and soldiers, with attendants.
	(b)	Portuguese official or nobleman on a horse with attendants.
	(c)	Rich Portuguese in a palanquin with attendants.
	(d)	Vessels used by the Portuguese and the inhabitants of Malabar to wage war and conduct trade, by Baptista (?).
p. 48	(a)	Portuguese woman in a palanquin with attendants.
	(b)	Portuguese woman in a palanquin with attendants.
	(c)	Various Portuguese women in different dresses.
	(d)	Portuguese couple with attendants visiting a church at night.
p. 58	(b)	Wedding procession in the Western Ghats near Goa.
	(e)	Small Indian vessels used in Goa and Cochin for fishing and trade.
	(f)	Envoy of the 'King of the Western Ghats' with attendants in Goa.
p. 64	(a)	Muslims of Cannanore and inhabitants of the pepper-growing areas of the Malabar Coast.
	(b)	King of Cochin on an elephant with a number of Nayars.

De Bry, *Achter Theil der Orientalische Indien*

plate 4	The Dutch concluding a peace treaty with the Zamorin of Calicut, accompanied by his retinue (plate 15 in the Latin edition of 1607).

Commelin, *Begin ende voortgangh*, Vol. 2

part 1, p. 8	(a)	Zamorin of Calicut and his palace.
	(b)	Reception of the VOC by the Zamorin.

Van Purmerendt, *Journael, ofte een Oost-Indische reys-beschrijvinghe*

p. 31 (?) View of the fleet off the coast of Mozambique and the capture of a Portuguese carrack near Goa.

Journael van ... Steven van der Hagen

p. 5 Ships near the bay of Goa.
p. 6 View of a procession arriving at Goa.
p. 8 Ships near the coast of Calicut.
p. 9 Meeting with the Zamorin of Calicut.
p. 10 View of Cochin.

Von der Behr, *Diarium*

p. 40 View of the roadstead of Goa with Dutch and Portuguese ships (?).
p. 112 Marketplace in Malabar (?).

Herport, *Eine kurtze Ost-Indianische Reisz-Beschreibung*

p. 122 Bird's-eye view of Cochin, with local people, by Wilhelm Stettler and Conrad Meyer, 1669.
p. 140 Bird's-eye view of Cannanore, with local people, by Wilhelm Stettler and Conrad Meyer, 1669.
p. 198 Indian trees and houses, with inset showing a plan of the battle with the King of 'Peremin' (bordering Kayankulam and Purakkad?), February 1665, by Wilhelm Stettler and Conrad Meyer.

Andersen and Iversen, *Orientalische Reisebeschreibunge*

p. 78 Inhabitants of Malabar, including Nayars and 'Polyas'.

Saar, Evertsz and Herport, *Verhaal van drie voorname reizen*

p. 188 VOC Admiral stating his terms to the King of 'Petemin' (bordering Kayankulam and Purakkad).

Baldaeus, *Nauwkeurige beschryvinge*

part 1, p. 70 (b) Map and bird's-eye view of Goa.
part 1, p. 100 View of the town and bay of Cannanore.
part 1, p. 105 Reception of Vasco da Gama by the Zamorin of Calicut.
part 1, p. 109 Portuguese factory at Calicut being assaulted by Indians.
part 1, p. 110 Four views of Cranganur.
part 1, p. 114 Four views of Cochin.
part 1, p. 121 Entry of Rijklof van Goens Junior into Cochin, by G. Appelmans.
part 1, p. 122 Two maps of Cochin at the time of its conquest by the

	Dutch, 1663, and in its present state, scale *c.* 1:5000.
part 1, p. 142	Map of Quilon.
part 2, p. 51	View of the naval battle between the Dutch and the Portuguese near Goa in 1638.

Dapper, *Asia*

p. 354	View of Bijapur, with elephants and dromedaries.
p. 356	View of the bay and town of Dabhol.

Schouten, *Oost-Indische voyagie*

part 1, p. 188	View of Quilon being conquered by the Dutch (?), by C. Decker.
part 1, p. 192	View of a battle between the Portuguese and the Dutch off the Malabar coast.
part 1, p. 194	View of a battle between Nayars and the Dutch.
part 1, p. 200	View of Cranganur, by J. Kip.

Van Reede tot Drakestein, *Hortus Indicus Malabaricus*

throughout the volumes	Plants from Malabar, with names in Latin, Malayalam, Arabic and Sanskrit (?).

Nieuhof, *Gedenkwaerdige zee- en lant-reize*

p. 117	View of Quilon, by Kip.
p. 124	Dutch victory at Cochin, by C. Decker.
p. 139	Nieuhof's audience at the Queen of Quilon.
p. 145	Malabar man and woman, by Gilliam vander Gouwen.
p. 159	Malabar snake charmers, by Gilliam vander Gouwen.
p. 162	Palm trees and other flora, probably in Malabar.
p. 181	Jackals and bats, probably in Malabar.

De Vries, *Curieuse aenmerckingen*

Vol. 1, p. 46	Palm trees from Malabar (and other places?) with local people.
Vol. 1, p. 128	Pepper plants from various places, including Kanara.

Van den Bos, *Leeven en daden*

p. 123	Naval battle with the Portuguese at Goa, by Jan Luyken.

Hermann, *Horti academici*

p. 689	Plant from Malabar.

Schweitzer, *Journal- und Tage-Buch*

p. 72	Method of fishing at the Malabar coast.

Allard, *Orbis habitabilis*

plate 45	View of Cochin.
plate 46	Two inhabitants of Cochin, with the town in the background, by A. Meijer.
plate 47	View of Goa, by Allard (?).
plate 48	View of a man and woman, with servant, from Goa, with the town in the background, by Allard and A. Meijer.

Bógaert, *Abraham Bógaerts historische reizen*

p. 365	Inhabitants of Malabar, by J. Harrewyn.

De Bruin, *Reizen over Moskovie*

p. 352	(a) Fish from Malabar.
	(b) View of Cochin.

Kaempfer, *Amoenitatum exoticarum*

p. 459	Inhabitants of Malabar and some temples, by F.W. Brandshagen.

Valentijn, *Oud en nieuw Oost-Indiën*, Vol. IV, part 2

1st section, p. 234	Portrait of Nur Jahan, Queen of Bijapur, by J. Lamsveld.
1st section, p. 239	Plan of the factory at Vengurla and its vicinity, with legend, scale *c.* 1:500.
1st section, p. 245	Portrait of 'Adil Shah' of Bijapur.
1st section, p. 248	(a) Portrait of Shivaji, Maratha ruler.

Valentijn, *Oud en nieuw Oost-Indiën*, Vol. V, part 2

1st section, p. 2	Map of the southern Malabar Coast, scale *c.* 1: 1,100,000.
1st section, p. 6	Plan of the factory at Barcelore as surveyed in 1686 by Engineer L.N. van Duyvendaal, with legend, by order of *Commandeur* Adam van der Duijn (1708-9), 1709, scale *c.* 1:250.
1st section, p. 8	(a) Plan of the fort at Cannanore, with profile of the defence works and legend, by Joh. van Braam and G. onder de Linden, by order of *Commandeur* Adam van der Duijn, 1709, scale *c.* 1:1400.
	(b) View of Cannanore.
1st section, p. 10	Plan of the fort at Cranganur, its defences and its vicinity, with legend, by Joh. van Braam and G. onder de Linden, by order of *Commandeur* Adam van der Duijn, 1709, scale *c.* 1:1750.
1st section, p. 12	(a) Bird's-eye view of Cochin and its surroundings, with inset of the defences at the fort.

(b) Plan of the fort at Quilon, with profile of the defence works and legend, by Joh. van Braam and G. onder de Linden, scale *c.* 1:1750.
(c) View of Dabhol.
(d) View of the coast at Dabhol, with legend.

Picart, *Naaukeurige beschryving*

Vol. 2, p. 227 (b) Procession of the inquisition at Goa, by Picart, 1723.
Vol. 2, p. 229 (or 219?) (b) Banner of the inquisition at Goa, by Picart, 1722.

Seba, *Naaukeurige beschryvinge*

Vol. 1, plate 36, no. 10 Plant from Malabar.
Vol. 2, plate 54, no. 1, plate 94, no. 1 Snakes from Malabar.
Vol. 2, plate 114, no. 34 'Milk stones' from Malabar.

Heydt, *Allerneuester Geographisch- und Topographisher Schau-Platz*

p. 289 View of Cochin from the sea, by Heydt.

De Bucquoy, *Aanmerkelyke ontmoetingen*

p. 110 View of the Malabar coast and the travellers' escape by boat.

Worms, *Ost-Indian- und Persianische Reisen*

p. 875 Soldier and another person from Malabar, and Portuguese and Malabar women.

Du Bois, *Historische beschryving*

Vol. 1, p. 45 Three different small Indian vessels used off the Malabar Coast, by J. v. Schley.
Vol. 1, p. 49 Reception of Vasco da Gama by the Zamorin of Calicut, by J. v. Schley.
Vol. 1, p. 92 View of the King of Cochin on an elephant, accompanied by his Nayars, by J. v. Schley.
Vol. 12, p. 253 View of Goa, by J. v. Schley.
Vol. 12, p. 255 Bird's-eye view of Goa, by J. van Schley.
Vol. 15, p. 6 Plan of the fort at Cannanore, by J. v. Schley.
Vol. 15, p. 186 (a) View of the coast near Dabhol, by J. v. Schley.
(b) View of Dabhol, by J. v. Schley.
Vol. 16, p. 4 (a) View of the harbour of Cannanore, by J. v. Schley.
(b) View of Cannanore, by J. v. Schley.
(c) Plan of the fort at Cranganur, with defensive works and projection of new fortifications dating from 1709, by J. v. Schley.

	(d) Plan of the fort at Quilon, by J. v. Schley.
Vol. 16, p. 7	Bird's-eye view of Cochin and surroundings, by J. v. Schley.

De Marre and Van Keulen, *De nieuwe groote lichtende zee-fakkel*

p. 12 (no. 17)	Map of the mud bay of Cranganur, with soundings, scale *c.* 1:30000.
p. 76 (no. 50)	Map of the coasts of Konkan, Kanara and Malabar, with soundings, scale *c.* 1:1,500,000.

Conradi and Van der Plaats, *Nederlandsche reizen*

Vol. 3, p. 62	Bird's-eye view of Goa, with some elephants.
Vol. 4, p. 104	View of the harbour of Cannanore.
Vol. 9, p. 27	Bird's-eye view of the roadstead of Cannanore.

4. Ceylon
(including Fishery Coast and Maldives)

't Historiael journael

title page	Joris van Spilbergen shaking hands with King Vimala Dharma Suriya I of Kandy in 1602, with hunters in the background.
p. 28	Map of Ceylon.
p. 30	Bird's-eye view of the reception of Joris van Spilbergen by the King of Kandy at Batticaloa in 1602.
p. 33	Bird's-eye view of 'Vintana' (Alutnuwara), up the river of Trincomalee.
p. 36	Bird's-eye view of the arrival of Van Spilbergen in Kandy.
p. 39	Bird's-eye view of the ships of Van Spilbergen in the bay of Batticaloa.
p. 48	(a) Worshipping of the god of the 'King of Batticaloa'.
	(b) Blazon of the 'King of Ceylon' (Batticaloa?).

De Bry, *Achter Theil der Orientalische Indien*

plate 8	King of Batticaloa and his retinue meeting the Dutch.
plate 9	Vice-admiral Sebald de Weert and his retinue being killed (by the King of Kandy?).

Commelin, *Begin ende voortgangh*, Vol. 1

part 10, p. 24	See *'t Historiael journael*, p. 30 (above).
part 10, p. 28	See *'t Historiael journael*, p. 33 (above).
part 10, p. 30	See *'t Historiael journael*, p. 36 (above).
part 10, p. 32	See *'t Historiael journael*, p. 39 (above).

part 10, p. 42	(a) See *'t Historiael journael*, p. 48 (a-b) (above).
	(b) Map of Ceylon.
part 11, p. 20	Murder of Admiral Sebald de Weert by the King of Kandy.

Journael van ... Joris van Spilbergen

p. 25 View of the court of Batticaloa, with elephants, during the visit of Van Spilbergen.
p. 29 Bird's-eye view of the arrival of Van Spilbergen at 'Vintana' (Alutnuwara) or Kandy (?).

Saar, *Ost-indianische funfzehen-jährige Kriegs-Dienst*

2nd section, p. 50	Ceylonese family.
2nd section, p. 58	Catching of elephants.
2nd section, p. 61	Baptising and naming of three elephants.
2nd section, p. 63	Saar and some comrades being attacked by a snake.
2nd section, p. 67	Catching of crocodiles.
2nd section, p. 87	Cornelis Salvegad being executed by an elephant.
2nd section, p. 136	Pearl diving near Jaffna (?).

Von der Behr, *Diarium*

pp. 49, 51	Coconut trees with people working or resting (on Ceylon?).
p. 54	Cinnamon tree with people working.
p. 102	Elephant hunt (on Ceylon?).

Herport, *Eine kurtze Ost-Indianische Reisz-Beschreibung*

p. 172	Bird's-eye view of Colombo, with local and Dutch people, by Wilhelm Stettler and Conrad Meyer.
p. 184	Catching of elephants, by Wilhelm Stettler and Conrad Meyer, 1669.
p. 214	Dutch entry into Colombo after the expedition to Cochin, 1665, by Wilhelm Stettler and Conrad Meyer, 1669.

Andersen and Iversen, *Orientalische Reisebeschreibunge*

p. 83	Map of Ceylon.

Saar, Evertsz and Herport, *Verhaal van drie voorname reizen*

p. 35	Saar's friend being attacked by a crocodile near Negombo, and the catching of another crocodile.
p. 37	Jan Ruppert fighting with a tiger.
p. 47	Cornelis Salvegad being executed by an elephant.
p. 181	Catching of elephants.

Baldaeus, *Nauwkeurige beschryvinge*

part 1, p. 150	Bird's-eye view of Tuticorin.
part 2, title page	Map of Ceylon, with soundings, scale *c.* 1:1,500,000.
part 2, p. 4	Usurper stoned to death.
part 2, p. 10	Pedro Lopes welcoming 'Doña Catharina, Empress of Ceylon'.
part 2, p. 12	Murder of King 'Janiere' by the Portuguese.
part 2, p. 15	Building of a fortress at Kandy by Portuguese prisoners of war.
part 2, p. 18	Audience given by the King of Kandy to Sebald de Weert.
part 2, p. 20	Murder of Sebald de Weert.
part 2, p. 32	Two views of the funeral of a prince of Kandy.
part 2, p. 54	Bird's-eye view of the fort at Batticaloa.
part 2, p. 56	Impaling of some rebels.
part 2, p. 60	(a) Dutch conquest of Galle. (b) View of Galle.
part 2, p. 61	View of the fort at Kalutara.
part 2, p. 105	Entry of Gerard Hulft into Kandy.
part 2, p. 106	Audience given by the King of Kandy to Gerard Hulft.
part 2, p. 108	Portrait of Gerard Hulft, commander of the forces sent to Ceylon, by Govert Flinck and Abraham Blooteling, with an ode by Joost van Vondel.
part 2, p. 142	Murder of Willem Jacobsz Koster by the Sinhalese.
part 2, p. 128	Map of Colombo.
part 2, p. 144	View of Negombo.
part 2, p. 148	Dutch conquest of Mannar Island in 1658.
part 2, p. 150	Map of Mannar Island.
part 2, p. 153	Dutch conquest of Jaffna.
part 2, p. 154	Map of the Jaffna peninsula, scale *c.* 1:500,000.
part 2, p. 155	Bird's-eye view of fort Hammenhiel and surroundings.
part 2, p. 156	Bird's-eye view of the fort at Jaffna.
part 2, p. 160	Execution of Portuguese traitors.
part 2, p. 161	View of the church at Tellippalai.
part 2, p. 162	Four views of the churches at Mallakam, Myleddi, Acchaveli and Uduvil.
part 2, p. 163	View of the church at Vaddukoddai.
part 2, p. 164	Four views of the churches at Pantattarippu, Chankanai, Manipay and Vannarponnai.
part 2, p. 165	View of the church at Nallur.
part 2, p. 166	(a) View of the church at Chundukkuli. (b) Four views of the churches at Kopay, Navatkuli, Putur and Chavakachcheri.

part 2, p. 167	View of the church at Kachchai.
part 2, p. 168	(a) View of the church at Varani. (b) Four views of the churches at Eluthumadduval, Kattaiveli, Udupiddi and Point Pedro.
part 2, p. 169	Tamarind tree under which sermons are given, at the roadstead of Point Pedro.
part 2, p. 170	(a) Elephants throwing down palm trees.. (b) Four views of the churches at Puloppalai, Tampakamam, Mukamalai and Mullipattu.
part 2, p. 172	Catching of horses in Jaffna.
part 2, p. 173	Map of Nainativu, Analaitivu, Punkudutivu and some other islands.
part 2, p. 176	Inhabitants of Jaffna.
part 2, p. 177	Velalas threshing.
part 2, p. 178	Velalas making butter.
part 2, p. 189	Bird's-eye view of the fort and harbour of Trincomalee.
part 2, p. 190	Map of the fort of Trincomalee.
part 2, p. 192	Procession of Ceylonese monks with an elephant.
part 2, p. 195	Peeling of cinnamon.
part 2, p. 198	Catching of elephants.
part 2, p. 202	VOC soldier catching a snake.
part 2, p. 204	Map of the siege of Colombo under the command of Gerard Hulft.

Schouten, *Oost-Indische voyagie*

part 1, p. 184	View of Colombo, by J. Kip.
part 1, p. 186	View of a pearl fishery.
part 1, p. 306	View of Galle.
part 1, p. 309	View of the reception of Joris van Spilbergen in Kandy (?).
part 2 (or part 1), at the back	Map of Ceylon, with soundings, by O. Lindeman, scale *c.* 1:1,800,000. Only in the edition of 1775.

Breynius, *Exoticarum aliarmque*

pp. 52, 140, 142, 180	Plants from Ceylon.

Nieuhof, *Gedenkwaerdige zee- en lant-reize*

p. 190	View of a pearl fishery with Tuticorin in the background, by Kip.

De Vries, *Curieuse aenmerckingen*

Vol. 1, p. 123	Cinnamon trees and their processing.

Hermann, *Horti academici*

pp. 63, 97, 171, 175, 435, 643, 653, 683, 687, 693 Plants from Ceylon.

Schweitzer, *Journal- und Tage-Buch*

p. 78	Palanquin, with plan of a fortress in the background.
p. 110	Ceylonese woman, with fortifications and crocodiles in the background, by Melchior Haffner.

Knox, *'t Eyland Ceylon in sijn binnenste*

title page	View of the Kandyan court (?).
p. 1	Map of Ceylon, showing the itinerary of Robert Knox.
p. 13	(a) Method of ploughing.
	(b) Method of threshing and the use of 'Talipot' leaves.
p. 31	Ceylonese death-sentences by elephant trampling and impaling.
p. 35	(a) 'Rillow' and 'Wanderow' monkeys.
	(b) Method of fishing.
p. 46	King Rajasinga of Kandy being honoured.
p. 109	(a) 'Tirinanx', highest Ceylonese priest.
	(b) Veddah, member of a Ceylonese tribe.
p. 132	(a) Ceylonese noble woman and man dressed in their best clothes.
	(b) Manner of eating and drinking.
p. 155	Method of demanding fines.
p. 174	Burning of dead bodies.

Allard, *Orbis habitabilis*

plate 43	View of a man and woman from Batticaloa, with the town in the background, by A. Meijer (?).
plate 44	Bird's-eye view of Colombo.

Commelin, Ruysch and Kiggelaar, *Horti Medici Amstelodamensis*

Vol. 1, pp. 11, 69, 73, 75, 97, 99, 101, 117, 219	Plants from Ceylon.
Vol. 2, pp. 41, 170	Plants from Ceylon.

Parthey, *Ost-Indianische und Persianische Neun-jährige Kriegs-Dienste*

p. 59	Bird's-eye view of Colombo.
p. 67	Parthey being wounded (on Ceylon?).
p. 69	Elephant hunt near Galle.
p. 76	View of Adam's Peak with dead wrapped up bodies lying at its foot.
p. 113 or 114	Map of Ceylon.
pp. 127, 129	Ceylonese trees.
p. 130	Pearl fishery off the Ceylonese coast.

Hermann, *Paradisus Batavus*

pp. 72, 73, 78, 105, 107, 217, 238	Plants from Ceylon.

Ruysch, *Thesaurus animalium primus*

p. 38, plate 1, no. 1A	Ceylonese bird.
p. 39, plate 3, no. 1A	Ceylonese fish.
p. 42, plate 7, no. A	Ceylonese fish.

Bógaert, *Abraham Bógaerts historische reizen*

p. 334	Sinhalese and their way of dressing, by J. Harrewyn.
p. 388	Franciscus Xavierus and his servants baptising *Paravas*, by J. Harrewyn

De Bruin, *Reizen over Moskovie*

p. 354	View of Adam's Peak from the sea.
p. 359	Mestiza on Ceylon.

Valentijn, *Oud en nieuw Oost-Indiën*, Vol. V, part 1

3rd section, p. 22	(a)	Map of Ceylon, by François Valentijn, J. van Braam and G. onder de Linden, scale *c.* 1:900,000.
	(b)	View of Galle.
	(c)	Map of Galle, with legend, scale *c.* 1:5500, and plan and profile of the fort at Mannar, scale *c.* 1:1500.
3rd section, p. 24	(a)	View of the Governor's residence at Colombo and plan of the garden behind the residence, by M. Balen and Dirk Jongman, scale *c.* 1:500.
	(b)	View of a part of the Governor's residence seen from the back garden, view of the 'playing house' by the sea in front of the Governor's 'fore house' at Colombo, and two views of the Governor's country house, by D. Jongman.
3rd section, p. 30	(a)	Bird's-eye view of Jaffna.
	(b)	Plan of the fort at Jaffna, scale *c.* 1:3800, and architectural view of the church at Jaffna, scale *c.* 1:380, by I.C. Philips.
3rd section, p. 32	(a)	View of Batticaloa.
	(b)	Sinhalese man and woman, by O. Elliger Junior, and plan of the fort at Batticaloa in 1698, with legend, by Engineer J.G. Worzee (J.C. Toorzee?), scale *c.* 1:2500.
3rd section, p. 47		Bird's-eye view of the elephant hunting in the 'Alutcoer Corle' at 'Horregelle' in 1717, with explanatory note.

3rd section, p. 62	Lion attacking the King's daughter.
3rd section, p. 77	Killing of the 'emperor of Ceylon' by the Portuguese, by M. Balen and Dirk Jongman.
3rd section, p. 79	Humiliation of King 'Jaja Vira' by the Portuguese, by M. Balen and O. Elliger Junior.
3rd section, p. 81	Murder of the King of the seven 'corles', by M. Balen and Dirk Jongman.
3rd section, p. 97	Don Pedro (de Sousa) and the 'empress of Ceylon' in captivity, by M. Balen and Dirk Jongman.
3rd section, p. 111	Murder of the Prince of 'Oeval', by M. Balen and Dirk Jongman.
3rd section, p. 199	Flight of Rajasinga (?) and others with an elephant, by M. Balen and Dirk Jongman.
3rd section, p. 211	Some Sinhalese men and one woman having been put to work by Commander De Grauwe, by M. Balen and Dirk Jongman.
3rd section, p. 360	(a) Plan of Fort Oostenburg in the Bay of Trincomalee and surroundings, scale *c.* 1:2800, and map of the coast between Batticaloa and Trincomalee and up to the 'Palvakaar' River, scale *c.* 1:70000. (b) Plan of the fort at Trincomalee with the adjacent 'temple mountain', scale *c.* 1:4500. (c) Map of the Bay of Trincomalee, with soundings and legend, scale *c.* 1:50000.
3rd section, p. 380	View of Adam's Peak and people climbing to 'Adam's foot' at its top.
3rd section, p. 403	Group of priests with 'Stacy'.

Seba, *Naaukeurige beschryvinge*

Vol. 1, plate 10, no. 1, plate 11, no. 1, plate 18, no. 3, plate 22, nos 5, 12, plate 26, no. 2	Ceylonese plants.
Vol. 1, plate 10, no. 2, plate 11, no. 2, plate 33, nos 5-6, plate 35, no. 4, plate 43, nos 4-5, plate 94, nos 7-9, plate 95, no. 5, plate 100, no. 4, plate 109, no. 1	Ceylonese snakes and their eggs.
Vol. 1, plate 32, nos 7-8	Ceylonese tiger 'foetuses'.
Vol. 1, plate 33, no. 4, plate 34, no. 1, plate 35, nos 1-2, plate 47, no. 1	Ceylonese sloths.
Vol. 1, plate 41, no. 1	Ceylonese 'kwasje' (rodent?).
Vol. 1, plate 48, no. 3	Ceylonese monkey.
Vol. 1, plate 54, no. 1	Ceylonese armadillo.

Vol. 1, plate 69, nos 1-2	Ceylonese spiders.
Vol. 1, plate 69, no. 5	Ceylonese bird.
Vol. 1, plate 70, no. 4	Ceylonese scorpion.
Vol. 1, plate 79, no. 3, plate 80, no. 4	Ceylonese tortoises or turtles.
Vol. 1, plate 82, no. 3	Ceylonese chameleon.
Vol. 1, plate 90, no. 7, plate 93, no. 2, plate 94, nos 4-5, plate 95, nos 3-4, plate 99, no. 2, plate 100, no. 3, plate 105, nos 1-2, plate 109, no. 2	Ceylonese lizards.
Vol. 1, plate 103, no. 1, plate 104, nos 10-12, plate 105, nos 3-4	Ceylonese crocodiles and their eggs.
Vol. 1, plate 108, nos 1-2	Ceylonese geckos.
Vol. 2, throughout the volume	Ceylonese snakes.
Vol. 2, plate 2, no. 9, plate 14, no. 4, plate 32, no. 3, plate 41, no. 6, plate 49, no. 2	Ceylonese lizards.
Vol. 2, plate 8, nos 1-2	Ceylonese snake eating a mouse.
Vol. 2, plate 12, no. 7	Ceylonese salamander or gecko.
Vol. 2, plate 25, no. 4	Ceylonese centipede.
Vol. 2, plate 32, no. 4	Ceylonese caterpillar.
Vol. 2, plate 110, no. 2	Internal parts of a Ceylonese salamander or gecko.
Vol. 2, plate 113, no. F	Bezoar stone grown inside a Ceylonese lizard.
Vol. 2, plate 113, no. N	Gallstone of a Ceylonese elephant.
Vol. 2, plate 114, no. 19	Black Ceylonese 'snake stone'.
Vol. 4, plate 102, nos 26-7	Ceylonese ores and minerals (?) containing gold and silver.

Burmannus, *Thesaurus Zeylanicus*

throughout the volume Ceylonese plants.

Heydt, *Allerneuester Geographisch- und Topographisher Schau-Platz*

p. 142	View of the castle and roadstead of Colombo from the sea, by Heydt and Andreas Hoffer, 1734.
p. 145	View of the castle and harbour of Colombo from the sea, by Heydt and Andreas Hoffer, 1735.
p. 148	View of a courtyard and Adam's Peak from a window in 'Hülffsdorf', four hours from Colombo, by Heydt and Andreas Hoffer, 1736.
p. 151	View of the 'hall of pleasure' (courtyard) from another window in 'Hülffsdorf', by Heydt and Andreas Hoffer, 1736.
p. 154	View of 'Hülffsdorf' and the 'hall of pleasure' (courtyard), by Heydt and Andreas Hoffer, 1736.
p. 157	View of the hill of 'Calana' (Kelaniya?), one 'good mile' from Colombo, by Heydt and Andreas Hoffer.
p. 160	View of the fort at Hanwella, by Heydt, 1736.
p. 163	Another view of the fort at Hanwella, by Heydt.
p. 166	Plan of the fort at Hanwella, by Heydt.
p. 169	View of the fort at Negombo, by Heydt, 1736.
p. 172	Plan of the fort at Negombo and surroundings, by Heydt.
p. 175	View of the fort at Kalutara, by Heydt.
p. 178	Plan of the fort at Kalutara, by Heydt, scale *c.* 1:1000.
p. 181	View of the surroundings of Sitwaka, with some Ceylonese, by Heydt.
p. 184	Map of the *dissavony* of Colombo, by Heydt, 1736, scale *c.* 1:600,000.
p. 187	View of the fortifications and harbour of Galle, by Heydt, 1736.
p. 190	View of the fortifications of Galle seen from the sea, by Heydt, 1737.
p. 193	View of the fortifications and part of the harbour of Galle, by Heydt, 1736.
p. 196	View of the fortifications of Galle and some ships at its harbour, by Heydt, 1736.
p. 199	View of Galle from within, by Heydt, 1737.
p. 202	View of the garden of the Preacher Marinus near Galle, seen in the direction of Adam's Peak, by Heydt.
p. 205	Plan of Galle, by Heydt, scale *c.* 1:4500.
p. 208	View of the fort and river at Matara, by Heydt.
p. 211	Another view of the fort at Matara, by Heydt.
p. 214	Plan of the fort at Matara, by Heydt, scale *c.* 1:2800.
p. 217	View of the fort at Katuwana, by Heydt, 1736.
p. 220	Plan of the fort at Katuwana and surroundings, by Heydt, 1736, scale *c.* 1:1100.

p. 223	View of Adam's Peak and surroundings, with a note on the curiosities to be found on the mountain, by Heydt.
p. 226	View of the main sacrificial spot on Adam's Peak, by Heydt.
p. 229	Characters in an unidentified script to be found on Adam's Peak, by Heydt, 1736.
p. 232	View of a space with a reclining Buddha, other statues and murals, as well as Ceylonese musicians, by Heydt.
p. 235	View of Adam's Peak and surroundings seen from 'Kawatta', by Heydt, 1736.
p. 238	View of Adam's Peak and surroundings seen from 'Kawatta', by Heydt, 1735.
p. 241	View of the pearl fishery near Mannar or Arippu, by Heydt.
p. 244	View of the fort at Hammenhiel, by Heydt, 1736.
p. 247	Plan of the fort at Hammenhiel, by Heydt, scale *c.* 1:100.
p. 250	View of the fort at Jaffna with the tower, stalls and roadstead seen from the sea, by Heydt.
p. 253	View of the fort at Jaffna with the tower seen from the land side, by Heydt, 1736.
p. 256	View of the interior of the fort at Jaffna, by Heydt, 1735.
p. 259	View of the church at Jaffna, by Heydt.
p. 262	View of the interior of the church at Jaffna, by Heydt.
p. 265	View of the so-called 'mountain or coast of death' and surroundings, with some game, near 'Attipetty', by Heydt, 1736.
p. 268	Bird's-eye view of the town of Kandy and the arrival of a VOC envoy (probably Daniel Agreen), and view of the royal residence, by Heydt, 1736.
p. 271	View of the retinue of the VOC envoy Daniel Agreen marching to Kandy, by Heydt, 1736.
p. 274	View of the audience granted to the VOC envoy at the court of Kandy, by Heydt.
p. 277	View of the meal offered by the King of Kandy to the VOC envoy and his retinue, by Heydt.
p. 280	View of several elephants, by Heydt.
p. 286	View of Tuticorin seen from the sea, by Heydt, 1736.

Worms, *Ost-Indian- und Persianische Reisen*

p. 500	Deer hunt at night.

Du Bois, *Historische beschryving*

Vol. 12, p. 233	Map of the Maldives, by J. v. Schley.
Vol. 13, p. 134	Map of Ceylon, by N. Bellin and J. v. Schley, 1750.
Vol. 13, p. 156	(a) Ceylonese way of burning the dead, by J. v. Schley. (b) Ceylonese death-sentences by elephant trampling, hanging and impaling, by J. v. Schley.

Vol. 13, p. 158	King Rajasinga of Kandy and the 'Titinanxi', High Priest of the Sinhalese, by J. v. Schley.
Vol. 13, p. 161	Some Ceylonese sheltering from the rain under the leaves of a 'Talipot' tree, by J. v. Schley.
Vol. 13, p. 163	Sinhalese nobles and ladies around the holy 'Bogahah' tree, by J. v. Schley.
Vol. 13, p. 165	Various types of Ceylonese monkeys, by J. v. Schley.
Vol. 13, p. 170	(a) Map of Galle, by J. v. Schley.
	(b) View of Galle from the sea, by J. v. Schley.
Vol. 13, p. 174	(a) Bird's-eye view of Jaffna and surroundings, by J. v. Schley.
	(b) Map of the Bay of Trincomalee, with soundings, by J. v. Schley.
	(c) View of Batticaloa from the sea, by J. v. Schley.
Vol. 13, p. 178	View of Adam's Peak and people climbing to 'Adam's foot' at its top, by J. v. Schley.
Vol. 14, p. 276	Catching of elephants, by J. v. Schley.
Vol. 20, p. 169	Portrait of Governor Joan Maetsuyker (1646-50), depicted as Governor-General, by J. v. Schley.
Vol. 20, p. 246	Portrait of Governor Rijcklof van Goens Senior (1662-3, 1665-75), depicted as Governor-General, by J. v. Schley.
Vol. 20, p. 379	(a) The Lord's Prayer in Sinhalese.
	(b) Portrait of Governor Gustaaf Willem van Imhoff (1736-40), depicted as Governor-General, by J. v. Schley.

De Marre and Van Keulen, *De nieuwe groote lichtende zee-fakkel*

p. 10 (no. 15)	Landfalls of the northern islands of the Maldives, various parts of Cape Comorin, Adam's Peak and several other mountains and hills on Ceylon.
p. 10 (no. 16)	Map of the coast around Kayalpatnam and Punneikayal, with landfall and soundings, scale *c.* 1:130,000, and map of the coast near Tuticorin, with soundings, scale *c.* 1:35000.
p. 16 (no. 19)	Map of 'Aria' (Ari?) Atoll (western Maldives), scale *c.* 1:200000.
p. 20 (no. 23)	Map of the coast around Kalpitiya, with soundings, scale *c.* 1:140,000.
p. 20 (no. 24)	Map of the harbour of Colombo, with soundings, scale *c.* 1:2000.
p. 22 (no. 25)	Map of the coast around Galle, with soundings, scale *c.* 1:90000, and map of the bay of Nilwala, with soundings, scale *c.* 1:27000.
p. 22 (no. 26)	Map of the Bay of Trincomalee, with soundings, scale

	c. 1:75000, and map of Vandeloos Bay, with soundings, scale *c.* 1:100,000.
p. 76 (no. 51)	Map of the Maldives, scale *c.* 1:2,250,000.
p. 76 (no. 52)	Map of Ceylon, with soundings, scale *c.* 1:600,000.

Fybrants and Philipsz, Het Heylige Evangelium

title page	View of three figurines and an angel in front of Colombo fort.

Conradi and Van der Plaats, *Nederlandsche reizen*

Vol. 3, p. 168	Bird's-eye view of the roadstead of Galle.
Vol. 3, p. 202	View of Adam's Peak.
Vol. 12, p. 110	Bird's-eye view of Jaffna and its roadstead.

Vosmaer, *Natuurkundige beschryving*

1st section, part 12, p. 6	'Wood dog' (wild dog?) from Ceylon, by A. Schouman.
2nd section, part 7, p. 10	Parrot, called 'big purple-red Loeri', from Ceylon, by A. Schouman and S. Fokke.
2nd section, part 9, p. 12	'Cinnamon pigeon' from Ceylon, by A. Schouman and S. Fokke.

Haafner, *Lotgevallen op eene reize*

title page	Haafner arriving on the island Karaitivu, by Haafner and R. Vinkeles.

Haafner, *Reize te voet*

title page	View of a Dutch fort on Ceylon (Hammenhiel?).
p. 72	Encounter with a bear, by Haafner and R. Vinkeles.
p. 140	*Mudaliyar*, 'Sinhalese general', by Haafner and R. Vinkeles.
p. 408	'Pambourahja' snake attacking Haafner, by Haafner and R. Vinkeles.

5. Coromandel

De Vries, *Korte historiael*

p. 76	De Vries travelling in a palanquin to Vishakhapatnam or Bimlipatam (?).
p. 79	Young woman committing *sati* at Vishakhapatnam.

Saar, *Ost-indianische funfzehen-jährige Kriegs-Dienst*

2nd section, p. 106	Widow-burning in Coromandel.

Journael van ... Steven van der Hagen

p. 57	Audience with the Governor of Petapoli (?).
p. 59	Reception at Masulipatam (?), with dancing girls.

Baldaeus, *Nauwkeurige beschryvinge*

part 1, p. 154	(b) Bird's-eye view of Nagappattinam, scale *c.* 1:3000.
part 1, p. 158	Bird's-eye view of Fort Geldria at Pulicat.
part 1, p. 160	View of Masulipatam, with people and an elephant in the foreground.

Schouten, *Oost-Indische voyagie*

part 1, p. 180	(a) Two views of Teganapatam (upper one possibly Thiruppapuliyar), by J. Kip. (b) View of Nagappattinam.
part 1, p. 182	Fight between Coromandel women and Schouten and his companions.
part 2, p. 4	Atrocities committed by the inhabitants of the Andaman Islands against the Dutch.

Nieuhof, *Gedenkwaerdige zee- en lant-reize*

p. 106	View of St. Thome, by Kip.
p. 112	Bird's-eye view of Pulicat and Fort Geldria, with people being executed and cattle in the foreground.
p. 113	Mestiza at Pulicat, by Hen. Cause.

De Vries, *Curieuse aenmerckingen*

Vol. 3, p. 596	View of the Golkonda court, with the Sultan, nobles, the harem, etc., as well as some Dutchmen.

Havart, *Op- en ondergang*

title page	Golkonda military troops and camp, and a man prostrating himself in front of the King.
part 1, p. 86	Map of the area between Nagappattinam, Teganapatam and Ariyalur.
part 1, p. 91	View of the holy bird mountain at Tirukkalukundram, where two birds are daily fed by a 'priest'.
part 1, p. 105	Map of Pulicat, scale *c.* 1:4000.
part 1, p. 144	Plan of the factory at Masulipatam, scale *c.* 1:350.
part 1, p. 191	King of Golkonda visiting the Dutch church.
part 2, p. 17	Plan of the lodge in Nagulvancha, scale *c.* 1:300.

part 2, p. 57	Stoning of two women who have poisoned their husbands.
part 2, p. 93	Plan of the factory at Golkonda, scale *c.* 1:3500.
part 2, p. 155	Reception of Ambassador Laurens Pit at the gate of Golkonda in March 1686.
part 2, p. 158	Reception of Pit by King Abul-Hasan Qutb Shah of Golkonda.
part 2, p. 208	Plan of the walls and tanks of Golkonda fort.
part 2, p. 210	Portrait of King Abdullah Qutb Shah of Golkonda, with verse by Havart.
part 2, p. 214	Portrait of King Abul-Hasan Qutb Shah of Golkonda, with verse by Havart.
part 2, p. 219	Portrait of Madanna, *Majmuadar* (collector) of the King of Golkonda, with verse by Havart.
part 2, p. 220	Portrait of Akkanna, *Shahnawis-i qalamraw-i Sultan* (chief bookkeeper of the crown estate) and *Sar-lashkar* (commander-in-chief) of Golkonda, with verse by Havart.
part 2, p. 224	Exhibition of the bodies of Madanna and Akkanna after their assassination.
part 2, p. 226 (or 234?)	Portrait of Muhammad Ibrahim, *Sar-khail* (chancellor) and *Sar-lashkar* (commander-in-chief) of Golkonda, with verse by Havart.
part 2, p. 238	King of Golkonda having the treacherous Secretary Itimad Rao beaten to death in his presence.
part 3, p. 4	Plan of the lodge at Palakollu.
part 3, p. 48	Plan of the lodge at Draksharama, scale *c.* 1:4500.
part 3, p. 76	Plan of the lodge at Bimlipatam, scale *c.* 1:400.

Parthey, *Ost-Indianische und Persianische Neun-jährige Kriegs-Dienste*

p. 132	Burning of a dead man and his wife committing *sati* in Coromandel.

Valentijn, *Oud en nieuw Oost-Indiën*, Vol. V, part 1

1st section, p. 12	View of St. Thome, by J.C. Philips, and map of St. Thome, scale *c.* 1:12500.
1st section, p. 17	View of the grave of Anthonia Nilo Steelandt, wife of Governor Johannes van Steelandt (1705-10), at Nagappattinam, December 1709, by Matijs Baale and P. Tanjee, 1725, and view of the storm at Nagappattinam, November 1715.

Seba, *Naaukeurige beschryvinge*

Vol. 2, plate 112, no. 3	Bezoar stone, grown inside a sea cow or walrus, from Coromandel.

Du Bois, *Historische beschryving*

Vol. 13, p. 291	View of Masulipatam from the land side, by J. v. Schley.
Vol. 15, p. 29	Bird's-eye view of Fort Geldria at Pulicat, by J. v. Schley.
Vol. 16, p. 116	Map of the theatre of war in south Coromandel, by J. v. Schley.
Vol. 16, p. 136	Plan of Pondicherry in 1741, by J. v. Schley.
Vol. 16, p. 150	'Princess mother' of the Nawab of Arcot and some servants, by J. v. Schley.
Vol. 16, p. 177	Plan of Madras and surroundings after being captured by the French in September 1746, by J. v. Schley.
Vol. 16, p. 265	(a) Plan of Tranquebar and Fort Dansborg, by J. v. Schley.
	(b) Views of Fort Dansborg from the east and the south, by J. v. Schley.
	(c) Views of Fort Dansborg from the north and the west, by J. v. Schley.
	(d) Map of the area under the jurisdiction of Tranquebar, by J. v. Schley.
Vol. 16, p. 276	(a) Plan of the fort at St. Thome, by J. v. Schley.
	(b) View of the ruins at St. Thome, by J. v. Schley.
Vol. 20, p. 159	Portrait of Governor Carel Reniers (1636-8), depicted as Governor-General, by J. v. Schley.
Vol. 20, p. 263	Portrait of Governor Cornelis Janszoon Speelman (1663-5), depicted as Governor-General, by J. v. Schley.
Vol. 20, p. 343	Portrait of Governor Dirck van Cloon (1723-30), depicted as Governor-General, by J. v. Schley.
Vol. 20, p. 398	Portrait of Governor Jacob Mossel (1738-43), depicted as Governor-General, by J. v. Schley.

De Marre and Van Keulen, *De nieuwe groote lichtende zee-fakkel*

p. 26 (no. 27)	Map of Teganapatam, with soundings, scale *c.* 1:90000, and map of the coast around Pulicat, with soundings, scale *c.* 1:330,000.
p. 76 (no. 53)	Map of the coast of Coromandel, with soundings, scale *c.* 1:1,900,000.

Conradi and Van der Plaats, *Nederlandsche reizen*

Vol. 7, p. 71	Reception of Pieter van den Broeck at Masulipatam.

Haafner, *Lotgevallen op eene reize*

p. 202	Meeting with the *Jamadar* at Alambaram, by Haafner and R. Vinkeles.

Haafner, *Reize in eenen palanquin*

part 1, p. 134	Fortune-teller, by Haafner and R. Vinkeles.
part 1, p. 142	Rest house and some Indians at 'Darma-oer', by Haafner and R. Vinkeles.
part 1, pp. 210, 218	*Devadasis* (female temple dancers), by Haafner and R. Vinkeles.
part 1, p. 430	Mendicant, by Haafner and R. Vinkeles.
part 2, p. 96	Haafner meeting 'Mamia' near a Hindu temple at 'Nababpeent' (Nawabpet?), by Haafner and R. Vinkeles.
part 2, p. 392	Mestiza with servants going to church, by Haafner and R. Vinkeles.
part 2, p. 427	The five *Rathas* (temples) at Mamallapuram (Mahabalipuram), by Haafner and R. Vinkeles.

6. Bengal
(including Bihar)

Van der Heiden and Kunst, *Vervarelyke schip-breuk*

title page	Shipwreck off the Bengal coast.
p. 8	Castaways leaving the wrecked ship by raft.
p. 10	Raft near the coast, by D. Bosboom.
pp. 13-14, 32	Castaways trying to survive and catching animals ashore, by D. Bosboom.
p. 29	Building a new raft.
p. 30	Resting near a waterway, by D. Bosboom.
p. 40	Raft entangled in the branches of a tree (at high tide?), by D. Bosboom.
p. 42	Unburying a dead man to be eaten, by D. Bosboom.
pp. 68, 71, 73	Battle between Nawab 'Maesmachaen' (Mir Jumla) and Assam (?), with elephants and ships.

Schouten, *Oost-Indische voyagie*

part 2, p. 10	Traders from Arakan selling Bengal slaves to the Dutch at Pipli.
part 2, p. 12	View of the fortifications and defences at Pipli, and its Governor negotiating with enemies from Arakan.
part 2, p. 62	Washing and praying of Bengalis in the Ganges or Hooghly River and a Bengali being attacked by a tiger.
part 2, p. 74	View of the court of the Muslim Governor of Bengal.
part 2, p. 78	Bengali Muslims celebrating the festival of 'Hassan and Hossein' (Muharram?).
part 2, p. 80	Muslim wedding procession in Bengal.
part 2, p. 110	Hindu deity being carried around in his *rath* (car) (at Pipli?).
part 2, p. 114	Bengali jugglers.

Hermann, *Horti academici*

p. 625	Plant from Bengal.

Commelin, Ruysch and Kiggelaar, *Horti Medici Amstelodamensis*

Vol. 1, pp. 35, 119	Plants from Bengal.

De Graaff, *Reisen*

p. 92 (or 91?)	Bird's-eye view of the court and garden of Prince Shah Shuja (?) at Rajmahal, and map of Monghyr.
p. 105	Jan van Oosterwyk being treated for his illness by a male and a female doctor at 'Soupra' (Chhapra?), by C. Huberts and J. Lux.

Bógaerts, *Abraham Bógaerts historische reizen*

p. 406	Bengali Muslims mourning the dead.

Valentijn, *Oud en nieuw Oost-Indiën*, Vol. V, part 1

1st section, p. 146	Map of the Bengal 'kingdom', with soundings, by Joh. van Leenen, J. van Braam and G. onder de Linden, by order of *Directeur* Mattheus van den Broucke (1658-63), scale *c.* 1:2,300,000.
1st section, p. 162	Bird's-eye view of Hooghly, with legend, scale *c.* 1:1700.
1st section, p. 166	Portrait of Nawazish Khan, Governor at Rajmahal.

Heydt, *Allerneuester Geographisch- und Topographisher Schau-Platz*

p. 295	View of Hooghly from the river, by Heydt.

Du Bois, *Historische beschryving*

Vol. 15, p. 50	Map of the Bengal 'kingdom', by J. v. Schley.
Vol. 15, p. 52	Bird's-eye view of the palace and garden of Prince Shah Shuja of Rajmahal, and plan of Monghyr, by J. v. Schley.
Vol. 16, p. 286	Bird's-eye view of the factory at Hooghly and surroundings, by J. v. Schley.
Vol. 20, p. 346	Portrait of *Directeur* Abraham Patras (1724-7), depicted as Governor-General, by J. v. Schley.

De Marre and Van Keulen, *De nieuwe groote lichtende zee-fakkel*

p. 36	Map of the coast north of Palmyras Point up to Bandel on the Hooghly River, with soundings, scale *c.* 1:2,400,000.
p. 76 (no. 54)	Map of the Ganges River down from Patna and the northern part of the Bay of Bengal, with soundings, scale *c.* 1:390,000.

Defence de la Compagnie Unie

p. 125	Sketch of the fortress 'Makwatanna' (on p. 135 in the Dutch trans.).

Stavorinus, *Reize van Zeeland*

part 2, p. 3	Map of the Hooghly River from Hijili to Bandel and beyond, by C. van Baarsel, 1793, scale *c.* 1:1,200,000.

Vosmaer, *Natuurkundige beschryving*

1st section, part 6, p. 20	Five-fingered sloth from Bengal, by A. Schouman and S. Fokke.
1st section, part 11, p. 10	Crocodile-killer called 'Ichneumon' from Bengal, by A. Schouman.

Haafner, *Reize naar Bengalen*

title page	View of the tomb of Bahadur Sahib on the Hooghly River, by Haafner, J. Smies and P. Velyn.
p. 127	View of the Hooghly River, some buildings on its bank and a few boats, by Haafner, J. Smies and P. Velyn.
p. 201	*Chobdar* (stick-bearer) and *peon* (servant and guard), by J. Smies and P. Velyn.

Appendix II: Addresses and Information

Note that at the time of writing, in most provinces the provincial state archives and the municipal archives of the provincial capital (and sometimes other municipalities and organizations) were in a process of merger to become so-called Regional Historical Centres. This may cause some materials to be transferred. For up-to-date information on governmental archives and a large number of other repositories, see for instance the following web sites:

- www.archiefnet.nl
- www.archieven.nl
- archief.pagina.nl
- www.hum.uva.nl/nhl/bizon/mateboer_repertorium.htm
- iias.leidenuniv.nl/bib/collections.html
- www.museum.nl
- www.maritiemdigitaal.nl

Most repositories are closed on national holidays: 1 January, Easter (two days), 30 April, 5 May, Ascension Day, Whitsun (two days), 25 and 26 December. Most repositories in Leiden are also closed on 3 October.

1. Government Archives

1.1. *Regionaal Archief Alkmaar*
Regional Archives in Alkmaar

Hertog Aalbrechtweg 5, Alkmaar / P.O. Box 9232, 1800 GE Alkmaar
Tel: 072-5662626, fax: 072-5662633
Internet: www.archiefalkmaar.nl, e-mail: regionaal@archiefalkmaar.nl
visiting hours: Tuesday 8.45-21.15 (June-August: 8.45-16.45), Wednesday-Friday 8.45-16.45

1.2. *Gemeentearchief Amsterdam*
Municipal Archives of Amsterdam

Amsteldijk 67, Amsterdam / P.O. Box 51140, 1007 EC Amsterdam
(from summer 2006 onward: Vijzelstraat 32, Amsterdam)
Tel: 020-5720202, fax: 020-6750596
Internet: www.gemeentearchief.amsterdam.nl, e-mail: secretariaat@gaaweb.nl
visiting hours: Monday-Friday 10.00-17.00

1.3. *Gelders Archief*
Archives of Guelderland

Markt 1, 6811 CG Arnhem
Tel: 026-3521600, fax: 026-3521699
Internet: www.geldersarchief.nl, e-mail: info@geldersarchief.nl
visiting hours: Tuesday-Friday 9.00-17.00, Saturday 9.00-13.00 (except for July-August)

1.4. *Drents Archief*
Archives of Drenthe

Brink 4, Assen / P.O. Box 595, 9400 AN Assen
Tel: 0592-313523, fax: 0592-314697
Internet: www.drentsarchief.org, e-mail: info@drentsarchief.org
visiting hours: Monday 13.30-17.00, Tuesday 9.00-21.00 (July-September: 9.00-17.00), Wednesday, Thursday and Friday 9.00-17.00

1.5. *Regionaal Historisch Centrum Bergen op Zoom*
Regional Historical Centre Bergen op Zoom

Blokstallen 2, Bergen op Zoom / P.O. Box 35, 4600 AA Bergen op Zoom
Tel: 0164-241931, fax: 0164-254096
Internet: www.archboz.nl, e-mail: archiefdienst@bergenopzoom.nl
visiting hours: Tuesday 10.00-21.00, Wednesday-Friday 10.00-17.00

1.6. *Gemeentearchief Delft*
Municipal Archives of Delft

Oude Delft 169, 2611 HB Delft
Tel: 015-2602341, fax: 015-2602355
Internet: www.delft.nl/archief, e-mail: archief@delft.nl
visiting hours: Tuesday-Friday 9.00-17.00

1.7. *Streekarchief Midden-Holland*
Regional Archives Central Holland

Groeneweg 30, 2801 ZC Gouda
Tel: 0182-521821 / 516135, fax: 0182-589829
Internet: www.groenehartarchieven.nl/middenholland.asp,
e-mail: middenholland@groenehartarchieven.nl
visiting hours: Tuesday-Friday 9.30-17.00, Tuesday 18.30-21.00 (except for June-August)

1.8. *Groninger Archieven*
Archives of Groningen

Cascadeplein 4, Groningen / P.O. Box 30040, 9700 RM Groningen
Tel: 050-5992000, fax: 050-5992050
Internet: www.groningerarchieven.nl, e-mail: info@groningerarchieven.nl
visiting hours: Tuesday 9.00-22.00, Wednesday-Friday 9.00-17.00, Saturday 9.00-13.00 (July-August: Tuesday-Friday 9.00-17.00)

1.9. *Archiefdienst voor Kennemerland*
Archival Service for Kennemerland

Jansstraat 40, 2011 RX Haarlem
Tel: 023-5113320, fax: 023-5113447
Internet: www.haarlem.nl, e-mail: avk@haarlem.nl
visiting hours: Tuesday-Friday 9.00-17.00, Thursday 9.00-21.00

1.10. *Rijksarchief in Noord-Holland*
State Archives in North Holland

Kleine Houtweg 18, 2012 CH Haarlem
Tel: 023-5172700, fax: 023-5172720
Internet: www.noordhollandsarchief.org,
e-mail: info@noordhollandsarchief.nl
visiting hours: Tuesday-Friday 9.00-1700, Saturday 9.00-17.00 (except for July-August)

1.11. *Haags Gemeentearchief*
Municipal Archives of The Hague

Spui 70, 2511 BT The Hague
Tel: 070-3537003 / 3537013, fax: 070-3537010
Internet: www.gemeentearchief.denhaag.nl, e-mail: postbus@hga.denhaag.nl
visiting hours: Monday-Saturday 9.30-17.00

1.12. *Streekarchivariaat Noordwest-Veluwe: Harderwijk*
Regional Archives Northwest Veluwe: Harderwijk

Havendam 56, Harderwijk / P.O. Box 149, 3840 AC Harderwijk
Tel: 0341-411454, fax: 0341-425895
Internet: www.streekarchivariaat.nl, e-mail: info@streekarchivariaat.nl
visiting hours: Monday-Thursday 13.00-17.00, and by appointment

1.13. *Streekarchivariaat Noord-Veluwe: Hattem*
Regional Archives North Veluwe: Hattem

Markt 1, Hattem / P.O. Box 93, 8050 AB Hattem
Tel: 038-4431616, fax: 038-4446839
Internet: www.hattem.nl, e-mail: gemeente@hattem.nl
visiting hours: Tuesday, Friday, Wednesday in even weeks, by appointment

1.14. *Historisch Informatiecentrum Helmond*
Historical Information Centre Helmond

Molenstraat 121, Helmond / P.O. Box 191, 5600 AD Eindhoven
Tel: 040-2649940, fax: 040-2649977
Internet: www.rhc-eindhoven.nl, e-mail: info@rhc-eindhoven.nl
visiting hours: Tuesday-Friday 9.00-17.00, Thursday 9.00-21.00

1.15. *Brabants Historisch Informatie Centrum: Den Bosch*
Historical Information Centre of Brabant: Den Bosch

Zuid-Willemsvaart 2, 's-Hertogenbosch (a.k.a. Den Bosch) / P.O. Box 81, 5201 AB 's-Hertogenbosch
Tel: 073-6818500, fax: 073-6146439
Internet: www.bhic.nl, e-mail: info@bhic.nl
visiting hours: Tuesday 9.00-21.00, Wednesday-Friday 9.00-17.00, Saturday 9.00-13.00 (July-August: closed on Tuesday evening and Saturday)

1.16. *Westfries Archief*
Archives of West Friesland

Nieuwe Steen 1, Hoorn / P.O. Box 603, 1620 AR Hoorn
Tel: 0229-252200, fax: 0229-252040
Internet: www.westfriesarchief.nl, e-mail: info@westfriesarchief.nl
visiting hours: Tuesday-Friday 9.00-17.00, second and fourth Thursday of every month 19.00-21.45 (except for July-August)

1.17. *Gemeentearchief Zaanstad*
Municipal Archives of Zaanstad

Hoogstraat 34, 1541 KZ Koog aan de Zaan
Tel: 075-6552233, fax: 075-6553205
Internet: www.zaanstad.nl/gemeentearchief,
e-mail: gemeentearchief@zaanstad.nl
visiting hours: Tuesday-Friday 9.00-16.30, Monday 18.30-21.00 (except for June-August)

1.18. *Tresoar, Frysk Histoarysk en Letterkundich Sintrum*
Tresoar, Friesian Historical and Literary Centre

Boterhoek 1, Leeuwarden / P.O. Box 2637, 8901 AC Leeuwarden
Tel: 058-7890789, fax: 058-7890777
Internet: www.tresoar.nl, e-mail: info@tresoar.nl
visiting hours: Monday 13.00-17.00, Tuesday-Wednesday 9.00-21.00, Thursday-Friday 9.00-17.00, Saturday 9.00-13.00 (July-August: closed Tuesday and Wednesday evening, and Saturday)

1.19. *Regionaal Archief Leiden*
Regional Archives of Leiden

Boisotkade 2A, Leiden / P.O. Box 16113, 2301 GC Leiden
Tel: 071-5165355, fax: 071-5164950
Internet: www.leidenarchief.nl, e-mail: info@leidenarchief.nl
visiting hours: Monday 13.00-17.00, Tuesday-Friday 9.30-17.00, Saturday 9.00-13.00

1.20. *Rijksarchief in Limburg*
State Archives in Limburg

Sint Pieterstraat 7, 6211 JM Maastricht
Tel: 043-3217051, fax: 043-3255640
Internet: www.rijksarchieflimburg.nl, e-mail: info@rijksarchieflimburg.nl
visiting hours: Monday 13.00-17.00, Tuesday-Friday 9.00-17.00, Saturday 9.00-15.00
(this repository will be part of the Regionaal Historisch Centrum Limburg / Regional Historical Centre Limburg, www.rhcl.nl)

1.21. *Zeeuws Archief*
Zeeland Archives

Hofplein 16, Middelburg / P.O. Box 70, 4330 AB Middelburg
Tel: 0118-678800, fax: 0118-628094
Internet: www.zeeuwsarchief.nl, e-mail: info@zeeuwsarchief.nl
visiting hours: Tuesday-Friday 9.00-17.00, Saturday 9.00-1700 (except for July-August)

1.22. *Gemeentearchief Rotterdam*
Municipal Archives of Rotterdam

Hofdijk 651, Rotterdam / P.O. Box 71, 3000 AB Rotterdam
Tel: 010-2434567, fax: 010-2434666
Internet: www.gemeentearchief.rotterdam.nl
e-mail: info@gar.rotterdam.nl
visiting hours: Monday 13.00-17.00, Tuesday-Friday 9.00-17.00, Wednesday until 21.30 (except for July-August)

1.23. *Het Utrechts Archief*
The Archives of Utrecht

Alexander Numankade 199-201, 3572 KW Utrecht
Tel: 030-2866611, fax: 030-2866600
Internet: www.hetutrechtsarchief.nl,
e-mail: secretariaat@hetutrechtsarchief.nl
visiting hours: Tuesday, Wednesday, Friday 9.00-17.00, Thursday 9.00-21.00

1.24. *Stads- en Streekarchief Zutphen*
Town and Regional Archives of Zutphen

Spiegelstraat 13-17, 7201 KA Zutphen
Tel: 0575-512157, fax: 0575-510719
Internet: www.streekarchiefzutphen.nl
e-mail: streekarchief@zutphen.nl
visiting hours: Tuesday 9.00-21.00, Wednesday-Friday 9.00-17.00 (June-August: Tuesday 9.00-17.00)

1.25. *Historisch Centrum Overijssel*
Historical Centre Overijssel

Eikenstraat 20, Zwolle / P.O. Box 1510, 8001 BM Zwolle
Tel: 038-4266300, fax: 038-4266333
Internet: www.historischcentrumoverijssel.nl, e-mail: info@hcov.nl
visiting hours: Tuesday-Friday 9.00-17.00, Saturday 9.00-17.00 (except for July-August)

2. Universities

2.1. *Universiteit van Amsterdam, Artis Bibliotheek*
University of Amsterdam, Artis Library

Plantage Middenlaan 45, 1018 DC Amsterdam
Tel: 020-5255898, fax: 020-5256612
Internet: www.uba.uva.nl/bijzondere collecties, e-mail: bibpb@science.uva
visiting hours: Wednesday-Friday 10.00-15.00

2.2. *Universiteit van Amsterdam, Universiteitsbibliotheek*
University of Amsterdam, University Library

Singel 425, Amsterdam / P.O. Box 19185, 1000 GD Amsterdam
Tel: 020-5252473 (manuscripts) / 5252354 (maps), fax: 020-5252311
Internet: www.uba.uva.nl,
e-mail: specialcollections-uba@uva.nl, maps-uba@uva.nl
visiting hours: manuscripts Monday-Friday 9.30-17.00, maps Tuesday-Friday 13.00-17.00

2.3. *Vrije Universiteit Amsterdam, Bibliotheek*
Vrije Universiteit Amsterdam, Library

De Boelelaan 1105, Amsterdam / De Boelelaan 1103, 1081 HV Amsterdam
Tel: 020-5985184 (manuscripts, old books) / 5985188 (maps) / 5985200 (general), fax: 020-5985259
Internet: www.ubvu.vu.nl, e-mail: www@ubvu.vu.nl
visiting hours: Monday-Friday 9.00-12.30, 13.00-16.45

2.4. *Bibliotheek Technische Universiteit Delft*
Delft University of Technology Library

Afdeling Trésor
Prometheusplein 1, Delft / P.O. Box 98, 2600 MG Delft
Tel: 015-2783240 / 2785678, fax: 015-2785706
Internet: www.library.tudelft.nl, e-mail: tresor@library.tudelft.nl
visiting hours: Monday-Friday 9.00-17.00, by appointment

2.5. *Theologische Universiteit Kampen, Universiteitsbibliotheek*
Theological University of Kampen, University Library

Oudestraat 6, Kampen / P.O. Box 5021, 8260 GA Kampen
Tel: 038-3371653, fax: 038-3371613
Internet: www.thuk.nl, e-mail: bibliotheek@mail.thuk.nl
visiting hours: Monday-Friday 8.30-17.00 (September-June Thursday until 18.30)

2.6. *Universiteit Leiden, Instituut Kern*
Leiden University, Kern Institute

Nonnensteeg 1-3, Leiden / P.O. Box 9515, 2300 RA Leiden
Tel: 071-5272502 / 5272619, fax: 071-5272956
Internet: www.instituutkern.leidenuniv.nl, e-mail: kernlib@let.leidenuniv.nl
visiting hours: Monday-Friday 11.00-17.00

2.7. *Universiteit Leiden, Universiteitsbibliotheek*
Leiden University Library

Witte Singel 27, Leiden / P.O. Box 9501, 2300 RA Leiden
Tel: 071-5272857 / 5272857, fax: 071-5272836
Internet: ub.leidenuniv.nl, e-mail: specialcollections@library.leidenuniv.nl
visiting hours: Monday-Friday 9.30-13.00, 13.30-16.45

2.8. *Bibliotheek Universiteit Tilburg*
Tilburg University Library

Warandelaan 2 (Gebouw L), Tilburg / P.O. Box 90153, 5000 LE Tilburg
Tel: 013-4662865 / 4662124, fax: 013-4662996
Internet: www.uvt.nl/bibliotheek, e-mail: library@uvt.nl
visiting hours: Monday-Friday 9.00-17.00

2.9. *Universiteit Utrecht, Faculteit Ruimtelijke Wetenschappen*
Utrecht University, Faculty of Geosciences

University Library, Kaartenzaal, Heidelberglaan 3, Utrecht / P.O. Box 80124, 3508 TC Utrecht
Tel: 030-2534401 / 2535156, fax: 030-2538398
Internet: kaartenzaal.geog.uu.nl, e-mail: r.oddens@geog.uu.nl
visiting hours: Monday-Friday 9.00-17.00

2.10. *Universiteit Utrecht, Universiteitsbibliotheek*
Utrecht University Library

Leeszaal Bijzondere Collecties, Heidelberglaan 3, Utrecht / P.O. Box 80124, 3508 TC Utrecht
Tel: 030-2536633, fax: 030-2538398
Internet: www.library.uu.nl, e-mail: lszbijzcol@library.uu.nl
visiting hours: Monday-Friday 9.00-17.00

2.11. *Bibliotheek Wageningen Universiteit en Researchcentrum*
Wageningen University and Research Centre Library

Jan-Kopshuis Library, Generaal Foulkesweg 19 (building 356), Wageningen / P.O. Box 9100, 6700 HA Wageningen
Tel: 0317-482701, fax: 0317-484761
Internet: library.wur.nl/speccol
e-mail: speccol.library@wur.nl
visiting hours: Monday-Friday 9.00-12.30

3. Ecclesiastical Organizations

3.1. *Archief Bisdom 's-Hertogenbosch*
Archives Diocese 's-Hertogenbosch

Parade 11, 's-Hertogenbosch (a.k.a. Den Bosch) / P.O. Box 1070, 5200 BC 's-Hertogenbosch
Tel: 073-6125488, fax: 073-6136850
Internet: www.bisdomdenbosch.nl, e-mail: info@bisdomdenbosch.nl
visiting hours: Monday-Friday 9.00-16.00, by appointment

3.2. *Archief van de Nederlandse provincie der Jezuïeten*
Archives of the Netherlands province of the Jesuits

Houtlaan 4, 6525 XZ Nijmegen
Tel: 024-3554219, fax: 024-3558712
Internet: www.jezuieten.org, e-mail: archief@jezuieten.org
visiting hours: Monday-Friday 9.00-15.30, by appointment

4. Museums and Other Public Institutions

4.1. *Stedelijk Museum Alkmaar*
Municipal Museum of Alkmaar

Canadaplein 1, 1811 KE Alkmaar
Tel: 072-5489789, fax: 072-5151476
Internet: www.stedelijkmuseumalkmaar.nl, e-mail: museum@alkmaar.nl
visiting hours: Tuesday-Friday 10.00-17.00, Saturday-Sunday 13.00-17.00

4.2. *Koninklijk Instituut voor de Tropen (KIT)*
Royal Tropical Institute

P.O. Box 95001, 1090 HA Amsterdam
Internet: www.kit.nl
Kenniscentrum:
Mauritskade 63, Amsterdam
Tel: 020-5688462, fax: 020-6654423
e-mail: library@kit.nl
visiting hours: Monday-Friday 10.00-16.45

Museum Library:
Linnaeusstraat 2, Amsterdam
Tel: 020-5688254 / 5688623, fax: 020-5688331
e-mail: tropenmuseum@kit.nl
visiting hours: Monday-Friday, Sunday 10.00-16.45

4.3. *Nederlandsch Economisch-Historisch Archief (NEHA)*
Netherlands Economic-Historical Archives

Cruquiusweg 31, 1019 AT Amsterdam
Tel: 020-6685866, fax: 020-6654181
Internet: www.neha.nl, e-mail: info@neha.nl
visiting hours: Monday-Friday 9.00-17.00

4.4. *Nederlands Scheepvaartmuseum Amsterdam*
Netherlands Maritime Museum Amsterdam

Kattenburgerplein 1, 1018 KK Amsterdam
Tel: 020-5232211, fax: 020-5232213
Internet: www.scheepvaartmuseum.nl
Library:
e-mail: bibliotheek@scheepvaartmuseum.nl
visiting hours: Tuesday-Friday 10.00-16.45
Museum:
e-mail: info@scheepvaartmuseum.nl
visiting hours: Tuesday-Sunday 10.00-17.00 (between mid-June and mid-September also on Monday)

4.5. *Rijksmuseum Amsterdam*
Rijksmuseum Amsterdam

P.O. Box 74888, 1070 DN Amsterdam
Tel: 020-6747000, fax: 020-6747001
Internet: www.rijksmuseum.nl, e-mail: info@rijksmuseum.nl
Rijksprentenkabinet and Library:
Jan Luijkenstraat 1a, Amsterdam
visiting hours: Tuesday-Saturday 10.00-17.00
Museum:
Stadhouderskade 42 / Hobbemastraat 19, Amsterdam
visiting hours: daily 10.00-17.00

4.6. *Museum Bronbeek*
Bronbeek Museum

Velperweg 147, 6824 MB Arnhem
Tel: 026-3763555, fax: 026-3763590
Internet: www.bronbeek.nl, e-mail: ktomm.bronbeek@army.dnet.mindef.nl
visiting hours: Tuesday-Sunday 10.00-17.00

4.7. *Dordrechts Museum*
Museum of Dordrecht

Museumstraat 40, Dordrecht / P.O. Box 1170, 3300 BD Dordrecht
Tel: 078-6482148, fax: 078-6141766
Internet: www.dordrechtsmuseum.nl,
e-mail: dordrechtsmuseum@dordrecht.nl
visiting hours: Tuesday-Sunday 11.00-17.00

4.8. *Simon van Gijn - Museum aan huis*
Simon van Gijn - Museum at home

Nieuwe Haven 29-30, 3311 AP Dordrecht
Tel: 078-6398200, fax: 078-6317913
Internet: www.simonvangijn.nl, e-mail: simonvangijn@dordrecht.nl
visiting hours: Tuesday-Sunday 11.00-17.00

4.9. *Groninger Museum*
Museum of Groningen

Museumeiland 1, Groningen / P.O. Box 90, 9700 ME Groningen
Tel: 050-3666555 / 0900-8212132, fax: 050-3120815
Internet: www.groninger-museum.nl, e-mail: info@groninger-museum.nl
visiting hours: Tuesday-Sunday 10.00-17.00 (in July and August also Monday 13.00-17.00)

4.10. *Teylers Museum*
Teyler's Museum

Spaarne 16, 2011 CH Haarlem
Tel: 023-5319010, fax: 023-5342004
Internet: www.teylersmuseum.nl, e-mail: info@teylersmuseum.nl
visiting hours (reading room): by appointment

4.11. *Centraal Bureau voor Genealogie (CBG)*
Central Office for Genealogy

Prins Willem-Alexanderhof 22, The Hague / P.O. Box 11755, 2502 AT The Hague
Tel: 070-3150500 / 3150570, fax: 070-3478394
Internet: www.cbg.nl, e-mail: algemeen@cbg.nl
visiting hours: Monday-Friday 9.30-17.00, Tuesday 9.30-21.30, Saturday 9.00-13.00 (except for Saturdays preceding national holidays)

4.12. *Koninklijke Bibliotheek (KB)*
Royal Library

Prins Willem-Alexanderhof 5, The Hague / P.O. Box 90407, 2509 LK The Hague
Tel: 070-3140322 / 3140310, fax: 070-3140655
Internet: www.kb.nl, e-mail: info@kb.nl
visiting hours: Monday-Friday 9.00-17.00, Saturday 9.00-13.00

4.13. *Museum Meermanno*
Meermanno Museum

Prinsessegracht 30, 2514 AP The Hague
Tel: 070-3462700, fax: 070-3630350
Internet: www.meermanno.nl, e-mail: bibliotheek@meermanno.nl
visiting hours: Tuesday-Friday 11.00-12.30, 13.00-16.45, by appointment

4.14. *Koninklijk Instituut voor Taal-, Land- en Volkenkunde (KITLV)*
Royal Institute of Linguistics and Anthropology

Reuvensplaats 2, Leiden / P.O. Box 9515, 2300 RA Leiden
Tel: 071-5272473 / 5272637 / 5272295, fax: 071-5272638
Internet: www.kitlv.nl, e-mail: collections@kitlv.nl
visiting hours: Monday-Friday 9.00-17.00

4.15. *Museum Boerhaave*
Boerhaave Museum

Information Centre
Lange St. Agnietenstraat 10, Leiden / P.O. Box 11280, 2301 EG Leiden
Tel: 071-5214224, fax: 071-5120344
Internet: www.museumboerhaave.nl,
e-mail: informatie@museumboerhaave.nl
visiting hours: Monday-Friday 9.00-12.30, 13.30-17.00

4.16. *Nationaal Herbarium Nederland - Universiteit Leiden*
National Herbarium of the Netherlands - Leiden University

Van Steenis Gebouw, Einsteinweg 2, Leiden / P.O. Box 9514, 2300 RA Leiden
Tel: 071-5273513 / 5273514 / 5273515, fax: 071-5273511
Internet: www.nationaalherbarium.nl
e-mail: library@nhn.leidenuniv.nl
visiting hours: Monday-Friday 8.15-12.30, 13.00-16.45

4.17. *Naturalis, Nationaal Natuurhistorisch Museum*
Naturalis, National Museum of Natural History

Library
Darwinweg 2, Leiden / P.O. Box 9517, 2300 RA Leiden
Tel: 071-5687668 / 5687600, fax: 071-5687666
Internet: www.naturalis.nl, e-mail: library@naturalis.nnm.nl
visiting hours: Tuesday-Saturday 10.00-16.30

4.18. *Rijksmuseum voor Volkenkunde*
National Museum of Ethnology

Steenstraat 1, Leiden / P.O. Box 212, 2300 AE Leiden
Tel: 071-5168800, fax: 071-5128437
Internet: www.rmv.nl, e-mail: info@rmv.nl
visiting hours: Tuesday-Friday 10.00-12.30, 13.30-16.30, by appointment

4.19. *Zeeuwse Bibliotheek / Zeeuws Documentatiecentrum*
Zeeland Library / Zeeland Documentation Centre

Kousteensedijk 7, Middelburg / P.O. Box 8004, 4330 EA Middelburg
Tel: 0118-654285, fax: 0118-654001
Internet: www.zeeuwsebibliotheek.nl,
e-mail: zbdoc@mail.zeeuwsebibliotheek.nl
visiting hours: Monday 17.30-21.00, Tuesday-Friday 10.00-21.00, Saturday 10.00-13.00

4.20. *Zeeuws Museum*
Zeeland Museum

Abdij 3, Middelburg / P.O. Box 378, 4330 AJ Middelburg
Tel: 0118-653000, fax: 0118-653099
Internet: www.zeeuwsmuseum.nl, e-mail: info@zeeuwsmuseum.nl
visiting hours: unknown at the time of writing (the museum will reopen *c.* 2007)

4.21. *Slot Zuylen*
Zuylen Castle

Tournooiveld 1, 3611 AS Oud-Zuilen
Tel: 030-2440255, fax: 030-2443907
Internet: www.slotzuylen.com, e-mail: info@slotzuylen.com
visiting hours: by appointment

4.22. *Atlas van Stolk*
Van Stolk Atlas

Korte Hoogstraat 31, 3011 GK Rotterdam
Tel: 010-2176767 / 2176724, fax: 010-4334499
Internet: www.atlasvanstolk.nl, e-mail: info@atlasvanstolk.nl
visiting hours: by appointment

4.23. *Centrale Bibliotheek Rotterdam*
Central Library of Rotterdam

Special collections
Hoogstraat 110, 3011 PV Rotterdam
Tel: 010-2816188 / 2816100, fax: 010-2816181
Internet: www.bibliotheek.rotterdam.nl,
e-mail: informatie@bibliotheek.rotterdam.nl,
erasmuszaal@bibliotheek.rotterdam.nl
visiting hours: Monday-Friday 10.00-17.00, by appointment

4.24. *Maritiem Museum Rotterdam*
Maritime Museum Rotterdam

Library
Leuvehaven 1, Rotterdam / P.O. Box 988, 3000 AZ Rotterdam

Tel: 010-4132680, fax: 010-4137342
Internet: www.maritiemmuseum.nl, www.maritiemdigitaal.nl
e-mail: info@maritiemmuseum.nl
visiting hours: Tuesday-Friday 10.00-17.00, first Saturday of every month 10.00-17.00

4.25. *Museum Boijmans Van Beuningen*
Boijmans Van Beuningen Museum

Museumpark 18-20, 3015 CX Rotterdam
Tel: 010-4419456 / 4419400, fax: 010-4360500
Internet: www.boijmans.rotterdam.nl, e-mail: info@boijmans.rotterdam.nl
visiting hours: Tuesday-Saturday 11.00-16.30, by appointment

5. Companies, Private Organizations and Individuals

5.1. Feikema

J.D. Feikema, Stephensonstraat 53, 3817 JB Amersfoort
Tel: 033-4612278
e-mail: j.d._feikema@heineken.nl
visiting hours: by appointment

5.2. Six collection

Amstel 218, 1017 AJ Amsterdam
visiting hours: by appointment

5.3. Tutein Nolthenius

C. Tutein Nolthenius, Park Boswijk 306, 3941 AC Doorn
e-mail: genealogy@tuteinnolthenius.org
visiting hours: by appointment

5.4. De Lannoy

Deventer
For more information, one should contact the Secretariat of the *Centraal Register van Particuliere Archieven*, c/o *Nationaal Archief*, P.O. Box 90520, 2509 LM The Hague
Tel: 070-3315400 / 3315444, fax: 070-3315499

5.5. Heyning

The Hague
For more information, one should contact the Secretariat of the *Centraal Register van Particuliere Archieven*, c/o *Nationaal Archief*, P.O. Box 90520, 2509 LM The Hague
Tel: 070-3315400 / 3315444, fax: 070-3315499

5.6. *Koninklijk Huisarchief*
Archives of the Royal Family

Paleis Noordeinde, Hoge Wal 17, The Hague / P.O. Box 30412, 2500 GK The Hague
Tel: 070-3624701, fax: 070-3659348
Internet: www.koninklijkhuis.nl
e-mail: koninklijk.huisarchief@dkh.nl
visiting hours: Monday-Friday 9.30-16.30, by appointment

5.7. *Orde van Vrijmetselaren onder het Grootoosten der Nederlanden*
Fraternity of Freemasons under the Grand East of the Netherlands

Cultureel Maçonniek Centrum 'Prins Frederik' (CMC), Jan Evertstraat 9, The Hague / P.O. Box 11525, 2502 AM The Hague
Tel: 070-3461676, fax: 070-3641237
Internet: www.vrijmetselarij.nl, e-mail: bibliotheek.cmc@vrijmetselarij.nl
visiting hours: Monday-Friday 9.30-12.30, 13.30-17.00, by appointment

5.8. *Stichting kunstbezit Koninklijke Nedlloyd*
Royal Nedlloyd art collection foundation

Boompjes 40, Rotterdam / P.O. Box 487, 3000 AL Rotterdam
Tel: 010-4007111 / 4007666
visiting hours: by appointment

5.9. Karting

A. Karting, Van Lugtenburgstraat 6, 2274 KB Voorburg
Tel: 070-3870564
visiting hours: by appointment

Supplements to Volume 1

SUPPLEMENT I: BIBLIOGRAPHY

1. GENERAL

1.1. PRIMARY SOURCES

1 'Appendix II: Dutch Records from The Hague', trans. C.C. Remmerswaal, in Balkrishna, *Shivaji the Great*, Vol. 1 (pt. 2) (Bombay, 1932).

2 'Appendix III: Dutch Records at Batavia', trans. E.C. Godée Molsbergen, in Balkrishna, *Shivaji the Great*, Vol. 1 (pt. 2) (Bombay, 1932).

3 Bógaert, Abrahamus, *Abraham Bógaerts historische reizen door d'oostersche deelen van Asia* (Amsterdam, 1711).

4 Bois, J.P.J. du, *Historische beschryving der reizen of nieuwe en volkoome verzameling van de aller-waardigste en zeldsaamste zee- en landtochten / Histoire générale des voyages, ou nouvelle collection de toutes les relations de voyages par mer et par terre, qui ont été publiées jusqu'á présent dans les différentes langues de toutes les nations connues* (The Hague and Amsterdam, 1747-67 / 1747-80).

5 Bol, Pieter, *De wispelturige adjudant of de ongelukkige lotgevallen van den heer Pieter Bol en desselfs voorvaderen* (Rotterdam, n.d. [second half eighteenth century]).

6 Bolling, Frederik Andersen, *Oost-Indiske Reise-bog hvor udi befattis hans Reise til Oost-Indien saa vel og eendeel Platzers Beskrifvelse med en Andtall Hedningers Ceremonier ... end og negotierne med de regierendis itzige Hollandske Herrers andtkomst, gage, promotion og politie ...* [= East Indian travel book containing his journey to the East Indies as well as the description of some places with a number of heathens' ceremonies ... and also of the trade with the currently governing Dutch gentlemen's arrival, salary, promotion and police ...] (Copenhagen, 1678), trans. J. Visscher, ed. G.P. Rouffaer, 'Oost-Indisch Reisboek', *Bijdragen tot de Taal-, Land- en Volkenkunde van Nederlandsch-Indië*, 68 (1913).

7 Bos, Lambert van den, *Leeven en daden der doorlughtige zee-helden* (Amsterdam, 1683).

8 Bruin, Cornelis de, *Reizen over Moskovie, door Persie en Indie* (Amsterdam, 1711).

9 Commelin, Johan, Frederik Ruysch and François Kiggelaar, *Horti Medici Amstelodamensis rariorum tam Orientalis, quam Occidentalis Indiae, aliarumque peregrinarum plantarum / Beschryvinge en curieuse afbeeldingen van rare vreemde Oost-, West-Indische en andere gewassen*

vertoont in den Amsterdamsche Kruyd-hof, 2 vols [Vol. 2 slightly different title] (Amsterdam, 1697, 1701-2).

10 Cramer, Pieter, *De uitlandsche kapellen voorkomende in de drie waereld-deelen Asia, Africa en America*, 4 vols (Amsterdam and Utrecht, 1779-82).

11 Daalmans, Aegidius, *De nieuw hervormde genees-konst, gebouwt op de gronden van 't Acidum en Alcali waar in klaar en kortelijk na de nieuwe practijk alle siektens met weynig omslag genesen werden. Beneffens de gedenkweerdigste aanmerkinge van verscheyde siektens. Die op het eylant Cylon, in de stadt Colombo, Batavia op de cust Coromandel, ten tyden des autheurs verblijf aldaar zijn voor-gevallen* (Amsterdam, 1694); part. trans. F.H. de Vos, 'Indian Notes (Aug. 1687 to Feb. 1689) of Aegidius Daalmans, M.D.', *Ceylon Literary Register*, 2, 35-8 (1888), W.G. van Dort, 'Observations on the Diseases of Ceylon and India', *Monthly Literary Register and Notes and Queries for Ceylon*, 1, 4 (1888) [see *Dutch Sources on South Asia*, Vol. 1, Bibliography, no. 539].

12 Daalmans, Aegidius, 'Kort relaas van een ongedrukt schrift van Indiaanse aanteikeningen, geschreven door Aegidius Daalmans', ed. M.D.H.C. Millies, *Kronijk van het Historische Genootschap*, 24 (1868) [concerning Ceylon and Coromandel (among other areas) *c.* 1690].

13 Diemen, Antonio van, Hendrik Brouwer and Johan Carstensz, 'Stukken betreffende den handel van Perzië en den Golf van Bengalen. 1633 [and 1632]', ed. P.A. Leupe, *Kronijk van het Historisch Genootschap*, 10 (1854).

14 Doys, G.J., a.o., *Staat der generale Nederlandsche Oost-Indische Compagnie, behelzende rapporten van de heeren ... G.J. Doys, baron van der Does ... P.H. van de Wall J. Rendorp ... en H. van Straalen*, 2 vols (Amsterdam, 1792).

15 '[Dutch Records]', trans. R.D. Vadekar, in *Sivaji Nibandhavali*, Vol. 1 [English section] (Poona, 1930); partial and modified edition, 'Appendix I: Dutch Records from The Hague', trans. R.D. Vadekar and E.C. Godée Molsbergen, in Balkrishna, *Shivaji the Great*, Vol. 1 (pt. 2) (Bombay, 1932).

16 Eschelskroon, Adolf, *Beschrijving van het eiland Sumatra, inzonderheid ten aanzien van deszelfs koophandel ... waar bij gevoegd is een aanhangzel, behelzende eene beknopte bescrijving der eilanden Borneo, Banda, Amboina en Ceylon, benevens die van eenige Nederlandsche comptoiren aan de kust van Malabar, en veele bijzonderheden betreffende den specerij-handel in Oostindien* (Haarlem, 1783).

17 'Extracts from Dutch Records', ed. S.N. Sen, in *Foreign Biographies of Shivaji* (Extracts and Documents Relating to Maratha History, 2) (Calcutta, 1927).

18 Goens, Rijcklof van, Senior, 'Rijklof van Goens, gouverneur-generaal van Nederlandsch Indie. 1678-1681', ed. P.A. Leupe, *Berigten van het Historisch Genootschap*, 5, 2 (1856).

19 Graaff, Nicolaus de, *Reisen van Nicolaus de Graaff, na de vier gedeeltens*

des werelds, als Asia, Africa, America en Europa (Hoorn, 1701); reprint J.C.M. Warnsinck (ed.) (Werken Linschoten Vereniging, 33) (The Hague, 1930).

20 Havart, Daniel, *Hondert en vyftig grafschriften* (Rotterdam, 1718).

21 Heeck, Gijsbert, *Een Bunschoter VOC-chirurgijn. 'Dagelijkse aantekeningen' van de reis naar Oost-Indië in 1654*, ed. O. Dekkers (Bunschoten, 2001).

22 Hermann, Paul, *Horti academici Lugduno-Batavia catalogus* (Leiden, 1687).

23 Huysers, Ary, *Beknopte beschryving der oostindische etablissementen, verzeld van eenige bylagen, zeer dienstig voor lieden die zig in den dienst van de Ooster-maatschappy begeeven* (Utrecht, 1789).

24 *Journael van de Voyagie, gedaen met twaelf scheepen naer Oost-Indien, onder 't beleydt van den Heer Admirael Steven van der Hagen, waer in verhaelt wordt ... de reyse van 't schip Delft ... van Bantam naer de kuste van Choromandel* (Amsterdam, *c.* 1663-70).

25 Lacombe, Jean de, *A Compendium of the East Being an Account of Voyages to the Grand Indies, Made by the Sieur Jean de Lacombe of Quercy, Formerly Captain at Arms in the Service of the Company of the Indies of Holland*, trans. S. Clark and D. Clark, ed. A. Gibson (London, 1937).

26 Linschoten, Jan Huygen van, *Icones, habitus gestusque Indorum ac Lusitanorum per Indiam viventium, templorum, aedium, arborum, fructuum, herbarum, aromatum, mores item gentium circa sacrisicia, politiam acrem familiarem* (Amsterdam, *c.* 1604).

27 Linschoten, Jan Huygen van, *Een zestiende-eeuwse Hollander in het verre Oosten en het hoge Noorden. Leven, werken, reizen en avonturen van Jan Huyghen van Linschoten (1563-1611)*, ed. A. van der Moer (The Hague, 1979) [see *Dutch Sources on South Asia*, Vol. 1, Bibliography, nos 35-6].

28 Linschoten, Jan Huygen van, *Jan Huygen van Linschoten and the Moral Map of Asia. The Plates and Text of the 'Itinerario' and 'Icones, habitus, gestusque Indorum ac Lusitanorum per Indiam viventium'; with a study of Ernst van den Boogaart* (London, 1999).

29 Millius, D., 'Miscellanea Orientalia', in D. Millius, *Dissertationes selectae* (Leiden, 1743).

30 '"Monumenta Historiae Indiae". Extracts from the Dutch Diaries of the Castle of Batavia ...', ed. B.A. Fernandes, *Journal of the Bombay Historical Society*, 1-4 (1928-31) [see *Dutch Sources on South Asia*, Vol. 1, Bibliography, no. 11].

31 *Nederlandsch India, in haaren tegenwoordigen toestand beschouwd, of waar en grondig berigt van haare regeering, derzelver bestier en handelingen, haare bezittingen, haare militie, haar' kwijnenden handel, enz* (Batavia, *c.* 1780).

32 Neyn, P. de, *Lust-hof der huwelyken, behelsende verscheyde seldsame ceremonien en plechtigheden, die door desen by verscheyde natien en*

volckeren soo in Asia, Europa, Africa als America in gebruyck zyn geweest, als wel die voor meerendeel noch hedendaegs gebruykt ende onderhouden werden (Amsterdam, 1681).

33 Picart, Bernard, *Ceremonies et coutumes religieuses de tous les peuples du monde*, 6 vols (Amsterdam, 1723-37).

34 Purmerendt, Cornelis Claesz van, *Journael, ofte een Oost-Indische reys-beschrijvinghe ... verhalende veel besondere vreemdigheden van landen, lieden het belegeren van Mosambiecke en Goa ...* (Amsterdam, 1651); reprint A. de Booy (ed.), *De derde reis van de V.O.C. naar Oost-Indië onder het beleid van admiraal Paulus van Caerden, uitgezeild in 1606* (Werken Linschoten Vereniging, 70) (The Hague, 1968).

35 Radermacher, J.C.M., 'Korte schets van den tegenwoordigen staat van het half-eiland, beöosten de Ganges', *Verhandelingen van het Bataviaasch Genootschap van Kunsten en Wetenschappen*, 4 (1786) [see *Dutch Sources on South Asia*, Vol. 1, Bibliography, no. 45].

36 Radermacher, J.C.M., 'Korte schets van den tegenwoordigen staat van het Hindostansche Ryk, en het half-eiland, bewesten de Ganges', *Verhandelingen van het Bataviaasch Genootschap van Kunsten en Wetenschappen*, 4 (1786) [see *Dutch Sources on South Asia*, Vol. 1, Bibliography, no. 44].

37 Roeper, V., and R. van Gelder (eds), *In dienst van de Compagnie. Leven bij de VOC in honderd getuigenissen [1602-1799]* (Amsterdam, 2002).

38 *Seder Tefilot, Shevahot we shirin ... kefi minhage anshe Singili ... weqahal qadosh beqogin* [= Order of the prayers, hymns and songs ... according to the customs of the Sinhalese ... and the holy community at Cochin] (Amsterdam, 1757).

39 *Seder Tefilot ... kefi minhage anshe Singili ... kol 'eleh nishtalhu mi ... qogin* [= Order of the prayers ... according to the customs of the Sinhalese ... all sent from ... Cochin] (Amsterdam, 1769).

40 Stavorinus, Johan Splinter, *Reize van Zeeland over de Kaap de Goede Hoop, naar Batavia, Bantam, Bengalen, enz. gedaan in de jaaren MDCCLXVIII tot MDCCLXXI* (Leiden, 1793) [see *Dutch Sources on South Asia*, Vol. 1, Bibliography, no. 50].

41 Stoll, Casper, *Natuurlyke en naar 't leeven naauwkeurig gekleurde afbeeldingen en beschryvingen der cidaden en wantzen ... / Représentation exactement colorée d'après nature des cigales et des punaises ...*, 4 vols [with slightly different titles] (Amsterdam, 1780-1813).

42 Valentijn, Francois, *Oud en nieuw Oost-Indiën*, 5 vols in 8 parts, reprint (Franeker, 2002) [see *Dutch Sources on South Asia*, Vol. 1, Bibliography, no. 56].

43 Velse, Hendrik, *Naauwkeurige berigten nopens de grondvesting des Christendoms onder de heidenen op de kust van Choromandel en Malabaar, door de Deensche missionarissen op Tranquebar; behelzende ook veel aanmerckelyke byzonderheden aangaande het land, den aart, godsdienst, gewoontens, kunsten en wetenschappen der Malabaaren* (The Hague, 1739).

44 'Verdere brieven van overzee (1737-1743) gericht aan Balthazar [Nolthenius]', in R.P.J. Tutein Nolthenius (ed.), *Het geslacht Nolthenius (Tutein Nolthenius)* (Haarlem, 1914, 1930), Vol. 2, part 2.

45 Vosmaer, Aernout, *Natuurkundige beschryving eener uitmuntende verzameling van zeldsaame gedierten, bestaande in Oost- en Westindische viervoetige dieren, vogelen en slangen, weleer leevend voorhanden geweest zijnde buiten den Haag op het Kleine Loo van Z.D.H. den Prins van Oranje Nassau* (Amsterdam, 1766-1804).

46 Vries, Simon de, *Curieuse aenmerckingen der bijsonderste Oost- en West-Indische verwonderens-waerdige dingen*, 4 vols in 2 parts (Utrecht, 1682).

47 Wurmb, F. von, *Merkwürdigkeiten aus Ostindien. Die Länder- Völker-Kunde und Naturgeschichte betreffend. Aus den Papieren der Holländischen Compagnie gestandenen Herrn von Wurmb und andern sichern Quellen herausgegebn vom Major von Wurmb* (Gotha, 1797) [see also *Dutch Sources on South Asia*, Vol. 1, Bibliography, no. 775].

48 *Zamenspraak weegens de oorzaaken van het bederf der Nederl. O.-I. Compagnie* (Rotterdam, 1773).

1.2. Secondary Sources

1.2.1. *Archives, bibliographies and historiography*

49 Balk, L., and F. van Dijk, *Inventaris van het archief van de gouverneur-generaal en raden van Indië (Hoge Regering) van de Verenigde Oostindische Compagnie en taakopvolgers, 1612-1811* (Jakarta, 2002).

50 Bes, L., 'Hundreds of Rosetta Stones and Other Patient Papers. The Dutch Records at the Tamil Nadu Archives, Chennai (Madras)', *Itinerario*, 27, 1 (2003).

51 Das Gupta, A., 'Dutch Materials and Modern Indian History', *Quarterly Review of Historical Studies*, 3 (1963-4).

52 Goonewardena, K.W., 'Dutch Historical Writing on South Asia', in C.H. Philips (ed.), *Historians of India, Pakistan and Ceylon* (London, 1961).

53 Nat, J., *De studie van de oostersche talen in de 18e en de 19e eeuw* (Amsterdam, 1929).

54 Rietbergen, P.J.A.N., 'De VOC herdenken?', *Tijdschrift voor Geschiedenis*, 115, 4 (2002).

55 Roosegaarde Bisschop, W., 'Onderzoek van stukken in het India Office', *Bijdragen tot de Taal-, Land- en Volkenkunde van Nederlandsch-Indië*, 47 (1897).

56 *Tentoonstelling Sanskritkunde in de Nederlanden en in Europa in historisch perspectief* (Leuven, 1966) [includes: 'Bibliografisch repertorium der vertalingen uit het Indisch en der geschriften der Voorindische beschaving betreffende en daardoor beïnvloed in het Nederlands'].

57 Tutein Nolthenius, R.P.J., 'De brieven van Overzee', in idem (ed.), *Het geslacht Nolthenius (Tutein Nolthenius)* (Haarlem, 1914, 1930), Vol. 2, part 1.

58 Veen, E. van, and D. Klijn, *A Guide to the Sources of the History of Dutch-Portuguese Relations in Asia (1594-1797)* (Leiden, 2001).

59 Vogel, J.Ph., *The Contribution of the University of Leiden to Oriental Research* (Leiden, 1954).

1.2.2. *General surveys*

60 A.V.L., 'Grafschriften van Nederlanders in Voor-Indië en elders', *De Navorscher*, 55 (1905).

61 Akveld, L., and E.M. Jacobs (eds), *De kleurrijke wereld van de VOC. Nationaal Jubileumboek VOC 1602 / 2002*, trans. *The Colourful World of the VOC. National Anniversery Book VOC 1602 / 2002* (Bussum, Amsterdam and Rotterdam, 2002).

62 Arasaratnam, S, 'Politics and Society in Tamil Nad 1600-1800. A View in Historical Perspective', in *Proceedings of the Third International Conference Seminar of Tamil Studies* (Pondicherry, 1973).

63 Balkrishna, 'The Rise and Fall of the Dutch in India', in H.S. Bhatia (ed.), *Mahrattas, Sikhs and Southern Sultans of India. Their Fight against Foreign Terror* (New Delhi, 1992) [see *Dutch Sources on South Asia*, Vol. 1, Bibliography, no. 101].

64 Bijlsma, R., 'De aan Nederland gebleven bescheiden van de etablissementen in Voor-Indië', *Nederlandsch Archievenblad*, 3/4 (1931-2).

65 Boeren, J., and L. de Brouwer, 'Tilburg in de koloniën, de koloniën in Tilburg. De relatie van de gebroeders Bles met Indië en Suriname', *Tijdschrift Tilburg*, 1 (2001).

66 Bonke, H., *De zeven reizen van de Jonge Lieve. De biografie van een VOC-schip, 1760-1781* (Nijmegen, 1999).

67 Cotton, J.J., *List of Inscriptions on Tombs or Monuments in Madras, Possessing Historical or Archaeological Interest* (Madras, 1905).

68 Dekker, F., *Voortrekkers van Oud-Nederland. Uit Nederland's geschiedenis buiten de grenzen* (The Hague, 1938).

69 Epen, D.G. van, 'Grafschriften in Voor-Indië', *De Wapenheraut*, 1 (1897).

70 Everaert, J., 'Soldiers, Diamonds and Jesuits. Flemings and Dutchmen in Portuguese India (1505-90)', in A. Disney and E. Booth (eds), *Vasco da Gama and the Linking of Europe and Asia* (New Delhi, 2000).

71 Gaastra, F.S., *De geschiedenis van de VOC*, special edition (Zutphen, 2002), trans. *The Dutch East India Company. Expansion and Decline* (Haarlem, 2003) [see *Dutch Sources on South Asia*, Vol. 1, Bibliography, no. 112].

72 Goens, R. van, *Met de V.O.C. naar Voor-Indië* (Amsterdam and Batavia, 1938).

73 Goor, J. van, 'India and the Indonesian Archipelago from the *Generale Missiven der VOC* (Dutch East India Company)', *Itinerario*, 16, 2 (1992).

74 Goor, J. van, *Indische avonturen. Opmerkelijke ontmoetingen met een andere wereld* (The Hague, 2000).

75 Greig, D., *The Reluctant Colonists. Netherlanders Abroad in the 17th and 18th Centuries* (Assen, Maastricht and Wolfeboro, 1987).

76 *Jaarboek van het Centraal Bureau voor Genealogie 2002* (The Hague, 2002) [VOC theme issue].

77 Kemp, P.H. van der, *De teruggave der Oost-Indische koloniën, 1814-1816, naar oorspronkelijke stukken* (The Hague, 1910).

78 Neve, R.G. de, 'Dormieux en aanverwanten in dienst der VOC op Coromandel en Ceylon eind 17e tot eind 18e eeuw', *De Indische Navorscher*, 3 (1990).

79 Neve, R.G. de, 'De gezagdragers op de buitencomptoiren in Azië sedert 1795 tot aan de Engelse verovering van Java', *De Indische Navorscher*, 8 (1995).

80 Oers, R. van, *Dutch Town Planning Overseas during VOC and WIC Rule (1600-1800)* (Zutphen, 2000).

81 Overvoorde, J.C., 'Hollandsche monumenten in Britsch-Indië', *Bulletin, uitgegeven door den Nederlandschen Oudheidkundigen Bond* (1911).

82 Poonen, T.I., *Dutch Beginnings in India Proper (1580-1615)* (Madras, 1933).

83 Putten, L.P. van, *Ambitie en onvermogen. Gouverneurs-generaal van Nederlands-Indië, 1610-1796* (Rotterdam, 2002).

84 Schaik, A. van, 'Vergane Hollands glorie in India', *Archeologie*, 8 (2000).

85 Stevens, H., *De VOC in bedrijf 1602-1799 / Dutch Enterprise and the VOC 1602-1799* (Zutphen, 1998).

86 Teltscher, K., *India Inscribed. European and British Writing on India 1600-1800* (Delhi, 1995).

87 Temminck Groll, C.L., a.o., *The Dutch Overseas. Architectural Survey. Mutual Heritage of Four Centuries in Three Continents* (Zwolle, 2002).

88 Vanvugt, E., *Zwartboek van Nederland overzee. Wat iedere Nederlander moet weten* (Soesterberg, 2002).

89 Wennekes, W., *Gouden handel. De eerste Nederlanders overzee, en wat zij daar haalden* (Amsterdam and Antwerp, 1996).

90 Wevers, L.B., 'Sadras en Wingurla. Bouwgeschiedenis van een tweetal gefortificeerde VOC-factorijen in India', in M.H. Bartels, E.H.P. Cordfunke and H. Sarfatij (eds), *Hollanders uit en thuis. Archeologie, geschiedenis en bouwhistorie gedurende de VOC-tijd in de Oost, de West en thuis. Cultuurhistorie van de Nederlandse expansie* (Hilversum, 2002).

91 Wiechen, P. van, *Vademecum van de Oost- en West-Indische Compagnie* (Utrecht, 2002).

92 Wijnaendts, H., 'Nederlandsche grafsteden in Voor-Indië', *De Nederlandsche Leeuw*, 58-9 (1940-1).

93 Wijnaendts van Resandt, W., 'De tak van het geslacht Van Teylingen in India, Ceylon en Java', *De Nederlandsche Leeuw*, 71, 8 (1954).

94 Woodhouse, E., 'Influence of the Portuguese and Dutch Languages on the Sinhalese and the Tamil', *Orientalist*, 1-2 (1884-6).

95 Zandvliet, K., 'Kolonisatie en cartografie in de Oost. De rol van militaire ingenieurs', in P. van Mil and M. Scharloo, *De VOC in de kaart gekeken.*

Cartografie en navigatie van de Verenigde Oostindische Compagnie 1602-1799 (The Hague, 1988).

96 Zandvliet, K., *Mapping for Money. Maps, Plans and Topographic Paintings and Their Role in Dutch Overseas Expansion during the 16th and 17th Centuries* (Amsterdam, 1998).

97 Zandvliet, K., 'Vestingbouw in de Oost', in G. Knaap and G. Teitler (eds), *De Verenigde Oost-Indische Compagnie tussen oorlog en diplomatie* (Verhandelingen van het Koninklijk Instituut voor Taal-, Land- en Volkenkunde, 197) (Leiden, 2002).

98 Zandvliet, K. (ed.), *De Nederlandse ontmoeting met Azië 1600-1950 / The Dutch Encounter with Asia 1600-1950* (Amsterdam and Zwolle, 2002).

1.2.3. *Commerce*

99 Arasaratnam, S., 'Some Notes on the Dutch in Malacca and the Indo-Malayan Trade', *Journal of South-East Asian History*, 10, 3 (1969).

100 Barendse, R.J., *The Arabian Seas. The Indian Ocean World of the Seventeenth Century* (Armonk, 2002) [see *Dutch Sources on South Asia*, Vol. 1, Bibliography, no. 151].

101 Das Gupta, A., *The World of the Indian Ocean Merchant 1500-1800. Collected Essays of Ashin Das Gupta*, ed. U. Das Gupta and S. Subrahmanyam (New Delhi, 2001).

102 Dijk, W.O., 'The VOC's Trade in Indian Textiles with Burma, 1634-80', *Journal of Southeast Asian Studies*, 33, 3 (2002).

103 Gaastra, F.S., 'The Dutch East India Company and its Intra-Asiatic Trade in Precious Metals', reprint in O. Prakash (ed.), *European Commercial Expansion in Early Modern Asia* (An Expanding World, 10) (Aldershot, 1997) [see *Dutch Sources on South Asia*, Vol. 1, Bibliography, no. 163].

104 Jacobs, E.M., *Koopman in Azië. De handel van de Verenigde Oost-Indische Compagnie tijdens de 18de eeuw* (Zutphen, 2000); English translation forthcoming.

105 Jacobs, E.M., 'De Verenigde Oost-Indische Compagnie: een veelkantig handelsbedrijf', *Tijdschrift voor Geschiedenis*, 115, 4 (2002).

106 Prakash, O., 'European Private Traders in the Eastern Indian Ocean Trading Network in the Early Modern Period', in J. Parmentier and S. Spanoghe (eds), *Orbis in Orbem. Liber Amicorum John Everaert* (Gent, 2001).

1.2.4. *Politics and law*

107 Alexandrowicz, C.H., 'The Discriminatory Clause in South Asian Treaties in the Seventeenth and Eighteenth Centuries', in idem, *The Indian Year Book of International Affairs*, Vol. 6 (Madras, 1957).

108 Blussé, L., and G. Winius, 'The Origins and Rhythm of Dutch Aggression against the Estado da India, 1601-1661', in T.R. de Souza (ed.), *Indo-Portuguese History. Old Issues, New Questions* (New Delhi, 1985).

109 Boxer, C.R., 'Naval Actions between the Portuguese and the Dutch in India, 1654', *The Mariner's Mirror*, 14, 3 (1928).

110 Boxer, C.R., 'The Third Dutch War in the East (1672-4)', *The Mariner's Mirror*, 16, 4 (1930).

111 Gaastra, F.S., 'Dutch, French and English Rivalry in Asia, 1688-1714', in *Guerres maritimes 1688-1713. IVes journées franco-brittanniques d'histoire de la marine, Portsmouth 1-4 avril 1992* (Vincennes, 1996).

112 Goor, J. van, 'De koopman als diplomaat. Hofreizen als spiegel van Europees-Aziatische verhoudingen', in J. Parmentier and S. Spanoghe (eds), *Orbis in Orbem. Liber Amicorum John Everaert* (Gent, 2001).

113 Hoek, I.H.J., *Het herstel van het Nederlandsche gezag over Java en onderhoorigheden in de jaren 1816-1819* (The Hague, 1862).

114 Jacob, H.K. s', 'Rijcklof Volckertsz van Goens, 1619-1682. Kind van de Compagnie, diplomaat en krijgsman', in G. Knaap and G. Teitler (eds), *De Verenigde Oost-Indische Compagnie tussen oorlog en diplomatie* (Verhandelingen van het Koninklijk Instituut voor Taal-, Land- en Volkenkunde, 197) (Leiden, 2002).

115 Kraan, A. van der, 'A Merchant Armed. The Van Goens Mission to Ceylon and India, 1653-54', *The Great Circle. Journal of the Australian Association for Maritime History*, 21, 1-2 (1999).

116 Penkala, E., 'An Expensive Dutch Embassy', *Geographic Magazine* (1959).

117 Raben, R., 'Het Aziatisch legioen. Huurlingen, bondgenoten en reservisten in het geweer voor de Verenigde Oost-Indische Compagnie', in G. Knaap and G. Teitler (eds), *De Verenigde Oost-Indische Compagnie tussen oorlog en diplomatie* (Verhandelingen van het Koninklijk Instituut voor Taal-, Land- en Volkenkunde, 197) (Leiden, 2002).

118 Winius, G., 'Luso-Nederlandse rivaliteit in Azië', in G. Knaap and G. Teitler (eds), *De Verenigde Oost-Indische Compagnie tussen oorlog en diplomatie* (Verhandelingen van het Koninklijk Instituut voor Taal-, Land- en Volkenkunde, 197) (Leiden, 2002).

1.2.5. *Art, intellectual life, religion, travel*

119 Arnolli, G., and S. Wille-Engelsma, *Sits. Exotisch textiel in Friesland*, 2 vols (Zwolle, 1990).

120 Baas, P., 'De VOC in Flora's Lusthoven', in L. Blussé and I. Ooms, *Kennis en Compagnie. De Verenigde Oost-Indische Compagnie en de moderne Wetenschappen* (Leiden, 2002).

121 Barend-van Haeften, M., *Oost-Indië gespiegeld. Nicolaas de Graaff, een schrijvend chirurgijn in dienst van de VOC* (Zutphen, 1992).

122 Bergvelt, E., M. Jonker and A. Wiechmann (eds), *Burgers verzamelen 1600-1750. Schatten in Delft* (Zwolle and Delft, 2002).

123 Beumer, W.G.M., 'Philippus Baldaeus en Gerrit Mosopatam: een buitengewoon portret', *Bulletin van het Rijksmuseum*, 47, 2/3 (1999).

124 Boogaart, E. van den, *Het verheven en verdorven Azië. Woord en beeld in*

het Itinerario *en de* Icones *van Jan Huygen van Linschoten* (Amsterdam and Leiden, 2000).

125 Bruijn, M. de, and R. Raben (eds), *The World of Jan Brandes 1743-1808. Drawings of a Dutch Traveller in Batavia, Ceylon and Southern Africa* (Amsterdam and Zwolle, 2003).

126 Buddingh, S.A., *Naamlijst der predikanten in Neerlands Oost-Indie, van 1615 tot 1857, benevens van die te Ceylon van 1623 tot 1807, van die te Choromandel van 1625 tot 1784, van die te Malabaar van 1663 tot 1751* ... (Batavia, 1857).

127 Buitenen, J.A.B. van, and P.C. Ganeshsundaram, 'A Seventeenth-Century Dutch Grammar of Tamil', *Bulletin of the Deccan College Research Institute (Poona)*, 14 (1952-3).

128 Christiaans, P.A., 'De loges in de buitengewesten', *De Indische Navorscher*, 7, 3 (1994) [pertaining to the Freemasonry].

129 Eliëns, T.M. (ed.), *Wonen op de Kaap en in Batavia 1602-1795 / Domestic Interiors at the Cape and in Batavia 1602-1795* (Zwolle and The Hague, 2002).

130 Goetz, H., 'An Indian Element in 17th Century Dutch Art', *Oud-Holland. Tweemaandelijksch Tijdschrift voor Nederlandsche Kunstgeschiedenis*, 54, 5 (1937).

131 Goetz, H., *The Indian and Persian Miniature Paintings in the Rijksprentenkabinet (Rijksmuseum) Amsterdam* (Amsterdam, 1958).

132 Goor, J. van, 'Dutch Calvinists on the Coromandel Coast and in Sri Lanka', reprint in M.N. Pearson and I.B. Watson (eds) *Asia and Europe. Commerce, Colonialism and Cultures. Essays in Honour of Sinnappah Arasaratnam* (Armidale, 1996) [see *Dutch Sources on South Asia*, Vol. 1, Bibliography, no. 248].

133 Hartkamp-Jonxis, E., 'Voor-Indische sitsen voor Groninger families', *Bulletin van de Vereniging van vrienden van het Gronings Museum*, 6 (1980).

134 Harvard, W.M., *A Narrative of the Establishment and Progress of the Mission to Ceylon and India* (London, 1823).

135 Honoré-Naber, S.P. l', 'Onthullingen uit Centraal-Azië', *Tijdschrift van het Koninklijk Nederlandsch Aardrijkskundig Genootschap*, 3rd series, 42 (1925).

136 Jaffer, A., *Furniture from British India and Ceylon* (London and Salem, 2001).

137 Jennes, J., *Invloed der Vlaamsche prentkunst in Indië, China en Japan* (Leuven, 1943).

138 Kinze, C.C., 'Rehabilitation of *Platanista Gangetica* (Lebeck, 1801) as the Valid Scientific Name of the Ganges Dolphin', *Zoologische Mededelingen*, 74, 11 (2000).

139 Kley, E.J. van, 'Asian Religions in Seventeenth-Century Dutch Literature', *Itinerario*, 25, 3/4 (2001).

140 Loos-Haaxman, J. de, *Johannes Rach en zijn werk* (Batavia, 1928).

141 Lunsingh Scheurleer, P., 'Hoofse Snuisterijen uit India', *Aziatische Kunst.*

Mededelingenblad van de Vereniging van Vrienden der Aziatische Kunst, 21, 3 (1991).

142 Mollema, J.C., *Voor den stroom en op de klippen. De lotgevallen van Frans en Pieter Bol* (Haarlem, 1929).

143 Ormeling Sr., F.J., 'De reizen van Samuel van de Putte', *Caert-thresoor. Tijdschrift voor de geschiedenis van de kartografie in Nederland*, 17, 1 (1998).

144 Peters, M., 'Nicolaes Witsen and Gijsbert Cuper. Two Seventeenth-Century Dutch Burgomasters and Their Gordian Knot', *Lias. Sources and Documents Relating to the Early Modern History of Ideas*, 16 (1989).

145 Pilleri, G., 'William Roxbrugh (1751-1815), Heinrich Julius Lebeck (†1801) and the Discovery of the Ganges Dolphin (*Platanista Gangetica* Roxburgh, 1801)', *Investigations on Cetacea*, 9 (1978).

146 Rietbergen, P.J.A.N., 'Varieties of Asia? European Perspectives, *c.* 1600-*c.* 1800', *Itinerario*, 25, 3/4 (2001).

147 Rissink, W.G.F.C., 'Drie voorwerpen uit India en Ceylon', *Verslagen en Aanwinsten* (Stichting Cultuurgeschiedenis van de Nederlanders Overzee) (1961-5).

148 Rissink, W.G.F.C., 'Een arkientje', *Verslagen en Aanwinsten* (Stichting Cultuurgeschiedenis van de Nederlanders Overzee) (1966-7).

149 Rissink, W.G.F.C., 'Een reukwaterflacon', *Verslagen en Aanwinsten* (Stichting Cultuurgeschiedenis van de Nederlanders Overzee) (1974-5).

150 Schultink, R., 'Nederlandse Vrijmetselarij in India en Ceylon in de tweede helft van de 18de eeuw', *Thoth. Tijdschrift voor Vrijmetselaren*, 38, 5 (1987).

151 Schutte, G.J. (ed.), *Het Indisch Sion. De Gereformeerde kerk onder de Verenigde Oost-Indische Compagnie* (Hilversum, 2002).

152 Sliggers, B.C., and M.H. Besselink (eds), *Het verdwenen museum. Natuurhistorische verzamelingen 1750-1850* (Blaricum and Haarlem, 2002).

153 Terwen-de Loos, J., *Nederlandse schilders en tekenaars in de oost, 17de-20ste eeuw* (Amsterdam, 1972).

154 Troostenburg de Bruyn, C.A.L. van, *De Hervormde Kerk in Nederlandsch Oost-Indië onder de Oost-Indische Compagnie (1602-1795)* (Arnhem, 1884).

155 Troostenburg de Bruyn, C.A.L. van, *Biografisch woordenboek van Oost-Indische predikanten* (Nijmegen, 1893).

156 Veenendaal, J., 'Een zilveren sirihbladhouder', *Bulltin van het Rijksmuseum*, 35, 1 (1987).

157 Verbeek, J., 'Een zilveren papkom', *Verslagen en Aanwinsten* (Stichting Cultuurgeschiedenis van de Nederlanders Overzee) (1972-3).

158 'Verslag over het jaar [1961-83]', *Verslagen en Aanwinsten* (Stichting Cultuurgeschiedenis van de Nederlanders Overzee) (1961-83) [partially concerning the present state of Dutch buildings in South Asia].

159 Vos, A., 'Hanske, "Rembrandts olifant"', *'s-Hertogenbosch*, 2, 5 (1994).

160 Walle, A. van de, '"Soete dieren en stinkende swartinnen". Beeldvorming

en representatie van de Oost-Indische vrouw in de Nederlandse reisliteratuur', in J. Parmentier and S. Spanoghe (eds), *Orbis in Orbem. Liber Amicorum John Everaert* (Gent, 2001).

161 Wille-Engelsma, S.I.E., 'Een derde wapen-palempore voor het Fries Museum', *Vrije Fries*, 71 (1991).

2. SURAT
(including Sind and Hindustan)

2.1. Primary Sources

162 Brouwer, C.G., 'Rediscovered after More than Three Centuries: Pieter van den Broecke's Original *Resolutieboeck* Concerning Dutch Trade in Northwest India, Persia and Southern Arabia, 1620-1625', *Manuscripts of the Middle East*, 1 (1986); also published in C.G. Brouwer, *Dutch-Yemeni Encounters. Activities of the United East India Company (VOC) in South Arabian Waters since 1614* (Amsterdam, 1998).

163 Carstensz, Johan, 'Stukken over den handel van Persië en den Golf van Bengalen. 1634', ed. P.A. Leupe, *Kronijk van het Historisch Genootschap*, 10 (1854).

164 *Copije van eenen brief uyt Zuratten, leggende in Oost-Indien, hoe dat aldaer, ende die plaetsen daer ontrent, groote, noyt gehoorden, vreesselijcken honger geleden wort* (Delft, 1633).

165 Corsi, Francisco, 'A Dutch Translation of an Unknown Letter of Francisco Corsi S.J.: Missionary to the Great Mogul', *Karnataka Historical Review* (1940).

166 'Hongersnood in Suratta anno 1631', ed. A.J. Servaas van Rooijen, *De Navorscher*, 37 (1887).

2.2. Secondary Sources

167 Alam, I., 'Rented Housing in Mughal India. The Dutch and English Experience', in K.M. Shrimali (ed.), *Reason and Archaeology* (Delhi, 1998).

168 Auboyer, J., 'Un maître hollandais du XVIIe siècle s'inspirant des miniatures mogholes', *Arts Asiatiques*, 2, 4 (1955).

169 Bellasis, A.F., *An Account of the Old Tombs in the Cemeteries of Surat* (Bombay, 1868).

170 B[loys] v[an] T[reslong] P[rins], [P.C.], 'Hollandsche oudheeden te Ahmadabad', *De Indische Navorscher*, 3 (1937).

171 Bodewitz, H.W., 'Ketelaar and Millius and their Grammar of Hindustani', *Bulletin of the Deccan College Post Graduate and Research Institute*, 54-5 (1994-5).

172 Bredius, A., 'Hindostan'sche teekeningen in Nederland in de XVIIe eeuw', *Oud Holland*, 29 (1911).

173 Broos, B.P.J., 'Rembrandts Indische miniaturen', *Spiegel Historiael* (1980).

174 Gelder, H.E. van, 'Wollebrandt Geleynsz. de Jongh, "De Alkmaarder Wees"', reprint in *Alkmaarse opstellen* (Alkmaar, 1960) [see *Dutch Sources on South Asia*, Vol. 1, Bibliography, no. 350].

175 Gelder, R. van, *Naporra's omweg. Het leven van een VOC-matroos (1731-1793)* (Amsterdam, 2003).

176 Gupta, V.B., 'Dutch East India Company in Gujarat Trade, 1660-1700. A Study of Selected Aspects' (Unpublished PhD thesis, Delhi University, 1991).

177 'De Hollandsche grafmonumenten te Surat', *De Indische Navorscher*, 4 (1938).

178 Jacobs, E.M., 'De Verenigde Oostindische Compagnie als ondernemer in Azië. Directe handelscontacten tussen Suratte en Canton (1744-1755)', in *Nederlandse ondernemers over de grenzen*, special edition of *Bijdragen en Mededelingen betreffende de Geschiedenis der Nederlanden*, 108, 4 (1993).

179 Lunsingh Scheurleer, P., 'De Maharana van Udaipur ontvangt de V.O.C.-gezant J.J. Ketelaar in het voorjaar van 1711, India, Udaipur, ca 1711', *Bulletin van het Rijksmuseum*, 37, 3 (1989).

180 Lunsingh Scheurleer, P., 'De Moghul-miniaturen van Rembrandt', in H.J. 't Hart-van den Muyzenberg and Th. de Bruin (eds), *Waarom Sanskrit? Hondervijfentwintig jaar Sanskrit in Nederland* (Kern Institute Miscellanea, 4) (Leiden, 1991).

181 Ouden, J.H.B. den, *De factorij der Verenigde Oostindische Compagnie te Surat: in het bijzonder tot ongeveer 1632* (Amsterdam, 1961).

182 Pott, P.H., 'Gouden gedachtenispenning voor Daniël Parvé', *Verslagen en Aanwinsten* (Stichting Cultuurgeschiedenis van de Nederlanders Overzee) (1974-5).

183 Santen, H.W. van, 'Trade between Mughal India and the Middle East, and Mughal Monetary Policy', reprint in O. Prakash (ed.), *European Commercial Expansion in Early Modern Asia* (An Expanding World, 10) (Aldershot, 1997) [see *Dutch Sources on South Asia*, Vol. 1, Bibliography, no. 365].

184 Santen, H.W. van, 'Meesters ter zee. De VOC in Mughal India', in A. Huussen, J. de Jong and G. Prince (eds), *Cultuurcontacten. Ontmoetingen tussen culturen in historisch perspectief* (Historische Studies, 4) (Groningen, 2001).

185 Santen, H.W. van, *VOC-dienaar in India. Geleynssen de Jongh in het land van de Groot-Mogol* (Franeker, 2001).

186 Santen, H.W. van, 'Shah Jahan Wore Glasses. Remarks on the Impact of the Dutch East India Company on Northern India and Some Suggestions for Further Research', in J. Gommans and O. Prakash (eds), *Circumambulations in South Asian History. Essays in Honour of Dirk H.A. Kolff* (Leiden, 2003).

187 S[nouckaert] v[an] S[chauburg], W., 'Opschriften op grafsteden van Nederlanders te Suratte en Ahmedabad', *De Nederlandsche Leeuw*, 17 (1899).

188 Topsfield, A., 'Ketelaar's Embassy and the Farangi Theme in the Art of Udaipur', *Oriental Art*, 30 (1984-5).

189 Welings, Y., 'Gejaagd door de wind. Een geval van desertie aan het einde van de achttiende eeuw', *Zeeland. Tijdschrift van het Koninklijk Zeeuwsch Genootschap der Wetenschappen*, 2, 4 (1993).

190 Wortel, Th.P.H., 'Wollebrand Geleynssen de Jongh in Burhanpur', *Oud Alkmaar*, 5, 2 (1981).

3. MALABAR (including Kanara and Konkan)

3.1. Primary Sources

191 Bucquoy, Jacob de, *Aanmerkelyke ontmoetingen in de zestien jaarige reize naa de Indiën, gedaan door Jacob De Bucquoi* (Haarlem, 1744).

192 Burmannus, Joannes, *Flora Malabarica, sive Index in omnes tomos Horti Malabarici, quem juxta normam a botanicishujus aevi receptam conscripsit, et ordine alphabetico digessit Joannes Burmannus* (Amsterdam, 1769).

193 Cellarius, Johan Adam, 'Aantekening over de spraak, weetenschappen en kunsten der Mallabaaren', *Verhandelingen van het Bataviaasch Genootschap van Kunsten en Wetenschappen*, 3 (1787); also in *Verhandelingen van het Bataviaasch Genootschap van Kunsten en Wetenschappen*, 3 (1824).

194 Commelin, Casparus, *Flora Malabarica, sive horti Malabarici catalogus* (Leiden, 1696).

195 'Het doop/trouwboek van Cochin', eds C.H. van Wijngaarden a.o., *Gens Nostra. Maandblad der Nederlandse Genealogische Vereniging*, 47, 1-3, 7/8 (1992).

196 *The Dutch in Malabar Being a Translation of Selections nrs. 1 and 2 with Introduction and Notes* (Selections from the Records of the Madras Government, Dutch Records, 13), ed. A. Galletti, A.J. van der Burg and P. Groot, reprint (New Delhi, 1984) [see *Dutch Sources on South Asia*, Vol. 1, Bibliography, no. 383].

197 'Mathys Hendricksz. Quast voor Goa', ed. P.A. Leupe, *Bijdragen tot de Taal-, Land- en Volkenkunde van Nederlandsch Indië*, 6 (2) (1859).

198 Noronha, Miguel de, and Pieter Vlak, 'Belangrijke Portugeesche brieven van den onderkoning van Goa don Miguel de Noronha, conde de Linhares, onderschept door Pieter Vlak, raad van Neerlandsch Indie. 1634', ed. P.A. Leupe, *Kronijk van het Historisch Genootschap*, 9 (1853).

199 Paiva, Mosseh Pereyra de, *Notisias dos Judeos de Cochim* (Amsterdam, 1687).

200 Smith, W., 'Sterrekundige waarnemingen, gedaan ter bepalinge van de breedte en lengte van Cochin, op de kust van Malabar, genomen aldaar', *Verhandelingen uitgegeven door het Zeeuwsch Genootschap der Wetenschappen te Vlissingen*, 6 (1778), 9 (1782).

3.2. Secondary Sources

201 Balbian Verster, J.F.L. de, 'De verrassing van Goa (1639)', *Eigen Haard* (1904).

202 Balbian Verster, J.F.L. de, 'De zeeslag voor Goa in 1638. Schilderij van Abraham van Beerstraten', *Eigen Haard* (1905).

203 Christiaans, P.A., 'Inwoners van Cochin in april 1814', *De Indische Navorscher*, 5 (1992).

204 Dillwyn, L.W., *A Review of the References to the Hortus Malabaricus of Henry van Rheede tot Draakenstein* (Swansea, 1839).

205 Jacob, H.K. s', *The Rajas of Cochin, 1663-1720. Kings, Chiefs and the Dutch East India Company* (New Delhi, 2000).

206 Lanman, J.T., 'Life on a Portuguese Nao. Linschoten's Voyage to India, 1583', *Revista da Universidade de Coimbra, Série Separatas*, 169 (1985); also in *Revista da Universidade de Coimbra*, 33 (1986) (?).

207 Land, J.P.N., 'De smeekschriften der Malabaarsche christenen, 1709-1728', *Bijdragen tot de Taal-, Land- en Volkenkunde van Nederlandsch Indië*, 18 (6) (1871).

208 Lannoy, M. de, 'Rama Varma, koning van Travancore (1758-1798) en de VOC', in A. Huussen, J. de Jong and G. Prince (eds), *Cultuurcontacten. Ontmoetingen tussen culturen in historisch perspectief* (Historische Studies, 4) (Groningen, 2001).

209 Lannoy, M. de, 'The Trials of Captain Hackert and Engineer Andries Leslorant at the Malabar Council of War', in J. Gommans and O. Prakash (eds), *Circumambulations in South Asian History. Essays in Honour of Dirk H.A. Kolff* (Leiden, 2003).

210 Luttervelt, R. van, 'Een nieuwe aanwinst voor de Historische Afdeling van het Rijksmuseum: een schilderij van J.B. Weenix', *Bulletin van het Rijksmuseum*, 3, 1 (1955).

211 Miedema, H., 'Het stadsklavecimbel van Amsterdam', *Bulletin van het Rijksmuseum*, 48, 4 (2000).

212 Nicolson, D.H., C.R. Suresh and K.S. Manilal, *An Interpretation of Van Rheede's Hortus Malabaricus* (Regnum Vegetabile, 119) (Königstein, 1988).

213 Oers, R. van, 'Stadsplanning en het behoud van VOC-structuren', in L. Blussé and I. Ooms, *Kennis en Compagnie. De Verenigde Oost-Indische Compagnie en de moderne Wetenschappen* (Leiden, 2002).

214 Poonen, T.I., 'The South Indian Pepper Trade under the Protection of the Ships Blockading Goa, 1636-1644', *Ceylon Historical Journal*, 1, 4 (1952).

215 Vaidyanadhan, R., *Communication History of the Dutch in India* (Madras, 1997).

216 Warner, M.F., 'The Dates of Rheede's Hortus Malabaricus', *The Journal of Botany, British and Foreign*, 63 (1920).

4. CEYLON
(including Fishery Coast and Maldives)

[For an almost complete survey of the contents of the *Journal of the Dutch Burgher Union of Ceylon*, see www.geocities.com/Athens/Styx/6497/JDBUC.html]

4.1. Primary Sources

217 *De algemeene Sendbrieven der heiligen Apostelen ... uyt de oorspronkelyke Grixe taale in de Singaleesche spraake overgeset ... door Henricus Philipsz predikant op Colombo* (Colombo, 1766).

218 Baldaeus, Philippus, 'Description of the Grand Island of Ceylon', trans. P. Brohier, ed. R.L. Brohier and G.V. Grenier, *Journal of the Dutch Burgher Union of Ceylon*, 47, 1-4 (1957), 48, 2-4 (1958), 49, 1-4 (1959); part. trans. P. Brohier, 'The Siege of Colombo (by the Dutch) Described by the Portuguese', *Journal of the Dutch Burgher Union of Ceylon*, 41, 3-4 (1951), 42, 1-4 (1952); P. Brohier, 'The Siege of Colombo by the Dutch', ed. R.L. Brohier and G.V. Grenier, *Journal of the Royal Asiatic Society, Ceylon Branch*, new series, 8, 1 (1962) [see *Dutch Sources on South Asia*, Vol. 1, Bibliography, no. 450].

219 Bekker, Hendrik, 'The Dutch and Devil Worship in Ceylon', *Ceylon Literary Register*, 2, 1 (1887).

220 Bell, H.C.P., 'Excerpta Maldiviana. No. 2, Sultan's Missives: A.C. 1713; 1819', *Journal of the Ceylon Branch of the Royal Asiatic Society*, 29 (1923).

221 Bell, H.C.P., 'Excerpta Maldiviana. No. 11, Dutch Intercourse with the Maldives, Seventeenth Century', *Journal of the Ceylon Branch of the Royal Asiatic Society*, 32 (1932).

222 Bell, H.C.P., 'Excerpta Maldiviana. No. 13, Some Polyglot Missives of Sultan Ibrahim Iskandar II', *Journal of the Ceylon Branch of the Royal Asiatic Society*, 33 (1934).

223 Bochouwer, Marcellus de, 'Transactions between the Dutch and the King of Kandy. The Remonstance of Marcellus de Bochouwer', trans. D. Ferguson, *Ceylon Literary Register*, 1, 1-3, 5-7, 9, 11-12 (1931), 2, 1, 5-6, 9-12 (1932), 3, 1-3 (1933).

224 Borstius, Jacobus, *Kort begryp der Christelyke religie, voor die zig willen begeven tot des Heeren heilig avondmaal; ten dienste der kerken en schoolen, in de Tamulsche spraak overgezet ... door Sigisbertus Abrahamsz Bronsveld* (Colombo, 1754).

225 Breynius, Jacob, *Jacobi Breynii Gedanensis exoticarum aliarmque minus cognitarum plantarum centuria prima, cum figuris aeneis summo studio elaboratis* (Gdansk, 1678).

226 Breynius, Johannes Philippus, *Dissertatio Botanico-medica, de Radice Gin-sem, seu Nisi, et Chrysanthemo Bidente Zeylanico Acmella dicto* (Leiden, 1700).

227 'A Brief Notice of Robert Knox and his Companions in Captivity in

Kandy for the Space of Twenty Years Discovered among the Dutch Records Preserved in the Colonial Secretary's Office, Colombo', ed. and trans. J.R. Blake, *Journal of the Royal Asiatic Society, Ceylon Branch*, 4, 14 (1867-70).

228 'Brieven gewisseld tusschen den Portugeeschen goeverneur van Colombo en den bevelhebber van Gale', ed. J.A. Grothe, *Bijdragen en Mededeelingen van het Historisch Genootschap*, 10 (1887).

229 Bronsveld, Sigisbertus Abrahamsz, *Dissertatio Academica, de procuranda Indorum salute* (n.p., 1747).

230 Bronsveld, Sigisbertus Abrahamsz, *Catechismus, ofte onderweyzing in de Christelicke leere, die in de hervormde kerken en schoolen geleerd word, ten dienst der kerken en schoolen, in de Tamulsche spraak overgezet ... door Sigisbertus Abrahamsz Bronsveld, bedienaar des H. Evangeliums in Christi Gemeinte te Columbo* (Colombo, 1754).

231 Bronsveld, Sigisbertus Abrahamsz, *Tamulsch kinder-catechismus ... ten dienste der schoolen in een vervolg en uitgegeven door Sigis. Abrah. Bronsveld* (Colombo, 1768); revision Mattheus Jurgen Ondaatje (Colombo, 1788).

232 Bystervelt, Henricus van, 'Henricus van Bystervelt (Ambassador to Kandy, Feb. 1671)', *Ceylon Literary Register*, 2, 19 (1887).

233 Bystervelt, Henricus van, 'Henricus van Bystervelt's Embassy to Kandy (1671 A.D.)', trans. F.H. de Vos, *Journal of the Royal Asiatic Society, Ceylon Branch*, 11, 40 (1890) [see *Dutch Sources on South Asia*, Vol. 1, Bibliography, no. 690].

234 Caen, Anthony, 'The Capture of Trincomalee A.D. 1639', trans. F.H. de Vos, *Journal of the Ceylon Branch of the Royal Asiatic Society*, 10, 35 (1887).

235 Caen, Anthony, 'The Dutch Designs on Ceylon in 1639', *Ceylon Literary Register*, 2, 23 (1887) [letter to *Directeur* Barend Pietersz of Surat].

236 'The Campaign of 1764 (Van Eck's Expedition to Kandy)', trans. J.R. Blaze, *Journal of the Dutch Burgher Union of Ceylon*, 50, 1-4 (1960).

237 'Capitulation of Colombo by the Dutch to the English (the Twenty-six Articles)', *Journal of the Dutch Burgher Union of Ceylon*, 44, 1 (1954).

238 Caron, François, 'François Caron and the French East-India Company', trans. F.H. de Vos, *Journal of the Royal Asiatic Society, Ceylon Branch*, 18, 55 (1904).

239 'Ceilonsch volksrecht, opgeteekend in 1707', ed. C. van Vollenhoven, *Bijdragen tot de Taal-, Land- en Volkenkunde van Nederlandsch-Indië*, 75 (1919).

240 'Ceylon in 1640-41. Extracts from the Journal (Dag-Register) Kept in the Fort of Batavia, A.D. 1640-41', trans. F.H. de Vos, *Ceylon Literary Register*, 2, 42-50, 52 (1888).

241 'Ceylon under the Dutch East India Co. in 1778-84 (Extracts from Company's Despatches and Minutes of Positive and Permanent Orders for the Use of the Company in General and the Factory of Batticaloa in Particular, Received from 19 Dec 1778-June 1784)', *Ceylon Literary Register*, 2, 53-4 (1888).

242 *Os CL psalmos d'el Rey e Propheta David como taõbem outros Canticos espirituaes uzadas 'na Igreja Reformada compostos pelo muy reverendo Padre d'a Igreja Portugeza 'na cidade Batavia Jacobus op den Akker e agora para uzo d'a Igreja Portugeza d'esta cidade com autoridade e licença de magistrado d'esta ilha de novo imprimidos pela cuidade de Sigisb. Abrah. Bronsveld* (Colombo, 1763); another edition with partially different title (Colombo, 1768).

243 Cleghorn, Hugh, 'Notes from Mr. Cleghorn's Minute Dated 1st June 1799, on the Administration of Justice and of the Revenues under the Dutch Government', *Ceylon Almanac and Annual Register* (1855); reprint, 'Dutch Administration in Ceylon', *Ceylon Literary Register*, 6, 6-7 (1891).

244 Cleghorn, Hugh, 'Administration of Justice and of Revenue on the Island of Ceylon under the Dutch Government', ed. R. Pieris, *Journal of the Royal Asiatic Society, Ceylon Branch*, new series, 3, 2 (1954).

245 'Correspondence Relating to the Surrender of Colombo by the Dutch, 1795', *Ceylon Literary Register*, 2, 39-41 (1888).

246 Coster, Willem Jacobsz, 'The Capture of Batticaloa by the Dutch in 1638', *Ceylon Literary Register*, 2, 6 (1887) [letter to Governor-General Antonio van Diemen].

247 Coster, Willem Jacobsz, 'The Occupation of Batticaloa by the Dutch in 1638', *Ceylon Literary Register*, 2, 7 (1887) [letters to Governor-General Antonio van Diemen].

248 Croocq, Paulusz, 'The Struggle between the Dutch and the Portuguese for the Possession of Ceylon', *Ceylon Literary Register*, 2, 13 (1887) [letter from Vengurla to *Directeur-Generaal* Philip Lucasz at Colombo].

249 Cuylenberg, R.A. van, 'Extracts from the Records of the Dutch Government in Ceylon', *Journal of the Ceylon Branch of the Royal Asiatic Society*, 5, 19 (1874) [concerning the years 1658-69].

250 Danielsz, 'Diary of a Visit to the King of Kandy in 1739, for the Purpose of Curing His Imperial Majesty of Certain Disorders under Which He Was Suffering', trans. W. Goonetilleke, *Ceylon Examiner Literary Supplement*, 1, 4 (1863).

251 'Diary of a Dutch Ambassador to the Court of Kandy in 1721', trans. E. Reimers, *Ceylon Observer Annual* (1948).

252 Diemen, Antonio van, 'The Embassy from the King of Kandy to the Dutch Governor-General in 1638', *Ceylon Literary Register*, 2, 8 (1887) [letter to the King of Kandy].

253 Diemen, Antonio van, Philip Lucaszoon and Adam Westerwolt, 'The Occupation of Batticaloa by the Dutch in 1638', *Ceylon Literary Register*, 2, 10 (1887) [letter to Willem Jacobsz Coster].

254 Diemen, Antonio van, Anthony Caen and Cornelis van der Lijn, 'The Dutch-Sinhalese Alliance against the Portuguese in 1639', *Ceylon Literary Register*, 2, 15 (1887) [letter to Patria].

255 'Donatie die gedaen heeft den Coningh van Ceylon Dom Joan Pereapander', *Orientalist*, 3 (1888-9).

256 'The Dutch and British Cinnamon Monopolies. A Rare Unpublished Report of an East India Company Inspector, 1823', ed. J.A.W. Perera, *Ceylon Causerie*, 26, 12 (1960).

257 'The Dutch Landraad House at Galle', *Ceylon Literary Register*, 2, 52 (1888).

258 Eck, Lubbert Jan van, 'Journal of Governor Van Eck's Expedition against the King of Kandy, 1765', trans. A.E. Buultjens, *Journal of the Ceylon Branch of the Royal Asiatic Society*, 16, 50 (1899).

259 *Eenige psalmen des koninglyken prophete Davids, en andere lofzangen, uyt den Nederduytschen in Tamulschen digte overgeset door Philippus de Melho* (Colombo, 1755).

260 *Het eerste boek Moses genaamt Genesis, inde Singaleesche tale overgeset ... door Henricus Philipsz, predikant te Colombo* (Colombo, 1783).

261 'Extracts from Dutch Registers, Resolutions, etc.', *Ceylon Literary Register*, 2, 15 (1887).

262 'Extracts from the Diary of the Commandeur of Galle, 1667', trans. F.H. de Vos, *Ceylon Literary Register*, 4, 16-18 (1889).

263 'Extracts Relating to Ceylon from the Batavian Dag-Register A.D. 1653', trans. F.H. de Vos, *Ceylon Literary Register*, 2, 54 (1888).

264 'Extracts Relating to Ceylon from the Dag Register[s], Batavia [1678-1680, 1673, 1624-1629, 1642]', trans. F.H. de Vos, *Journal of the Ceylon Branch of the Royal Asiatic Society*, 26, 3-4 (1918), 28, 1-4 (1919), 30, 1-4 (1925-6).

265 Falck, Iman Willem, 'Bericht wegens de kaneel, opgemaakt uit de toegezondene beschryving', *Verhandelingen uitgegeeven door de Hollandse Maatschappy der Weetenschappen te Haarlem*, 15 (1774).

266 Falck, Iman Willem, 'Instructions of Governor Falck to the Chief of the District of Batticaloa, the Titular Junior Merchant Francke', *Asiatic Journal and Monthly Register for British India and its Dependencies*, 13 (1822).

267 Feber, Jan Jurgen, 'Dutch Retreat from Kandy, 1765. Justification of Colonel Feber', *Ceylon Literary Register*, 3rd series, 3, 11 (1934).

268 Feber, Jan Jurgen, and Johan Gerard van Angelbeek, 'Looting of the Palace at Kandy 1765', *Ceylon Literary Register*, 3, 12 (1934).

269 Figueiredo, Simao de, 'Historical Records of the Society of Jesus. (3) The Portuguese and the Dutch in Galle', trans. S.G. Perera, *Ceylon Antiquary and Literary Register*, 3, 3 (1918).

270 Foenander, P., 'Report of the Engineer Foenander Respecting the Dam of Molleriawe, 1789-90', trans. G. Lee, in R.L. Brohier (ed.), *Ancient Irrigation Works in Ceylon*, Vol. 3 (n.p., 1935).

271 Forbes, John G., 'Rajakariya in the Matara District under the Dutch Government', *Ceylon Literary Register*, 4, 10 (1889).

272 Forster, J.R., *Indische Zoologie oder systematische Beschreibungen seltener und unbekannter Thiere aus Indien* (Halle, 1781).

273 Frankena, A., and P. Dufflo, 'The Dutch Retreat from Kandy, 1765. Report of Majors A. Frankena and P. Dufflo, 20th September 1765', *Ceylon Literary Register*, 3rd series, 3, 10 (1933-4).

274 Frankena, A., and P. Dufflo, 'What is the Latin for Arrack?', trans. S.G. Perera, *Aloysian*, 6, 3 (1946-50).

275 Gelynsen de Jonge, Wollebrant, 'The Murder of the Dutch Commander Coster by the Sinhalese in 1641', *Ceylon Literary Register*, 2, 5 (1887) [extract from a letter to Patria].

276 Gelynsen de Jonge, Wollebrant, 'The Recapture of Negombo by the Dutch in 1644', *Ceylon Literary Register*, 2, 9 (1887).

277 Goens, Rijcklof van, Junior, 'Some Sinhalese Royal Families', ed. and trans. J.H.O. Paulusz, *Journal of the Ceylon Branch of the Royal Asiatic Society*, new series, 2, 1 (1952).

278 Goens, Rijcklof van, Senior, 'Brief van Rijkloff van Goens, raad van Indië, super-intendent en admiraal over Ceilon enz., aan den gouverneur generaal Maetsuycker, in het belang van den Engelschen vice-commandeur Jonas Handid. 1673', ed. P.A. Leupe, *Bijdragen en mededelingen van het Historisch Genootschap*, 2 (1879).

279 Greevings, 'Greevings Diary', trans. T.H. Kriekenbeek, ed. V.M. Methley, *Journal of the Royal Asiatic Society, Ceylon Branch*, 26, 3-4 (1918) [concerning Kandy in 1803].

280 Grimm, Hermann, *Laboratorium chymicum, gehouden op het voortreffelycke eylandt Ceylon, soo in 't animalische, vegetabilische, als mineralische ryck* (Batavia, 1677); reprint F.A.H. Peeters (ed.) (Tilburg, 1982).

281 Haafner, Jacob, *Travels on Foot through the Island of Ceylon*, reprint (New Delhi, 1995) [see *Dutch Sources on South Asia*, Vol. 1, Bibliography, no. 463].

282 *De Handelingen der Apostelen ... in de Singaleesche tale overgezet door de twee Singaleese taalkundige tolken onder opzigt van den wel eerwaarden Simon Cat*, ed. Johan Joachim Fybrands and Henricus Philipsz (Colombo, 1771).

283 Hemme, S.A., 'Report on the Pearl Banks of Ceylon, from Mannar to Negumbo, Addressed to His Excellency Jan Schreuder', *Colombo Journal*, 122 (1833).

284 Hermann, Paul, *Paradisus Batavus* (Leiden, 1698).

285 Hermann, Paul, *Musaeum Zeylanicum, sive catalogus plantarum, in Zeylana sponte nascentium, observatarum & descriptarum* (Leiden, 1717).

286 Herport, Albrecht, 'Travels in the East Indies (Account of Ceylon 25th March 1663-12 October 1663)', *Ceylon Literary Register*, 1, 47-8 (1887); reprint, *Journal of the Dutch Burgher Union of Ceylon*, 43, 1 (1953) [see *Dutch Sources on South Asia*, Vol. 1, Bibliography, nos 46, 461, 465].

287 Heydt, Johann Wolfgang, 'Galle as Seen by Heydt', ed. Gallean, *Aloysian*, 3, 2-3 (1929-30).

288 *Het Heylige Evangelium onses Heeren en Zaligmakers Jesu Christi, na de beschryvinge van de mannen Gods en h. Evangelisten Mattheus, Marcus, Lucas en Joannes, uyt het oirspronkelyke Grieks in de Singaleesche tale overgebragt*, trans. Willem Konijn, ed. Johannes Philippus Wetzelius (Colombo, 1739); revd edn with partially different

title by Johan Joachim Fybrants and Henricus Philipsz (Colombo, 1780).

289 *Het Heylige Evangelium onzes Heeren en Zaligmakers Jesu Christi, na de beschryvinge van den heiligen Apostel en Evangelist Mattheus uyt de oorspronkelyke Griekse, in de Mallabaarse tale overgebragt*, trans. [into Tamil] Adolphus Cramer (Colombo, 1741).

290 *Het Heylige Evangelium onzes Heeren ende Zaligmakers Jesu Christi, na de beschryvinge, van de mannen Gods, en de h. Evangelisten, Mattheus, Marcus, Lucas, ende Johannes ... uit het oorspronkelyk Grieks, in de Tamulsche tale overgebragt* (Colombo, 1748).

291 'The Hobart Papers. The Capitulation of Colombo, 15th February, 1796', *Ceylon Literary Register*, 3rd series, 1 (1931).

292 Hofstede, Petrus, *Oost-Indische Kerkzaken, zoo oude als nieuwe, meest alle, uit oorspronglyke en ongedrukte stukken by een versameld, in orde gebragt, en beredeneerd*, 2 vols (Rotterdam, 1779-80).

293 Houel, J.P.L.L., *Histoire naturelle des deux éléphans, mâle et femelle, du Muséum de Paris, venus de Hollande en France en l'an VI* (Paris, 1803).

294 Imhoff, Gustaaf Willem van, 'Ceylon in 1740', comp. and trans. G. Lee, *Ceylon Magazine*, 2, 14 (1841); reprint, *History of Ceylon by John Ribeyro* (1847) [see *Dutch Sources on South Asia*, Vol. 1, Bibliography, no. 472].

295 Imhoff, Gustaaf Willem van, 'The Giant's Tank. Extract from the Journal of H.E. the Governor Van Imhoff, Kept in the Year 1739', *Ceylon Miscellany*, 2 (1843); reprint in R.L. Brohier (ed.), *Ancient Irrigation Works in Ceylon*, Vol. 2 (n.p., 1935).

296 Imhoff, Gustaaf Willem van, 'Copy of the Will of Governor Gustaaf Willem Baron van Imhoff, obiit 1st Nov. 1750', *Ceylon Literary Register*, 2, 4-5 (1887).

297 'Instructions from the Respective "Landraaden" of this Government (Extract from the Dutch Political Council Minutes of 25 June, 1789)', trans. S.A.W. Mottau, ed. T. Nadaraja, *Journal of the Dutch Burgher Union of Ceylon*, 55, 1-4 (1965).

298 'Instructions to the Dutch Disawe of Colombo, Issued by Governor Cornelis Joan Simons, in 1707', ed. and trans. G.P.S.H. de Silva, *Ceylon Historical Journal*, 19 (1969-70).

299 'Jaffna Burial Ground. Report on the Scriba's Visit', *Journal of the Dutch Burgher Union of Ceylon*, 24, 4 (1935).

300 Jong, Jacob de, 'Galle Two Centuries Ago. Memoir of Jacob de Jong, Commander of Galle, for his Successor, 18 May 1748', trans. S.A.W. Mottau, *University of Ceylon Review*, 6, 2 (1948).

301 *Journael van de Voyagie gedaen met drie schepen, uyt Zeelandt, naer Oost-Indien, onder het beleydt van den Commandeur Joris van Spilbergen, zijn eerste Reyse, uytghevaren in de jare 1601, 1602, 1603, en 1604* (Amsterdam, *c.* 1648?).

302 Kerckhoven, Simon van den, *Historisch verhael, der wonderlike ende seer zeldsame voor-vallen, den gene bejegent die met het re-tour-schip Aernhem, van Batavia na het Vaderland verreist zijn den 23. Decem. 1661* (Middelburg, 1663); slightly different re-edition, Johannes van

Kerckhoven [= Simon], *Wijtloopig breede en waerachtige beschrijvinge van de ongeluckige voyage van 't schip Aernhem ... na het Eylant Zylon ...* (Amsterdam, 1664).

303 Konijn, Willem, *De Heydelbergse Catechismus, in de Singaleese tale overgeset door d'eerwaarde Willem Konyn* (Colombo, 1741); reprinted as *Catechismus ofte onderwysinge in de Christelyke leere, die in de kerken ende schoolen der Nederlandsche Gereformeerde Kerken geleert word, in de Singaleese taale overgeset door den eerwaarden Willem Konyn* (Colombo, 1761, 1780).

304 Konijn, Willem, *Vier praedicaatsien ... overgeset in de Singaleese taal ten dienste van de Christelijke Singaleesche gemeentens door den praedicant Wilhelmus Konyn* (Colombo, 1746).

305 *Kort uittrekzel van de leere der waarheid die na de godsaaligheid is. Ten dienste der schoolen uit de Hollandsche in de Tamulsche taale overgezet door Mattheus Jurgen Ondaatje, proponent in de hervormde gemeente, en geredíveerd door den mede proponent Mattheus Jurgen Ondaatje, in de Tamulsche gemeente, en door de taalkundigen Philip Jansz. en Adrian Frans Farnando* (Colombo, 1789).

306 *Korte beschryving van Adams, en Evaas graf, en graf-zark*, ed. Christiaan Hansz (Middelburg, n.d. [first half eighteenth century]).

307 Langhansz, Christoph, 'Ceylon in 1695', ed. D. Ferguson, *Ceylon Literary Register*, 4, 1-2 (1935) [see *Dutch Sources on South Asia*, Vol. 1, Bibliography, no. 32].

308 Langius, Joachim, *Joachimi Langii colloquiorum centuria in usum et utilitatem juventutis ad primae Ceilanae cura et studio Wilhelmi Jurgen Ondaatje Columboniensis Seminarii Rectoris* (Colombo, 1770).

309 Lannoy, Juliana Cornelia de, 'Grafschrift op mijnen geëerden neef Lubbert Jan Baron van Eck ... Gouverneur en Directeur van Ceylon. Overleeden te Colombo ... Overwinnaar van het Candiesche Rijk', in idem, *Dichtkundige werken* (Leiden, 1780).

310 Lebeck, Heinrich Julius, 'An Account of the Pearl Fishery in the Gulph of Manar, in March and April 1797', *Asiatick Researches or Transactions of the Society, Instituted in Bengal for Inquiring into the History and Antiquities, the Arts, Sciences, and Literature of Asia*, 5 (1798); reprint in J. Steuart (ed.), *An Account of the Pearl Fisheries of Ceylon* (n.p., 1843).

311 Lebeck, Heinrich Julius, 'Bemerkungen über einige Ceylonische Fossilien und ihre Schleifmethode', *Der Naturforscher*, 28 (1799).

312 Linnaeus, Carolus, *Flora Zeylanica sistens plantas Indicus Zeylonae* (Amsterdam, 1748).

313 *Liturgie der Gereformeerde Kerken ... uit de Hollandsche in de Tamulsche taale overgezet ten dienste van de Christelyke Tamulsche gemeenten, door Philippus de Melho* (Colombo, 1760).

314 Loten, Joan Gideon, 'Kasagal Vihara', ed. and trans. E.R. Gunaratna, *Journal of the Ceylon Branch of the Royal Asiatic Society*, 8, 29 (1884) [letter to the Siamese priest Upali].

315 'Louis XVI Indents on the Dutch at Colombo in 1786 for Two Ceylon Elephants', *Ceylon Literary Register*, 2, 3 (1887).

316 *Mallebaars Catechismus en gebede-boek* (Colombo, 1739) [in Tamil].

317 Martins, Antonio, 'A Spanish Captain on Ceylon at the Beginning of the 17th Century', trans. D. Ferguson, *Monthly Literary Register and Notes and Queries for Ceylon*, 4, 7 (1896) [letter to Philip III of Spain].

318 Mascarenhas, Philip, and Jan Thysz, 'Letters between Don Philip Mascarenhas (Portuguese General at Colombo) and Jan Thysz (Captain of Dutch Fort at Galle) 27 May 1641 and 8 June 1641', *Ceylon Literary Register*, 2, 3 (1887).

319 Melho, Philippus de, *Triumph der waarheid zynde eene beknopte en kragtige wederlegging van de voornaamste dwaalingen der Roomsche kerke ... in de Tamulsche taale opgesteld, ten dienste van de Christelyke Tamulsche gemeenten, door Philippus de Melho, beroepen praedicant te Jaffanapatnam* (Colombo, 1753).

320 Melho, Philippus de, *Vier praedicatien: door de liefhebbers der waarheyd in de Singaleesche taal overgeset* (Colombo, 1753).

321 Mello de Castra, 'The Dutch Embassy to Kandy in 1637', *Ceylon Literary Register*, 2, 9 (1887).

322 *Memoirs and Instructions of Dutch Governors, Commandeurs, etc., and Selections from the Dutch Records of the Ceylon Government*, trans. E. Reimers and S. Anthonisz-Pieters, reprint in 5 vols (Clifton (New Jersey), 1971) [see *Dutch Sources on South Asia*, Vol. 1, Bibliography, no. 472].

323 Metzlar, Jacob Caspar, 'Bericht aangaande een Singalees, die, op het eiland Ceilon, iets van dat geene aan zyn hoofd hadt, het welk naar de Plica Polonica of Poolsche Vlecht geleek', *Verhandelingen uitgegeeven door de Hollandse Maatschappy der Weetenschappen te Haarlem*, 24 (1787).

324 Mottau, S.A.W., 'Documents on Ceylon History (2), Documents Relating to the Tombo Registration of the Dutch Administration in Ceylon: Instructions Issued to the Tombo Commissioners', *Ceylon Historical Journal*, 3, 2 (1953).

325 Mudiyanse, N., 'A Sinhalese Record of a Dutch Embassy to Kandy', *Journal of the Vidyalankara University of Ceylon*, 1, 2 (1972) [*c.* 1753].

326 Nagel, T., T. Williams, A. Moyaart and C.F. Ebell, 'Dutch Administration in Ceylon. The Jaffna Peninsula (from a Report Made in 1794, Part of It Destroyed)', *Ceylon Literary register*, 1, 50-1 (1887).

327 Nagel, Thomas, 'Tanks and Irrigation in the Northern Province in the Time of the Dutch', trans. G. Lee, *Ceylon Literary Register*, 1, 17 (1886).

328 Nagel, Thomas, 'Account of the Vanni, 1793', *Journal of the Royal Asiatic Society, Ceylon Branch*, 38, 106 (1948).

329 *Het Nieuw Testament, ofte alle de boeken des nieuwen verbonds van onsen Heer Jesus Christus ... uit de oirspronglyke Grieksche taal in de Tamulsche spraak overgezet* (Colombo, 1759).

330 *Noodzakelyke verdediging, wederlegging en ophelderinge, voor het belang*

van de Nederlandsche Oost-Indische Compagnie, tegens eene nooit gehoorde traverseering en eindelyk geheele vernietiging van een project aangaande de landbouw en de verbeetering des lands ... aantoonende verder wat considerabel nadeel hier door aan de Edele Compagnie en dies onderhoorigen, op het wyduitgestrekte eiland Ceylon is toegebragt [by Casparus de Jong?] (n.p., *c.* 1768).

331 'Novas da India oriental. Ano de 1655. Portugueses e Holandeses, relacao contemporanea', ed. C.R. Boxer, *Arqueologia e Historia, orgao de Associacao dos Arqueologos Portugueses*, 6 (1928).

332 'The Outbreak of the Kandyan-Dutch War of 1761 and the Great Rebellion', trans. J.H.O. Paulusz, *Journal of the Ceylon Branch of the Royal Asiatic Society*, new series, 3, 1 (1953).

333 Perera, S.G., 'Two Letters of the Dutch to Rajasinha', *Ceylon Literary Register*, 3rd series, 1 (1931).

334 Philip III of Spain, 'Don Jeronimo de Azevedo, Governor of Ceylon 1594-1611 A.D.', trans. and ed. A.E. Buultjens, *Journal of the Ceylon Branch of the Royal Asiatic Society*, 15 (1898) [based on a seventeenth-century Dutch translation of a letter to Azevedo].

335 Pielat, Bartholomeus, *Insulae Ceyloniae thesaurus medicum, vel laboratorium Ceylonicum* (Amsterdam, 1679).

336 Pielat, J.C., 'A Tamil Document Relating to Changes in the Value of Currency of the Dutch Period in Ceylon', trans. and ed. S. Thananjaya-rajasingham, *Vidyodaya Journal of Arts, Science and Letters*, 3, 1 (1970); reprint, *Proceedings of the Second International Conference Seminar of Tamil Studies*, Vol. 2 (1971).

337 Prins, Francois Albertus, 'Prins's Embassy to the Kandyan Court, 1770. Introduction and Report', trans. and ed. A.N. Weinman, *Journal of the Dutch Burgher Union of Ceylon*, 53, 1-4 (1963).

338 Pybus, John, *Account of Mr. Pybus's Mission to the King of Kandy in 1762. Printed from the Records of the Madras Government* (Colombo, 1862) [see *Dutch Sources on South Asia*, Vol. 1, Bibliography, no. 482].

339 'The Recapture of Negombo by the Dutch in 1643', *Ceylon Literary Register*, 2, 11 (1887) [commission to François Caron].

340 *Het regt gebruik van des Heeren H. Avondmaal ... door G. Drelincourt, P. du Moulin en andere godsgeleerde mannen, in de Nederduitsche taal opgesteld, en de zelve ten dienste van de Tamulsche gemeente in derzelve taale, overgezet door Jan Franciscus proponent in de hervormde Tamulsche gemeente te Colombo* (Colombo, 1775).

341 Reimers, E. (ed.), 'Capitulation of Colombo, 1796. Some Dutch Official Documents Relating thereto', *Ceylon Antiquary and Literary Register*, 8, 2 (1922).

342 'A Report on the Giant's Tank Made in the Year 1791', *Ceylon Miscellany*, 2 (1843).

343 'Resolutions and Sentences of the Council of the Town of Galle, 1640-1644 (Being the Translation of Vols. I and II of the Galle Dutch Records,

Made for the Society in Holland)', ed. and trans. R.G. Anthonisz, *Journal of the Ceylon Branch of the Royal Asiatic Society*, 17, 53 (1902).

344 Rhee, Thomas van, 'Extracts from a Memoir Left by the Dutch Governor Thomas van Rhee to his Successor Governor Gerrit de Heer, 1697', trans. R.A. van Cuylenberg, *Journal of the Royal Asiatic Society, Ceylon Branch*, 5, 17 (1871-2) [see *Dutch Sources on South Asia*, Vol. 1, Bibliography, no. 472].

345 Ribeiro, Joao, 'Ribeiro's Account of the Capture of Mannar and the Siege and Capitulation of Jaffna in 1658', trans. D. Ferguson, *Ceylon Literary Register*, 5, 26 (1891).

346 Ribeiro, Joao, 'Ribeiro's Account of the Siege of Colombo in 1655-56', trans. D. Ferguson, *Journal of the Ceylon Branch of the Royal Asiatic Society*, 12, 42 (1891).

347 Ruëll, Joannes, *Grammatica off Singalese taal-kunst, zijnde eene korte methode om de voornaamste fondamenten van de Singaleese spraak te leeren* (Amsterdam, 1708).

348 Sanden, Jacques Fabrice van, 'Journal Kept during a Tour in the Districts of Koetjaer, Tamblegam and Kattoekolompattoe by the Junior Merchant Jacques Fabrice van Sanden, Governor of Trincomalie, in the Year 1786', *Ceylon Miscellany*, 3, 2 (1844).

349 Schreuder, Jan, 'Ceylon in 1762. Summary of the Memoir Left by Governor Schreuder for the Guidance of his Successor L.J. van Eck', comp. and trans. G. Lee, *Ceylon Magazine*, 2, 16 (1841); reprint, *History of Ceylon by John Ribeyro* (1847) [see *Dutch Sources on South Asia*, Vol. 1, Bibliography, no. 472].

350 *De Sendbrieven van den heilige Apostel Paulus geschreven aan de Corinthen en Galaten uyt de oorspronkelyke Griexe taale in de Singaleesche spraake overgeset door Henricus Philipsz predikant op Kolombo* (Colombo, 1773).

351 *De Sendbrieven van den heiligen Apostel Paulus geschreven aan de Ephesen, Philippensen, Kolossensen, Thessalonicensen, b'nevens die aan Thimotheus, Titus, Philemon en aan de Hebreen uit de oorspronkelyke Griexe taale in de Singaleese spraake overgeset ... door Henricus Philipsz predikant op Kolombo* (Colombo, 1775).

352 *De Sentbrief van den heiligen Apostel Paulus geschreven aan de Romynen uyt de oorspronkelyke Griexe taale in de Singaleesche spraake overgeset door Henricus Philipsz predikant op Kolombo* (Colombo, 1772).

353 *Singaleesch formulier boek. Behelsende vier formulieren, namentlyk: van de kinderen, bejaarden, 't houwelyk ende H. Avondmaal; item der sieken-troost; mitsgaders eenige gebeeden, soo voor ende na de praedicaatsie, als ook voor ende na de leere des Catechismi; waarop ten laatsten volgd, de zeegen des Heeren, die over de gemeynte uitgesproken word, by 't eynde van de godsdienst* (Colombo, 1744) [possibly by Johannes Philippus Wetzelius].

354 *Singaleesch gebeede-boek* (Colombo, 1737) [attributed to Johannes

Philippus Wetzelius]; reprinted as *Singaleesch belydenis boek[je]* (Colombo, 1738, 1742).

355 *Singaleesch school-boek behelsende korte vragen en antwoorden, nopens de grond-beginselen van de waare leere der Christelyken religie* (Colombo, 1742).

356 'A Short History of the Principal Events', ed. and trans. F.H. de Vos, *Journal of the Ceylon Branch of the Royal Asiatic Society*, 9, 38 (1889) [concerning the Dutch presence on Ceylon, 1602-1757].

357 'A Slaafbrief 156 Years Old', *Journal of the Dutch Burgher Union of Ceylon*, 14, 4 (1925).

358 *Some Documents Relating to the Rise of the Dutch Power in Ceylon, 1602-1670, from the Transactions at the India Office*, ed. P.E. Pieris (Colombo, 1929) [see *Dutch Sources on South Asia*, Vol. 1, Bibliography, no. 479].

359 Spaan, Gerrit van, *De Aziaansche weg-wijzer, vertoonende verscheide landstreken, ten dienste van die gene, dewelke haar geluk in andere gewesten moeten zoeken* (Rotterdam, 1695).

360 Spilbergen, Joris van, 'The Visit of Spilbergen to Ceylon, Translated from Admiral Joris van Spilbergen's Relation', trans. D. Ferguson, *Journal of the Royal Asiatic Society, Ceylon Branch*, 30 (1927).

361 Strachan, 'An Account of Taking and Taming Elephants in Zeylan', *Philosophical Transactions*, 277 (1702).

362 *Summaria relacam dos prodigiosos feitos que as armas portuguesas obrarão na ilha de Ceilão contra os olandeses e chingalas, no anno passado de 1655* (Lisbon, 1656).

363 'Summaries of the Proceedings of the Secret War Committee of the Dutch Political Council of Ceylon during the War with Kandy, 1762-1766', trans. and ed. S.A.W. Mottau and R.L. Brohier, *Journal of the Dutch Burgher Union of Ceylon*, 56, 1-4 (1966).

364 'Summary of the Revenue and Expenditure of Ceylon under the Dutch Government, from the Year 1739-40 to 1760-61, Inclusive', comp. and trans. G. Lee, *Ceylon Magazine*, 2, 13 (1841); reprint, *History of Ceylon by John Ribeyro* (1847).

365 'The Surrender of Trincomalie in 1795', trans. F.H. de Vos, *Journal of the Dutch Burgher Union of Ceylon*, 11, 1-2 (1918).

366 Tennekoon, 'Raja Simha, his Military and Other Resources', trans. J.H.O. Paulusz, *Journal of the Royal Asiatic Society, Ceylon Branch*, new series, 5, 2 (1957).

367 'Three Tamil Proclamations Issued under the Dutch Rule in Ceylon', trans. and ed. S. Thananjayarajasingham, *Acta Orientalia*, 36 (1974).

368 Thunberg, Carl Peter, 'Aanmerkingen over de kaneel op Ceylon', *Verhandelingen uitgegeven door het Zeeuwsch Genootschap der Wetenschappen te Vlissingen*, 12, 1 (1786).

369 Thunberg, Carl Peter, *Resa uti Europa, Africa, Asia, förrättad åren 1770-1779* [= Travels to Europe, Africa, Asia, made in the years 1770-1779]

(Upsala, 1788-93); part. trans., 'Voyage to Ceylon', *Monthly Literary Register and Notes and Queries for Ceylon*, 1, 1-4 (1893).

370 Thysz, Jan, 'Galle in 1641', *Ceylon Literary Register*, 2, 1 (1887) [letter to Governor Arent Gardenijs of Coromandel].

371 Thysz, Jan, 'The Capture of Negombo and Galle by the Dutch in 1640', *Ceylon Literary Register*, 2, 10 (1887) [extract from a letter to Governor Arent Gardenijs of Coromandel].

372 Tornbauer, J.G., 'Kantalay Tank at the End of the Eighteenth Century', trans. G. Lee, *Ceylon Literary Register*, 1, 1-2 (1886).

373 'Transactions between the King of Kandy and the Dutch 1609-1617', trans. D. Ferguson, *Ceylon Literary Register*, 3rd series, 1-3 (1931-4).

374 'Translation of a (Dutch) Proclamation by the Governor in Council of Ceylon, Dated 11 August, 1686', *Journal of the Royal Asiatic Society of Great Britain and Ireland*, 5 (1839).

375 'Translation of a *slaafbrief* of 1791', *Journal of the Dutch Burgher Union of Ceylon*, 21, 2 (1931).

376 'Translation of an Historical Account of the Voyage to the East-Indies with 15 Ships under Wybrant van Waerwijck, Admiral, and Sebaald de Weert, Vice Admiral', trans. F.H. de Vos, *Orientalist*, 3 (1888-9) [see *Dutch Sources on South Asia*, Vol. 1, Bibliography, no. 9].

377 'Treaty of Peace between the Dutch and the Sinhalese, Dated 14 February, 1766', trans. H.C.P. Bell, *Orientalist*, 3 (1888-9).

378 Turner, L.J.B., 'The Capitulation of Colombo, 1796. Some Dutch Official Documents Relating thereto', *Ceylon Antiquary and Literary Register*, 8, 2 (1922).

379 *Het tweede boek Moses genaamt Exodus, inde Singaleesche tale overgeset ... door Henricus Philipsz, predikant te Colombo* (Colombo, 1786).

380 Valentijn, Francois, 'The Dutch in Ceylon - Spilbergen', trans. A.E. Buultjens, *Orientalist*, 2 (1885-6), 3 (1888-9) [see *Dutch Sources on South Asia*, Vol. 1, Bibliography, no. 484].

381 Valentijn, Francois, '(Pieter de) Bucquoy', *Ceylon Literary Register*, 2, 19 (1887) [see *Dutch Sources on South Asia*, Vol. 1, Bibliography, no. 484].

382 Valentijn, Francois, 'The Dutch in Ceylon', trans. A.E. Buultjens, *Orientalist*, 4, 3-4 (1891) [see *Dutch Sources on South Asia*, Vol. 1, Bibliography, no. 484].

383 Valentijn, Francois, 'Francois Valentijn's Description of Ceylon [Chapters 16-17])', trans. S.A.W. Mottau, *Journal of the Dutch Burgher Union of Ceylon*, 61-2, (1983-5) [see *Dutch Sources on South Asia*, Vol. 1, Bibliography, no. 484].

384 Vriest, Philippus de, *Sestien praedicatien overgeset in de Tamulsche taal, ten dienste van de Christelyke Tamulsche gemeentens, door den praedicant Philippus de Vriest* (Colombo, 1747).

385 Wermelskircher, Matthias (ed.), *Singaleesch-gezangboekje ... in den jaare 1723, door de Modliaars Anthony Perera en Louis de Seram op de digt-*

en-zangmaat Petri Datheni gestelt en van den kerken-raad oover-gezien en goedgekeurt zynde (Colombo, 1755); reprinted as Sigisbertus Abrahamsz Bronsveld (ed.), *Singaleesche psalmen en lofzangen op de gewoone zangmaate onzer kerke overgezet en bereimd, en tot stigtinge der Singaleesche Christenen* (Colombo, 1768).

386 Wetzelius, Johannes Philippus, *Kort ontwerp van de leere der waarheid die na de godsaligheyd is, overgeset in de Singaleese tale ten dienste van de Christelyke Singaleesche Gemeentens door den praedicant Johannes Philippus Wetzelius* (Colombo, 1744); 2nd edn revised by Henricus Christoffel Philipsz (Colombo, 1790).

387 Wezel, Cornelis Taay van, 'A Pertinent Account and Detailed Description of the Character, Nature, Coitus, and Production of Elephants in the Great Island of Ceylon ... and also How They are Stalled and Tamed and Sold on Account of the Hon. Dutch East India Co. ... Ao 1713', trans. F.H. de Vos, *Journal of the Royal Asiatic Society, Ceylon Branch*, 15, 49 (1898).

388 White, H., and H.A. Loos (eds), *A Revised Edition of the Legislative Enactments of Ceylon, 1656-1900*, 3 vols (Colombo, 1900); supplements F.G. Smith a.o. (eds) (Colombo, 1907-23).

4.2. Secondary Sources

389 A.C., 'The Conquest of Jaffna, by the Dutch', *Ceylon Literary Register*, 1, 41-2 (1887).

390 Abeyasinghe, T.B.H., 'Princes and Merchants. Relations between the Kings of Kandy and the Dutch East India Company in Sri Lanka (1688-1740)', *The Sri Lanka Archives*, 2 (1984).

391 Abeyasinghe, T.B.H., 'The Kingdom of Kandy. Foundations and Foreign Relations to 1638', in K.M. de Silva (ed.), *History of Sri Lanka* (University of Peradeniya), Vol. 2 (*c.* 1500 to *c.* 1800) (Peradeniya, 1995).

392 Abeydeera, A., 'Kartografie als een essentieel element van bestuur door het Hollandse koloniale gouvernement van Sri Lanka's kustgebieden tussen 1658 en 1796', *Kartografisch tijdschrift*, 17, 1 (1991).

393 Altendorff, D.V., 'Genealogies of Dutch Families in Ceylon', *Journal of the Dutch Burgher Union of Ceylon*, 23, 3 (1934) - 53, 1-2 (1963).

394 Amerasinghe, Ch.F., *Aspects of the Actio Iniuriarum in Roman-Dutch Law* (Colombo, n.d. [1966]).

395 Anthonisz, R.G., 'Some Old Dutch Churches', *Ceylon Literary Register*, 6, 32, 36 (1892) [concerning Galle, Ambalangoda and Bentota].

396 Anthonisz, R.G., 'The Disuse of the Dutch Language in Ceylon', *Journal of the Dutch Burgher Union of Ceylon*, 1, 1 (1908).

397 Anthonisz, R.G., 'The Dutch Burgher Union of Ceylon', *Journal of the Dutch Burgher Union of Ceylon*, 1, 1 (1908).

398 Anthonisz, R.G., 'Wolvendaal Church', *Journal of the Dutch Burgher Union of Ceylon*, 1, 3 (1908).

399 Anthonisz, R.G., 'The Dutch Church at Galle', *Journal of the Dutch Burgher Union of Ceylon*, 1, 4 (1908).

400 Anthonisz, R.G., 'Heraldry as Represented in Dutch Seals and Monuments in Ceylon', *Journal of the Dutch Burgher Union of Ceylon*, 2, 1-2 (1909).

401 Anthonisz, R.G., 'Some Early Marriages in Colombo A.D. 1661-1699', *Journal of the Dutch Burgher Union of Ceylon*, 2, 4 (1909), 3 (1910).

402 Anthonisz, R.G., 'The Dutch Burgher Union of Ceylon. A Retrospect', *Journal of the Dutch Burgher Union of Ceylon*, 3 (1910).

403 Anthonisz, R.G., 'The Dutch at Matara', *Journal of the Dutch Burgher Union of Ceylon*, 4 (1911).

404 Anthonisz, R.G., 'A Dutch Educational Report', *Journal of the Ceylon Branch of the Royal Asiatic Society (Notes and Queries)*, 24, 5 (1916).

405 Anthonisz, R.G., 'Johan Gerard van Angelbeek', *Journal of the Dutch Burgher Union of Ceylon*, 9, 1 (1916).

406 Anthonisz, R.G., 'Gerard Hulft', *Journal of the Dutch Burgher Union of Ceylon*, 9, 3 (1916).

407 Anthonisz, R.G., 'Dutch Governors who Died in Ceylon', *Journal of the Dutch Burgher Union of Ceylon*, 10, 4 (1918).

408 Anthonisz, R.G., 'Adam Westerwolt', *Journal of the Dutch Burgher Union of Ceylon*, 14, 1 (1924).

409 Anthonisz, R.G., 'More about Governor Van Angelbeek', *Journal of the Dutch Burgher Union of Ceylon*, 14, 1 (1924).

410 Anthonisz, R.G., 'A Hundred Years Ago', *Journal of the Dutch Burgher Union of Ceylon*, 14, 4 (1925).

411 Anthonisz, R.G., 'History in the Making. The Murder of Willem Jacobsz Coster', *Journal of the Dutch Burgher Union of Ceylon*, 15, 1 (1925).

412 Anthonisz, R.G., 'The Burghers of Ceylon', *Journal of the Dutch Burgher Union of Ceylon*, 17, 1 (1927); reprint (Colombo, 1927).

413 Anthonisz, R.G., 'Some Marriages in Colombo from A.D. 1700 to 1750', *Journal of the Dutch Burgher Union of Ceylon*, 17, 2-4 (1927-8), 18, 1-4 (1928-9), 19, 1-2 (1929).

414 Anthonisz, R.G., 'Lansi (the Burghers)', *Journal of the Dutch Burgher Union of Ceylon*, 14, 3 (1928).

415 Anthonisz, R.G., 'The Government Archives', *Journal of the Dutch Burgher Union of Ceylon*, 18, 4 (1929).

416 Anthonisz, R.G., 'The Dutch Political Council. A Sketch of its Constitution and Functions and an Outline of the System of Government under the Dutch East India Company', *Journal of the Dutch Burgher Union of Ceylon*, 19, 1 (1929).

417 Anthonisz, R.G., 'The Dutch Burgher Union of Ceylon. A Review', *Journal of the Dutch Burgher Union of Ceylon*, 21, 1 (1931).

418 Anthonisz, R.G., 'The Dutch Governors of Ceylon: Ryclof van Goens, 1663-1675', *Journal of the Dutch Burgher Union of Ceylon*, 21, 2 (1931).

419 Anthonisz, R.G., *The Dutch of Ceylon. Glimpses of Their Life and Times* (Colombo, 1905); reprint, *Journal of the Dutch Burgher Union of Ceylon*, 24, 3-4, 25, 1-2 (1935) [see *Dutch Sources on South Asia*, Vol. 1, Bibliography, no. 494].

420 Anthonisz, R.G., F.H. de Vos and E.B.F. de Sueter, 'Dutch Inscription,

Colombo', *Journal of the Royal Asiatic Society, Ceylon Branch (Notes and Queries)*, 23, 2 (1913).

421 Anthonisz, V.R.L., 'The Dutch Reformed Church. A Short Historical Narrative', *Journal of the Dutch Burgher Union of Ceylon*, 45, 1 (1955).

422 Arasaratnam, S., 'Keystones in Ceylon's History. 2, Reverend Baldaeus and his Work on Ceylon', *Journal of the Dutch Burgher Union of Ceylon*, 51, 4 (1961).

423 Arasaratnam, S., 'The Consolidation of Dutch Power in the Maritime Regions 1658-1687', in K.M. de Silva (ed.), *History of Sri Lanka* (University of Peradeniya), Vol. 2 (*c.* 1500 to *c.* 1800) (Peradeniya, 1995).

424 Arasaratnam, S., 'Sri Lanka's Trade, Internal and External in the 17th and 18th Centuries', in K.M. de Silva (ed.), *History of Sri Lanka* (University of Peradeniya), Vol. 2 (*c.* 1500 to *c.* 1800) (Peradeniya, 1995).

425 Ardagh, J., 'Paul Hermann's Ceylon Herbarium and Icones', *Journal of Botany*, 69 (1931).

426 Balen, J.H. van, *De Trompetter van admiraal Spilbergh. De eerste Nederlanders op Ceylon, 1601-1604* (Amsterdam, 1882).

427 Bartholomeusz, C.H., 'A Lieutenant of Outpost in Dutch Times', *Journal of the Burgher Association of Ceylon*, 3, 1 (1936) [pertaining to Andreas Amabert].

428 Bartholomeusz, C.H., 'The Coming of the Dutchmen to Ceylon', *Journal of the Burgher Association of Ceylon*, 3, 2 (1936).

429 Bartholomeusz, F., 'The Story of Hendala', *Journal of the Dutch Burgher Union of Ceylon*, 32, 4, 33, 1 (1943).

430 Bell, H.C.P., 'Letter from the Kandyan Court: 1726', *Ceylon Antiquary and Literary Register*, 1, 2 (1915-16).

431 Bell, H.C.P., 'Andreas Amabert', *Ceylon Antiquary and Literary Register*, 1, 4 (1916).

432 Bellamy, C.V., 'The Fort of Jaffna', *Monthly Literary Register and Notes and Queries for Ceylon*, 3, 5 (1895).

433 Bes, L., 'The Setupatis, the Dutch, and Other Bandits in Eighteenth-Century Ramnad (South India)', *Journal of the Economic and Social History of the Orient*, 44, 4 (2001); for the correct accompanying map, see *JESHO*, 45, 1 (2002).

434 Blaze, L.E., 'Joan Maatzuyker', *Journal of the Dutch Burgher Union of Ceylon*, 17, 4 (1928).

435 Blaze, L.E., 'The Catalogue of the Dutch Archives', *Journal of the Dutch Burgher Union of Ceylon*, 33, 2 (1943).

436 B[loys] v[an] T[reslong] P[rins], [P.C.], 'Hollandsche grafsteen, in januari 1934 gevonden op Ceylon', *De Nederlandsche Leeuw*, 52 (1934).

437 B[loys] v[an] T[reslong] P[rins], P.C., 'Oude grafsteenen te Colombo', *De Indische Navorscher*, 1 (1934-5).

438 Bosch, R.P. van den, 'Ceylon tijdens het Nederlandsch Bestuur onder de Oost-Indische Compagnie van 1656 tot en met 1796. Historische-genealogische-heraldieke aanteekeningen', *Algemeen Nederlandsch*

Familieblad, 12 (1895); also in *De Wapenheraut*, 1-5 (1897-1901).

439 Boudens, R., 'The Sources for a History of the Catholic Church in Ceylon under the Dutch Rule', *The Ceylon Historical Journal*, 2, 1-2 (1952).

440 Boudens, R., 'The Catholic Church in Ceylon from 1658 to 1687', *The Ceylon Historical Journal*, 2, 3-4 (1953).

441 Boudens, R., 'Christian Reaction to the Dutch Persecution in Ceylon', *The Aloysian Herald*, 4, 4 (1953).

442 Boudens, R., 'Negombo, un centre de résistance catholique à Ceylan sous l'occupation hollandaise', *Neue Zeitschrift für Missionswissenschaft*, 11 (1955).

443 Boxer, C.R., 'Portuguese and Dutch Colonial Rivalry, 1641-1661', *Studia*, 2 (1958).

444 Brohier, D., 'Who are the Burghers?', *Journal of the Royal Asiatic Society, Sri Lanka Branch*, new series, 30 (1985-6).

445 Brohier, R.L., 'The Assault on the Fortress of Colombo by the Dutch', *Journal of the Dutch Burgher Union of Ceylon*, 16 (1926).

446 Brohier, R.L., 'Vestiges of Dutch Occupation in the Hambantota District', *Journal of the Dutch Burgher Union of Ceylon*, 18, 4, 19, 1 (1929).

447 Brohier, R.L., 'Adam's Berg. Jottings of References to this Rock in Dutch Times', *Journal of the Dutch Burgher Union of Ceylon*, 20, 1 (1930).

448 Brohier, R.L., 'Former Dutch Maritime Possessions', *Ceylon Causerie*, 1, 11-12 (1930); reprint, *Ceylon Fortnightly Review*, 2, 23-4 (1950).

449 Brohier, R.L., 'A Fort which Replaced a Chapel', *Journal of the Dutch Burgher Union of Ceylon*, 20, 2 (1930); reprint, *Ceylon Causerie*, 2, 11 (1931); *Ceylon Fortnightly Review*, 2, 6, 8 (1949), 12, 7, 9 (1959) [pertaining to Kalpitiya].

450 Brohier, R.L., 'Relics of Dutch Times in Ambalangoda and Bentota', *Journal of the Dutch Burgher Union of Ceylon*, 21, 4 (1932).

451 Brohier, R.L., 'Relics of Dutch Times at Barberyn and Kalutara', *Journal of the Dutch Burgher Union of Ceylon*, 22, 1 (1932).

452 Brohier, R.L., 'Forts and Fortresses in Ceylon', *Ceylon Observer Annual* (1936).

453 Brohier, R.L., 'Land Tenure, Registration and Survey in Dutch Times', *Journal of the Dutch Burgher Union of Ceylon*, 27, 1 (1937).

454 Brohier, R.L. (ed.), *De Wolvendaalsche Kerk* (Colombo, 1938); revd edn (Colombo, 1957) [see *Dutch Sources on South Asia*, Vol. 1, Bibliography, no. 532].

455 Brohier, R.L., 'European Chairs in Ceylon in the 17th and 18th Centuries', *Journal of the Ceylon Branch of the Royal Asiatic Society*, 28 (1938).

456 Brohier, R.L., 'The Dutch Period of the Church in Ceylon', *Journal of the Dutch Burgher Union of Ceylon*, 28 (1938).

457 Brohier, R.L., 'North Ceylon in Dutch Times. Relics of War', *Journal of the Dutch Burgher Union of Ceylon*, 29, 4 (1940).

458 Brohier, R.L., 'Glimpses of Old Social Customs', *Journal of the Dutch Burgher Union of Ceylon*, 34, 2 (1944).

459 Brohier, R.L., 'The Dutch Canal System between Kalutara and Colombo',

Journal of the Dutch Burgher Union of Ceylon, 37, 2 (1947).

460 Brohier, R.L., 'A Notable Bi-centenary. Wolvendaalsche Kerk', *Ceylon Fortnightly Review*, 1, 17 (1949).

461 Brohier, R.L., 'Legacies of the Colonial Dutch Engineer', *Transactions of the Engineering Association of* Ceylon (1949); reprint, *Journal of the Dutch Burgher Union of Ceylon*, 40, 3 (1950).

462 Brohier, R.L., 'Ceylon-Dutch Domestic Art', *Kalamanjari*, 1 (1950-1).

463 Brohier, R.L., 'The Events Leading to the Capitulation of 1796. A Statement Based on Documents in the Madras Record Office', *Ceylon Historical Journal*, 2 (1952).

464 Brohier, R.L., 'Links with History which Will Soon Be No More', *Journal of the Dutch Burgher Union of Ceylon*, 42, 3 (1952) [concerning Dutch graves].

465 Brohier, R.L., 'The Events Leading to the Capitulation of 1796. A Restatement', *Ceylon Historical Journal*, 2, 3-4 (1953).

466 Brohier, R.L., 'New Light on an Old Controversy: Has the Story of the Decline of the Dutch Power in Ceylon Been Fully Covered', *Journal of the Dutch Burgher Union of Ceylon*, 43, 1 (1953).

467 Brohier, R.L., 'Dutch Forts and Fortresses in Ceylon', *Ceylon Fortnightly Review*, 6, 20, 23, 7, 1 (1954).

468 Brohier, R.L., 'Dutch Canals', *Ceylon Fortnightly Review*, 7, 5, 7 (1954).

469 Brohier, R.L., 'Reflections on Forts and Fortresses in Ceylon', *Journal of the Dutch Burgher Union of Ceylon*, 44, 1 (1954).

470 Brohier, R.L., 'Dutch Colonial Furniture in Ceylon', *Journal of the Dutch Burgher Union of Ceylon*, 50, 1-2 (1960).

471 Brohier, R.L., 'Armorial Bearings of Ceylon in the Dutch Era', *Times of Ceylon Annual* (1956); reprint, *Journal of the Dutch Burgher Union of Ceylon*, 50, 3-4 (1960).

472 Brohier, R.L., 'A Historical Facet - Witnessing the Past', *Journal of the Dutch Burgher Union of Ceylon*, 51, 3-4 (1961) [concerning Colombo Fort and the Wolvendaal Church].

473 Brohier, R.L., 'Historical Links between the Netherlands and Ceylon', *Journal of the Dutch Burgher Union of Ceylon*, 53, 3-4 (1963).

474 Brohier, R.L., 'Vignettes from the Past. Look Back from Pettah to "Oude Stad"', *Journal of the Dutch Burgher Union of Ceylon*, 55, 1-4 (1965).

475 Brohier, R.L., 'Vignettes from the Past. IV, When Temple Trees Was a Dutch Distillery', *Journal of the Dutch Burgher Union of Ceylon*, 56, 1-4 (1966).

476 Brohier, R.L., 'Memories are Revived', *Ceylon Observer Pictorial* (1971) [pertaining to Dutch furniture].

477 Brohier, R.L., 'Dutch Churches in Ceylon', *The Herald*, 61, 3-10 (1972).

478 Brohier, R.L., 'Changing Face of Colombo (1505-1972)', in I. Raheem (ed.), *Views of Colombo (1518-1900)* (Colombo, 1984) [see *Dutch Sources on South Asia*, Vol. 1, Bibliography, no. 656].

479 Brohier, R.L., and S.A.W. Mottau, 'The Dutch Records in Ceylon. A

Symposium. 1, The Origin of the Archives; 2, The Memoirs of Dutch Governors', *Journal of the Dutch Burgher Union of Ceylon*, 52, 1-2 (1962).

480 Bruggen, A.C. van, and F.F.J.M. Pieters, 'Notes on a Drawing of Indian Elephants in Red Crayon by Petrus Camper (1786) in the Archives of the Rijksmuseum van Natuurlijke Historie', *Zoologische Mededelingen*, 63, 19 (1990).

481 Bruin, E.R.V. de, 'Sidelights on the term "Burgher"', *Journal of the Burgher Association of Ceylon*, 3, 2 (1936).

482 Bruin, E.R.V. de, 'Who is a "Burgher"?', *Journal of the Burgher Association of Ceylon*, 3, 3 (1937).

483 Burgh, R.J. van den, 'Joris van Spilbergen. "Reijs-broeder van de son, der Castillianen tergher"', *De Waterschans. Geschiedkundig tijdschrift en mededelingenblad*, 23, 1 (1993).

484 'The Burghers of Ceylon. A Flashback', *Journal of the Dutch Burgher Union of Ceylon*, 47, 1 (1957).

485 Buultjens, A.E., 'On Some Dutch Words Commonly Used by the Sinhalese', *Orientalist*, 3 (1888-9); reprint, *Journal of the Dutch Burgher Union of Ceylon*, 19, 2 (1929).

486 Cannegieter, H.G., 'The Dutch in Ceylon', *Journal of the Dutch Burgher Union of Ceylon*, 22, 3 (1933).

487 Capper, J., 'The Revenue and Expenditure of the Dutch Government in Ceylon during the Last Years of Their Administration', *Journal of the Ceylon Branch of the Royal Asiatic Society*, 1, 3 (1847-8).

488 Capper, J., 'Expenditure on Public Works in Ceylon', *Journal of the Ceylon Branch of the Royal Asiatic Society*, 3 (1858-9).

489 Capper, J., 'Dutch Colombo', *Journal of the Dutch Burgher Union of Ceylon*, 40, 3 (1950).

490 Capper, J., and P. Munnich, 'De inkomsten en uitgaven van het Hollandsche gouvernement op Ceylon, gedurende de laatste jaren van deszelfs bestuur: voorgelezen den 26sten februarij 1848, in een wetenschappelijk genootschap', *Tijdschrift voor Nederlandsch Indië*, 12, 1 (1850).

491 Casie Chitty, S., 'Ceylon Celebrities. Philip de Melho, 1723-1790', *Ceylon Literary Register*, 3rd series 2, 2 (1932).

492 'Ceylon-Dutch Domestic and National Artistry', *Journal of the Dutch Burgher Union of Ceylon*, 43, 4 (1953).

493 'Ceylon in 1762', *The Literary Association Magazine*, 1, 3 (1863) [pertaining to Pybus' embassy to Kandy].

494 Chandrahasan, N., 'Roman-Dutch Law in Ceylon', *The Colombo Law Review*, 3 (1972).

495 Codrington, H.W., 'A Recent Find of Coins', *Journal of the Ceylon Branch of the Royal Asiatic Society*, 23 (1913).

496 Codrington, H.W., 'Dutch Pagodas and Fanams of Ceylon', *Journal of the Ceylon Branch of the Royal Asiatic Society (Notes and Queries)*, 23, 4 (1914).

497 Codrington, H.W., *Ceylon Coins and Currency*, reprinted as *V.O.C. Coins in Ceylon* (Amsterdam, 1980) [see *Dutch Sources on South Asia*, Vol. 1, Bibliography, no. 535].

498 Colin-Thomé, P., 'The Portuguese Burghers and the Dutch Burghers of Sri Lanka', *Journal of the Dutch Burgher Union of Ceylon*, 62 (1985).

499 Cooray, A.B., 'The Roman-Dutch Law in Ceylon', *Ceylon Law Students Magazine* (1939).

500 Cooray, L.J.M., 'The Reception of Roman-Dutch Law in Ceylon', *The Comparative in International Law Journal of Southern Africa*, 7 (1974).

501 Crino, S., 'Carte e piante inedite del secolo XVII riguardante l'isola di Ceylon rinvenute nel Palazzo Pitti, nel Museo degli strumenti Antichi di Firenze e nel British Museum di Londra', *La Bibliofilia. Rivista di storia del libro e delle arti grafiche di bibliografia ed erudizione*, 36, 1-2 (1934) [concerning a Dutch map].

502 Croo de Vries, A.B.R. du, 'Joan Gideon Loten (1710-1789). Gouverneur van Ceylon', in J. Aalbers a.o. (eds), *Utrechtse biografieën. Levensbeschrijvingen van bekende en onbekende Utrechters*, Vol. 1 (Amsterdam and Utrecht, n.d.).

503 Cumaraswamy, A., 'Education in Dutch Ceylon', *Ceylon Teacher*, 11, 57 (1948).

504 Dekker, F., 'The Dutch in Ceylon', *Journal of the Dutch Burgher Union of Ceylon*, 27, 1-3 (1937-8), 28, 3 (1939).

505 Dewaraja, L.S., *A Study of the Political, Administrative and Social Structure of the Kandyan Kingdom of Ceylon, 1707-1760* (Colombo, 1972).

506 Dewaraja, L.S., 'The Kandyan Kingdom. The Secret of its Survival', *Journal of the Royal Asiatic Society of Sri Lanka*, new series, 30 (1985-6).

507 Dewaraja, L.S., 'The Kandyan Kingdom 1638-1739. A Survey of its Political History', in K.M. de Silva (ed.), *History of Sri Lanka* (University of Peradeniya), Vol. 2 (*c.* 1500 to *c.* 1800) (Peradeniya, 1995).

508 Dewaraja, L.S., 'The Kandyan Kingdom and the Nayakkars, 1739-1796', in K.M. de Silva (ed.), *History of Sri Lanka* (University of Peradeniya), Vol. 2 (*c.* 1500 to *c.* 1800) (Peradeniya, 1995).

509 Dewaraja, L.S., 'The Social and Economic Conditions in the Kandyan Kingdom in the 17th and 18th Centuries', in K.M. de Silva (ed.), *History of Sri Lanka* (University of Peradeniya), Vol. 2 (*c.* 1500 to *c.* 1800) (Peradeniya, 1995).

510 Dewaraja, L.S., S. Arasaratnam and D.A. Kotelawele, 'Administrative Systems: Kandyan and Dutch', in K.M. de Silva (ed.), *History of Sri Lanka* (University of Peradeniya), Vol. 2 (*c.* 1500 to *c.* 1800) (Peradeniya, 1995).

511 Diehl, K.S., 'Ceylon Students Abroad in the Eighteenth Century' in idem (ed.), *Historical Essays. Primary Printed and Manuscript Sources for Sixteenth to Nineteenth Century Available in Sri Lanka* (Colombo, 1976).

512 Diehl, K.S., 'Simon Kat, Translator 1624-1704', *Ceylon Historical Journal*, 25 (1978).

513 'A Dip into the Past', *Journal of the Dutch Burgher Union of Ceylon*, 38, 1 (1943).

514 'Dutch Cypher Codes Used in Ceylon', *Ceylon Literary Register*, 2, 53 (1888).

515 'Dutch Inscription in the Bentota Church', *Ceylon Literary Register*, 1, 9 (1886).

516 'Dutch Inscription on Gold Medals in Ceylon', *Ceylon Literary Register*, 2, 36 (1888).

517 'Dutch Inscriptions', *Ceylon Literary Register*, 2, 15 (1887).

518 'Dutch Schools in Ceylon', *Journal of the Dutch Burgher Union of Ceylon*, 42, 4 (1952).

519 'Dutch Visits to Ceylon in the 17th Century', *Ceylon Literary Register*, 7, 5 (1892).

520 E.M.L., 'Christopher Fryke. A Surgeon to the Dutch East-India Company in the 17th Century', *British Medical Journal* (1931); reprints, *Ceylon Fortnightly Review*, 7, 7 (1954); *Journal of the Dutch Burgher Union of Ceylon*, 44, 1 (1954).

521 'Education in Ceylon. (2) Under the Dutch. (3) The Pet Institution (under the Dutch)', *Ceylon Friend*, 3rd series, 18-19 (1886).

522 F., L., 'Arippu', *Ceylon Observer Christmas Number* (1921).

523 Ferdinand, D., 'Trincomalee Saga, 1709-1957', *Journal of the Dutch Burgher Union of Ceylon*, 48, 2-4 (1958).

524 Ferdinand, M., 'Spotlight on the Dutch Administrative System', *Journal of the Dutch Burgher Union of Ceylon*, 40, 3 (1950).

525 Ferguson, D., 'The Revd. Philippus Baldaeus and his Book on Ceylon', *Monthly Literary Register and Notes and Queries for Ceylon*, 3, 6-8 (1895); reprints (Colombo, 1895); *Ceylon Literary Register*, 4, 7-10 (1936).

526 Ferguson, D., 'Alagiyavanna Mohattala, the Author of Kusajataka Kavyaya', *Journal of the Royal Asiatic Society, Ceylon Branch*, 16, 50 (1899).

527 Ferguson, D., 'Joan Gideon Loten, F.R.S., the Naturalist Governor of Ceylon (1752-1757), and the Ceylonese Artist De Bevere', *Journal of the Royal Asiatic Society, Ceylon Branch*, 19, 58 (1907-8) [see *Dutch Sources on South Asia*, Vol. 1, Bibliography, no. 549].

528 Ferguson, D., 'Mulgiri-Gala', *Journal of the Royal Asiatic Society, Ceylon Branch*, 22, 64 (1911).

529 Fernando, C.N., 'Christianity in Ceylon in the Portuguese and the Dutch Periods', *University of Ceylon Review*, 6, 4 (1948); reprint, *Journal of the Dutch Burgher Union of Ceylon*, 39, 2-3 (1949).

530 'First Establishment and Present State of the Dutch Church in Ceylon', *Colombo Religious and Theological Magazine*, 1, 2 (1833).

531 'Flash-back on Dutch Rule', *Journal of the Dutch Burgher Union of Ceylon*, 40, 2 (1950).

532 Fonseka, M., 'Areas of Concern, Old Colombo, Sri Lanka', *Monumentum*, 25, 2 (1982).

533 Forrer, M., 'Vijfjarige Ceylonese olifant en zijn twee begeleiders gezien tegen de Baai van Nagasaki', *Bulletin van de Vereniging Rembrandt*, 10, 2 (2000).

534 Gaastra, F.S., 'Ceylon als "handelscomptoir" van de V.O.C.', in R. Kromhout (ed.), *Het Machtige Eyland. Ceylon en de V.O.C.* (The Hague, 1988).

535 Gaastra, F.S., '"Sware continuerende lasten en groten ommeslagh". Kosten van de oorlogsvoering van de Verenigde Oost-Indische Compagnie', in G. Knaap and G. Teitler (eds), *De Verenigde Oost-Indische Compagnie tussen oorlog en diplomatie* (Verhandelingen van het Koninklijk Instituut voor Taal-, Land- en Volkenkunde, 197) (Leiden, 2002).

536 Gallicus, 'Javanese Exiles to Ceylon in the 18th Century', *Tropical Agriculturist Literary Register Supplement*, 18 (1898).

537 Geer, W. van, *De opkomst van het Nederlands gezag over Ceilon* (Leiden, 1895).

538 Gert, A. van der, 'A Nursery of Dutch History in South Ceylon. Bicentenary of the Church in Galle', *Journal of the Dutch Burgher Union of Ceylon*, 42, 4 (1952).

539 Godée Molsbergen, E.C., *Report on the Dutch Records in the Government Archives at Colombo* (Sessional Paper, 9) (Colombo, 1929).

540 Gooneratna, C.F.W., 'Some Historical Aspects of Leprosy in Ceylon during the Dutch Period 1658-1796', *Medical History*, 15, 1 (1971).

541 Gooneratne, F.E., 'A Story of a Dutch Noble Family of Old', *Ceylon Christian Herald*, 8, 8 (1917).

542 Gooneratne, F.E., *The Landhesi Kaaleya or the Dutch Times* (n.p. [Colombo], 1922).

543 Goonetileke, H.A.I., 'Another Mr. Knox in Dutch Ceylon', *Times of Ceylon Annual* (1973).

544 Goonewardena, K.W., 'Moors in the Dutch Period', *Al-Eslam* (1967); reprint in A.I.L. Marikar, A.L.M. Lafir and A.H. Macan Makar (eds), *Glimpses from the Past of the Moors of Sri Lanka* (Colombo, 1976).

545 Goonewardena, K.W., 'Muslims under Dutch Rule up to the Mid-Eighteenth Century', in M.A.M. Shukri (ed.), *Muslims of Sri Lanka. Avenues to Antiquity* (Beruwala, 1986).

546 Goor, J. van, 'Protestantism and Other Religions under the Dutch in Sri Lanka', in E.C.T. Candappa and M.S.S. Fernandopulle (eds), *Don Peter Felicitation Volume. Tribute to a Sri Lankan Scholar, Educator and Historian on his Sixty-fifth Birthday* (Colombo, 1983).

547 Goor, J. van, 'De V.O.C. op Ceylon', in R. Kromhout (ed.), *Het Machtige Eyland. Ceylon en de V.O.C.* (The Hague, 1988).

548 Graaf, H.J. de, 'De laatste Nederlandse Residenten te Tuticorin', *Verslagen en Aanwinsten* (Stichting Cultuurgeschiedenis van de Nederlanders Overzee) (1972-3).

549 'Grafzerken van Nederlandsche goeverneurs van Ceylon, te Colombo', *De Wapenheraut*, 11 (1907).

550 Gratiaen, L.J., 'Colombo in the 17th Century', *Ceylon Antiquary and Literary Register*, 8, 4 (1923).

551 Grenier, G.V., 'Early Colonisation - and Later Developments', *Journal of the Dutch Burgher Union of Ceylon*, 50, 3-4 (1960); reprint, *Ceylon Fortnightly Review*, 13, 22 (1961).

552 Grenier, G.V., 'Seven Tragic Months, when Portuguese Colombo was Besieged by the Dutch', *Journal of the Dutch Burgher Union of Ceylon*, 52, 1-2 (1962).

553 Grenier, G.V., '"Burgher" Etymology and Some Relevant Reflections', *Journal of the Dutch Burgher Union of Ceylon*, 16, 1-4 (1966).

554 Gunawardhena, D.C., 'Medical and Economic Plants of the Museum Zeylanicum of Paul Hermann', *Journal of the Royal Asiatic Society of Sri Lanka*, new series, 19 (1975).

555 Hardy, Ch.F., 'Dutch Tobacco Boxes and the Calendar', *Ceylon Antiquary and Literary Register*, 4, 4 (1919).

556 Haubourdin, R.M., 'Landmeters in dienst van de Verenigde Oostindische Compagnie (Batavia, Ceylon en de Kaap), 1691-1791', in E. Muller and K. Zandvliet (eds), *Admissies als landmeters in Nederland voor 1811* (Alphen aan den Rijn, 1987).

557 Haughton, S., 'The San Pedro Round Tower in Mannar Island', *Ceylon Antiquary and Literary Register*, 5, 1 (1919).

558 Hazelhoff Roelfzema, H., 'De vestingwerken van de V.O.C.', in R. Kromhout (ed.), *Het Machtige Eyland. Ceylon en de V.O.C.* (The Hague, 1988).

559 Heniger, J., 'Botanisch onderzoek op Ceylon in de V.O.C.-tijd', in R. Kromhout (ed.), *Het Machtige Eyland. Ceylon en de V.O.C.* (The Hague, 1988).

560 Hesseling, D.C., 'Remnants of the Dutch in Ceylon', in idem, *On the Origin and Formation of Creoles. A Miscellany of Articles*, ed. and trans. T.L. Markey and P.T. Roberge (Ann Arbor, 1979).

561 Horst, M.H.J. van den, *Compensation for Improvement. The Roman Dutch Law in Sri Lanka* (Amsterdam, 1989).

562 Horst, M.H.J. van den, and L. Hovy, 'Recht en rechtspraak', in R. Kromhout (ed.), *Het Machtige Eyland. Ceylon en de V.O.C.* (The Hague, 1988).

563 'In the days of the Dutch in Ceylon', *Ceylon Observer Annual* (1934) [concerning the water colours of C. Steiger].

564 'Index to the Legislative Acts of the Dutch Government of the Island of Ceylon', in *A Collection of Legislative Acts of the Ceylon Government from 1796-1851*, 2 vols (Colombo, 1853-4).

565 Jayasena, R.M., 'Katuwana. Archeologisch onderzoek van een VOC-fort in Sri Lanka', in M.H. Bartels, E.H.P. Cordfunke and H. Sarfatij (eds), *Hollanders uit en thuis. Archeologie, geschiedenis en bouwhistorie*

gedurende de VOC-tijd in de Oost, de West en thuis. Cultuurhistorie van de Nederlandse expansie (Hilversum, 2002).

566 Jayawardene, A., *The Roman-Dutch Law, as it Prevails in Ceylon. How Much of it is Applicable, and in what Localities?* (Colombo, 1901).

567 Jongens, E., 'Nederlands museum in Colombo', *Verslagen en Aanwinsten* (Stichting Cultuurgeschiedenis van de Nederlanders Overzee) (1976-7).

568 Jongens, E., 'Gebouwen uit de Nederlandse tijd in Sri Lanka', *Verslagen en Aanwinsten* (Stichting Cultuurgeschiedenis van de Nederlanders Overzee) (1980-1).

569 Jongens, E., 'De Nederlandse erfenis op Sri Lanka', in R. Kromhout (ed.), *Het Machtige Eyland. Ceylon en de V.O.C.* (The Hague, 1988).

570 Jongens, E., *Het Nederlands-Ceylonese erfgoed. Vierhonderd jaar betrekkingen tussen Nederland en Ceylon/Sri Lanka* (The Hague, 2002).

571 Joseph, S.P., 'Katuwana Fort', *Journal of the Dutch Burgher Union of Ceylon*, 23, 1 (1933).

572 Jurriaanse, M.W., 'Empty Tummies. The Ceylon Elephant in Dutch Times', *Loris, a Journal of Ceylon Wild Life* (1940).

573 Jurriaanse, M.W., 'The Story of Francina van Reede', *Journal of the Dutch Burgher Union of Ceylon*, 32, 1, 3 (1942-3) [concerning an inscription at Trincomalee].

574 Jurriaanse, M.W., 'The Compilation of the Customary Law of Jaffna (Thesawalamai in 1707)', *Bijdragen tot de Taal-, Land- en Volkenkunde van Nederlandsch-Indië*, 110 (1954).

575 K.V.S., 'Lapidarium Zeylonicum, Being a Collection of Monumental Inscriptions of the Dutch Churches of Ceylon ...', *De Navorscher*, 32 (1882).

576 Kalff, S., 'Nederlanders te Colombo', *De Navorscher*, 58 (1909).

577 Kan, J. van, 'The Government Archives, Colombo', *Journal of the Dutch Burgher Union of Ceylon*, 21, 4 (1932) [trans. of the section on Ceylon in Van Kan's *Compagnies bescheiden en aanverwante archivalia in Britsch-Indië en op Ceylon*, see *Dutch Sources on South Asia*, Vol. 1, Bibliography, no. 75].

578 Kanapathypillai, V., 'Dutch Rule in Maritime Ceylon, 1766-1796' (Unpublished PhD thesis, University of London, 1969).

579 Kanapathypillai, V., 'Helen or Costly Bride. The VOC and the Cinnamon Trade of Sri Lanka 1766-1796', reprint in C.R. de Silva and S. Kiribamune (eds), *K W Goonewardena Felicitation Volume* (Peradeniya, 1989) [see *Dutch Sources on South Asia*, Vol. 1, Bibliography, no. 583].

580 Kekulawala, S.L., 'Some Linguistic Features of the Eighteenth Century Sinhala Placaaten of the Dutch. A Preliminary Survey', in K.S. Diehl (ed.), *Historical Essays. Primary Printed and Manuscript Sources for Sixteenth to Nineteenth Century Available in Sri Lanka* (Colombo, 1976).

581 Keuneman, A.E., 'The Judiciary - Past and Present', *Journal of the Dutch Burgher Union of Ceylon*, 38, 1 (1948).

582 Keuneman, H., 'At the End of the Road', *Ceylon Observer Pictorial* (1952).

583 Keuneman, H., 'The Forts of Ceylon', *Times of Ceylon Annual* (1967).

584 Kleyn, A.R., 'Gouverneur-Generaal Von Imhoff', *Sibbe. Maandblad van het Nederlandsch Verbond voor Sibbekunde*, 3, 6 (1943).

585 Knaap, G.J., 'Coffee for Cash. The Dutch East India Company and the Expansion of Coffee Cultivation in Java, Ambon and Ceylon 1700-1730' in J. van Goor (ed.), *Trading Companies in Asia 1600-1830* (Utrecht, 1986).

586 Koppius, W.J., 'Wat Nederland aan Ceilon heeft verloren', *De Indische gids*, 57-8 (1935-6).

587 Kotelawele, D.A., 'The Dutch in Ceylon 1743-1766' (Unpublished PhD thesis, University of London, 1968).

588 Kotelawele, D.A., 'Value of the Proclamations (Placaaten) Issued by the Dutch Government of Ceylon [for the] History of the 17th and 18th Centuries. Some Preliminary Observations', in K.S. Diehl (ed.), *Historical Essays. Primary Printed and Manuscript Sources for Sixteenth to Nineteenth Century Available in Sri Lanka* (Colombo, 1976).

589 Kotelawele, D.A., 'Some Notes on the Dutch Interest in Native Medicine in Sri Lanka', *Journal of the Netherlands Alumni Association of Sri Lanka* (1982).

590 Kotelawele, D.A., 'Muslims under Dutch Rule in Sri Lanka, 1638-1796', in M.A.M. Shukri (ed.), *Muslims of Sri Lanka. Avenues to Antiquity* (Beruwala, 1986).

591 Kotelawele, D.A., 'Some Aspects of Social Change in the South West of Sri Lanka, *c.* 1700-1833', *Social Science Review*, 4 (1988).

592 Kotelawele, D.A., 'The VOC in Sri Lanka 1688-1766. Problems and Policies', in K.M. de Silva (ed.), *History of Sri Lanka* (University of Peradeniya), Vol. 2 (*c.* 1500 to *c.* 1800) (Peradeniya, 1995).

593 Kotelawele, D.A., 'The VOC in Sri Lanka, 1658-1796. Social and Economic Change in the Maritime Regions', in K.M. de Silva (ed.), *History of Sri Lanka* (University of Peradeniya), Vol. 2 (*c.* 1500 to *c.* 1800) (Peradeniya, 1995).

594 Kuiper, F.B.J., 'Dutch Students of Tamil', *Proceedings of the First International Conference Seminar of Tamil Studies*, Vol. 2 (Kuala Lumpur, 1969).

595 Kuruppu, I. and G. Wijesuriya, 'The Conservation of the Galle Fort and its Environs', *Ancient Ceylon. Journal of the Department of Archaeology, Sri Lanka*, 15 (1992).

596 Kuruppu, S.B., 'A Dutch Inscription on a Medal', *Ceylon Literary Register*, 2, 25 (1888).

597 Lee, G.W., 'Ceylon Archives at the Cape of Good Hope', *Journal of the Royal Asiatic Society, Ceylon Branch*, 22, 65 (1912).

598 Leembruggen, H.U., 'The Dutch Reformed Church in Ceylon 1642-1796 and after', *Journal of the Dutch Burgher Union of Ceylon*, 32, 2 (1942).

599 Leupe, P.A., 'Cornelis Houtman's tweede reis naar Indië, 1598', *Bijdragen tot de Taal-, Land- en Volkenkunde van Nederlandsch-Indië*, 28 (4) (1880).

600 Lewis, J.P., 'Dutch Rule in Ceylon', *Ceylon Literary Register*, 2-3 (1888-9); reprint *Ceylon Literary Register*, 3rd series, 4 (1935).

601 Lewis, J.P., 'Old Matara', *Ceylon Literary Register*, 3, 38-9, 41 (1889).

602 Lewis, J.P., 'Dutch Inscriptions - Negombo', *Ceylon Literary Register*, 3, 44 (1889).

603 Lewis, J.P., 'Old Negombo', *Ceylon Literary Register*, 4, 3-8 (1889).

604 Lewis, J.P., 'Dutch Memorial Stone', *Proceedings of the Journal of the Royal Asiatic Society (Ceylon Branch)* (1889-90) [concerning Negombo].

605 Lewis, J.P., 'Calpentyn Inscriptions', *Monthly Literary Register and Notes and Queries for Ceylon*, 4, 12 (1896).

606 Lewis, J.P., 'The Dutch Church at Jaffna', *Journal of the Dutch Burgher Union of Ceylon*, 2, 3 (1909).

607 Lewis, J.P., 'Dutch Extracts and the Dutch Method of Transliterating Sinhalese', *Journal of the Dutch Burgher Union of Ceylon*, 2 (1909).

608 Lewis, J.P., 'Forged Dutch Extracts in the Matara District', *Journal of the Dutch Burgher Union of Ceylon*, 2 (1909).

609 Lewis, J.P., 'Dutch Furniture in Ceylon', *Times of Ceylon Christmas Number* (1911).

610 Lewis, J.P., *List of Inscriptions on Tombstones and Monuments in Ceylon* (Colombo, 1913); reprint (New Delhi, 1994).

611 Lewis, J.P., 'Some Old Dutch Colonial Furniture', *Connoisseur*, 37, 146 (1913).

612 Lewis, J.P., 'Dutch Tobacco Boxes in Ceylon', *Times of Ceylon Christmas Number* (1916).

613 Lewis, J.P., 'The Portuguese-Dutch Churches of Jaffna', *Ceylon Antiquary and Literary Register*, 2, 1, 3 (1916-17).

614 Lewis, J.P., 'A Mysterious Dutch Tobacco Box', *Times of Ceylon Christmas Number* (1917).

615 Lewis, J.P., 'Dutch Tobacco Boxes', *Ceylon Antiquary and Literary Register*, 5, 3 (1920).

616 Lewis, J.P., 'The Old Forts and Military Posts of Ceylon', in P.M. Bingham (ed.), *History of the Public Works Department, Ceylon, 1796-1896*, Vol. 2 (n.p., 1922).

617 Lewis, J.P., 'Slavery Traffic under the Dutch East India Company', *Ceylon Antiquary and Literary Register*, 9, 2 (1923).

618 Lewis, J.P., and R.G. Anthonisz, 'Tombstones in the Cemetery of the Parish of Colpetty', *Journal of the Dutch Burgher Union of Ceylon*, 6, 1 (1913).

619 Liefkes, F., 'Twee schrijfcassettes uit Ceylon', *Verslagen en Aanwinsten* (Stichting Cultuurgeschiedenis van de Nederlanders Overzee) (1972-3).

620 Liefkes, F., 'Een houten juwelenkistje', *Verslagen en Aanwinsten* (Stichting Cultuurgeschiedenis van de Nederlanders Overzee) (1974-5).

621 Lingen, J., 'Muntslag op Ceylon', in R. Kromhout (ed.), *Het Machtige Eyland. Ceylon en de V.O.C.* (The Hague, 1988).

622 'List of Books Translated and Published under the Dutch Government for

Promoting Christian Knowledge among the Heathens', *Ceylon Magazine*, 1, 3 (1840).

623 'Lives of the Dutch Governors-General of Netherlands India: Jean Maatzuiker (Ex-Governor of Ceylon)', *Ceylon Literary Register*, 1, 21 (1886).

624 Lorenz, Ch.A., 'Dutchmen and the Dutch Church', *Young Ceylon*, 1, 2 (1850).

625 Lourteigh, A., 'l'Herbier de Paul Hermann, base du Thesuarus Zeylanicus de Johan Burman', *Taxon*, 15 (1966).

626 M.H.S., 'Watering Point, Galle', *Aloysian*, 3, 3 (1930).

627 Mahroof, M.M.M., 'Islamic Law in a Roman-Dutch Law / English Law Environment of Sri Lanka', *Journal of the Pakistan Historical Society*, 44, 2 (1996).

628 Marshall, Ch., 'Law Courts in Ceylon in the Time of the Dutch', *Ceylon Literary Register*, 1, 16 (1886).

629 Marshall, Ch., 'Dutch Law Courts in Ceylon', *Ceylon Law Students Magazine*, 1, 4 (1927).

630 McGilvray, D.B., 'Dutch Burghers and Portuguese Mechanics. Eurasian Ethnicity in Sri Lanka', *Comparative Studies in Society and History*, 24 (1982).

631 McMurtrie, D.C., *Memorandum of the First Printing in Ceylon* (Chicago, 1931).

632 Mendis, G.C., 'The Importance of Dutch Rule in Ceylon', *Journal of the Dutch Burgher Union of Ceylon*, 45, 4 (1955).

633 Meuron, G. de, *Le Régiment Meuron, 1781-1816* (Lausanne, 1982).

634 'Monumental Inscription of Francina van Rheede', *Ceylon Literary Register*, 1, 14 (1886) [at Trincomalee?].

635 'The Moravian Mission in Ceylon (in the Eighteenth Century)', *Ceylon Literary Register*, 1, 10 (1886).

636 'Moravian Mission to Ceylon in 1740', *Colombo Religious and Theological Magazine*, 1, 2-4 (1833).

637 Moss, A.S., 'Valentyn's Account of Adam's Peak', *Journal of the Ceylon Branch of the Royal Asiatic Society*, 7, 23 (1881).

638 Mottau, S.A.W., 'Governor Van Imhoff and his Scheme of Inland River Communication in the Colombo *Disavany*', *University of Ceylon Review*, 5, 1 (1947).

639 Mottau, S.A.W., 'The Memoirs of the Dutch Governors', *Journal of the Dutch Burgher Union of Ceylon*, 52, 1-2 (1962).

640 Mottau, S.A.W., 'Archival Collections for Studies of the Dutch in Ceylon', in *Historical Essays* (Colombo, 1976) [see *Dutch Sources on South Asia*, Vol. 1, Bibliography, no. 617].

641 Nadaraja, T., 'New Light on Cleghorn's Minute on Justice and Revenue', *Journal of the Ceylon Branch of the Royal Asiatic Society*, new series, 10 (1966).

642 Nadaraja, T., 'The Administration of Justice in Ceylon under the Dutch

Government, 1656-1796 (Cleghron's Minute)', *Journal of the Ceylon Branch of the Royal Asiatic Society*, new series, 12 (1968); re-edition in R.L. Brohier (ed.), *Links between Sri Lanka and the Netherlands. A Book of Dutch Ceylon* (n.p. [Colombo], 1978) [see *Dutch Sources on South Asia*, Vol. 1, Bibliography, nos 531, 620].

643 Nell, A., 'Colombo Fort in A.D. 1757', *Ceylon Literary Register*, 3rd series, 1 (1931).

644 Nell, L., 'An Explanatory List of Dutch Words Adopted by the Sinhalese', *Orientalist*, 3 (1888-9).

645 '"Nossa Senhora dos Milagres". The Fort of Jaffna', *Times of Ceylon Christmas Number* (1927).

646 'An Old Dutch Burial Ground', *Ceylon Review*, new series, 1, 1-2 (1895).

647 'Old Dutch Copper Coins', *Journal of the Dutch Burgher Union of Ceylon*, 1, 4 (1908), 20, 3 (1931).

648 'Onbekende wapens', *Sibbe. Maandblad van het Nederlandsch Verbond voor Sibbekunde*, 3 (1943).

649 'The Origin of the Ceylon Elephant Establishment (under the Dutch)', *Ceylon Literary Register*, 6, 18 (1891).

650 Oostroom, S.J. van, 'Hermann's Collection of Ceylon Plants in the Rijksherbarium (National Herbarium) at Leyden', *Blumea*, Supplement 1 (J.J. Smith Jubilee Vol.) (1937).

651 Paesie, R., *Het VOC-retourschip Ravesteyn. De laatste reis van een Zeeuwse Oostindiëvaarder* (Amsterdam, 1999) [pertaining to the Maldives].

652 Palm, J.D., 'The Education Establishments of the Dutch in Ceylon', *Journal of the Royal Asiatic Society, Ceylon Branch*, 1, 2 (1846-7); reprint, *Journal of the Dutch Burgher Union of Ceylon*, 28, 4, 29, 1-2 (1939) [see *Dutch Sources on South Asia*, Vol. 1, Bibliography, no. 628].

653 Palm, J.D., 'An Account of the Dutch Church in Ceylon, Collected from the Local Records Deposited in the Wolfendahl Church, Colombo', *Journal of the Royal Asiatic Society, Ceylon Branch*, 1, 2-3 (1846-8) [see *Dutch Sources on South Asia*, Vol. 1, Bibliography, no. 629].

654 Paranavitana, K.D., *Land for Money. Dutch Land Registration in Sri Lanka* (Colombo, 2001).

655 Paranavitana, K.D., and R.K. de Silva, *Maps and Plans of Dutch Ceylon. A Representative Collection of Cartography from the Dutch Period* (Colombo, 2002).

656 Parthesius, R., 'Het wrak van het VOC-schip *Avondster* in de haven van Galle (Sri Lanka). Een potentiële bron van kennis over de Europese expansie in Azië', in M.H. Bartels, E.H.P. Cordfunke and H. Sarfatij (eds), *Hollanders uit en thuis. Archeologie, geschiedenis en bouwhistorie gedurende de VOC-tijd in de Oost, de West en thuis. Cultuurhistorie van de Nederlandse expansie* (Hilversum, 2002).

657 Paulusz, J.H.O., 'A Dutch Doctor at Kandy in 1739', *Journal of the Dutch Burgher Union of Ceylon*, 20, 4 (1931).

658 Paulusz, J.H.O., 'Prince Crumpty-Pippit and Governor Van Eck', *Journal of the Dutch Burgher Union of Ceylon*, 21, 2 (1931).

659 Paulusz, J.H.O., 'History of the Ceylon Government Archives', *Journal of the Royal Asiatic Society, Ceylon Branch*, 36, 97 (1944).

660 Paulusz, J.H.O., 'Pieter van Dam's Account of Ceylon, 1701', *Journal of the Royal Asiatic Society, Ceylon Branch*, 37, 101 (1946).

661 Paulusz, J.H.O., 'The Rebellion of 1665 against Rajasinha', *Journal of the Royal Asiatic Society, Ceylon Branch*, new series, 7, 2 (1961) [see *Dutch Sources on South Asia*, Vol. 1, Bibliography, no. 638].

662 Peacock, O., 'The Burghers of Sri-Lanka during Dutch and British Regime. A Socio-Economic-Political Profile', *South Asian Studies*, 19, 2 (1984).

663 Pearson, J., 'Dutch Furniture', *Transactions of the Engineering Association of Ceylon* (1930).

664 Peeters, L., and P.B. Sannasgala, 'Dutch Loan Words in Sinhala', *Spektator. Tijdschrift voor Neerlandistiek*, 5, 4 (1976).

665 Peiris, E., 'Sinhalese Christian Literature of the 17th and 18th Centuries', *Journal of the Ceylon Branch of the Royal Asiatic Society*, 35, 96 (1943).

666 Peiris, E., 'Paul Hermann, the Father of Ceylon Botany', *Journal of the Ceylon Branch of the Royal Asiatic Society*, new series, 2, 1 (1952).

667 Perera, J.A., 'Services Rendered to the Vereenigde Oost-Indische Compagnie by Castes and Classes in the Southern Province', *Young Ceylon*, 3, 10-11 (1935); reprint, 'In the Days of the Dutch. Caste, Land Tenure, Customs and Other Services in Matara District', *Ceylon Fortnightly Review*, 1, 10, 14 (1948).

668 Perera, S.G., 'French Expeditions against Trincomalee. 1, The French versus the Dutch, 1761', *Ceylon Antiquary and Literary Register*, 5, 3 (1920).

669 Perera, S.G., 'An Embassy to the Court of Kandy in 1736', *Aloysian*, 3, 1 (1928).

670 Perera, S.G., 'The Zwart Fort, Galle', *Ceylon Causerie*, 2, 7 (1930); reprint, *Ceylon Fortnightly Review*, 1, 2 (1948).

671 Perera, S.G., 'Michael de St. Amand', *Ceylon Literary Register*, 2, 1 (1932).

672 Perera, S.G., 'Ceylon Documents at The Hague', *Ceylon Literary Register*, 2, 12 (1932).

673 Perera, S.G., 'Ceylon Documents at The Hague—A Latin S.O.S. from Kandy, 1765', *Ceylon Literary Register*, 3, 2 (1933).

674 Perera, S.G., 'Narendrasinha, the Dutch and a Catholic Priest, 1734', *Ceylon Literary Register*, 3rd series, 4 (1935-6).

675 Perniola, V., *The Catholic Church in Sri Lanka. The Dutch Period*, 3 vols (Dehiwala, 1983-5) [see *Dutch Sources on South Asia*, Vol. 1, Bibliography, no. 645].

676 'Philip Baldaeus Found Out', *Ceylon Literary Register*, 3, 7 (1934).

677 Pieris, P.E., 'Notes on a Dutch Medal', *Journal of the Ceylon Branch of the Royal Asiatic Society*, 18, 54 (1903), 22, 65 (1912).

678 Pieris, P.E., 'Inscriptions at St. Thomas's Church, Colombo', *Journal of the Ceylon Branch of the Royal Asiatic Society*, 22, 65 (1912).

679 Pieris, P.E., 'A Dutch Gold-Medal', *Spolia Zeylanica. Bulletin of the National Museums of Ceylon*, 8, 30 (1912).

680 Pieris, P.E., 'Some Dutch Medals', *Spolia Zeylanica. Bulletin of the National Museums of Ceylon*, 8, 32 (1913).

681 Pieris, P.E., 'The "Madura Dynasty"', *Journal of the Ceylon Branch of the Royal Asiatic Society (Notes and Queries)*, 26 (1917).

682 Pieris, P.E., 'A Gift from Van der Parra', *Journal of the Ceylon Branch of the Royal Asiatic Society (Notes and Queries)*, 28 (1921).

683 Pieris, P.E., 'A Dutch House for Ceylon', *Journal of the Ceylon Branch of the Royal Asiatic Society*, 35 (1940).

684 Pieris, P.E., 'A Report on Buddhism in Siam A.C. 1689 (Tr. from the Sinhalese, Notes by Sir Josiah Crosby', *Journal of the Ceylon Branch of the Royal Asiatic Society*, 36 (1945).

685 Pieris, P.E., 'The Dutch Embassy to Kandy in 1731-32 Translated from the Sinhalese', reprint in *Sir Paul E. Pieris' Selected Writings* (New Delhi, 1995) [see *Dutch Sources on South Asia*, Vol. 1, Bibliography, no. 646].

686 Pieris, P.E., *Ceylon and the Hollanders, 1658-1796*, reprint (New Delhi and Madras, 1999) [see *Dutch Sources on South Asia*, Vol. 1, Bibliography, no. 648].

687 Pieris, R. (ed.), 'Administration of Justice and Revenue on the Island of Ceylon under the Dutch Government ("The Cleghorn's Minute")', *Journal of the Ceylon Branch of the Royal Asiatic Society*, new series, 3, 2 (1953).

688 Ploeger, J., 'Ceilon tydens die V.O.C.-tydperk en daarna', *Simon van der Stel Foundation, Bulletin*, 6 (1963).

689 Pott, P.H., 'Een Sirih-kistje met ivoor- en zilverbeslag', *Verslagen en Aanwinsten* (Stichting Cultuurgeschiedenis van de Nederlanders Overzee) (1970-1).

690 Puype, J.P., 'Oorlogvoering op Ceylon in de V.O.C.-tijd', in R. Kromhout (ed.), *Het Machtige Eyland. Ceylon en de V.O.C.* (The Hague, 1988).

691 R.E.H., 'Nederlanders op Ceylon begraven', *Algemeen Nederlandsch Familieblad*, 7 (1890).

692 Raat, A.J.P., 'Joan Gideon Loten (1710-1789) en zijn collectie aquarellen van planten en dieren uit Ceylon', in R. Kromhout (ed.), *Het Machtige Eyland. Ceylon en de V.O.C.* (The Hague, 1988).

693 Raben, R., 'Trade and Urbanization. Portuguese and Dutch Urban Attitudes in Ceylon. Colombo: Mirror of the Colonial Mind', *Mare Liberum*, 13 (1997).

694 Raheem, I., 'Dutch Colonial Period Architecture in Sri Lanka and its Heritage', in R. Kromhout (ed.), *Het Machtige Eyland. Ceylon en de V.O.C.* (The Hague, 1988).

695 Raven-Hart, R., *Ceylon 200 Years Ago* (n.p., 1952).

696 Raven-Hart, R., 'Notes on Hermannus', *Journal of the Royal Asiatic Society, Ceylon Branch*, new series, 2, 2 (1952) [hospital inspector].

697 Raven-Hart, R., 'The Great Road [Parts 1-2]', *Journal of the Royal Asiatic Society, Ceylon Branch*, new series, 4, 2 (1955), 8, 1 (1962) [pertaining to Dutch missions to Kandy].

698 Raven-Hart, R., 'Once upon a Time', *Ceylon Observer Pictorial* (1955) [concerning Dutch forts].

699 Raven-Hart, R., 'Kandy - in a Flashback', *Times of Ceylon Annual* (1957) [pertaining to the mission of Daniel Agreen to Kandy in 1736].

700 Raven-Hart, R., 'With Van Eck to Kandy (in 1764)', *Times of Ceylon Annual* (1958).

701 Raven-Hart, R., 'Mr. Pybus Goes to Kandy (in 1762)', *Times of Ceylon Annual* (1962).

702 Raven-Hart, R., *Ceylon, History in Stone* (Colombo, 1964).

703 Raven-Hart, R., 'Wolf's "Journey to Ceylon (1756-95)"', *Africa Notes and News* (1968).

704 Reimers, E., 'The Burghers of Ceylon', *Journal of the Dutch Burgher Union of Ceylon*, 13, 1-2 (1921).

705 Reimers, E., 'Old Dutch Panel', *Journal of the Royal Asiatic Society, Ceylon Branch*, 28, 74 (1921) [concerning Colombo harbour].

706 Reimers, E., 'The Coming of the Dutch', in *Ceylon. Its History, People ...* (n.p., 1924); reprints, *Outdoor Life* (1929, 1933) [see *Dutch Sources on South Asia*, Vol. 1, Bibliography, no. 663].

707 Reimers, E., 'Watering Point, Galle', *Aloysian*, 2, 4 (1925).

708 Reimers, E., 'Old Matara and the Rebellion of 1760-61', *Journal of the Dutch Burgher Union of Ceylon*, 15, 1-3 (1925-6).

709 Reimers, E., 'How the Dutch Captured Colombo', *Ceylon Observer Christmas Number* (1929).

710 Reimers, E., 'Krediet-brieven and Kas-briefjes', *Journal of the Dutch Burgher Union of Ceylon*, 20, 1 (1930).

711 Reimers, E., 'Van Imhoff's Tour in the Matara District', *Ceylon Literary Register*, 1, 1-2 (1931).

712 Reimers, E., 'Early Dutch Views of Ceylon. Photographs Taken in the Rijks-Museum at Amsterdam of Water-Colours Painted in Ceylon about 1710', *Times of Ceylon Christmas Number* (1936) [concerning C. Steiger].

713 Reimers, E., 'Colonial Dutch Furniture', *Journal of the Royal Asiatic Society, Ceylon Branch*, 34, 91 (1938).

714 Reimers, E., 'Kandy at War with the Dutch', *Times of Ceylon Annual* (1948).

715 Reimers, E., 'The Portuguese and Dutch in Ceylon. Military and Economic Penetration', in *Independent Ceylon. The First Year Feb. 4, 1948-Feb. 4, 1949* (Colombo, 1949).

716 Reimers, E., 'The Treaty of 1766 between the King of Kandy and the Dutch', *Ceylon Historical Journal*, 2, 1-4 (1952-3), 3, 2 (1953).

717 *Report on the Dutch Archives* (Colombo, 1938).

718 Rhede van der Kloot, M.A., 'Het wapen van Colombo op Ceylon', *De Navorscher*, 60 (1911).

719 Rhede van der Kloot, M.A., 'De wapens van Ternate en Colombo', *De Nederlandsche Leeuw*, 30 (1912).

720 Roberts, M., I. Raheem and P. Colin-Thomé, *People Inbetween. The Burghers and the Middle Class in the Transformations within Sri Lanka, 1790s-1960s* (Ratmalana, 1989).

721 Roncière, M. de la, 'Un document inédit de la V.O.C.. Une représentation cartographique de l'île de Ceylan, en 1666', in M. Mollat (ed.), *Sociétés et compagnies de commerce en Orient et dans l'Ocean Indien* (Actes de Huitième Colleque International d'Histoire Maritime) (Paris, 1970).

722 Ronkel, P.S. van, 'Verklaring der inheemsche termen in de beschrijving van het Ceilonsch volksrecht', *Bijdragen tot de Taal-, Land- en Volkenkunde van Nederlandsch-Indië*, 75 (1919).

723 Rooy, W.E.V. de, 'A Review of the Early History of the Union', *Journal of the Dutch Burgher Union of Ceylon*, 35, 3 (1946).

724 Ros, J.E., 'Testamenten Ceylon 1690-1787', *Gens Nostra. Maandblad der Nederlandse Genealogische Vereniging*, 57, 11 (2002).

725 Ros, J.E., 'Uittreksels uit de archieven van de VOC bewaard in het "National Archives of Sri Lanka"', *Gens Nostra. Maandblad der Nederlandse Genealogische Vereniging*, 57, 11 (2002).

726 Rott, N., 'Archivalia van de V.O.C. op Ceilon', *De Indische Gids*, 59 (1937).

727 Rott, N., 'Nederlandsche archivalia op Ceilon', *De Indische Gids*, 59 (1937).

728 Sansoni, B., 'Some Notes on Old Furniture', *Times of Ceylon Annual* (1962).

729 Schrikker, A., 'Een ongelijke strijd? De oorlog tussen de Verenigde Oost-Indische Compagnie en de koning van Kandy, 1760-1766', in G. Knaap and G. Teitler (eds), *De Verenigde Oost-Indische Compagnie tussen oorlog en diplomatie* (Verhandelingen van het Koninklijk Instituut voor Taal-, Land- en Volkenkunde, 197) (Leiden, 2002).

730 Schutte, G.J., 'Een hutje in den wijngaard. Gereformeerd Ceylon', in idem (ed.), *Het Indisch Sion. De Gereformeerde kerk onder de Verenigde Oost-Indische Compagnie* (Hilversum, 2002).

731 Scott, J., 'The Sampeturu Round Tower', *Ceylon Antiquary and Literary Register*, 5, 4 (1920).

732 Shaw, G., *The South Asia and Burma Retrospective Bibliography. Stage 1: 1556-1800* (London, 1987).

733 Silva, A.V. de, *The Dutch in Ceylon (Being a History of the Island in the Seventeenth and Eighteenth Centuries)* (Dehiwala, 1919).

734 Silva, C.R. de, 'Expulsion of the Portuguese from Sri Lanka', in K.M. de Silva (ed.), *History of Sri Lanka* (University of Peradeniya), Vol. 2 (*c.* 1500 to *c.* 1800) (Peradeniya, 1995).

735 Silva, G.P.S.H. de, 'The Indian Possessions of the Dutch Government

during the Dutch Period 1657-1796', *The Indian Archives*, 34, 2 (1985) [pertaining to the Fishery Coast].

736 Silva, M.U. de, 'Land Tenure, Caste System and Rajakariya under Foreign Rule. A Review of Change in Sri Lanka under Western Powers, 1592-1832', *Journal of the Royal Asiatic Society, Sri Lanka Branch*, 37 (1992-3).

737 'A Sinhalese Cannon in the Ryks Museum at Amsterdam', *Ceylon Literary Register*, 2, 1 (1932).

738 'A Slab Inscription from Colombo', *Epigraphical Notes*, 9 (1972).

739 Slatkes, L.J., 'Rembrandt's Elephant', *Simiolus. Netherlands Quarterly for the History of Art*, 11 (1980).

740 Somaratne, G.P.V., 'The History of the Sinhala Bible', *Journal of the Royal Asiatic Society of Sri Lanka*, new series, 34 (1991).

741 'Some Dutch Legislation', *Ceylon Review*, new series, 1, 11 (1896).

742 Srinivasachari, C.S., 'Dutch Intervention in the Southern Poligar Wars', *Proceedings of the Indian Historical Congress*, 7 (1944).

743 Stapelveld, E., 'Een brief van een 18e-eeuwse voorvader', *Gens Nostra. Maandblad der Nederlandse Genealogische Vereniging*, 57, 11 (2002) [pertaining to Johan Gerard van Angelbeek].

744 Steinmetz, C., 'Een koerier van Ceilon naar Amsterdam (1674)', *Historia*, 15 (1950).

745 Sueter, E.B.F., 'Dutch Inscription', *Journal of the Royal Asiatic Society, Ceylon Branch (Notes and Queries)*, 24, 6 (1916) [concerning Colombo].

746 Talens, J., 'Prestatie en tegenprestatie. Gouverneur Vuyst en de sociale relatie met Kandy (1726-1729)', *Aanzet*, 6, 3 (1987-8).

747 Tambiah, H.W., 'The Roman-Dutch Law in Ceylon', *Ceylon Law Society Review*, 13, 2 (1951).

748 Tambiah, H.W., 'The Roman-Dutch Text Books in the Library of the Courts in Ceylon during the Dutch Regime', *Ceylon Law College Review* (1960-1).

749 Tammita-Delgoda, S., 'The English East India Company and Sri Lanka 1760-1796', in K.M. de Silva (ed.), *History of Sri Lanka* (University of Peradeniya), Vol. 2 (*c.* 1500 to *c.* 1800) (Peradeniya, 1995).

750 Temminck Groll, C.L., 'De huidige toestand van de Nederlandse monumenten in Sri Lanka', *Bulletin KNOB [Koninklijke Nederlandse Oudheidkundige Bond]*, 94, 1 (1995).

751 Terwen-de Loos, J., 'Een Ceylonese wieg', *Bulletin van het Rijksmuseum*, 15, 4 (1967).

752 Thananjayarajasingham, S., *A Critical Study of a Seventeenth Century Tamil Document Relating to a Commercial Treaty* (Peradeniya, 1968) [concerning Ramnad].

753 Thananjayarajasingham, S., 'The Language of a Tamil Plakkaat of the Eighteenth Century', in *Proceedings of the First International Conference Seminar of Tamil Studies*, Vol. 2 (Kuala Lumpur, 1969); also in *University of Ceylon Review*, 23, 1-2 (1965).

754 Thananjayarajasingham, S., 'Some Dutch Loan-Words in the Jaffna Dialect of Tamil', in *Proceedings of the First International Conference Seminar of Tamil Studies*, Vol. 2 (Kuala Lumpur, 1969).

755 Thananjayarajasingham, S., 'A Descriptive Analysis of a Tamil Document of the Eighteenth Century', in *Proceedings of the Second International Conference Seminar of Tamil Studies*, Vol. 1 (Madras, 1971).

756 Thananjayarajasingham, S., 'A Tamil Biljet Relating to the Obligatory Services of Certain Subjects of the Dutch Government in Ceylon', in *Proceedings of the Second International Conference Seminar of Tamil Studies*, Vol. 2 (Madras, 1971).

757 Thananjayarajasingham, S., 'A Tamil Plakkaat Relating to Trade in Arecanuts under the Dutch in Ceylon', *Bijdragen tot de Taal-, Land- en Volkenkunde*, 128, 3 (1972).

758 Theophilus [C.M. Enriquez], 'Tombstones in Ceylon', *Times of Ceylon Christmas Number* (1928).

759 Toll, J. van, 'Ceylon's regeering onder de O.I.C.', *Sibbe. Maandblad van het Nederlandsch Verbond voor Sibbekunde*, 3, 6 (1943).

760 Toll, J. van, 'Sterkte van het Compagnie-personeel op Ceylon', *Sibbe. Maandblad van het Nederlandsch Verbond voor Sibbekunde*, 3, 6 (1943).

761 Toll, J. van, 'Lijst van geborenen op Ceylon en in 1823 op Java wonenden', *Sibbe. Maandblad van het Nederlandsch Verbond voor Sibbekunde*, 3, 6 (1943).

762 Toll, J. van, 'Ceylon in de Nederlandsche genealogische tijdschriften', *Sibbe. Maandblad van het Nederlandsch Verbond voor Sibbekunde*, 3, 8 (1943).

763 Toll, J. van, 'Notabelen te Ceylon in het jaar 1760', *Sibbe. Maandblad van het Nederlandsch Verbond voor Sibbekunde*, 3, 8 (1943).

764 Toussaint, J.R., 'The Dutch Connection with Batticaloa', *Journal of the Dutch Burgher Union of Ceylon*, 19, 2 (1929).

765 Toussaint, J.R., 'Batticaloa between 1766 and 1796', *Journal of the Dutch Burgher Union of Ceylon*, 20, 3 (1931).

766 Toussaint, J.R., 'Major Jan van der Laen', *Journal of the Dutch Burgher Union of Ceylon*, 20, 3 (1931).

767 Toussaint, J.R., 'Iman Willem Falck', *Ceylon Literary Register*, 1, 2 (1931).

768 Toussaint, J.R., 'Wolvendaal Church in Early Times', *Journal of the Dutch Burgher Union of Ceylon*, 28, 2 (1938).

769 Toussaint, J.R., 'The Burghers in Early British Times', *Journal of the Dutch Burgher Union of Ceylon*, 25, 2 (1935), 29 (1939).

770 Toussaint, J.R., 'John Christopher Wolf in Ceylon', *Journal of the Dutch Burgher Union of Ceylon*, 28, 4 (1939).

771 Toussaint, J.R., 'The Dutch Burghers of Ceylon', *Journal of the Dutch Burgher Union of Ceylon*, 29, 1 (1939).

772 Toussaint, J.R., 'Dutch Ladies who Lived in Ceylon', *Journal of the Dutch Burgher Union of Ceylon*, 29, 2 (1939).

773 Toussaint, J.R., 'Disuse of the Dutch Language in Ceylon', *Journal of the Dutch Burgher Union of Ceylon*, 32, 2 (1942).

774 Toussaint, J.R., 'Undeserved Criticisms of the Dutch in Ceylon', *Journal of the Dutch Burgher Union of Ceylon*, 33, 2-3 (1943-4).

775 Trimen, H., 'Hermann's Ceylon Herbarium and Linnaeus' "Flora Zeylanica"', *Journal of the Linnean Society, Botany*, 24 (1887).

776 Troostenburg de Bruyn, C.A.L. van, 'The Dutch Reformed Church in Ceylon, 1602-1795', trans. F.H. de Vos, *Journal of the Dutch Burgher Union of Ceylon*, 30, 1-4, 31, 1-2 (1940-1).

777 V., 'Old Dutch Tombstones at Galle', *Monthly Literary Register and Notes and Queries for Ceylon*, 1, 2 (1893).

778 Vanderstraaten, J.L., 'A Brief Sketch of the Medical History of Ceylon', *Journal of the Ceylon Branch of the Royal Asiatic Society*, 9, 32 (1886).

779 Veeger, L., 'Het verlies van Ceylon aan de Engelsen', in R. Kromhout (ed.), *Het Machtige Eyland. Ceylon en de V.O.C.* (The Hague, 1988).

780 Verkerk Pistorius, A.W.P., *Ceylon. Indische Volksbelangen* (The Hague, 1874).

781 Vermeulen, A.J.C., '"Op het tapijt gebragt". Ceylon en de kaartenmakers van de V.O.C.', in R. Kromhout (ed.), *Het Machtige Eyland. Ceylon en de V.O.C.* (The Hague, 1988).

782 Vink, M.P.M., 'Church and State in Seventeenth-Century Colonial Asia. Dutch-Parava Relations in Southeast India in Comparative Perspective', *Journal of Early Modern History*, 4, 1 (2000).

783 Vink, M.P.M., 'The Temporal and Spiritual Conquest of the Fishery Coast. The Portuguese-Dutch Struggle over the Parava Community of Southeast India, *c.* 1640-1700,' *Portuguese Studies Review*, 9, 1/2 (2001).

784 Vink, M.P.M., 'Between the Devil and the Deep Blue Sea. The Christian Paravas. A "Client Community" in Seventeenth-Century Southeast India', *Itinerario*, 26, 2 (2002).

785 Vogelaar, W.Th., 'Sprokkelhout. Nog een Nederlandsche familie van Ceylonschen oorsprong: het geslacht Vogelaar', *Sibbe. Maandblad van het Nederlandsch Verbond voor Sibbekunde*, 3, 8 (1943).

786 Vos, C.E., 'The Dutch Predikants of Ceylon', *Journal of the Dutch Burgher Union of Ceylon*, 5, 2, 4 (1912), 6, 2-4 (1913-14), 7, 1-4 (1914), 8, 1 (1915), 9, 1-3 (1916), 10, 1-2 (1917), 14, 3-4 (1925), 15, 1-2, 4 (1925-6), 16, 1 (1926) [see *Dutch Sources on South Asia*, Vol. 1, Bibliography, no. 688].

787 Vos, A. de, 'Dutch Period Museum, Prince Street, Pettah', *The Journal of the Netherlands Alumni Association of Sri Lanka* (1979).

788 Vos, A. de, and G. Wijesuriya, *Preservation of the Historic City Centre of Galle* (Colombo, 1986).

789 Vos, F.H. de, 'Galle. The Dutch Fort of Galle', *Ceylon Literary Register*, 2, 42-3 (1888).

790 Vos, F.H. de, 'Old Dutch Epitaphs', *Ceylon Literary Register*, 3, 47-8 (1889).

791 Vos, F.H. de, 'Genealogische en heraldische aanteekeningen aangaande Hollandsche familien te Ceylon', *De Navorscher*, 48-57 (1898-1908),

792 Vos, F.H. de, 'Genealogie van het geslacht De Vos (van Ceylon)', *De Navorscher*, 49 (1899).

793 Vos, F.H. de, 'Notes on a Dutch Medal', *Journal of the Ceylon Branch of the Royal Asiatic Society*, 18, 56 (1905).

794 Vos, F.H., 'Genealogien', *Journal of the Dutch Burgher Union of Ceylon*, 1, 2 (1908)-14, 1 (1924) [concerning the Van Ranzow, Roosmale and Cocq families].

795 Vos, F.H. de, *Genealogy of the Family De Vos of Ceylon* (Galle, 1911).

796 Vos, F.H. de, 'Sergeant', *Journal of the Ceylon Branch of the Royal Asiatic Society (Notes and Queries)*, 23 (1914).

797 Vos, F.H. de, 'Andreas Amabert—Claude Antoine's Coffier', *Ceylon Antiquary and Literary Register*, 2, 1 (1916).

798 Vos, F.H. de, 'Dutch Inscription in Galle Fort—Anthony Johannes', *Journal of the Royal Asiatic Society, Ceylon Branch (Notes and Queries)*, 24, 5 (1916).

799 Vos, F.H. de, 'Trekels', *Journal of the Royal Asiatic Society, Ceylon Branch (Notes and Queries)*, 24, 7 (1916).

800 Vos, F.H. de, 'Dutch Colonisation of the East', *Journal of the Dutch Burgher Union of Ceylon*, 12, 1-4 (1920).

801 Vos, F.H. de, 'The Dutch Origin of Some Familiar Sinhalese Names', *Journal of the Dutch Burgher Union of Ceylon*, 29, 2 (1939).

802 Vos, F.H. de, 'Begrafenisstoet van Robertus Cramer', *Sibbe. Maandblad van het Nederlandsch Verbond voor Sibbekunde*, 3, 8 (1943).

803 Vos tot Nederveen Cappel, H.A.E. de, 'De dienaren van de V.O.C. teelden in Ceylon vele kinderen bij Europese, Mestiesen, Castiesen, Toepassen, swarte, Bandanese, Maleise en Singalese vrouwen', *Gens Nostra*, 33 (1978).

804 Vroom, W.H., 'Jan Brandes, de Landraad te Colombo in 1785', *Bulletin van het Rijksmuseum*, 37, 3 (1989).

805 Wagenaar, L, 'Knielen of buigen? De gezantschappen van de Compagnie naar Kandy na het vredesverdrag van 1766', in C.A. Davids, W. Fritschy and L.A. van der Valk (eds), *Kapitaal, ondernemerschap en beleid. Studies over economie en politiek in Nederland, Europa en Azië van 1500 tot heden* (Amsterdam, 1996).

806 Wall, V.I. van de, *Het Hollandsche koloniale barokmeubel. Bijdrage tot de kennis van het ebbenhouten meubel omstreeks het midden der XVIIde en het begin der XVIIIde eeuw* (Antwerp and The Hague, 1939).

807 Wall, E.H. van der, 'The Dutch in Ceylon', *Journal of the Dutch Burgher Union of Ceylon*, 13, 1-2 (1921).

808 Wall, E.H. van der, 'The Dutch Cemetery at Matara', *Journal of the Dutch Burgher Union of Ceylon*, 22, 1 (1932).

809 Wall, E.H. van der, 'The Contribution of the Dutch to the Making of Ceylon', *Journal of the Dutch Burgher Union of Ceylon*, 22, 2 (1932); reprint (Colombo, 1932).

810 Wall, E.H. van der, 'Dutch Words in the Sinhalese Language', *Journal of the Dutch Burgher Union of Ceylon*, 22, 4 (1933).

811 Wall, E.H. van der, 'The Dutch Cemetery at Kalutara', *Journal of the Dutch Burgher Union of Ceylon*, 23, 2 (1933).

812 Wall, E.H. van der, 'Genealogies of Dutch Families', *Journal of the Dutch Burgher Union of Ceylon*, 23, 2 (1933)-25, 3 (1936) [concerning the Van der Wall and Spaar families].

813 Wall, E.H. van der, 'A Dutch Tombstone', *Journal of the Dutch Burgher Union of Ceylon*, 23, 4 (1934) [concerning Kalutara].

814 Wall, E.H. van der, 'The Gajanayakas of the Elephant Department (in Dutch Times)', *Journal of the Dutch Burgher Union of Ceylon*, 24, 3 (1935).

815 'Wapens in kerken', *De Navorscher*, 25 (1875) [pertaining to Galle].

816 Weaver, J.N., 'The Fort of Galle', *Aloysian*, 2, 2 (1923).

817 Weinman, A.N., 'The "Great Sins". A Proclamation by Governor Falck', *Journal of the Dutch Burgher Union of Ceylon*, 18, 4 (1929).

818 Weinman, A.N., 'Remains of Dutch Governors. The Torch Light Funeral Procession in 1813 on the Removal of the Remains of the Dutch Governors and Others from the Old Church on the Site of the Present Gordon Gardens to the Wolvendaal Church', *Journal of the Dutch Burgher Union of Ceylon*, 19, 5 (1930).

819 Wellmer, H., *The Underground Drainage System in the Fort of Galle* (Heidelberg, 1986).

820 White, H., 'Exports from Ceylon in 1688', *Ceylon Antiquary and Literary Register*, 3, 2 (1917).

821 Wickramasuriya, S., 'The Beginnings of the Sinhalese Printing Press', in L. Prematilleke, K. Indrapala and J.E. van Lohuizen-de Leeuw (eds), *Senarat Paranavitana Commemoration Volume* (Leiden, 1978).

822 Wijnmalen, Th.Ch.L., 'De drukpers te Colombo. Proeve eener Singaleese bibliographie', *Bibliographische Adversaria*, 4 (1879).

823 Wijnmalen, Th.Ch.L., 'The Printing Press at Colombo. A Tentative Ceylon Dutch Bibliography', *Ceylon Literary Register*, 2, 13 (1887).

824 Wille, G.A., 'The Dutch Reformed Church in Ceylon', *The Brighter Ceylon Annual* (1933).

825 Wolff, M.P., 'Meubels en kostelijk kleingoed', in R. Kromhout (ed.), *Het Machtige Eyland. Ceylon en de V.O.C.* (The Hague, 1988).

826 'The Wolvendal Dutch Church, Colombo', *Ceylon Literary Register*, 6, 12 (1891).

827 Woolf, B.S., 'Tulips and Palmyrahs', *Times of Ceylon Christmans Number* (1934) [pertaining to Jaffna].

828 Wttewaall van Wickerburgh, B.W., 'Uit de laatste dagen der Ned. Oost-Indische Compagnie', *Bijdragen tot de Taal-, Land- en Volkenkunde van Nederlandsch-Indië*, 34 (10) (1885).

829 Wynaendts van Resandt, W., 'Nederlandsche families op Ceylon', *Sibbe. Maandblad van het Nederlandsch Verbond voor Sibbekunde*, 3, 6 (1943).

830 X., 'The Ambalangoda Resthouse', *Ceylon Literary Register*, 2, 10 (1887) [concerning a Dutch inscription].

831 Young, J.D., 'Dutch Epitaphs', *Ceylon Literary Register*, 3, 49 (1889).
832 'De zilveren bruiloft', *Journal of the Dutch Burgher Union of Ceylon*, 2, 1 (1909) [concerning wedding medals].

5. COROMANDEL

5.1. Primary Sources

833 Hooyman, J., 'Kort verhaal van de Deensche zending op de Kust Chormandel', *Verhandelingen van het Bataviaasch Genootschap van Kunsten en Wetenschappen*, 2 (1780).
834 'Lijst der oude boeken van de voormalige Nederlandsche Oost-Indische Compagnie ter kuste Coromandel / List of Records of the Dutch East India Company Settlement on the Coromandel Coast 1702-1795', ed. J. van Kan, *Verhandelingen van het Koninklijk Bataviaasch Genootschap van Kunsten en Wetenschappen*, 71 (1932) [see *Dutch Sources on South Asia*, Vol. 1, Bibliography, no. 751].

5.2. Secondary Sources

835 Alam, M., and S. Subrahmanyam, 'Exploring the Hinterland. Trade and politics in the Arcot *Nizamat* (1700-1732)', modified edition by Subrahmanyam, 'Commerce, Politics and the Early Arcot State', in S. Subrahmanyam, *Penumbral Visions. Making Polities in Early Modern South India* (New Delhi, 2001) [see *Dutch Sources on South Asia*, Vol. 1, Bibliography, no. 721].
836 Arasaratnam, S., 'The Dutch East India Company and its Coromandel Trade 1700-1740', reprint in O. Prakash (ed.), *European Commercial Expansion in Early Modern Asia* (An Expanding World, 10) (Aldershot, 1997) [see *Dutch Sources on South Asia*, Vol. 1, Bibliography, no. 724].
837 Bhattacharya, B., 'Nagapatnam and the Commercial Revolution in the Bay of Bengal', in J. Parmentier and S. Spanoghe (eds), *Orbis in Orbem. Liber Amicorum John Everaert* (Gent, 2001).
838 B[loys] v[an] T[reslong] P[rins], [P.C.], 'Het graf van de echtgenote van den Gouverneur Generaal Jacob Mossel', *De Indische Navorscher*, 1 (1934-5).
839 Bos, P., 'Voor de VOC naar Batavia, Makassar en Negapatnam 1763-1783', *Gens Nostra. Maandblad der Nederlandse Genealogische Vereniging*, 57, 11 (2002).
840 Crucq, K.C., 'Begraafplaats te Pulicat', *De Indische Navorscher*, 5 (1939).
841 H. de V.v.d.S., 'Een grafschrift', *De Navorscher*, 58 (1909).
842 'Een Hollandsch graf aan de kust van Coromandel', *De Indische Navorscher*, 4 (1938).
843 Houte de Lange, C.E.G. ten, 'Ten tijde van de V.O.C., 17e eeuw. Pieter Adriaensz. de Lange in Voor-Indië (circa 1650-1656 en 1661-1667)', in idem, *Het Alkmaarse regentengeslacht De Lange* (Rotterdam and Zeist, 1996).

844 Kruijtzer, G., 'Madanna, Akkanna and the Brahmin Revolution. A Study of Mentality, Group Behaviour and Personality in Seventeenth-Century India', *Journal of the Economic and Social History of the Orient*, 45, 2 (2002).

845 Lingen, J., 'Paliakatten: VOC-ropijen van de Coromandelkust in India', *Beeldenaar*, 24, 2 (2000).

846 Nilakanta Sastri, K.A., 'Two Negapatam Grants from the Batavia Museum', reprint in *South India and South East Asia. Studies in their History and Culture* (Mysore, 1978) [see *Dutch Sources on South Asia*, Vol. 1, Bibliography, no. 755].

847 Nilakanta Sastri, K.A., 'Shivaji's Charter to the Dutch on the Coromandel Coast', *Proceedings of the Indian History Congress* (Calcutta, 1939).

848 Peters, M. and F. André de la Porte, *In steen geschreven. Leven en sterven van VOC-dienaren op de Kust van Coromandel in India* (Amsterdam, 2002).

849 Poonen, T.I., *Early History of the Dutch Factories of Masulipatam and Petapoli, 1605-1636* (n.p., 1937).

850 Rissink, W.G.F.C., 'Een zilveren gedachtenisbord met een tragische achtergrond', *Verslagen en Aanwinsten* (Stichting Cultuurgeschiedenis van de Nederlanders Overzee) (1968-9) [pertaining to Governor Johannes van Steelandt].

851 Son, H.J.A. van, *Geschiedenis en genealogie van het geslacht Van Son*, Part 3 (Vol. 2) (n.p, n.d. [Dordrecht, 1951]).

852 Stapel, F.W., 'Cornelis Janszoon Speelman', *Bijdragen tot de Taal-, Land- en Volkenkunde van Nederlandsch-Indië*, 94 (1936).

853 Subrahmanyam, S., 'The "Pulicat Enterprise". Luso-Dutch Conflict in South-Eastern India, 1610-1640', *South Asia*, new series, 9, 2 (1986); reprint in idem, *Improvising Empire. Portuguese Trade and Settlement in the Bay of Bengal 1500-1700* (Delhi, 1990).

854 Subrahmanyam, S., 'Persians, Pilgrims and Portuguese. The Travails of Masulipatnam Shipping in the Western Indian Ocean, 1590-1665', *Modern Asian Studies*, 22, 3 (1988).

855 Subrahmanyam, S., 'An Eastern *El-Dorado*. The Tirumala-Tirupati Temple-Complex in Early European Views and Ambitions, 1540-1660', in D. Shulman (ed.), *Syllables of Sky. Studies in South India Civilization in Honour of Velcheru Narayana Rao* (Delhi, 1995); modified edition, 'Of Pagodas and Politics. Tirupati as El-Dorado', in S. Subrahmanyam, *Penumbral Visions. Making Polities in Early Modern South India* (New Delhi, 2001).

856 Varadarajan, L., 'Golconda Cotton Dyeing and a Dutch Grant Dated A.D. 1720', *Itihas. Journal of the Andhra Pradesh State Archives*, 8, 2 (1980).

857 Wada, I., 'Oranda Higashi Indo Gaisha ni-yoru daiyamondo koeki. J.P. Coen no shokanshu wo chushin ni [= Dutch diamond trade in the 17th century. Mainly based on J.P. Coen's *Bescheiden*]', *The Shirin*, 81, 6 (1998).

6. BENGAL (including Bihar)

6.1. Primary Sources

858 *Defence de la Compagnie Unie, de Marchands d'Angleterre Commerçans aux Indes Orientales, et de ses employés (particulièrement de ceux au Bengale) contre les plaintes de la Compagnie Hollandoise des Indes Orientales ... / Verdeediging der O.I. Comp. van Engeland, en haarer bediendens, dien van Bengale byzonderlyk, tegens de klagten van de Hollandsche O.I. Comp. ...* (The Hague, 1762).

859 Francken, Jacob, *Rampspoedige reize van het O.I. schip de Naarstigheid, in de terugreize van Batavia over Bengale naar Holland ... waar in vervat is een korte beschryving der Bengaalsche kust, de tegenwoordige oorlog tusschen de Engelschen en Mooren ...* (Haarlem, 1761).

860 Lebeck, Heinrich Julius, 'Beschreibung eines langarmigen, ungeschwänzten Affen aus dem Inneren von Bengalen', *Der Naturforscher*, 28 (1799).

861 Vos, Jacobus Reinier, 'Begin, voortgang, toevallen en genezing der cholera morbus, zoo als zij zich, sedert het jaar 1817, in Bengalen vertoonde', *Verhandelingen van het Bataviaasch Genootschap van Kunsten en Wetenschappen*, 10 (1825).

6.2. Secondary Sources

862 Beames, J., 'Old Dutch Hatchments in Chinsurah Church', *Proceedings of the Asiatic Society of Bengal* (1883)

863 Chatterjee, N., 'Anglo-Dutch Disputes during Verelst's Administration in Bengal (1767-69)', *Proceedings of the Indian Historical Congress*, 3 (1939).

864 'Colonel Milles, Soldier of Fortune and the Ostend East India Company' [by Milles?], *Bengal: Past and Present*, 34 (1927).

865 Cotton, E., 'A Forgotten Sea-fight in the "Bengal River"', *Bengal: Past and Present*, 53 (1937).

866 Datta, K., 'Situation of the Dutch in Bengal, 1740-1756 A.D. (Part I, Early Relationships; Part II, Critical Months 1756-57; Part III, Alarums and Excursions after Plassy)', *Bengal: Past and Present*, 43-4 (1932).

867 Datta, K., 'The Dutch in Bengal after Bedara', *Indian Historical Quarterly*, 14 (1938).

868 Datta, K., 'The Ostend Company in Bengal', *Indian Historical Quarterly*, 16 (1940).

869 Datta, K., 'Capture of the Dutch Settlements in Bengal and Bihar 1781', *Journal of the Bihar and Orissa Research Society*, 27 (1941).

870 Datta, K., 'A Memorial of the Dutch to Warren Hastings and the Council in Calcutta', *Proceedings of the Indian Historical Records Commission*, 18 (1942).

871 Derozario, M., *The Complete Monumental Register: Containing all the Epitaphs, Inscriptions, &c. &c. &c. in the Different Churches and Burial-Grounds, in and about Calcutta* (Calcutta, 1815).

872 Gaastra, F.S., 'British Capital for the VOC in Bengal', in O. Prakash and D. Lombard (eds), *Commerce and Culture in the Bay of Bengal, 1500-1800* (New Delhi, 1999).

873 Gaastra, F.S., 'De VOC en EIC in Bengalen aan de vooravond van de Vierde Engelse Oorlog (1780-1784)', *Tijdschrift voor Zeegeschiedenis*, 20, 1 (2001).

874 Gaastra, F.S., *Particuliere geldstromen binnen het VOC-bedrijf 1640-1795* (Van Gelder-lezingen 1) (Leiden, 2002).

875 Gosselink, M., 'Schilderijen van Bengaalse VOC-loges door Hendrik van Schuylenburgh', *Bulletin van het Rijksmuseum*, 46, 4 (1998).

876 Heyning, E., *Een Hollandse familie overzee. Drie eeuwen belevenissen van de familie Heijning* (Delft, n.d. [*c.* 1995]).

877 Hobbs, H., 'Clive's Quarrel with the Dutch in 1759', *Bengal: Past and Present*, 50 (1935), 51 (1936).

878 'Een Hollandsch graf aan de kust van Coromandel [*sic*]', *De Indische Navorscher*, 4 (1938) [pertaining to Chhapra].

879 Jacob, H.K. s', 'Bedara Revisited. A Reappraisal of the Dutch Expedition of 1759 to Bengal', in J. Gommans and O. Prakash (eds), *Circumambulations in South Asian History. Essays in Honour of Dirk H.A. Kolff* (Leiden, 2003).

880 Kalff, S., 'Een Indisch portret in het Rijksmuseum', *Eigen Haard*, 50-2 (1897) [pertaining to Mattheus van den Broucke].

881 Kühne-van Diggelen, W., 'De wapenserviezen van Jan Albert Sichterman', *Vormen uit vuur*, 176, 3 (2001).

882 Lequin, F., *Isaac Titsingh (1745-1812). Een passie voor Japan. Leven en werk van de grondlegger van de Europese Japanologie* (Alphen aan den Rijn, 2002).

883 Lutter, A.A., and P.A. Christiaans, 'Vrijmetselaren in Bengalen', *De Indische Navorscher*, 7, 3 (1994).

884 Rookmaaker, L.C., 'Captive Rhinoceroses in Europe from 1500 until 1810', *Bijdragen tot de Dierkunde*, 43, 1 (1973).

885 Rookmaaker, L.C., 'De neushoorn van 1741', *Ons Amsterdam*, 30, 1 (1978).

886 Verheij, I., *Op reis met Clara. De Geschiedenis van een bezienswaardige neushoorn* (Rotterdam, 1992).

887 Wilson, C.R., 'Dutch Monumental Inscriptions', *Journal of the Asiatic Society of Bengal* (1904).

Author Index

Supplement II: Archival Guide to the National Archives

Nationaal Archief (formerly *Algemeen Rijksarchief*)

Prins Willem-Alexanderhof 20, The Hague / P.O. Box 90520, 2509 LM The Hague
Tel: 070-3315400 / 3315444, fax: 070-3315499
Internet: www.nationaalarchief.nl, e-mail: info@nationaalarchief.nl
visiting hours: Tuesday 9.00-21.00, Wednesday-Friday 9.00-17.00, Saturday 9.00-13.00

Note that as this guide went to press, the inventories of most archives and collections of the *Nationaal Archief* that pertain to the VOC were being made accessible on its web site or on www.tanap.net. These include the tables of contents of each volume of the *overgekomen brieven en papieren* series of both the Amsterdam and Zeeland Chambers of the Company. In addition, updated inventories of VOC materials kept at the National Archives of Sri Lanka at Colombo, the Tamil Nadu Archives at Chennai (Madras), the Arsip Nasional Republik Indonesia at Jakarta, the Cape Town Archives Repository and the British Library (Oriental and India Office Collections) at London were also being made available on the above-mentioned web sites.

1. *Verenigde Oostindische Compagnie*
Dutch East India Company

Access no.:	1.04.02
Inv. nos:	1-14933
Size:	*c.* 1270 metres
Period:	(1597) 1602-1811
Inventory:	M.A.P. Meilink-Roelofsz, *De archieven van de Verenigde Oostindische Compagnie / The Archives of the Dutch East India Company (1602-1795)* (The Hague, 1992), with introductions, appendices and indices

These are the archives of the VOC's board of directors (*Heeren XVII*, Gentlemen XVII) and its six offices (*kamers*, chambers) in the Dutch Republic, located in Amsterdam, Zeeland (Middelburg), Delft, Rotterdam, Hoorn and Enkhuizen. These archives are an exceptionally rich and voluminous source for the history of South Asia. The bulk of the relevant materials in these archives has been described in Vol. 1 of *Dutch Sources on South Asia* (1.1, 1.2, 1.7.10, 2.1, 2.2, 3.1, 3.2, 3.7, 4.1, 4.2, 4.7, 5.1, 5.2, 5.7, 6.1, 6.2 and Appendix I).

VOC 54	*Resoluties* (proceedings) of the ordinary and extraordinary meetings of the Gentlemen XVII, 1755-6, including an *eis* (order for supply) for Bengal of October 1756, containing a sample of *doeras* cloth to be purchased from Dhaka (on f. 13 at the back of the volume). Described and reproduced in Stevens, *De VOC in bedrijf / Dutch Enterprise and the VOC*, p. 60 (see Supplement I: Bibliography, no. 85).
VOC 1055, ff. 187-8	Including instructions to Carolus de Lannoy concerning his mission to Kandy, 1610.
VOC 3715, ff. 603-6	Petition of 'Ghennessam' *c.s.* concerning a security for the former *Directeur* Johannes Mattheus Ross (1776-81) of Bengal, 1787. In Persian (with translation), with gold-leaf decorations.
VOC 3821, f. 811	Letter from Hooghly concerning the war with the British 1784. In Armenian.
VOC 9640, ff. 336-7	Plan of the French fort at Karaikal, 1739. Manuscript, coloured.
VOC 9712, ff. 634-9	Maps of Punneikayal and plan of the factory there, with legend, 1720. Manuscript, coloured.
VOC 9732, ff. 183-4	Map of Coromandel between Teganapatam, Pulicat, Vellore, Gingee and Tiruvannamalai (?), indicating European settlements and including some remarks concerning politics and trade, part of the appendices to a letter from the *Independent Fiscaal* Hendrick Becker to the Gentlemen XVII, 1703. Manuscript, coloured.
VOC 9733	Case files of the Council of Justice in Coromandel concerning deserters, 1759-60. One volume (erroneously referred to as inv. no. 7434 in Vol. 1 of *Dutch Sources on South Asia*).
VOC 9734	Papers concerning the extortion of Frederik Jan Lovernaar, *Opperhoofd* at Jagannathapuram, 1765. One volume (erroneously referred to as inv. no. 7435 in Vol. 1 of *Dutch Sources on South Asia*).
VOC 9809, ff. 721-4	Six drawings depicting various stages of forestry (including the growing of cinnamon trees) in 'Hina corla' at Alutgama and in 'Henegam corla' at 'Degambedde' on Ceylon, with legend, by Christiaan Boomgaard (?), 1720. Coloured.
VOC 9817, ff. 507-19	Plan of the fort at Colombo, indicating the location of the powder magazine, with accompanying text, by Christiaan Boomgaard a.o., 1722. Manuscript, coloured.
VOC 11346	Various documents concerning equipage, including sailing instructions for routes between Bengal,

Coromandel, the Fishery Coast, the Maldives, Ceylon, Malabar, Surat and other regions in Asia, 1760 (?). One volume, printed.

2. *Hoge Regering te Batavia*
High Government at Batavia

Access no.: 1.04.17
Inv. nos: 1-1011
Size: 20 metres
Period: 1602-1827
Inventory: in typescript, with introduction and index

The collection consists of papers that were transferred from Batavia to the Netherlands in 1862-3. The documents relate mainly to the settlements in Asia that were abandoned by the Dutch since the eighteenth or early nineteenth century. The bulk of the material in this collection concerning South Asia has been described in Vol. 1 of *Dutch Sources on South Asia* (1.3.1, 2.3, 2.7, 3.3, 3.7, 4.3, 4.7, 5.3, 5.7, 6.3 and Appendix I, 3).

2 Various proclamations, 1667-1770, including orders for the guards and garrisons on Ceylon, signed by Johan Gerard van Angelbeek, 1767. One folder, printed.

40-3 Papers deriving from Johannes Bacherus, Commissioner to the Coromandel Coast during the period 1684-93, largely in various Indian languages, mostly Persian and Telugu. For a description of Bacherus' career, the majority of the papers in his archives and their custodial history, see *Dutch Sources on South Asia*, Vol. 1, Appendix I, 3. Also including:

40, folder 59 Document possibly concerning bookkeeping. In Tamil, 232 palm leafs or fragments thereof, tied together by a ribbon, in a separate box.

40, folder 60 Part of a letter received (according to the Dutch text on the envelope in the same folder) from Mustafa Quli Khan, *Sar-lashkar* of Srikakulam on 8 August 1691 AD. In Telugu, palm leaf in a separate folder (erroneously mentioned as belonging to inv. no. 41 in Vol. 1 of *Dutch Sources on South Asia*).

41 (no number) Five documents, separated by the *Nationaal Archief* from the rest of the Bacherus archives, probably for exhibition purposes. One folder.

110 *Wajib al-arz* (petition) directed to Bacherus, in Persian, endorsed on the back by the petitioners, including the *Dubash* Nagosa, in Devanagari, Modi and Telugu script.

111 Letter to Bacherus, in Persian.

112 Letter in Telugu, marked H. Possibly belonging

with a Persian letter from Maasum Khan to Bacherus in inv. no. 41, folder 3.

113 Letter in Telugu, marked I. Possibly belonging with a Persian document in inv. no. 41, folder 83.

114 Letter in Telugu, marked J. Possibly belonging with a Persian letter from Mustafa Quli Khan, *Sar-lashkar* of Srikakulam, to Bacherus in inv. no. 41, folder 57.

805 Two plans of the Surat factory, appended to letters from the Surat Resident to Batavia, 1820-3. One volume.

3. *Factorij in Canton*
Factory in Canton

Access no.:	1.04.20
Inv. nos:	1-390
Size:	9.1 metres
Period:	1742-1826
Inventory:	J.L. Parani, 'Inventaris van het archief van de Nederlandse factorij te Canton 1742-1826' (1972), with introduction, index and appendix

After a period of occasional visits to China, the VOC regularly sailed to the south-eastern Chinese city of Canton (present-day Guangzhou) from 1729 onward. Initially directly connected to the Dutch Republic, the factory came under the supervision of Batavia in 1734. The trade, bartering Indonesian spices for tea, silk and chinaware, was seasonal and so was the VOC's actual stay in Canton. The Company's staff annually resided in a rented building there between *c.* September and February and spent the rest of the year at nearby Macao. The management of the factory was in the hands of the *Commercie Raad* (Council of Commerce), consisting of an *Opperhoofd*, later a *Directeur*, and the so-called *Supercargas* (superintendents of trade), who generally speaking operated relatively independently from the GG&C. In 1756, the administration of the trade was taken over by the China Committee based at The Hague. In addition to the usual shipping link with Batavia, a special connection between Canton and Surat was maintained between 1744 and 1755, exchanging chinaware, star anise and sugar for cotton. In the nineteenth century the factory was changed into a consulate. Its archives were transferred from Batavia to The Hague in the years 1862-5. As a result of the shipping connection with Surat, most of the relevant documents concern that region. One should note that many other inv. nos than the ones mentioned below are very likely to include references to South Asia (in particular Surat) as well.

3, 10-11, 13-14, 17 *Resoluties* (proceedings) of the *Commercie Raad*, including *resoluties* and reports of the combined meetings of the *Supercargas* of Canton and Surat, 1744, 1748-9, 1750-4. Six volumes.

15	*Resoluties* of the *Commercie Raad*, including reports of the secret meetings with the council of Surat, 1751-2. One volume.
39	*Resoluties* of the *Commercie Raad*, including a letter to the Governor and council at Goa (no. 30), 1776-7. One volume.
104-5	Instructions, *resoluties* and minutes of the GG&C, mostly concerning the trade between Canton and Surat, 1743-9. Two volumes.
108-9, 111	Letters received from various places, including Surat, Colombo (or Ceylon) and Cochin, 1747-53. Three volumes.
110	Papers received from Batavia with instructions concerning the trade between China and Surat, 1749-51. One volume.
112	Instructions for a *Supercarga*, travelling from Batavia to China and Surat, 1751. One volume.
113	Letter from Batavia concerning shipping and administrative matters with regard to the trade between China and Surat, 1751. One volume.
179	Papers received from Batavia, including extracts from letters from Bengal, 1795. One volume.
202, 208	Reports with annexes by the *Supercargas* of the trade between Surat and China, D.W. van Nimwegen, E. de Wendt and R. Blok, 1750, 1752. Two volumes.
313	Letters to various VOC factories, with appendices, 1744-9, including two letters to Surat and one to Colombo. One volume.
314-15	Letters concerning the trade between China and Surat, exchanged between Canton, Surat, Batavia and other places, also containing references to other establishments in South Asia, 1748-52. Two volumes.
318	Letters to the Gentlemen XVII and various VOC factories, 1755, including one letter to Surat. One volume.

4. *Factorij in Japan*
Factory in Japan

Access no.:	1.04.21
Inv. nos:	1-1952
Size:	39.9 metres
Period:	1609-1862
Inventory:	M.P.H. Roessingh, 'Het archief van de Nederlandse factorij in Japan, 1609-1860 / The archives of the Dutch factory in Japan, 1609-1860' (1964), with an extensive introduction, table of contents and appendix in English

Nine years after the first Dutch-Japanese contacts in 1600, the VOC established a factory on the island of Hirado (or Firando), west of Kyushu. In 1641 the settlement was moved to the artificial island of Deshima in the Nagasaki harbour. It was governed by an *Opperhoofd* and council. In Japan, the Company exchanged Chinese silk for bullion (gold, silver and copper), which, in turn, was used to purchase textiles in India. In 1639, the Japanese authorities expelled all Europeans other than the Dutch. The VOC servants were not allowed to leave their factory, however, except for the annual mission to the capital Edo (modern-day Tokyo). Until 1854, when Japan was forced to reopen its borders, the Dutch settlement provided the country's only contact with the rest of the world. After 1840 the factory slowly grew into a diplomatic post and officially became a consulate-general in 1860. The first part of the archives (dating from the period 1609-1842) was shipped to Batavia in 1852 and 1860. The years 1862-3 saw its transfer to The Hague.

276-349	Correspondence with the GG&C, Japanese authorities and various VOC settlements, including factories in South Asia, 1614-1736. 73 volumes, one folder.
354	Letters from Coromandel, 1655-8. One folder.
355	Letters from Bengal, 1656-60. One folder.
482-99	Letters to the GG&C, Japanese authorities and various VOC settlements, including factories in South Asia, 1623-1786. 18 volumes.
501	Two letters to Bengal, 1725, 1729. Two pieces.
648	Memorandum of news from Coromandel, Bengal, Colombo and other places, drawn up for the Japanese, *c.* 1690. One piece.

5. *Staten-Generaal*, 1576-1796
   States General

Access no.:	1.01.03
Inv. nos:	1-12697
Size:	1030 metres
Period:	1550-1796
Inventory:	in typescript in several volumes, numbered 1.01.02 (table of contents) to 1.01.08

The overall supervision of the VOC and the colonies lay with the States General of the Dutch Republic. They granted the charters to the Company and appointed its high officials, such as the Governor-General at Batavia. The bulk of the material in this collection concerning South Asia has been described in Vol. 1 of *Dutch Sources on South Asia* (1.4.2, 2.4 and 4.4).

12576, folder 83, 1	Papers concerning the disagreement between the VOC and the EIC about the ships Hopewell and Luijpaert sent by the English to Malabar, 1663-4. One folder.
12577, folders 38 & 39, 1	Papers concerning the disagreement with the Portuguese about Cochin and Cannanore, 1666-7. One folder, one piece.

6. *Extra aanwinsten Raad van State*
   Extra acquisitions of the Council of State

Access no.: 1.01.19.02
Inv. nos: 1-59
Size: 3.35 metres
Period: 16th-18th centuries
Inventory: in typescript (1999), with short introduction

The *Raad van State* (established in 1588) was the most important advisory board to the government of the Dutch Republic. This collection of acquisitions probably originated from the Representatives of the town of Delft in the meetings of the States of Holland, the main governmental body of this province during the VOC period.

40 Various papers concerning the VOC, including an extract of a *resolutie* (proceedings) of the States of Holland concerning hostilities of VOC servants against the EIC in Bengal, 1761, and a request by Johannes Haselkamp, former factor at Nagappattinam, to the Gentlemen XVII to have a sum of money returned, 1769.

7. *Gedeputeerden van Haarlem ter Dagvaart*
   Convened Representatives of Haarlem

Access no.: 3.01.09
Inv. nos: 1-1295
Size: 9.4 metres
Period: 1245-1793
Inventory: 'Inventaris van het archief van de Gedeputeerden van Haarlem ter Dagvaart van de Staten van Holland (1589) 1603-1787', with extensive introduction, appendices and index

These are the archives of the representatives of the town of Haarlem in the meetings of the States of Holland, the main governmental body of this province during the VOC period. In addition to the document described below, inv. nos 539-49 also concern the Company.

7 Notes of Jacobus van Veckhoven, Pensionary of Haarlem, about various subjects, including a letter from envoy Hop concerning a ship on the Hooghly River, 1731. Four pieces.

8. *Raad der Aziatische Bezittingen en Etablissementen*
   Council of Asian Possessions and Establishments

Access no.: 2.01.27.02
Inv. nos: 1-407
Size: 36 metres
Period: 1793-1806
Inventory: in typescript, with a brief introduction and index

The Council was the second in the line of successors to the VOC management in the Netherlands. It functioned from 1800 to 1806. The bulk of the material in the archives concerning South Asia has been described in Vol. 1 of *Dutch Sources on South Asia* (1.4.5, 4.4 and 5.4).

398 m Request of Johannes Kuper, former servant at Surat, with appendices including letters from Surat, late eighteenth century and 1805. One quire, one piece.

9. *Hollandse Staatscommissies tot de Zaken van de Oost-Indische Compagnie*
Holland State Commissions regarding the East India Company

Access no.: 3.02.33
Inv. nos: 1-26
Size: 3.1 metres
Period: 1790-6
Inventory: Th.H.P.M. Thomassen, 'Inventaris van de archieven van de twee Hollandse Staatscommissies tot de Zaken van de Oost-Indische Compagnie, 1790-1796' (1983), with introduction, appendices and index

When, because of the fourth Anglo-Dutch war (1780-4), the financial situation of the VOC had greatly deteriorated, the Province of Holland was the most important party to stand surety for the Company. Holland had to invest large sums of money in an attempt to prevent its bankruptcy. The Province took in pledge all merchandise and revenues of the VOC and set up (on its own or with the Province of Zeeland) four consecutive commissions to support and control the Company's administration, in particular its finances. The archives described here were created by the third and fourth of these institutions: the *Hollands-Zeeuwse Staatscommissie tot de Zaken van de Oost-Indische Compagnie* (Holland and Zeeland State Commission regarding the East India Company), 1790-5 (inv. nos 1-23), and, after the great political changes in 1795, the *Committé tot de Zaken van de Oost-Indische Compagnie* (Committee regarding the East India Company), 1795-6 (inv. nos 24-6). The latter was disbanded when, after the dissolution of the VOC, the *Comité tot de Zaken van de Oost-Indische Handel en Bezittingen* (Committee regarding East Indian Trade and Possessions) was established in 1796 as the successor of the VOC direction in the Netherlands (see Vol. 1 of *Dutch Sources on South Asia*, 1.4.4).

1-2 Minutes of the State Commission, 1790-5. Two volumes. See also inv. no. 21, below.

3-20 Appendices to the minutes of the State Commission (including incoming and outgoing letters, reports, memorandums etc.), with many general documents partly concerning South Asia. 18 volumes. See also inv. nos 22-3, below. Including:

3C, no. 58 Letter to Governor Willem Jacob van de Graaff of Ceylon, 1791.

3C, no. 414 Letter to Johan Carel Lodewijk Blume, factor at Hooghly, 1794.

12, no. 9 & 13, no. 19B Litt. V append. G (220-2) & 15, no. 68 & 17, no. 116	Papers concerning the possessions in Malabar in general and the possible sale of Cochin in particular, 1789-92.
13, no. 19B Litt. S (172-6) & 15, no. 74	Papers concerning the expenses and use of the Meuron and Württemberg Regiments, 1790-1.
13, no. 19B Litt. V & V append. C, E	*Resolutie* (proceedings) of the Gentlemen XVII concerning a plan to leave the trade of Bengal and Coromandel textiles to private persons, 1791, with appendices concerning the Bengal and Coromandel trade, 1770-80. Printed.
13, no. 19B Litt. V append. C1-C5 (218-19)	Papers concerning the Ceylonese trade during the period 1781-9. Printed.
17, no. 109 & 20, no.192	Papers concerning the imminent conflict with Kandy, 1791-4.
19, no. 170 & 20, no. 191	Memoir of Johan Carel Lodewijk Blume at Hooghly concerning the revenues and the general condition of the VOC, 1774, with accompanying letters of Blume to Governor-General Willem Arnold Alting and the State Commission, 1792-4.

21 Alphabetical and chronological repertory to the minutes of the State Commission, 1795. Four folders. See inv. nos 1-2, above.

22 Alphabetical and chronological repertory to the outgoing letters, 1795. One folder. See inv. nos 3-20, above.

23 Table of contents of the appendices to the minutes of the State Commission, 1795. One volume. See inv. nos 3-20, above.

24 Minutes of the Committee, 1795-6, and appendices, 1795. One volume.

25 Appendices to the minutes of the Committee, 1795-6. One volume. Including:

nos 417, 419	Letter from Jean van Maseyk, Dutch Consul at Aleppo, to VOC *Advocaat* P.J. Guépin, concerning his efforts not to let letters addressed to VOC officials in Bengal and Surat (and sent to Maseyk) be confiscated by the British, 1795.
no. 713	Letter of Richard Muilman & Co., VOC correspondent in London, to the Amsterdam Chamber partly concerning the transfer of VOC forts on Ceylon to the British, 1796.

10. *Legatie Portugal*
Consulate General at Lisbon, Portugal

Access no.: 1.02.18
Inv. nos: 1-137
Size: 3.9 metres
Period: 1702-1804
Inventory: in J.C.M. Pennings and Th.H.P.M. Thomassen (eds), *Archieven van Nederlandse gezanten en consuls to 1813. Deel 1: Overgedragen brieven van gezanten en consuls in de Christelijke wereld* (The Hague, 1994), pp. 369-78, with introduction and index

These papers originate from the Dutch Consulate General at Lisbon (1780-1809) and three envoys who served at the Portuguese capital: Jan Willem Hogguer (1783-90), Gerrit Carel van Spaen tot Voorstonden (1791-4) and Charles Henri van Grasveld (1801-4). The papers of Hogguer include a relevant document. Another paper in this collection concerning South Asia has been described in Vol. 1 of *Dutch Sources on South Asia* (3.4).

27 Memorandum of association of a Portuguese mercantile house intending to conduct trade in Malabar, 1787. One piece.

11. *Overige Gezanten en Legatiearchieven Diversen*
Other Envoys, Embassies and Consulates

Access no.: 1.10.110
Inv. nos: 1-189
Size: 1 metre
Period: 1569-1791
Inventory: in typescript, with short introduction and appendices

This collection consists of papers originating from Dutch representative bodies or people abroad that were erroneously added to other archives and now have (temporarily?) been put together. The documents deriving from the representatives in Great Britain include some relevant papers.

156 Papers concerning the military expeditions of the French to Trincomalee (copies made by the so-called Holland Enquiry Commission from a file of Fagel, see sections 20 and 30 in this Supplement), 1789. One folder.

12. *Verspreide West-Indische Stukken*
Scattered papers concerning the West Indies

Access no.: 1.05.06
Inv. nos: 1-1410
Size: 6.25 metres
Period: 1614-1795
Inventory: I. Guicherit, 'Collectie verspreide West-Indische stukken' (1989), with introduction, appendices and index

This collection consists of papers deriving from or concerning the *Westindische Compagnie* (WIC, West India Company) that in the course of time were separated from the archives they originally belonged to and were never put back.

934 Extracts from *resoluties* (proceedings) of the Gentlemen XIX (board of directors of the WIC) and other papers concerning the claim by the WIC of a part of the sum of money that Portugal promised to pay when it made peace with the Dutch Republic in 1661, which was actually never paid, however, while afterwards the VOC conquered Cochin and Cannanore, 1665-1711. Three pieces.

13. *Nederlandse Hervormde Kerk, Synode, 1566-1816*
Dutch Reformed Church, Synod

Access no.: 2.19.064
Inv. nos: 1-793 (1583 catalogue nos)
Size: *c.* 24 metres
Period: 1566-1816
Inventory: A. Fris, 'Inventaris van de archieven van het Convent van Wesel, 1568; Nationale Synode, 1571-1619 (1668); Commissies op Nationaal Niveau, 1619-1805; Synode van Holland en Zeeland, 1574; Provinciale Synode van Holland, 1582; Particuliere Synode van Zuid-Holland, (1566) 1579-1816' (1991), with introduction, cross-references, appendices and index

The bulk of these archives consists of documents of the *Particuliere Synode van Zuid-Holland* (Private (provincial) Synod of South Holland). These include a substantial number of papers with regard to the activities of the Dutch Reformed Church in the East Indies, as the Synod played an advisory and supportive role in this field. The Synod of South Holland supervised a number of Classes, among which were those of Delft and Schieland (the latter also known as Rotterdam). Documents relevant for South Asia mostly concern Ceylon. These archives have been deposited at the *Nationaal Archief* only temporarily and in the future may be transferred to *Het Utrechts Archief* (see 1.1.23).

320 Forty-six documents with correspondence between the Church Council of Colombo and the Deputies *ad res Indicas* (committee regarding East Indian church affairs) of the Delft, Schieland and Amsterdam Classes, with annual statements about the state of affairs of the church on Ceylon and reports concerning the seminaries at Colombo and Jaffna, with a table of contents, 1700-40. One volume (catalogue no. 1327). The microfiches kept at the *Centraal Bureau voor Genealogie* (The Hague) referred to as *Doop-, Trouw-, Begraaf- en Lidmatenregisters (DTBL):*

voormalige Nederlandse koloniën, 'Ceylon ref' are probably copies, see 4.4.

321, ff. 81-174 — Nineteen letters from the Church Council of Batavia concerning the state of affairs of the church in the East Indies, with sections on South Asia, 1675-1700 (catalogue no. 1326).

321, ff. 207-364 — Eight documents concerning the early return to the Dutch Republic of Johannes Ruyterus, priest at Nagappattinam, because of his dissatisfaction with corruption in the church in the East Indies, the immoral behaviour of church members there and overdue payments, 1684-90 (catalogue no. 1335).

322 — Correspondence between the Church Council of Batavia and the Synod of South Holland and the Deputies *ad res Indicas* of the Delft and Schieland Classes, with annual statements about the state of affairs of the church in the East Indies, including sections on South Asia, with table of contents, 1701-40. One volume (catalogue no. 1328).

323, ff. 213-20, 863-70, 927-34 — Three documents with correspondence with appendices between the Church Council of Colombo and the Deputies *ad res Indicas* of the Delft and Schieland Classes, with annual statements about the state of affairs of the church on Ceylon, 1733-4, 1745, 1747 (catalogue no. 1327).

323, ff. 385-404, 665-734, 755-862, 871-926, 947-94 — Twenty-seven documents with correspondence between the Church Council of Batavia and the Synod of South Holland and the Deputies *ad res Indicas* of the Delft and Schieland Classes, with annual statements about the state of affairs of the church in the East Indies, including sections on South Asia, with table of contents, *c.* 1739-51 (?) (catalogue no. 1328).

323, ff. 935-46 — Defence of Henricus Saakens, priest at Colombo, against a treatise by Sijbert Abrahams in which priests in Coromandel and Ceylon are accused of being lazy and neglecting their duty, 1748 (catalogue no. 1351).

437 — Notes with advice and remarks received from

the Classes of South Holland, the Synods of Utrecht and North Holland, and the Deputies, in response to reports about the state of affairs of the church in the East Indies, including some references to Ceylon, late eighteenth century. One folder (catalogue no. 1332).

438 Reports received from the Deputies *ad res Indicas*, including some references to Ceylon, 1777, 1805-6. One folder (catalogue no. 1330).

544 Declarations received from the Deputies *ad res Indicas* of the Delft and Schieland Classes, including some references to Ceylon, 1805-6, 1808. One folder (catalogue no. 1331).

610 Correspondence with appendices between the Church Council of Colombo and the Deputies *ad res Indicas* of the Delft and Schieland Classes, with annual statements of the state of affairs of the church on Ceylon, 1751-75. One folder (catalogue no. 1327).

611 Annual statements of the number of priests and church members in the East Indies per congregation, with accompanying letters from the Church Council of Batavia, including sections on South Asia, 1753-94. One bundle (catalogue no. 1329).

14. *Nederlandse Hervormde Kerk, losse handschriften*
Dutch Reformed Church, separate manuscripts

Access no.: 2.19.082
Inv. nos: 1-219
Size: *c.* 3 metres
Period: 16th-20th centuries
Inventory: J.A.A. Bervoets, 'Inventaris van de voorlopige lijst van de verzameling losse handschriften van de Nederlandse Hervormde Kerk 16e-20e eeuw' (1991), with short introduction and index

These miscellaneous papers include some documents concerning the Dutch Reformed Church in South Asia, in particular Ceylon. Part of the materials has suffered badly from water damage. These papers have been deposited at the *Nationaal Archief* only temporarily and in the future may be transferred to *Het Utrechts Archief* (see 1.1.23).

79 Various papers concerning church affairs in the East Indies, including Ceylon, with table of contents, 1614-1757. One volume. Including:
ff. 387-98 Correspondence between the Church Councils of Batavia

and Ceylon concerning the promotion of a *Krankenbezoeker* (visitor to patients) to *Proponens* (ordinand), 1667.

ff. 407-34 Extract from a consideration by the priest Simon Kat concerning a Sinhalese seminary for the vicinity of Colombo and 'Mutrire', 1690.

ff. 463-513 Various papers concerning the seminary at Jaffna, 1690-2.

ff. 514-30 Translation of some Hindu (?) texts in Tamil (?) for youngsters, with an indication of how certain offensive sections have been altered.

ff. 531-56 Letter with appendices from the Church Council of Ceylon to the Gentlemen XVII, 1691.

ff. 568-75 Extract from the memorandum by Commissioner Pielat to Governor Diederik van Domburg of Ceylon, 1734.

80 Extracts from the *resoluties* (proceedings) of the Church Council at Batavia, with table of contents, 1699-1741. One volume. Including:

ff. 1, 7-8, 11 Concerning Colombo, Jaffna and the situation of the (Dutch Reformed?) religion on Ceylon, *c.* 1700.

f. 15 Concerning the death of the *Krankenbezoeker* Domingo Abrahams and his succession by Gerrit Grevens at Malabar (?).

81 Extracts from letters of the Gentlemen XVII to the GG&C concerning church affairs, partly with regard to Ceylon, 1633-1776. One volume.

15. *Johan van Oldenbarnevelt*

Access no.: 3.01.14
Inv. nos: 1-3622
Size: 13 metres
Period: 1586-1619
Inventory: H.J.Ph.G. Kaajan, 'Archief van Johan van Oldenbarnevelt 1586-1619 (voorlopige inventaris)' (1984), with introduction and index

Johan van Oldenbarnevelt (1547-1619) held many high political functions in the Dutch Republic, including *Advocaat van den Lande* (grand pensionary) of Holland. He played an important role in the merger of the early Dutch East India Companies into the VOC. Inv. nos 3054-118 concern the VOC and its predecessors.

3069 Memorandum of Augustijn Stalpaert van der Wiele to the Directors of one of the early East India Companies concerning commodities to be shipped from the Dutch Republic to the East Indies for trade, and a memorandum regarding the towns in Asia where textiles can be purchased, including a few references to Ceylon, Pulicat, St. Thome, Nagappattinam, Masulipatam, Bengal and possibly other locations in South Asia, 1600. One folder.

3118 Two copies of an extract from letters and recommendations of the Directors of the VOC to the States General concerning the trade and war in the East Indies, including sections on Pulicat, Masulipatam, Ceylon, Malabar and possibly other locations in South Asia, 1604. One folder.

16. *Hugo van Zuylen van Nyevelt*

Access no.: 2.21.179.01
Inv. nos: 1-13
Size: 4.3 metres
Period: *c.* 1600, 1803-48
Inventory: in typescript

This collection consists of papers deriving from Hugo Baron van Zuylen van Nyevelt (1781-1853), who held several diplomatic functions.

13 Various documents concerning the 'cruel, treacherous and hostile' activities of the Portuguese in the East Indies in the late sixteenth, early seventeenth century, including a few references to places in South Asia, such as Goa and Batticaloa (?), early seventeenth century. One volume.

17. *Wollebrandt Geleynssen de Jongh(e)*

Access no.: 1.10.30
Inv. nos: 1-320
Size: 2 metres
Period: 1612-48
Inventory: in *VROA*, 35 (1912), pp. 94-135, and *VROA*, 36, 1 (1913), pp. 96-104

During the years 1623-31 and 1636-40, Wollebrandt Geleynssen de Jongh (1594-1674) served the VOC in Surat and some of its subaltern factories. For a more extensive description of his activities and the bulk of the material in this collection concerning South Asia, see 1.1.1 and Vol. 1 of *Dutch Sources on South Asia* (1.5.2, 2.5, 3.5, 4.5, 5.5 and 6.5, as well as 1.6.1 and 2.6).

35 Letter received by Geleynssen at Bharuch on 14 November 1625 from Hendrick Vapoer at Lahore, including a drawing by Vapoer of an Indian couple in Mughal clothing. One piece. Drawing described and reproduced in Van Santen, *VOC-dienaar in India*, p. 67 (see Supplement I: Bibliography, no. 185), and Lunsingh Scheurleer, 'Hoofse Snuisterijen uit India', p. 6 (Bibl., no. 141).

18. *Cornelis de Groot*

Access no.: 1.10.34
Inv. nos: 1-40
Size: 0.86 metres
Period: 1622-96
Inventory: in *VROA*, 25 (1902), pp. 36-41

Cornelis de Groot was Secretary of the *Admiraliteit van het Noorderkwartier* (Admiralty of the Northern Quarter).

15 Liquidations of the Admiralty and the VOC, partly concerning contacts

with the Portuguese in South Asia, 1635-52. Three pieces.

19. *Van Hardenbroek family*

Access no.: 1.10.37
Inv. nos: 1-210
Size: 2.6 metres
Period: 1480-1791
Inventory: in typescript (1985), with introduction, genealogical trees and index

The papers derive from various members of the Van Hardenbroek family, including Pieter (1593-1658), who held high political functions in and on behalf of the province of Utrecht.

29 Report by *Advocaat* Pieter van Dam on behalf of the Directors of the VOC submitted to the States General concerning the return fleet and other Company affairs, including sections on Coromandel, Bengal, Orissa, Ceylon, Cochin and Vengurla, 1664.

20. *Casper Fagel*

Access no.: 3.01.18
Inv. nos: 1-497
Size: 9.6 metres
Period: 1669-88
Inventory: L. Strasser, 'Inventaris van het archief van Raadpensionaris Gaspar Fagel 1672-1688' (1995), with extensive introduction, appendices and index

Like many of his relatives, Caspar (or Gaspar) Fagel (1634-88) became *Griffier* (clerk) of the States General in 1670. Between 1672 and 1688 he served as *Raadpensionaris* (grand pensionary) of the States of Holland, the main governmental body of this province during the VOC period.

58 Letters (with appendices) to the States of Holland and Casper Fagel from various people, including Quirijn van Rhijn at Patna, 1680.

21. *Van Schinne family*

Access no.: 1.10.75.01
Inv. nos: 1-209
Size: 2.5 metres
Period: 1683-1855
Inventory: in typescript, with genealogical trees and index to personal and geographical names

The archives of the Van Schinne family include some papers deriving from Isaac I (1640-86) who served as chief-factor in Japan.

6 List of relatives and friends staying in the Indies at the time Isaac I and

his wife Aletta de Bitter (1654-1708) left Batavia, including people concerned with South Asia, 1684. One piece.

22. *d'Ablaing van Giessenburg family*

Access no.: 2.21.183.01
Inv. nos: 1-104
Size: 8 metres
Period: 1380-1906
Inventory: in typescript (1980)

These family papers include documents originating from the related Six family. One of its members was Willem Six (*c.* 1667-1718), who sailed to the East Indies in 1693 and became second-in-command at Surat in 1701. After his departure in 1706, he held several other high functions in Asia.

84 Papers deriving from the Six family, including two letters from Willem Six at Surat to his sister Agatha Cornelia Six and her husband Bernardus Muijskens, 1698, 1700. One folder.

23. *Teding van Berkhout family*

Access no.: 3.20.59
Inv. nos: 1-2278
Size: 21.6 metres
Period: 1578-1994
Inventory: O. Schutte, 'Het archief van de familie Teding van Berkhout' (1974), with introduction, appendices, genealogical trees, index and supplement (*c.* 2000)

Several members of this family held high political functions in the province of Holland during the VOC period. Some of them, including Jan Teding van Berkhout (1713-66), served as Directors of the Delft Chamber of the Company. Inv. nos 121, 164, 276-8 and 363-7 (partly) concern the VOC.

363 Notes by Jan Teding van Berkhout concerning the VOC since 1669, continued until 1779, including a short anonymous memorandum about a journey from Batavia to Bengal, Ceylon, Malabar and Coromandel (among other places), *c.* 1750, a few remarks regarding Jaffna and *Commandeurs* Deleg (?) and Arnoldus de Lij of Galle, and some more notes concerning South Asia. One folder.

24. *Radermacher family*

Access no.: 1.10.69
Inv. nos: 1-638
Size: 6.5 metres
Period: 1601-1800
Inventory: in typescript, with introduction

These papers include documents deriving from Samuel Radermacher, Director in the Zeeland Chamber of the VOC between 1730 and 1761, and his son and successor Daniël Radermacher. The bulk of the relevant materials in this collection has been described in Vol. 1 of *Dutch Sources on South Asia* (1.5.27, 2.5, 3.5, 4.5, 5.5 and 6.5).

86 Papers concerning the calling at various ports, 1683-90, including a printed survey of the Bay of Galle by the Pilots Frans Prins and Cornelis Coppe, 1690. Three pieces.

382 Various printed instructions, regulations, edicts, etc., with table of contents, 1647-1760, including sailing instructions for the route from the Cape of Good Hope to Malabar, the Fishery Coast and Ceylon (in particular the bays of Galle and Nilwala), 1665-8 (in the first volume), and for the route from the Hooghly River to Batavia, *c.* 1757 (second volume). Two volumes.

391 Newsletters concerning the East Indies, including news from Surat, Cochin and Ceylon, printed at Amsterdam, 1744-5. Three pieces.

420 Instructions for the sailing from the Cape of Good Hope to Ceylon during all seasons, 1714-17, 1746, 1759. One folder, partly printed.

25. *Van Schmid*

Access no.: 2.21.153
Inv. nos: 1-24
Size: 0.3 metres
Period: 1741-1855
Inventory: in typescript

These documents were collected by W.J.M. van Schmid (1806-84) in his capacity as official at the *Algemene Secretarie* (General Office of the Government of the Dutch East Indies) at Batavia.

3 Replies of the VOC Directors to complaints about hostilities of VOC servants against the British in Bengal, 1761. Printed.

26. *Boreel family, supplement*

Access no.: 1.10.105
Inv. nos: 1-82
Size: 2.9 metres
Period: 1608-1797
Inventory: in typescript, with index

These papers are a supplement to the archives of the Boreel family (access no.: 1.10.10), see Vol. 1 of *Dutch Sources on South Asia* (1.5.8 and 4.5). Documents relevant for South Asia (mostly pertaining to Bengal) probably originate from Jacob Boreel Jansz (1711-78) who served as Councillor Fiscal to the Admiralty at Amsterdam. Access is restricted, for further information one should contact the staff of the *Nationaal Archief*.

36 Various papers including documents from, to and concerning the Nawab of Bengal and the British, sent to or from Hooghly, Cossimbazar and Coromandel, with a drawing of the flag of the British ship Pitt, *c.* 1759. Partly in French, one folder (old no. D5).

57 Report with appendices of the EIC to the King of Great Britain concerning the conclusions of an investigation into the conflicts between the Dutch and British in Bengal, including a plan of the fort at 'Makvatanna' (?) and its vicinity, 1759. In French, one folder (old no. G7).

65 Letters from the *Raadpensionaris* (grand pensionary) P. Steijn to J. (Jacob?) Boreel Jz., envoy at London, partly concerning conflicts between the VOC and the EIC in connection with the treaty with the Nawab of Bengal, 1762. Partly in French, one bundle (old no. H5).

69 Letters to J. (Jacob?) Boreel Jz. from various people including the Directors of the VOC concerning the delegation of representatives to London to solve the conflicts with the EIC in Bengal, 1762. Partly in French, one folder (old no. I4).

27. *Joachim Ammema van Plettenberg*

Access: 1.10.67
Inv. nos: 1-43
Size: 0.34 metres
Period: 1780-8
Inventory: in typescript

Joachim Ammema van Plettenberg went to the East Indies in 1764 and served the VOC until *c.* 1783. He never stayed in South Asia. Most of the relevant materials in these archives has been described in Vol. 1 of *Dutch Sources on South Asia* (1.5.18 and 5.5).

26 *Memorie van overgave* (final report) of *Directeur* Louis Taillefert of Bengal to his successor George Lodewijk Vernet, 1763. One volume.

28. *Calkoen family*

Access no.: 1.10.16.01
Inv. nos: 1-1803
Size: 11 metres
Period: 1131-1953
Inventory: G.W.G. van Bree, 'Inventaris van het archief van de familie Calkoen' (1966), partly in manuscript, with introduction and genealogical notes

The archives of the Calkoen family, textile traders and high officials at Amsterdam, include some documents regarding *Directeur* Jan Huygens of Bengal (1744-50).

1618 Papers concerning the liquidation of the estate of Jan Huygens, 1749-65. One folder.

29. *Van Vredenburgh family*

Access no.: 1.10.83
Inv. nos: 1-16
Size: 1.2 metres
Period: 1602-1779
Inventory: in manuscript

The collection consists of papers deriving from Adriaan (1680-1759) and Gerard (1710-84) van Vredenburgh, both of whom were Director of the Delft Chamber of the VOC. See also section 35 in this Supplement.

6 Index to the *resoluties* (proceedings) of the Gentlemen XVII, 1602-1759, compiled by Gerard van Vredenburgh, including entries concerning South Asia.
7 Notes concerning the history of the trade in the East Indies, including sections on South Asia with profits, losses, commodities and number of servants, 1683-1755. One volume.
9-14 Various papers concerning the VOC, including *resoluties*, letters, notes, etc., partially concerning South Asia, in particular Ceylon and Bengal, 1678-1766. Six volumes.
15 Various papers concerning the VOC, consisting of a part of inv. no. 7 (see above). One volume.
16 Notes, arranged alphabetically, concerning Asian flora and commodities, with an index, eighteenth century. One volume.

30. *Fagel family, supplement*

Access no.: 1.10.94
Inv. nos: 1-993
Size: *c.* 48 metres
Period: 1524-1795
Inventory: in typescript (1990), with appendices

These papers are a supplement to the archives of the Fagel family (access no.: 1.10.29), see Vol. 1 of *Dutch Sources on South Asia* (1.5.25, 2.5, 3.5, 4.5 and 6.5). Members of this family held high offices from the mid-seventeenth century onward and some served as *Griffiers* (clerks) to the States General between 1672 and 1795. In addition to the papers mentioned below, inv. nos 11, 277-82 also concern the VOC.

12 Letters received by the *Griffiers* Fagel from *Directeur* Martinus Joan Boschman (1768-76) and the factor Abraham Josias Sluysken at Surat, 1769. Two pieces.

31. *Thomas and Jan Hope*

Access: 1.10.46
Inv. nos: 1-120
Size: 5 metres

Period: 1602-1782
Inventory: in typescript (1994), with introduction

Thomas Hope was a banker and representative of Stadtholder William V with the VOC from 1766 to 1770. His son Jan or John was a Director of the Amsterdam Chamber of the Company between 1770 and 1784. The bulk of the relevant materials in this collection has been described in Vol. 1 of *Dutch Sources on South Asia* (1.5.17, 2.5, 3.5, 4.5, 5.5 and 6.5).

11 Notes concerning Bengal, extracted from the *Haagse Verbaal* (general summary of letters and papers received from the East Indies and drafts of replies), with index, 1711-40. One volume.

12 Extracts from the *memorie van overgave* (final report) of *Directeur* Louis Taillefert of Bengal (1755, 1760-3) to his successor (Adriaan Bisdom?), 1755. One volume.

13-21 Various surveys concerning the VOC administration, trade, bookkeeping, shipping, etc., with sections on Surat, Malabar, Ceylon, Coromandel and Bengal, 1602-1769. Nine volumes.

24 Letters sent by Thomas Hope to VOC officials in the East Indies, 1763-70, with register, including Governor Iman Willem Falck of Ceylon, 1766-9, Willem Jacob van de Graaff on Ceylon, 1767, Governor Pieter Haksteen of Coromandel, 1766-8, and *Directeur* George Lodewijk Vernet of Bengal, 1765-8. One volume.

28-36 Letters and other papers sent to Thomas Hope by VOC officials in the East Indies, including many functionaries in South Asia, partly with register, 1755-71. Eight volumes, one folder.

32. *Jan Wttewaal and Hendrik van Staveren*

Access no.: 1.10.86
Inv. nos: 1-136
Size: 0.9 metres
Period: 1758-1804
Inventory: in *VROA*, 42, 1 (1919), pp. 195-204, with introduction

The collection consists of papers originating from Jan Wttewaal (born in 1734), who stayed in Batavia and Ternate between 1755 and 1774, and Hendrik van Staveren (d. 1777), serving on Sumatra between 1756 and 1770.

42 Letters to Wttewaal from C. de Cock at Colombo, 1776-7. One folder.

33. *Boelen family*

Access no.: 1.10.08
Inv. nos: 1-389
Size: 2.5 metres
Period: 1715-1958
Inventory: N.M. Brandt, 'Inventaris van het archief van de familie Boelen 1715-1958, met oudere stukken van aanverwante geslachten' (1981), with introduction, genealogical trees and index

The Boelen family, based at Amsterdam, was initially involved in the textile industry. Johannes Boelen (1710-91) became a wine merchant, as did his second son Jacobus (1752-1827). They both received several letters from Colombo.

45 Letters received by Johannes Boelen from his cousin Jan Hendrik Borwater, *Fiscaal* at Colombo, and the latter's wife Barbara Bregentina Lebeck, 1771-88. One folder.

46 Current account received by Johannes Boelen from Borwater and Lebeck, 1775. One piece.

47 List of receipts and expenses concerning the sale of wine received by Johannes Boelen from Borwater and Lebeck, 1778. One piece.

48 Bills of exchange of various persons on Ceylon to Johannes Boelen for the benefit of Borwater, 1780. One folder.

49 List of papers concerning payment bills sent by Borwater to his representatives in Batavia, 1782. One piece.

54 Letters received from Nicolaas Rijnders, Bookkeeper at Colombo, 1787, 1789. Two pieces.

86 Letters received by Jacobus Boelen from Borwater and Lebeck, 1777. One piece.

114 Letter received by Jacobus Boelen from Lebeck, widow of Borwater, 1787. One piece.

115 Letter received by Jacobus Boelen from Governor Willem Jacob van de Graaff (1785-94), 1788. One piece.

34. *Daniël Adriaan Meerman van der Goes*

Access no.: 1.10.57
Inv. nos: 1-262
Size: 1.7 metres
Period: 1755-95
Inventory: Ms Soemartini, 'Het archief Meerman van der Goes' (1968), with introduction, genealogical trees and appendices

Daniël Adriaan Meerman van der Goes (1748-1805) entered the service of the VOC in 1776 as *Adjunct-Advocaat* and functioned as second *Advocaat* between 1777 and 1784. From 1781 to 1795 he was also Pensionary of Amsterdam.

18 Correspondence of Meerman van der Goes with F.W. Boers and P.E. van de Perre at Paris, concerning Franco-Dutch military matters in Asia, partly with regard to Coromandel and Haidar Ali Khan, 1782-3. Partly in French, one folder.

34 Letters from the Gentlemen XVII with instructions for the Governor-General and the Governors of Ceylon and the Cape of Good Hope in connection with the war, 1782. Three pieces.

35 Letter from Meerman van der Goes to the Governors, Commissioners and other chiefs of the VOC settlements on Ceylon and Malabar with instructions, 1783. One piece.

36 Letters from the Gentlemen XVII to the Governor-General and the Governors of Ceylon and the Cape of Good Hope concerning the peace negotiations, 1783. One piece.

37 Letters from Meerman van der Goes to the Governor-General and the Governors of Ceylon and the Cape of Good Hope concerning the progress of the peace negotiations, 1783. Three pieces.

38 Letters from Meerman van der Goes to the Governor-General and the Governors of Ceylon, Malabar, Coromandel and the Cape of Good Hope concerning the signing of the peace negotiations, 1783. Two pieces.

57 Incomplete report received by Meerman van der Goes concerning VOC matters in Asia, partly regarding Bengal, 1777-9. One piece.

59 Letter to Meerman van der Goes from Abraham Josias Sluysken, second-in-command at Surat, 1779. Two pieces.

138 Memorandum concerning the claims of the VOC's brokers at Surat to the estate of the deceased second-in-command Bangeman, with appendices, 1779. One piece.

157 Extract from the register of *resoluties* (proceedings) of the States General concerning the private ship Antoinette in Bengal, equipped by the firm Robert Charnock at Vlissingen, 1789. One piece.

203 Note of bills of exchange drawn from Bengal at the expense of the VOC, payable in the fall of 1781 at the firm of Hope & Co, 1782. One piece.

223 Receipt of letters for Batavia, the Cape of Good Hope, Ceylon and Malabar from the Captain of the ship Goes, 1783. One piece.

232 Proclamations and regulations, printed at Batavia, including an ordinance concerning the exchange of rupees from Surat and Bengal (among other places), 1780. One folder.

235 List of qualified people in the service of the VOC in Asia, including various persons in South Asia, 1779. One piece.

35. *J.E. Heeres*

Access no.: 1.13.04
Inv. nos: 1-43
Size: 1.2 metres
Period: 1525-1893
Inventory: 'Plaatsingslijst van de Collectie Heeres', with introduction

J.E. Heeres (1858-1932) was employed at the *Algemeen Rijksarchief* (National Archives) at The Hague between 1888 and 1897. He subsequently became Professor of History of the East Indies in Delft and Leiden. His collection includes papers deriving from Gerard van Vredenburch (see section 29 in this Supplement), Professor G. Lauts and J.C. van der Meulen. Most documents concern the VOC. Inv. nos 35-41 consist of late nineteenth-century biographical notes and surveys by Heeres, Van der Meulen and others about Company personnel.

1 Alphabetical index to instructions, regulations, *resoluties* (proceedings)

and other documents of the Gentlemen XVII for the years 1602-1750 and 1739-55 (the latter period only up to the letter O), including entries concerning South Asia. One volume.

2 Glossary of foreign terms (mostly from Asian languages) appearing in VOC letters sent from the East Indies, including many entries pertaining to South Asia, 1758. One volume.

9 Three acknowledgements of debt of the *Director* Jan Kersseboom (1750-5) and Council at Hooghly to Indian merchants, 1751-2, and two receipts of silver to be minted for the VOC, drawn up at Calcutta (by the EIC?), 1790. One folder, partly in English.

13 Correspondence with various people and other papers deriving from or concerning Gerard van Vredenburgh. One volume. Including (in no particular order):

(a) Letters from *Commandeur* Arnoldus de Lij of Galle to Van Vredenburgh, 1767-72.

(b) Considerations by Nicolaas Schagen (*Directeur* of Bengal 1685-8) concerning the instructions of Hendrik Adriaan van Reede tot Drakenstein about trade in Bengal.

(c) Remarks by *Directeur* Jan Albert Sichterman of Bengal (1734-44) and advice of Governor Jacob Mossel of Coromandel (1738-43), both concerning the considerations of Gustaaf Willem van Imhoff about textile trade and coinage on the Fishery Coast, in fact regarding the whole of South Asia, 1739.

(d) Letter from De Lij at Galle to Prince William of Orange V, 1767.

(e) Letter from J.J. Francken at Galle to Van Vredenburgh, 1767.

(f) List of the *Commandeurs* of Galle during the period 1640-1723.

(g) Several letters from De Lij at Galle to the GG&C, 1769.

(h) Extracts from *resoluties* (proceedings) of Ceylon and from letters sent from Colombo and Galle, 1759-71.

(i) Letter from Iman Willem Falck on Ceylon.

(j) Letters from R. de Klerck at Batavia and Senff (?) at Cochin to De Lij at Galle, 1769.

(k) Letters from Nagappattinam to Van Vredenburgh, 1771.

(l) Letters from J. Gratiaen and G. van Angelbeek, both at Tuticorin, to De Lij at Galle, 1772.

18 Papers concerning free trade and shipping, serving as appendices to the *memorie van overgave* (final report) of *Directeur* Johannes Bacheracht of Bengal (1771-6), 1771-5. One volume, partly printed.

22 Various papers concerning the VOC, including printed conditions with respect to the shipping of cargo to South Asia, 1791, and extract of a letter of Governor Iman Willem Falck of Ceylon (1765-85) with bookkeeping regarding South Asia, 1779.

36. *Mackay van Ophemert family*

Access no.: 2.21.115
Inv. nos: 1-1689

Size: 41 metres (together with supplement)
Period: 1370-1968
Inventory: 'Beschrijving van een verzameling stukken afkomstig van het geslacht Mackay van Ophemert en van leden van aanverwante geslachten' (1967), with introduction and several supplements

The Mackay family, of Scottish descent, included many high military officers. Cornelis Anne Mackay (1769-1841) joined the Dutch navy in 1784 and sailed to the East Indies, including South Asia, around 1690. For a supplement to this collection, see section 37, below.

107-16 Journal by Cornelis Anne Mackay of the warship Zephir, sailing to and from the East Indies, 1788-93, with inv. nos 110-12 concerning Malabar, Ceylon and Coromandel. Ten volumes.

37. *Mackay van Ophemert family, supplement*

Access no.: 2.21.116
Inv. nos: 1690-1991
Size: 41 metres (together with main collection)
Period: 1370-1994
Inventory: 'Beschrijving van een verzameling stukken afkomstig van het geslacht Mackay van Ophemert en van leden van aanverwante geslachten, supplement II' (1977-2001), partially with index

This collection is a supplement to the papers originating from the Mackay family. For more information, see section 36, above.

1851 Letter from Ferdinand Dejaen to his father concerning his journey as VOC ship's doctor to Batavia and his travels in Asia, including short descriptions of his visits to Ceylon, Coromandel, Bengal, Surat and Malabar, 1763-7. One volume, in French.

38. *Nicolaus Engelhard*

Access no.: 2.21.004.21
Inv. nos: 1-181
Size: 1.9 metres
Period: 1620-1831
Inventory: in *VROA*, 39 (1916), pp. 358-77

Nicolaus Engelhard (1761-1831) sailed to the Southeast Asian Archipelago in 1777, where he held several offices in the course of time. The majority of the papers deriving from him concern the VOC and its successors. Despite the fact Engelhard never stayed in South Asia, some documents concern Bengal and Ceylon.

17 Letter from Engelhard to I. Schmaltz at Chandernagore, 1812. One piece.
135 Plea of the factor F. Schouwman stating that merchandise of 1795 sent

directly from Batavia is more profitable than when sent via Ceylon and China, 1795. One piece.

39. *D.F. van Alphen and Nicolaus Engelhard*

Access no.: 2.21.004.19
Inv. nos: 1-63, 94-374
Size: 7.4 metres
Period: 1584-1893
Inventory: in *VROA*, 19 (1896), 22 (1900)

The bulk of these papers, originating from the VOC officials Nicolaus Engelhard (see section 38, above) and D.F. Alphen (1744-1840), pertains to the VOC and its successors.

3 Various papers concerning colonial and overseas matters, seventeenth to nineteenth centuries, including some notes concerning South Asia. Nine pieces, in bad condition.

5 Warrant of Ph. Muykens of the Council of Justice at Batavia to Arnoldus Muyskens, former *Directeur* of Bengal (1688-96), 1699. One piece.

276 Letter from J. Muller at Chinsura to Governor-General G.A.G.Ph. van der Capellen, 1816. One piece.

278 Letter from Daniel Antonie Overbeek at Chinsura to Engelhard, 1817. One piece.

40. *Laurens Pieter van de Spiegel*

Access no.: 3.01.26
Inv. nos: 1-684
Size: *c.* 18 metres
Period: 1229-1816
Inventory: Hingman and Heeres, 'Inventaris van het archief en andere bescheiden en handschriften van den Raadpensionaris van Holland Mr. Laurens Pieter van de Spiegel, 1787-1795', copy of *VROA* (1895), pp. 54-61, 99-192, with introduction and additions in typescript and manuscript

These papers consist of the actual archives of Laurens Pieter van de Spiegel (1736-1800) as well as other documents concerning his activities. From 1759 onward, Van de Spiegel held several high governmental functions in Zeeland. During the years 1787-1795 he served as *Raadpensionaris* (grand pensionary). Inv. nos 99-127, 428-42 concern the VOC and the East Indies.

101-6 Memorandums by VOC *Advocaat* Sebastiaan Cornelis Nederburgh and Director A.C. van der Hoop, letters from former Major Jan Andries Duurkoop, Henry Hope at Amsterdam, Director W. Prins and the Amsterdam Chamber of the VOC, report by a commission consisting of Arnoldus Adrianus van Tets, Willem Cornelis Boers, Daniel Adriaan Meerman van der Goes and Jan Jager, and other documents, all concerning the state of the VOC, with appendices, including references to South Asia, 1788-9. Two volumes, four folders.

107 Letters and other documents of VOC Director A.S. van der Hoop concerning the state of the VOC and the East Indies during the years 1754-89, including extracts from letters sent by Governor Willem Jacob van de Graaff of Ceylon (1785-94), 1787, and from Bengal, 1788. One folder.

113 Letters and other documents by Jacob Voute and Henry Hope at Amsterdam, W.C.H. Baron van Lijnden of the Zeeland Admiralty, and Lampsins and Robert Charnock at Vlissingen about free trade in Bengal and the ship Antoinette that had brought goods there violating the monopoly of the VOC, 1788-90. Partly in French, one folder, partly printed.

114 Draft or account of a conversation with MacPherson, former EIC Governor of Bengal, 1789. One piece.

115 Letter from A.W.C. Baron van Nagell, Dutch envoy at London, to Van de Spiegel, with appendices, concerning claims of the VOC to goods confiscated by the British in Bengal., 1789. One folder.

116 Letters and other documents of Director Cornelis van der Oudermeulen concerning his negotiations in England about the relations with the British in the East Indies and the obstruction of American trade, 1789-90. One folder.

126 Letters received by Van de Spiegel from VOC Director E. Craeyvanger, VOC *Advocaat* P.J. Guepin and Gijsbert Karel van Hogendorp, Pensionary at Rotterdam, and documents of the States of Holland, including references to South Asia, 1791, 1794. One folder.

127 Various papers concerning the VOC, 1789-92, including a report about the relations with the King of Kandy, 1792, and extracts from letters from Cochin, 1789, and Ceylon, partly concerning Mysore, 1789-90. One folder.

429 Various papers concerning the VOC, including an extract from a *resolutie* (proceedings) of the States General concerning Bengal, Robert Charnock and the ship Antoinette, 1791, and a short note concerning the importance of Pulicat to the EIC, 1788. One folder.

433 Extracts of *resoluties* of the States General and the States of Holland concerning the VOC, including sections on Ceylon, 1789-94. One folder, partly printed.

434 Appendices to a report about the state of the VOC, including sections on Coromandel, Bengal, Malabar, Surat and Ceylon, 1791. One bundle, partly printed.

439 Letters, sent to and from Colombo and Trincomalee among other places, and reports partly concerning the French expedition to Trincomalee, 1788. One folder, partly in French.

41. *C.Ph.C.E. Steinmetz*

Access no.: 1.13.21
Inv. nos: 1A-Z
Size: *c.* 0.4 metres

Period: 1648-1951
Inventory: in typescript (1985), with short introduction

The bulk of this collection originates from C.Ph.C.E. Steinmetz, who was employed as archivist of family papers pertaining to the East Indies at the *Koninklijk Instituut voor de Tropen* (Royal Tropical Institute) at Amsterdam between 1941 and 1949. In addition to the documents below, many other papers concern the VOC.

1B Letters and other papers regarding the VOC and the East Indies, mostly collected because of the signatures on these documents, 1649-1816, with modern-day notes, including two extracts from letters dating from 1677 and 1716, sent by Governor Petrus Vuyst of Ceylon (1726-9) to the GG&C, 1728. One folder.

42. *Heijning family*

Access no.: 2.21.281.41
Inv. nos: 1-83
Size: 1.5 metres
Period: 1713-1986
Inventory: shelf list

Nicolaas Heijning (1686-1759) joined the VOC in 1704 and served at the Cape of Good Hope. His grandson Johannes Cornelis Heijning (1754-1810), known as Jan, sailed from the Cape to Chinsura in 1769 and married Elisabeth Gerardina Eilbracht, daughter of Governor Jacob Eilbracht of Coromandel (1790-5). Their son Jacob Daniël Heijning (1783-1832) also lived as a merchant at Chinsura as well as in 'Saatgong' (Chittagong?) after a stay in the Dutch Republic between 1790 and 1802. In 1817, he moved with his family to the Netherlands via the Cape. Most of the papers described below are in a bad physical condition. Some relevant drawings related to this collection are kept in private possession, see 1.5.5.

3-4 Letters from Johannes Cornelis Heijning at Chinsura to relatives and friends at the Cape of Good Hope and the Netherlands, former *Directeuren* Isaac Titsingh (1785-92) and Cornelis van Citters Aarnoutszoon (1792-5), and his son Jacob Daniël, partly concerning mercantile and financial matters and the situation in Bengal under the EIC, 1797-1810. One bundle, one folder.[1]

5-11 Letters from Jacob Daniël Heijning in Chinsura, other places in Bengal and the Netherlands to relatives, friends and other people at the Cape of Good Hope, in the Netherlands and in Bengal, partly with modern transcriptions, 1806-25. Partly in English, six folders, one volume.[1]

12 Account books of Jacob Daniël Heijning, kept in Bengal, 1815-17. One folder.[1]

[1] Described in Heyning, *Een Hollandse familie overzee*, pp. 51-80 (see Supplement I: Bibliography, no. 876).

43. *Uhlenbeck family*

Access no.: 2.21.165
Inv. nos: 1-222
Size: 2 metres
Period: 1744-1978
Inventory: J.A.A. Bervoets, 'Inventaris van het familiearchief Uhlenbeck 1744-1978' (1985), with introduction, appendices, genealogical trees and index

Johan Wilhelm Uhlenbeck (1744-1812) entered the service of the VOC on Ceylon in 1768. In 1775 he married Maria Wilhelmina Gildemeester (1757-1813). As Major-Commander at Galle, he was imprisoned by the British when Ceylon was surrendered to them. His son Christianus Cornelius Uhlenbeck (1780-1845), married in 1805 to Catharina Elisabeth Andringa (1789-1849), was also detained by the British. Soon, however, he took service with the EIC and, as such, represented the Dutch community in Ceylon. In 1820, he and his relatives, including his son Olke Arnoldus Uhlenbeck (1810-88), returned to the Netherlands.

2 Deeds of appointment of Johan Wilhelm Uhlenbeck during his military career on Ceylon, 1768-95. One folder.
3 Testament of Uhlenbeck and Maria Wilhelmina Gildemeester, drawn up by Notary Wilhelm Abraham Kriekenbeek at Colombo, 1809. One piece.
4 Inventory of Uhlenbeck's estate, drawn up at Colombo, 1811. One piece.
5 Account concerning the estate of Gildemeester, with a copy of her testament, drawn up at Colombo, 1813. Two pieces, partly in English.
6 Correspondence of Christianus Cornelius Uhlenbeck at Colombo with C.A. Lorentz, 1817. One folder, partly in English, in bad condition.
7 Portrait of Uhlenbeck, by P. Estraat, with coat of arms of the Uhlenbeck family, pencil drawings, 1816. Two pieces.
8 Papers concerning Uhlenbeck's departure from Ceylon, with acts drawn up by the Register Office on this occasion, his journey to the Netherlands and the financial settlement of his possessions on Ceylon, 1820-1. One folder, partly in English.
11 Certificates presented by the Masonic Lodge of 'Sint Jan' at Galle, called De Oprechtheid, 'daughter' of the 'national' Dutch Lodge at Colombo, with a cloth used by the chairman depicting Freemasons' emblems, 1798-1800. Three pieces.
16 Notes and poems by Catharina Elisabeth Andringa, made on Ceylon on the occasion of the birth of her daughters, 1789-1805. Three pieces.
20 Memories written by Olke Arnoldus Uhlenbeck about his life until 1830, with references to Ceylon, 1887. One folder.

44. *Gérard Jan Chrétien Schneither*

Access no.: 2.21.007.57
Inv. nos: 1-137
Size: 9 metres

Period: 1788-1835
Inventory: in *VROA*, 38, 1 (1915), pp. 366-79, with introduction

Gérard Jan Chrétien Schneither (1795-1877) held several administrative and judicial functions at Batavia between 1819 and 1832. He was the private secretary of the Governor-General from 1821 to 1826. The collection includes a few papers concerning trade between India and the Dutch East Indies.

18 Survey of the trade between Bengal and the Dutch East Indies between 1813 and 1822 and from Java to Bengal, Coromandel and England in 1822. One piece.
20 Letter from Wapper Melis, Director of duties, to the Governor-General concerning opium from Malwa and Dutch textiles, 1821-3. One folder.

45. *Du Bus de Gisignies family*

Access no.: 2.21.035
Inv. nos: 1-550
Size: 11 metres
Period: 1602-1901
Inventory: J. Steur, 'Inventaris van het archief Du Bus de Gisignies' (1967), with introduction and genealogical notes

These archives chiefly concern Léonard Pierre Joseph du Bus de Gisignies (1780-1849), who was appointed Commissioner General in the Dutch East Indies in 1825. Relevant documents concern the Dutch settlements in India around the time they were finally abandoned.

232 Essay concerning the late-eighteenth and early-nineteenth century history of the Dutch possessions in Bengal, Coromandel and Malabar, undated (probably after 1825). One volume.
253 Documents concerning the acquittal of pensions, received from the Governor-General, mostly by former servants of the factory at Chinsura, 1828. One folder.
450 Papers concerning the coinage of Java *ropijen* by the mint at Calcutta, Palmer & Co. (?), 1824. One folder.

46. *Jan Cock Blomhoff*

Access no.: 2.21.005.37
Inv. nos: 1-15
Size: 0.2 metres
Period: 1817-29
Inventory: in *VROA* (1907), p. 108, with short introduction and supplement from 1996

Jan Cock Blomhoff (1779-1853) served two periods in Deshima (Japan) and other Dutch settlements during the years 1805-24. Although he never functioned in South Asia, he collected some notes regarding India.

13 Notes concerning customs, institutions, products, etc., of various places in Asia. Seventeen pieces. Including:
   (4) Short description of Gujarat.
   (5) Note concerning diamonds in Golkonda (?).

47. *Johannes van den Bosch*

Access no.: 2.21.028
Inv. nos: 1-1250
Size: 13 metres
Period: 1627-1914
Inventory: in typescript, with introduction and index

Johannes van den Bosch (1780-1844) was installed as military officer in Batavia in 1798. Among several functions in both the East and West Indies, he served as Governor-General and Commissioner-General of the Dutch East Indies between 1828 and 1833. From 1834 to 1839 he was Minister of Colonial Affairs.

349 Registers comparing the budgets of the various local Dutch governments in the East Indies for the years 1819, 1825, 1831-5 and 1834, including India. One volume.
398 Papers concerning the activities of the financial commission for the plans of the Government of the Dutch East Indies to borrow money from Palmer at Calcutta and to change the monetary system, 1824-5. One folder.
495-6 Registers of Java's import and export to and from other areas, including 'West of the Indies' (British India) and Bengal over the years 1823-32, with accompanying papers, 1834. Two folders.
823 Extract from the *resoluties* (proceedings) of the Commissioners General of 27 May 1795 concerning the textile trade at Coromandel. One piece.

48. *Prins family*

Access no.: 2.21.317
Inv. nos: 1-62
Size: 0.5 metres
Period: 1656-20th century
Inventory: L. Bes, 'Plaatsingslijst van de collectie van de familie Prins, 1656-20ste eeuw' (2003), with introduction

This collection originates from the Ceylonese Prins family, which belonged to the community of *Burghers* (Dutchmen and their descendants who stayed on the Island after the British took over the VOC government). The family descends from the VOC servant Frans Prins, who was possibly related to the Rotterdam-based Prins family (see 1.1.22). He passed away at Trincomalee in 1694. François Albertus Prins, a member of this family too, functioned as envoy to Kandy in 1770. These papers were collected by Lorenz A. Prins (who died in 1953), seemingly as documentation for a family history he intended to write. All documents relate to the Dutch presence in Asia. Part of the collection consists of transcriptions, translations and notes of materials dating from the VOC period. Of these, only transcriptions and translations are listed below. Most papers concern Ceylon and chiefly pertain to church matters, real estate and genealogy. A large part of the collection is severely damaged, as a consequence of which access may be restricted.

1 Marriage registers of Negombo, 1667-78, Colombo, 1656-63, and unknown locations (probably including Galle), 1673, 1742, partly with transcriptions. One volume, three pieces.

2 Remarks concerning the propagation of Christianity on Ceylon, 1659. One folder.

3 *Resoluties* (proceedings) of the meetings of the *Scholarchen* at Colombo (?), 1674-8. One folder.

4 Decisions made at the meetings of the *Scholarchen* at Colombo with regard to school and church matters, with replies (?), 1674-80. One folder.

5 *Resolutie* of the extraordinary meeting (of the Church Council at Colombo?), 1685, with transcription and English translation. Three pieces.

6 Declaration concerning Salvadoor de Croes from Tuticorin, drawn up at Colombo, 1716. One piece.

7 *Resoluties* of the extraordinary meeting of the Church Council at Colombo, 1721. One folder.

8 Baptismal (and other?) registers of the Dutch Reformed Church (?) at an unknown place on Ceylon (probably Galle), *c.* 1730-1813. One volume.

9 Baptismal and marriage registers of various places on Ceylon, 1742-89. One folder.

10 Roll of members of the Dutch Reformed Church (?) (at Galle?), *c.* 1742-1830. One volume.

11 Report of the inspection of the pearl banks near Arippu by Martin Anthonisz, Bookkeeper at Mannar, drawn up at Colombo, 1747. One volume.

12 Private letter of the *vrijburger* (free merchant) Jacob Adamsz at Colombo to the *vrijburger* Petrus Soescan at Galle, 1749. One piece.

13 Proclamation of Governor Julius Valentijn Stein van Gollonesse of Ceylon (1743-51) concerning the supply of wild pepper. Printed, one piece.

14 Declaration of Jacob Gerrard Overbeek and Pierre Ferrand, members of the Council of Justice at Colombo, concerning the transfer to Dirk Blankert, *Kapitein der Burgerij*, of a garden on an island near Colombo by his father Pieter Blankert, factor and *Shah Bandar*, and of parts of the adjacent lake by Governor Joan Gideon Loten (1752-7), with small plan, 1758. One piece.

15 Declaration of Sigisb. Abraham Bronsveld, member of the Church Council at Colombo, addressed to the Christian community at Tuticorin, concerning the membership of Carel Lodewijk Weijland and his wife Elizabeth Heijk (?), 1761. One piece.

16 Declaration of Js. Erfson and Gilles (?), members of the Council of

Justice at Tuticorin, concerning the transfer of a house at Tuticorin to the chief 'Pattangatijn' Don Gabriel Gomes, 1763. Some fragments.

17 Declaration of Johannes Erfson and Diederich Thomas Fretz, members of the Council of Justice at Colombo, concerning the debt of Maria Mardappa, widow of the *Chetti* Jeronimus Rodrigo, to Christiaan Drijhaupt, former factor at Colombo, 1769. One piece.

18 Declaration of Hendrik Cramer and Bernard Isaak de Bellon, members of the Council of Justice at Tuticorin, concerning the sale of a house at Tuticorin to the *Parava* Saviel Henriko Mote, 1769. One piece.

19 Declaration of Adriaan Berghuijs and Jan Jacob Gilbert, members of the Council of Justice at Colombo, concerning the debt of the *Chetti* Daniel Casie Chittij to the Bookkeeper Julius Cornelis van der Sprang, 1775. One piece.

20 Declaration of Christiaan van Angelbeek and Dirk Jacob de Moor, members of the Council of Justice at Colombo, concerning the transfer of a house at Colombo to Henrikus van Essen, with small plan, 1783. One piece.

21 Declaration of Daniel Bodenschatz and Andries van Hek, members of the Council of Justice at Galle, concerning the transfer of the garden 'de Eendracht' at 'Galoepiadde' to Abraham Antonie Engelbrecht, with small plan, 1787. One piece.

22 *Resolutie* of the meeting of the Council of Justice (at Galle?), 1788. One piece.

23 Letter from P. Sluijsken (?) at Galle to Joung (?) at Colombo, 1790. One piece.

24 Declaration of Henrik Willem Francken and Fredrik Jacob Papo, members of the Council of Justice at Colombo, concerning the transfer of a house at Colombo by the Schoolmaster Philippus Harmanus Helmers to the *Voorlezer* and *Krankenbezoeker* (visitor to patients) Harmanus Helmers, with small plan, 1792. One piece.

25 Letter from the Bishop of Cochin to Xaddi Talavem Mor, 1792. In Portuguese, one piece.

26 Declaration of Petrus Gerardus de Vos, Bookkeeper at the 'secretariat of police' at Colombo, concerning the testament of Cornelis Johannes, Bookkeeper of the Council of Justice at Colombo, and his wife Agnieta Gerardina Muller, 1795. One piece.

27 Name list, probably mentioning Dutchmen on Ceylon, eighteenth century (?). One piece.

28 Request to August Friederich Caemmerer, missionary at the Lutheran community of Tranquebar, to baptise Wilhelm David Smith, son of Johan Godlieb Smith and Leonora Kempe, eighteenth century (?). One fragment.

30 Regulations of the church fund of the Dutch Reformed Church (?) at Colombo, printed by Frans de Bruin in 1803, with added notes in manuscript and some separate papers. One volume.

31 Letter, possibly sent from Batavia to Ceylon, 1807. One fragment.

32 Notes of August Carel Fredrik van Ranzow concerning his life up to 1807, kept at Colombo, with additions concerning relatives, dating from the late nineteenth century, and partial transcription. Two volumes.

33 Extract from the register of the minutes and resolutions of the *Opperhoofd* of Coromandel and the Fishery Coast, 1823. Some fragments.

35 List with questions and answers concerning the religion of the inhabitants of Kandy, nineteenth century (?). One folder.

36 Notes, letters and printed texts and pictures concerning the Dutch presence on Ceylon, nineteenth and twentieth century, including transcriptions of seventeenth-and eighteenth-century documents, mostly of a genealogical nature. One bundle.

37 Transcription of a diary (by Major Frankema?) kept at Kandy over the period April-September 1765, with some separate papers and a partial English translation, undated. One volume.

38 English translation of a diary kept by Johan Hendrik Muller during his journey to Kandy, the occupation of the city and subsequent events, over the period March-April 1765, undated. One volume.

39 Transcription of some documents dating from the period 1770-1 concerning the mission to Kandy by François Albertus Prins, twentieth century. One volume. For the original documents, see *Nationaal Archief*, archives of the VOC (access no. 1.04.02), inv. no. 3291. Prins' report of the mission published in Weinman, 'Prins's Embassy to the Kandyan Court, 1770' (see Supplement I: Bibliography, no. 337).

40 Transcriptions of the baptismal registers of the Dutch church at Galle over the periods 1677-1742 and 1788-98, undated. Two volumes.

42 English translation of (extracts from?) the *dagregister* (diary) of Colombo over the period December 1756-January 1757, undated. One folder.

43 Thirty declarations concerning the membership of various people of the Dutch Reformed Church and extracts from baptismal registers, *resoluties*, lists of transferred goods and letters regarding church matters, drawn up at Tuticorin, Galle, Colombo, Jaffna, Delft and Leerdam (?), partly with transcriptions (including some of which the originals are missing), 1747 (?), 1775-1807 and undated. One volume, six pieces.

44 Declaration concerning the transfer of 590.5 *rijksdaalders* between (representatives of) Gerrit Jetses, *Resident* at Manapadu, and the innkeeper Douwe Sites, drawn up by Justinus Rutgart Kriekenbeek at Colombo, with partial English translation, 1755 and undated. Two pieces.

45 Declaration of Johannes Erfson and Gilles Wouter Trek, members of the Council of Justice at Tuticorin, concerning the transfer of a house at Tuticorin to the *Parava* Casper de Croes, 1763. One piece.

46 Two declarations concerning the membership of Willem and Catharina de Jong and Elizabeth van Wageningen of the Dutch Reformed Church, drawn up at Galle and Colombo, with transcriptions, 1766 and undated. Three pieces.

47 Declaration concerning the ownership of some gardens and the administrative function of 'Nalandelege Don Abraham', *Lascorin* at

'Malerverwe' near Kalutara, drawn up at Hulftsdorp, with some printed and handwritten Sinhalese texts at the back, 1767. One piece.

48 Declaration in Tamil and Dutch of the *Opperhoofd* and council at Tuticorin concerning the severance of all relations between the Dutch Reformed Church and the *Parava* caste, with transcriptions of both the Tamil and Dutch texts and English translation, 1769 (?) and undated. Four pieces.

49 List of household goods transferred by the Deacon Johan Hendrik Smith to the Deacon Hendrik Cramer, drawn up at Tuticorin, with transcription, 1774 and undated. Two pieces.

50 Two declarations concerning the ownership of Wouter Gilles Trek of two Indian female slaves, drawn up by Arnoldus Lunel at Tuticorin, with contemporary translations of the deeds of purchase of the slaves, 1775-6. Two pieces.

51 Declaration concerning the ownership of Pieter Lambert Trek, Bookkeeper at Cape Comorin, of an Indian female slave, drawn up by Arnoldus Lunel at Tuticorin, with contemporary translation of the deed of purchase of the slave, 1776. One piece.

52 Declaration of Pieter Lambert Trek (?) concerning the sale of a female slave and her son to Johan Hendrik Smith, drawn up at Tuticorin, 1776. One piece.

53 Declaration concerning the ownership of Johannes Martinus Fruins, citizen at Cape Comorin, of an Indian female slave, drawn up by Arnoldus Lunel at Tuticorin, with contemporary translation of the deed of purchase of the slave, 1780. One piece.

54 List of goods received from Colombo by the Deacon Johan Hendrik Smith, drawn up at Tuticorin, 1786. One piece.

55 Letter from Carl Fridr. Ebde (?) at Jaffna to the Church Council at Tuticorin concerning the sending of some church goods, 1798. One piece.

56 Nineteen recipes for the baking of cakes, bread and the like (with some small drawings), probably used on Ceylon, apparently originating from the collection of R.G. Anthonisz, archivist at Colombo, with transcriptions, eighteenth century (?) and undated. One volume, five pieces.

57 Declaration concerning the debt of Mr Van der Wall to Gertruida Henrietta Barte... (?), widow of Diederick Thomas Fretz, and the pledging of some jewellery, drawn up by Notary Wilhelm Abraham Kriekenbeek at Colombo, 1816, 1821. One piece, part of the document is missing.

58 Notes concerning the history of the Ceylonese De Vos family from the early eighteenth century until 1827, nineteenth century (?). One volume.

59 Transcription of an extract from the *dagregister* of Colombo over the period January-February 1770 concerning the mission of François Albertus Prins to Kandy, 1925 (?). One piece.

60 Transcription of an English translation of a Dutch translation from 1794 of a Tamil letter from 1778, written by several indigenous inhabitants of Tuticorin to the Bookkeeper Johan Hendrik Smith (?), concerning the transfer of real estate, undated. One piece.

61 Transcription of a document drawn up by Commissioner Jacob Andries

van Braam at Sadras in 1818 concerning the relations between the Dutch and the *Paravas* at Tuticorin, undated. One piece.

49. *Raffles-Minto* (photocopies)

Access no.:	2.21.183.64
Inv. nos:	1-4
Size:	0.4 metres
Period:	1810-14
Inventory:	printed (1970), with introduction

The EIC official Thomas Stamford Raffles (1781-1826) functioned as Lieutenant-General of the Dutch East Indies between 1811 and 1816 during the British take-over of the region. Lord Minto was the Governor-General of India at that time. This collection consists of photocopies of letters (chiefly sent from Melaka and Java) by Raffles to Minto, kept in the India Office Library at London.

1, pp. 6-11 Letter from Raffles at Calcutta to Minto, 1810.

50. *W. Roosegaarde Bisschop (India Office, London)*

Access no.:	2.21.145
Inv. nos:	1-31
Size:	0.9 metres
Period:	1895-1913, concerning 1818-31
Inventory:	'Inventaris [van] stukken betreffende in het India Office te Londen aanwezig en op de Nederlandse koloniën betrekking hebbende bescheiden vervaardigd door mr. W. Roosegaarde Bisschop' (1978), with introduction

This collection consists of surveys and some copies of EIC documents kept at the India Office (part of the British Library) in London that concern the relations between Great Britain and the Netherlands with respect to Dutch settlements in the East Indies, including Bengal. The surveys and copies were made by W. Roosegaarde Bisschop under auspices of the *Koninklijk Instituut voor Taal-, Land- en Volkenkunde* (*KITLV*, Royal Institute of Linguistics and Anthropology) at Leiden, but were never completed because the Ministry of Colonial Affairs stopped its financial backing of the project. See also Roosegaarde Bisschop, 'Onderzoek van stukken in het India Office' (see Supplement I: Bibliography, no. 55).

1-22 Lists of archival material kept at the India Office in London concerning the Anglo-Dutch relations with regard to the settlements in the East Indies for the period 1818-31, compiled in 1895-9. In typescript, 22 folders. See also inv. nos 23-31 below. Including:

- 1 Bengal Board of customs, salt and opium, 1818-30 (range C and CI).
- 2 Bengal commercial and shipping consultations, 1818-30 (range CLVIII and CLIV).

- 3 Bengal criminal judicial consultations (Western and Lower Provinces), 1818-30 (range CXXXIII-CXXXIX).
- 4 Bengal civil judicial consultations (Western and Lower Provinces), 1818-30 (range CL and CLI).
- 5 Bengal commercial reports, 1818-31 (range CLXXXIV).
- 6 Bengal dispatches, 1818-30 (Vols 77-115).
- 7 Letters from the Court of Directors to the Board of Commissioners for the affairs of India, 1818-30 (Vols 6-10), and letters from the Board of Commissioners for the affairs of India, 1818-30 (Vols 5-8).
- 8 Bengal foreign consultations, 1818-30 (range CLXVI).
- 9 Bengal letters, original letters sent by the Governor General in Council at Fort William in Bengal to the Court of Directors of the EIC in London, 1818-30 (Vols 79-113).
- 10 Bengal military consultations, 1818-30 (range XXVIII-XXXIII).
- 11 Bengal public consultations, 1818-30 (range IX-XII).
- 12 Bengal political consultations, 1818-30 (range CXXI-CXXVI).
- 13 Bengal secret consultations, 1818-30 (Vols (296)-(309) and unnumbered).
- 14 Bengal secret letters, original letters sent by the Governor General in Council at Fort William in Bengal to the Court of Directors of the EIC in London, 1818-30 (Vols 18-20).

23 Alphabetical index to the lists in inv. nos 1-22 (see above), with references to Surat, Malabar, Ceylon, Coromandel and Bengal, compiled in 1913. One folder.

24-30 Copies of some papers mentioned in the lists in inv. nos 8, 11-13, 16-17 (see above), compiled in 1895-9. In typescript, seven folders. Including:

- 24 Bengal public consultations, 1819-29.
- 25 Bengal political consultations, 1819-20.
- 26 Bengal foreign consultations, 1825.
- 27 Bengal secret consultations, 1820-5.
- 30 Correspondence between the Governor General in Council and the Secret Committee of the Court of Directors in London, 1819-26.

31 Index cards referring to personal and geographical names and subjects in the papers mentioned in inv. nos 8, 11-13, 21 (see above), compiled in 1895-9. One box.

51. *Losse aanwinsten*
Separate acquisitions

Access no.: 1.11.01.01
Inv. nos: 1-2152
Size: 45 metres
Period: up to 1800
Inventory: in typescript, with introduction and index

This collection contains separately acquired papers that have not (yet) been relocated to any of the more substantial archives of the *Nationaal Archief*. The items are arranged according to the year of acquisition but have recently been given sequential inv. nos. The old numbers based on the year of acquisition are mentioned between brackets. The bulk of the material in this collection concerning South Asia has been described in Vol. 1 of *Dutch Sources on South Asia* (1.6.1, 1.7.10, 2.6, 3.6, 3.7, 4.6, 4.7, 5.6, 5.7, 6.6 and Appendix I, 6).

112 Ship's logs kept by Chief Steersman Michiel Gerritsz. Boos of the ships Maarsseveen, Naarden, Vlaardingen, Nieuwenhoven, Durgerdam, Diemermeer and Nusenborch, 1662-9, including a number of landfalls in Coromandel (?), Ceylon (Adam's Peak among other places) and Bengal (Balasore among other places), and maps (sometimes with landfalls) of the coasts around Masulipatam, roughly between San Thome and Pulicat, roughly between Negombo and Galle, around Cannanore, between Kayankulam and Cape Comorin, and roughly between Manapadu and Baipar (Vaypar), 1666-7. One volume (1866 A IV KA 58).

162 Papers deriving from the States General, the VOC and the town of Veere (Zeeland province) concerning various subjects, 1598-1799, including the journey of Pieter Isaacx Eyloff to Coromandel, 1608. One bundle (1876 01).

758 Memorandum (*memorie van overgave*?) from Governor Rijcklof van Goens Junior of Ceylon (1675-9) to the chief-factor Pieter Verwer at Nagappattinam, 1679. One piece (1897 LII 14).

838 Correspondence of Jan Warnar Falck, *Equipagemeester* (master of the equipage) and *Kapitein-Luitenant-ter-Zee* (captain lieutenant) at Surat, concerning private affairs, with some appendices mostly regarding bookkeeping, 1753-60. 14 volumes (1900 XXIX 02) (erroneously indexed under Iman Willem Falck in Vol. 1 of *Dutch Sources on South Asia*). Including:

2 A-I, K Correspondence with various people at Batavia, Tagal and Cirebon, 1753-60, with 2C including a letter from Joan Gideon Loten at Colombo, 1756.

2 L-M Correspondence with various people in Bengal, including Adriaan Bisdom, the latter's wife Amalia Constantia Falck (Jan Warnar's sister?), Jan Warnar's nephew Otto Willem Falck, N. Armanout, Louis Taillefert and Pieter Cramer, at Hooghly and Cossimbazar, with an envelope with a note on the back in an unidentified Indian script (Gujarati?), 1753-60.

2 N Correspondence with various people, including Hendrik Dirkse, Warner Florijn, A. van de Does, Johan Friedrich Hoffman, the Jew Ezekiel Rabbi and G. Feith (?) at Cochin, 1755-60, Steeven Baaden at Galle, 1759-60, and Pieter Nieuwenhuijsen at Colombo, 1760.

2 Q Correspondence with various people, including Pierre Antoine de Bellon, Barnard Zimmerman and N. de Wind, at Ahmadabad, Bharuch and 'Kera', 1756-9.

1004 Request of *Directeur* Isaac Titsingh of Bengal (1785-92) to the GG&C to be allowed to repatriate, *c.* 1793. One piece (1905 LIII 03).

1137 Papers concerning the fleet that sailed to the East Indies under Admiral Pieter Willemsz Verhoeven, 1607-10, with a ship's log (possibly of the ship Zeeland or Enkhuizen belonging to the fleet under Admiral Steven van der Hagen, departed in 1603) of a voyage in 1605 in the waters of Ceylon and Aceh. One volume (1910 XV 02).

1625 *Radicale beschrijving* (official review of the VOC's state of affairs) concerning Surat, by D. van Rheeden, 1758. One volume (1931 X 12). Published in *Bijdragen en Mededelingen Historisch Genootschap*, 6 (1883).

2066 Fragment of a ship's log kept by a chirurgeon sailing from the Cape of Good Hope to Bengal, 1761. Photocopies, one folder (1977 VIII).

52. *Nederlandse Hervormde Kerk Ceylon* (on microfilm)
Dutch Reformed Church on Ceylon

Access no.: 1.11.06.02
Size: 48 films
Period: 1620-1981
Inventory: in typescript

These papers are available at the *Nationaal Archief* on microfilm (nos 2118-65), whereas the originals (*c.* 6 metres) are kept at the Wolvendaal Church in Colombo. Most of the original papers are damaged, as a consequence of which the microfilms are sometimes badly legible. The series below have not been arranged entirely chronologically. See the inventory for more details about the contents of each film. The microfiches kept at the *Centraal Bureau voor Genealogie* (The Hague) referred to as *Doop-, Trouw-, Begraaf- en Lidmatenregisters (DTBL): voormalige Nederlandse koloniën*, 'Colombo (Wolvendaalkerk) ref', are probably copies of parts of these microfilms, see 4.4.

film no. 2118 (part 1-3) — Proceedings of the Synod of North and South Holland, parts of the school *tombos* (papers regarding land ownership) and correspondence concerning church matters, 1664-1837.

film no. 2119 (part 1) — Correspondence about church matters, *tombo* extracts, proclamations concerning private slave transactions, list of distributed catechisms at Colombo, list of people receiving charity, 1652-1825.

film nos 2119 (part 2)-2128 (part 3) — Proceedings of the Synod of North and South Holland, correspondence concerning church matters, and baptismal and marriage registers, 1620-1799.

film no. 2129 (part 1)	Reports of visits to schools and proceedings of the Synod of South Holland, 1681-1799.
film nos 2129 (part 2)-2130 (part 1)	Proceedings of the Synod of North and South Holland, parts of the school *tombos* and correspondence concerning church matters, 1660-1809.
film no. 2130 (part 2)	Proceedings of the Synod of North and South Holland, parts of the school *tombos*, correspondence concerning church matters and declarations of adoption, 1659-1823.
film nos 2130 (part 3)-2131 (part 1)	Baptismal and marriage registers, 1678-1812.
film nos 2131 (part 2)-2134 (part 3)	Proceedings of the Synod of North and South Holland, parts of the school *tombos* and correspondence concerning church matters, 1657-1913.
film nos 2135 (part 1)-2139 (part 2)	Requests for baptisms, 1806-61.
film nos 2139 (part 3)-2144 (part 6)	Requests for proclamations of prohibitions and permissions of marriages at Colombo, 1800-96.
film no. 2145 (part 1)	Baptismal register and requests for baptisms, 1806-23.
film nos 2146 (part 1)-2147 (part 3)	Baptismal registers of Colombo, 1743-1981.
film nos 2148 (part 1)-2150 (part 4)	Marriage registers of Colombo, 1743-1931.
film no. 2150 (part 5-6)	Baptismal and marriage registers of 'outer districts', 1708-1806.
film no. 2151 (part 1-3)	Baptismal and marriage registers of 'outer districts' and forms for adoption, 1757-1877.
film nos 2151 (part 4)-2152 (part 2)	Funeral registers of Colombo, concerning both the 'inner' and 'outer' cemetery, 1803-1915.
film no. 2152 (part 3)	Lists of 'funeral areas' in the Pettah quarter at Colombo, 1684-1889.
film no. 2153 (part 1)	Church member and other registers, 1787-1859.
film no. 2156 (part 1-2)	Various books with minutes, 1721-7.
film no. 2157 (part 1)	Correspondence of the Church Council of Colombo, 1726-42.
film nos 2157 (part 2)-2158 (part 2)	Books of outgoing letters of the Church Council of Colombo, 1743-98.

film nos 2158 (part 3)-2160 (part 1)	Books of incoming letters of the Church Council of Colombo, 1743-1806.
film nos 2160 (part 2)-2161 (part 1)	Lists of furniture and other possessions of the church, gifts and funds for the poor, 1796-1824.
film no. 2161 (part 2)	Various papers, 1824-52.
film nos 2161 (part 3)-2164 (part 2)	Correspondence of the Church Council of Colombo, 1815-84.
film no. 2165 (part 1)	Various papers, undated.
film no. 2165 (part 2)	Regulations of the church fund at Colombo and financial documents, 1803-26.
film no. 2165 (part 3)	Papers concerning the church fund at Colombo, 1803-6.

53. *Artus Gijsels* (on microfilm)

Access no.: 1.11.06.04
Inv. nos: 462-500
Size: 17 films
Period: 1602-47
Inventory:
- in typescript, with introduction (1992)
- E.F. Kossmann, 'Hollandsche handschriften te Karlsruhe', *De Nederlandsche Spectator*, 9 (1888)
- *Die Handschriften der grossherzoglich Badische Hof- und Landesbibliothek in Karlsruhe* (Die Karlsruher Handschriften, IV) (Karlsruhe, 1896)
- *Zeitschrift für die Geschichte des Oberrheins*, 41 (1887), pp. 129-200

These papers are available at the *Nationaal Archief* on microfilm (nos 3698-714), whereas the originals are kept at the *Badische Landesbibliothek* (including the documents pertaining to South Asia) and the *Generallandesarchiv*, both in Karlsruhe, Germany. Artus (also Aert or Arnout) Gijsels (*c.* 1593-1676), born in the province of Guelderland, took service with the VOC at the age of sixteen. He stayed in Asia during the periods *c.* 1609-21 and 1629-38 and became Governor of Ambon. Later, he served as advisor to the Elector of Brandenburg in Germany. Virtually all papers in this microfilm collection concern the VOC.

462-73, 487, 489-90	General and private letters and instructions, by Gijsels and the GG&C, including references to South Asia, 1629-37. Film nos 3698-702, 3709-10.
478	Remonstrance of Gijsels, Commander of the return fleet, to the Gentlemen XVII, including sections on Surat, Goa, Bijapur and Vengurla, Ceylon, Coromandel and Bengal, 1638. Film no. 3704.

482-3 Declaration concerning the state of affairs in the East Indies during the government of Governor-General Antonio van Diemen, including references to South Asia, 1636-7. Film no. 3706.

485 Various papers, including a general description of the East Indies, remonstrance to the GG&C and report about the mission to Bijapur, all by the chief-factor and *Fiscaal* Johan van Twist, remonstrance concerning Malabar and notes regarding a journey to or in Bengal, 1635-7 and undated. Film no. 3708.

495 Various papers, including descriptions of regions, towns and villages between Golkonda and Aleppo by several travellers, *c.* 1600 (?), and a treaty concluded with the Zamorin of Calicut (?), 1610. Film no. 3712.

54. *Jacob Mossel* (on microfilm)

Access no.: 1.11.06.03
Inv. nos: 1-20
Size: 1 film
Period: 1699-1801
Inventory: in typescript (1971), with introduction

These papers are available at the *Nationaal Archief* on microfilm (no. 3697), whereas the originals are kept as part of the Mossel family collection. Jacob Mossel (1704-61) became *Onderkoopman* (assistant merchant) in 1730 at Nagappattinam and functioned as Governor of Coromandel between 1738 and 1743. From 1750 to his death in 1761 he was Governor-General. The rest of the material in this collection concerning South Asia has been described in Vol. 1 of *Dutch Sources on South Asia* (1.6.2 and 6.6).

3 Letters from Jacob Mossel at Nagappattinam to his mother and sister, 1734, 1736. Two pieces.

55. *Verzameling buitenlandse kaarten, Leupe* (VEL)
Foreign maps collection, Leupe

Access no.: 4.VEL
Inv. nos: A-BB, 1-2175 (2831 items)
Period: 16th-19th centuries
Inventory: P.A. Leupe, *Inventaris der verzameling kaarten berustende in het Rijksarchief*, Vol. 1 (The Hague, 1867), geographically arranged (inconsistent), with introduction

This collection consists of maps and drawings that mostly originate from the secretarial offices of the Amsterdam and Zeeland Chambers of the VOC and the WIC (West India Company). Some maps and drawings originate from other authorities, for instance the *Staten-Generaal* (States General) and the *Staten van*

Holland (States of Holland). The entire collection has been put on microfiche. The bulk of the material in this collection concerning South Asia has been described in Vol. 1 of *Dutch Sources on South Asia* (1.7.1, 2.7, 3.7, 4.7, 5.7 and 6.7).

968 Plan of the projected changes of the fortifications of Colombo, by De la Lustrière, 1787. Two sheets.

56. *Verzameling buitenlandse kaarten, supplement, Leupe-l'Honoré Naber* (VELH)
Foreign maps collection, supplement, Leupe-l'Honoré Naber

Access no.: 4.VELH
Size: 844 items
Period: 16th-19th centuries
Inventory: S.P. l'Honoré Naber, *Inventaris der verzameling kaarten berustende in het Rijksarchief*, First Supplement (The Hague, 1914), geographically arranged (inconsistent), with introduction and indices to personal and geographical names

This collection consists of foreign maps and charts that were acquired by the *Nationaal Archief* in the years 1867-86. A supplement to this collection concerns the *Atlas Vingboons*. The bulk of the material in this collection concerning South Asia (including most of the relevant maps in the *Atlas Vingboons*) has been described in Vol. 1 of *Dutch Sources on South Asia* (1.7.2, 2.7, 3.7, 4.7, 5.7 and 6.7).

619 *Verzameling van paskaarten dienende tot de vaart naar Oost- en West-Indien*, or *Atlas Vingboons*, i.e. collection of compass maps, designed for the voyages to the East and West Indies, by Johannes Vingboons, *c.* 1660. Including:
24 View of Batticaloa from the sea.
115 Bird's-eye view of Colombo.

57. *Ministerie van Oorlog, buitenlandse plans van vestigingen* (OBPV)
Ministry of War, foreign plans of fortifications

Access no.: 4.OBPV
Size: 708 items
Period: 17th-19th centuries
Inventory: copied from typescript index cards, geographically arranged (inconsistent)

This collection consists of maps and drawings of fortifications abroad. The rest of the material in this collection concerning South Asia has been described in Vol. 1 of *Dutch Sources on South Asia* (1.7.5 and 4.7).

3.354 Map of Pondicherry, based on the memory of Dupleix, who defended it in 1748, *c.* 1760. In French.

3.355 Map of Pondicherry, indicating the attacks by the British in 1778, by Josephus Jones, 1784. In French, coloured.

58. *J.W. Janssens* (JSF)

Access no.: 4.JSF
Inv. nos: 1-164
Period: 1748-1825
Inventory: R.M. Haubourdin, 'Plaatsingslijst van de verzameling kaarten en tekeningen afkomstig van J.W. Janssens (1762-1838)' (1993), with introduction, appendix and index to personal names

J.W. Janssens (1762-1838) functioned as Governor-General at the Cape of Good Hope between 1802 and 1806, and at Batavia from 1810 to 1811. During the period 1807-9 he was Minister of War. The maps in this collection were collected by him in his capacity of these positions.

84 Map of Colombo and its environs, with the British camp commanded by Colonel Stuard, 1796. Manuscript, in English, scale *c.* 1:7160.

59. *Library*

Size: *c.* 50000 items
Period: 17th century–up to the present
Inventory: – data base
– index cards

The collection of the library consists chiefly of books and magazines, and focuses on Dutch history and archival subjects. It includes a few printed items that may be considered archival material.

53 H 13 Letter of the Directors of the VOC concerning the ship Antonetta, which sailed under the Dutch flag to Calcutta, 1789. Partly in English

56 H 20 Letter of the Directors of the VOC concerning the question to which extent the Dutch trade to Bengal can be considered to be lost, 1791.

Index to Chapters 1-6, Appendix I and Supplement II

Following Dutch rule, personal names with a prefix such as 'van' or 'de' are to be found under their full, second name.